AAMC
Tomorrow's Doctors, Tomorrow's Cures®

Minority Student Opportunities

in United States Medical Schools

2007

Learn

Serve

Lead

18th Editon

Edited by Lily May I. Johnson
Division of Diversity Policy and Programs

Association of
American Medical Colleges

32/98

To order additional copies of this publication, please contact:

Association of American Medical Colleges
Customer Service/Order Fulfillment
2450 N Street, NW
Washington, DC 20037
Phone: 202-828-0416
Fax: 202-828-1123
www.aamc.org/publications

Price: $15, plus shipping
(Item code: MSOUSMS07)

Remittance or institutional purchase order must accompany order.

AAMC

Acknowledgments

The editor thanks Darrell G. Kirch, M.D., president of the Association of American Medical Colleges (AAMC), and Charles Terrell, Ed.D., vice president, Division of Diversity Policy and Programs at the AAMC, for their support. She also thanks the medical school officials who provided the information for this book. Thanks also go to AAMC staff, especially Kehua Zhang, Ph.D., Angela Moses, and Ann Steinecke, Ph.D., for providing invaluable advice and support throughout the process of revising and laying out the book.

Preface

Medical schools supply the information in this book in response to a questionnaire from the AAMC's Division of Diversity Policy and Programs. The questionnaire asks schools to update the information published in the previous edition of *MSOUSMS* in 2005. Unless otherwise noted by an asterisk, all schools submitted updated information on their programs and policies related to minority student opportunities in medical schools.

In the Table of Contents, medical schools are listed both alphabetically and by geographical location to help readers locate information about specific medical schools. Most entries cover seven topics: (1) recruitment, (2) admissions, (3) academic support programs, (4) enrichment programs, (5) student financial assistance, (6) educational partnerships, and (7) other pertinent information. Each school's entry also contains a table showing the most recent data on applicants and matriculants by gender and race, ethnicity.

In addition to the schools' entries, two appendices present (1) selected AAMC data of interest and (2) a table consolidating enrichment activities at medical schools. For more detailed information regarding any program, policy, or procedure please contact the school in which you are interested. Contact information is provided for each medical school.

We want to introduce you to Aspiring Docs.org. AspiringDocs.org was launched in 2006 by the AAMC to provide students with the information, encouragement, and support they need to choose careers in medicine. Although targeted to minority students, the interactive Web site contains features and information that will be valuable to any student considering a career in medicine.

Our hope is that prospective applicants will find this book useful, along with other resources such as AspiringDocs.org, in determining where to apply to medical school. Among the items to examine when making a decision are a medical school's program and philosophy, geographic location, state residency requirements, and the cost of attending. Be sure to discuss this and other information with a premedical advisor at your undergraduate institution, as well as with the minority affairs representatives at the medical schools to which you are applying. This book should be used in conjunction with the *Medical School Admission Requirements (MSAR™)*, which is also published by the AAMC and is available for purchase at *(http://www.aamc.org/students/amcas/start.htm)*.

Policies and procedures regarding recruitment and admissions programs described in this book are those of each medical school, not those of the AAMC.

AAMC

AAMC Division of Diversity Policy and Programs

The AAMC's Division of Diversity Policy and Programs (formerly the Division of Community and Minority Programs) was established in 1988. The division works within the AAMC and with our constituents—the nation's medical schools and teaching hospitals—to promote diversity in medicine. The division's vision is to change the face of medicine to reflect the face of the nation as a means of achieving quality health care for all. Our mission is to be a principal source of ideas, policies, research, programs, and services that

- Build diversity in the medical education and physician workforce pipeline,
- Make the case for the benefits of diversity in medical education and medical practice, and
- Support the AAMC's Group on Student Affairs-Minority Affairs Section (GSA-MAS) as a strategic resource for academic medicine.

Within these strategic initiatives, the division develops and supports programs, conducts research, provides constituent services, and develops publications for those working to advance diversity throughout medical education. Below are some of the division's programs and resources that will be useful to students considering medical school.

AspiringDocs.org
Comprehensive Web-based marketing campaign to increase diversity in medicine

Amy Addams, 202-828-0531
aaddams@aamc.org

Calendar of Events
Online calendar students can easily search for recruitment events at schools in their state or in a specific date range
(http://services.aamc.org/jsp/GSA-MAS/)

Angela Mose, 202-862-6203
amoses@aamc.org;
Lily May Johnson, 202-828-0573
lmjohnson@aamc.org

Cultural Competence
Information about cultural competence education and delivery of care

Norma Poll, Ph.D., 202-862-6115
npoll@aamc.org
Ann Steinecke, Ph.D., 202-862-6296
asteinecke@aamc.org

Group on Student Affairs-Minority Affairs Section (GSA-MAS)
Support for Minority Affairs officers at U.S. medical schools

Lily May Johnson, 202-828-0573
lmjohnson@aamc.org
Juan Amador, 202-862-6149
jamador@aamc.org

Health Care Disparities
Efforts to address health care disparities through education and research

Ann Steinecke, Ph.D., 202-862-6296
asteinecke@aamc.org

Health Professions for Diversity Coalition
Coalition of organizations dedicated to improving health care for all by promoting diversity in the health professions

Ruth Beer Bletzinger, 202-828-0585
rbletzinger@aamc.org

Holistic Admissions and Enhancing Diversity Project
Tools and information on individualized holistic review of applicants

Ruth Beer Bletzinger, 202-828-0585
rbletzinger@aamc.org

Information for Students
- Enrichment programs at U.S. medical schools
- Medical Minority Applicant Registry (Med-MAR): The Med-MAR is a self-identification registry that prospective medical students can choose to join once they have taken the Medical College Application Test (MCAT). Students who identify themselves as minority or disadvantaged supply the Med-MAR with their biographical information. The Med-MAR then distributes this information to minority affairs and admission offices of AAMC members and certain health-related agencies interested in increasing opportunities for students.

Angela Moses, 202-862-6203
amoses@aamc.org

GSA-MAS Directory
Searchable database (name, location, institution) of the Group on Student Affairs-Minority Affairs Section (GSA-MAS) Administrators at U.S. medical schools *(http://services.aamc.org/minorityaffairsdirectory/)*

Angela Moses, 202-862-6203
amoses@aamc.org
Lily May Johnson, 202-828-0573
lmjohnson@aamc.org

Minority Faculty Career Development
Professional development for junior minority faculty

Lily May Johnson, 202-828-0573
lmjohnson@aamc.org
Laura Castillo-Page, Ph.D., 202-828-0579
lcastillopage@aamc.org

Minority Student Medical Career Fair
Annual career fair for high school and college students held at the AAMC's Annual Meeting

Juan Amador, 202-862-6149
jamador@aamc.org

Association of American Medical Colleges, 2007

Nickens Awards
Annual outstanding achievement awards for medical school leadership, faculty, and students

Juan Amador, 202-862-6149
jamador@aamc.org

Publications
• *Diversity Research Forum Proceedings*
• *Facts & Figures* series
• *Minority Student Opportunities at U.S. Medical Schools (MSOUSMS)*

Ann Steinecke, Ph.D., 202-862-6296
asteinecke@aamc.org

Research and Data
Data, research support, and resources related to diversity in medical education

Laura Castillo-Page, Ph.D., 202-828-0579
lcastillopage@aamc.org
Kehua Zhang, Ph.D., 202-828-0578
kzhang@aamc.org

Summer Medical and Dental Education Program (SMDEP), funded by the Robert Wood Johnson Foundation
The Division of Diversity Policy and Programs co-directs the national program office of the Summer Medical and Dental Education Program (SMDEP) with the American Association of Dental Education. SMDEP programs are held at 12 sites across the country—nine combined medical and dental school sites, and three medical-school only sites. Each site offers a six-week summer enrichment program that strengthens the academic proficiency of minority college students (freshmen and sophomores) from disadvantaged backgrounds who are interested in pursuing careers in medicine and dentistry.

Norma Poll, Ph.D., 202-862-6115
npoll@aamc.org

Vice President
Charles Terrell, Ed.D., 202-828-0584
cterrell@aamc.org

Division of Diversity Policy and Programs Staff

Charles Terrell, Ed.D., *Vice President*

Amy Addams, *Program Coordinator*

Dexter Allen, *Administrative Assistant*

Juan Amador, *Senior Staff Associate*

Ruth Beer Bletzinger, *Director*

Laura Castillo-Page, Ph.D., *Assistant Vice President*

Dee Corley, *Senior Staff Associate*

Daniel Curl, *Part-Time Administrative Assistant*

Charnell Edwards, *Temporary Processing Assistant*

Vivian Harriday, *Administrative Assistant*

Lily May Johnson, *Manager*

Sakima Jones, *Processing Assistant*

Angela Moses, *Administrative Assistant*

Norma Poll, Ph.D., *Director SMDEP*

Michelle Reynolds, *Processing Assistant*

Ann Steinecke, Ph.D., *Senior Staff Associate*

Oswald Umuhoza, *Intern*

Angela Walker, *Outreach Coordinator*

Kehua, Zhang, Ph.D., *Senior Research Analyst*

Group on Student Affairs–Minority Affairs Section (GSA-MAS) Coordinating Committee 2007

Chair
Marvin (Ted) Williams, Ph.D.
University of South Florida
College of Medicine

Chair Elect
Cynthia E. Boyd, M.D., M.B.A.
Rush Medical College of Rush
University Medical Center

Chair, Central Region
Gloria V. Hawkins, Ph.D.
University of Wisconsin School
of Medicine and Public Health

Chair Elect, Central Region
Wanda D. Lipscomb, Ph.D.
Michigan State University College
of Human Medicine

Chair, Northeast Region
Gary C. Butts, M.D.
Mount Sinai School of Medicine
of New York University

Chair Elect, Northeast Region
Carlyle H. Miller, M.D.
Cornell University Joan and Sanford I.
Weill Medical College and Graduate
School of Medical Sciences

Chair, Southern Region
Karen A. Lewis
Meharry School of Medicine

Chair Elect, Southern Region
Brenda A. Latham-Sadler, M.D.
Wake Forest University Health Sciences

Chair, Western Region
Linda K. Don, M.Ed.
University of Arizona College of Medicine

Chair Elect, Western Region
Valerie Romero-Leggott, M.D.
University of New Mexico School
of Medicine

Ex Officio Members
Past MAS National Chair
James L. Phillips, M.D.
Baylor College of Medicine

Group on Student Affairs (GSA) National Chair
Dwight Davis, M.D.
Pennsylvania State University College
of Medicine

MAS Liaison to GSA Committee on Admissions (COA)
Sunny Nakae-Gibson, M.S.W.
Northwestern University
The Feinberg School of Medicine

MAS Liaison to GSA Committee on Student Affairs (COSA)
Virginia D. Hardy, Ph.D.
The Brody School of Medicine
at East Carolina University

MAS Liaison to GSA Committee on Student Financial Assistance (COSFA)
Martha C. Trujillo
Stanford University School of Medicine

MAS Liaison to GSA Committee on Student Records (COSR)
Sonia Beasley
University of Maryland School
of Medicine

Organization of Student Representatives (OSR) Liaison to MAS
Nathan T. Chomilo
University of Minnesota Medical School

National Association of Advisors for the Health Professions (NAAHP) Liaison to MAS
Saundra Herndon Oyewole, Ph.D.
Trinity University (Washington, DC)

AAMC Division of Diversity Policy and Programs Staff Support
Charles Terrell, Ed.D
Lily May Johnson, M.S.
Juan Amador
Angela Moses

Table of Contents

Association of American Medical Colleges, 2007

Alphabetical Listing of Medical Schools

Association of American Medical Colleges, 2007

AAMC

Association of American Medical Colleges, 2007

Geographical Listing of Medical Schools

Association of American Medical Colleges, 2007

Association of American Medical Colleges, 2007

Association of American Medical Colleges, 2007

Foreword

The publication of the 2007 edition of *Minority Student Opportunities in United States Medical Schools (MSOUSMS)* coincides with the 50th anniversary of the desegregation of Central High School in Little Rock, Arkansas by nine exceptional young people who acted with courage and poise beyond their years. When we think about the struggles and events that have filled the time since their first day of high school, we can say truthfully that much has changed. Still, minority students remain underrepresented in our country's medical schools, and the Division of Diversity Policy and Programs at the Association of American Medical Schools (AAMC) remains committed to changing the face of medicine to reflect the face of the nation as a means of achieving quality health care for all.

One important new project begun since the last edition of *MSOUSMS* is Aspiring Docs.org, which you will see referred to throughout this book. AspiringDocs.org is a comprehensive marketing campaign to increase diversity in medicine by directing information and resources to the students who need it the most. The centerpiece of this campaign is an interactive Web site AspiringDocs.org that features the most up-to-date information on preparing for, applying to, and financing medical education. In addition to inspiring stories about medical students and physicians who have made it, the site allows users to "Ask the Experts" and discuss "Hot Topics" on timely issues related to medical school. For example, recent features have covered "Preparing for the MCAT" (January 2007) and "Preparing a Winning Medical School Application" (June 2007). In addition to the Web site, pilot programs at four universities, California State University, Fresno; Rutgers University; University of Arizona; and University of Pittsburgh are exploring the best ways to deliver the most useful information to minority students considering careers in medicine. We recommend you use *MSOUSMS* in combination with the resources featured on AspiringDocs.org.

Another AAMC initiative to enhance access for students from underrepresented groups is the Holistic Admissions and Enhancing Diversity Project. The project's purpose is to support medical schools in their efforts to create and sustain diversity at their institutions. Its focus is on the application and admissions processes and how these link to medical schools' missions and goals, as well as to related diversity-building programs, such as outreach, recruitment, financial aid, and retention. AAMC staff from the Division of Diversity Policy and Programs and the Division of Medical School Affairs —working with the recommendations of a constituent working group—are supporting an advisory committee of constituents and experts to develop tools and information about holistic admissions that medical schools can adopt or adapt to suit their institution-specific mission and goals, culture, and constraints.

Minority Student Opportunities in United States Medical Schools (MSOUSMS), itself, remains an important tool for increasing minority student representation in medicine. Produced by the Division of Diversity Policy and Programs, *MSOUSMS* contains information on each medical school, including school-specific data on minority student enrollments, applicants, acceptances, and graduates, as well as other useful medical school information. This information is crucial for assisting students, their families, and their advisors with decision-making about the possibilities for careers in medicine.

We wish you luck in your pursuit, and we welcome any suggestions or ideas that will make this publication more useful to you in the future.

Charles Terrell, Ed.D.
Vice President
Division of Diversity Policy and Programs
AAMC

Selected AAMC Web-Based Resources

AAMC Homepage
www.aamc.org

AAMC Diversity Web Site
http://www.aamc.org/diversity/

Academic Medicine
www.academicmedicine.org

AspiringDocs
www.AspiringDocs.org

Enrichment Programs on the Web
http://services.aamc.org/summerprograms

Facts & Figures Data Series
www.aamc.org/factsandfigures

Minorities in Medicine Web Site
www.aamc.org/students/minorities/start.htm

Summer Medical and Dental Education Program (SMDEP)
www.smdep.org

Student Portal (Information about the Medical School Process)
www.tomorrowsdoctors.org

U.S. Medical School Applicant, Matriculant, and Graduate Data
www.aamc.org/data/facts/start.htm

U.S. Medical School Faculty Data
www.aamc.org/data/facultyroster/reports.htm

Association of American Medical Colleges, 2007

AAMC
Tomorrow's Doctors, Tomorrow's Cures®

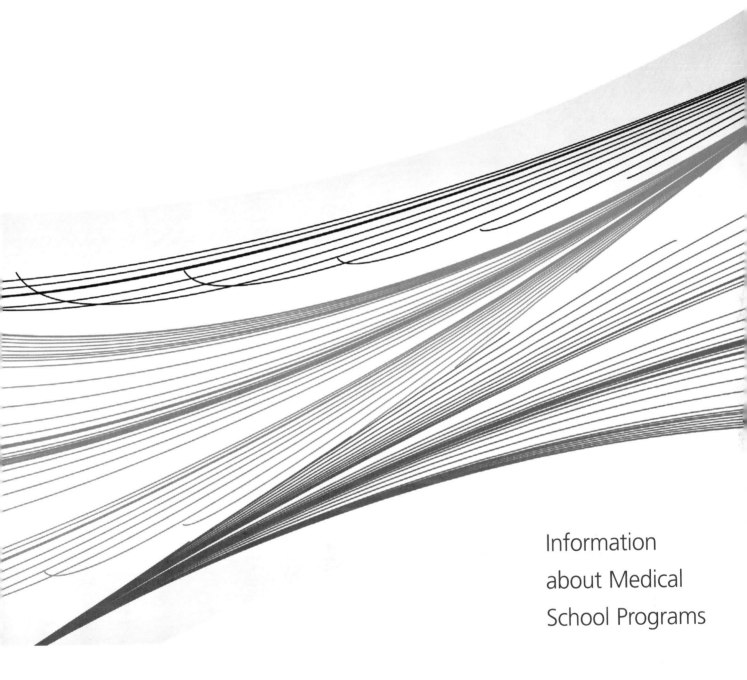

Information
about Medical
School Programs

Association of
American Medical Colleges

AAMC

University of Alabama School of Medicine

Dr. John W. Scott, Assistant Dean
for Minority Education,
University of Alabama
School of Medicine
Medical Student Services
1530 3rd Avenue S, VH P100
Birmingham, AL 35294-0019
205-934-7975, 800-707-3579
205-996-2575 Fax
jscott@uasom.meis.uab.edu

Recruitment

The University of Alabama School of Medicine (UASOM) has a fundamental commitment to the identification, recruitment, retention, and career advisement of minorities and students from disadvantaged populations. Staff of the Office of Medical Student Services and the Office of Minority Enhancement, a division of the Office of Medical Student Services, participate in high school and college recruitment activities throughout Alabama. Other recruitment activities include participation in local and national conferences such as the Minority Access to Research Careers/Minority Biomedical Research Support annual conference. Minority and disadvantaged students interested in the study of medicine are identified, provided literature, and offered counsel. A relationship with the identified students is maintained through their academic advisors. Visits to appropriate college campuses are made at least once each year by recruitment officers and, when possible, by minority medical students. Through these visits, information on the admissions process, curriculum, financial aid, and personal development programs is given to interested students. Individual conferences are arranged, especially with junior-level college students.

Admissions

Applications submitted by minorities and students from disadvantaged backgrounds are reviewed by members of the Admissions Committee. Particular emphasis is placed on students who are residents of Alabama, and all students so designated are offered on-campus interviews. Area interviews are offered, when possible, and are frequently coordinated with the college visitation program. Considerable effort is expended to make the interview process convenient for the student.

Academic Support Programs

Enrichment and academic aid programs designed to assist minorities and disadvantaged groups are offered on an as needed basis. The School of Medicine maintains a sophisticated and extensive educational development office that prepares, evaluates, and administers self-development instructional materials. Other study aids and tutorial assistance are also available to students. The tutorial sessions are available to all students upon request, and as the need is identified by the faculty. Considerable effort is made to identify minority tutors.

Student Financial Assistance

The university waives application fees for disadvantaged students upon verification of need. The Mineral District Medical Society (MDMS), a community-based association of practicing minority physicians, awards scholarships annually to minority medical students. In support of the University of Alabama School of Medicine's goals to increase the number of minorities that enter and graduate from the UASOM, the university has developed merit scholarships for incoming students.

Educational Partnerships

In an effort to facilitate minority access, a positive mentoring relationship has been developed between the UASOM and the MDMS.

University of Alabama School of Medicine, 2006
Applicants and Matriculants by Gender, Race and Ethnicity

Race and Ethnicity	Applicants			Matriculants		
	Women	Men	Total	Women	Men	Total
Hispanic/Latino						
Cuban	4	3	7	0	0	0
Mexican American	8	3	11	0	0	0
Puerto Rican	3	2	5	0	0	0
Other Hispanic	18	25	43	0	2	2
Multiple Hispanic*	1	1	2	0	0	0
Subtotal	34	34	68	0	2	2
Non-Hispanic/Latino**						
Black	178	75	253	9	5	14
Native American/Alaska Native	3	2	5	0	0	0
Native Hawaiian/Other Pacific Islander	2	0	2	1	0	1
White	502	699	1,201	44	85	129
Asian	111	152	263	9	17	26
Other Race	0	2	2	0	0	0
Multiple Race*	24	20	44	1	2	3
Unknown	3	4	7	0	0	0
Subtotal	823	954	1,777	64	109	173
Foreign	12	12	24	1	0	1
Total	869	1,000	1,869	65	111	176

*Since 2002, students can select more than one race and / or ethnicity. **Those who did not choose 'Hispanic/Latino' or 'Non-Hispanic/Latino' are counted under 'Non-Hispanic/Latino'.
Data Source: AAMC Data Warehouse: Applicant-Matriculant File, as of 5/9/2007.

Association of American Medical Colleges, 2007

These mentors serve as role models and student advisors to UASOM minority medical students.

Other Pertinent Information

In support of the institution's goals of increased minority participation at the UASOM, an Office of Minority Enhancement was developed to assist minority students in preparing to enter and graduate from the University of Alabama School of Medicine. As a component of the Office of Medical Student Services, the Office of Minority Enhancement can assist students in utilizing the full range of services available to medical students. Programs and activities include:

- counseling and support for academic and personal concerns;
- tutorial programs as needed;
- financial assistance;
- assistance with finding and securing research opportunities; and
- liaison activities among the UASOM, minority students, and medical organizations.

University of South Alabama College of Medicine

Dr. Hattie M. Myles
Assistant Dean—Student Affairs and Educational Enrichment
University of South Alabama
College of Medicine
307 University Blvd., 1005 MSB
Mobile, AL 36688-0002
251-460-7313; 251-460-6761 Fax
hmyles@usouthal.edu
http://www.southalabama.edu/com/specialcourses.shtml

Recruitment

Representatives from the Admissions Office and the Office of Student Affairs visit colleges in Alabama, and adjoining service areas in Mississippi and Florida, to provide pre-professional students with information on preparing for medical school. When possible, medical students participate in these recruitment visits. Disadvantaged underrepresented medical students are especially encouraged to visit the Historically Black Colleges and Universities to share their experiences in the College of Medicine with prospective minority applicants. Interested pre-medical students are interviewed, and their academic record, background, and financial resources are reviewed for further consideration for special programs and medical school preparation activities.

Admissions

All applicants are evaluated by the Admissions Committee of the College of Medicine. This committee is composed of faculty, members of the local community (medical and non-medical), and medical

University of South Alabama College of Medicine, 2006
Applicants and Matriculants by Gender, Race and Ethnicity

Race and Ethnicity	Applicants			Matriculants		
	Women	Men	Total	Women	Men	Total
Hispanic/Latino						
Cuban	3	4	7	1	0	1
Mexican American	7	1	8	0	0	0
Puerto Rican	2	4	6	0	0	0
Other Hispanic	10	9	19	1	1	2
Multiple Hispanic*	2	1	3	0	0	0
Subtotal	24	19	43	2	1	3
Non-Hispanic/Latino						
Black	79	26	105	7	2	9
Native American/Alaska Native	2	1	3	0	0	0
Native Hawaiian/Other Pacific Islander	1	0	1	0	0	0
White	266	396	662	24	29	53
Asian	49	88	137	2	6	8
Multiple Race*	12	13	25	0	1	1
Unknown	1	3	4	0	0	0
Subtotal	410	527	937	33	38	71
Foreign	19	19	38	0	0	0
Total	453	565	1,018	35	39	74

*Since 2002, students can select more than one race and / or ethnicity. **Those who did not choose 'Hispanic/Latino' or 'Non-Hispanic/Latino' are counted under 'Non-Hispanic/Latino'.
Data Source: AAMC Data Warehouse: Applicant-Matriculant File, as of 5/9/2007.

Association of American Medical Colleges, 2007

students. There are no special admissions procedures for any applicants. Selection is made on a competitive basis using academic qualifications, Medical College Admission Test (MCAT) scores, and personal qualities and abilities such as maturity, leadership, determination, and motivation for a career in medicine.

Academic Support Programs

Because of the relatively small size of the College of Medicine classes, academic assistance is readily available to all students. This assistance is provided both by other medical students and by faculty. Tutorials, academic and personal counseling, and other support can be obtained by the individual or coordinated through the Office of Student Affairs. Study skills information, including specialized preparation for board exams, are also available through this office.

Enrichment Programs

Biomedical Enrichment and Recruitment (BEAR) Program. The University of South Alabama College of Medicine offers this special summer program designed for disadvantaged underrepresented undergraduates who are first-time sophomores. It offers a direct process for conditional acceptance into the University of South Alabama College of Medicine. Summer students participate in MCAT preparation sessions and are introduced to the first year of medical school through a series of medical courses, lectures, seminars, and clinical experiences by medical school faculty and staff. They also receive information for applying to medical school and for financial aid.

The Office of the Dean Summer Research Program. A limited number of research positions are available for incoming first-year students and rising second-year students. The program provides students with the opportunity to work with clinical and basic science faculty on a variety of

research projects. These projects are presented in August at Student Research Day, and abstracts from these presentations are published in the *Alabama Journal of Medical Sciences.*

Student Financial Assistance

State scholarships and a variety of federal loan programs are available to qualified applicants. These programs are handled through the Office of Financial Aid of the College of Medicine. Each year, a limited number of tuition waiver scholarships are available to qualified disadvantaged underrepresented medical school matriculants.

Educational Partnerships

The relationship between the University of South Alabama College of Medicine and the historically black colleges of Alabama allows priority consideration to their students for participation in the summer programs and regards these schools as primary feeders for disadvantaged underrepresented students.

Association of American Medical Colleges, 2007

University of Arizona College of Medicine

Dr. Ana María López, Associate Dean
Ms. Linda K. Don, Director
Outreach and Multicultural Affairs
University of Arizona
College of Medicine
P.O. Box 245140
1501 North Campbell Avenue, Room 1119B
Tucson, AZ 85724-5140
520-621-5531; 800-841-5948
520-626-2895 Fax
www.diversity.medicine.arizona.edu

Jonathan P. Robles, Director, Phoenix Office
Outreach and Multicultural Affairs
550 East Van Buren Street
Phoenix, AZ 85004-2230
602-827-2027
602-827-2127 Fax

Note: The University of Arizona College of Medicine, beginning in 2007, has two campuses, in Tucson (total enrollment 440) and Phoenix (total enrollment 24).

Recruitment

The University of Arizona (UA) College of Medicine is strongly committed to the recruitment, admission, education, and graduation of an increased number of individuals from ethnic minority groups that are underrepresented in medicine. The school also has a strong interest in individuals who intend to practice in medically underserved areas of Arizona. Applications can only be accepted from Arizona residents, highly qualified applicants who are Western Interstate Commission on Higher Education (WICHE)-certified, and American Indians who live on reservations contiguous with the state of Arizona. A combined M.D./M.P.H. program, with opportunities to concentrate on health disparities issues, is offered through collaboration with the Mel and Enid Zuckerman College of Public Health. Information about this program can be obtained by contacting the College of Public Health directly. For more information, please visit the website, *(www.publichealth.arizona.edu)*.

Outreach and Multicultural Affairs (OMA) works closely with the Office of Admissions. Like the admissions office, OMA has two locations, one at each campus. OMA offers recruitment and pre-admissions activities such as mock interviews, workshops, and the Arizona Applicant Academy. Additionally, mock Medical College Admission Tests (MCATs) are offered in collaboration with OMA's statewide pre-health professions student organization, Fostering and Achieving Cultural Equity and Sensitivity (F.A.C.E.S.) in the Health Professions. F.A.C.E.S. encourages any student who is interested in diversity issues in health professions education to participate in its activities. There are F.A.C.E.S. chapters on various campuses in the state, offering opportunities to develop leadership skills, volunteer with health care projects that target underserved populations, and shadow community physicians.

Admissions

The University of Arizona College of Medicine accepts only Arizona residents; highly qualified WICHE applicants and Native Americans who reside on reservations contiguous with the state of Arizona. In evaluating applicants, the Admissions Committee considers many factors including the applicant's entire academic record, performance on the MCAT, personal statement, interviews, and letters of recommendation. Applicants are chosen on the basis of their career goals, motivation, academic ability, integrity, maturity, altruism, communication skills, and leadership abilities. Clinical, research, or community service experience is viewed favorably. The Admissions Committee strives to accept a student body with diverse backgrounds in order to best meet the medical needs of the people of Arizona. Priority consideration is given to applicants who demonstrate a

University of Arizona College of Medicine, 2006
Applicants and Matriculants by Gender, Race and Ethnicity

Race and Ethnicity	Applicants			Matriculants		
	Women	Men	Total	Women	Men	Total
Hispanic/Latino						
Cuban	2	0	2	0	0	0
Mexican American	28	24	52	9	5	14
Puerto Rican	1	1	2	0	0	0
Other Hispanic	10	13	23	2	1	3
Multiple Hispanic*	1	0	1	0	0	0
Subtotal	42	38	80	11	6	17
Non-Hispanic/Latino**						
Black	21	8	29	4	1	5
Native American/Alaska Native	10	4	14	1	1	2
Native Hawaiian/Other Pacific Islander	1	2	3	0	0	0
White	225	265	490	35	35	70
Asian	54	48	102	10	5	15
Other Race	0	1	1	0	0	0
Multiple Race*	11	9	20	0	1	1
Unknown	2	2	4	0	0	0
Subtotal	324	339	663	50	43	93
Foreign	3	2	5	0	0	0
Total	369	379	748	61	49	110

*Since 2002, students can select more than one race and / or ethnicity. **Those who did not choose
Hispanic/Latino' or 'Non-Hispanic/Latino' are counted under 'Non-Hispanic/Latino'.
Data Source: AAMC Data Warehouse: Applicant-Matriculant File, as of 5/9/2007.

willingness to practice in medically under-served areas of Arizona. No preference is given to any particular type of undergraduate major. Since many of the patients who receive care at the Arizona Health Sciences Center and its affiliated clinics and hospitals speak Spanish as their primary language, it would be useful for the University of Arizona medical students to be conversant in Spanish.

Academic Support Programs
The staff of the Office of Student Development offers extensive individual and small-group sessions that help students adjust their study skills for successful completion of the curriculum. Special attention is given to the transition into medical school in a week-long Medical Student Bridge Program for non-traditional students. Additionally, the Student Development staff provide support for preparation for all steps of the United States Medical Licensing Exam (USMLE), including a six-week, structured review for those students needing to repeat the USMLE Step 1.

Enrichment Programs
OMA operates summer programs for high school and college students. Med-Start, on the University of Arizona campus in Tucson, offers five weeks of educational enrichment activities for Arizona high school students to explore health professions career opportunities and experience the academic demands of college life. Maricopa Med-Start, in partnership with Arizona State University, provides a similar five-week program in Phoenix. Additional information can be found at *(www. medstart.arizona.edu)*.

Arizona Maximizing Medical Education Potential (AZ MMEP) is a six-week summer academic program for college pre-medical students. It is particularly helpful for students who are from ethnic groups that are underrepresented in medicine, first in their families to graduate from college,

economically/educationally disadvantaged, and/or from rural or reservation communities. AZ MMEP offers challenging educational activities designed to strengthen academic performance, prepare them for medical education, and increase understanding of and planning for the pathway to medical school. Clinical and cultural competency experiences are also included in AZ MMEP.

The College of Medicine has offered a post-baccalaureate program in past years. The program is currently being revised. It is anticipated that the program will resume operations in Fall 2008. Please continue to check the Admissions Office Web page for information as it becomes available, *(http://www.admissions.medicine.arizona.edu/)*.

Student Financial Assistance
The College of Medicine assesses each individual's financial need and attempts to meet it through a package tailored for that student. All applicants are sent financial aid information and request forms in January following receipt of their American Medical Application Service (AMCAS) form. The University of Arizona Financial Aid Office has assigned three staff members, located at the College of Medicine, to work exclusively with the medical students. This permits a high degree of personalized service for students as they seek financial assistance for their medical education. Students who are willing to repay their debt by practicing in a medically-underserved area in Arizona upon completion of residency may be eligible for the Arizona Medical Student Loan Program. The College of Medicine is also able to award scholarship support through the federal assistance program for disadvantaged students.

Educational Partnerships
OMA and other programs work together to provide a comprehensive academic and social support network for Arizona pre-medical and medical students. The College of Medicine is a charter member of the Hispanic-Serving Health Professions Schools, (HSHPS) Inc. and has been recognized nationally for its enrollment and support of Hispanic and American-Indian medical students. For example, *Hispanic Business Magazine* has recognized the College of Medicine for the past two years as one of the top-ten medical schools for Hispanics. The Arizona Hispanic Center of Excellence provides a resource network to support Hispanic pre-medical and medical students, as well as Hispanic faculty. The University of Arizona and Inter Tribal Council of Arizona Indians into Medicine (INMED) Program offer students academic advising and tutoring, health career forums, and talking circles, as well as funding to attend Association of American Indian Physicians (AAIP) conferences and workshops. INMED is directed by Dr. Yvette Roubideaux, a former AAIP president and nationally renowned authority on diabetes and American-Indian health.

University of Arkansas for Medical Sciences College of Medicine

Dr. Billy R. Thomas,
Associate Dean,
Center for Diversity Affairs
University of Arkansas
College of Medicine
4301 West Markham,
Slot 625 Little Rock,
AR 72205-7199
501-686-7299;
501-686-7439 Fax
www.uams.edu/com/edu

Recruitment

The Center for Diversity Affairs (CDA) assists in the early identification, recruitment, and retention of minority students for the University of Arkansas for Medical Sciences (UAMS) College of Medicine. The CDA conducts programs designed to identify, inform, motivate, and assist prospective candidates for medical school admission. These programs pay special attention to minority and disadvantaged students in the state.

Over the years, high school counselors and pre-medical advisory personnel at undergraduate institutions have worked with the CDA staff to inform academically gifted and academically disadvantaged students of opportunities offered at UAMS. This network of dedicated and committed individuals provides the College of Medicine with young and enthusiastic minority students from which to increase the applicant pool.

The Associate Dean, Directors, and Project Coordinator in the Center for Diversity Affairs are responsible for recruitment. In previous years, the CDA staff focused primarily on college and university students; however, over the last few years, the staff have developed a recruitment module for junior and senior high school students. The CDA staff members visit junior high schools, high schools, and colleges, throughout the state that have high concentrations of African-American and other underrepresented minority students. Resources for reaching these students include counselor recommendations, Health Career Occupation classes, science classes, National Merit semifinalists and finalists, school visitations, College Day Programs, Governor's School attendees, and tours of the University of Arkansas campus. These sources have provided an extensive and ever-expanding list of students for follow-up counseling. Lastly, in an effort to increase our applicant pool the recruitment efforts of the CDA have been expanded through the addition of a Director of Diversity and Recruitment for all five UAMS colleges.

Retention

The Minority Recruitment and Retention Committee, appointed by the Dean of the College of Medicine, consists of faculty members, students, and Center for Diversity Affairs staff. This committee reviews the recruitment and retention strategies of the Center for Diversity Affairs and the College of Medicine and offers recommendations to ensure diversity and fairness of treatment for minority applicants and students. Once a student has applied to the College of Medicine, every assistance is given to her/him in the processing of the necessary forms to complete the admissions process. Information concerning financial aid availability and procedures is covered in detail later. Members of this committee also serve as advisors to, and advocates for, minority students.

The Dean's Minority Advisory Committee is another committee appointed by the Dean of the College of Medicine, with the advice of the staff of the CDA and members of the Arkansas Medical, Dental, and Pharmaceutical Association (AMDPA)— an association composed of minority health care professionals in Arkansas. This committee meets four times each

University of Arkansas for Medical Sciences College of Medicine, 2006
Applicants and Matriculants by Gender, Race and Ethnicity

Race and Ethnicity		Applicants			Matriculants		
		Women	Men	Total	Women	Men	Total
Hispanic/Latino							
Cuban		3	5	8	0	0	0
Mexican American		7	6	13	1	0	1
Other Hispanic		8	10	18	1	0	1
Multiple Hispanic*		2	2	4	0	0	0
	Subtotal	20	23	43	2	0	2
Non-Hispanic/Latino**							
Black		49	18	67	3	1	4
Native American/Alaska Native		4	5	9	0	1	1
White		228	354	582	52	75	127
Asian		67	90	157	7	12	19
Other Race		0	2	2	0	0	0
Multiple Race*		11	19	30	1	1	2
Unknown		1	2	3	0	0	0
	Subtotal	360	490	850	63	90	153
Foreign		4	7	11	0	0	0
	Total	384	520	904	65	90	155

*Since 2002, students can select more than one race and / or ethnicity. **Those who did not choose Hispanic/Latino' or 'Non-Hispanic/Latino' are counted under 'Non-Hispanic/Latino'.
Data Source: AAMC Data Warehouse: Applicant-Matriculant File, as of 5/9/2007.

Association of American Medical Colleges, 2007

ear and has the responsibility of advising the dean on recruitment, retention, and problems that may be encountered by minority students. Members of this committee, and of AMDPA, serve as mentors for medical students and often provide them with counsel and financial assistance.

Admissions

The Admissions Committee is composed of 15 members appointed by the Board of Trustees of the University of Arkansas and selected from a list submitted by the Dean of the College of Medicine. The committee is subject to the approval of the Vice President of Health Sciences, the President of the University System, and the Board of Trustees. Six of the committee members are on the faculty of the College of Medicine; two members are appointed from each of the four Congressional Districts, as established by ACT 337 of 1971, and are apportioned on the basis of members from each district; and one member is appointed from the state-at-large. All members of the committee serve one-year terms and may be reappointed for not more than three consecutive terms. All medical school applicants are reviewed by this committee.

Academic Support Programs
The progress of each student is carefully monitored and, when additional help is needed, it is made available on an individual basis. Each department has review and tutorial sessions available for any student.

Counseling is available for all students by the Office of the Dean, Center for Diversity Affairs, the Office of the Associate Dean for Academic Affairs, and the Office of Educational Development. The latter is an instructional support agency at UAMS that works directly with students to help them to be successful in their educational experiences. The staff works with the students in areas such as enhancing learning strategies, improving test-taking skills, managing

time effectively, improving interpersonal skills, note-taking, and establishing efficient study habits.

Four different retention activities are offered to medical students:

- A four-week summer pre-matriculation program for incoming minority/disadvantaged students. Students are selected based on Medical College Admission Test (MCAT) scores, grade-point average (GPA), and other criteria for disadvantaged (rural background and socioeconomic conditions) status. Lectures in microanatomy, gross anatomy, biochemical and physiological aspects of cellular function, learning and test-taking skills, and other seminars are given;
- A five-week preparation/review program for at-risk sophomore students who are required to pass United States Medical Licensing Examination (USMLE) Step 1 before entering into the junior year of medical school. At-risk students are those whose basic science course grades are marginal and those who have relatively low MCAT scores and undergraduate GPA. This course is taught by faculty of the College of Medicine and basic science courses are reviewed;
- A five-week intense science review program for students who failed, for the first time, the USMLE Step 1 examination. Key features of this program are lectures and frequent testing of students; and
- A four-week clinical science review program for students who fail to pass the USMLE Step 2 examination. This program is taught by College of Medicine faculty and reviews all clerkships taken in the clinical years.

Enrichment Programs
Due to cuts in Title VII funding (e.g. Health Careers Opportunity Program) the number and length of academic enrichment programs supported by the CDA have been reduced.

Undergraduate Summer Science Enrichment Program (USSEP). This program, funded by the Health Careers Opportunity Program (HCOP) in the College of Medicine, is designed to acquaint college students with the rigors of the first-year medical school curriculum. The five-week program provides students with an opportunity to work with basic science and clinical faculty in encapsulated versions of the courses taken by freshman. Mock exams, labs, study skills, test-taking skills, and reading skills are integral parts of this program. Sophomore students focus mainly on academics; whereas with junior and senior students the major emphasis is on test-taking skills and MCAT review. Students are also given the opportunity to shadow minority practitioners at least five mornings each year during the program to gain firsthand knowledge of the medical practice. This year a total of 15-20 students will participate in the program.

Bridging the Gap Program (BTG). This is a junior high school outreach program that provides mechanisms for continually reaching 11th- and 12th-grade students. The objectives of this program are to increase and nurture minority tenth- and 11th-grade high school students' interest in pursuing careers in biomedical research and the health professions, to enhance the academic skills and preparation of students who will matriculate into colleges/universities, and to continue to familiarize students on the health careers opportunities at UAMS. Schools in Arkansas are visited throughout the academic year. In addition, 25 to 30 students are selected each summer to participate in a six-week on-campus program. Activities in the program are designed to enhance basic academic skills and the conduct of science projects. *Due to a loss of HCOP funding this program has been reduced to a three-week ACT/SAT Prep Program.*

Middle School Summer Camp for Disadvantaged Students. This program was originally supported through funds from the Arkansas Department of Higher Education. All funding is now provided by the College of Medicine. The purpose of this program is to familiarize or enhance minority students' knowledge of opportunities that exist at UAMS or careers in the health care professions health-related professions, nursing, pharmacy, and medicine. Last year the CDA staff visited 20 junior high schools, and they contacted and placed in the College of Medicine's database more than 5,000 students. Other major activities conducted for junior high school students (K7-9) include tours of the UAMS campus.

Summer Science Discovery Program (SSDP). In addition to programs targeting middle schools, high schools, and undergraduate schools, the CDA has been able to develop a program targeting K-sixth grade students, the Summer Science Discovery Program (SSDP). The program is concentrated during the summer and has a primary objective of exposing students to science and the possibility of a career in health care. A total of 200 students participate in the program each summer.

Student Financial Assistance
The medical school participates in the American Medical College Application Service and, under its fee waiver program, will waive the $10 UAMS application fee. Financial assistance is available to all students and is based on individual need. Need is determined in consideration of previous educational debts, parental resources, dependent siblings, and retirement status. In addition to the standard sources, there are other institutional funds administered on either an academic or need-based measurement.

Educational Partnerships
The College of Medicine has an educational partnership with three schools from the public school system in Little Rock, the Museum of Discovery, Greater Friendship Incorporated (a community-based organization), two local historically Black colleges, a local community college, and a majority undergraduate institution that is strategically located in the Northeast corner of the state. In addition, the College of Medicine, the AMDPA, and the Arkansas Mentoring and Networking Association (AMNA) have an educational partnership. The AMDPA is an association whose membership includes minority physicians and pharmacist. Members of the association serve as advisors to the Dean of the College of Medicine, and as mentors and external support persons for medical students. The AMNA is an association whose membership includes local community leaders, faculty members from local universities, and individuals from multiple health care specialties.

Contact: Dr. Billy Thomas, Associate Dean or Mr. Bill E. Bauknight, Director of the Center for Diversity Affairs, University of Arkansas, College of Medicine, 4301 West Markham, Slot 625, Little Rock, AR 72205. *(www.uams.edu/com/eda)*

AAMC

David Geffen School of Medicine at UCLA

Ms. Patricia Pratt, Director, Academic Enrichment and Outreach
David Geffen School
of Medicine at UCLA
10833 LeConte Ave, Suite 13-154CHS
Los Angeles, CA 90095-6990
310-825-3575; 310-206-7180 Fax
ppratt@mednet.ucla.edu
www.medstudent.ucla.edu/prospective

Recruitment

The David Geffen School of Medicine at UCLA is firmly committed to attracting and educating qualified disadvantaged students. The school's interest in promoting quality and equity in medical education has led to the development of a continuum of support extending from early pre-medical contact with disadvantaged students, to medical school admissions, through graduation, postgraduate medical education, minority faculty development, and alumni networking. Recruitment, support services, and retention are the primary elements that structure the scope of work of the Office of Academic Enrichment and Outreach (OAE&O).

In addition, OAE&O offers a six-week summer enrichment program UCLA PREP, a nationally recognized program that was established in 1982, and the UCLA ReApplicant Program, established in 2000 (see Enrichment Programs).

Faculty, administrators, and medical students are actively engaged in various aspects of the recruitment process. They participate in national, regional, and local conferences and programs for students in the medical education pipeline. David Geffen School of Medicine at UCLA encourages campus visits and can often arrange visits to acquaint prospective students and groups with current medical students and the School of Medicine's facilities. In compliance with the current California legislation prohibiting the consideration of race, ethnicity, or gender in the admissions of students, the David Geffen School of Medicine at UCLA has increased its efforts to maintain the excellent diversity within its student body. The OAE&O also provides technical support, conferences, and workshops designed to increase the number of underrepresented minorities in the national physician work force.

Admissions

The David Geffen School of Medicine at UCLA's Admissions Committee is composed of subcommittees, one of which is devoted to the consideration of applicants with disadvantaged backgrounds and/or who are from historically underserved communities. This subcommittee is primarily composed of faculty and medical students who have themselves overcome socioeconomic and/or educational disadvantages and who have experience in evaluating the non-cognitive aspects of these applications.

The subcommittee evaluates all applications on the basis of academic performance, Medical College Admission Test (MCAT) scores, letters of recommendation, and personal comments—as does the full Admissions Committee. In addition, the subcommittee carefully considers those factors that might have affected the applicant's past academic record or future achievement. Course requirements are the same for all applicants. Special consideration is given to each applicant's potential contribution to the university's goals and society's needs.

Academic Support Programs

The Office of Academic Enrichment & Outreach monitors individual student

David Geffen School of Medicine at UCLA, 2006
Applicants and Matriculants by Gender, Race and Ethnicity

Race and Ethnicity	Applicants			Matriculants		
	Women	Men	Total	Women	Men	Total
Hispanic/Latino						
Cuban	17	9	26	0	1	1
Mexican American	120	117	237	6	5	11
Puerto Rican	14	9	23	0	0	0
Other Hispanic	80	76	156	3	2	5
Multiple Hispanic*	11	13	24	0	0	0
Subtotal	242	224	466	9	8	17
Non-Hispanic/Latino**						
Black	111	78	189	4	4	8
Native American/Alaska Native	5	6	11	0	0	0
Native Hawaiian/Other Pacific Islander	13	10	23	0	0	0
White	977	1,220	2,197	19	32	51
Asian	835	895	1,730	22	20	42
Other Race	3	4	7	0	0	0
Multiple Race*	98	96	194	1	1	2
Unknown	19	32	51	0	1	1
Subtotal	2,061	2,341	4,402	46	58	104
Foreign	91	87	178	0	0	0
Total	2,394	2,652	5,046	55	66	121

*Since 2002, students can select more than one race and / or ethnicity. **Those who did not choose Hispanic/Latino' or 'Non-Hispanic/Latino' are counted under 'Non-Hispanic/Latino'.
Data Source: AAMC Data Warehouse: Applicant-Matriculant File, as of 5/9/2007.

performance in the medical curriculum in order to identify and address problems as early as possible. Services offered include confidential counseling; learning skills diagnosis; study skills consultation; a United States Medical Licensing Examination (USMLE) review course; tutoring, stress, and anxiety reduction strategies; and a summer pre-entry course.

Enrichment Programs
UCLA Prep, an intensive six-week summer program, provides pre-medical and pre-dental students from disadvantaged backgrounds with a means of strengthening their ability and readiness to study medicine and dentistry. Program participants are exposed to the rigors of academic medicine, with hands-on clinical preceptorships in clinical and research settings and are mentored by accomplished medical students.

UCLA ReApplicant Program (UCLA RAP) is a comprehensive program designed to assist promising students from disadvantaged backgrounds who have unsuccessful in gaining admission to any U.S. medical school. The 11-month program is conducted in two sessions that begin with an intensive six-week summer session focused on MCAT preparation. Distinguished guest lecturers provide workshops discussing academic skills, extensive science reviews, self development, time management, financial planning, medical school re-application, and interviewing skills. Each participant is given a study-skills diagnostic assessment to aid in developing a successful plan for academic achievement. An individualized academic-year program of a science coursework follows, and participants work in close consultation with program advisors to select courses through UCLA Extensions or a local California Sate University.

Prologue to Medicine. The optional summer pre-entry course, Prologue to Medicine, is conducted for a one-week period immediately preceding the first year of medical

school. Prologue has been designed to help students from non-traditional backgrounds and with a wide variety of learning styles to navigate UCLA's problem-based learning curriculum. The interdisciplinary approach and small-group study sessions lend themselves well to the introduction of the major basic sciences. The faculty consists of members of the basic science and clinical departments, enabling students not only to sample various styles, but more importantly, to know some of their professors before fall semester. Subject matter, per se, is secondary to the development of learning behavior that will enable students to cope with the new rigors of medical education. The pace, although slower at first, builds up to that which will be encountered when medical school actually begins in the fall. The aim is to make the experience as realistic as possible, permitting the students and faculty to anticipate possible trouble spots and work toward early solutions. Participation is open to accepted students from non-traditional and disadvantaged backgrounds.

Celebrations in Diversity. From the first day of class and throughout the four years of medical training, students participate in activities to promote appreciation and effective communication with many diverse cultures. Each year a multimedia theatrical presentation, "A Slice of Rice, Frijoles and Greens," serves as the foundation for the cultural competency components of the medical curriculum. "Standing on the Shoulders of Giants: A Survey of 5,000 years of Contributions by Blacks to Health, Healing and Medicine" is a permanent exhibit, which is displayed annually. Hispanic Heritage Month activities include a variety of events including a film festival, food sharing, and community health fairs. Similar activities are sponsored by student organizations including the annual city-wide "Minority Health Conference," sponsored by the Asian Pacific American Medical Student Association, the Latino Medical Student Association, and the Student National Medical Association.

Guest Lecture Series. Each year the School of Medicine hosts a guest lecture inviting a distinguished leader in medicine, who is from an underrepresented minority background, to address the student body and faculty.

Student Financial Assistance
The Admissions Committee makes an effort to seek out qualified applicants. If a supplemental application is requested, a processing fee of $40 is required. Fee waivers, based solely on economic need, are granted to approximately 3 percent of UCLA's applicants.

The School of Medicine provides assistance towards meeting the financial needs of admitted economically disadvantaged students from university funds that have been authorized to support students in the School of Medicine, as well as private scholarship and loan money from a variety of sources. The financial needs for living and medical school expenses, as evaluated from the scholarship-loan application forms, can be met in several ways. Students eligible for campus-based aid are generally offered a combination or package of various types of aid (loans, grants, and scholarships).

Educational Partnerships
Through the outreach programs conducted by the Office of Academic Enrichment and Outreach and in individual departments of the School of Medicine, UCLA has established educational partnerships that are designed to facilitate minority access to medical careers:

- "The Magic of Medicine" Undergraduate UCLA Course;
- UCLA PREP, Summer Pre-medical Enrichment Program;
- UCLA Re-Application Program (RAP);
- Educational Affiliation Agreements with targeted local feeder colleges, community colleges, high schools, and middle schools;
- Affiliation with Charles R. Drew University of Medicine and Science;

Association of American Medical Colleges, 2007

- Combined-degree programs with other UCLA professional schools; and
- Academic Advancement Program on the UCLA undergraduate campus.

UCLA RAP is a member of the California Postbac Consortium that includes all five of the University of California medical schools.

Keck School of Medicine of the University of Southern California

Ms. Althea Alexander
Assistant Dean, Office of Diversity
Keck School of Medicine of the University of Southern California
1333 San Pablo Street, MCH51C
Los Angeles, CA 90033-9152
323-442-1050; 323-442-3575 Fax
aalexand@usc.edu

Recruitment

Consistent with the premise that the choice of a career in the health professions requires early academic preparation and planning, the Keck School of Medicine of the University of Southern California's recruitment effort is multifaceted and multi-leveled. Throughout the *Med-Cor Program*, which is concerned with identifying interested and talented high school and college students, an intensive program is conducted. The program consists of weekly science enrichment sessions throughout the school year and is directed by Dr. John Davis. During the summer months, students work in health-related jobs in the Los Angeles County (LAC) and University of Southern California Medical Center. At the undergraduate level, an active recruitment program is conducted through regular visits to local colleges and universities, as well as liaison with pre-medical advisors and student organizations.

Admissions

The Committee on Admissions considers all qualified applicants. Each applicant is assessed on the basis of his/her potential

Keck School of Medicine of the University of Southern California, 2006
Applicants and Matriculants by Gender, Race and Ethnicity

Race and Ethnicity	Applicants			Matriculants		
	Women	Men	Total	Women	Men	Total
Hispanic/Latino						
Cuban	19	9	28	1	0	1
Mexican American	120	122	242	3	9	12
Puerto Rican	14	16	30	0	0	0
Other Hispanic	79	82	161	2	4	6
Multiple Hispanic*	18	10	28	1	0	1
Subtotal	250	239	489	7	13	20
Non-Hispanic/Latino**						
Black	169	105	274	3	5	8
Native American/Alaska Native	7	9	16	0	1	1
Native Hawaiian/Other Pacific Islander	18	14	32	0	0	0
White	1,269	1,606	2,875	44	46	90
Asian	1,023	1,003	2,026	19	13	32
Other Race	3	6	9	0	0	0
Multiple Race*	117	103	220	5	1	6
Unknown	29	40	69	1	0	1
Subtotal	2,635	2,886	5,521	72	66	138
Foreign	144	154	298	2	2	4
Total	3,029	3,279	6,308	81	81	162

*Since 2002, students can select more than one race and / or ethnicity. **Those who did not choose Hispanic/Latino' or 'Non-Hispanic/Latino' are counted under 'Non-Hispanic/Latino'.
Data Source: AAMC Data Warehouse: Applicant-Matriculant File, as of 5/9/2007.

as a physician. The Assistant Dean of the Office of Diversity is a member of the Admission and Screening Committee. All qualifying minority students are interviewed at the Keck School of Medicine of the University of Southern California. Great care is taken to ensure that qualified students from disadvantaged backgrounds are accepted. There are 18 members of the admissions committee and student representatives from second, third, and fourth year also sit on the committee. The Assistant Dean of the Office of Diversity is a permanent member of the Admissions Committee.

Academic Support Programs

Throughout the academic year, tutoring services are provided for all students. Complete advisement and retention activities are offered to all medical school matriculants.

Enrichment Programs

Summer Program. In the summer, the Keck School of Medicine offers a three-week Bridge Program for incoming freshman students that will give them an overview of the curriculum and introduce them to gross anatomy.

Student Financial Assistance

The dean has provided 11 four-year scholarships and limited monies are available for tuition through privately endowed scholarships. Students have access to several low-interest loan funds. The dean has also committed a significant amount of money to be set aside for minority students' scholarships.

Educational Partnerships

The School of Medicine has partnerships with many universities, colleges, and high schools throughout Southern California to encourage and support interest in the health professions. They include tutorial programs with local high schools (Bravo Medical Magnet, Stevenson, and Bell Gardens) and campus tours coordinated

with pre-medical organizations: Minority Association of Pre-Health Students (MAPS) at nearby undergraduate institutions (California State University at Long Beach and San Bernadino, Fresno and also at University of Nevada at Las Vegas). Two student organizations, Latino Medical Student Association and Student National Medical Association, conduct health fairs at the local high schools; hold monthly meetings at two elementary schools, one in the Black community and one in the Latino community; and sponsor annual pre-medical conferences. The medical school visits with the following high schools to promote interest in health professions: Manual Arts, Loyola, Sacred Heart, and Dorsey.

AAMC

Loma Linda University School of Medicine*

Dr. Daisy D. DeLeón
Assistant to the Dean for Diversity
Loma Linda University
School of Medicine
Dean's Office, Coleman Pavilion
Loma Linda, CA 92350
909-558-2757; 909-558-0475 Fax
ddelwon@som.llu.edu

Recruitment

The recruitment of disadvantaged students to the Loma Linda University School of Medicine is part of a commitment that extends throughout the school system sponsored by the Seventh Day Adventist Church. High school students are encouraged to pursue careers in science, and undergraduate college students are encouraged to pursue careers in medical and paramedical fields. A high school summer research program provides funds for minority students to spend time in research labs and thus gain valuable exposure to the medical field. The School of Medicine also sponsors a week-long summer Health Careers Workshop (*Careers in Medicine*) for college and/or senior high school students to acquaint them with medicine and other health careers. Minority students are brought on campus for a week to meet physicians, medical students and other medical staff; attend lectures; and tour laboratories and medical facilities, such as the operating room, in an effort to better acquaint them with the opportunities medicine has to offer. Travel grants and tuition waivers for those wishing to participate in the program but without the financial resources to do so are available for a limited number of interested students.

Admissions

Minority applicants are reviewed by the entire Admissions Committee and the Admissions Office staff. The committee includes student representation and minority faculty, as well as the School of Medicine's Director of Diversity and the Loma Linda University President's Assistant for Diversity. Assessment of all applicants is based on the overall academic record, pattern of academic performance, motivation, extracurricular activities, ability to relate to people, emotional stability, and life styles that are in accordance with the standards and policies of the school.

Academic Support Programs

All students matriculating at the Loma Linda University School of Medicine have access to tutoring, study-skills help, and other academic aid services. These services are provided by a qualified professional counseling center, selected faculty, graduate students and, quite often, by interested and competent students such as those in the Early Selection Program. There is also available a Teaching Learning Center (TLC) that helps students improve their reading, study and learning skills. Students can attend the TLC after admission but prior to starting classes or they can choose to attend once enrolled at the school. In addition, the School of Medicine holds a study-skills workshop, SILVER, that teaches advanced, graduate-level study-skills techniques. These resources provide support to the student who is identified as needing such assistance at the time of admission to the medical school, those students interested in improving their performance, and those students who may experience academic difficulty.

Student Financial Assistance

Application fees may be waived for disadvantaged students when requested in writing. Travel expenses for interviews can be minimized as members of the School of

Loma Linda University School of Medicine, 2006
Applicants and Matriculants by Gender, Race and Ethnicity

Race and Ethnicity	Applicants			Matriculants		
	Women	Men	Total	Women	Men	Total
Hispanic/Latino						
Cuban	13	8	21	0	0	0
Mexican American	77	70	147	4	2	6
Puerto Rican	16	11	27	0	1	1
Other Hispanic	59	52	111	8	7	15
Multiple Hispanic*	10	8	18	1	2	3
Subtotal	175	149	324	13	12	25
Non-Hispanic/Latino**						
Black	115	90	205	3	1	4
Native American/Alaska Native	5	5	10	1	0	1
Native Hawaiian/Other Pacific Islander	12	9	21	0	0	0
White	660	957	1,617	32	54	86
Asian	561	544	1,105	18	22	40
Other Race	3	5	8	0	0	0
Multiple Race*	53	57	110	2	2	4
Unknown	11	18	29	0	4	4
Subtotal	1,420	1,685	3,105	56	83	139
Foreign	100	108	208	4	8	12
Total	1,695	1,942	3,637	73	103	176

*Since 2002, students can select more than one race and / or ethnicity. **Those who did not choose Hispanic/Latino' or 'Non-Hispanic/Latino' are counted under 'Non-Hispanic/Latino'.

Data Source: AAMC Data Warehouse: Applicant-Matriculant File, as of 5/9/2007.

Medicine Admissions Committee regularly travel to college sites throughout the nation.

Financial support is available to students on the basis of scholarship (academic performance) and demonstrated need. A variety of funds are available for disadvantaged and minority students. A special fund for disadvantaged students can provide a four-year, partial tuition scholarship. In addition, for students who qualify for the Medical Scientist Training Program (M.D.–Ph.D.), a full scholarship with stipend is available for the duration of the student's graduate and medical education at Loma Linda University School of Medicine.

Educational Partnerships

Early Acceptance Program. The School of Medicine has established partnership programs with colleges in Alabama, California, Massachusetts, Michigan, and Puerto Rico. The program identifies sophomore students at partnership colleges who have an interest in medicine and have exhibited an academic performance that makes them good potential candidates for medical school. Once selected into the program, students participate in a summer research program, and one semester of graduate science school classes at Loma Linda University. Students who meet pre-determined performance criteria can qualify for early decision acceptance to the Loma Linda University School of Medicine. Students accepted through this program receive the benefits of the enrichment components of the program, as well as a financial package commensurate with their scholarship and financial need. The School of Medicine also benefits as these students can function as tutors and Problem-Based Learning Course Facilitators for all School of Medicine students.

Stanford University School of Medicine

Dr. Ronald Garcia
Assistant Dean for Minority Affairs
Stanford University School of Medicine
Center of Excellence
251 Campus Drive, MSOB x361 Stanford, CA 94305-5404
650-725-0354; 650-725-7855 fax
Ron.garcia@stanford.edu
http://coe.stanford.edu

Recruitment

The Stanford University School of Medicine sends recruiters—faculty and students—to visit a number of summer programs in which minority pre-medical students are enrolled. In addition, the medical school participates in career day programs throughout the country. The Center of Excellence, the Office of Admissions, and Stanford University Minority Medical Student Alliance co-sponsor a pre-medical students conference, "SUMMA," in early February.

Yearly, specially prepared brochures describing the medical school program are sent to a large number of minority students on the Medical Minority Applicant Registry list. The medical school students are encouraged to inform minority students at their own undergraduate colleges about the program.

Admissions

Stanford is committed to being a premier research-intensive medical school that improves health through leadership, collaborative discoveries, and innovation in patient care, education, and research. We will identify, accept, and recruit the future leaders of medicine. In particular, we seek individuals whose leadership will result in

Stanford University School of Medicine, 2006
Applicants and Matriculants by Gender, Race and Ethnicity

Race and Ethnicity	Applicants			Matriculants		
	Women	Men	Total	Women	Men	Total
Hispanic/Latino						
Cuban	17	13	30	0	0	0
Mexican American	102	102	204	2	1	3
Puerto Rican	13	22	35	0	0	0
Other Hispanic	86	84	170	2	4	6
Multiple Hispanic*	9	8	17	1	0	1
Subtotal	227	229	456	5	5	10
Non-Hispanic/Latino**						
Black	149	106	255	3	1	4
Native American/Alaska Native	8	9	17	0	0	0
Native Hawaiian/Other Pacific Islander	11	5	16	0	0	0
White	1,269	1,708	2,977	20	19	39
Asian	789	907	1,696	16	7	23
Other Race	2	5	7	0	0	0
Multiple Race*	98	110	208	3	2	5
Unknown	24	39	63	0	0	0
Subtotal	2,350	2,889	5,239	42	29	71
Foreign	131	160	291	1	4	5
Total	2,708	3,278	5,986	48	38	86

*Since 2002, students can select more than one race and / or ethnicity. **Those who did not choose Hispanic/Latino' or 'Non-Hispanic/Latino' are counted under 'Non-Hispanic/Latino'.
Data Source: AAMC Data Warehouse: Applicant-Matriculant File, as of 5/9/2007.

AAMC

significant advances in the ability to care for patients. Whether through careers in basic biomedical research, in clinical research, in health policy research, or in community and/or international service based on original scholarship, Stanford's medical students will contribute uniquely and importantly.

We are committed to ensuring that each graduate has fully explored his/ her potential as a student and as a scholar. Key goals of the curriculum are the melding of 21st century laboratory and medical sciences, and helping each student build in-depth expertise in an area of personal, scholarly interest. While traditional courses and clerkships are required for graduation, the duration of study leading to the M.D. degree may vary from four to six years. All M.D. candidates must satisfactorily complete at least 13 quarters of academic work. Fees for additional quarters are nominal. Courses are graded pass/fail.

Scholarly concentrations provide medical students with independent, creative scholarly experiences in areas of personal interest. This required component of the curriculum develops critical thinking, skills in evaluation of new data, and hands-on experiences with the methods by which new scholarly information is generated.

Stanford does not discriminate on the basis of race, religion, national origin, sex, marital status, age, or disability. The applicant's state of residence is irrelevant in the selection process. Applicants whose Medical College Admission Test (MCAT) scores are below the national mean are highly unlikely to be admitted to the medical school.

For more details, please see *Medical School Admissions Requirements,* published by the AAMC.

Academic Support Programs

Stanford has a formal, required curriculum that includes two years of basic pre-clinical training followed by two years of clinical experience. However, the curricular plan gives students the option of extending their period of study to five or more years. This arrangement allows students to enrich their training with research or other types of experience and, in addition, offers them the possibility of adjusting their academic load according to their individual needs and capacities.

If academic difficulties arise, tutorial assistance is available to help students improve their performance. Instruction is also available on the general problems of time management and study skills. Peer study groups are also an important source of help to minority students.

Center of Excellence in Cultural Diversity.
The Center of Excellence (COE) promotes diversity in the medical school's student body, residency, fellowship programs, and faculty. The program also seeks to increase research and information on health problems impacting minority populations and to integrate this information into the medical school's curriculum.

The Center of Excellence sponsors numerous activities, including minority student recruitment and retention projects, the Early Matriculation Program, United States Medical Licensing Examination Review Course, and minority health grand rounds. Community health pre-clinical and clinical electives are offered in local minority communities.

In addition, the COE sponsors student and faculty research on topics related to minority health issues and health care disparities. A faculty development program is offered to increase the recruitment and retention of minority faculty. The COE sponsors a breadth of educational activities that promote cultural competence.

Summer Premedical Student Program (SPSP)
The SPSP is a six-week in-residence program at Stanford designed to increase diversity in the medical school applicant pool. The program combines course work in anatomy, cell biology, and research with a variety of workshops, which demystify the medical school admission process. Stanford faculty, staff, and students create a very supportive environment and offer many opportunities for mentorship and interactions with role models. (Note: *This program was formerly known as the Summer HCOP program.*)

Community College Outreach
This program is designed to reach out to students attending community colleges. It provides an opportunity for students at community colleges to learn about how to prepare for medical school and other health professions. Staff visit community colleges, conduct admission workshops, and provide individual and group advising sessions. In addition, guidance is offered in developing leadership activities and establishing premedical student health profession clubs.

Cultural Competence

Stanford adopted cultural competence as an educational objective in 2001: "To promote cultural competency in the science and practice of medicine." This has resulted in a variety of activities related to cultural competence in the curriculum beginning with a presentation during orientation, "Faces of the Community," which introduces students to the diversity of the student community. Throughout the curriculum, presentations, workshops, and courses are offered that examine the role of culture in the context of medical care. Cultural competence is an area that continues to expand each year.

Enrichment Programs
Early Matriculation Summer Program.
In 1984, Stanford University School of Medicine started an early matriculation

summer program designed for disadvantaged students who have been accepted and will attend Stanford. The summer program includes pre-clinical course work and opportunities to engage in research activities with faculty members. Further information may be obtained by contacting the Center of Excellence: *(http://coe.stanford.edu).*

Student Financial Assistance

Available grant and loan funds are awarded to students on the basis of demonstrated need. For federal aid, students are considered independent. For university-based aid, students are considered dependent up until the age of 30, and the school will consider the student's parents' ability to contribute to the cost of financing the student's education in determining eligibility for loans and grants. Foreign students must complete a certification of finances reflecting an escrow account of funds to cover the cost of education for the M.D. degree.

Other Pertinent Information

The Stanford University School of Medicine provides an environment where the individual is judged on intellectual and academic merits. Training is rigorous and every student is expected to develop a sound basis of professional competence. However, Stanford does not wish to mold its students into a specific kind of professional person; instead the aim is to help students achieve and sharpen their own unique professional capabilities and to develop an inquiring and critical approach to medicine in tune with their individual interests. Because of the school's commitment to seeing increased representation of minorities on medical school faculties in the future, special efforts are made to increase students' awareness of the opportunities open to them in careers in academic medicine.

The Admissions Committee recruits outstanding minority applicants with a potential for leadership in medicine and makes every effort to identify those with promise for an eventual academic career.

Stanford University School of Medicine is situated on the campus of the university, and it is possible for medical students to take academic work in other schools on campus concurrently with their medical studies.

It is hoped that students will make use of this opportunity, together with the flexibility of the medical school curricular schedule, to develop other academic interests relevant to their long-term goals in medicine.

Stanford is world-renowned for the quality of its clinical care. It receives referral cases on a worldwide basis. It offers medical students excellent opportunities for clinical training through clerkships, not only at the Stanford University Hospital but also at the Santa Clara Valley Medical Center, a county hospital; the Palo Alto Veterans Administration Medical Center; the Packard Childrens' Hospital; and the Kaiser Permanente Hospital, an HMO hospital. Overall, these facilities provide nearly 2,100 teaching hospital beds. Students also have the opportunity to take clerkships in other approved institutions either in the United States or abroad. They may also gain experience of primary care at community clinics, including the Drew Clinic and the Alviso Clinic, which mainly serve Black and Chicano populations. These clinical experiences have allowed Stanford minority students to enter some of the most prestigious residency training programs in the United States.

Association of American Medical Colleges, 2007

AAMC

UCLA/Drew Medical Education Program

Dr. Daphne Calmes
Dean for Student Affairs
Charles R. Drew University
of Medicine and Science
173 East 120th Street
Los Angeles, CA 90059
323-563-4957 Fax
www.cdrewu.edu

Recruitment

Recruitment for the Drew/UCLA Medical Education Program is done through a range of campus visits, participation in SMDEP programs, career fairs, professional conferences and associations, and with the support of undergraduate, graduate and medical student organizations; particularly those that are historically underrepresented in medicine and that work with medically underserved communities. Faculty, state alumni and medical students participate in the recruitment activities for the medical education program.

Admissions

The Drew/UCLA Medical Education Program admits individuals who are committed to its mission of service to underrepresented and underserved communities. The Admissions Committee seeks intelligent, mature, and highly motivated candidates who show promise of becoming leaders and innovators in the medical field. The committee carefully considers personal qualities, including integrity, professionalism, personal stability, and potential to succeed. Other factors, including academic record, Medical College Admission Test (MCAT) scores, record of activities and accomplishments, community service, recommendations from pre-medical communities and science teachers, as well as the ability to overcome personal obstacles are also reviewed by the Admissions Committee. The personal interview is also an integral part of the process.

The Drew/UCLA Medical Education Program is committed to ensuring diversity through adequate representation of women and minority groups. All applicants are given consideration without regard to sex, race, age, religion, national origin, sexual orientation, or financial status. To be considered for admission, applicants must demonstrate excellence and successful completion of all pre-medical requirements.

Application Process

Applicants who seek admission to the Drew/UCLA Medical Education Program are required to apply through the American Medical College Application Service (AMCAS). An application and fee information may be obtained by writing to the Association of American Medical Colleges, 2450 N Street, NW, Washington, DC 20037-1127. Information can also be found on the association's Web site at (www.aamc.org/amcas). For questions about the process, contact AMCAS directly at 202-828-0600.

Academic Support Programs

The Office of Medical Student Affairs is committed to ensuring all medical students have the necessary needed to successfully complete medical school. Students who encounter academic difficulties are referred to various faculty who have expertise and extensive experience. Learning skills specialists are available to test, assess, counsel, and work with students who may encounter academic difficulties. Tutoring and other retention interventions are available through the office of Academic Enrichment and Outreach the David Geffen School of Medicine at UCLA.

Students' career directions are congruent with the mission and goals of the school.

UCLA/Drew Medical Education Program, 2006
Applicants and Matriculants by Gender, Race and Ethnicity

Race and Ethnicity	Applicants			Matriculants		
	Women	Men	Total	Women	Men	Total
Hispanic/Latino						
Cuban	8	1	9	0	0	0
Mexican American	80	60	140	3	3	6
Puerto Rican	6	1	7	0	0	0
Other Hispanic	49	38	87	1	1	2
Multiple Hispanic*	6	7	13	0	0	0
Subtotal	149	107	256	4	4	8
Non-Hispanic/Latino**						
Black	135	96	231	3	2	5
Native American/Alaska Native	1	2	3	0	0	0
Native Hawaiian/Other Pacific Islander	10	8	18	0	0	0
White	268	282	550	2	1	3
Asian	284	258	542	1	3	4
Other Race	1	3	4	1	0	1
Multiple Race*	32	29	61	1	2	3
Unknown	8	10	18	0	0	0
Subtotal	739	688	1,427	8	8	16
Foreign	29	27	56	0	0	0
Total	917	822	1,739	12	12	24

*Since 2002, students can select more than one race and / or ethnicity. **Those who did not choose Hispanic/Latino' or 'Non-Hispanic/Latino' are counted under 'Non-Hispanic/Latino'.
Data Source: AAMC Data Warehouse: Applicant-Matriculant File, as of 5/9/2007.

Academic advising and career exploration are fostered through many mechanisms including preceptorships, special interests groups, and faculty mentors. The Drew/UCLA Medical Education Program is bolstered by its association with several of UCLA's professional schools. Students interested in obtaining a Masters in Business Administration or Public Health are encouraged to apply. The flexibility in the program allows students to conduct research at any accredited university across the country or participate in international health, social service, and community service.

Enrichment Programs

MCAT Preparation Program. The Drew/UCLA Center of Excellence Program offers two eight-week workshop series in preparation for the April and August administration of the MCAT. Both series are free of charge and conducted at Charles R. Drew University of Medicine and Science. The workshop series is not a content review course. *As such, preference for admission is given to those students who have completed their pre-medical course requirements.*

The workshops focus on test taking, study skills, and problem solving taught against the backdrop of the material included in two practice examinations (published by the Association of American Medical Colleges) taken in each series. The materials offered in the two series will complement each other and workshop participants will work extensively in small groups on the practice exams.

Medical students and past participants act as tutors and mentors for the workshop participants who are drawn from local schools including the California State Universities, University of California schools, and various independent colleges and universities.

Interested workshop candidates must submit an electronic application online through the following Web site, *(http://www.cdrewu.edu/com2002/departments/coe/mcat_prep.htm).*

PRIME. PRIME is a required pre-entry program for students admitted to the Drew/UCLA Medical Education Program. The program is organized and facilitated with the assistance of the second- year medical students and introduces students to the first weeks of the medical curriculum. Additionally, activities are planned for the incoming class to interact in social settings and learn about the community served by Drew University. Students will attend clinically relevant lectures on genetics, cell signaling, membrane potentials, hematology, inflammation, immunology, oncology, and histology. Past topics covered in PRIME include biochemistry, gross anatomy, orientation to primary care (visiting clinics and community facilities), physiology, stress reduction, and study skills.

Student Financial Assistance

Federal grants and scholarships from the university and private donors are used to meet a portion of a students needs. Most scholarships are based on academic achievements and financial need.

In addition, students are encouraged to apply for competitive private scholarships and research grants. Over the past several years, Drew/UCLA medical students have been awarded grants from the National Institutes of Health, Howard Hughes Medical Institute, and other prestigious agencies.

Financial aid for the Drew/UCLA medicine Education Program is coordinated through the David Geffen School of Medicine at UCLA. Skilled financial counselors meet with students to offer guidance and support.

University of California, Davis, School of Medicine

Dr. Mark Henderson
Associate Dean, Admissions & Outreach
Office of Medical Education
University of California, Davis
School of Medicine
4610 X Street, Suite 1202
Sacramento, CA 95817
916-734-4800; 916-734-4050
medadmsino@ucdavis.edu

Recruitment

The School of Medicine at the University of California (UC), Davis remains committed to providing opportunities in medical education for students from educationally and socioeconomically disadvantaged backgrounds.

Recruitment and undergraduate student development efforts include high school outreach activities, recruitment at targeted community colleges and universities, a Medical College Admission Test (MCAT) preparation program, and various pre-medical applicant training through conferences and workshops. A year-long postbaccalaureate program is also offered for applicants to medical school.

Faculty, staff, community-based physicians, medical school students, and residents are all involved in the school's recruitment efforts. This involvement ranges from visiting undergraduate campuses for pre-medical advising to offering mentor relationships, academic support, and clinical exposure.

Admissions

The School of Medicine selects students for admission with a view to meeting the needs of the medical profession, the school, and society at large. Because we live in a pluralistic society, it is felt that medical training and practice is enhanced by the interaction of students from various backgrounds. The school has become a leader in attracting and maintaining such diversity in its student body. This is reflected in the school's continuing commitment to expanding opportunities in medical education for individuals from groups traditionally underserved in medicine and to increasing the number of physicians practicing in medically underserved areas.

With a founding mission that emphasizes community service, UC Davis School of Medicine recently launched a new program to help increase health care access for underserved populations living in rural areas.

Called "Rural-PRIME," this unique program is designed to train the best and the brightest students for a fulfilling career in rural primary care medicine. It is an opportunity that offers a range of experiences, from public health and community service to the use of leading-edge medical technologies like telemedicine.

Rural-PRIME is a combined, five-year M.D. and master's degree program. It focuses on developing physicians who can become leaders and advocates for improving health care delivery throughout the state's smaller, more isolated communities.

The Admissions Committee is composed of individuals from a variety of backgrounds and abilities, and represents a broad spectrum of medical disciplines. The committee evaluates applicants on the basis of the following factors: academic accomplishment; experience in the health care field; research experience; and such personal traits as character, motivation, capacity for work, career objectives, and the motivation of the individual to make a positive contribution to society, the profession, the discipline, and the school.

University of California, Davis, School of Medicine, 2006
Applicants and Matriculants by Gender, Race and Ethnicity

Race and Ethnicity	Applicants			Matriculants		
	Women	Men	Total	Women	Men	Total
Hispanic/Latino						
Cuban	9	3	12	0	0	0
Mexican American	108	100	208	1	2	3
Puerto Rican	12	10	22	0	0	0
Other Hispanic	83	60	143	1	1	2
Multiple Hispanic*	10	8	18	0	0	0
Subtotal	222	181	403	2	3	5
Non-Hispanic/Latino**						
Black	93	56	149	2	0	2
Native American/Alaska Native	6	4	10	0	0	0
Native Hawaiian/Other Pacific Islander	17	9	26	0	0	0
White	850	981	1,831	27	21	48
Asian	767	777	1,544	19	9	28
Other Race	4	6	10	0	0	0
Multiple Race*	91	69	160	8	1	9
Unknown	22	28	50	0	1	1
Subtotal	1,850	1,930	3,780	56	32	88
Foreign	63	67	130	0	0	0
Total	2,135	2,178	4,313	58	35	93

*Since 2002, students can select more than one race and / or ethnicity. **Those who did not choose Hispanic/Latino' or 'Non-Hispanic/Latino' are counted under 'Non-Hispanic/Latino'.
Data Source: AAMC Data Warehouse: Applicant-Matriculant File, as of 5/9/2007.

The faculty has set specific academic requirements and policies to govern the evaluation of candidates for admission. The Admissions Committee seeks those applicants who have demonstrated academic potential for a lifetime of self-directed study. It also seeks those individuals who are cognizant of the physician's role and its demands, have demonstrated ability in effective interpersonal relations, have leadership potential, and who show promise of serving the needs of our evolving society. As our society increases in diversity, it is felt that physicians should reflect a similarly diverse spectrum. The school, through its Admissions Committee, actively seeks out individuals from a wide variety of backgrounds and interests who can share experiences and knowledge of representative population groups.

The University of California, in compliance with Titles VI and VII of the Civil Rights Act of 1964, Title IX of the Education Amendments of 1972 (45 CFR 86), and Sections 503 and 504 of the Rehabilitation Act of 1973, does not discriminate on the basis of race, color, national origin, religion, sex, or handicap in any of its policies, procedures, or practices; nor does the university, in compliance with the Age Discrimination in Employment Act of 1967 and Section 402 of the Vietnam Era Veterans Readjustment Act of 1974, discriminate against any employees or applicants for employment on the basis of their age or because they are disabled veterans or veterans of the Vietnam era. This nondiscrimination policy covers admission, access, and treatment in university programs and activities, and application for university employment.

Academic Support Programs

UC, Davis offers a wide variety of support services to all of its students. Because of the relatively small class size of approximately 105 students, close and frequently collegial relationships between faculty and students are possible. In addition, each student has a faculty advisor who serves as a source of guidance and support. Students at UC Davis also have the option to extend the first two years of the curriculum to three years, in order to make use of the additional time to individualize their educational program.

In addition to these offerings, the Office of Medical Education provides an array of supplemental academic support services to its medical students.

Academic tutoring is available to all students upon request. Tutoring is offered by peers who excel in the subject, particularly in the first two years of the curriculum. Faculty members also provide tutorial assistance.

Academic assistance is offered to aid in such areas as test taking, time management, and study skills for those students wishing such instruction. A preclinical retention program is also available for medical students to assist them in making the transition from the preclinical to clinical years. This is an academic, year-round program for students who are in their first two years of medical school, and is conducted at one of five student-run, community-based clinics in Sacramento. These clinics, Clinica Tepati, Paul Hom Asian Clinic, Shifa Clinic, Joan Viteri Memorial Clinic, and the Imani Clinic, operate under the auspices of the UC, Davis Department of Family Practice and Division of Medicine.

To prepare second-year students for the United States Medical Licensing Examination (USMLE) Step 1, various review activities are offered including small-group tutorials, intensive test-taking skills sessions, content review sessions, and self-study guidance. In addition, the Office of Medical Education Opportunity Programs offers supplemental support for students experiencing difficulty with academic coursework and USMLE.

Enrichment Programs

Summer Pre-Entry Program (SPEP). The school offers a special pre-matriculation program for all interested incoming disadvantaged students. Anatomy, Physiology, Biochemistry, and Introduction to the Physical Examination are taught by UC, Davis faculty. Financial assistance my be available to cover students' living expenses over the duration of the program. The SPEP Program is voluntary; however, students are strongly urged to attend.

Post-Baccalaureate Program. Beginning in the summer and extending through the spring quarter, this program is designed to assist educationally and socioeconomically disadvantaged applicants gain admission to medical school through a variety of structured offerings ranging from an intensive summer MCAT prep program to upper division science course work during the school year.

Student Financial Assistance

The School of Medicine will waive the application fee for disadvantaged students who qualify under the American Medical College Application Service (AMCAS) fee waiver guidelines. If a waiver is not granted by AMCAS, a waiver request may be completed for this institution separately along with a letter from the Financial Aid Office of the undergraduate college and/or graduate school confirming the student's financial situation. Upon receipt of the application and letter, the fee waiver is generally granted.

Although no financial help is available to offset the cost of interview trips, an attempt is made to arrange for overnight accommodations with current medical students, as needed.

Financial aid programs are administered through the School of Medicine Financial Aid Office and are primarily provided on the basis of need. In addition to a variety

AAMC

of federal, state, and private programs, the School of Medicine offers two types of grants/scholarships. Regents Scholars are selected on the basis of academic excellence and involve a stipend of $7,500 renewable for all four years. Chancellor Grants are awarded to academically promising students from disadvantaged backgrounds and include a scholarship of up to $7,500 per year, renewable for four years. In addition, Smith Scholars are awarded to students with proven academic excellence and have proven achievement in the areas of research, leadership, community service, athletics, and the arts of public service. These scholarships are awarded up to $7,500 for four years.

University of California, Irvine, School of Medicine

Dr. Ellena Peterson, Associate Dean
Gayle Pierce, Director, Admissions
University of California
Irvine School of Medicine
Berk Hall
P.O. Box 4089
Irvine, CA 92697-4089
949-24-388, 800-824-5388;
949-824-2485 Fax

Recruitment

The University of California, Irvine (UCI) School of Medicine has demonstrated a strong commitment to identify and recruit applicants from socio-economically disadvantaged backgrounds. Outreach efforts are designed to incorporate a variety of educational institutions, including high schools, community colleges, and universities within California. In addition, presentations and information are provided at career fairs, pre-medical club meetings, health professions conferences, and other appropriate recruitment venues.

The Office of Admissions and Outreach participates in local, state, and national conferences to discuss the school's efforts to attract and retain our diverse student population. Also, each fall in partnership with the UCI School of Medicine student organizations, a pre-medical conference is held that includes seminars, panel discussions, and interactive workshops aimed at informing potential applicants on the admissions process. Topics include the American Medical College Application Service (AMCAS) application, MCAT preparedness, interview skills, post-baccalaureate programs, and personal essays. In addition upon request,

University of California, Irvine, School of Medicine, 2006
Applicants and Matriculants by Gender, Race and Ethnicity

Race and Ethnicity	Applicants			Matriculants		
	Women	Men	Total	Women	Men	Total
Hispanic/Latino						
Cuban	9	6	15	0	0	0
Mexican American	109	106	215	5	5	10
Puerto Rican	9	10	19	0	0	0
Other Hispanic	76	57	133	1	0	1
Multiple Hispanic*	10	7	17	0	0	0
Subtotal	213	186	399	6	5	11
Non-Hispanic/Latino**						
Black	74	54	128	1	0	1
Native American/Alaska Native	2	3	5	1	0	1
Native Hawaiian/Other Pacific Islander	16	11	27	0	0	0
White	743	888	1,631	18	27	45
Asian	769	749	1,518	20	16	36
Other Race	3	7	10	0	0	0
Multiple Race*	84	82	166	2	5	7
Unknown	21	26	47	2	1	3
Subtotal	1,712	1,820	3,532	44	49	93
Foreign	33	29	62	0	0	0
Total	1,958	2,035	3,993	50	54	104

*Since 2002, students can select more than one race and / or ethnicity. **Those who did not choose Hispanic/Latino' or 'Non-Hispanic/Latino' are counted under 'Non-Hispanic/Latino'.
Data Source: AAMC Data Warehouse: Applicant-Matriculant File, as of 5/9/2007.

admission counselors visit campuses that otherwise may not have access to pre-medical conferences and resources.

Admissions

The Admissions Committee is composed of faculty, medical students, and community representatives. This committee reviews all applications for admission. Approximately one third of the applicant pool is invited to submit a secondary application. Applicants granted interviews are chosen by the Admissions Committee from those submitting a secondary application. The factors emphasized in the selection of applicants for admissions from those interviewed are academic strength, clinical and/or research experiences, community commitment, motivation, interpersonal skills, and leadership.

Program in Medical Education for the Latino Community (PRIME-LC). PRIME-LC is a five-year M.D./M.P.H. or M.D./M.B.A. program in which 12 students per class are invited to participate. The primary goal of the program is to develop leaders that will serve the underserved Latino community in California. Students receive immersion courses in Spanish, Latin-American culture, geography, and history. Throughout their medical training they work with Spanish-speaking patients and in areas with a predominance of underserved Latino patients. PRIME-LC students host a number of community service events as part of their training.

Academic Support Programs
Academic Monitoring Program
This ongoing program, beginning with enrollment, is coordinated by the Office of Educational Affairs to assist students in achieving academic success in their course work and to ensure the availability and utilization of all resources. Advisors are assigned to all students to provide academic advisement. Students are invited to participate in the Clinical Mentorship Program

beginning with year one. A Peer Tutoring Program is available to all medical students to provide tutorial assistance in the basic and clinical sciences. Tutoring services are provided by second- and third-year medical students. A Learning Skills Specialist, who aids with study skills training, as well as a Clinical Psychologist are available to provide additional support services to students. A United States Medical Licensing Examination Review Course is also offered on campus.

Enrichment Programs
Post-baccalaureate Program. The UCI School of Medicine Post-baccalaureate Program is composed of students that have not yet applied to medical school, reapplicants, and those chosen by the Admissions Committee to be granted a conditional acceptance. The purpose of this program is to give individuals from underserved communities and/or disadvantaged backgrounds the opportunity to become a successful medical school applicant. It is also a goal of these programs to eventually increase the number of underrepresented and disadvantaged students who, upon completion of their M.D. degree, will practice in medically underserved areas of California.

The post-baccalaureate program is composed of two phases. In Phase I, students are given a battery of diagnostic tests and participate in an intense six-week summer Medical College Admissions Test (MCAT) Review Course. In Phase II, students are placed in upper division courses chosen after taking into consideration the individual's academic need. Since the programs are tailored to strengthen the student's deficiencies, the curricula vary. The UCI School of Medicine has had over 20 years of experience with this and other educational initiatives that are exemplary models of outreach and enrichment programs. In particular, the UCI School of Medicine Post-baccalaureate Program has an 85

percent success rate in the placement of participants who complete the program and are accepted into medical and/or osteopathic schools.

Student Financial Assistance
Financial assistance is available to all students based primarily on financial need. The School of Medicine participates in all publicly recognized financial aid programs. The aid programs consist of scholarships, grants, and loans. Currently, 80 percent of the students receive aid of some type. In addition, the School of Medicine has a limited amount of scholarships from private and discretionary funds for disadvantaged students and funds that may be used for emergency situations.

Other Pertinent Information
The Office of Educational Affairs provides proactive programmatic experiences for medical students at different points during the process of medical education in order to enrich students' personal and professional development. Examples of programs include: workshops on stress management, interpersonal relations, and career development; professional and peer counseling; and student/faculty colloquia. A variety of speaker series and support for students through professional organizations have been benchmarks for a positive medical school educational experience.

University of California, San Diego, School of Medicine

Dr. Sandra Daley, Assistant
Dean of Diversity &
Community Partnerships
University of California San Diego
School of Medicine
9500 Gilman Drive, MC 0927
La Jolla, CA 92093-0927
619-681-0675; 619-681-0666 Fax
somdiversity@ucsd.edu
http://meded.ucsd.edu/diversity/index.html
http://meded.ucsd.edu/HCOE
http://som.ucsd.edu

Recruitment

Recruitment is conducted by University of California, San Diego, (UCSD) School of Medicine's medical students, faculty, and administrators who are representatives themselves of disadvantaged backgrounds. Conferences, seminars, and workshops are held on campus to inform and encourage students, counselors, and pre-medical advisors of current opportunities in medicine and health-related fields. Speakers visit schools with high disadvantaged student populations and high interest in health-related careers. On campus, the Office of Community Outreach of the medical school serves as a focal point for information pertinent to the health sciences, in general, and the UCSD School of Medicine, in particular.

Admissions

The Recruitment and Admissions Committee (RAC) screens applications, selects applicants to invite for an interview, and interviews selected applicants. Within the RAC, there is an Executive Committee whose membership consists of faculty from disadvantaged and other backgrounds and medical students with voting privileges. The Executive Committee has the consideration of applicants with disadvantaged and/or special backgrounds as one of its functions. This committee makes recommendations on students to the Admissions Committee which, in turn, makes admissions decisions on all students.

Academic Support Programs

After matriculation to UCSD School of Medicine, ongoing tutorial services are available, and the use of these services is encouraged. Tutorial services, in various basic science areas, are performed by professionals who are intimately familiar with the lecture material. Special student guides and study programs have been developed by the tutorial services. Similar programs, services, and assistance are available in preparation for the United States Medical Licensing Examination Step 1. These services are individualized to meet specific needs. The students also have access to learning skills experts who can analyze and treat learning problems.

Enrichment Programs

The primary goal of the UCSD School of Medicine's (UCSD SOM) academic enrichment programs is to train a new generation of health care providers who are prepared to address issues confronting populations at risk for health disparities. These programs include:

The Community Outreach Partnership Center (Grades seven-12). This program sparks an interest in scientific research in young students from disadvantaged backgrounds through advanced instruction and involvement in scientific research, COPC students have a 100 percent high school graduation rate.

UniversityLink Medical Sciences Program (Community College Grades 13-14) improves community college transfer, retention, and graduation rates for students from disadvantaged background interested in health sciences through a

University of California, San Diego, School of Medicine, 2006
Applicants and Matriculants by Gender, Race and Ethnicity

Race and Ethnicity	Applicants			Matriculants		
	Women	Men	Total	Women	Men	Total
Hispanic/Latino						
Cuban	17	9	26	0	0	0
Mexican American	111	126	237	6	4	10
Puerto Rican	15	17	32	0	0	0
Other Hispanic	87	90	177	0	3	3
Multiple Hispanic*	11	9	20	1	0	1
Subtotal	241	251	492	7	7	14
Non-Hispanic/Latino**						
Black	92	64	156	0	0	0
Native American/Alaska Native	8	7	15	0	0	0
Native Hawaiian/Other Pacific Islander	15	10	25	0	0	0
White	1,115	1,384	2,499	24	32	56
Asian	837	872	1,709	28	17	45
Other Race	4	6	10	0	0	0
Multiple Race*	109	111	220	0	4	4
Unknown	23	33	56	0	3	3
Subtotal	2,203	2,487	4,690	52	56	108
Foreign	32	24	56	0	0	0
Total	2,476	2,762	5,238	59	63	122

*Since 2002, students can select more than one race and / or ethnicity. **Those who did not choose
Hispanic/Latino' or 'Non-Hispanic/Latino' are counted under 'Non-Hispanic/Latino'.
Data Source: AAMC Data Warehouse: Applicant-Matriculant File, as of 5/9/2007.

Association of American Medical Colleges, 2007

summer residential and year-long academic skill building and mentoring program. Ninety three percent of program participants transfer to university compared to the 66 percent national transfer rate.

The Research Training Lab (Grades 11-16) trains students from disadvantaged backgrounds in basic and advanced biological laboratory techniques and places them with mentors in research environments.

The First-Time Applicant and Re-applicant Post Baccalaureate Program assists highly motivated students to acquire the academic skills needed to succeed in medical school, prepare for the MCAT, complete a competitive application to a health professions school and prepare for the admission interview. Students in the post-baccalaureate program are two times more likely to gain admission to a medical school than students who did not participate in the program.

The Conditional Acceptance Program is the only program of its kind in a medical school in California. Students must be selected by the Admissions Committee of the UCSD School of Medicine to participate in this program. They are enrolled in a one-year post-baccalaureate program and are guaranteed admission into the School of Medicine if they maintain a GPA of 3.5 in designated courses. All the students (20) who have participated in this program have entered medical school.

The Pre-matriculation, Cognitive Strategies, and United States Medical Licensing Examination (USMLE) Review programs provide quality instruction in study skills, time management, standardized test-taking, reading speed, and comprehension for students in medical, pharmacy, and graduate schools as well as students in undergraduate academic enrichment and post-baccalaureate programs.

Student Financial Assistance
Financial aid is awarded to students

on the basis of demonstrated need. Intensive efforts are made to provide ample support for individuals from groups traditionally underrepresented in medicine. A Support Scholarship has been instituted, with the support of the financial aid officer, as an incentive to recruit students from disadvantaged backgrounds who show great promise. This is being provided as a stimulus in securing an early decision from applicants to matriculate into UCSD School of Medicine and not to hold multiple acceptances. These students will have the highest priority for funding throughout their stay at UCSD School of Medicine.

Educational Partnerships
The goal of UCSD's educational partnerships is to significantly increase the number of qualified educationally, socially, and/or economically disadvantaged students from urban and rural areas that enter the region's health care work force. The objectives include: developing a competitive applicant pool; recruiting talented students for participation in academic enrichment and research training programs; and providing career awareness and exposure to community-based primary health care services. UCSD SOM has established partnerships with:

• The San Diego State University Pre-College Institute (PCI) and School of Public Health
• The San Diego Border Area Health Education Center (SD/AHEC)
• Nine Community Colleges in San Diego and Los Angeles County
• The Health Careers Opportunity Program, San Diego Regional Consortium
• 14 "feeder" middle and high schools
• UCSD Moores Cancer Center
• San Diego County Health and Human Services Department of Public Health
• San Diego Police Department Multicultural Relations Office

University of California, San Francisco, School of Medicine

Dr. David Wofsy
Associate Dean for Admissions
University of California, San Francisco
521 Parnassus, Room C-200, Box 0408
San Francisco, CA 94143-0408
415-476-4044
admissions@medsch.ucsf.edu
www.medschool.ucsf.edu/admissions

Dr. Alma M. Martínez
Director of Outreach and
Academia Advancement
http://www.medschool.ucsf.edu/outreach

Recruitment

The School of Medicine has a long-standing commitment to increasing the number of underrepresented racial/ethnic groups (African American, Mexican American, Native American, Hispanic, and mainland Puerto Rican) enrolled at the University of California, San Francisco (UCSF). As a result, UCSF has had, over the last 30 years, one of the highest minority enrollments of continental U.S. medical schools.

The Office of Outreach & Academic Advancement at UCSF directs the outreach efforts for the School of Medicine. Outreach is targeted toward undergraduate and postgraduate individuals who have an interest in pursuing careers in the health sciences. Faculty, staff, and students of the School of Medicine participate in a number of formal and informal recruitment activities throughout the year. They serve as speakers and resource persons at pre-medical conferences, summer programs, and scientific symposia. The school works with various student organizations to assist underrepresented applicants who are interviewed at UCSF. The Office of Outreach and Academic Advancement directs the UCSF Post-Baccalaureate Program for individuals from disadvantaged backgrounds. This office also offers a yearly Admissions Workshop for interested pre-medical students and pre-medical advisors to provide information regarding applications to medical school. The office also directs a Mentoring Program for UIM (underrepresented in medicine) medical students during the academic year. Additional information for these activities can be found at (*http://www.medschool.ucsf.edu/outreach*).

Admissions

All applicants are evaluated by members of the Admissions Committee. Selection is based on an appraisal of both intellectual and personal characteristics, which the Admissions Committee regards as desirable for prospective medical students and physicians. Each application is reviewed individually. Screening, based on the information provided in the American Medical College Application Service application, occurs shortly after its receipt. Academic performance is evaluated in relation to background, with the aim of determining the influence of external factors on this parameter; therefore, non-traditional applicants are encouraged to apply. Applicants granted further consideration are requested to provide letters of recommendation, which play a significant role in the selection process. Completed files are evaluated and a limited number of applicants are selected for interview. Personal interviews are required of applicants who pass the second screening. It is to an applicant's advantage to be interviewed at UCSF, and limited funds are available to assist disadvantaged minority applicants with travel expenses. If this is not possible, interview reports from other medical schools are acceptable. Non-residents, as well as California residents, are encouraged to apply.

University of California San Francisco, School of Medicine, 2006
Applicants and Matriculants by Gender, Race and Ethnicity

Race and Ethnicity	Applicants			Matriculants		
	Women	Men	Total	Women	Men	Total
Hispanic/Latino						
Cuban	14	12	26	1	1	2
Mexican American	119	119	238	6	9	15
Puerto Rican	14	20	34	1	0	1
Other Hispanic	94	75	169	2	1	3
Multiple Hispanic*	10	10	20	0	1	1
Subtotal	251	236	487	10	12	22
Non-Hispanic/Latino**						
Black	126	68	194	5	4	9
Native American/Alaska Native	7	10	17	0	1	1
Native Hawaiian/Other Pacific Islander	16	7	23	1	1	2
White	1,274	1,458	2,732	36	25	61
Asian	832	873	1,705	16	22	38
Other Race	2	6	8	0	0	0
Multiple Race*	110	102	212	5	1	6
Unknown	25	40	65	2	0	2
Subtotal	2,392	2,564	4,956	65	54	119
Foreign	70	78	148	0	0	0
Total	2,713	2,878	5,591	75	66	141

*Since 2002, students can select more than one race and / or ethnicity. **Those who did not choose Hispanic/Latino' or 'Non-Hispanic/Latino' are counted under 'Non-Hispanic/Latino'.
Data Source: AAMC Data Warehouse: Applicant-Matriculant File, as of 5/9/2007.

Association of American Medical Colleges, 2007

Successful applicants tend to have solid academic records; firm and clear motivation for medicine that is manifested in their work experience, activities, or interests; and outstanding personal qualities.

Academic Support Programs
Upon enrollment, medical students are assigned to one of four Advisory Colleges. The colleges, led by faculty mentors, serve as communities for student well-being and personal and professional advising. The colleges help students through all transitions of medical school, and mentors connect students with additional resources and opportunities. Additional information may be found at *(http://www.medschool. ucsf.edu/professional_development).*

Individual tutors are provided, as necessary, during any quarter. Instruction in study skills is offered to those students who need and wish such instruction.

UCSF Medical Scholars Program (MSP). The Office of Outreach directs the Underrepresented in Medicine Mentorship Program. The program provides medical students with the opportunity to meet physicians from diverse fields of medicine in both academic and community settings. Participating physicians includes academic and research UCSF faculty, community physicians, as well as residents and fellows throughout the School of Medicine. The mentors provide academic and personal support as well as career planning advice to medical students.

Information about other programs at UCSF is available by contacting the programs directly.

Summer programs at UCSF:

Science & Health Education Partnership University of California, San Francisco 100 Medical Center Way Woods Bldg, Upper Level San Francisco, CA 94143-0905 Telephone: 415-476-0300 Fax: 415-502-4846

Daly Ralston Resource Center: 415-514-0585 *(http://biochemistry.ucsf.edu/~sep/ interns.html)*

UCSF Department of Pediatrics High School Summer Internship Program in Biomedical and Health Sciences *(http://www.pediatrics.medschool.ucsf.edu/ youth/training/intern.aspx)* Paid internships. Check Web for deadline dates.

Student Financial Assistance
The School of Medicine awards a number of special scholarships, based on academic achievement. General financial support is available through the Financial Aid Office. Aid packages consist of a combination of loans, grants-in-aid, and scholarships. Financial Aid Information may be found at *(http://saawww.ucsf.edu/financial).*

AAMC

University of Colorado School of Medicine

Maureen J. Garrity, Ph.D.
Associate Dean Student Affairs
Steven Lowenstein, MD, MPH
Associate Dean Faculty Affairs
4200 East Ninth Avenue, Box C292
Denver, CO 80262
303-315-7678;303-315-1778 FAX

Recruitment
The School of Medicine at the University of Colorado at Denver and Health Sciences Center has a standing committee on Diversity. There is also an Office of Diversity serving the School of Medicine, School of Dentistry, School of Nursing, and School of Pharmacy as well as other programs at the Health Sciences Center. The School of Medicine's standing committee consists of faculty and students committed to recruitment, retention, and support of a diverse faculty and student body. The Office of Diversity has three basic objectives: to discover, motivate, develop, and sustain the interest of postsecondary minority and disadvantaged students in a health sciences career track; to increase the numbers of qualified minority students admitted to the health sciences programs; and to support the schools in providing optimal conditions for these students to successfully complete their training.

Admissions
The Admissions Committee for the School of Medicine is composed of approximately 80 basic science, and clinical faculty members and community practitioners. The faculty members have a variety of educational, cultural, and professional backgrounds. The committee is chaired by the Associate Dean of Admissions, School of Medicine. One hundred fifty six students are admitted to UCDHSC's School of Medicine each year. There is a strong commitment to admit and graduate ethnic minority and disadvantaged students.

Both cognitive and non-cognitive factors are considered in the admissions process. Specifically, criteria such as overall grade-point average (GPA), science GPA, senior year GPA, Medical College Admission Test scores, ethnicity, medically related work experience, and two personal interviews are quantified and integrated into an overall evaluation of each applicant. There is flexibility in the process in that the students with the highest scores, both minority and non-minority alike, are not necessarily the individuals who ultimately matriculate into UCDHSC's School of Medicine.

Student Support Programs
The Office of Student Affairs assists students with personal, academic, and financial concerns and makes referrals to appropriate campus and community services. This Office has access to many resources for assisting students who have academic difficulties, including tutoring. The services provided are available to all medical students; however special focus is given to minority and disadvantaged students. Students also have access to staff in the Office of Diversity for assistance.

Student Financial Assistance
Financial aid generally consists of a combination of long-term, low-interest loans, grants and, in some cases, part-time employment. All financial aid is awarded on the basis of financial need. Financial need is defined as the difference between the cost of attendance as defined by the institution (tuition and fees, books and supplies, room and board, transportation, and essential incidental expenses) and total resources available to the student. All applicants for aid must be admitted to a professional program or be degree candidates and registered as full-time students to be eligible for financial aid.

University of Colorado School of Medicine, 2006
Applicants and Matriculants by Gender, Race and Ethnicity

Race and Ethnicity	Applicants			Matriculants		
	Women	Men	Total	Women	Men	Total
Hispanic/Latino						
Cuban	9	7	16	0	0	0
Mexican American	53	31	84	5	2	7
Puerto Rican	5	3	8	0	0	0
Other Hispanic	29	35	64	0	1	1
Multiple Hispanic*	5	4	9	0	1	1
Subtotal	101	80	181	5	4	9
Non-Hispanic/Latino**						
Black	45	21	66	2	1	3
Native American/Alaska Native	9	8	17	0	0	0
Native Hawaiian/Other Pacific Islander	7	2	9	0	0	0
White	870	1,107	1,977	54	68	122
Asian	173	203	376	7	4	11
Other Race	3	1	4	0	0	0
Multiple Race*	43	39	82	8	1	9
Unknown	7	12	19	0	0	0
Subtotal	1,157	1,393	2,550	71	74	145
Foreign	22	25	47	1	0	1
Total	1,280	1,498	2,778	77	78	155

*Since 2002, students can select more than one race and / or ethnicity. **Those who did not choose
Hispanic/Latino' or 'Non-Hispanic/Latino' are counted under 'Non-Hispanic/Latino'.
Data Source: AAMC Data Warehouse: Applicant-Matriculant File, as of 5/9/2007.

Association of American Medical Colleges, 2007

Financial aid applications can be obtained in the Office of Financial Aid. Applications are not available to students who have not been officially accepted to a program at the Health Sciences Center. The deadline for submitting applications for financial aid is April 1 preceding the academic year for which assistance is desired or 30 days after the date of the letter of acceptance for entering students. Late applications will be accepted and considered after those received by the deadlines. For inquiries and requests contact: Office of Financial Aid, University of Colorado Health Sciences Center, 4200 East 9th Avenue, Box A-088, Denver, CO 80262 or call 303-315-8364.

Educational Partnerships

The Office of Diversity works to develop K-12 linkages to the Health Sciences Center programs. The School of Medicine has developed two new scholarships designed to recruit students. The Florence Sabin Scholarship for Commitment to Community Health honors the famous Colorado public health pioneer Florence Sabin and is for a student who has shown a commitment to community health and who has plans related to community health as a physician. The Justina Ford Scholarship for Commitment to the Underserved honors the first African-American woman physician in Colorado and is for a student who has demonstrated commitment to the underserved and who has future plans relating to care of the underserved.

University of Connecticut School of Medicine

Dr. Marja M. Hurley
Associate Dean and Director
Department of Health Career
Opportunity Programs
University of Connecticut
School of Medicine
Farmington, CT 06030-3920
860-679-3483;860-679-1875 Fax
http://medicine.uchc.edu/
departments/hcop

Recruitment

The University of Connecticut School of Medicine recruits a diverse group of applicants nationally through the Department of Health Career Opportunity Programs (HCOP). Visits to area colleges and to Historically Black Colleges and

Universities, attendance at recruitment programs, use of community resources, and summer enrichment programs are some of the methods used to interest qualified applicants to the School of Medicine's programs. The Student National Medical Association and other students enrolled at the School of Medicine are actively encouraged to participate in the recruitment program.

Admissions

Applications from candidates for admissions receive a thorough and sensitive review and are selected on a competitive basis. Minority candidates invited for an interview meet with the staff of the Department of Health Career Opportunity Programs and with minority medical students who answer questions in an informal setting. The Department of Health Career

University of Connecticut School of Medicine, 2006
Applicants and Matriculants by Gender, Race and Ethnicity

Race and Ethnicity	Applicants			Matriculants		
	Women	Men	Total	Women	Men	Total
Hispanic/Latino						
Cuban	5	5	10	0	0	0
Mexican American	17	8	25	0	0	0
Puerto Rican	11	9	20	0	1	1
Other Hispanic	43	32	75	1	2	3
Multiple Hispanic*	4	8	12	1	1	2
Subtotal	80	62	142	2	4	6
Non-Hispanic/Latino**						
Black	136	74	210	7	2	9
Native American/Alaska Native	2	5	7	0	0	0
Native Hawaiian/Other Pacific Islander	3	1	4	0	0	0
White	696	756	1,452	32	20	52
Asian	310	253	563	4	3	7
Other Race	5	2	7	0	0	0
Multiple Race*	40	36	76	2	2	4
Unknown	11	17	28	1	0	1
Subtotal	1,203	1,144	2,347	46	27	73
Foreign	105	105	210	0	1	1
Total	1,388	1,311	2,699	48	32	80

*Since 2002, students can select more than one race and / or ethnicity. **Those who did not choose Hispanic/Latino' or 'Non-Hispanic/Latino' are counted under 'Non-Hispanic/Latino'.
Data Source: AAMC Data Warehouse: Applicant-Matriculant File, as of 5/9/2007.

Opportunity Programs is represented on the Admissions Committee.

Academic Support Programs

Academic support is available on an individual basis through the Associate Dean and Director of the Department of Health Career Opportunity Programs. Academic advising and counseling are provided. The "HCOP Newsline," a monthly publication of the department, publishes intramural and extramural academic opportunities available to medical students. A time management, test-taking skills course is provided on an individual basis and is available for all incoming freshman students.

Student Financial Assistance

The application fee may be waived. The financial aid program available to all students has in the past been able to meet approximately 85-90 percent of estimated financial needs. Financial aid packages typically consist of scholarships, tuition remissions, and loans.

Educational Partnerships

The University of Connecticut Health Center, in collaboration with the Hartford School District, Central Connecticut State University, University of Connecticut at Storrs, and Wesleyan University, has designed a comprehensive program of educational enrichment and support activities for disadvantaged students from Connecticut. Its goal is to increase the number of these students applying to professional and graduate programs in medicine, dental medicine, biomedical research, allied health, nursing, and pharmacy. Implementation of the program is through the formal educational consortium consisting of the University of Connecticut Health Center and the universities and school district.

Health Careers Discovery Program. The Health Careers Discovery Program is a six-week summer science camp for 11th- and 12th-grade disadvantaged high school students. The program provides a holistic view of mathematics and science with the goal of encouraging students to pursue the more challenging courses offered subsequent to participation in the summer camp. Scheduled activities throughout the day include science labs, mathematics, computer science, language arts, and guidance/counseling.

Bulkeley and Weaver High School Health Professions Centers of Excellence. The Center of Excellence operates as a school-within-a-school, clustering students with a common interest in health professions in classes each day and taught by a team of the same teachers from year to year. The Center of Excellence is a magnet program that also takes students from outside the district through the Choice Program. The advantages offered by the center over regular programs include programs geared to the interests and abilities of individual students; development of an integrated curriculum focusing on health careers; dedicated teachers working as a team to meet student needs; enhanced learning activities that will allow students to relate what they learn to health careers; extensive opportunities for job shadowing, internships, field trips, and work experience in health care; and the opportunity to earn college credits while in high school.

Jumpstart Program. The Jumpstart Program is an enrichment program for ninth and tenth grade students attending Hartford public and/or magnet schools. This program is comprised of an academic-year session and a six-week summer session. The program consists of:

- Enrichment experiences both in and outside of the classroom.

- Daily classes in language arts, math, science, career and college awareness preparation, integrating CAPT strategies and support across the curriculum.
- Assessments and evaluations throughout a student's affiliation with Jumpstart, including pre, mid, and post testing; student and parent surveys, mid and final progress reports, etc.
- 20 Saturday Academics during the academic year, where students continue to strengthen their academic skills and college preparation, and are exposed to careers in the health professions.

Juniors Doctors Academy. The Juniors Doctors Academy is a 36-week Saturday academic-year program. The academic components focus on math, language arts, and proven test-taking strategies to increase SAT scores. Student participants are registered to take the SAT, with clear emphasis on career and college preparation. Criteria for admission include:

- Minimum of B- average in science, math and language arts,
- Interest in health careers,
- Entering 11th grade,
- Submission of a 150-word essay explaining interest in joining the program, and
- Two letters of recommendation from Science or English teachers or guidance counselors.

High School Student Research Apprentice Program. The High School Student Research Apprentice Program (HSSRAP) is a six-week summer program for Connecticut high school students who have completed their junior or senior year, and have indicated an interest in medicine, dental medicine, or biomedical research. This program provides the students with a research experience in one of the basic science or clinical laboratories at the university of Connecticut Health Center, the

University of Connecticut at Storrs or Central Connecticut State University. Students report the results of their research in a presentation before faculty, preceptors, other program participants, and invited guests during the final week of the program. Selected participants must be able to commute daily to the University of Connecticut Health Center or Central Connecticut State University or to reside at the University of Connecticut at Storrs. Students who are selected to participate in the summer research program also have the opportunity to participate in the High School Mini Medical/Dental School Program during the following academic year.

Pre-College Enrichment Program. The Pre-College Enrichment Program (PCEP) is a six-week summer program for college pre-freshmen who will matriculate in one of the partner colleges and is designed to provide sound development of scientific, mathematical, communications, problem-solving and test-taking skills. The purpose of this program is to enhance the preparation of high school seniors for college and to increase the retention of freshmen already admitted to one of the partner college. The program consists of 30 hours per week of formal lecture, laboratory, and directed study, addressing the needs of college pre-freshmen respectively. Lectures in each of the following subjects are provided: biology, general chemistry, English, reading, and mathematics. A study skills course focusing on problem solving and test taking is conducted. Seminars on topics related to the health professions is presented. Room and board and a stipend are provided.

Priority consideration is given to former program participants. *College Enrichment Program.* The College Enrichment Program (CEP) is a six-week summer program for college freshmen and sophomores designed to provide sound development of scientific and mathematical

skills. The purpose of this program is to increase the retention of freshmen and sophomores admitted to college. The program consists of 30 hours per week of formal lecture, laboratory, and directed study, addressing the needs of college freshmen or sophomores. Courses in biology, calculus, organic/biochemistry, and physics are offered. Room and board and a stipend are provided. Priority consideration is given to former program participants.

Clinical College Enrichment Program. The Clinical College Enrichment Program is an alternative to the traditional College Enrichment Program and is designed for students seeking an in-depth clinical experience. This is a six-week summer program that includes:

- Direct clinical contact with patients where possible,
- Participation in departmental meetings, orientation and lectures, and
- Presentations and/or attendance at departmental seminars on special research topics.

Medical/Dental Preparatory Program. The Medical/Dental Preparatory Program (MDPP) is a six-week summer program designed to provide a reinforcement and enrichment experience for students from disadvantaged backgrounds who expect to apply to professional schools of medicine and dental medicine. The purposes of the program are to (a) facilitate the entry of these students into professional school by improving their performance on admissions tests and through professional development activities and, (b) to increase the retention of successful matriculants to professional school through early exposure to professional education. Two tracks are available. *Track One-MCAT/DAT Prep Course* is for students who will be taking the Medical College Admission Test

(MCAT) or Dental Admissions Test (DAT) in the fall. The program will focus on MCAT/DAT test preparation, clinical interaction with preceptors, and introduction to problem based learning through case studies. *Track Two-Basic Medical Science Course* is for all other students not on Track One. This track consists of basic medical science courses emphasizing essential principles of cell and molecular biology correlated to problem-based learning case studies. Clinical experiences and professional development exercises are also presented. The program provides room and board and a stipend. Priority considerations is given to former program participants.

Summer Research Fellowship Program. The Summer Research Fellowship Program is a 10-week program designed to provide a research enrichment experience and some exposure to clinical medicine or dental medicine to undergraduate college students who are interested in a career in medicine, dental medicine, or biomedical research. Applicants should have completed some college coursework in biology and chemistry (preferably through organic chemistry). A variety of research projects are available. A faculty sponsor will be identified for each student. Faculty develop and make available suitable project descriptions. The student will meet with the faculty sponsor and develop a research protocol in April or May. The student will commit approximately 30 hours per week for the project and will work with the faculty sponsor or his/her designates. Approximately 10 hours per week will be set aside for required clinical experiential and other requirements. Minority Access to Research Careers (MARC) students are encouraged to apply. A stipend will be provided.

Priority consideration is given to former program participants.

Post-Baccalaureate Program. The School of Medicine, in cooperation with the College of Arts and Sciences at the University of Connecticut, offers two non-degree study programs for capable college graduates wishing to prepare for application to medical schools. One program serves the non-traditional students who have little or no science preparation. It is intended to provide an opportunity for these students to complete medical school science prerequisites. The second program is intended to provide these students an opportunity to demonstrate academic excellence in upper division science coursework. To apply, a student must have completed a baccalaureate degree program from an accredited college or university. Admitted students normally present at least a B-/B+ average each semester. Courses available to students participating in these programs are normal course offerings of the University of Connecticut. Counseling for the program course selection is available on an individual basis from the Pre-Professional Evaluation Committee and representatives of the School of Medicine.

Science Teacher Summer Fellowship Program. The Science Teacher Summer Fellowship Program is open to Connecticut elementary, middle, junior high, and high school science teachers who teach life sciences to a significant number of disadvantaged students. The program is also open to Connecticut college students who are from disadvantaged backgrounds, meet all eligibility criteria, have a high probability of fulfilling the social and educational goals of this program, and who plan to teach life sciences to a significant number of disadvantaged students. The purpose of the program is to allow science teachers to participate in a basic science research project for six weeks during the summer in order to update their knowledge and skills in modern research tools and techniques. A faculty sponsor will be identified for each teacher. Faculty will develop and make available suitable project descriptions. The science teacher will meet with the faculty member prior to the start of the program to develop a research protocol. The teacher will commit approximately 30 hours per week to the project and will work with the faculty sponsor or his/her designates. A stipend will be provided.

Other Pertinent Information

The University of Connecticut School of Medicine is a small institution, 80 per class, where the student does not get lost in the institutional shuffle. A counseling and adult development program is available to all students. A student-based tutorial program is also available.

Association of American Medical Colleges, 2007

Yale University School of Medicine

Dr. Forrestor A. Lee
Professor of Medicine
Assistant Dean of Multicultaral Affairs
Yale University School of Medicine
P.O. Box 208036
367 Cedar Street, ESH 320
New Haven, CT 06520-8036
203-785-7545; 203-737-5507 Fax
omca@yale.edu/
http://www.med.yale.edu/omca

Recruitment

Yale University School of Medicine seeks to achieve diversity among students and actively recruits qualified students from groups underrepresented in medicine. Programs to increase student diversity are centered in the Yale Office of Multicultural Affairs (OMCA).

Yale University School of Medicine employs a variety of activities to assist in carrying out its recruitment efforts. Direct mailings are sent to students identified from the AAMC Medical Minority Applicant Registry. Campus visits are made, with special attention given to those colleges/universities with large enrollments of underrepresented student groups. These visits are made by the director and staff of the Office of Multicultural Affairs and by Yale medical students to inform prospective applicants and advisors about Yale University School of Medicine and its programs. Minority group students and premed advisors may visit the Yale University School of Medicine to meet with medical students, admissions office staff, members of the Admissions Committee, faculty, and financial aid representatives.

Admissions

Minority applications are considered by the same general procedures as all applications. The Admissions Committee composition at Yale University School of Medicine has good representation from minority faculty members, students, and women. At least one of a minority applicant's interviews is with a minority member of the Committee. When interviewing, minority applicants are invited to meet and have lunch with members of the minority student body and to meet with the Dean and staff of the Office of Multicultural Affairs. All minority applicants are contacted prior to their interview dates by the OMCA and offered overnight hosting with an on-board minority student if they wish to do so.

Academic Support Programs

Any student who has difficulty or wishes assistance during his/her time at the medical school can receive tutorial assistance from students or a faculty member. The Yale *Programs of Medical Education* offer the student considerable flexibility for individual curriculum planning. Grades are not given and rank order is not established during the first two years. Exams are offered but taken anonymously. Written evaluation of performance in the first two years is provided by the faculty based primarily based on faculty–student interactions and engagement in small-group sessions. More traditional evaluation and grading systems are in place for the final two years. All Yale students submit a research thesis as a requirement for graduation. Students work directly with faculty mentors who supervise research activities, which may include any health-related area of inquiry.

Enrichment Programs

The Office of Multicultural Affairs conducts three summer academic enrichment programs for college and high school students interested in careers in medicine and

Yale University School of Medicine, 2006
Applicants and Matriculants by Gender, Race and Ethnicity

Race and Ethnicity	Applicants			Matriculants		
	Women	Men	Total	Women	Men	Total
Hispanic/Latino						
Cuban	15	12	27	0	0	0
Mexican American	42	48	90	1	1	2
Puerto Rican	17	23	40	1	0	1
Other Hispanic	50	65	115	0	1	1
Multiple Hispanic*	6	8	14	0	0	0
Subtotal	130	156	286	2	2	4
Non-Hispanic/Latino**						
Black	155	123	278	2	2	4
Native American/Alaska Native	0	7	7	0	0	0
Native Hawaiian/Other Pacific Islander	7	5	12	0	0	0
White	974	1,292	2,266	23	32	55
Asian	560	626	1,186	11	6	17
Other Race	3	5	8	0	0	0
Multiple Race*	80	70	150	4	1	5
Unknown	18	38	56	1	2	3
Subtotal	1,797	2,166	3,963	41	43	84
Foreign	154	160	314	6	5	11
Total	2,081	2,482	4,563	49	50	99

*Since 2002, students can select more than one race and / or ethnicity. **Those who did not choose Hispanic/Latino' or 'Non-Hispanic/Latino' are counted under 'Non-Hispanic/Latino'.
Data Source: AAMC Data Warehouse: Applicant-Matriculant File, as of 5/9/2007.

Association of American Medical Colleges, 2007

science. These programs are designed to increase the numbers of students from groups underrepresented in biomedical science careers.

BioSTEP (Biomedical Science Training and Enrichment Program). Introduced in 1992, this program is designed to provide intensive, short-term training in research for college students underrepresented in biomedical science. The program has been supported continuously by grants from the National Heart, Lung, and Blood Institute. Over 300 trainees have participated in the program with 95 percent of participants progressing into graduate or professional biomedical science training and education programs after completing college. Many BioSTEP students have entered Yale as M.D. and M.D./Ph.D. students.

Trainee selection is competitive. Program participants carry out research projects in the laboratories and training sites of Yale University School of Medicine. Each trainee works in the laboratory of a Yale faculty member who serves as the trainee's mentor. Investigative opportunities ranging from fundamental molecular biology to applied clinical research.

The ten-week program conducted from early-June to mid-August is open to students who have completed at least one year of undergraduate work at an accredited college or university. Each student participant receives a stipend, travel allowance, and lodging.

SMDEP (Summer Medical and Dental Education Program). Yale University School of Medicine is one of the 12 sites of SMDEP, a national program of The Robert Wood Johnson Foundation. Approximately 80 students attend Yale each summer. The program provides an intensive six-week curriculum of college biology, chemistry, organic chemistry, and physics and limited exposure to clinical shadowing. The academic program also provides instruction in writing and communications along with career planning and counseling pertinent to applying to medical and dental school. Yale SMDEP exposes students to an academic environment that emphasizes collaborative, group-facilitated learning. In classroom and seminar settings, teachers cover topics in basic and clinical sciences and provide highly individualized instruction in writing and verbal communication skills. Students develop a foundation of knowledge and skills needed to become successful medical and dental school applicants and future physicians.

Yale S.C.H.O.L.A.R (Science Collaborative Hands-on Learning and Research). This is a tuition-free, summer science academic enrichment program for students enrolled at New Haven's magnet science high school —the Hill Regional Career High School. The goals of the program are 1) to reinforce and sustain students' interest in the sciences by providing a fun, intensive educational experience that will academically prepare students for higher level science courses and 2) to increase the success of Career High School students in pursuing health and science-related careers. Approximately 60 students participate each summer. Yale students and faculty serve as instructors and advisors in the program.

Student Financial Assistance
The application fee may be waived upon request. All applicants, including international students, are eligible for need-based financial assistance. Ample scholarship support is available to cover need not met by personal or family resources. To assure equitable distribution of aid, all applicants are required to provide parental financial information and all recipients are required to borrow an annually determined minimum amount (or base loan) before becoming eligible for institutional scholarship funds. The financial aid office collects and evaluates financial information from FAFSA, the Need Access Application, and a Yale financial aid application.

The George Washington University School of Medicine and Health Sciences

Dr. Yolanda C. Haywood
Assistant Dean for Student Affairs
The George Washington
University School of Medicine
and Health Sciences
2300 I Street, N.W.
Washington, D.C. 20037
202-994-4242; 202-994-1753 Fax
emdych@gwumc.edu

Recruitment

The committee has targeted the traditionally Black colleges and universities, Hispanic and Native-American communities, and several MED-PREP programs around the country for visits by members of the committee, to discuss the School of Medicine and Health Sciences' program with minority students.

Admissions

The Committee on Admissions seeks a balanced but heterogeneous student body of gifted, sensitive, mature individuals who will excel in the art, as well as the science, of medicine. In order to identify a diverse group of individuals best suited to the school's program of medical education, admissions decisions are based on a multiplicity of factors. There is no discrimination in the selection process because of race, sex, color, religion, or national or regional origin. The School of Medicine and its Committee on Admissions is committed to increasing numbers and proportions of students from ethnic, racial, and socioeconomic groups currently underrepresented in the field of medicine, and to continuing to seek out qualified applicants from the District of Columbia.

The admissions brochure explicitly describes the selection process. A copy of this brochure is sent to all applicants. Applicants may write to the Office of Admissions for a copy of this brochure prior to application or review our Web site.

Applicants should submit applications and all requested materials as early as possible. In this way, the committee has ample time to review their biographical data and personal comments, and evaluate non-cognitive factors such as motivation, interest in medicine, and dedication. Personal comments are an important element in the evaluation of the applicant's personal characteristics.

Academic Support Programs

The Committee on Admissions attempts to select those applicants, minority or otherwise, who demonstrate the academic promise and commitment to successfully complete the course of study. This policy, as well as active participation of students and faculty, has kept low the number of students who experience academic difficulties. Second-year students mentor first-year students. Students with difficulties are evaluated by the Assistant Dean for Student Affairs, who can then guide the student to the appropriate support services (e.g., tutoring, or counseling center). In order to offer students with great personal promise but less well proven academic ability an opportunity to study medicine, the School of Medicine has a five-year decelerated program. Students are registered in the School of Medicine Special Program Division and take the first year of medical school course work over two years. Students who perform satisfactorily in the decelerated program are promoted into the second year of the M.D. program. There is no separate application process for this program. Students admitted to this program are chosen from a group of applicants who have demonstrated a commitment to service, a high level of self awareness, and the commitment to successfully complete the rigorous medical school curriculum.

George Washington University School of Medicine & Health Sciences, 2006
Applicants and Matriculants by Gender, Race and Ethnicity

Race and Ethnicity	Applicants			Matriculants		
	Women	Men	Total	Women	Men	Total
Hispanic/Latino						
Cuban	41	31	72	0	1	1
Mexican American	88	88	176	2	0	2
Puerto Rican	36	32	68	0	0	0
Other Hispanic	149	113	262	2	2	4
Multiple Hispanic*	15	9	24	0	0	0
Subtotal	329	273	602	4	3	7
Non-Hispanic/Latino**						
Black	433	180	613	17	3	20
Native American/Alaska Native	5	9	14	0	0	0
Native Hawaiian/Other Pacific Islander	28	22	50	1	0	1
White	2,952	3,156	6,108	41	48	89
Asian	1,474	1,404	2,878	31	19	50
Other Race	10	9	19	2	0	2
Multiple Race*	171	127	298	0	1	1
Unknown	52	51	103	3	2	5
Subtotal	5,125	4,958	10,083	95	73	168
Foreign	169	183	352	1	1	2
Total	5,623	5,414	11,037	100	77	177

*Since 2002, students can select more than one race and / or ethnicity. **Those who did not choose Hispanic/Latino' or 'Non-Hispanic/Latino' are counted under 'Non-Hispanic/Latino'.
Data Source: AAMC Data Warehouse: Applicant-Matriculant File, as of 5/9/2007.

Association of American Medical Colleges, 2007

University Counseling Center services help students resolve personal social, career, and study problems that can interfere with their academic progress and success. Services include workshops and groups on topics such as time management, study skills, procrastination prevention, family and relationship issues, stress management, conflict management, and self-esteem. Clinical services including crisis intervention and brief personal counseling for issues related to university life are also available.

Enrichment Programs
Students can mentor minority high school students through programs such as the American Medical Student Association's Students Teaching Aids to Students, Science in Our Lives, SHAPED (Study Health and Promote an Education Degree), a Latin American youth health care program, and Upward Bound. The Interdisciplinary Student Community Oriented Patient Education Service (ISCOPES) is currently an elective program designed to provide hands-on experience and training in population-based community-oriented health promotion activities. Over a year and a half period an interdisciplinary team of medical, physician assistant, nurse practitioner, health administration, and public health students works closely with their community site to develop a health promotion project that will be of benefit to the population or community served by the site. Both university and community faculty serve as team supervisors. The team presents its work at an ISCOPES Poster Session twice each year.

Through the Interdisciplinary Student Community Oriented Patient Education Service (ISCOPES), students enhance their understanding of community-oriented primary care and cultural competency. Needs of the community are addressed.

A combined M.D./M.P.H. program is offered.

Student Financial Assistance
Financial aid is awarded to students on the basis of need. The school's financial aid funds are limited, but the services of the Financial Aid Office are available to assist accepted students to develop plans to meet their financial obligations. There are a limited number of merit-based scholarships available. The application fee is waived for disadvantaged students. The Admissions Committee will utilize regional interviews to avoid having disadvantaged applicants travel to the medical center from substantial distances.

All students are required to attend financial planning workshops.

Educational Partnerships
The Upward Bound Program is a partnership with the D.C. public school system designed to encourage students to pursue careers in the sciences.

Georgetown University School of Medicine

Joy Phinizy Williams
Associate Dean for Students
Georgetown University
School of Medicine
14 Butler Annex, 3900 Reservoir Rd., NW
Washington, D.C. 20057-1423
202-687-1645; 202-687-7660 Fax
williamsj@georgetown.edu

Admissions

The Committee on Admissions reviews all applications to the School of Medicine and evaluates them based on established academic parameters and fair and equitable guidelines. Each application is considered individually to enable the committee to have an opportunity to select persons who will add diversity and strength to the class.

The Committee on Admissions is made up of Georgetown University faculty and student representatives. Invited applicants are interviewed individually by a member of the faculty, alumni, or a fourth-year medical student. The School of Medicine and the committee are committed to maintaining a diverse student body and to increasing the numbers of physicians from groups currently underrepresented in the field of medicine.

Academic Support Programs

The Georgetown University Experimental Medical Studies Program (GEMS). GEMS is a one-year post-baccalaureate course of study. Its primary purpose is to offer highly motivated, underrepresented minority students, with modest pre-medical academic records, an opportunity to demonstrate their academic capabilities by passing selected courses taught to first-year students at Georgetown University School of Medicine.

In concert with this primary objective:

- GEMS students must be United States citizens who are either from minority groups that have been traditionally underrepresented in medicine (African Americans, mainland Puerto Ricans, Mexican Americans, and Native Americans) or others who meet all other criteria and show evidence of their ability to satisfy the social and educational goals of this program.
- Special consideration is given to residents of the District of Columbia.
- Applicants to the GEMS Program must have successfully completed one year each of general chemistry, organic chemistry, biology, physics, and college mathematics. Appropriate preparation in the laboratory will be required in biology, chemistry, and physics.
- All applicants must show evidence of having earned a baccalaureate degree from an accredited college or university.
- Participants take courses selected from the first-year medical school curriculum and are graded on the same basis as other students enrolled in these courses. The GEMS course requirements are equivalent to half the full-time, first-year course requirements. GEMS students who successfully complete the program are encouraged to apply to the School of Medicine. If accepted, these students will take the remaining first year courses the following academic year.

For additional information about the GEMS Program, telephone 202-687-1406, or write GEMS Program, Georgetown University School of Medicine, 3900 Reservoir Rd., NW Washington, DC 20057-1423. Contacts for the GEMS Program are Joy P. Williams, Associate Dean for Student Affairs and Special Programs, 202-687-1645 or David Taylor, GEMS Program, Senior Facilitator, 202-687-5411 or Dr. Shyrl Sistrunk, Senior Clinical Advisor, 202-687-1406.

Georgetown University School of Medicine, 2006
Applicants and Matriculants by Gender, Race and Ethnicity

Race and Ethnicity	Applicants			Matriculants		
	Women	Men	Total	Women	Men	Total
Hispanic/Latino						
Cuban	31	22	53	1	0	1
Mexican American	70	83	153	2	1	3
Puerto Rican	28	26	54	1	1	2
Other Hispanic	119	100	219	4	0	4
Multiple Hispanic*	15	6	21	0	0	0
Subtotal	263	237	500	8	2	10
Non-Hispanic/Latino**						
Black	322	161	483	8	4	12
Native American/Alaska Native	6	4	10	0	0	0
Native Hawaiian/Other Pacific Islander	13	19	32	0	0	0
White	2,251	2,626	4,877	61	67	128
Asian	1,111	1,106	2,217	15	14	29
Other Race	2	5	7	0	0	0
Multiple Race*	135	122	257	5	3	8
Unknown	37	50	87	0	3	3
Subtotal	3,877	4,093	7,970	89	91	180
Foreign	180	184	364	1	0	1
Total	4,320	4,514	8,834	98	93	191

*Since 2002, students can select more than one race and / or ethnicity. **Those who did not choose
Hispanic/Latino' or 'Non-Hispanic/Latino' are counted under 'Non-Hispanic/Latino'.
Data Source: AAMC Data Warehouse: Applicant-Matriculant File, as of 5/9/2007.

Association of American Medical Colleges, 2007

The faculty of the School of Medicine is strongly committed to the academic development of all students, and individual faculty members are generally available to conduct group and individual tutorials.

Student Financial Assistance
Application fees may be waived upon request and justification of need for financially disadvantaged applicants.

Education Partnerships
Georgetown University School of Medicine has a partnership agreement with Eastern Senior High School, Health and Human Services Academy, a magnet program in the District of Columbia public schools for students who aspire to careers in health and or human services.

Howard University College of Medicine*

Dr. Dawn L. Cannon, Associate Dean for Student Affairs & Admissions
Judith Walk, Admissions Director
Ann Finney, Admissions Officer
Howard University College of Medicine
Washington, D.C. 20059
202-806-6279; 202-806-7934 Fax
jwalk@howard.edu

Recruitment
Recruitment activities are coordinated by the Associate Dean for Student Affairs and the staff of the Admissions Office. Efforts are made to achieve more effective communication between the college, pre-medical students, and their advisors. The college conducts year-round undergraduate pre-medical student recruitment efforts, including travel to colleges and universities in various geographic locations across the

nation. These efforts are aimed at identifying potential student applicants at an early stage in their college careers and at working to increase the representation of minority students underrepresented in the medical profession.

Another important facet of recruitment is the highlighting of Howard's special programs (e.g., the B.S./M.D. Program, academic reinforcement programs for admitted and enrolled students, M.D./Ph.D programs, the Human Genome Center, the Center for Sickle Cell Disease, the Howard University Cancer Center), and other related programs that may be of particular interest to applicants. The university's Center for Preprofessional Education sponsors two workshops for pre-medical students that serve as an orientation to the medical school application process and allow participants to interact with medical

Howard University College of Medicine, 2006
Applicants and Matriculants by Gender, Race and Ethnicity

Race and Ethnicity	Applicants			Matriculants		
	Women	Men	Total	Women	Men	Total
Hispanic/Latino						
Cuban	14	13	27	1	0	1
Mexican American	48	43	91	0	0	0
Puerto Rican	19	15	34	0	1	1
Other Hispanic	82	63	145	1	1	2
Multiple Hispanic*	10	7	17	0	0	0
Subtotal	173	141	314	2	2	4
Non-Hispanic/Latino**						
Black	1,094	492	1,586	36	38	74
Native American/Alaska Native	1	2	3	1	0	1
Native Hawaiian/Other Pacific Islander	21	11	32	1	0	1
White	423	542	965	3	5	8
Asian	573	580	1,153	8	4	12
Other Race	3	4	7	0	0	0
Multiple Race*	64	52	116	0	4	4
Unknown	16	19	35	0	0	0
Subtotal	2,195	1,702	3,897	49	51	100
Foreign	202	178	380	6	8	14
Total	2,570	2,021	4,591	57	61	118

*Since 2002, students can select more than one race and / or ethnicity. **Those who did not choose Hispanic/Latino' or 'Non-Hispanic/Latino' are counted under 'Non-Hispanic/Latino'.
Data Source: AAMC Data Warehouse: Applicant-Matriculant File, as of 5/9/2007.

school representatives from across the nation. Although recruitment activities have operated primarily at the undergraduate college level, some efforts are aimed at the secondary school student.

Since Howard University is the oldest and largest predominantly minority medical school in the country, it is concerned with the preparation of pre-medical students in underrepresented minority group communities. The College of Medicine has a sincere commitment to identify, at the earliest stage of undergraduate training, the highly motivated and academically qualified minority student who has expressed an interest in pursuing a medical career.

Admissions

The primary mission of the College of Medicine is to train physicians to practice in medically underserved communities and facilities. The college's admissions policies and procedures are in accord with this mission. The college is an historically Black institution, yet has one of the most diverse student bodies in the country. Candidates for admission and alternates are selected from those applicants who have competitive academic credentials and desirable personal and social traits, and who are most likely to practice in communities or facilities needing physician services.

The college participates in the American Medical College Application Service (AMCAS). The deadline for filing the completed AMCAS application is December 15 of the year immediately preceding the year the applicant expects to enter. All applicants to the college must also take the Medical College Admission Test (MCAT) no earlier than three years prior to the year of expected matriculation. Letters of recommendation from a health professions committee, or from two science faculty, a secondary application form, and an application fee of $45 are required, as is a personal interview. The application fee cannot be waived.

Academic Support Programs

An academic support program for all basic science courses has existed at the Howard University College of Medicine since 1963. Sessions are sponsored and coordinated by the Office of Medical Education.

Each freshman student is assigned two advisors: a faculty advisor and a student advisor. The faculty advisor is a member of the college's faculty who will serve as a counselor throughout the years of medical study. The student advisor is a second-year student who provides support and important study materials and helps guide the entering student through the transition to undergraduate medical education. Additionally, students are assigned a Senior Faculty Advisor, who will assist them in their transition to postgraduate medical education.

During freshman orientation week, and periodically throughout the year, workshops are offered presenting techniques for understanding and memorizing information, taking lecture notes, taking multiple-choice examinations, and managing time in the medical curriculum. Counseling is offered to all students in academic difficulty. These students may receive tutorial support, assistance with learning skills, or referral to other university services. Aid in preparing for the United States Medical Licensing Examination (USMLE) Step 1 is provided through a commercial review course.

Freshman and sophomores may remove one or two course deficiencies through reexamination or by attending the Summer Directed Study Program and then passing an examination administered at the end of the program.

Enrichment Programs

Preliminary Academic Reinforcement Program (PARP). PARP was organized during 1971 for a small group of incoming medical freshmen and has continued each successive summer. PARP is a six-week

summer program that introduces selected entering freshmen to the basic medical sciences, strengthens their learning skills, and provides some measure of their ability to handle the freshman medical curriculum. The subjects taught mirror the blocks of the new integrated curriculum: structure and function, molecules and cells, and medicine and society. Satisfactory completion of the program, a requirement for students selected, is determined on the basis of examinations, attendance, and professionalism. No credit is offered for PARP courses, and the program neither satisfies course prerequisites for medical school nor replaces any courses in the freshman medical curriculum. Participating students may be given some assistance with expenses for room and board. No tuition is charged. Limited funds may be available for out-of-town students to help defray travel expenses to and from the program.

Students for this program are selected by the Admissions Committee from the pool of AMCAS applicants. *No direct application to the PARP program is possible.*

SMDEP is a free (full tuition, housing, and meals) six-week summer medical and dental school preparatory program that offers eligible students intensive and personalized medical and dental school preparation

The mission of the Howard University Summer Medical Dental Education Program (SMDEP) is to provide an educational experience of exceptional quality that will strengthen the overall academic preparation of underrepresented minority, disadvantaged, and low-income students who express interest in admission to medical or dental school.

SMDEP strives to enhance the Universitys ability to contribute well-qualified, socially conscious medical and dental school candidates committed to improving the health and quality of life for all communities throughout this nation and the world,

AAMC

specially those communities underserved by the health professions.

Student Financial Assistance

About 85 percent of the students enrolled in the College of Medicine receive some sort of financial assistance. Financial aid awards are based on an analysis of the student's need and academic scholarship. Financial aid applicants are required to file the Free Application for Federal Student Aid.

Several kinds of financial aid are available to the student in need. Scholarships are awarded by the college and are applied to the cost of tuition. Guaranteed and non-guaranteed student loans are available from a number of sources, including the university. While the college attempts to ensure that all its students have financial resources to meet the cost of attendance, we cannot provide financial assistance for application or interview travel.

Educational Partnerships

The College of Medicine is a partner with the Center for Preprofessional Education of the Howard University College of Arts and Sciences in preparing underrepresented minority and disadvantaged students for medical school. In addition to providing counseling and support for pre-medical students, the Center for Preprofessional Education sponsors several special programs. Among these are the B.S./M.D. Program; a Post-Baccalaureate Pre-medical Program; a summer program for undergraduate pre-medical students; and the MED-DENT START Program.

B.S./M.D. Program. This program enables highly qualified students to complete requirements for the B.S. degree and for the M.D. degree within six years after graduation from high school. Students in this program can complete all requirements for admission to the College of Medicine by the end of their sophomore undergraduate year and may at that point be admitted to the College of Medicine. The B.S. degree is awarded to these students upon the successful completion of the sophomore year in medical school, and the M.D. degree is awarded upon successful completion of the final two years of the medical curriculum.

Preprofessional Advanced Enrichment Program. The Center for Preprofessional Education offers this six-week summer program to prepare undergraduate college students for the MCAT; to introduce them to basic medical science courses as taught by medical school faculty; to provide clinical hospital experience; and to improve communication, reading, analytical, and exam-taking skills.

MED-DENT START Program. This program provides pre-medical and pre-dental students with supervised and planned clinical experiences in the Howard University Hospital. Staffed largely by minority physicians, the Howard University Hospital is the largest minority-owned and run health care facility in the country and serves a large minority population.

For further information regarding any of the above programs offered by the Center for Preprofessional Education, in cooperation with the College of Medicine, please contact:

Dr. Georgiana F. Aboko-Cole, Director, Center for Preprofessional Education, College of Arts and Sciences, P.O. Box 473, Howard University, Washington, D.C. 20059, 202-238-2363.

Florida State University College of Medicine

Dr. Eugene A. Trowers, Jr.
Assistant Dean for Diversity and Outreach
Florida State University
College of Medicine
1115 West Call Street
Tallahassee, FL 32306-4300
850-644-4607; 850-644-5766 Fax
eugene,trowers@med.fsu.edu
http://med.fsu.edu

Recruitment

The Florida State University (FSU) College of Medicine was created to train physicians to serve the health care needs of underserved populations in Florida. Because of this unique mission, the FSU College of Medicine (FSUCOM) actively recruits individuals from rural, inner city, and other underrepresented population groups throughout the state. In 1993, prior to the establishment of the FSUCOM, the FSU Program in Medical Sciences implemented the outreach program, Science Students Together Reaching Instructional Diversity and Excellence (SSTRIDE). SSTRIDE was developed to increase the interest and achievement in science and mathematics of a diverse group of middle and high school students. Because of this very successful recruitment program, SSTRIDE has expanded its outreach to include college and post-baccalaureate programs at FSU, and programs for middle and high school students in surrounding rural counties. In cooperation with educational, professional, and physician partnerships, outreach/recruitment activities include in-school coursework in anatomy and physiology, after-school mentoring and tutoring, standardized test preparation, career-shadowing experiences, and pre-medical advising.

SSTRIDE programs run continuously throughout the academic year, and an on-campus residential summer program is available to upcoming 11th- and 12th-grade students from nearby rural areas. Students are encouraged to remain in the SSTRIDE program until graduation from college, thereby creating a recruiting pipeline to FSU's medical school and other higher education programs. SSTRIDE outreach/recruitment programs are sponsored and implemented by administrators and pre-health professions advisors within the Division of Student Affairs, Admissions, and Outreach at the FSUCOM and the Big Bend Area Health Education Center (AHEC). Representatives from FSU College of Medicine, Division of Student Affairs regularly attend pre-medical and pre-health forums throughout the state of Florida, particularly those targeting underrepresented groups, to recruit students to health care professions. Students enrolled in the College of Medicine also aid in recruitment efforts through active participation with SSTRIDE, and inner city and rural schools, giving guest lectures to address health issues, career in health professions, and biomedical research.

Admissions

Consistent with its mission, the FSU College of Medicine Admissions Committee is especially interested in students who have demonstrated consistent motivation for service to others. Students from underrepresented minority groups, rural and inner city, and non-traditional backgrounds are of particular interest to the committee.

Academic Support Programs

During orientation and throughout the year, FSUCOM students are provided information regarding study skills, coping skills, and instructional support materials. Students are assigned a specific faculty

Florida State University College of Medicine, 2006
Applicants and Matriculants by Gender, Race and Ethnicity

Race and Ethnicity	Applicants			Matriculants		
	Women	Men	Total	Women	Men	Total
Hispanic/Latino						
Cuban	49	55	104	0	1	1
Mexican American	10	14	24	0	0	0
Puerto Rican	21	14	35	0	0	0
Other Hispanic	74	54	128	2	2	4
Multiple Hispanic*	7	7	14	0	0	0
Subtotal	161	144	305	2	3	5
Non-Hispanic/Latino**						
Black	150	63	213	11	4	15
Native American/Alaska Native	2	3	5	0	0	0
Native Hawaiian/Other Pacific Islander	4	2	6	0	0	0
White	400	474	874	42	22	64
Asian	164	181	345	6	5	11
Other Race	1	1	2	0	0	0
Multiple Race*	22	31	53	3	0	3
Unknown	5	9	14	2	0	2
Subtotal	748	764	1,512	64	31	95
Foreign	12	14	26	0	0	0
Total	921	922	1,843	66	34	100

*Since 2002, students can select more than one race and / or ethnicity. **Those who did not choose Hispanic/Latino' or 'Non-Hispanic/Latino' are counted under 'Non-Hispanic/Latino'.
Data Source: AAMC Data Warehouse: Applicant-Matriculant File, as of 5/9/2007.

advisor upon matriculation and another is assigned when students relocate to a regional campus. With the help of faculty, student performance is monitored. If a student is identified as not performing at the appropriate level in course work, counseling and tutoring are provided. Study groups are formed early in the first semester but are very fluid as students' academic needs change or emerge. Full-time student support staff is available throughout the four years of medical school. All intervention services and counseling are coordinated by the Director of Student Development and Program Initiatives who works in conjunction with the Student Support Coordinators assigned to each medical class. To facilitate the success of the medical students and to support the unique mission of the College of Medicine, small-group, problem-based instruction with early and extensive clinical experiences are part of the curriculum delivery throughout the four-year program of study. Students are also part of learning communities (consisting of 25-30 students) that have designated facilities conducive to the dialogue of learning and information assimilation.

The Post-Baccalaureate Bridge Program is designed to provide assistance for a small number of identified students who apply to medical school but whose backgrounds may place them at an academic disadvantage for immediate entry into medical school. These students are enrolled in a year-long program, which allows them to take selected medical school courses; enroll in upper level science, bioethics, and psychosocial courses; take personal skills development workshops; and develop and participate in a community service activity to prepare for entry into medical school. Successful completion of this structured program will ensure entry into the next College of Medicine class.

Individualized intervention activities are possible and utilized by all students regardless of background or ethnicity. The student learning communities provide social and educational opportunities for students. Each community is served by a student support coordinator, who can, along with the help of the Director of Student Development and Program Initiatives and peer counselors from the senior classes, identify any psychological issues that may emerge and can direct students to help from university and private resources.

Enrichment Programs

Through SSTRIDE, middle and high school students are exposed to enrichment activities that include an elective anatomy and physiology course offered during the school day, science and mathematics tutorials, hands-on laboratory activities, career shadowing, science and math competitions, and test preparation activities. During the summer months 11th- and 12th-grade students from the Rural SSTRIDE program are provided an intensive three- week residential experience called RIPE (Rural Introduction to Premedical Education). RIPE is designed to motivate students to excel academically, expose students to a variety of clinical sites and training opportunities, teach students about scholarships and university based mentoring programs, expose them to college campuses, and inspire students to consider careers in health care professions in medically underserved communities

Undergraduate students from FSU and Florida A & M University (FAMU), minority students, non-traditional students, and students from rural/inner city backgrounds participate in the Multicultural Association of Pre-health Students (MAPS) and in the College of Medicine's pre-health advising program. These students are offered academic advisement, test preparation activities, mathematics and science tutorial services, study group activities, interview workshops, career workshops, review of personal statements, and participation in local and national pre-health conferences. They can also apply to participate in the Physician Partnership Program and a medical assistant training program sponsored by the College of Medicine and Big Bend Area Health Education Center (AHEC) with Lively Vocational Technical College. After medical assistant training, these students, many of whom must work to support themselves, are able to find employment in a health care setting, obtain valuable medical experiences, and confirm their commitment to medicine. Web site: (http://www.med.fsu.edu/ StudentAffairs/default.asp).

Student Financial Assistance

A number of need-based and minority scholarships are available to students. In addition, emergency loans are extended to students who are having difficulty meeting living expenses and tuition fees. During orientation and throughout the year, a financial aid liaison in the College of Medicine provides individual budget counseling to help students develop personal budgets and access to available resources.

Educational Partnerships

Educational partnerships exists between FSUCOM and school districts in Leon, Gadsden, Okaloosa, and Madison County schools. In addition, we have partnerships with the Big Bend AHEC, Lively Vocational Technical Center, Kaplan Educational Testing Center, Princeton Review,

Putzer's Review Incorporated, Project Motivational Math, Tallahassee Orthopedic Surgical Center, The Children's Clinic, Wakulla County Health Department, Neighborhood Health Services, Shand's Hospital, and numerous community physicians. Partnerships for third- and fourth-year clinical training exist with physicians, health plans, and hospitals and physician offices in Pensacola, Sarasota, Orlando, and Tallahassee.

University of Florida College of Medicine

Dr. Donna M. Parker
Dr. Kendall M. Campbell
Assistant Deans for Minority Affairs
University of Florida
College of Medicine
P.O. Box 100202
Gainesville, FL 32610-0202
352-273-6656; 352-392-5647 Fax
dparker@dean.med.ufl.edu
kmarvinc@dean.med.ufl.edu
http://www.med.ufl.edu/oma

Recruitment

The College of Medicine actively recruits undergraduate students from underrepresented groups for its medical, physician assistant, and interdisciplinary biomedical science research programs. Visits are made by the Assistant Deans for Minority Affairs and students to undergraduate colleges, including several located in the southeast with predominant underrepresented student populations.

Admissions

The Medical Selection Committee reviews applications and compares the applicant's Medical College Admission Test scores and grade-point average with those of other medical students who attend their undergraduate college or are currently enrolled in the College of Medicine. In addition, the applicant's record of clinical experience, research, and volunteerism is taken into consideration. The College does not have a separate minority admissions committee. The College of Medicine is aware of underrepresentation of many groups in the health care workforce, and it is committed to helping to alleviate this problem. Hence, the committee looks critically at applicants' experiences in serving the underserved.

Academic Support Programs

Advisor/Mentor Programs. All incoming medical students are paired with a clinical faculty member who shares the student's area of specialty interest. Students have the opportunity to shadow their advisor and/or participate in their research. Mostly the advisor/mentor introduces students to a career in medicine and provides them with individual support and guidance. During the third year, students may select a new advisor/mentor upon determining the specialty area they wish to pursue for residency training.

Office of Student Counseling and Development. Confidential counseling and workshops are offered to help students with personal issues (e.g., stress, anxiety, depression), academic issues (e.g., study skills, test taking), and career issues (e.g., medical specialty decision making, residency application, and interviewing). In addition, support groups for spouses and significant others meet weekly when there is sufficient interest.

Tutoring. The Offices of Medical Education and Student Counseling and Development coordinate tutorial services for students who are referred for this assistance.

The services listed above are conducted by Dr. Beverly Vidaurreta.

Enrichment Programs

Health Care Summer Institute. The Office of Minority Affairs and the Area Health Education Centers co-sponsor a four-week summer camp for rising high school seniors interested in health care careers. Participants attend workshops in study skills and test taking and also shadow several health care professionals. Health professions students who serve as the camp counselors also provide mentoring.

Summer Research Program. The Short-Term Summer Research Training for Minority Students Program is funded by the National Institutes of Health to

University of Florida College of Medicine, 2006
Applicants and Matriculants by Gender, Race and Ethnicity

Race and Ethnicity	Applicants			Matriculants		
	Women	Men	Total	Women	Men	Total
Hispanic/Latino						
Cuban	55	52	107	4	3	7
Mexican American	19	12	31	0	0	0
Puerto Rican	24	21	45	0	1	1
Other Hispanic	89	57	146	1	2	3
Multiple Hispanic*	7	9	16	0	0	0
Subtotal	194	151	345	5	6	11
Non-Hispanic/Latino**						
Black	141	70	211	3	1	4
Native American/Alaska Native	3	2	5	0	1	1
Native Hawaiian/Other Pacific Islander	2	4	6	0	0	0
White	494	583	1,077	41	38	79
Asian	183	195	378	12	13	25
Other Race	1	1	2	0	0	0
Multiple Race*	25	29	54	2	0	2
Unknown	9	10	19	0	2	2
Subtotal	858	894	1,752	58	55	113
Foreign	5	5	10	0	0	0
Total	1,057	1,050	2,107	63	61	124

*Since 2002, students can select more than one race and / or ethnicity. **Those who did not choose Hispanic/Latino' or 'Non-Hispanic/Latino' are counted under 'Non-Hispanic/Latino'.
Data Source: AAMC Data Warehouse: Applicant-Matriculant File, as of 5/9/2007.

increase the number of ethnic minority students entering research and academic careers. Preference is given to undergraduates; however, the program is also open to the professional students and others wishing to pursue graduate education. Students are compensated with a stipend, housing, and travel allowance.

Advisement. The Assistant Deans for Minority Affairs serve as the faculty advisors to the Student National Medical Association (SNMA) and Minority Association of Pre-medical Students (MAPS). The MAPS is organized under the umbrella of the SNMA. Our local SNMA chapter is very active and also provides advisement and mentoring to the members of MAPS.

Student Financial Assistance
A partial- or full-tuition scholarship is available to all qualified underrepresented students. Every effort is made to meet each student's total financial need through additional scholarships and loans.

University of Miami, Miller School of Medicine

Dr. Astrid K. Mack, Associate
Dean for Minority Affairs
University of Miami
Miller School of Medicine
P.O. Box 016960 (R-128)
Miami, FL 33101
305-243-5998, 305-243-2938 Fax
amack@med.miami.edu
www.miami.edu/minority_affairs

Recruitment
Students, faculty, and members of the administration visit various college campuses in the southeast to recruit students. In addition to this, the Associate Dean for Minority Affairs tries to visit the predominantly Black colleges and universities in the state of Florida, as well as some of the institutions in the southeast, to recruit minority and disadvantaged students. These visits may occur on *career days*, depending upon the convenience of the schools and the schedule of the Associate Dean for Minority Affairs. At these visits an attempt is made to have pre-medical and science major students present, along with faculty advisors, science teachers, etc., to discuss with the group the requirements for admission to medical schools, the planning of necessary courses prior to taking the Medical College Admission Test (MCAT), etc.

Admissions
Applicants for admission must complete an American Medical College Application Service (AMCAS) application. The AMCAS application is used to identify applicants about whom the Admissions Committee

University of Miami Miller School of Medicine, 2006
Applicants and Matriculants by Gender, Race and Ethnicity

Race and Ethnicity	Applicants			Matriculants		
	Women	Men	Total	Women	Men	Total
Hispanic/Latino						
Cuban	68	67	135	5	6	11
Mexican American	35	22	57	0	0	0
Puerto Rican	43	39	82	0	0	0
Other Hispanic	112	90	202	1	3	4
Multiple Hispanic*	15	10	25	1	2	3
Subtotal	273	228	501	7	11	18
Non-Hispanic/Latino**						
Black	182	94	276	7	4	11
Native American/Alaska Native	5	4	9	0	0	0
Native Hawaiian/Other Pacific Islander	8	5	13	0	0	0
White	920	1,183	2,103	38	53	91
Asian	354	455	809	20	25	45
Other Race	1	2	3	0	0	0
Multiple Race*	57	51	108	4	3	7
Unknown	13	22	35	2	2	4
Subtotal	1,540	1,816	3,356	71	87	158
Foreign	32	23	55	0	0	0
Total	1,845	2,067	3,912	78	98	176

*Since 2002, students can select more than one race and / or ethnicity. **Those who did not choose Hispanic/Latino' or 'Non-Hispanic/Latino' are counted under 'Non-Hispanic/Latino'.
Data Source: AAMC Data Warehouse: Applicant-Matriculant File, as of 5/9/2007.

Association of American Medical Colleges, 2007

would like more information. These applicants will be invited to complete a supplemental application, which includes letters of recommendation, a photograph, and a residency statement and validation form, among other information. An evaluation interview, conducted by a member of the Committee on Admissions, is an integral part of the selection process. Interviews are conducted only by an invitation extended by the Committee on Admissions. The Committee on Admissions gives careful consideration to many factors when evaluating a candidate for admission. Some of these factors are scholastic aptitude, interpersonal skills, intellectual curiosity, maturity, motivation, and compassion. Applications from women and socioeconomically disadvantaged candidates are especially encouraged, as are those from older applicants who have had several years of work experience or graduate study. It has long been a policy of the school to admit students with widely differing backgrounds in order to meet the many needs of medicine.

Special efforts and programs are in place to achieve our goal of increasing the enrollment, retention, and graduation of underrepresented minority students.

Academic Support Programs
A system of volunteer tutors, from the faculty and student body, has been established for one-to-one tutorial sessions with all currently enrolled students.

Enrichment Programs
Minority Students Health Careers Motivation Program. In 1976, the school established a summer enrichment program for minority students interested in health careers. This program, referred to as the *Minority Students Health Careers Motivation Program ("Motivation Program")* is the university's priority program for facilitation of entry of minority students to medical school.

The Motivation Program is a seven-week, full-time program for college students, particularly juniors and seniors, who are interested in health careers, primarily medicine. Occasionally, a few college graduates are accepted to the program. Generally, the students selected are majors in one of the biological or physical sciences. Priority is given to Florida residents. The main goal of the Motivation Program is to facilitate the entry of minority/disadvantaged students, particularly Blacks, into health professions schools. This goal is met in part by providing the participants with a challenging curriculum composed of several pre-clinical medical school courses (biochemistry, histology, gross anatomy, and microbiology). An intensive reading and study-skills course accompanies the science curriculum. Clinical correlation conferences and visits to designated clinical areas give students opportunities to learn and also expose them to a wide variety of clinical activities. Seminars and workshops are presented to participants desiring to attend *Preparing for Medical School* (which includes the planning of credentials, application process, interviewing, the personal statement, reapplying, and alternative careers). Each of the participating students receives a stipend. The Associate Dean for Minority Affairs is the Project Director.

A seven-week, full-time nonresidential *Medical College Admission Test (MCAT) preparation program* is offered to underrepresented minority students who plan to take the MCAT the following August. The goal of the program is to have 70 percent of each group of participants score no less than eight (8) on the verbal reasoning, and physical and biological sciences sections of the test and a score no less than N on the writing sections. The form of the comprehensive review program consists of several components designed to keep participants alert and involved. They include small classes, trained instructors, comprehensive

science sessions, unparalleled verbal reasoning and writing programs, five full-length tests and detailed diagnostic score reports, and a comprehensive set of course review and practice materials. The course is offered at no cost to Florida residents living within commuter distance to the University of Miami/Jackson Memorial Medical Center.

Student Financial Assistance
Considerable financial aid is provided to students who demonstrate financial need through the Office of Financial Assistance Services. *(www.mededu.miami.edu/osfa)*

Educational Partnerships
The Office of Minority Affairs at the University of Miami Miller School of Medicine has entered into formal, written partnership agreements with Miami-Dade County Area Health Education Center (M-DCAHEC), University of Miami Schools of Arts and Sciences and Medicine, Miami-Dade County Public Schools Division of Schools of Choice: 100 Black Men of South Florida, Inc. and Miami-Dade Chapter, and the National Medical Association. Each agreement specifies the resources and support the entity will contribute to our comprehensive programs. Our programs provide assistance to is advantaged/minority students aspiring to careers in medicine and other health professions. These programs create an array of activities commencing early in the educational pipeline, supporting the career aspirations of disadvantaged/minority students, and allowing for a greater likelihood of successful entry into health professions careers.

University of South Florida College of Medicine

Dr. Suzanne Jackson
Director, Office of Student
Diversity & Enrichment
813-974-2562; 813-396-9463
s.jackson@health.usf.edu
www.hsc.usf.edu/medicine/osde
Dr. Nazach Rodriguez-Snapp
Coordinator, Office of Student
Diversity & Enrichment
University of South Florida College
of Medicine
12901 Bruce B. Downs, Blvd. MDC 24
Tampa, FL 33612
813-974-7592; 813-396-9463
nazrodri@hsc.usf.edu
www.hsc.usf.edu/medicine/osde

Recruitment

The Office of Student Diversity and Enrichment encourages and promotes an environment at the USF College of Medicine that welcomes and embraces diversity in the student body. We strive to ensure that all students feel supported and accepted in order to optimize their educational experience. The Office of Student Diversity and Enrichment participates in all major recruitment activities in the state of Florida and at selected schools through out the United States. Recruitment activities are held during the summer and academic years. Minority pre-medical student organizations are encouraged to invite the OSDE director and coordinator to present at meetings and conferences.

Admissions

Applicants are encouraged to apply early and complete applications as soon as possible. We will begin to interview applicants with completed files in late September. Since we operate on a weekly "rolling admissions" environment, our Admissions Committee may vote to admit highly qualified applicants in such a way that the class could be filled earlier than the final application deadline. Once the class is filled, interviewed applicants will be able to enter the class via the wait-list process.

Students applying for admission to the USF College of Medicine MD Program must complete the requirements for a bachelor's degree at an accredited university or college by the time of matriculation. Applicants will be evaluated on the basis of personal attributes and achievements, academic record, performance on the MCAT, personal references, interviews, and their demonstrated motivation for medicine and helping others. These motivations are mainly demonstrated by a consistent history of medical and community service, volunteering, some physician shadowing, teamwork, leadership, and basic science-related research. Applicants who are currently pursuing graduate-level work toward a Ph.D. degree or other professional degree are obligated to complete all degree requirements prior to matriculation into the MD Program.

To be considered for an interview applicants should have both a science (BCPM) GPA and overall GPA of at least 3.0 on a 4.0 scale and a minimum MCAT score of 24. Over the last three years the matriculating class averaged GPAs and MCATs at about 3.65 (BCPM), 3.70 (overall), and 30, respectively.

You must be a U.S. citizen or Permanent Resident Alien (PRA) with a Green Card in your possession before we will consider your application for a possible interview.

The College of Medicine is committed to the principle of a diverse classroom. According to the AAMC our program is in the top 25 percent of medical schools in the nation for ethnic and racial diversity. But diversity means much more and

University of South Florida College of Medicine, 2006
Applicants and Matriculants by Gender, Race and Ethnicity

Race and Ethnicity	Applicants			Matriculants		
	Women	Men	Total	Women	Men	Total
Hispanic/Latino						
Cuban	53	56	109	2	3	5
Mexican American	17	11	28	2	3	5
Puerto Rican	22	18	40	2	0	2
Other Hispanic	80	56	136	3	3	6
Multiple Hispanic*	12	9	21	0	1	1
Subtotal	184	150	334	9	10	19
Non-Hispanic/Latino**						
Black	136	64	200	5	0	5
Native American/Alaska Native	3	2	5	0	0	0
Native Hawaiian/Other Pacific Islander	4	1	5	0	0	0
White	488	509	997	39	30	69
Asian	149	172	321	13	13	26
Other Race	2	1	3	0	0	0
Multiple Race*	21	30	51	0	1	1
Unknown	4	6	10	0	0	0
Subtotal	807	785	1,592	57	44	101
Foreign	15	13	28	0	0	0
Total	1,006	948	1,954	66	54	120

*Since 2002, students can select more than one race and / or ethnicity. **Those who did not choose
Hispanic/Latino' or 'Non-Hispanic/Latino' are counted under 'Non-Hispanic/Latino'.
Data Source: AAMC Data Warehouse: Applicant-Matriculant File, as of 5/9/2007.

includes factors such as gender, various educational degrees from varied institutions, life experiences, rural, city, and disadvantaged backgrounds, and many more.

Applicants should clearly indicate their state of residency. The MD Program is state-supported and a vast majority of our matriculating class will be Florida residents. But since the entering class of 2004, a growing number of non-Florida residents have matriculated into this program.

A Florida resident, for purposes of admission, lower tuition, and other university classification needs, is one whose parents or guardian (if the applicant is dependent) or the applicant (if independent) is a citizen of the U.S. or a PRA, and has established legal residence and resided permanently in Florida for at least 12 months preceding registration at the university. The owning of property in Florida, while being physically located in another state does not qualify a person to claim Florida residence. In those instances where residency is in question, an applicant is requested to submit a Declaration of Domicile one year in advance of matriculation for tuition purposes. Please visit *(http://www.registrar. usf.edu/Residency/Definitions.php)* for additional residency requirement information.

Interview invitations for all applicants are at the discretion of the Admissions Committee. An invitation to interview means only that the initial evaluation is sufficient to warrant further consideration by the committee. An accepted applicant is given two weeks to reply to an admissions offer to the MD Program. That response must be a written statement of intent to attend with an original signature. If an accepted applicant is later offered a position by another medical program, the applicant is obligated to notify each program of their intent to attend/withdraw as rapidly as possible. Any offer of acceptance is provisional pending the satisfactory completion of all requirements and

conditions of admission. An acceptance offer may be canceled failing to meet requirements or failure to maintain high scholastic standards.

Academic Support Programs

Academic Enhancement Services: The goal of this program is to improve student grades in historically difficult courses and to foster an environment of learning, where seeking academic assistance is not seen as remediation, but rather than a critical component of academic success.

The program is intended help medical, doctorate of physical therapy, and Interdisciplinary Medical Science degree (IMS) students who are in need of academic assistance. Students do not have to be experiencing academic difficulty to participate in this program. We encourage all students to take advantage of this program.

Tutors are available at no cost to students. The Office of Academic Enrichment pays 100 percent of the tutor fees.

In most cases, tutoring will be one-on-one. The type of tutoring sessions(s) will depend on available tutors. It is the responsibility of the student to set up appointments with the tutor.

Current medical or doctorate of physical therapy students who have been deemed course competent in the subject matter he/she will render tutelage facilitate academic assistance sessions. Students are recommended or endorsed by the Course Director(s) of the course in which he/she will render tutelage.

There is no limit to the number of hours you can receive tutoring services.

Enrichment Programs

Pre-medical Summer Enrichment Program (PSEP). The PSEP is an intensive six-week full-time summer program for highly motivated students who are preparing for medical school. The program will help participants to enhance the science and

communication skills needed for quality performance on the MCAT; explore test-taking strategies to enhance learning skills; provide exposure to medicine through clinical experiences; and offer medical school admissions information through interaction with medical school faculty, staff and students. The program is designed for undergraduates interested in medical school. To be eligible, students must have completed a minimum of 60 hours with an overall GPA no less than 3.0 prior to May 4, 2007. Applicants whose overall GPA is less than 3.0 will not be considered. Students receive a $1,500 stipend for participation in the PSEP program. Stipends are paid out in two installments. Students participate in the following five areas:

1. Academic Enhancement:

- Biology, Chemistry and Physics: Participants will be provided the opportunity to review and enhance their comprehension of concepts in biology, general and organic chemistry, and physics.
- Verbal Reasoning and Writing Skills: Participants will be provided the opportunity to enhance their reading and reading-inference skills as well as gain writing experience through personal essays and other assignments.
- Test Preparation: Participants will take science-based pre- and post-half tests and simulated MCAT exams during the program.

2. Test-Taking Strategies:

- Participants will work closely with L.E.A.R.N. Program faculty in the areas of reading skills, test-taking skills, etc. Utilizing a proven model of metacognition and intentional learning, students utilize the results of such assessments to develop individualized plans to improve or enhance essential learning skills.

AAMC

. Clinical Experience:

- Participates will be paired with physicians in the local community and you will have the opportunity to develop an appreciation of the "real world of medicine" through weekly clinical experiences.

. Clinical Seminars:

- Participants will take part in one hour per week of exposure to the "real world of medicine" through clinical topics such as health disparities, obesity, diabetes, heart disease and more.

. Workshop Series:

- Participants will participate in one hour per week of workshops on admissions procedures, financial planning, study skills, test taking, time management, stress management and interviewing techniques.
http://health.usf.edu/medicine/osde/psep.html)

Pre-matriculation Program: The purpose of this course is to introduce students to the rigor of a medical education, to provide a modest increase in your specific knowledge and to enhance the tools available to you for success in medical school. This program may benefit students who identify themselves as:

- First-generation college student
- English as a second language
- Non-traditional students (second career, returned to school after an absence, non-science major)
- Economically disadvantaged

The instructional methods to be used are threefold:

1. Case based education – This method of instruction was selected to provide for input of members of the basic science departments of the College of Medicine. The faculty members participating in this course are experienced instructors representing each of the basic science departments in the College of Medicine.

2. Lectures provided by selected faculty on Fridays after completion of the individual case study are intended to provide information necessary for complete understanding of the case.

3. Assessment of skills—Students will receive individual evaluations with regard to factors that are well recognized as significant in a successful medical school career. Specifically, each student will be evaluated with regard to their learning style, their reading skills and their test-taking talents. Individual programs will be designed for the students to enhance their competences in reading, studying and test taking. Laboratory exercises will be provided to accomplish these academic enhancements.

Interdisciplinary Medical Science degree (IMS). The Interdisciplinary Medical Science degree (IMS) is designed to provide qualified students with advanced training in the science basic to the practice of medicine. Students successfully completing the program will have a foundation that fosters opportunities in the private sector, teaching, or the pursuit of further advance degrees. A primary goal of this concentration is to provide promising medical school applicants an opportunity to develop the knowledge, skills, and attitudes that would enable them to have a career in the medical sciences. This concentration creates a unique opportunity for students interested in graduate work with a broad medical base. Students will take courses that, while not identical to the first year of medical school will provide the same level of depth, breadth, and intensity, allowing successful participants to demonstrate their readiness for the rigors of a medical school curriculum. Alternatively, appropriate selection of elective courses will allow any student who completes the program to tailor their educational experience to best suit their future plans and aspirations.
(http://health.usf.edu/medicine/oae/pre matriculation.html)

Student Financial Assistance
In addition to federal loan programs and National Medical Fellowships, the university has two special grant funds that are designated for minority students. These are the Delores A. Auzenne Fellowship and the University of South Florida College of Medicine Minority Tuition Scholarship.

Association of American Medical Colleges, 2007

Emory University School of Medicine*

Dr. Robert Lee
Associate Dean and Director
Multicultural Medical Student Affairs
1440 Clifton Road, NE
Ste. 310 WHSCAB
Atlanta, GA 30322
404-727 0016; 404-727 0045 Fax
rlee08@emory.edu

Recruitment

College Students. The Associate Dean for Multicultural Medical Student Affairs visits eight to ten college campuses per year to meet with students and faculty to discuss careers in medicine, answer their questions, and encourage them to apply to Emory University School of Medicine.

We make use of the Medical Minority Applicant Registry (Med-MAR) to provide information to candidates who have taken the April Medical College Admission Test (MCAT). By writing to selected candidates, we encourage them to apply for the following entering class. Generally, 1,000 potential candidates are encouraged to apply, resulting in an applicant pool of students-of-color and from disadvantaged backgrounds totalling almost 750 per year. The Committee on Admissions is very supportive and active in the efforts to recruit these men and women.

Middle and High School Students. The Summer Science Discovery Camp (Grades eight to ten) and The Science Academy (Grades 11 and 12) are designed to introduce and encourage students to explore the areas of science common in the life of humans. Starting with the principles that

- science is all around us,
- people-of-color and persons who are female are capable of learning, understanding, and excelling in scientific careers, and
- it is OK to be academically smart and well prepared in the sciences,

our six-week programs introduce students to the areas of biology, anatomy, chemistry, diseases common to humans, and neural science. Our programs are taught by medical students, residents, and medical school faculty. Guest lecturers also teach periodically during the summer programs.

Increased numbers of visitation to high school/middle school career days by the Associate Dean for Multicultural Medical Student Affairs and members of the Student National Medical Association (SNMA) provide the programs and careers in the health sciences increased visibility for these students.

Admissions

All candidates to Emory University School of Medicine must apply to through the American Medical College Application Service (AMCAS) and authorize this school to receive their application. Our AMCAS school code is #121. October 15th of each year is our AMCAS deadline, and December 1st is the deadline for the completion of our Supplemental Application. Candidates are *strongly* urged to complete and submit the AMCAS and Emory Supplemental Applications well in advance of the announced deadline dates. The following factors are considered in the review of applications:

- Science and non-science grades and grade trends;
- Scores on the Medical College Admission Test;
- Extracurricular and leadership activities of the candidate;

Emory University School of Medicine, 2006
Applicants and Matriculants by Gender, Race and Ethnicity

Race and Ethnicity	Applicants			Matriculants		
	Women	Men	Total	Women	Men	Total
Hispanic/Latino						
Cuban	24	16	40	0	0	0
Mexican American	39	31	70	0	1	1
Puerto Rican	22	15	37	0	0	0
Other Hispanic	71	64	135	4	3	7
Multiple Hispanic*	7	4	11	0	0	0
Subtotal	163	130	293	4	4	8
Non-Hispanic/Latino**						
Black	463	187	650	3	5	8
Native American/Alaska Native	6	7	13	0	0	0
Native Hawaiian/Other Pacific Islander	5	3	8	0	0	0
White	1,440	1,605	3,045	39	36	75
Asian	542	577	1,119	13	5	18
Other Race	1	3	4	0	0	0
Multiple Race*	78	71	149	1	0	1
Unknown	17	20	37	0	0	0
Subtotal	2,552	2,473	5,025	56	46	102
Foreign	131	124	255	2	2	4
Total	2,846	2,727	5,573	62	52	114

*Since 2002, students can select more than one race and / or ethnicity. **Those who did not choose Hispanic/Latino' or 'Non-Hispanic/Latino' are counted under 'Non-Hispanic/Latino'.
Data Source: AAMC Data Warehouse: Applicant-Matriculant File, as of 5/9/2007.

Letters of recommendation by faculty, administrators, and mentors who have known the candidate; and personal interview, if authorized, by the Committee on Admissions.

Our interview season begins on October 1st and concludes on the last day of February. No decisions regarding interviews will be made until the application is completed. If candidates take or re-take the August MCAT, a decision will be rendered when the scores arrive and all other supporting documentation is received. Applicants are reminded that the submission of an application, receipt of an invitation to apply, and/or an invitation to interview is not a guarantee of being accepted at Emory University School of Medicine. We practice "rolling admissions" and announce decisions each month following the meeting of the Committee on Admissions.

The Office of Multicultural Medical Student Affairs sponsors the *Emory Revisited Program* beginning the third Wednesday of March each year. Successful candidates from underrepresented groups who are admitted by that time are invited to return for a "second look" at Emory. Hosted by members of the Emory SNMA Chapter, faculty, and administrators, this program allows face-to-face, one-on-one opportunities to meet members of the Emory family and other candidates who have been accepted and learn more about the school, the university, and the City of Atlanta. Expenses for this program are paid by the Office of Multicultural Medical Student Affairs. Participants are reimbursed up to $150.00 for transportation. All other expenses are covered.

Academic and Personal Support

We believe that all candidates admitted to Emory University School of Medicine are prepared and able to succeed, based on the review of academic credentials and personal interview. On the occasion where a student may encounter academic difficulty, faculty are available for one-on-one tutoring, extra personal and/or small-group "help sessions," and personal counseling. Personal counseling is available through the Office of Multicultural Medical Student Affairs, the Executive Associate Dean for Medical Education and Students Affairs, the students' Medical Society Leaders at Emory, as well as Student Counseling. As warranted, students can be seen in the Student Counseling Center of Emory University. It has been our experience that difficult personal situations may be manifested in academic performance. In the event a student becomes medically ill, the mandatory health insurance covers the medical needs, including hospitalization and care by a psychiatrist or psychologist.

Student Financial Assistance

Need-based financial aid is available to students to help pay for his/her medical education and related expenses. Grants and loans are available to help meet need. Accepted students must file the Free Application for Federal Student Financial Aid (FAFSA) (beginning January 1st) and the CSS Financial Aid PROFILE® (beginning October 1st). Early submission is encouraged!

There are two scholarships of note:

The Woodruff Scholarship—Seven are awarded in the School of Medicine, with five for students in the regular M.D. degree program and two for students in the M.D./Ph.D. Program.

The Dean's Scholarship—The number varies from year to year. Scholarships are awarded to students from diverse backgrounds (e.g., educational, financial, and geographical areas of the country).

We encourage students to borrow only the amount of money they need to avoid excess debt. Students find that having a roommate helps to keep their debt as low as possible. Financial aid is administered centrally at Emory and financial aid advisers are available to assist students.

Medical College of Georgia School of Medicine

Wilma A. Sykes-Brown
Assistant Dean
Office of Educational
Outreach and Partnerships
Medical College of Georgia
School of Medicine
CB 1801, Research & Education Building
Augusta, GA 30912-1900
706-721-2522; 706-721-8203 fax
wsykes@mail.mcg.edu
http://www.mcg.edu/careers/specop/

Recruitment

The Medical College of Georgia conducts an extensive recruitment program utilizing the team approach to assure that students benefit from a targeted recruitment strategy as well as multiple contact persons who may be able to assist them as they prepare for medical school. Faculty and staff in the Office of Educational Outreach and Partnerships, in the Office of Admissions in the School of Medicine, enrolled medical students, and Clinical Faculty, visit colleges through-out Georgia, especially colleges with a preponderance of underrepresented students. Additionally, visits are made to out-of-state colleges that have large enrollments of Georgia residents who are underrepresented in the health professions.

Admissions

Applications to the first-year class of the Medical College of Georgia (MCG) are considered on the basis of the assessment of potential for meeting the health care needs of Georgia, the applicants' motivation and potential for serving as a physician, personal interviews, and academic ability and achievement as measured through college grades and scores on the Medical College Admissions Test (MCAT).

The Admissions Committee is composed of 18 voting members including 12 faculty, three medical students, one community member, one physician from the community, and the Associate Dean for Admissions. There is no application fee to apply for Admission to the Medical College of Georgia. Application through the Early Decision Program is encouraged for Georgia residents. The MCG School of Medicine encourages qualified students from groups underrepresented in medicine to apply.

Academic Support Programs

The Office of Educational Outreach and Partnerships sponsors academic enrichment programs designed to meet the special needs of underrepresented, non-traditional, and disadvantaged students at the pre-admission, pre-matriculation, and matriculation stages of the educational pipeline. Additionally, academic support services are available to all students enrolled in each of MCG's five colleges to enhance student retention and graduation from their specific programs of study.

The Office of Educational Outreach and Partnerships administers the following programs:

- The *Student Educational Enrichment Programs (SEEP)*, a seven-week summer program for high achieving pre-college and college students, designed to enrich their academic backgrounds and strengthen test-taking abilities in preparation for careers in the health professions;
- The *Supplemental Instruction Program (SIP)*, a retention program for matriculating underrepresented, non-traditional, disadvantaged, and other students in need of academic assistance;
- The *Prematriculation Program,* a six-week summer program for students who have been accepted into our Schools of Medicine, Dentistry and Graduate Studies. The program is designed to facilitate the academic adjustment of underrepresented, non-traditional, and disadvantaged students

Medical College of Georgia School of Medicine, 2006
Applicants and Matriculants by Gender, Race and Ethnicity

Race and Ethnicity	Applicants			Matriculants		
	Women	Men	Total	Women	Men	Total
Hispanic/Latino						
Cuban	4	9	13	0	0	0
Mexican American	7	2	9	0	0	0
Puerto Rican	8	6	14	2	0	2
Other Hispanic	31	31	62	0	2	2
Multiple Hispanic*	4	4	8	0	0	0
Subtotal	54	52	106	2	2	4
Non-Hispanic/Latino**						
Black	229	77	306	5	3	8
Native American/Alaska Native	3	1	4	0	0	0
Native Hawaiian/Other Pacific Islander	0	2	2	0	0	0
White	472	526	998	65	78	143
Asian	149	167	316	21	11	32
Other Race	1	1	2	0	0	0
Multiple Race*	20	27	47	2	1	3
Unknown	1	4	5	0	0	0
Subtotal	875	805	1,680	93	93	186
Foreign	46	29	75	0	0	0
Total	975	886	1,861	95	95	190

*Since 2002, students can select more than one race and / or ethnicity. **Those who did not choose
Hispanic/Latino' or 'Non-Hispanic/Latino' are counted under 'Non-Hispanic/Latino'.
Data Source: AAMC Data Warehouse: Applicant-Matriculant File, as of 5/9/2007.

Association of American Medical Colleges, 2007

and to increase retention of students in the targeted groups. The program is held the summer immediately prior to the beginning of students' first fall semester.

Student Financial Assistance
The Medical College of Georgia's Office of Student Financial Aid assists students in financial planning for meeting educational expenses. Approximately 80 percent of all medical students receive some form of financial aid. Financial assistance includes loans, scholarships, and part-time employment. Non-federal scholarships administered by the Medical College of Georgia are awarded by the School of Medicine Scholarship Committee. Financial aid application materials are distributed electronically via the internet at *(www.mcg.edu/ students/finaid)*. Students are encouraged to apply for financial aid as soon as possible after January 1 and to complete the process by March 31. For more information, contact the Office of Student Financial Aid, Medical College of Georgia, AA-2013, Augusta, GA 30912-7320; 706-721-4901; email: *(cparks@mail.mcg.edu)*.

Educational Partnerships
The Medical College of Georgia partners with local high schools and colleges throughout Georgia, with the Statewide Area Health Education Centers (AHECs), and with non-Georgia colleges with large numbers of Georgia residents, to assure that underrepresented, non-traditional, and disadvantaged students have access to health career opportunities. The Office of Educational Outreach and Partnerships has established formal Affiliation Agreements with the following colleges: Augusta State University, Clark Atlanta University, Fort Valley State University, Georgia College and State University, Paine College, Savannah State University, and Valdosta State University. Formal agreements have also been formed with the Richmond County School District, National Science

Center—Fort Discovery, and a community-based entity under the auspices of Beulah Grove Baptist Church. Informal collaborations are also maintained with Albany State, Georgia Southern, Morehouse College, Hampton University, Spelman College, State University of West Georgia, University of Georgia, Xavier University, and the Boys and Girls' Club of Augusta. The Assistant Dean, Office of Educational Outreach and Partnerships, serves as Faculty Advisor for MCG student organizations that include the Student National Medical Association and the Junior Medical League.

Other Pertinent Information
The Medical College of Georgia is the Health Science University of the state of Georgia. It is strategically located in Augusta, the second largest city in the State, and is 2.5 hours from Atlanta, 2 hours from Savannah, 2.5 hours from Charleston, and 55 minutes from Columbia, South Carolina.

AAMC

Mercer University School of Medicine*

Rachel M.A. Brown
Assistant Dean for
Student Affairs; Minority Affairs
Mercer University School of Medicine
1550 College Street
Macon, GA 31207
478-301-2542; 478-301-2547 Fax
Brown_rm@mercer.edu

Recruitment
Mercer University School of Medicine makes a significant effort to recruit among minority groups underrepresented in medicine. Annually, admissions officers visit Georgia universities and colleges with predominantly underrepresented minority student bodies. In addition, staff lecture to pre-medical students and organizations, and participate in career day programs and fairs.

Admissions
The Admissions Committee is committed to admitting qualified individuals from groups underrepresented in medicine. The academic record and non-cognitive variables are given equal weight in the admissions process. Compliance with the school's mission is emphasized. Therefore, experience relative to health care for Georgia's medically underserved, community service, and leadership are emphasized.

Academic Support Programs
The Office of Study Skills assists all students who have personal or academic problems. Programs for underrepresented minority students are embodied in the overall operations of the Study Skills Office.

Enrichment Programs
Summer Pre-matriculation Program. Introduction to Basic Medical Sciences is a cross-section of advance biology topics that represent the introductory material encountered in the first three phases (blocks) at Mercer University School of Medicine. The goal of this course is to provide an overview of the essential elements of biochemistry, histology, cell biology, microbiology, and immunology for first-year medical students. Advanced topics presented in the first year of medical school require a basic understanding of key biological concepts. By previewing some of these concepts before entering medical school the student should enhance his/her chances of academic success. Students are expected to have successfully completed a college general biology course and organic chemistry.

Student Financial Assistance
The application fee is waived for applicants with an American Medical College Application Service (AMCAS) fee waiver. There is a faculty endowed scholarship for minority students. Low interest loans and state scholarships are also available.

Educational Partnerships
Faculty work with students in the community on their science fair projects as well as participate in the science fairs. Students also have an opportunity to work in the laboratories with research faculty.

Other Information
The mission of Mercer University School of Medicine is to educate physicians and health professionals to meet the primary care and health care needs of rural and medically underserved areas of Georgia. The principal need is for physician specialists in the areas of family practice, internal

Mercer University School of Medicine, 2006
Applicants and Matriculants by Gender, Race and Ethnicity

Race and Ethnicity		Applicants			Matriculants		
		Women	Men	Total	Women	Men	Total
Hispanic/Latino							
Cuban		2	1	3	0	0	0
Mexican American		4	0	4	0	0	0
Puerto Rican		3	2	5	0	0	0
Other Hispanic		12	12	24	0	0	0
Multiple Hispanic*		3	0	3	0	0	0
	Subtotal	24	15	39	0	0	0
Non-Hispanic/Latino**							
Black		100	35	135	1	1	2
Native American/Alaska Native		1	0	1	0	0	0
White		175	204	379	24	27	51
Asian		64	54	118	2	3	5
Other Race		1	1	2	0	0	0
Multiple Race*		10	9	19	2	0	2
Unknown		1	0	1	0	0	0
	Subtotal	352	303	655	29	31	60
Foreign		2	0	2	0	0	0
	Total	378	318	696	29	31	60

*Since 2002, students can select more than one race and / or ethnicity. **Those who did not choose
'Hispanic/Latino' or 'Non-Hispanic/Latino' are counted under 'Non-Hispanic/Latino'.
Data Source: AAMC Data Warehouse: Applicant-Matriculant File, as of 5/9/2007.

medicine and pediatrics, obstetrics and gynecology, general surgery, psychiatry, and Emergency Medicine and these are recognized as career choices consistent with the mission of the school of medicine. Mercer School of Medicine does not accept out-of-state students.

Morehouse School of Medicine

Dr. Ngozi Anachebe
Interim Assistant Dean for Student Affairs
Assistant Professor of Clinical Ob/Gyn
Morehouse School of Medicine
720 Westview Drive, S.W.
Atlanta, GA 30310-1495
404-752-1651; 404-752-1824 Fax
nanachebe@msm.edu

Recruitment

Recruitment is conducted by the Office of Admissions and Student Affairs. The admissions officer and other student affairs staff members, administrators, faculty, and students participate in the recruitment process.

The recruitment efforts—to identify, inform, and encourage prospective minority and disadvantaged candidates—are multifaceted. Approaches designed to accomplish this include: recruitment visits at state and private colleges and universities; seminars and conferences within the Atlanta University Center; contacts made with pre-medical advisors and counselors; and participation in many local, state, and national conferences and career fairs. Arrangements can be made to tour Morehouse School of Medicine on an individual or group basis through the Office of Admissions.

Admissions

The primary mission of Morehouse School of Medicine is to admit and educate students who will become primary care physicians for medically underserved rural areas and inner cities, including low-income and minority communities. The Admissions Committee seeks candidates who possess the academic qualifications judged necessary for the successful study and

Morehouse School of Medicine, 2006
Applicants and Matriculants by Gender, Race and Ethnicity

Race and Ethnicity	Applicants			Matriculants		
	Women	Men	Total	Women	Men	Total
Hispanic/Latino						
Cuban	11	10	21	0	0	0
Mexican American	25	11	36	0	0	0
Puerto Rican	15	13	28	0	1	1
Other Hispanic	44	46	90	1	1	2
Multiple Hispanic*	6	5	11	0	0	0
Subtotal	101	85	186	1	2	3
Non-Hispanic/Latino**						
Black	863	406	1,269	24	11	35
Native American/Alaska Native	5	7	12	0	0	0
Native Hawaiian/Other Pacific Islander	7	5	12	0	0	0
White	289	361	650	3	4	7
Asian	319	333	652	3	4	7
Other Race	3	4	7	0	0	0
Multiple Race*	44	29	73	1	0	1
Unknown	5	11	16	0	0	0
Subtotal	1,535	1,156	2,691	31	19	50
Foreign	56	40	96	0	0	0
Total	1,692	1,281	2,973	32	21	53

*Since 2002, students can select more than one race and / or ethnicity. **Those who did not choose Hispanic/Latino' or 'Non-Hispanic/Latino' are counted under 'Non-Hispanic/Latino'.
Data Source: AAMC Data Warehouse: Applicant-Matriculant File, as of 5/9/2007.

practice of medicine. Equally important, but less tangible, are personal factors such as character, maturity, integrity, perseverance, and motivation.

Because of the urgent need for physicians in the state of Georgia, preferential consideration will be given to qualified residents of Georgia. However, Morehouse School of Medicine welcomes applications from well qualified out-of-state students.

Applicants must apply through the American Medical College Application Service (AMCAS) and request that their application, along with Medical College Admission Test scores, be forwarded to Morehouse School of Medicine. The school's code number is GA825. Each application received from AMCAS is reviewed individually. Following the initial screening, applicants granted further consideration are requested to submit supplementary materials. Only completed applications are then evaluated for interview. A completed application consists of an AMCAS application form, all supplementary materials, and the $50 application fee. Applications not completed by given deadlines are withdrawn from consideration.

Academic Support Programs

Complete advisement and retention activities are offered to all medical school matriculants. Upon matriculation, each student is assigned to a faculty advisor. Available to all students are a wide range of academic support services such as student tutors, study-skills and test-taking strategies, the Kaplan Board preparation program, and personal counseling from Counseling Services. Retention activities are designed to meet the needs of the individual student and may include a flexible curriculum schedule.

Enrichment Programs

Summer Pre-matriculation Program. The Morehouse School of Medicine offers a five-week summer pre-matriculation program for rising seniors and post-baccalaureate students. This program includes courses in human morphology, biochemistry, epidemiology/ bio-statistics, test taking and study skills, and time management. This program is identical to the curriculum of the first-year students and begins approximately the first week of July. The 11-month curriculum for first-year students also begins at this time.

Student Financial Assistance

A non-refundable processing fee of $50 is required with submission of the Online Supplemental Application. If a student has received a waiver of the AMCAS application fee, that student is eligible for a waiver of the $50 fee. The school does not have funds available to help with interview trips. Morehouse uses a needs-analysis system to determine students' eligibility for financial aid. The demonstration of need is the key factor in all financial aid awards. The School of Medicine's scholarships are awarded to qualified applicants on the basis of established criteria and in accordance with the stipulation of the donors.

Educational Partnerships

Below are existing programs for elementary, middle, and high school students.

Benjamin Carson Science Academy.

Partnerships: Morehouse School of Medicine and metro Atlanta schools.

The Benjamin Carson Science Academy consists of a summer science camp and a Saturday science component. It provides an enrichment program for elementary and middle school students to enhance their knowledge of science, mathematics, and health careers. The students are involved in hands-on interactive activities that are designed to challenge them while

making the learning of science fun. The students also have an opportunity to explore health careers, participate in educational field trips, and participate in recreational activities. These recreational activities include chess, martial arts, and dance. Students are recruited for the program after completion of the third grade and continue until they complete the eighth grade.

Medical Post Explorers Program.

Partnerships: Morehouse School of Medicine, Boy Scouts of America, and metro Atlanta public school districts.

The Medical Post Explorers (MedPost) Program was established at Morehouse School of Medicine in conjunction with the Boy Scouts of America in 1991. The program was designed to introduce and encourage high school students to pursue a college education in the sciences that will ultimately lead to a career in the medical, biomedical science, allied health, or technologies fields. Current Morehouse School of Medicine medical students and MedPost alumni volunteer their time to assist Med-Post students during the 'hands-on science' laboratory experiments; they also serve as tutors, mentors, and positive role models for the participants.

Vivien Thomas High School Research Program.

Partnerships: Morehouse School of Medicine and metro Atlanta public school districts.

The Vivien Thomas Summer Research Program for high school students was established in 2001 to provide experiences in the research laboratories at the Morehouse School of Medicine. The students conduct research under the direction of a medical school faculty member and learn the content, process, and methodology involved in inquiry science. They serve as apprentices in biomedical research laboratories and conduct scientific research in conjunction with real research being investigated by Morehouse School of Medicine faculty, research professors, and laboratory technicians. At the end of this summer experience the students present their research findings to the faculty and staff at Morehouse School of Medicine Priority is given to rising ninth- and tenth-grade students who have participated in the Benjamin Carson Science Academy or the MedPost Program.

*Existing Programs for
College Undergraduates.*

SNMA/MAPS Mentoring Program
Partners: Morehouse School of Medicine, Atlanta University Center Schools, Georgia State, and University of Georgia.
Location: Morehouse School of Medicine.
Participants: Undergraduate students of Atlanta University Center Schools, Georgia State, and University of Georgia.

The SNMA/MAPS Mentoring Program is conducted by Morehouse School of Medicine medical students who are members of the Student National Medical Association (SNMA) and the Minority Association of Pre-medical Students (MAPS). They serve as mentors for undergraduate students. Students in the Morehouse School of Medicine college cohort are enrolled in this program.

*Public Health Fellowship Program
for Minority Students.*

The Public Health Fellowship Program for Minority Students is a summer program that provides rising college seniors or recent graduates a hands-on experience in public health. The program includes opportunities in epidemiological or community intervention research under the supervision of a mentor. One Example of research is surveying mothers of preschool children in public health clinics regarding risk factors for lead poisoning.

Other Pertinent Information
Morehouse School of Medicine, as a two-year basic medical science institution, admitted its charter class in 1978. In 1985 the school received full accreditation by the Liason Committee on Medical Education and awarded its first M.D. degrees on May 17, 1985.

Students are required to pass the United States Medical Licensing Examination (USMLE) Step 1 for promotion into the clinical phase of the curriculum. Passage of the USMLE Step 2 examination is required to receive the M.D. degree.

Morehouse School of Medicine also offers academic programs leading to the Ph.D. in the Biomedical Sciences and the Master of Public Health Degrees. For more information, contact the admissions office at 404-752-1650.

University of Hawai'i at Mānoa John A. Burns School of Medicine

Dr. Satoru Izutsu
Senior Associate Dean and Chair
Admissions Committee
University of Hawai'i at Mānoa
John A. Burns School of Medicine
651 Iola Street
Honolulu, HI 96813
808-692-0890; 808-692-1247 Fax
sizutsu@hawaii.edu

Recruitment

Significant recruitment efforts at the University of Hawai'i at Mānoa John A. Burns School of Medicine are directed towards increasing the number of individuals from educationally, socially, or economically disadvantaged backgrounds who have demonstrated a commitment to serve areas of need in Hawaii and the Pacific. Priority is given to applicants with strong ties to the State of Hawaii and the Pacific.

An extensive network has been established with key officials in local public and private schools, scholarship officers, local legislators, mass media, and college students studying in the United States. Recruitment is conducted by the faculty and staff alumni and students who serve as role models and help to encourage and motivate the men and women of Hawaii to pursue health careers.

Admissions

Applicants are screened by an Admissions Committee composed of faculty and medical practitioners. All applicants are considered without discrimination on the basis of age, sex, race, creed, national origin, or handicap. Standards are high, and the criteria are both objective and subjective. Judgements are made on an individual basis, the intent being to select the candidates deemed most likely to become humanistic physicians. Important in the selection process is an evaluation of what the potential student might contribute to the welfare of the people of Hawaii and the Pacific. Preference is given to the residents of Hawaii. For further information see our Web site: *(http://hawaiimed.hawaii.edu).*

Academic Support Programs

In medical school, all first-year students are assigned faculty advisors. All students are offered assistance in study skills, test-taking skills, speaking and writing skills. Students are screened for learning differences. All students are assessed for learning styles. The progress of all students is reviewed regularly and help is offered as needed.

Enrichment Programs

The Imi Ho'ola Post-Baccalaureate Program. The University of Hawai'i at Mānoa John A. Burns School of Medicine conducts a post-baccalaureate program designed to provide medical educational opportunities for individuals from disadvantaged backgrounds who are deemed capable of succeeding in medical school. This program prepares students for the academic rigors of medical school and provides individual counseling, tutoring, and support. Each year, up to ten students are selected to participate in the 12-month program. Upon successful completion, they will matriculate into the first-year class at the John A. Burns School of Medicine.

The Native Hawaiian Center of Excellence (NHCOE) is one of 37 Centers of Excellence in the U.S. funded by the Division of Health Professions Diversity, Bureau of Health Professionals, Health Resources Services Administration, Department of Health and Human Services. The mission of the center is to

University of Hawai'i at Mānoa John A. Burns School of Medicine, 2006
Applicants and Matriculants by Gender, Race and Ethnicity

Race and Ethnicity	Applicants			Matriculants		
	Women	Men	Total	Women	Men	Total
Hispanic/Latino						
Cuban	6	10	16	0	0	0
Mexican American	13	15	28	0	0	0
Puerto Rican	4	5	9	1	1	2
Other Hispanic	31	20	51	3	0	3
Multiple Hispanic*	5	1	6	0	0	0
Subtotal	59	51	110	4	1	5
Non-Hispanic/Latino**						
Black	25	16	41	0	0	0
Native American/Alaska Native	1	4	5	0	0	0
Native Hawaiian/Other Pacific Islander	22	12	34	5	3	8
White	286	424	710	3	4	7
Asian	244	266	510	16	14	30
Other Race	2	2	4	0	0	0
Multiple Race*	60	67	127	3	9	12
Unknown	3	9	12	0	0	0
Subtotal	643	800	1,443	27	30	57
Foreign	41	35	76	0	0	0
Total	743	886	1,629	31	31	62

*Since 2002, students can select more than one race and / or ethnicity. **Those who did not choose Hispanic/Latino' or 'Non-Hispanic/Latino' are counted under 'Non-Hispanic/Latino'.
Data Source: AAMC Data Warehouse: Applicant-Matriculant File, as of 5/9/2007.

improve the health and wellness of Native Hawaiians through research, leadership training, faculty and curriculum development, cultural competency, information resources, and networking. Programs and activities include:

- Continuing Education—Focusing on Native Hawaiian health and cultural competency
- Fellowship and Faculty Training Program
- Oral History Project
- Secondary School Recruitment Program
- Rural Placement Services
- Student Retention Program
- Native Hawaiian Research Elective
- Historic Medical Documents Reprint Series
- Native Hawaiian Health Database Resource

Administratively, the Imi Hoʻola Program and Center are under the Department of Native Hawaiian Health, chaired by Dr. Marjorie Mau.

Student Financial Assistance
Financial status is not a factor in considering applicants for acceptance. Efforts are made to assist students in obtaining loans and scholarships whenever possible. Students in financial need are eligible for assistance from funds administered by the University of Hawaiʻi's Financial Aid Office. Organizations and governments outside the university and the state offer assistance, especially to students of Hawaiian, Samoan, Micronesian, and Filipino ancestry.

Other Pertinent Information
- The John A. Burns School of Medicine (JABSOM) is one of the most ethnically diverse medical schools in the United States.
- The principal mode of instruction at JABSOM is problem-based learning (PBL). This innovative method of instruction is well suited to the learning styles of many minority students.

Chicago Medical School at Rosalind Franklin University of Medicine and Science

Dr. Timothy R. Hansen
Vice President for Academic Affairs
Rosalind Franklin University of Medicine and Science
3333 Green Bay Road,
North Chicago, IL 60064
847-578-8734; 847-775-6537 Fax
tim.hansen@rosalindfranklin.edu
www.rosalindfranklin.edu

Recruitment
Recruitment is conducted primarily through field visitations and visits to local universities with large minority enrollments. Groups of students from these universities are invited to visit the medical school campus for group discussions and individual conferences with the Admissions Office staff and the Minority Affairs Officer. Minority students enrolled at the medical school are very much involved in this process. Administrative persons taking part in these programs are the Assistant Dean of Educational Affairs and the Director of Admissions. Considerable contact is maintained between these officials and many of the special minority programs offered both within the university and by other schools.

Admissions
A separate committee for minority applicants is not utilized. All applicants are processed in the same manner. The Admissions Office and the Office of Educational Affairs both respond to admission information requests from minority applicants. Additionally, efforts are made to facilitate contact between minority applicants and interviewees with

Chicago Medical School at Rosalind Franklin University of Medicine and Science, 2006
Applicants and Matriculants by Gender, Race and Ethnicity

Race and Ethnicity	Applicants			Matriculants		
	Women	Men	Total	Women	Men	Total
Hispanic/Latino						
Cuban	22	18	40	0	0	0
Mexican American	71	70	141	1	1	2
Puerto Rican	15	14	29	0	0	0
Other Hispanic	82	77	159	0	0	0
Multiple Hispanic*	17	6	23	0	0	0
Subtotal	207	185	392	1	1	2
Non-Hispanic/Latino**						
Black	197	108	305	3	3	6
Native American/Alaska Native	3	6	9	0	0	0
Native Hawaiian/Other Pacific Islander	17	15	32	0	2	2
White	1,584	1,947	3,531	30	49	79
Asian	1,111	1,123	2,234	32	46	78
Other Race	8	7	15	0	1	1
Multiple Race*	102	91	193	0	2	2
Unknown	18	33	51	1	0	1
Subtotal	3,040	3,330	6,370	66	103	169
Foreign	220	228	448	5	9	14
Total	3,467	3,743	7,210	72	113	185

*Since 2002, students can select more than one race and / or ethnicity. **Those who did not choose Hispanic/Latino' or 'Non-Hispanic/Latino' are counted under 'Non-Hispanic/Latino'.
Data Source: AAMC Data Warehouse: Applicant-Matriculant File, as of 5/9/2007.

minority students of the medical school by direct introduction during visits to the university, exchange of phone numbers, or letters.

Academic Support Programs
Academic skills programs are available (optional) to all students early in their first term. Academic skills counseling, tutoring, personal counseling, and time management information are available to all students. These services are presented through academic departments and several Chicago Medical School offices, including Educational Affairs and Student Affairs, and the University Division of Student Development. Students who encounter academic problems are counseled by the Senior Associate Dean for Student Affairs and referred to the appropriate university office for assistance. Modifications to the medical school program, which may or may not require an extended period of medical study, can be designed.

Enrichment Programs
Pre-matriculation Program. Rosalind Franklin University, in collaboration with the Chicago Area Health and Medical Careers Program (CAHMCP), offers a Pre-matriculation Program for minority students working in the CAHMCP program. Students recommended by CAHMCP and selected by Rosalind Franklin University of Medicine and Science for this program are enrolled in selected courses with first-year medical students and are given access to all the support services of the university. Demonstration of academic excellence in this curriculum is seen as a strong indicator of success by the Chicago Medical School (CMS) Admissions Committee.

Student Financial Assistance
Low interest living expense loans are available to students who have minimal personal and family resources and/or, because of academic status, do not have access to state and federal financial aid programs. In addition, disadvantaged students are given consideration for deferral of tuition payments for a limited period. All students are encouraged to discuss their needs with the Financial Aid Office, in advance of matriculation, to obtain a realistic view of their needs and the availability of funds.

Educational Partnerships
Chicago Area Health and Medical Careers Program (CAHMCP). Rosalind Franklin University is an active participant in the CMS and CAHMCP partnership, which presents the Pre-matriculation Program noted above.

Loyola University of Chicago Stritch School of Medicine

Dr. Julita McPherson, Assistant Professor of Family Medicine
Loyola University of Chicago Stritch School of Medicine, Office of Admissions
Bldg. 120, Room 200
2160 South First Avenue
Maywood, IL 60153
708-216-3229; 708-216-9160 Fax

Recruitment

Loyola University of Chicago Stritch School of Medicine welcomes applications from students with diverse backgrounds, including those who are economically disadvantaged or belong to a group that is underrepresented in medicine. Loyola's efforts to recruit and encourage minority and disadvantaged students to pursue scientific and health-related careers include participation in community outreach programs and promotion of reciprocal campus visitation programs. Faculty, medical students, and administration all contribute to the success of Loyola's recruitment efforts.

Admissions

Successful applicants to the Stritch School of Medicine demonstrate academic competence and the potential to satisfactorily complete Stritch's four-year interdisciplinary curriculum. Loyola's Committee on Admissions, composed of basic and clinical science faculty, administrators, and students, reviews all applications. In the evaluation process, committee members look not only at an applicant's academic ability, but also at his/her ability to solve problems, handle responsibility, and work effectively with others. Ideal candidates for admission to the Stritch School of Medicine demonstrate leadership, involvement in community service, and the ability to work with a diverse patient population.

Academic Support Programs

The Stritch School of Medicine's Office of Student Affairs supports students in their studies through academic counseling and referral to a network of faculty and other resources. To help students adjust to the rigor of the curriculum, the Stritch Teaching and Learning Center sponsors workshops and offers materials on topics such as effective study strategies, problem-solving techniques, memorization, time management, test taking, and the use of computer applications for learning and testing. Students are encouraged to meet with the program's director to talk about particular concerns, either in a small-group setting or one on one. Through all four years, students are paired with mentors and role models within the curriculum or in tandem with it. During the first year, students are assigned to a clinical faculty advisor who helps guide their academic pursuits and progress. Loyola's faculty is noted for its accessibility to students, and their interest in fostering formal and informal learning and professional growth.

Enrichment Programs

The Summer Enrichment Program (SEP) at Loyola University of Chicago Stritch School of Medicine is a six-week experience for pre-medical students. The program offers students a variety of educational experiences including academic courses, clinical experiences, and service activities to enhance their preparation for a career in medicine. The program targets students who have the potential to enrich the diversity of our medical student community. SEP participants will develop an understanding and appreciation of the skills and attributes needed to deliver compassionate health care through the basic ideals of Jesuit education. These ideals include striving for excellence, care and concern

Loyola University of Chicago Stritch School of Medicine, 2006
Applicants and Matriculants by Gender, Race and Ethnicity

Race and Ethnicity	Applicants			Matriculants		
	Women	Men	Total	Women	Men	Total
Hispanic/Latino						
Cuban	26	22	48	0	1	1
Mexican American	87	86	173	3	2	5
Puerto Rican	20	18	38	0	0	0
Other Hispanic	89	97	186	1	2	3
Multiple Hispanic*	13	13	26	1	0	1
Subtotal	235	236	471	5	5	10
Non-Hispanic/Latino**						
Black	166	96	262	4	2	6
Native American/Alaska Native	5	5	10	0	0	0
Native Hawaiian/Other Pacific Islander	18	12	30	0	0	0
White	2,334	2,658	4,992	52	53	105
Asian	1,056	1,071	2,127	7	10	17
Other Race	8	8	16	0	0	0
Multiple Race*	112	98	210	2	0	2
Unknown	21	31	52	0	0	0
Subtotal	3,720	3,979	7,699	65	65	130
Foreign	9	10	19	0	0	0
Total	3,964	4,225	8,189	70	70	140

*Since 2002, students can select more than one race and / or ethnicity. **Those who did not choose
Hispanic/Latino' or 'Non-Hispanic/Latino' are counted under 'Non-Hispanic/Latino'.
Data Source: AAMC Data Warehouse: Applicant-Matriculant File, as of 5/9/2007.

Association of American Medical Colleges, 2007

for the individual, service to the poor, and reflection on the human experience.

Student Financial Assistance

A fee waiver is granted to applicants who have received a fee waiver from the American Medical College Application Service, or who submit a letter explaining their situation from a college financial aid officer. The Stritch Financial Aid Office has been successful in funding minority and disadvantaged students through need-based financial aid programs, including Loyola Stritch grant and loan funds.

Northwestern University, The Feinberg School of Medicine

Sunny Gibson, M.S.W.
Director, Minority and Cultural Affairs
303 East Chicago Avenue,
Morton 1-658
Chicago, IL 60611
312-503-0461; 312-503-4474 Fax
s-gibson@nothernwestern.edu
www.medschool.northwestern.edu

Recruitment

Student recruitment is conducted at the college level, primarily, with emphasis placed on candidates who have distinguished themselves academically, personally and professionally, and come from a multiplicity of backgrounds and interests. The medical school facilitates recruitment through visits to the institution, pre-arranged group tours of the medical school, premedical enrichment programs and advising, and extensive communication by mail, email and telephone. Feinberg is committed to diversity and excellence, which go hand in hand in enrolling the best and brightest students.

Admissions

Applications to the Medical School are reviewed and evaluated by a diverse group of faculty and students, who compose the Committee on Admissions. The admission of minority student applicants is determined on a competitive basis with the same process used to evaluate all applicants. Inclusive in the evaluation process is attention to trends in performance, employment history, extracurricular involvement, scholarly activities, the

Northwestern University the Feinberg School of Medicine, 2006
Applicants and Matriculants by Gender, Race and Ethnicity

Race and Ethnicity	Applicants			Matriculants		
	Women	Men	Total	Women	Men	Total
Hispanic/Latino						
Cuban	17	13	30	1	0	1
Mexican American	70	63	133	1	1	2
Puerto Rican	14	12	26	0	0	0
Other Hispanic	69	64	133	2	2	4
Multiple Hispanic*	8	6	14	0	0	0
Subtotal	178	158	336	4	3	7
Non-Hispanic/Latino**						
Black	171	101	272	8	4	12
Native American/Alaska Native	2	2	4	0	0	0
Native Hawaiian/Other Pacific Islander	11	9	20	0	0	0
White	1,699	1,989	3,688	38	46	84
Asian	886	982	1,868	26	23	49
Other Race	2	4	6	0	0	0
Multiple Race*	98	79	177	5	5	10
Unknown	30	31	61	3	2	5
Subtotal	2,899	3,197	6,096	80	80	160
Foreign	149	172	321	3	4	7
Total	3,226	3,527	6,753	87	87	174

*Since 2002, students can select more than one race and / or ethnicity. **Those who did not choose Hispanic/Latino' or 'Non-Hispanic/Latino' are counted under 'Non-Hispanic/Latino'.

Data Source: AAMC Data Warehouse: Applicant-Matriculant File, as of 5/9/2007.

personal comments of the applicant, and the evaluations included from letters of recommendation. Please see the admissions website for specifics: *(http://www. medschool.northwestern.edu/admissions/md/ index.html)* or contact admissions at: *(med-admissions@northwestern.edu).*

Academic Support Programs

All students at Feinberg have the full support of the Feinberg community: course directors, assigned mentors, associate deans, fellow students, and staff. In addition, the Director of Academic and Career Counseling in the Office of Student Programs provides workshops and one-on-one assistance to students seeking additional academic guidance. Every effort is made to ensure that students have the tools to successfully meet their academic and career goals. Third-and fourth-year students also offer formal and informal advice and support to first- and second-year students as they progress.

Enrichment Programs

Pre-Matriculation Program. Beginning in the summer of 2007, the Office of Minority and Cultural Affairs will sponsor selected underrepresented matriculating students to participate in an individualized prematriculation program in bench research, clinical research, or community/educational partnerships. Students will receive a stipend, have the opportunity to acclimate to the medical school environment and meet fellow students and faculty early on, as well as acclimate to the City of Chicago community.

Ongoing Activities: The Feinberg School of Medicine is regularly involved in providing information, resources, and guidance to college, post-baccalaureate students, and occasionally high school students interested in pursuing medical school. The medical school also nurtures a community partnership infrastructure that allows us to invest more heavily in the surrounding Chicago neighborhoods and still maintain

continuity as our students progress from year to year. Please see our Web site: *(http://www.medschool.northwestern.edu)* for updates on our program development.

Student Financial Assistance

Supplemental application fees are waived upon receipt of a fee waiver from the American Medical College Application Service, or upon written request from the applicant's undergraduate college financial aid officer. Any applicant experiencing financial hardship and needing assistance in the admissions process should call or e-mail the Office of Minority and Cultural Affairs to explore possible solutions.

Cultural Competency and Diversity

Cultural Dynamics in Medicine (CDM): CDM was added as a part of the Patient, Physician, and Society curriculum in 2004. This six-week course is mandatory for first-year students and focuses on fundamental cultural competency skills. Throughout the curriculum, issues of cultural competency are addressed including communication and language barriers, healthcare disparities, and how personal biases can impact patient care.

Diversity. The Medical School has active chapters of the Student National Medical Association (SNMA), Latino Cultural Medical Association (LCMA), Asian Pacific American Medical Student Association (APAMSA), South Asian Medical Student Association (SAMSA), Queers and Allies (Q&A), and American Medical Women's Association (AMWA). Our student groups are involved in outreach in the surrounding community, both educational and clinical. For a full list of student groups, please visit: *(http://www.medschool.northwestern.edu/ studentprograms/orgs/studorgs.html.)*

Rush Medical College of Rush University Medical Center

Sharon D. Gates, Director, Rush University Community Services
Director of Multicultural Affairs
Rush Medical College
600 South Paulina Street, Suite 1080K
Chicago, IL 60612
312-942-3670; 312-942-3127 Fax
sharon_gates@rush.edu

Recruitment

Rush Medical College seeks to attract candidates who can help make the student body more representative of our national population and more realistically informed about social problems affecting the delivery of health care in this country. Rush welcomes applications without regard to race, creed, national origin, or sex.

Minority pre-medical groups are encouraged to visit the Rush University Medical Center to meet with students and faculty to see the facilities. Such visits can be arranged through the Office of Admissions.

Academic Support Programs

Each student is assigned a carefully selected and trained academic advisor who will provide counseling and guidance throughout all four years of medical school. Students experiencing academic difficulty are provided a range of assistance including: individual and group instruction in time management, study skills, and test-taking strategies; peer tutors; and individualized instruction. Students have the option of modifying and extending their schedules so as to proceed at a slower pace during the pre-clinical years.

Student Financial Assistance

Financial aid, in the form of loans and non-refundable aid, is available to all students based primarily on need and accrued educational debt. The application fee is waived for applicants meeting the requirements for fee waivers by American Medical College Application Service. Financial assistance for interview trips is not available.

Rush Medical College of Rush University Medical Center, 2006
Applicants and Matriculants by Gender, Race and Ethnicity

Race and Ethnicity	Applicants			Matriculants		
	Women	Men	Total	Women	Men	Total
Hispanic/Latino						
Cuban	10	8	18	0	0	0
Mexican American	49	38	87	1	0	1
Puerto Rican	8	10	18	0	0	0
Other Hispanic	45	38	83	0	1	1
Multiple Hispanic*	11	5	16	0	1	1
Subtotal	123	99	222	1	2	3
Non-Hispanic/Latino**						
Black	144	84	228	3	3	6
Native American/Alaska Native	1	0	1	0	0	0
Native Hawaiian/Other Pacific Islander	11	7	18	2	1	3
White	1,267	1,357	2,624	45	39	84
Asian	674	664	1,338	22	18	40
Other Race	3	4	7	0	0	0
Multiple Race*	58	54	112	0	3	3
Unknown	14	25	39	1	0	1
Subtotal	2,172	2,195	4,367	73	64	137
Foreign	15	27	42	0	0	0
Total	2,310	2,321	4,631	74	66	140

*Since 2002, students can select more than one race and / or ethnicity. **Those who did not choose
'Hispanic/Latino' or 'Non-Hispanic/Latino' are counted under 'Non-Hispanic/Latino'.
Data Source: AAMC Data Warehouse: Applicant-Matriculant File, as of 5/9/2007.

Association of American Medical Colleges, 2007

Southern Illinois University School of Medicine

Dr. Wesley G. Robinson-McNeese
Executive Assistant to
the Dean for Diversity
and Minority Affairs
P.O. Box 19620
Springfield, IL 62794-9620
217-545-6012; 217-545-0786 Fax
wmcneese@siumed.edu

Recruitment

Members of the Southern Illinois University (SIU) School of Medicine's Office of Student Affairs routinely visit regional college campuses and minority student groups to discuss the programs and curricula offered at SIU. We also participate in statewide and regional recruitment fairs, taking medical students with us whenever possible. In addition, elementary, high school, and college students are invited to orientation visits and Career Days at the school's Carbondale and Springfield campuses. SIU medical students also participate in various educational events at local and area schools.

Our school sponsors a non-degree, post-baccalaureate Medical/Dental Education Preparatory Program (MEDPREP) on the Carbondale campus. MEDPREP is designed to assist students from groups currently identified by the AAMC as underrepresented in their preparation for medical school. Illinois rural white applicants from disadvantaged educational or economic backgrounds, as well as other minority group members, are considered for the program on a space-available basis.

MEDPREP students are recruited nationwide. That recruitment process includes visits to campuses by MEDPREP personnel. It also includes attending national recruitment fairs held in conjunction with national meetings such as National Association of Minority Medical Educators and AAMC. Also, the admissions officers at many other health professional schools help identify likely candidates for MEDPREP.

Admissions

Academically qualified U.S. citizens and foreign citizens with permanent resident visas who are residents of the State of Illinois are encouraged to apply to the SIU School of Medicine. A limited number of out-of-state residents are considered for the M.D./J.D. program.

All applicants must present scores from the Medical College Admission Test (MCAT). Applicants are expected to have a good foundation in the natural sciences, social sciences, and humanities and demonstrate facility in writing and speaking the English language.

A minimum of 90 semester hours of undergraduate work in an accredited, degree-granting college or university is required. At least 60 semester hours must be completed at a U.S. or Canadian college or university. Preference is given to those applicants who will have earned a baccalaureate degree by the time of matriculation to medical school and who have had sufficient and recent academic activity to demonstrate a potential for successful completion of the rigorous medical school curriculum.

Before issuing an acceptance to an applicant, the Admission Committee looks beyond proven scholastic ability for evidence of responsibility, maturity, integrity, compassion, proper motivation, identification with the goals of the school, exploration of medicine as a career, service orientation, and good interpersonal skills. Meeting the admission requirements does not insure admission, as the school is limited to a freshmen class of 72 students. Although the Admissions Committee

Southern Illinois University School of Medicine, 2006
Applicants and Matriculants by Gender, Race and Ethnicity

Race and Ethnicity	Applicants			Matriculants		
	Women	Men	Total	Women	Men	Total
Hispanic/Latino						
Cuban	0	3	3	0	0	0
Mexican American	11	11	22	0	1	1
Puerto Rican	3	4	7	1	0	1
Other Hispanic	7	4	11	1	0	1
Multiple Hispanic*	2	1	3	0	0	0
Subtotal	23	23	46	2	1	3
Non-Hispanic/Latino**						
Black	68	37	105	6	1	7
Native Hawaiian/Other Pacific Islander	2	0	2	0	0	0
White	309	301	610	30	28	58
Asian	156	151	307	1	3	4
Other Race	0	1	1	0	0	0
Multiple Race*	6	11	17	0	0	0
Unknown	1	4	5	0	0	0
Subtotal	542	505	1,047	37	32	69
Foreign	4	0	4	0	0	0
Total	569	528	1,097	39	33	72

*Since 2002, students can select more than one race and / or ethnicity. **Those who did not choose
Hispanic/Latino' or 'Non-Hispanic/Latino' are counted under 'Non-Hispanic/Latino'.
Data Source: AAMC Data Warehouse: Applicant-Matriculant File, as of 5/9/2007.

uses no quotas, active efforts are made to recruit qualified applicants from groups traditionally underrepresented in the medical profession.

Students interested in MEDPREP may obtain application forms and information from that program's Admission Coordinator. There is no application fee to MEDPREP. Invited MEDPREP applicants come to the Carbondale campus for an Admissions Day, which includes a series of tests, interviews with the faculty, and meetings with MEDPREP students in order to learn more about the program.

All students enrolled in MEDPREP must have completed at least two years of college coursework and maintained an overall grade-point average (GPA) of 2.0 and a math/science GPA of 2.0; a majority of MEDPREP participants are post-baccalaureate students. Each year, approximately 60 minority and disadvantaged students participate in MEDPREP. Most students participate in the program for two academic years.

Acceptance to, or success in, MEDPREP does not guarantee admission to Southern Illinois University School of Medicine or any other medical school. MEDPREP does, however, use the MEDPREP Alliance Program as a portal to the SIU School of Medicine. MEDPREP students who are Illinois residents and meet the Alliance criteria are guaranteed admission to Southern Illinois University School of Medicine. Two-thirds of MEDPREP students have been accepted to, and matriculated at, Southern Illinois University School of Medicine, and/or one of 95 other health professional schools.

The Southern Illinois University School of Medicine Admissions Committee, separate and apart from the MEDPREP Admissions Committee, is composed of basic science and clinical faculty from the Carbondale and Springfield campuses. Medical students

are also voting members on this committee. The Office of Student Affairs and Admissions encourages minority applicants to make application to the Southern Illinois University School of Medicine, and a particular effort is made to interview those minority students who apply.

Academic Support Programs
The curriculum is designed to prepare students for careers as health care professionals in a rapidly changing field, while providing a means for developing the knowledge and skills necessary for licensure, residency, and future accreditation examinations. The emphasis of the curriculum is on developing self-directed and lifelong learning skills that will help students maintain their knowledge and experience throughout their careers.

Students are assigned to mentors who work with them as they develop and build their clinical skills. In year four, students mentor second-year students as part of a *Doctoring Curriculum* that runs throughout the entire four years. Year-four students also choose an Electives Advisor to work with them as they choose and participate in electives that will most appropriately prepare them for their chosen specialties.

Every student must attain the predefined levels of competence established by the faculty. Evaluations are designed to measure levels of competence in knowledge, skills, and attitudes, not to compare students. Decisions regarding student progress are made on the basis of whether students demonstrate the prescribed levels of competency. Determining whether students demonstrate appropriate attitudes, concepts, and skills is accomplished through oral and computer-based examinations, faculty evaluation of cognitive and non-cognitive attributes, and performance based examinations.

The school's *Student Progress System (SPS)* prescribes the standards of academic

conduct that must be met by students in order to graduate. The SPS also describes how student academic performance and professional conduct are evaluated. A Student Progress Committee, composed of students, faculty and administrators, monitors the student progress decision process.

Counseling services are available for all medical students, with an emphasis on academic and personal guidance as needed.

MEDPREP offers a series of tutorials, courses, and seminars covering many phases of pre-professional preparation for medical education. The curriculum is tailored for students as determined by analytic tests, a review of previous academic history, student preferences, and the admissions requirements of the medical schools to which the student plans to apply. MEDPREP and other university courses are available for developmental and advanced work in both basic sciences and learning skills. Students have an opportunity to prepare for the Medical College Admission Test (MCAT), the Dental Admissions Test (DAT), and are exposed to the medical school faculty and curriculum. MEDPREP emphasizes small classes and close faculty interaction and supervision.

Enrichment Programs
Southern Illinois University School of Medicine invites high school students to its campuses on a regular basis throughout the school year, setting up Career Day-type experiences. Similar tours and workshops are arranged for college students, especially pre-medical students.

The School of Medicine also participates in a High School Research Apprenticeship Program that brings students to Carbondale and Springfield to participate in a paid, six-week research experience. The students make a formal presentation of their research project at summer's end.

AAMC

The Office of Student Affairs supports and coordinates cultural and ethnic observances throughout the school year. These functions are spearheaded by student organizations in cooperation with local community groups.

MEDPREP (Post-baccalaureate Program). This two-year program, as noted above, is an enrichment program, which begins in June and runs through the entire year. Every attempt is made to make the student aware of areas of strength and weakness. A major purpose is to promote student self-learning. During the second year of the MEDPREP experience, enrichment courses in areas such as cardiovascular physiology, hormonal regulation, and medical immunology are taught. The enrichment courses offer the student advanced medical school level work. Contact: Vera Felts, 618-453-1554.

Student Financial Assistance
Approximately 85 percent of the students at Southern Illinois University School of Medicine rely upon financial assistance to meet their educational costs.

Southern Illinois University School of Medicine participates in all major Federal Student Aid programs. All applications for financial assistance must include a summary of the family's financial situation. This summary is analyzed by an approved need analysis service to determine the expected family contribution. SIU School of Medicine utilizes the Free Application for Federal Student Aid (FAFSA) for this purpose.

The School of Medicine assists students in developing their financial aid package and works to provide the difference between the student's total educational expenses and the existing resources. Most financial need is met by combining various loan programs. Scholarship and grant aid is generally limited to students who demonstrate exceptional need. A limited number of institutional and outside scholarships are available and offer students a means of minimizing their educational debt.

Educational Partnerships
MEDPREP. The MEDPREP Alliance Program is a partnership with the SIU School of Medicine. MEDPREP students who meet predetermined criteria are admitted to the SIU School of Medicine. Additionally, more than a dozen admissions officers from various medical schools across the country visit MEDPREP each year. Students from MEDPREP are often admitted to those medical schools. In a typical year, about 30 MEDPREP students matriculate to health professional school; those 30 students are accepted to 20-25 different schools around the country.

Other Pertinent Information
Questions about medical school minority student affairs should be directed to: Dr. Wesley G. Robinson-McNeese, Executive Assistant to the Dean for Diversity, Southern Illinois University School of Medicine, P.O. Box 19620, Springfield, IL 62794-9620, 217/545-6012, *(wmcneese@siumed.edu)*. Questions about MEDPREP should be directed to Vera Felts, Admissions Coordinator, MEDPREP, Southern Illinois University, School of Medicine, 210 Wheeler Hall, Mail Code 4323, Carbondale, IL 62901-4323, 618-453-1554, *(vfelts@siumed.edu)*.

University of Chicago Division of the Biological Sciences Pritzker School of Medicine

Dr. William A. McDade
Associate Dean for Multicultural Affairs
Rosita Ragin, Assistant Dean for
Multicultural and Student Affairs
University of Chicago
Pritzker School of Medicine
924 East 57th Street, BSLC 104
Chicago, IL 60637-5416
773-702-1939; 773-702-2598 Fax
sickledoc@aol.com
rragin@uchicago.edu

Recruitment
The University of Chicago, located on the south side of Chicago, is an integral part of an ethnically diverse neighborhood. It has a long-standing tradition of academic excellence and places particular emphasis on recruiting students who seek to be leaders in research and clinical care. Both the university and the Pritzker School of Medicine are involved in a studious effort to increase minority representation at all levels. Significant strides have been made in attracting underrepresented minority students into the medical school, residency programs, and into faculty positions. High levels of effort continue in all three areas and are showing tangible results. The percentage of minority students entering medical school at Pritzker has more than doubled in the last three years.

The Pritzker School of Medicine is particularly interested in seeking diversity among its students and is sensitive to society's need for an increasing number of minority men and women as physicians. It sends representatives, including enrolled minority students, to regional and national events to recruit underrepresented minority students and offers numerous campus tours and discussions. Students are encouraged to come to the campus for a variety of programs offered during the summer and throughout the academic year. Increased effort has been directed toward community outreach with medical students.

The Pritzker School of Medicine has had a long standing presence at national meetings of minority pre-medical Society for Advancement of Chicanos and Native Americans in Science and Annual Biomedical Research Conference for Minority Students and medical school meetings of the Student National Medical Association (SNMA). Multiple recruitment trips are made annually to college campuses to connect with minority pre-medical students.

Admissions
The University of Chicago utilizes the AAMC Medical Minority Applicant Registry to contact prospective students. The Admissions Committee is composed of a diverse group of faculty, students, and administrators who value diversity within the medical school class. Students who are invited for interviews will, under most circumstances, be given the opportunity to meet with the Associate or Assistant Dean for Multicultural Affairs and a minority faculty member or student as part of the admissions interview day. Housing is typically available with student hosts from SNMA.

Academic Support Programs
All students are assigned to a Career Advisor through their membership in one of the four Pritzker Societies. The Pritzker Societies provide a context and opportunity for gaining advice over time from a broad array of individuals such as peer students, students who are farther along in

University of Chicago Pritzker School of Medicine, 2006
Applicants and Matriculants by Gender, Race and Ethnicity

Race and Ethnicity	Applicants			Matriculants		
	Women	Men	Total	Women	Men	Total
Hispanic/Latino						
Cuban	20	19	39	0	0	0
Mexican American	62	69	131	4	1	5
Puerto Rican	21	17	38	1	0	1
Other Hispanic	76	73	149	1	2	3
Multiple Hispanic*	13	6	19	0	0	0
Subtotal	192	184	376	6	3	9
Non-Hispanic/Latino**						
Black	191	129	320	1	4	5
Native American/Alaska Native	3	6	9	0	0	0
Native Hawaiian/Other Pacific Islander	13	5	18	0	0	0
White	1,831	2,202	4,033	33	30	63
Asian	994	1,067	2,061	11	13	24
Other Race	4	7	11	0	0	0
Multiple Race*	104	93	197	0	0	0
Unknown	26	32	58	0	0	0
Subtotal	3,166	3,541	6,707	45	47	92
Foreign	183	189	372	3	2	5
Total	3,541	3,914	7,455	54	52	106

*Since 2002, students can select more than one race and / or ethnicity. **Those who did not choose
Hispanic/Latino' or 'Non-Hispanic/Latino' are counted under 'Non-Hispanic/Latino'.
Data Source: AAMC Data Warehouse: Applicant-Matriculant File, as of 5/9/2007.

their training, and faculty. In addition to the academic advising societies, the students are offered scheduled quarterly meetings with the deans to discuss well-being issues and academic plans. Additional opportunities are provided by the Bowman Society and its bimonthly lecture series that covers career development and the development of a biomedical scientific community interested in health care disparities. This positive networking provides both basic information and a valuable framework for assisting students in understanding the best ways to negotiate the four years at Pritzker. It also reduces the isolation students may initially feel, while additionally identifying any individuals who might benefit from personal counseling or other types of assistance. Faculty are strongly committed to each student's success.

Enrichment Programs

Young Scientist Training Program (YSTP) is a high school/college program sponsored by the National Institute of Diabetes, Digestive Diseases and Kidney Disease designed to help develop minority students' interest in biomedical research. Ten students are recruited locally and commute to the university to work with distinguished minority faculty mentors for ten weeks during the summer. Students are selected from the most outstanding cohort of science-oriented high school freshmen through college seniors. Stipends are paid to participants. An annual symposium participation experience is required. *(http://pritzker.bsd.uchicago.edu/about/diversity/pipeline/ysp.shtml)*

Summer Research Program (SRP) is sponsored by the National Heart, Lung and Blood Institute. This program provides an 11-week research experience for 15 entering underrepresented minority medical students and those students who have completed their first year at Pritzker. Participation in weekly research-cluster interest groups and an end of summer

symposium is required. Participants engage in basic science and clinical research projects. stipend is paid to participants.

Pritzker School of Medicine Experience in Research (PSOMER) is a residential program for minority junior and senior college students. Students are recruited from around the United States, and for eight weeks in the summer they are mentored by University of Chicago faculty, work on research projects that range from bench to clinical projects, and attend various seminar relevant to medical education. Participants augment their research work with weekly colloquiums. All participants are required to present their work at a poster session at the end of the program. Stipends are paid to the participants. *(http://pritzker.bsd.uchicago.edu/about/diversity/pipeline/psomer.shtml)*

The Chicago Academic Medicine Program (CAMP) is a non-residential six-week summer program for minority freshman or sophomore pre-medical students or graduating high school seniors. The goal of the program is to build the academic success skills of the students by providing group-learning and team-building projects using a curriculum that covers three organ systems in a mini-medical school style format. The curriculum is enhanced by daily medical education and learning skills seminars, weekly book club sessions, and clinical experiences held one morning each week. Participants are provided with various opportunities to meet the faculty by attending group meetings with professors and mentors and individual meetings with the deans. Students are selected locally or must have a local residence to reside at during the program. This tuition free program also provides a stipend and funding for local transportation. *(http://pritzker.bsd.uchicago.edu/about/diversity/pipeline/camp.shtml)*

Academic Support Programs

Minority students are welcomed to the Pritzker School of Medicine at a reception where students, housestaff, and faculty are invited, thus building an informal network of academic support. Mentorship of regular academic advisement is provided by the Office of Multicultural Affairs. The Pritzker Societies provides an opportunity for students to obtain advice over time from peer students, students who are farther along in their training, and faculty. All current students are equally divided into four societies, each with a head and five adjunct faculty advisors. Each class at Pritzker has an annual symposium/retreat that has a diversity component.

Student Financial Assistance

The University of Chicago has a variety of resources (both scholarships and low interest loans) to help students meet their educational expenses. Pritzker's support of students is need-based, and the new Dean's Promise Scholarships is offered to outstanding candidates. As a private institution, our student indebtedness is below the median for all graduating seniors with debt. Applicants who receive fee waivers from the American Medical College Application Service (AMCAS) will automatically receive a fee waiver for the Pritzker Supple-mental Application. Students without an AMCAS fee waiver may petition to waive Pritzker's fee with appropriate documentation from their college's financial aid office.

Other Pertinent Information

Students obtain early exposure to clinical medicine as they begin patient contact the first week of medical school. During the first two years, students develop important clinical skills that give them confidence in placing their focus on the patient while a full-time clinical student in the third year. The six junior-year clerkships, as well as the largely elective fourth year, give students an excellent background with which to enter residency and ultimately the practice of medicine.

The Summer Research Program, student/faculty dinners, and a number of organizations give students opportunity to work closely with faculty mentors. Students interested in obtaining the Masters in Business Administration, Masters in Public Policy, Masters in Health Studies, or Masters in Public Realm are encouraged to do so. Currently six students are enrolled in combined degree programs pursuing Ph.D. degrees in science. Six MSTPS students are in the Medical Scientist Training Program, one is on an NIH Pediatrics Growth and Development Training Grant, and one is on an NIH Minority Predoctoral Fellowship.

The Office of Multicultural Affairs created the Bowman Society Lecture Series, which is named in honor of one of Pritzker's outstanding minority emeritus professors, Dr. James E. Bowman. Dr. Bowman's legacy is one of excellence and distinguished service, and he has been a role model to many Pritzker students. The Bowman Society features nationally renown faculty presenters in a bimonthly lecture series followed by a meeting of the Society whose membership includes faculty, graduate and medical students, fellows, and housestaff where the principal topics of discussion are career development and forging a strong biomedical scientific community interested in health care disparities.

Students are active in community health centers and neighborhood schools to disseminate health information or provide care directly. Underrepresented minority students who attend Pritzker traditionally assume leadership roles during and after their medical school experience. The University of Chicago Hospital is a major health care provider to residents of the south side of Chicago, and as such, the diversity in patient population is large.

There is a significant outreach program in geriatrics care, where students are involved in a senior companion program. Students also volunteer in two community health centers. Some student-led outreach groups include Remedy Cuba/Peru, Maria Shelter, Washington Park Clinic, Community Health Clinics, Adolescence Substance Abuse Program, Prostate Cancer Awareness Program, HIPCORPS, Doctors Back to School Program, and Project Brotherhood. In addition, many of our enrichment activities involve mentorship of younger students by older medical students and provide excellent leadership and teaching experience for our minority medical student population. Numerous opportunities exist for students to initiate other outreach programs where they may perceive a need to exist.

A wide variety of student organizations sponsor programs and activities on numerous topics, including cultural sensitivity and diversity. Organizations such as the Student National Medical Association (SNMA) are dedicated to increasing the awareness of serving the unique health care needs of minority communities and working toward the abolition of the barriers that obstruct the fulfillment of those needs. The last two national presidents of SNMA (past and current) are from the University of Chicago. Pritzker students have won one of the ten national AMA Minority Scholar Awards in both the past and current academic year. They specifically focus on educating students and physicians about problems facing minority communities, recruiting and supporting minority medical students, and improving the health status of these communities. Students are also encouraged to attend a variety of annual festivals and events highlighting the arts, publications, and politics of a wide variety of communities.

AAMC

University of Illinois at Chicago College of Medicine*

Lillye A. Hart, Associate Dean
for Administration & Director
Urban Health Program
University of Illinois at
Chicago College of Medicine
1853 West Polk St., Rm 145 CMW
Chicago, IL 60612-7333
312-996-6491; 312-996-3548 Fax

Recruitment

Primarily, staff of the Urban Health Program conduct recruitment activities targeted at underrepresented minority and/or disadvantaged students. Recruitment activities are carried out in the community, at the high school and undergraduate levels. Recruitment efforts consist of providing workshops and seminars to a wide range of audiences, as well as participation in local and national conferences aimed at targeting pre-medical students. Minority medical students and faculty in the college also actively participate in the recruitment efforts. The Urban Health Program administers an intensive local outreach program, as well as visits other states to encourage out-of-state underrepresented minority and/or disadvantaged students to apply.

Admissions

In order to be considered for admissions, students must apply to the University of Illinois College of Medicine (UIC-COM) through the American Medical College Application Service (AMCAS). When the college receives the application from AMCAS, a determination is made of whether the applicant is to receive the college's supplemental application. All applicants must meet minimum academic criteria to be offered a supplemental application. Upon the college's receipt of the supplemental application and three letters of recommendation (or school's composite letter), the application is initially screened by a panel composed of members of the full Admissions Committee. Following the review of the application, a recommendation is made to the full Admissions Committee. All candidates being considered for admission must participate in an interview. The 244 medical students who are currently enrolled in the college are proof of the success of the admissions policies. With interns and residents, the number of minority students in training at University of Illinois facilities exceeds 900. Minority candidates are encouraged to contact staff members of the Urban Health Program for assistance before and during the process.

Academic Support Programs

Academic Assistance Program. The Urban Health Program developed the Academic Assistance Program to identify and aid students with the challenges of the medical curriculum. Academic Skills Specialists (one at each of the four campuses) work with faculty and administrators to identify appropriate interventions (i.e., test-taking skills, group and/or individualized tutoring, crisis management, etc.).

Retention programming activities include a comprehensive orientation to introduce the rigors of medical education and to provide information regarding resources and multiple approaches to overcoming academically related obstacles. The Learning and Study Skills Inventory (LASSI) is used to assist in identifying factors that are predictive of success in medical school.

The two minority medical student organizations at the College of Medicine campus, National Network of Latin American Medical Students-La Raza Medical Student Association (NNLAMS-LaRAMA) and the

University of Illinois at Chicago College of Medicine, 2006
Applicants and Matriculants by Gender, Race and Ethnicity

Race and Ethnicity	Applicants			Matriculants		
	Women	Men	Total	Women	Men	Total
Hispanic/Latino						
Cuban	17	17	34	1	1	2
Mexican American	110	92	202	10	10	20
Puerto Rican	16	11	27	2	1	3
Other Hispanic	87	70	157	9	13	22
Multiple Hispanic*	15	11	26	3	1	4
Subtotal	245	201	446	25	26	51
Non-Hispanic/Latino**						
Black	271	157	428	16	10	26
Native American/Alaska Native	6	3	9	0	0	0
Native Hawaiian/Other Pacific Islander	17	8	25	0	0	0
White	1,326	1,630	2,956	66	71	137
Asian	813	885	1,698	51	49	100
Other Race	3	5	8	0	0	0
Multiple Race*	71	59	130	3	5	8
Unknown	16	25	41	1	1	2
Subtotal	2,523	2,772	5,295	137	136	273
Foreign	8	6	14	0	0	0
Total	2,776	2,979	5,755	162	162	324

*Since 2002, students can select more than one race and / or ethnicity. **Those who did not choose
'Hispanic/Latino' or 'Non-Hispanic/Latino' are counted under 'Non-Hispanic/Latino'.
Data Source: AAMC Data Warehouse: Applicant-Matriculant File, as of 5/9/2007.

Student National Medical Association (SNMA), also provide academic assistance to first- and second-year students through reviews and mock practicals.

Enrichment Programs

Underrepresented minority and/or disadvantaged students can take advantage of the following summer and enrichment programs.

The *Summer Pre-matriculation Program (SPP)* is a six-week program offered to students who have been admitted to the College of Medicine, either traditionally or conditionally. The purpose of the program is to introduce students to the first-year curriculum. Preview courses in biochemistry, gross anatomy, tissue biology, and physiology are offered. Faculty and upper-class medical students organize lectures and laboratory sessions for the participants.

In addition, the Urban Health Program offers summer programs for college and high school students. The *Medical College Admission Test (MCAT) Review Program* is a seven-week summer program designed to provide participants with an intensive review of the basic sciences in preparation for the MCAT examination. The *Verbal Reasoning Workshop* is a supplement to the MCAT Review Program. The workshop is an eight-session academic year program, which offers participants an opportunity to focus on enhancing reading, comprehension, and writing skills in preparation for the MCAT.

The *Post-baccalaureate Admission Program (PAP)* is an invitation-only program. To be considered, one must apply for traditional admission through the AMCAS. The PAP is a 14-month, guaranteed admission program designed to provide an opportunity for 15 students each year to demonstrate their academic abilities in preparation to matriculate to medical school.

For high school students, the Urban Health Program offers a six-week *Summer Preparation Program*, designed to help high school students prepare for the ACT and expose them to health profession and biomedical careers. For more information, contact the Urban Health Program.

Student Financial Assistance

All students are awarded financial assistance based on need as the sole criterion. Personal need of each accepted applicant is reflected in the award. To make it financially feasible for out-of-state underrepresented minority applicants to attend the University of Illinois, students may apply to have the non-resident portion of their tuition waived through tuition differential coverage. It is important to apply for financial aid early in the process, even if an acceptance offer has not been made.

Educational Partnerships

The activities of the Urban Health Program are funded in part by a grant from the U.S. Department of Health and Human Services—Division of Health Professions Diversity. This comprehensive grant project promotes formal partnership with several high schools in the Chicago Public School system; a Chicago Community College; two community-based organizations; two Illinois state four-year colleges; and our own undergraduate institution on two campuses. The partnerships foster collaborative efforts to facilitate summer and academic-year program activities designed to facilitate access to medical school for students from underrepresented minority and disadvantaged backgrounds.

AAMC

Indiana University School of Medicine

Krystal Ardayfio
Director of Multicultural Affairs
Indiana University School of Medicine
535 Barnhill Drive, MS 166
Indianapolis, IN 46202-5120
317-278-3097; 317-274-4309
kardayfi@iupui.edu

Recruitment

The Indiana University School of Medicine (IUSM) is committed to expanding its efforts to identify, advise, and recruit underrepresented minority individuals who have potential and promise for education and training in medicine. The school's efforts include contact with appropriate administrators, teachers, and advisors in Indiana high schools, colleges, and universities.

Recruitment activities are developed and implemented through the admissions office. Such activities consist of on-campus visitations to conduct pre-medical seminars and converse with students on a one-to-one basis or in small groups. The school participates in high school career opportunity programs and also reaches out to the community through information sheets or brochures, visual aids, and tours of the medical center. The tours are available to students and small groups by appointment. Minority medical students share their experiences with local high school students through a "Doctor Back to School" program and through a partnership with a local "Center for Leadership Development Program" for high school students.

Admissions

The School of Medicine's Admissions Committee evaluates all applicants, minority and non-minority, on the basis of scholarship, character, personality, references, performance on the Medical College Admission Test (MCAT), and a personal interview. It is essential that all students apply early, follow appropriate admissions procedures, and promptly return necessary materials. The well-qualified students may expect early action on their applications.

Academic Support Programs

The Indiana University School of Medicine currently makes use of several academic reinforcement programs for disadvantaged students. Matriculants are mentored by upperclassmen through the Student National Medical Association (SNMA). The Assistant Dean for Cultural Diversity personally meets with each underrepresented minority student twice each year for face-to-face support, in addition to encouragement e-mails after the first semester.

Special Tutorial Programs. These programs are offered on a regularly scheduled basis by the faculty of each of the basic science courses for all students whose academic performance is below par.

Enrichment Programs

Master of Science in Medical Science Program. The Master of Science in Medical Science (MSMS) Program was established in 1995 at Indiana University School of Medicine to expand the pool of successful medical school applicants from underrepresented minority and disadvantaged backgrounds. The program enhances the preparation and confidence of its students to be successful in a medical curriculum. The Admissions Committee at IUSM identifies and selects MSMS students from its pool of medical school applicants.

Indiana University School of Medicine, 2006
Applicants and Matriculants by Gender, Race and Ethnicity

Race and Ethnicity	Applicants			Matriculants		
	Women	Men	Total	Women	Men	Total
Hispanic/Latino						
Cuban	4	8	12	1	0	1
Mexican American	31	38	69	4	2	6
Puerto Rican	7	9	16	1	2	3
Other Hispanic	29	37	66	4	3	7
Multiple Hispanic*	2	6	8	0	0	0
Subtotal	73	98	171	10	7	17
Non-Hispanic/Latino**						
Black	136	79	215	11	7	18
Native American/Alaska Native	3	3	6	0	2	2
Native Hawaiian/Other Pacific Islander	4	5	9	0	0	0
White	768	937	1,705	85	127	212
Asian	230	295	525	9	15	24
Multiple Race*	31	35	66	2	0	2
Unknown	6	10	16	0	1	1
Subtotal	1,178	1,364	2,542	107	152	259
Foreign	88	95	183	2	2	4
Total	1,339	1,557	2,896	119	161	280

*Since 2002, students can select more than one race and / or ethnicity. **Those who did not choose Hispanic/Latino' or 'Non-Hispanic/Latino' are counted under 'Non-Hispanic/Latino'.
Data Source: AAMC Data Warehouse: Applicant-Matriculant File, as of 5/9/2007.

Association of American Medical Colleges, 2007

The MSMS Program's two-year curriculum includes graduate medical science courses taught by IUSM faculty, collaborative problem-based learning courses, and a research experience. Students must maintain a B (3.0) average in the program and complete 35 credits to obtain the MSMS degree. The curriculum of the MSMS Program was designed to allow first- and second-year students to apply for medical school admission. Students who are admitted to medical school after one year in the program may apply 11 credits of basic medical science course work with grades of at least "B" toward completion of the requirements for the MSMS degree. The university underwrites a major portion of the cost, but tuition is charged. Financial aid is available.

Medical College Application Test Preparation Program. The MCAT Preparation Program begins in June as an intensive ten-week academic experience. The goal of the program is to enhance and reinforce academic skills that are essential for both improved MCAT performance and success in rigorous graduate course work. Approximately 30 hours per week are spent in class, with an emphasis on cooperative learning in small groups. Subject matter includes biology, chemistry, organic chemistry, physics, verbal reasoning, and writing. Critical thinking skills are stressed. Physical conditioning is encouraged. At least three hours per week of regularly scheduled physical exercise is strongly recommended. Enrollment in the MCAT Preparation Program is limited to students admitted to the MSMS Program. For more information, visit *(www.msms.iu.edu)*.

Student Financial Assistance

Indiana University School of Medicine has one endowment scholarship from American States Insurance Company. The amount available annually is $10,000 committed to one student over four years.

The Eli Lilly Company Scholarships support several tuition scholarships annually. Endowed in 1993 by the Eli Lilly Company, the dean appropriates $150,000 annually to support renewals as well as select new recipients. In 1998, Lilly agreed to fund two additional scholarships to cover tuition, fees, books, and a stipend. A distribution is made by the Eli Lilly Company each year to cover these commitments. This is in addition to what is awarded through the endowed funds.

The Wishard Memorial Foundation provides tuition scholarships to one or two underrepresented minority students from Indiana each year in the form of four-year renewable scholarships. The George H. Rawls Scholarship began in 1998 in an effort to increase the number of minority physicians in the Indianapolis area. The scholarship commits the recipient to practicing within the area of Indianapolis. There is no specialty restriction.

The George and Lula Rawls Academic Excellence Award totals approximately $1,400 and is divided into three awards. The first award is given to a student with the highest academic performance in the MSMS Program; the second one is awarded to a second-year medical student with the highest academic performance after the first year; and a final award is given to a student in the upper second-to-fourth years with the highest academic performance.

The Indiana University School of Medicine's Dean's General Funds, used to recruit Indiana's best and brightest students, provides 20 percent-100 percent tuition scholarships. Among those students being recruited are URM's that fall in the top 30-40 entering students.

The Aesculapian Medical Society awards three external scholarships annually ($2,000 each) in the spring semester. The scholarships target students with the highest academic performance in the first and second year as well as a student in the final two years. This is not a school scholarship, although Indiana University School of Medicine assists the Aesculapian Society in identifying the recipients. The Aesculapian Society annually solicits its membership to fund the scholarships.

Educational Partnerships

IUSM has a partnership with the Center for Leadership Development *(www.cldinc.org)*.

Through the student-created Crispus Attucks Medical Magnet High School interest group, medical students have the opportunity to present medicine as a career to high school students.

The Bridges to the Doctorate initiative, funded by the National Institutes of Health, represents a formal partnership between Jackson State University (JSU), a historically black institution, and Indiana University-Purdue University at Indianapolis (IUPUI). The purpose of the partnership is to enhance the quality and quantity of underrepresented minority students who are being trained as the next generation of scientists by providing a structured "bridge" between the JSU Master's program and the IUPUI doctoral program. This program guarantees a 12 month stipend and fee remission for all Bridges students *(http://www.iupui.edu/~bridges/index.htm)*.

University of Iowa Roy J. and Lucille A. Carver College of Medicine

Barbara Barlow, Program Associate for Student Affairs
University of Iowa Roy J. and Lucille A. Carver College of Medicine
124 CMAB
Iowa City, IA 52242-1101
319-335-8057; 319-335-8049 Fax
barbara-barlow@uiowa.edu

Recruitment

The University of Iowa Roy J. and Lucille A. Carver College of Medicine maintains a long tradition of identifying, admitting, and graduating qualified applicants from ethnic groups underrepresented in U.S. medicine. This commitment has been demonstrated by the number of underrepresented minority students who have successfully entered and graduated from the college. Since 1970, more than 300 students have earned their M.D. degree and entered their chosen medical specialty.

The College of Medicine actively encourages minority students to seek information regarding its programs and welcomes applications to the college of medicine. Efforts to promote minority applications include:

- Faculty and administrative staff visits to undergraduate campuses and minority summer programs to present information and speak informally with individual students;
- Visits by students who hold membership in the Student National Medical Association to high schools and colleges for the purpose of presenting and sharing information related to medical education;
- Information packets mailed to selected registrants of the Medical Minority Applicant Registry; and
- Diversity weekend held the first weekend in December for students interviewing who would like to learn more about programs promoting diversity at Iowa.

Admissions

The College of Medicine participates in the American Medical College Application Service (AMCAS). Personal interviews are conducted and generally begin in early fall. There is no geographical restriction placed upon the selection of candidates.

The Admissions Office staff screens all applications forwarded to the College of Medicine by AMCAS. Students are asked to complete a University of Iowa College of Medicine application, arrange for the submission of three evaluation forms, and respond to several short essay topics. AMCAS applications should be submitted as early as possible to allow time for the return of supplementary materials and subsequent committee evaluation. Supplemental application materials must be on file in the College of Medicine by December 15.

All applicants must meet the high standards of the Admissions Committee to be offered admission to the College of Medicine. Selection for admission is based upon a careful review of each applicant's academic performance and potential, as well as a number of non-cognitive characteristics considered to be important in future physicians.

Academic Support Programs

The Office of Student Affairs and Curriculum provides individual and/or group counseling for all medical students. Services provided include career development, academic planning, personal advising, financial need and planning, and debt management counseling.

University of Iowa Roy J. and Lucille A. Carver College of Medicine, 2006
Applicants and Matriculants by Gender, Race and Ethnicity

Race and Ethnicity	Applicants			Matriculants		
	Women	Men	Total	Women	Men	Total
Hispanic/Latino						
Cuban	4	6	10	0	0	0
Mexican American	39	45	84	4	3	7
Puerto Rican	5	5	10	0	0	0
Other Hispanic	25	24	49	0	1	1
Multiple Hispanic*	1	4	5	0	0	0
Subtotal	74	84	158	4	4	8
Non-Hispanic/Latino**						
Black	84	51	135	5	3	8
Native American/Alaska Native	4	1	5	0	0	0
Native Hawaiian/Other Pacific Islander	2	1	3	0	0	0
White	720	1,003	1,723	61	42	103
Asian	211	249	460	10	6	16
Other Race	1	2	3	0	0	0
Multiple Race*	34	39	73	3	3	6
Unknown	6	6	12	0	1	1
Subtotal	1,062	1,352	2,414	79	55	134
Foreign	1	2	3	0	0	0
Total	1,137	1,438	2,575	83	59	142

*Since 2002, students can select more than one race and / or ethnicity. **Those who did not choose Hispanic/Latino' or 'Non-Hispanic/Latino' are counted under 'Non-Hispanic/Latino'.
Data Source: AAMC Data Warehouse: Applicant-Matriculant File, as of 5/9/2007.

Students are encouraged to utilize these services throughout their matriculation in the College of Medicine.

Free tutorial assistance is available for all first- and second-year courses, starting in the first two weeks of class. With their tutors (upper-class students, medical fellows and/or residents), students discuss their needs and determine a schedule of meetings. Sessions are conducted on a one-to-one basis or in small groups.

Students who have personal or academic difficulty can ask to have their academic schedule modified. Any required or necessary deviation from the curriculum schedule is determined by the dean and reviewed on an individual basis.

United States Medical Licensing Examination (USMLE) Study Groups. These groups are available for students registered to take the USMLE Step 1. Groups, consisting of six or seven students, meet weekly and are led by M3 or M4 students who scored high on the exam. There is no charge to participants.

Enrichment Programs
Summer Programs. All students accepted to the University of Iowa College of Medicine are invited to participate in this program during the summer preceding their entry into the college. The program introduces new students to the medical curriculum, provides personal and career development information, and conducts seminars emphasizing study skills, time management, and test-taking strategies. Orientation activities and assistance in adjusting to the local community are included. Tuition is free, and a grant from the university is provided to cover books and living expenses.

Early Mentoring Program. A program has been established with upper-class students and with clinical faculty. Each summer program student is matched with a second-year student and a clinical faculty

mentor. Effective mentoring programs, combined with a supportive campus environment, assist new students in adjusting more readily to unfamiliar surroundings. This, in turn, helps in learning.

Student Financial Assistance
The university will waive the admission application fee, upon request, for economically disadvantaged students who received a fee waiver from AMCAS. All students desiring consideration for financial aid must complete the Free Application for Federal Student Aid (FAFSA). The information provided on this application will be used to do a need assessment and to determine the level of financial assistance that can be awarded to each student. To assist students in meeting additional demonstrated need, other federal or national foundation grants are also utilized, as are loans from federal, collegiate, or private programs. Financial aid and debt management advising are available in the Office of Medical Student Affairs. College of Medicine staff strive to assist students in meeting 100 percent of demonstrated financial need so that every admitted student will be able to finance a medical education at the University of Iowa.

Other Pertinent Information
The College of Medicine's curriculum was redesigned beginning with the fall 1995 entering class. Major changes in emphasis include earlier patient exposure, increased integration and clinical relevance in the basic science courses, and community-based primary care in the clinical years. Running concurrently with the basic science courses found in the first two years will be a new course, Foundations of Clinical Practice, which will provide students with their first exposure to patients, to disciplines such as preventive medicine, and to critical appraisal skills. Major goals for this course include development of the interpersonal skills critical for patient

interactions and the facilitation of students' transition to an adult style of learning. Another unique feature of the revised curriculum is the greater emphasis placed on the skills and body of knowledge required by the generalist, which will coincide with the minimum core of material that the college envisions having all students master prior to graduation. One of the ways in which the new curriculum seeks to meet this goal is through the Generalist Core of Clerkships, including community-based primary care, family practice and internal medicine ambulatory care, general internal medicine, obstetrics and gynecology, and pediatrics. The inclusion of a Community-Based Primary Care six-week rotation will serve to further acquaint students with the settings in which generalist physicians practice medicine.

AAMC

University of Kansas School of Medicine

Ms. Gwendolyn Swoop
Executive Director
Office of Cultural
Enhancement and Diversity
University of Kansas
School of Medicine
Mail Stop 3022
3901 Rainbow Boulevard
Kansas City, KS 66160
913-588-1547; 913-588-8890 Fax
gswoop@kumc.edu
www2.kumc.edu/oced

Diversity is one of our core values at the University of Kansas School of Medicine, and we are deeply committed to creating the very best and stimulating educational environment for our students and delivering the best health care to our patients through diversity.

Recruitment

The Office of Cultural Enhancement and Diversity (OCED) was established in 1998 to address the cultural and diversity needs of the school. Objectives included in the office's mission are 1) to assist in recruiting a diverse student body; 2) to support an educational environment that fosters the vigorous exchange of ideas without fear of prejudice or persecution; 3) to train culturally and clinically skilled physicians and thereby improve access to high quality health care and biomedical research for underserved and special patient populations; and 4) to prepare students for leadership roles in the state of Kansas. In addition to recruitment, OCED accomplishes activities around diversity, such as retention, academic support services, cultural diversity and competency programming and education, and student career counseling and mentoring through several federally funded programs.

Admissions

Each August, the School of Medicine enrolls 175 students in the M.D. program. Prior to matriculation into the medical school, applicants must complete a course of studies leading to a baccalaureate degree as well as the following: (one year) general biology with lab; (one year) inorganic chemistry with lab; (one year) organic chemistry with lab; (one year) physics with lab; (one year) English composition or writing-intensive course; and (one semester) mathematics, college-level algebra, or above. In addition, applicants must take the Medical College Admission Test (MCAT). We believe that a diverse student body provides for the most optimal learning experience to prepare graduates for the success in their careers, and we consider a number of Diversity Characteristics during our review of applications and deliberations.

Diversity Characteristics Desired of School of Medicine Matriculants.

- Significant life experiences in rural, inner city urban, or diverse cultural communities.
- Significant life experiences in "non-western" countries or third-world countries.
- Bilingual or multilingual abilities.
- Previous careers before pursuing medicine.
- Success in overcoming financial, social, family, physical, or educational hardships.
- Success in overcoming adversity due to societal biases.
- Successful experience in scientific or social research as measured by first-author publications.
- Significant life experiences with individuals from cultural backgrounds other than their own.

University of Kansas School of Medicine, 2006
Applicants and Matriculants by Gender, Race and Ethnicity

Race and Ethnicity	Applicants			Matriculants		
	Women	Men	Total	Women	Men	Total
Hispanic/Latino						
Cuban	7	3	10	0	0	0
Mexican American	28	30	58	1	2	3
Puerto Rican	4	2	6	0	0	0
Other Hispanic	13	11	24	1	0	1
Multiple Hispanic*	1	2	3	1	0	1
Subtotal	53	48	101	3	2	5
Non-Hispanic/Latino**						
Black	59	33	92	5	3	8
Native American/Alaska Native	10	6	16	2	0	2
Native Hawaiian/Other Pacific Islander	1	0	1	0	0	0
White	449	622	1,071	61	69	130
Asian	126	193	319	10	13	23
Other Race	0	2	2	0	0	0
Multiple Race*	28	32	60	2	3	5
Unknown	3	2	5	1	0	1
Subtotal	676	890	1,566	81	88	169
Foreign	8	10	18	0	1	1
Total	737	948	1,685	84	91	175

*Since 2002, students can select more than one race and / or ethnicity. **Those who did not choose Hispanic/Latino' or 'Non-Hispanic/Latino' are counted under 'Non-Hispanic/Latino'.

Data Source: AAMC Data Warehouse: Applicant-Matriculant File, as of 5/9/2007.

Academic Support Programs

The Center of Excellence for Minority Medical Education (COE) is one of the federally funded programs administered by OCED. COE funds support the COE Learning Resource Center, which is located in close proximity to student classrooms. It contains a wealth of resources for students, serves as a gathering place used to discuss problems and exchange ideas, provides academic enrichment information, and provides an opportunity for students and OCED staff to interact on a regular basis. The Center employs a learning skills specialist, offers United States Medical Licensing Examination (USMLE) board preparation workshops, supports a minority faculty-student mentoring program, and supplemental instruction. The Center and staff support student-led research on minority health care issues in the Minority Students and Faculty Summer Research Training Program. In addition to these programs, which are specifically designed for students in our federally funded diversity programs, more services are available through the campus-wide Student Center *(http://www.kumc.edu/studentcenter/scess/).*

Enrichment Programs

The School of Medicine support and grows a continuous and vigorous K-20 Educational Pipeline Program. Developed in 1986, the University of Kansas Medical Center (KUMC) Health Careers Pathways Program (HCPP) has served 5,268 students via three Satellite Centers, Saturday Academy, and through the summer enrichment programs.

Educational Partnerships

The Greater Kansas City—Health Professions Pipeway Initiative (HPPI) is a visionary and innovative bi-state alliance between the KUMC (Schools of Nursing, Allied Health, and Medicine), the University of Missouri-Kansas City, United School District (USD) 500, KCMO School District and key churches *(http://www.gkc-hppi.org/).* This Pipeway provides educational and support programs to students and their teachers and families from kindergarten all the way through board examination, licensure, and employment, by linking with our other enrichment programs and community resources. The program's focus is on increasing the number of academically well-prepared underrepresented minority applicants in health care and other science-intensive careers. We have three church-based HPPI Cyber Learning Centers for partner families and their children *(http://www.gkc-hppi.org/cyber.htm).*

Student Financial Assistance

Several guaranteed federal student loan programs are available to medical students at the KUMC, including Stafford Loans, Perkins Loans, and Primary Care Loans. In addition, the University of Kansas Endowment Association provides scholarship and loan assistance to medical students. One of the ways the School of Medicine strives to ensure diversity in the student body is through the scholarship-awarding process. KUMC is the recipient of a NIH Endowment grant for increasing research and training capacity, through the National Center on Minority Health and Health Disparities, a program that assists in enabling us to do this. KUMC also awards the federal Scholarship for Disadvantaged Students annually. This scholarship is available to students from either economically or educationally disadvantaged backgrounds, as defined by program guidelines.

KUMC also offers the Kansas Medical Student Loan program. This program, created by the Kansas legislature, provides full tuition scholarships plus stipends in return for practice in rural and underserved parts of the state.

Other Pertinent Information

Multiple programs are available to support and educate students, faculty, and staff and impart cultural competence in this diverse learning environment.

There are close to 60 student organizations and interest groups that students have to choose from, and we encourage and support student participation in these important organizations. Among them are the Student National Medical Association, the Latino Midwest Medical Student Association, the Asian American Medical Students Association, the Muslim Student Organization, and Students Educating and Advocating for Diversity (SEAD). Medical students are also actively involved in providing health care to the uninsured residents of Wyandotte County at the student-run JayDoc Clinic and participate in Medical Mission trips several times a year through the International Outreach Program. Members of these organizations not only provide personal support to one another, but they also educate and enrich the campus and local communities through their outreach and service projects.

The Office of Cultural Enhancement and Diversity and the school support cultural immersion experiences within the state and abroad. The Nicodemus Project is one such program that takes place in rural Kansas in a unique setting—the only remaining all African American settlement founded by Exudusters in the post-civil-war era. Each summer descendants of the original settlers come together for a Homecoming Celebration, and our students participate by providing health screenings and prevention and health education as they learn about the culture of Nicodemus.

The Multicultural Health Care Information Resource Center (MIRC) houses, books, journals, posters, CDs, videos, and online access to its resource cache, as well as an electronic resource via the Dykes

Library Voyager online catalog and the MIRC Web site located at *(http://www2.kumc.edu/oced/mirc.htm)*. The MIRC Library has become a regional resource and clearinghouse, with its focus on health disparities and medical education opportunities for cultural minorities and underserved populations.

The Program on Diversity and Disparities in Health (PDDH), established within the Center of Excellence in Minority Medical Education in September 2001, was designed to enhance minority health research activities throughout KUMC. The program also sponsors a Distinguished Visiting Lectureship Series, which brings in speakers nationally and internationally renowned in health disparities research.

KUMC has a Diversity Initiative that includes a Diversity Advisory Council. This campus-wide initiative supported by a structure which is used to promote diversity *(http://www2.kumc.edu/hr/diversity/DefFiles/DivInt.htm)*.

University of Kentucky College of Medicine

Dr. Carol Elam
Associate Dean for Admissions and
Institutional Advancement
University of Kentucky
College of Medicine
800 Rose Street, MN 102, UKMC
Lexington, KY 40536-0298
859-323-6161; 859-257-3633 Fax
http://www.mc.uky.edu/medicine

Recruitment

The University of Kentucky has a commitment to provide health career information and counseling to high school and college students from minority and low-income groups in an effort to ensure such students have the opportunity to be admitted to, and succeed in, medical school. Special outreach programs designed to stimulate the interest of students from medically underserved populations in all health professions, especially medicine, have been developed for students attending Kentucky schools.

Additionally, the Center for Academic Resources and Enrichment Services (CARES) sponsors a yearly session for students on our undergraduate campus to meet with student affairs officers who can address their specific issues and concerns regarding their anticipated health profession. Medical center students also sponsor an annual Hispanic Health Fair.

Admissions

Academic considerations are the primary determinant of who receives an interview at our institution. Non-academic considerations include leadership, caliber of recommendations, exposure to medicine, interest in primary care research involvement, and willingness to establish practice in Kentucky.

University of Kentucky College of Medicine, 2006
Applicants and Matriculants by Gender, Race and Ethnicity

Race and Ethnicity	Applicants			Matriculants		
	Women	Men	Total	Women	Men	Total
Hispanic/Latino						
Cuban	4	3	7	0	0	0
Mexican American	8	8	16	0	0	0
Puerto Rican	0	2	2	0	0	0
Other Hispanic	8	10	18	0	0	0
Multiple Hispanic*	0	2	2	0	0	0
Subtotal	20	25	45	0	0	0
Non-Hispanic/Latino**						
Black	31	15	46	0	3	3
White	400	545	945	30	48	78
Asian	77	116	193	7	6	13
Other Race	2	0	2	0	0	0
Multiple Race*	20	16	36	2	0	2
Unknown	4	4	8	0	0	0
Subtotal	534	696	1,230	39	57	96
Foreign	37	38	75	2	5	7
Total	591	759	1,350	41	62	103

*Since 2002, students can select more than one race and / or ethnicity. **Those who did not choose
'Hispanic/Latino' or 'Non-Hispanic/Latino' are counted under 'Non-Hispanic/Latino'.
Data Source: AAMC Data Warehouse: Applicant-Matriculant File, as of 5/9/2007.

Non-cognitive factors play a role in the selection of all candidates.

The Committee on Admissions of the College of Medicine is composed of basic science and clinical faculty members, junior and senior medical students, and community practitioners.

Academic Support Programs

The Center for Academic Resources and Enrichment Services (CARES) administers a short pre-entry program for all entering health profession students in late July. The program emphasizes activities and mentor relationships with faculty and continuing students.

The Office of Medical Education provides all students of the College of Medicine with assistance in achieving their educational goals and in adjusting to the special demands of medical education. The following programs are available to students: individual and group counseling; educational resources; preparation for national licensure examinations; tutorial service; and specialized support services as required.

Student Financial Assistance

The College of Medicine works closely with students to establish a reasonable financial budget and to provide financial assistance within the resources available.

The College of Medicine participates in the following federal assistance programs for disadvantaged students:

- Scholarships for Disadvantaged Students (SDS)
- National Health Service Corps (NHSC) Scholarship (Service Commitment)
- Primary Care Loan

The following institutional programs provide limited assistance to disadvantaged/minority students enrolled in the College of Medicine:

- Parker Scholarship
- COM Diversity Scholarship
- Jonas Fields Scholarship
- Lyman T. Johnson Fellowship
- Provost Enhancement Scholarship

The College of Medicine also has institutional subsidized student loan programs to assist students in addition to federal financial aid.

Association of American Medical Colleges, 2007

AAMC

University of Louisville School of Medicine

Ms. Mary S. Joshua, Associate
Director, Special Programs Office
University of Louisville
School of Medicine
Health Sciences Center
Abell Administration Center
Room 502, 323 E. Chestnut Street
Louisville, KY 40202
502-852-7159; 502-852-8866 Fax
msjosh01@gwise.louisville.edu
www.louisville.edu/medschool/ahec/special.programs

Recruitment

To insure a quality education for our matriculants, an aggressive effort to identify and recruit a diverse student population is in place. Health career information and counseling are provided to high school and college students. A concerted effort is made to follow up with students from racial/ethnic groups underrepresented in medicine, counties underserved in health professions, and those with disadvantaged backgrounds. Also, information exchange occurs frequently with students and many pre-medical advisors throughout the United States.

The School of Medicine/Special Programs Office staff identifies high school and college students, encouraging them to participate in special summer preparatory programs to strengthen their academic skills and broaden their health career and research awareness. Throughout the year, mentorship activities, workshops and shadowing or visits with medical students, physicians, and basic science faculty are scheduled.

The Student National Medical Association and the Black Biomedical Graduate Student Organization assist with recruitment and retention of a diverse group of students.

Admissions

Applicants to the School of Medicine are considered individually and are selected based on merit. There is no separate admissions committee for screening applicants from underrepresented groups. However, there are individuals from underrepresented racial/ethnic groups who serve as members of the regular admissions committee.

The Admissions Committee evaluates an applicant's acceptability based on the entire academic record (undergraduate and graduate), Medical College Admission Test (MCAT) scores, and letters of recommendation. The applicant's personality and motivation are evaluated by interviews with members of the committee. Extracurricular activities and medical exposure are also important elements of the applicant evaluation.

The Medical Education Development (MED) Program provides a supplemental year for promising applicants who do not gain acceptance through the regular process. MED Program students are selected from the pool of regular applicants and are invited to take selected courses from the first-year medical school curriculum and graduate level courses. Upon passing these courses and completing other program requirements, MED Program participants are considered for admission to the medical school to take the remainder of the first-year courses. Preference is granted to denied applicants from the targeted recruitment groups.

Academic Support Programs

Services are available to assist students in achieving their educational and career goals. These activities include: a five-week pre-matriculation program prior to entry into medical school; relocation, housing,

University of Louisville School of Medicine, 2006
Applicants and Matriculants by Gender, Race and Ethnicity

Race and Ethnicity	Applicants			Matriculants		
	Women	Men	Total	Women	Men	Total
Hispanic/Latino						
Cuban	4	7	11	0	1	1
Mexican American	11	12	23	0	0	0
Puerto Rican	3	2	5	0	0	0
Other Hispanic	12	11	23	1	1	2
Multiple Hispanic*	0	2	2	0	0	0
Subtotal	30	34	64	1	2	3
Non-Hispanic/Latino**						
Black	68	35	103	5	3	8
Native American/Alaska Native	1	0	1	0	0	0
Native Hawaiian/Other Pacific Islander	1	0	1	0	0	0
White	504	730	1,234	44	71	115
Asian	133	185	318	9	7	16
Other Race	0	2	2	0	0	0
Multiple Race*	30	22	52	3	0	3
Unknown	4	5	9	1	2	3
Subtotal	741	979	1,720	62	83	145
Foreign	12	9	21	1	0	1
Total	783	1,022	1,805	64	85	149

*Since 2002, students can select more than one race and / or ethnicity. **Those who did not choose
Hispanic/Latino' or 'Non-Hispanic/Latino' are counted under 'Non-Hispanic/Latino'.
Data Source: AAMC Data Warehouse: Applicant-Matriculant File, as of 5/9/2007.

and financial aid information; individual counseling and faculty-student-resident interaction; a tutorial program; assistance in preparation for the United States Medical Licensing Examination; educational resource material; and other workshops and individualized support as needed.

Enrichment Programs
Go to *(www.louisville.edu/ medschool/ahec/special.programs)*.

Health Careers Adventure Program. This is an intensive effort of the NorthWest Area Health Education Center, which includes a four-week summer enrichment component for sixth-through tenth-grade students to encourage interest in a health career. Each summer, students participate and enhance academic skills in biology, math, chemistry, reading, and writing. They learn about health care and health careers through presentations and field trips to health care facilities with health professionals and professional students. Programs during the academic year, after-school, and Saturdays include tutoring, volunteer opportunities, and presentations.

The Pre-freshman Professional Education Preparation Program is a five-week residential academic program for graduating high school seniors interested in medicine or dentistry. Priority is given to graduating seniors from medically underserved counties in Kentucky and students from underrepresented groups. Students receive academic enrichment in math and science, study skills and test-taking strategies. They experience living away from home and adjusting to college life. Students are exposed to the health sciences and the undergraduate campus community.

Summer Medical and Dental Education Program (SMDEP). This innovative six-week residential academic program is for pre-medical and pre-dental students upon completion of one or two years of college.

Funded by The Robert Wood Johnson Foundation, the program introduces students to the academic realities of medical and dental education. The hallmark activity is a three credit-hour course entitled "Introduction to Fundamentals of Biomedical Sciences." Participants focus on integrating and applying the basic sciences utilizing team-based medial/dental applications for three academic credit hours, tuition-free. In addition to science enrichment, students receive intensive instruction and workshops centered on financial planning, career planning, health disparities, written and oral communication, learning-skills development, and cultural competency training. Students are divided into clusters with medical and dental students serving as Student Development Assistants and Cluster Leaders. The academic component is taught by Health Sciences Center faculty.

MCAT/DAT Training Conference. Pre-medical and pre-dental students, after completion of two years of college, may apply to a four-week summer residential program to assist them in preparation for the MCAT or the Dental Admission Test (DAT). Students review biology, general chemistry, organic chemistry, physics, verbal reasoning, and quantitative reasoning. Pre-dental students review an additional course in perceptual ability. In addition to review, students participate in professional and personal development workshops, clinical activities, and hospital tours. Supervised practice test sessions on the MCAT and DAT are conducted. Application, personal statement, and interview assistance are also provided.

Pre-matriculation Program. Upon their admission to the University of Louisville School of Medicine, students from disadvantaged backgrounds, underrepresented groups, or medically underserved counties are invited to participate in the five-week summer Pre-matriculation Program. This program is conducted

during the weeks immediately preceding the beginning of the school year. The areas of emphasis include human physiology, medical biochemistry, and anatomical science. Time is also devoted to overall orientation to medical school, study and test-taking skills, stress management, computing, financial management, practice opportunities, research options, and clinical activity. In addition to academic preparation, this program provides for the development of peer groups, establishment of support systems, familiarity with the city and school, dialogue with faculty and upper-level students, and an early establishment of day-to-day routine.

Student Financial Assistance
The University of Louisville School of Medicine waives the secondary application fee for disadvantaged students. Financial assistance for interview trips cannot be provided. The university offers scholarships for students with strong academic credentials. Based on available resources, the School of Medicine makes a concerted effort to assist students in meeting their financial needs. During the Pre-matriculation Program and academic year, workshops on debt management and financial planning are provided.

Educational Partnerships
University of Kentucky, State Council on Higher Education, Pikeville Osteopathic Medical School, Kentucky State University, Western Kentucky University

AAMC

Louisiana State University School of Medicine in New Orleans

Dr. Edward G. Helm
Associate Dean and Professor of Surgery
Louisiana State University School
of Medicine in New Orleans
Office of Community
& Minority Health Education
1901 Perdido Street
Suite 310, Box P3-2
New Orleans, LA 70112-1393
504-568-8501; 504-568-6319 Fax
http://www.medschool.lsuhsc.edu/cmhe/

Recruitment

The Louisiana State University (LSU) School of Medicine in New Orleans actively recruits minority and disadvantaged students. The Office of Community & Minority Health Education (CMHE) directs its retention activities at the K-12 and college level. Recruitment workshops are held annually at the health sciences center. Invitations are extended to all Louisiana college pre-medical advisors and students. A workshop consists of an overview of the medical school curriculum and presentations by the faculty and administrators. High school recruitment activities include working with high school science clubs, Career Awareness and Competition Days held at the health sciences center, and visits to high schools. Recruitment activities are carried out by the CMHE staff, medical students, and faculty. The school's recruitment efforts encompass an integrated program of visits, lectures, films, tours, and actual assistance in completing applications.

Admissions

The LSU School of Medicine in New Orleans is dedicated to providing the opportunity for an excellent medical education to all Louisiana applicants who are prepared to benefit from its curriculum and instruction. To this end, the Admissions Committee of the School of Medicine will strive to recruit and admit Louisiana residents from every geographic, economic, social, and cultural dimension of the state of Louisiana.

The primary goal of the School of Medicine in New Orleans is to produce competent, humanistic physicians. In order to achieve this goal, the School of Medicine finds that having a diverse student body is essential. Diversity in all its forms benefits students by creating a dynamic, productive, and positive learning environment that promotes better cross-cultural and cross-racial understanding. Ultimately the benefit of classroom diversity will help the School of Medicine produce individuals who are able to be effective clinicians within a multi-cultural environment.

Our present policy precludes us from accepting applications from individual who are not residents of Louisiana unless the applicant is the son/daughter of an alumnus of LSU School of Medicine in New Orleans who no longer resides in the state or an applicant who is applying to the M.D./Ph.D. program.* There is no discrimination because of race, religion, sex, age, disability, national origin, or financial status. Minority and disadvantaged students are strongly encouraged to apply. The Office of Community & Minority Health Education may be reached by calling 504-568-8501. Dr. Edward G. Helm is the associate dean for this office.

*If you are not sure of your residency status as it pertains to Louisiana or you would like information on the residency requirements, you should make an inquiry to W. Bryant Faust, Acting Registrar; LSU Health Sciences

Louisiana State University School of Medicine in New Orleans, 2006
Applicants and Matriculants by Gender, Race and Ethnicity

Race and Ethnicity	Applicants			Matriculants		
	Women	Men	Total	Women	Men	Total
Hispanic/Latino						
Cuban	3	8	11	0	0	0
Mexican American	5	5	10	1	2	3
Puerto Rican	1	3	4	0	0	0
Other Hispanic	14	16	30	0	2	2
Multiple Hispanic*	0	1	1	0	0	0
Subtotal	23	33	56	1	4	5
Non-Hispanic/Latino**						
Black	75	30	105	4	2	6
Native American/Alaska Native	1	2	3	0	1	1
Native Hawaiian/Other Pacific Islander	2	2	4	0	0	0
White	297	382	679	57	77	134
Asian	49	61	110	5	12	17
Other Race	1	0	1	0	0	0
Multiple Race*	5	10	15	0	4	4
Unknown	3	1	4	0	1	1
Subtotal	433	488	921	66	97	163
Foreign	6	8	14	1	0	1
Total	462	529	991	68	101	169

*Since 2002, students can select more than one race and / or ethnicity. **Those who did not choose
Hispanic/Latino' or 'Non-Hispanic/Latino' are counted under 'Non-Hispanic/Latino'.
Data Source: AAMC Data Warehouse: Applicant-Matriculant File, as of 5/9/2007.

Association of American Medical Colleges, 2007

Center, 433 Bolivar Street, New Orleans, LA 70112; 504-568-4829.

Rural Scholars Track. LSU School of Medicine in New Orleans has implemented a Rural Scholars' Track. The goal of this pathway is to identify and train physicians who will most likely practice medicine in rural settings, particularly in the state of Louisiana. This rural track is in response to the growing shortage of physicians in certain areas of Louisiana. The Rural Scholars' Track will improve the delivery and quality of the rural health care system through a combination of education, service, collaboration, and research specific to these underserved areas of the state.

The students admitted to this program will have to meet the same admissions criteria as all other students applying to the school. The students who are chosen to enter this track will be selected from applicants who have already been accepted into the entering class. Admission to this program will be limited to students coming from rural parishes defined as primary care shortage areas by the Louisiana State Board of Medical Examiners. In addition, students from parishes designated as rural by the Office of Rural Health Policy will be given further consideration.

Academic Support Programs
The School of Medicine has tutorial programs in the basic sciences, as well as in the clinical areas. In addition, the CMHE staff provides basic science course review sessions and study-skills workshops during the academic year for all minority/disadvantaged students. A structured four-week United States Medical Licensing Examination Step 1 review is available to all second-year LSU students.

Enrichment Programs
Science Enrichment Program (SEP). The SEP is an after-school program for 30 7th graders conducted at a New Orleans public middle school. SEP is for students who have expressed an interest in health careers and enjoy math and science. The classes, held two days per week for one-hour sessions, will not only sharpen science and mathematics skills but also improve test-taking skills for the eighth grade LEAP exam. High School Science Club members and LSU School of Medicine minority and disadvantaged medical students serve as SEP tutors.

Junior Summer Science Program (JrSSP). The JrSSP is a four-week summer hands-on research experience at LSU Health Sciences Center for 10 SEP students to apply learned science and mathematics principles in a biomedical hands-on laboratory setting. Minority and disadvantaged medial students assist the instructor for the program.

Summer Science Program (SSP). This eight-week enrichment program is for rising and graduating disadvantaged high school seniors who have demonstrated an interest in the health professions. The students must be Louisiana residents. The purpose of the program is to provide academically talented students an opportunity to interact with scientists, clinicians, and faculty of the Louisiana State University Health Sciences Center. This program provides classroom, as well as hands-on, laboratory experiences. Students are assigned sites in the university-affiliated hospitals, research laboratories of faculty, and clinical settings. Minority and disadvantaged medical students serve as program coordinators.

Medical College Admission Test (MCAT) Review. A comprehensive preparatory to review the MCAT is offered to potential applicants. This course includes a preliminary diagnostic examination, lectures in each area of the MCAT, a review of test-taking techniques, home-study materials, and access to the online data-based computer library. Upon completion of the course, a mock MCAT is given.

Pre-matriculation Program. The goal of the program is to provide entering disadvantaged medical students with experiences that will facilitate academic, environmental, and emotional adjustment to medical school. It is intended that participation in this program will enable the student to begin medical school with greater ease and competency. The program consists of lectures and lab experiences in histology, biochemistry, physiology, and gross anatomy. In addition, sessions in personal development, study skills, note taking, test-taking skills, memorization, and time management are also offered. Students will be given Career Exploration and Cultural Competency Workshops, a one-week rotation in a Community Health Clinic, and a two-week Primary Care Shadowing experience.

Student Financial Assistance
Incoming freshman students who are of the opinion that they are disadvantaged from an educational, economic, or social point of view are encouraged to apply for a scholarship. Members of the Medical School Scholarship Committee interview the applicants and the committee decides on who is most deserving for the award. A base award of $1,500-$3,000 per year is available for four years. The program is available for approximately 15 disadvantaged students/year.

Educational Partnerships
An educational network exists with the New Orleans Public School System (NOPS). Through this LSU–NOPS linkage, students receive information, support, and encouragement to explore health care fields as professions. School-based science clubs serve as the forum. Club sponsors—high school science teachers and counselors with LSU faculty—direct activities

AAMC

and field trips. Programmatic components of the network are Awareness Day, Competition Day, the High School Summer Science Program, and the Seventh Grade SEP and Junior Summer Science Program. In addition, CMHE has a *Young Healers Mentorship Program* with the Louisiana Medical Association. This program offers a variety of opportunities for African American medical students to work with practicing minority physicians.

In addition, partnerships with Louisiana Historically Black Colleges and Universities exist for the recruitment and facilitation of entry into the School of Medicine.

Louisiana State University School of Medicine at Shreveport

Shirley Roberson, Director
Multicultural Affairs
LSUHSC School of
Medicine in Shreveport
1501 Kings Highway
Shreveport, LA 71130-3932
(318) 675-5049; (318) 675-4332 Fax
srober1@lsuhsc.edu

Recruitment

The Director of Multicultural Affairs, along with the Assistant Dean of Admissions, visits college campuses in Louisiana each year with special attention given to the Historically Black Colleges and Universities in the state. Students are presented information pertaining to admissions procedures, scholarships, support systems,

student activities, curriculum, and other programs provided by the Louisiana State University Health Sciences Center School of Medicine. In an effort to inform pre-college students about the health care professions, visits to local high schools are made as requested. Minority medical students and faculty participate in both the interview and recruiting processes.

Admissions

The Louisiana State University Health Sciences Center School of Medicine in Shreveport is an American Medical College Application Service (AMCAS) affiliated school, and all applicants must apply through that agency. All Louisiana applicants completing the AMCAS process are sent a secondary application. Applicants who are granted a fee waiver from AMCAS can request a waiver of the $50 fee that normally accompanies the secondary

Louisiana State University School of Medicine in Shreveport, 2006
Applicants and Matriculants by Gender, Race and Ethnicity

Race and Ethnicity	Applicants			Matriculants		
	Women	Men	Total	Women	Men	Total
Hispanic/Latino						
Cuban	4	3	7	1	0	1
Mexican American	4	8	12	0	0	0
Puerto Rican	1	2	3	0	0	0
Other Hispanic	13	21	34	1	1	2
Multiple Hispanic*	0	2	2	0	0	0
Subtotal	22	36	58	2	1	3
Non-Hispanic/Latino**						
Black	72	31	103	2	1	3
Native American/Alaska Native	1	4	5	0	0	0
Native Hawaiian/Other Pacific Islander	1	1	2	1	0	1
White	286	399	685	43	59	102
Asian	52	82	134	3	6	9
Multiple Race*	5	14	19	0	0	0
Unknown	0	3	3	0	0	0
Subtotal	417	534	951	49	66	115
Foreign	6	8	14	0	0	0
Total	445	578	1,023	51	67	118

*Since 2002, students can select more than one race and / or ethnicity. **Those who did not choose Hispanic/Latino' or 'Non-Hispanic/Latino' are counted under 'Non-Hispanic/Latino'.
Data Source: AAMC Data Warehouse: Applicant-Matriculant File, as of 5/9/2007.

application filed directly with the Louisiana State University Health Sciences Center School of Medicine in Shreveport. Applicants are admitted to the Louisiana State University Health Sciences Center School of Medicine without regard to race, sex, marital status, disability, age, or creed. Students are evaluated on their scholastic records, Medical College Admission Test (MCAT) scores, interview evaluations, and letters of recommendation. Non-cognitive variables are also considered.

The Admissions Committee is composed of basic and clinical science faculty as well as physicians from the community. Minorities are represented on this committee.

Academic Support Programs

The Louisiana State University Health Sciences Center (LSUHSC) School of Medicine in Shreveport has a peer tutoring program for students experiencing academic difficulty. Academic progress of all students is monitored closely throughout the year by the Student Promotions Committee who are a part of the Medical Curriculum Counsel, which works closely with the Director of Multicultural Affairs. Academic and personal counseling is coordinated through the Offices of Student Affairs and Multicultural Affairs.

Student Financial Assistance

LSUHSC School of Medicine in Shreveport has re-established a scholarship program directed at medical students who come from disadvantaged backgrounds, educationally, economically, and/or socially. This program is designed to help reduce the educational debt incurred in medical school of those medical students who have lacked the traditional benefits available to most students in the areas of primary and secondary education, family income and assets, and social and cultural experiences. Students are also encouraged to compete for national merit and need-based awards and grants. There is an

emergency loan program funded by faculty donations to assist students who have an urgent need. All applicants are advised to be aggressive in making their financial needs known to medical school officials.

Other Pertinent Information

In addition to numerous intramural activities, there is a chapter of the Student National Medical Association (SNMA), a non-profit organization that is composed of minority medical, graduate and allied health students.

Association of American Medical Colleges, 2007

Tulane University School of Medicine

Dr. Ernest Sneed
Assistant Dean of Students
Office of Admissions and Student Affairs
Tulane University School of Medicine
1430 Tulane Avenue, SL 67
New Orleans, LA 70112
esneed@tulane.edu

Recruitment

The diversity of our student body is an important factor in ensuring that our students have an enriched learning environment and that they become culturally competent physicians. Members of our Office of Admissions and Student Affairs, along with student and faculty representatives, make visits to both local and national undergraduate institutions with significant minority populations to encourage interest in medicine in general and in our institution

in particular. Through the Student National Medical Association and the Office of Diversity, undergraduate and high school minority students from various colleges and local high schools visit our institution throughout the year. They interact with students, residents, and faculty while here and are encouraged to contact members of our medical community with any questions or concerns after they leave our campus. Tulane is a host site for the National Youth Leadership Forum on Medicine each summer, and we are able to encourage these exceptional high school students to return to Tulane for medical school. Tulane is also linked with the Center for Math and Science High School here in New Orleans, which also provides an opportunity to directly engage the interest of local, talented minority students.

Admissions

Tulane does not have a separate admissions process for minority students. Rather, all applications are considered individually, with race/ethnicity being only one of a number of factors that make up an individual's unique profile. We seek to admit a diversity of well-rounded, committed, involved students who will make positive contributions to our medical school and to the community in which they serve, and who will make competent, compassionate, and able physicians. The Admissions Committee always has at least three minority representatives (one student and two faculty) out of 25 total members. When minority students come for interviews, we routinely have our minority students and faculty available to interact with them, to answer any questions, and just to talk. We encourage the applicants to keep in touch after the interview process, and to feel free to contact anyone they have met here, or the Assistant Dean of Student Affairs, for specific questions. We have several Early Acceptance Programs with colleges in the area, which help to ensure that qualified minority students from those institutions choose our medical school to attend. We also have the Tulane Rural Medical Education (TRuMEd) program, which helps guide interested students to eventually practice in a rural and underserved setting.

Academic Support Programs

All students accepted to Tulane University School of Medicine are capable of excelling academically, and we monitor their progress via the Academic Performance Committee, whose purpose is to identify students with problems early on so that they can get the help they need to succeed. The course directors are proactive in assisting students with difficulties via individual or group tutoring by members of the department. Our Office of Education in the medical school, and the Educational

Tulane University School of Medicine, 2006
Applicants and Matriculants by Gender, Race and Ethnicity

Race and Ethnicity	Applicants			Matriculants		
	Women	Men	Total	Women	Men	Total
Hispanic/Latino						
Cuban	36	26	62	0	1	1
Mexican American	52	72	124	0	1	1
Puerto Rican	23	27	50	0	1	1
Other Hispanic	93	84	177	2	6	8
Multiple Hispanic*	10	13	23	0	0	0
Subtotal	214	222	436	2	9	11
Non-Hispanic/Latino**						
Black	283	119	402	6	5	11
Native American/Alaska Native	7	9	16	0	0	0
Native Hawaiian/Other Pacific Islander	12	15	27	0	1	1
White	1,857	2,262	4,119	37	66	103
Asian	815	838	1,653	13	15	28
Other Race	7	7	14	0	0	0
Multiple Race*	109	104	213	4	2	6
Unknown	26	29	55	1	0	1
Subtotal	3,116	3,383	6,499	61	89	150
Foreign	70	101	171	1	3	4
Total	3,400	3,706	7,106	64	101	165

*Since 2002, students can select more than one race and / or ethnicity. **Those who did not choose Hispanic/Latino' or 'Non-Hispanic/Latino' are counted under 'Non-Hispanic/Latino'.
Data Source: AAMC Data Warehouse: Applicant-Matriculant File, as of 5/9/2007.

Resource Center on the nearby undergraduate campus, are both available to assist with study skills and time management issues, as well as with testing for learning disabilities. A Peer Tutoring Program is in place that trains and funds upper-level students to work with first- or second-year students that are having course difficulties, and it has been very successful. There is also a system in place to assist any student with psychological or personal issues in a confidential and compassionate manner. We stress to all of our students that we will help in whatever way necessary to ensure their success in these often challenging medical school years.

Student Financial Assistance

Some application fee waivers are granted but no financial assistance is available for interview trips. Tulane offers financial assistance to qualified students through scholarships or loans, federal, private, or institutional. While most available financial aid is need-based, Tulane offers a limited number of scholarships that are awarded on the basis of academic achievement.

Inquires concerning financial aid should be directed to the Financial Aid Office, Tulane School of Medicine, New Orleans, LA 70112.

Johns Hopkins University School of Medicine

Dr. Crystal Simpson, Assistant Dean for Student Affairs/Office of Diversity
Johns Hopkins University
School of Medicine
Broadway Research Building, Suite 137
733 North Broadway
Baltimore, MD 21205
410-955-3416
410-955-0544 Fax
cfsimpson@jhml.edu

Recruitment

The Johns Hopkins University School of Medicine is committed to enrolling and educating individuals from disadvantaged groups. Minority faculty and students participate in all admissions and recruitment activities. Representatives of the Admissions Committee, faculty, student body, and the Assistant Dean for Student Affairs visit colleges throughout the country to provide pre-medical advisors and minority students with information about educational opportunities available at the Johns Hopkins medical institutions. This i followed by direct mailings to the students to encourage them to apply. Informal counseling is also available for pre-medical students. Tours of the medical school and hospital facilities are conducted for all applicants selected for interview, and similar tours can be conducted, upon request, to minority student groups interested in medical careers.

Admissions

There are no state residency requirements, and the Committee on Admission welcomes applications from minority students throughout the country. The B.A. degree,

Johns Hopkins University School of Medicine, 2006
Applicants and Matriculants by Gender, Race and Ethnicity

Race and Ethnicity	Applicants			Matriculants		
	Women	Men	Total	Women	Men	Total
Hispanic/Latino						
Cuban	18	22	40	0	1	1
Mexican American	56	64	120	0	1	1
Puerto Rican	23	16	39	1	1	2
Other Hispanic	69	74	143	1	3	4
Multiple Hispanic*	7	10	17	0	0	0
Subtotal	173	186	359	2	6	8
Non-Hispanic/Latino**						
Black	312	166	478	4	2	6
Native American/Alaska Native	4	7	11	0	1	1
Native Hawaiian/Other Pacific Islander	10	7	17	0	0	0
White	1,298	1,781	3,079	22	34	56
Asian	633	763	1,396	20	22	42
Other Race	3	4	7	0	0	0
Multiple Race*	89	82	171	0	2	2
Unknown	20	37	57	0	0	0
Subtotal	2,369	2,847	5,216	46	61	107
Foreign	138	129	267	3	2	5
Total	2,680	3,162	5,842	51	69	120

*Since 2002, students can select more than one race and / or ethnicity. **Those who did not choose Hispanic/Latino' or 'Non-Hispanic/Latino' are counted under 'Non-Hispanic/Latino'.
Data Source: AAMC Data Warehouse: Applicant-Matriculant File, as of 5/9/2007.

AAMC

or equivalent, must be received prior to matriculation. All students are encouraged to complete degrees in the liberal arts or sciences consistent with their undergraduate major. Admitted applicants may request a deferral of their admission for a period of up to three years. The Medical College Admission Test (MCAT) is required.

Minority students are considered on an equal basis with other candidates. Selection factors include: proven academic competence in college courses, strong personal qualities, demonstrated leadership, creative abilities, commitment to humanistic concerns, and supporting recommendations provided by pre-medical advisors or faculty members. Applications to the Johns Hopkins University School of Medicine are made through the American Medical College Application Service (AMCAS).

Academic Support Programs
The curriculum schedule emphasizes adequate time for self-study and exploration. In the first year, formal classroom activities end at 1:00 p.m. Students have the afternoon hours for further study or for extracurricular activities. Tutorial programs are provided in each of the courses and are subscribed to on a voluntary basis. Small-group sessions emphasize mentoring by individual faculty as well as open faculty office hours in the afternoon. The Student Assistance Program offers workshops on study skills, time management, and test taking. These programs are offered to all students on a voluntary basis. Programs emphasize individual students and are not targeted toward any subgroup in the student body.

Student Financial Assistance
All financial aid is need-based. Qualified aid applicants receive a package of scholarship and loan funds. Every aid recipient is first given a standard unit loan to meet their need. The amount of the unit loan

varies annually and is the same for every student. Remaining financial need above the unit loan is awarded in scholarship monies. The application fee can be waived if the applicant has received an AMCAS fee waiver or if a letter is sent from their financial aid officer or pre-medical advisor to certify their inability to pay the fee.

For several years, the average debt of our graduating seniors has been less than that for graduating seniors from state supported schools.

The financial aid office is actively searching for scholarships and grant awards for which our students are eligible and make application when such sources are identified. All funds received in this manner reduce the amount the student has to borrow or reduces their parents' contribution.

Enrichment Programs
Minority Summer Internship Program {Undergraduates}. This is a ten-week program for undergraduates interested in graduate biomedical research. Students accepted to the program are placed in the laboratories of faculty members and work on projects designed for them by faculty. While at Hopkins the students learn about the M.D./Ph.D admissions processes, interact with graduate students, and participate in a number of enrichment activities including journal clubs with faculty members and research seminars. The students receive full support in this program including stipend, housing, and travel.

Contact Person:
Dr. Peter Maloney, Director
Phone: 410-614-3385
FAX: 410-614-3386

High School Summer Research Placements. Each year five to ten students from local high schools are placed in research laboratories here at Johns Hopkins. The students are paired with advanced Ph.D. students who serve as their mentors for six to eight weeks. The high school students carry out

research projects designed for them by the Ph.D. student or faculty member and also participate in activities of the Minority Summer Internship Program for undergraduate students. These include journal clubs, seminar presentations, and field trips to the National Institutes of Health.

Summer Research Project. During the summer following first year of medical school, the students may participate in summer research fellowships with faculty from the school of medicine.

National Institute on Aging Summer Training in Aging Research. Medical students from all over the country spend six to 12 weeks performing a research project and rotating through clinical experiences in the Johns Hopkins School of Medicine Division of Geriatric Medicine & Gerontology. The students receive a stipend.

Contact Person:
Dr. Crystal Simpson, Director
Phone: 410-550-8686
Email: (cfsimpson@jhmi.edu)

Educational Partnerships
The Dunbar-Hopkins Health Partnership is Baltimore City's and Maryland's most strategically positioned school, university, and business-community partnership for the health professions. Dunbar Senior High School is a city-wide school that is envisioned as becoming a magnet health science school in the near future. This multifaceted collaboration involves Dunbar Senior High School; Johns Hopkins Schools of Medicine, Nursing, and Public Health; the Johns Hopkins Hospital; and the Johns Hopkins Center for the Social Organization of Schools. Under the direction of Dunbar's principal, the initiative prepares students for admission to college and to a variety of careers in the health professions. This goal is realized, in part, through a variety of programs and interventions, including: curricular view and consultation, faculty development,

field work and internships, grant writing, information technology donations and planning, longitudinal program evaluation, mentoring, public relations assistance, special seminars, and visiting scholars and faculty.

A critical element of the student's program at Dunbar High school is research. The initial research course, Scientific Research in Health Care Delivery Systems: Theory and Application, will be offered in the second year of high school. This course will provide the foundation for students who will learn to read, understand, and apply research to their pathway of study. Throughout the third and fourth year of high school, the students will continue to conduct more sophisticated research that will culminate in a senior project. This Senior Project for the Health Professions Majors will be a research project using all types of research resources, Internet, journals, and current unpublished research. The senior project will include an exhibition with a presentation to a panel of health care professionals, educators, and peers.

The Student National Medical Association of the Johns Hopkins University School of Medicine sponsors a tutorial program at the Dunbar Senior High School. Students are tutored from 3:30 p.m. to 4:30 p.m. once or twice weekly as their schedule permits. Students are tutored in mathematics, chemistry, physics, biology, history, English, and foreign languages. Special programs are also provided to prepare these students for college and to acquaint them with health career opportunities. This group of medical students also participates in a Teen Sex Education Program at the Dunbar Middle School.

In doing these things for the Dunbar Middle and High Schools, the minority medical students serve as role models to encourage disadvantaged youth to pursue careers in medicine.

Uniformed Services University of the Health Sciences F. Edward Hébert School of Medicine

Margaret Calloway, CDR, MC, USN
Associate Dean for Recruitment and Admissions, Acting Uniformed Services University of the Health Sciences
Office of Admissions
Bldg A Room A1041
4301 Jones Bridge Road
Bethesda, MD 20814-4799
301- 295-3383 Voice
301-295-3383 DSN
301-295-3542 Fax
mcalloway@usuhs.mil

The Uniformed Services University of the Health Sciences (USU) was established by Congress in 1972 to provide a comprehensive education in medicine to select young men and women who demonstrate potential for and commitment to careers as medical corps officers in the uniformed services. USU serves the uniformed services and the nation as an outstanding academic health sciences center with a worldwide perspective for education, research, service, and consultation. It is unique in relating these activities to military medical readiness, public health, disaster medicine, and humanitarian medical assistance worldwide. The university provides the nation with health professionals committed to careers in public service and scientists dedicated to inquiry, research, and technological advances that serve the common good.

USU is a tuition-free medical school. Students are commissioned as active duty reserve officers in one of the four branches of the uniformed services – Army, Navy,

Uniformed Services University of the Health Sciences School of Medicine, 2006
Applicants and Matriculants by Gender, Race and Ethnicity

Race and Ethnicity	Applicants			Matriculants		
	Women	Men	Total	Women	Men	Total
Hispanic/Latino						
Cuban	3	4	7	0	0	0
Mexican American	6	25	31	0	3	3
Puerto Rican	7	8	15	1	0	1
Other Hispanic	24	33	57	2	2	4
Multiple Hispanic*	4	4	8	0	0	0
Subtotal	44	74	118	3	5	8
Non-Hispanic/Latino**						
Black	62	36	98	0	1	1
Native American/Alaska Native	1	4	5	0	0	0
Native Hawaiian/Other Pacific Islander	6	7	13	0	1	1
White	271	730	1,001	30	102	132
Asian	122	226	348	6	15	21
Other Race	1	3	4	0	0	0
Multiple Race*	31	41	72	3	4	7
Unknown	4	5	9	0	2	2
Subtotal	498	1,052	1,550	39	125	164
Foreign	1	5	6	0	0	0
Total	543	1,131	1,674	42	130	172

*Since 2002, students can select more than one race and / or ethnicity. **Those who did not choose Hispanic/Latino' or 'Non-Hispanic/Latino' are counted under 'Non-Hispanic/Latino'.
Data Source: AAMC Data Warehouse: Applicant-Matriculant File, as of 5/9/2007.

Air Force, or Public Health Service—and afforded all of the pay and allowances, privileges and responsibilities of an active duty officer. In 2007, the annual average salary of a USU medical student was approximately $51,000, plus medical and dental benefits.

The Office of Recruitment and Admissions is instrumental in the recruitment and retention of a student body that mirrors the diversity of this nation through a multi-faceted approach to enhancing the cultural, ethnic, and experiential diversity within the university.

Recruitment

Seaman to Admiral Medical Corps Option (STA-21). This unique program was designed specifically with our nation's service members in mind. Its goal is to draw highly motivated, academically sound students from the current active duty community who are interested in pursuing military medical careers. The STA-21 Medical Corps Option, still in its infancy, will facilitate the completion of a baccalaureate degree, acceptance to medical school, and the completion of a Doctor of Medicine or Doctor of Osteopathy degree, by providing an opportunity for enlisted personnel to complete their education without a break in service, and finally to obtain a commission in the U.S. Navy. Current USU medical students would serve as mentors and tutors for this talented group of service members.

Student Ambassador Program. Representatives from USU attend various career fairs and national conferences, both as participants and exhibitors. First- and second-year students are invited to serve on medical student panels, admissions workshops, and other activities at many of these venues. USU students are encouraged to seek leadership positions in regional and national organizations and to attend the corresponding national meetings. Descriptive materials are mailed to prospective applicants and to undergraduate health professions advisors and career counselors nationwide. In conjunction with the Office of Recruitment and Admissions, current medical students often participate in workshops, seminars, and medical student panels throughout the United States.

Open House Tours. USU welcomes pre-medical and pre-health societies, undergraduate groups, health professions advisors, and high school classes or interest groups for tours of the campus and medical school. In cooperation with many different departments at the university and the National Naval Medical Center, the Office of Recruitment and Admissions coordinates a tour of the facilities, a meeting with the admissions counselors, and at least one hands-on activity for groups of three or more visiting prospective students, faculty, or advisors. Students from groups underrepresented in medicine and science are highly encouraged to take advantage of this opportunity.

Once matriculated, a student's academic progress is closely monitored. Academic issues in any course are immediately identified by faculty members and students are strongly encouraged to seek counsel in the Office of Student Affairs where a strategic plan of action is enacted.

Retention. Students accepted to the school of medicine are assigned current first- or second-year medical students as peer mentors in order to ease their transition into the military medical school environment. Later in the spring, official sponsors are assigned. In the immediate pre-matriculation time frame, incoming students are invited to attend impromptu sessions on time management, study skills, and other topics designed by volunteer faculty educators to prepare students for the academic rigors of the first year's course load.

The Office of Student Affairs (OSA) closely monitors the progress of all students. Individual counseling is provided as soon as problem areas are identified. Peer tutoring, faculty mentoring, study groups, and small tutorial sessions are available and tailored to the learning style and needs of the individual student. Higher performing classmates volunteer to lead study groups to clarify lecture or lab material. In addition, faculty volunteers assist students with preparation for exams, [including the United States Medical Licensing Exam (USMLE) Steps 1 and 2], complete with clinical diagnostic testing.

Admissions

Minority applicants follow the standard American Medical College Application Service (AMCAS) procedures. The Admissions Committee considers cognitive and non-cognitive factors in the evaluation and admissions process. Other than standard AMCAS fees, there are no additional charges for USU applications.

Academic Support Programs

Faculty Mentor Program. Early in each academic year, all students receive a form to request a faculty mentor. The overall goal of the mentor program is to allow the development of a personal and a professional relationship between the mentor and student such that the mentor is aware of all issues that may impact the student's professional and personal success.

Post-Baccalaureate Program. This unique program selects students from among the pool of candidates to the school of medicine who are not offered acceptance to the first-year class of the medical school by the full Admissions Committee because of some slight weakness in their dossier. Three students whose applications demonstrate significant potential are given the opportunity to attend USU as a civilian graduate student, taking a portion of the first-year courses, in an effort to better prepare them for the rigors of the school's full curriculum. Successful participants, maintaining a 3.00 or better in all classes, are offered commissioning and matriculation into the next entering class. (Students must meet commissioning physical standards prior to acceptance into the post-baccalaureate program).

Enrichment Programs
Center for Health Disparities. In 2004, the school of medicine received a substantial grant to conduct research in health disparities. The Center for Health Disparities offers a ten-week paid summer research internship for qualified college students through the graduate school. Participants also receive the benefit of faculty mentors who are pioneers in medical research. Applications are available online.

Educational Partnerships
USU has a close affiliation with many of the other federal institutions in the Washington Metropolitan Area, and several faculty members have dual appointments with the National Naval Medical Center, Malcolm Grow U.S. Air Force Medical Center, Walter Reed Army Medical Center, the Armed Forces Radiobiology Research Institute, the National Institutes of Health, the U.S. Army Institute of Research, the Naval Medical Research Command, and others. Medical students are welcome to participate in ongoing research programs through prior arrangement with faculty in any of these closely affiliated institutions.

Medical Student Professional Development. USU actively supports student-run organizations. The university provides administrative support as well as a modest amount of financial assistance for student officers to attend national or regional meetings of their respective organizations. It should be noted that all medical, graduate, and graduate nursing students and spouses are welcome to participate in any of the organizations supported by the medical school. This enhances the ethnic, cultural, and experiential diversity of the medical school.

Among the student groups at USU are:

Student National Medical Association (SNMA). This is the largest and most influential national organization for minority medical students. The USU chapter is active in recruitment of students for both the medical school as well as for science-related careers. SNMA members are involved in mentoring programs for high school students, and two members served as peer mentors for the 2004 S2M2 inaugural program. These students annually participate in the Pre-Medical Forum at the SNMA national meeting. Additionally, SNMA members serve as role models for elementary, middle, and high school students in the Washington Metropolitan Area.

Asian Pacific American Medical Student Association (APAMSA). Student leaders select activities and learning sessions that increase cultural awareness to both the USU community and the local medical community. As an active APAMSA chapter, USU students co-hosted the tenth annual conference at the Marvin Center on the George Washington University campus in 2003. These students also served as translators for a community-wide career awareness program at a local high school.

American Medical Student Association (AMSA). This chapter made AMSA history by presenting a resolution to establish a military medicine interest group at the AMSA national meeting. In addition to informing the membership of the many contributions of military medicine, the USU chapter leadership now serves as the point of contact for all military sponsored medical students nationwide.

Women in Medicine and Science (WIMS). Under student leadership with clinical faculty support, students are exposed to lectures and local events highlighting the accomplishments of women in medicine and science. Together with APAMSA and SNMA, WIMS co-sponsors monthly student activities at faculty members' homes including information sessions, professional development seminars, and team building exercises.

Other student-led organizations include the American Medical Association Medical Student Section (AMA-MSS), specialty interest groups (Surgery, Pediatrics, OB/GYN, Psychiatry, Internal Medicine and subspecialties, Aerospace Medicine, Wilderness Medicine, Dive Medicine, etc.), and the Alpha Omega Alpha Medical Honor Society. There are a host of additional intramural and county recreational league athletic teams composed of USU students and faculty members.

University of Maryland School of Medicine

Dr. Donna L. Parker, Associate Dean
for Student Affairs
University of Maryland
School of Medicine
655 West Baltimore Street
Room M-004
Baltimore, MD 21201
410-706-7476; 410-706-8311 Fax
dparker@som.umaryland.edu
www.umaryland.edu

Recruitment

The University of Maryland School of Medicine sponsors a number of undergraduate and high school programs that are designed to encourage, prepare, and facilitate the entry of minority students into the field of medicine. These include visits to undergraduate colleges and universities, seminars, workshops, and summer programs. An important focus of the school's recruitment effort is to provide information on admissions requirements, the admissions process, undergraduate preparation for medicine, the M.D./Ph.D. program, and other educational opportunities.

Applicants and prospective applicants are encouraged to contact the medical school admissions personnel. Visit our Web site at *(www.umaryland.edu)*. On the day of the interview, applicants have the opportunity to meet with medical students and faculty and tour the medical school.

Admissions

The University of Maryland School of Medicine participates in the American Medical College Application Service (AMCAS). Minority students from all states are encouraged to apply. The admissions procedure for minority students is the same as that for all applicants. Among the selection factors emphasized by the Admissions Committee are: undergraduate or graduate grade-point average, Medical College Admission Test scores, application essay, and personal characteristics of the applicant including work or research experience. The interview, letters of recommendation, and the applicant's life experiences help the committee to evaluate the subjective qualities. The University of Maryland does not grant extensions for the initial application.

Academic Support Programs

Retention services are available for all students through the Office of Medical Education and the Office of Student Affairs. Services provided include tutorials; academic monitoring; personal, academic, career, and financial counseling; interaction with faculty through the advisory system; and skills development workshops. Because of the school's commitment to recruiting and graduating increased numbers of students, a number of retention activities, such as the Pre-matriculation Summer Program, are available. The school's emphasis is on providing personalized services relative to the needs of each student.

Enrichment Programs

Pre-matriculation Summer Program (PSP). This program is offered to students who are scheduled to matriculate at the University of Maryland School of Medicine. The PSP provides an orientation to the medical school curriculum, gives a review of learning skills, and simulates the first semester schedule.

Short-Term Research Training Program. This program, which provides supervised full-time research experience, is offered to pre-matriculants. Students can participate in this program at any stage during the four-year curriculum. Both programs provide participants with a stipend, supervision, and support from both the faculty and administration.

University of Maryland School of Medicine, 2006
Applicants and Matriculants by Gender, Race and Ethnicity

Race and Ethnicity	Applicants			Matriculants		
	Women	Men	Total	Women	Men	Total
Hispanic/Latino						
Cuban	10	6	16	1	0	1
Mexican American	25	19	44	0	0	0
Puerto Rican	15	11	26	0	0	0
Other Hispanic	54	52	106	1	2	3
Multiple Hispanic*	6	7	13	1	1	2
Subtotal	110	95	205	3	3	6
Non-Hispanic/Latino**						
Black	291	127	418	13	5	18
Native American/Alaska Native	4	2	6	0	0	0
Native Hawaiian/Other Pacific Islander	8	8	16	0	0	0
White	1,089	1,164	2,253	57	34	91
Asian	492	485	977	21	15	36
Other Race	1	6	7	0	0	0
Multiple Race*	54	53	107	4	4	8
Unknown	18	28	46	1	0	1
Subtotal	1,957	1,873	3,830	96	58	154
Foreign	67	65	132	0	0	0
Total	2,134	2,033	4,167	99	61	160

*Since 2002, students can select more than one race and / or ethnicity. **Those who did not choose
Hispanic/Latino' or 'Non-Hispanic/Latino' are counted under 'Non-Hispanic/Latino'.
Data Source: AAMC Data Warehouse: Applicant-Matriculant File, as of 5/9/2007.

Association of American Medical Colleges, 2007

Student Financial Assistance

A variety of university, state, and federally funded programs provide financial aid to students in need. Students are encouraged to apply for financial aid as soon as applications become available—usually during the latter part of December to mid-January. Priority processing of financial aid applications is provided for those received prior to February 15th. Detailed information on programs and application procedures can be obtained by contacting the Student Financial Aid Office, 111 S. Greene Street, Suite 104, Baltimore, MD 21201, 410-706-7347.

Educational Partnerships

The University of Maryland School of Medicine is committed to increasing the number of underrepresented minority students (African American, American Indian/Alaskan Native, Mexican American/Chicano, and mainland Puerto Rican) at the medical school. The school has developed programs to increase the pipeline that supplies the minority applicant pool by developing partnerships with area high schools, colleges, and universities, and community programs, which will enhance the development/academic preparation of students through a variety of educational/professional experiences.

The High School Mini Medical School is an entertaining, educational program designed to provide high school students with interactive classroom instruction on a variety of medical subjects. Mini Medical School courses are taught by the University of Maryland School of Medicine Medical Students. Student participants, will learn directly from our medical students about many health subjects that impact them and specifically their communities. They also will get a chance to find out how they can break cycles of health care disparities and create positive changes in their families and communities. They will also learn how to take an active role in maintaining their own health.

Boston University School of Medicine

Dr. Jonathan Woodson, Associate Dean for Student and Minority Affairs
Boston University School of Medicine
715 Albany Street, Suite A407
Boston, MA 02118
617-638-4163; 617-638-4433 Fax
jwoodson@bu.edu

Recruitment

The Boston University School of Medicine (BUSM) is committed to the recruitment, admission, and retention of minority students. The Office of Minority Affairs (OMA) recruits nationwide for applicants to BUSM. The recruitment program involves visiting undergraduate schools to speak to individuals and groups. Staff also visit summer pre-medical programs to interview prospective applicants.

Admissions

BUSM has no special Admissions Committee for minority students. The OMA actively participates in the processing and screening of applications from minority students. The associate dean and director are active members of the Admissions Committee, participating in the medical school interviews and the selection process. Candidates for admission to BUSM must apply through the American Medical College Application Service, 2450 N Street, NW, Washington, DC 20037.

Academic Support Programs

All students receive group or individual tutorial assistance as the need arises. Academic counseling is offered by the associate dean, director, and other student affairs staff. In addition, each first-year student is assigned a faculty advisor. Various

Boston University School of Medicine, 2006
Applicants and Matriculants by Gender, Race and Ethnicity

Race and Ethnicity	Applicants			Matriculants		
	Women	Men	Total	Women	Men	Total
Hispanic/Latino						
Cuban	38	26	64	0	0	0
Mexican American	99	99	198	0	4	4
Puerto Rican	33	32	65	3	2	5
Other Hispanic	144	115	259	4	1	5
Multiple Hispanic*	18	12	30	1	1	2
Subtotal	332	284	616	8	8	16
Non-Hispanic/Latino**						
Black	264	142	406	17	3	20
Native American/Alaska Native	6	6	12	0	0	0
Native Hawaiian/Other Pacific Islander	17	9	26	0	0	0
White	2,663	2,751	5,414	41	47	88
Asian	1,369	1,267	2,636	22	16	38
Other Race	6	7	13	0	1	1
Multiple Race*	168	134	302	2	3	5
Unknown	44	54	98	0	1	1
Subtotal	4,537	4,370	8,907	82	71	153
Foreign	272	237	509	8	2	10
Total	5,141	4,891	10,032	98	81	179

*Since 2002, students can select more than one race and / or ethnicity. **Those who did not choose Hispanic/Latino' or 'Non-Hispanic/Latino' are counted under 'Non-Hispanic/Latino'.
Data Source: AAMC Data Warehouse: Applicant-Matriculant File, as of 5/9/2007.

seminars are conducted by the OMA to assist students in:

- developing their clinical acumen and interpersonal relationships;
- meeting faculty who can serve as mentors and role models; and
- selecting appropriate house officer training programs.

Students have available to them the alternative curriculum that permits them to take the first year over two years, or the second year over two years. Our policies state that a student must not take longer than three years to complete the first two years of the curriculum. We offer the students a variety of support services from the Office of Student Affairs, Office of Student Support Services, and the Office of Minority Affairs, including tutoring, counseling, testing, psychiatric evaluation and support, etc. Our objective is to help the student reach his/her full potential. Each student has a faculty advisor with whom they meet at least twice per year, and more if needed. In addition, the Associate Dean for Students and Minority Affairs is a member of all of the promotions committees and receives all students exam results throughout the year. This permits early intervention if needed.

Student Financial Assistance
Application fees are waived upon request when proof of need is submitted. The Office of Student Financial Management actively works with students in identifying sources of direct grants, loans, and service commitment programs.

Educational Partnerships
Early Medical School Selection Program (EMSSP). EMSSP was developed 13 years ago with a consortium of eight Historically Black Colleges and Universities. In order to further diversify the program, it was expanded to include students from colleges

with large Hispanic populations and the Indian Health Service. The program provides an early and more gradual transition into the medical school curriculum, through provisional acceptance into BUSM at the completion of the first two years of undergraduate study.

Students accepted into the program remain at their undergraduate colleges through their junior year and complete the maximum number of science courses required by their respective schools for graduation. Following their sophomore and junior years, the students take summer science courses at Boston University. The students complete their senior year at Boston University, taking first-year medical school courses at BUSM, while retaining bachelor degree candidacy at their home institutions. Applications may be requested from Boston University School of Medicine Office of Minority Affairs, 715 Albany Street Boston, MA 02118.

CityLab. This is a National Institutes of Health–Science Education Partnership Award and Howard Hughes Medical Institute-funded biotechnology learning laboratory designed to give high school students and their science teachers hands-on learning experiences. The laboratory is located within the Boston University Medical Center complex. A full-time high school teacher and laboratory manager coordinate laboratory experiences, including DNA fingerprinting, protein quantitation, and restriction analysis.

Boston University School of Medicine has a commitment to providing research training to underrepresented minorities through mentorship in Program Center Grants.

Short Term Research Training Program for Minority Students. This National Institutes of Health sponsored research training program is available to 5 undergraduate or graduate students for 10 weeks during the

summer. Students are placed in research laboratories for 10 weeks conducting research in such fields as AIDS, Sickle Cell Disease, Vitamin D metabolism, lipid metabolism, among others. Students are paid a stipend for the summer, as well as room, board and, round-trip airfare.

Boston University School of Medicine has as its flag-ship hospital the Boston Medical Center which serves a large diverse population in the City of Boston. Twenty six languages may be spoken on any given day. The staff and residents reflect the institutions commitment to diversity.

The Center for Community Health Education, Research, and Service (CCHERS) represents a consortium of 15 partners: 12 Boston neighborhood health centers, Boston University School of Medicine, Northeastern University College of Nursing, and Boston's Department of Health and Hospitals. CCHERS is an innovative model of community health care systems. It is an educational experience that not only satisfies the traditional medical school course objectives, but also achieves new goals that are fundamental to the health care provider in the 21st century—increasing the supply of generalist physicians and exposing students to community-based primary care.

Boston Area Health Education Center (BAHEC) is located at Boston City Hospital and affiliated with the Boston Department of Health and Hospitals, Boston University School of Medicine, and a network of neighborhood health centers. With a mission of alleviating health manpower shortages in medically underserved areas of Boston, BAHEC offers programs in three areas designed to make opportunities in health care available to minority populations, and to improve the quality of health care in Boston's inner-city neighborhoods.

Harvard Medical School

Dr. Alvin F. Poussaint, Faculty
Associate Dean for Student Affairs
Ms. Rosa Soler DaSilva, Program Director
Ms. Sherry Reddick, Program Coordinator
Office of Recruitment and
Multicultural Affairs
Harvard Medical School
260 Longwood Suite 244
Boston, MA 02115
617-432-2159; 617-432-0997 Fax
rosa-dasilva@hms.harvard.edu
http://www.hms.harvard.edu/orma/

Recruitment

Harvard Medical School (HMS) seeks diverse student populations. Our commitment to diversity is not only reflected in the variety of institutions from which students are accepted, but also in the ethnic and economic backgrounds of the student body. The Office of Recruitment and Multicultural Affairs was established in 1969. This office is responsible for recruiting and providing supportive services to individuals from groups underrepresented in medicine. HMS has been very successful in admitting and graduating students from these groups.

In the past 39 years, Harvard has graduated over 900 minority physicians. The medical school currently has 168 students from underrepresented groups (91 African Americans, 38 Mexican Americans, 12 Native Americans, 14 Puerto Ricans, 13 Hispanic).

The Office of Recruitment and Multicultural Affairs works closely with the minority student health organizations (The Multicultural Student Alliance composed of the Black Health Organization, Medical Students of Las Americas, and the Native American Health Organization), to recruit underrepresented minority students in medicine.

Students registered on the Medical Minority Applicant Registry list, published by the AAMC, receive admission information from the Office of Recruitment and Multicultural Affairs. The office coordinates campus visits for student organizations at other colleges and universities to meet HMS faculty, students, and staff. It also mails brochures and general information to undergraduate minority affairs and pre-medical advisors throughout the country.

Admissions

A student's entire record is evaluated when deciding on admission. The factors emphasized in the selection of applicants are academic strength, involvement in extracurricular activities, commitment to the community, and leadership potential. Research and comments contained in letters of recommendations are also considered.

Harvard Medical School does not have cutoff scores for grade-point averages and Medical College Admission Test (MCAT) scores. The grade-point averages of admitted students are within a broad range in keeping with the national average.

HMS students come from a variety of undergraduate institutions and academic backgrounds. The 2006 entering class came from several different colleges and universities. Forty nine percent were women and 20 percent were minorities. Although the majority of students admitted were science majors, non-science majors are given equal consideration.

Harvard Medical School, 2006
Applicants and Matriculants by Gender, Race and Ethnicity

Race and Ethnicity	Applicants			Matriculants		
	Women	Men	Total	Women	Men	Total
Hispanic/Latino						
Cuban	19	18	37	0	0	0
Mexican American	66	87	153	3	3	6
Puerto Rican	24	24	48	1	0	1
Other Hispanic	64	80	144	1	1	2
Multiple Hispanic*	7	10	17	0	0	0
Subtotal	180	219	399	5	4	9
Non-Hispanic/Latino**						
Black	229	169	398	7	7	14
Native American/Alaska Native	10	10	20	0	1	1
Native Hawaiian/Other Pacific Islander	6	5	11	0	0	0
White	1,262	1,791	3,053	45	31	76
Asian	662	764	1,426	17	23	40
Other Race	2	4	6	0	0	0
Multiple Race*	98	109	207	4	1	5
Unknown	19	45	64	2	1	3
Subtotal	2,288	2,897	5,185	75	64	139
Foreign	175	191	366	8	9	17
Total	2,643	3,307	5,950	88	77	165

*Since 2002, students can select more than one race and / or ethnicity. **Those who did not choose Hispanic/Latino' or 'Non-Hispanic/Latino' are counted under 'Non-Hispanic/Latino'.
Data Source: AAMC Data Warehouse: Applicant-Matriculant File, as of 5/9/2007.

AAMC

Academic Support Programs

Medical education at Harvard Medical School includes the following curricular elements: the biological and social sciences important to medicine, pathophysiology and mechanisms of disease, the patient-doctor relationship, clinical experiences in patient care, and electives. The first three elements form the common core of general medical education, which is taken by all students; the elective program encourages individual variation and emphasis.

The Academic Societies were established in 1987 to serve as the organizational framework for each student's experience in general medical education. Students in the Division of Health Science and Technology (HST) are members of its own society. All other students are assigned randomly to one of four societies: Cannon Society, Castle Society, Peabody Society, or Holmes Society. Each society is composed of faculty members including a Master, Associate Masters, Educators, Senior Fellows, Tutors, Preceptors, and Advisors, plus students from all four classes and administrative staff.

Members of a society share a society cluster area and classrooms in the Tosteson Medical Education Center (TMEC). Society-based academic activities support a problem-based learning approach and include the organization of tutorial groups, small-course evaluation and feedback sessions, and a mechanism for vertical integration of faculty and student curricular planning. Each society organizes a program of student advising, whose core is a four-year relationship between student and advisor to foster goals of self-assessment and professional development. The societies also plan para-curricular and social functions that bring faculty and students together.

Throughout its history, HMS has influenced the design of medical school education. From Harvard University President Charles Eliot's 19th century reform —developing the concept of a medical school as we know it today—to the ground breaking New Pathway curriculum of the 1980s, HMS has been in a continual process of growth and change. HMS recently redesigned its curriculum to meet the needs of 21st century medicine by integrating clinical and basic science across the curriculum, developing new models for clinical education, and engaging students in an in-depth scholarly experience.

The curriculum began mid-August 2006 with a new course, Introduction to the Profession, designed to introduce students to the profession, the practice of medicine, and the experiences that lie before them as they embark on the process of becoming physicians. Courses focused on the scientific basis of medical practice (basic, population, and behavioral sciences) and the patient-doctor relationship (professionalism, communication, physical diagnosis) span the first three and one-half semesters of the curriculum. In April of Year II, students begin making the transition from classroom to the clinical realm. Individual clerkships in the major disciplines of medicine (medicine, surgery, pediatrics, obstetrics and gynecology, psychiatry, neurology, radiology) are unified in a "Principal Clinical Experience," which will provide opportunities for longitudinal experiences with patients and faculty mentors as well as an interdisciplinary curriculum that integrates the scientific and clinical aspects of important diseases. Throughout the four years of medical school, students will have many opportunities to work one-on-one with faculty mentors. In this vein, a capstone experience for our students will be a several year, faculty-mentored, in-depth scholarly experience culminating in a written work product. This exploration of a topic in-depth will allow students to participate with faculty in the excitement of discovery and scholarship. The new HMS curriculum will prepare graduates to function in an increasingly multicultural landscape undergoing radical scientific, social, economic, and technological transformation. HMS seeks to ready students for this new world by providing them with the ideal educational environment and carefully integrated global experience to foster their growth as clinicians, scholars, discoverer, and leaders.

Students with a declared interest in a career in biomedical research or a strong interest and background in quantitative or molecular science may want to consider applying to Health Sciences and Technology (HST).

The following academic support services are provided for all students: tutorials for basic science courses, academic and personal counseling, and review materials and sessions for the United States Licensing Medical Examination.

The Faculty Associate Dean for Student Affairs is available to students for personal and academic counseling. There are no special academic programs or tracks for minority students since the attrition rate for minority students at HMS is negligible. All Harvard students go through the regular program.

Enrichment Programs

Pre-matriculation Summer Enrichment and Minority Faculty Development Program (PMSP). The Office of Recruitment and Multicultural Affairs sponsors this 8- to 10-week program for admitted HMS/HSDM underrepresented minority students. PMSP is directed to developing faculty from entering minority dental and medical students by fostering student interest in academic medicine and providing a mechanism for minority students and faculty to exchange ideas and interests. Through laboratory investigation seminars, site visits, and interaction with scientists and physicians, students gain a better understanding of career options in academic medicine. Participants receive a stipend, housing in the medical area dormitory, and payment for transportation to Boston.

Student Financial Assistance
Approximately 70 percent of all enrolled medical students receive some form of financial aid (grants and/or loans). All applications for admission are considered without regard to the financial resources of the applicant. Harvard awards financial aid according to need. There are several need-based scholarships and low-interest loans administered by the HMS Financial Aid Office. Parent information is an important component in determining eligibility for these programs.

Educational Partnerships
At present there are no formal educational partnerships that exist between Harvard Medical School and other institutions. However, there are several informal relationships between the medical school and city colleges, state colleges, and local high schools that have been established over the past years. Minority medical students volunteer as education counselors in local high schools and tutor high school students who attend after school programs.

Tufts University School of Medicine

Mrs. Colleen Romain, Director for Student Programs and Minority Affairs
Tufts University School of Medicine
136 Harrison Avenue
Boston, MA 02111
617-636-6576; 617-636-0375 Fax

Recruitment
Tufts University School of Medicine (TUSM) attracts students from all across the country. Approximately 51 percent of each class of 168 has been from the north-eastern U.S. The rest of the class is principally from the west and southwest. Most recruitment occurs at the undergraduate schools. Contacts are made by faculty, staff, students, and alumni through pre-medical organizations on individual campuses, as well as through national or regional student meetings, career day programs, and

by being in communication with summer and post-baccalaureate program staff.

Admissions
Minority student applications are evaluated by members of the Admissions Committee, which includes minority faculty. The committee is careful to evaluate the total person, including socioeconomic background, academic, and extracurricular accomplishments, and experience, as well as initiative, personal goals, and interests.

Academic Support Programs
Throughout the academic years, tutorial aid in the form of individualized or group instruction by faculty, graduate students, and upperclassmen has been provided to students who request it. In addition, workshops on study skills and stress management are offered. Students organize their own board reviews with support of faculty

Tufts University School of Medicine, 2006
Applicants and Matriculants by Gender, Race and Ethnicity

Race and Ethnicity	Applicants			Matriculants		
	Women	Men	Total	Women	Men	Total
Hispanic/Latino						
Cuban	32	18	50	1	0	1
Mexican American	62	68	130	1	1	2
Puerto Rican	34	29	63	0	0	0
Other Hispanic	115	80	195	3	1	4
Multiple Hispanic*	14	8	22	0	0	0
Subtotal	257	203	460	5	2	7
Non-Hispanic/Latino**						
Black	198	112	310	3	1	4
Native American/Alaska Native	7	7	14	0	1	1
Native Hawaiian/Other Pacific Islander	20	11	31	0	0	0
White	2,297	2,395	4,692	45	71	116
Asian	1,225	1,158	2,383	19	17	36
Other Race	8	5	13	0	0	0
Multiple Race*	153	113	266	2	2	4
Unknown	41	49	90	1	1	2
Subtotal	3,949	3,850	7,799	70	93	163
Foreign	151	163	314	0	1	1
Total	4,357	4,216	8,573	75	96	171

*Since 2002, students can select more than one race and / or ethnicity. **Those who did not choose Hispanic/Latino' or 'Non-Hispanic/Latino' are counted under 'Non-Hispanic/Latino'.
Data Source: AAMC Data Warehouse: Applicant-Matriculant File, as of 5/9/2007.

and staff and arrange for a simulated or practice Board exam during the month of March and April. Students are assigned both peer and faculty advisors. Workshops on specialty selection are made available to assist students in choosing a professional path. Carefully selected clinical faculty in each discipline work with third-year students to choose appropriate fourth-year courses and help plan the residency application process.

The Curriculum. Because rapid demographic, biomedical, technical, and scientific changes require that physicians confront new issues, practices, and information, Tufts initiated a new, integrated, cell to organism, interdisciplinary curricular model in 1985. The curriculum includes non-biological sciences relevant to health and health care delivery. A problem-based case study approach is closely coordinated with the material presented in each segment of the curriculum. Opportunities to participate in population health, primary care, and subspecialty clinical as well as research settings have also been accommodated in the regular curriculum.

M.D.-M.P.H. At Tufts it is possible to complete an M.D. and a Masters in Public Health within four years. The faculty have designed a challenging program for a very select group of students interested in examining the changes in population composition; the structure of health care delivery; or environmental, economic, and social factors that shape health services delivery.

M.D.-Ph.D. The Sackler School of Graduate Biomedical Sciences, in conjunction with the School of Medicine, offers an M.D.-Ph.D. degree program in biochemistry; pharmacology; cell, molecular, and developmental biology; cellular and molecular physiology; immunology, molecular biology, and microbiology; and neuroscience. Degree requirements are designed to be completed in approximately seven years.

The first two years include a modified first- and second-year medical school curriculum in which advanced graduate level courses, research experience, and seminars supplement the standard curriculum. The following three to four years are devoted to graduate courses and individual research. The dissertation and the final two years are devoted to the clinical portion of the M.D. curriculum.

M.D.-M.B.A. in Health Management. TUSM, in collaboration with the Florence Heller Graduate School for Advanced Studies in Social Welfare at Brandeis University and the Northeastern University Graduate School of Business Administration, now offers a combined M.D.-M.B.A. in Health Management degree. This program is believed to be the first in the nation to enable medical students to earn a Master of Business Administration (M.B.A.) in Health Management in the same four calendar years in which they earn the Doctor of Medicine (M.D.) degree. The program capitalizes on the strengths of three outstanding educational institutions—TUSM in medicine, Brandeis in health policy and social services, and Northeastern in business administration—to produce a new breed of physician capable of effectively participating in the planning and management of the changing health care environment.

Enrichment Programs

Pre-matriculation Summer Program. This program is a comprehensive introduction to courses, that are encountered in the first year of medical school. The areas of study include:

- Anatomy
- Biochemistry
- Histology
- Immunology
- Molecular Biology
- Physical Diagnosis
- Physiology
- Problem-Based Learning

Courses are taught by faculty members who are closely involved with the teaching of these general medical school courses, by graduate students in each of the disciplines, and by medical students who have recently completed the courses. Workshops run by upperclass students on such issues as surviving in medical school and preparing for classes, are also a part of the curriculum. The program runs for six weeks prior to the beginning of the first year.

An introduction to the new problem-based school curriculum, all explanation of Promotions and Evaluation Committee policies and procedures, as well as opportunities to meet with key staff (i.e., Deans, Financial Aid Counselors, the Registrar) are also incorporated into the program. Second-year students work with the new incoming students to familiarize them with the school and affiliated hospitals.

Students are given the opportunity to become involved in clinical exposure. These elective periods are over a three-week period and are under the supervision of mentor physicians. This can prove invaluable in providing an introduction to an environment in which exposure during medical school will help them in making informed career choices for graduate training.

Teachers and High School Students Program (TAHSS). Along with the traditional recruitment programs by faculty, alumni, and staff at the undergraduate level, Tufts focuses on the high school student. In 1988, TUSM started the Minority High School Program. The TAHSS is an integral part of the medical school's community outreach. The program's objectives are to motivate, guide, and advise high school students from disadvantaged backgrounds in the health and science professions. The program consists of presentations during the academic year and a seven-week summer research experience. These experiences are in bench research and clinical settings to further increase their knowledge of the health sciences. Faculty, students, and staff present career and financial planning information for college along with workshops on the health fields, courses in gross anatomy and, nutrition, and a special workshop for parents.

Student Financial Assistance

The application fee may be waived upon receipt of documentation from the American Medical College Application Service certifying that payment of the fee would constitute a financial burden. In certain cases, regional interviews may be scheduled.

Although scholarship resources are scarce, the dean provides a limited number of one-half scholarships for four years. In addition, the Financial Aid Office provides assistance to students in identifying sources of grants, low interest loans, and other programs.

University of Massachusetts Medical School

55 Lake Avenue North
Worcester, MA 01655
http://www.ummassmed.edu

Dr. Danna B. Peterson,
Assistant Dean
Student Affairs/
Diversity and Minority Affairs
508-856-3866; 508-856-5911 Fax
danna.peterson@umassmed.edu

Dr. Deborah Harmon Hines
Associate Vice Chancellor
for School Services
508-856-2444; 508-856-4888 Fax
Toll Free 877-395-3149 #1
Deborah-Harmon.Hines@umassmed.edu

Outreach Programs
508-856-2707; 508-856-6540 Fax
Toll Free 877-395-3149 #2
Outreach.programs@umassmed.edu

Introduction

Activities related to minority students are *pre-matriculation* activities and *matriculation* activities. All pre-matriculation activities reside in the Office of School Services under the direction of the Associate Vice Chancellor. They include the High School Health Careers Program, Summer Enrichment Program for Undergraduates, National Institutes of Health Funded Summer Research Fellowship Program for Minority Undergraduate Students, The Worcester Pipeline Collaborative, and all recruitment for University of Massachusetts Medical School (UMMS) programs. Matriculation activities are under the Assistant Dean for Students Affairs/ Diversity and Minority Affairs. They include career counseling, social activities, advising the UMMS Student National Medical Association (SNMA) Chapter, advising, and mentoring the progress of all minority students. Other matriculation

University of Massachusetts Medical School, 2006
Applicants and Matriculants by Gender, Race and Ethnicity

Race and Ethnicity	Applicants			Matriculants		
	Women	Men	Total	Women	Men	Total
Hispanic/Latino						
Cuban	0	1	1	0	0	0
Mexican American	1	0	1	0	0	0
Puerto Rican	2	1	3	0	0	0
Other Hispanic	11	9	20	0	0	0
Multiple Hispanic*	1	0	1	0	0	0
Subtotal	15	11	26	0	0	0
Non-Hispanic/Latino**						
Black	22	11	33	4	2	6
White	298	265	563	50	31	81
Asian	59	54	113	3	7	10
Multiple Race*	12	9	21	3	2	5
Unknown	4	2	6	1	0	1
Subtotal	395	341	736	61	42	103
Foreign	1	0	1	0	0	0
Total	411	352	763	61	42	103

*Since 2002, students can select more than one race and / or ethnicity. **Those who did not choose
Hispanic/Latino' or 'Non-Hispanic/Latino' are counted under 'Non-Hispanic/Latino'.
Data Source: AAMC Data Warehouse: Applicant-Matriculant File, as of 5/9/2007.

AAMC

support/activities are under the supervision of the Associate Vice Chancellor for School Services, Student Financial Aid, and Student Americans with Disabilities Act Services.

Recruitment

Recruitment to the University of Massachusetts Medical School is handled by the Office of School Services through recruitment visits to college fairs, recruitment events, high schools, colleges, and universities throughout the Commonwealth of Massachusetts. Recruitment is not conducted outside the Commonwealth because of very stringent residency requirements. Students who have graduated from Massachusetts high schools meet the residency requirements. Students attending colleges and universities may satisfy the residency requirement. Students can call 508-856-2323 for clarification.

Admissions

All applicants must complete an American Medical College Application Service (AMCAS) application. Upon receipt of the verified AMCAS application, the UMMS Admissions Office will send a UMMS Secondary Application and a proof of Massachusetts Residency form to all applicants. UMMS automatically waives application fees for students who have received fee waivers from AMCAS. All letters of recommendation should be sent directly to the Associate Dean for Admissions. A letter of recommendation from the Pre-medical Committee is preferred. If those are not available, two letters of recommendation should come from instructors in the pre-requisite courses. Applicants must have taken the Medical College Admission Test (MCAT) within the three years prior to application.

Selected applicants are invited for interviews. They are given the option of having one of two interviews at an off-campus site. A tour of the campus by students is also a part of the Interview Day. On the interview day, meetings are arranged for minority applicants and minority medical students, the Associate Vice Chancellor for School Services, and the Assistant Dean of Student Affairs/Diversity and Minority Affairs.

In the admission process service, volunteer activities and work with underserved populations are noted in all candidates as well as their academic achievement. The ability to work with diverse patients, professionalism, team work, communication, and leadership skills are key attributes for today's physicians. The interview process is geared towards assessing these and other non-cognitive factors. Both the Assistant Dean of Student Affairs/Diversity and Minority Affairs and the Associate Vice Chancellor for School Services are voting members of the Admissions Committee.

Academic Support Programs

There is a (pre-matriculation) Survival Skills Program available to all admitted first-year students during the week prior to the first week of classes. Tutorial services are available through the Office of Academic Achievement at no additional cost to the student. This includes content and skills tutoring. Students may elect to be in an extended program for a number of reasons. Such requests must be made in writing to the Associate Dean for Student Affairs. Participation in the Extended Program is aided by the fact that all students pay tuition for only four years. Each medical student is assigned to a faculty advisor and to a Second-Year Student Buddy by the Assistant Dean for Student Advising.

The faculty advisor monitors the student's academic progress. The Assistant Dean of Student Affairs/Diversity and Minority Affairs is closely involved with the minority students' academic progress. Both the Assistant Dean of Student Affairs/Diversity and Minority Affairs and the Associate Vice Chancellor/ Student Services are on the Academic Evaluation Boards. The Assistant Dean follows up on all academic issues related to matriculated students underrepresented in medicine. The Assistant Dean provides an additional advisory role for these students.

Enrichment Programs

For information on the following please contact:

(outreach.programs@umassmed.edu) for

- High School Health Careers Program (Massachusetts residents only) six weeks in the summer
- Summer Enrichment Program for Disadvantaged Undergraduate Students (Massachusetts residents only) four weeks in May/June
- Post-Baccalaureate Program for Disadvantaged Students (Massachusetts residents only) One year

(summer.research@umassmed.edu) for

- NIH Summer Research Program

Educational Partnerships

- Worcester Pipeline Collaborative: K-12 *(www.umassmed.edu/wpc)*
- Clark University's Worcester Education Partnership:*(http://www.clarku.edu/departments/hiattcenter/wep/about/index.shtml)*
- Partnership Advancing the Learning of Mathematics and Science K-12 (PALMS): *(http://www.umassmed.edu/rsrc/palms/)*

Student Financial Assistance

UMMS financial aid is need based. There is limited gift aid available. All students must file a Free Application Federal Student Aid (FAFSA) form. Also available to UMMS students is the Learning Contract. The Learning Contract, provided by the Massachusetts State Legislature, defers two-thirds of tuition annually for a service payback commitment of four years in the Commonwealth of Massachusetts. Service payback may be in the areas of 1) primary care, or 2) public service, or 3) community service, or 4) an underserved area. The Learning Contract is administered by the Office of School Services/Financial Aid.

Other Information
The Diversity and the Equal Opportunity Office sponsors annual celebrations for the Rev. Dr. Martin Luther King, Jr., Day and Black History Month (February).

The Office of School Services annually sponsors Latino Awareness Month (April).

UMMS is home to the statewide Area Health Education Office (AHEC).

In order to serve the increasingly changing diverse population of the Commonwealth, many UMMS students elect to participate in our growing International Program. Many of the people of Massachusetts are immigrants. UMMS students do electives in the countries of origins to learn language and social skills to assist them in serving our patient population.

Michigan State University College of Human Medicine

Dr. Wanda D. Lipscomb
Assistant Dean for Student Affairs and Services
Michigan State University College of Human Medicine
A-234 Life Sciences Building
East Lansing, MI 48824-1317
517-353-7140; 517-432-1051 Fax
lipscom3@msu.edu
www.mdadmissions.msu.edu

Recruitment

The Michigan State University (MSU) College of Human Medicine seeks a broadly diverse student body using a mission-based admission process that carefully evaluates applicants' non-academic attributes. Consistent with our motto, "Serving the People," we actively seek, consider, and maintain minority, disadvantaged, and students from underserved areas and populations in our applicant pool. The Office of Admissions works with our Student National Medical Association and Latino Medical Student Association groups to welcome accepted applicants using e-mail and phone contacts and hosts our Minority Recruitment Weekend that includes a reception with the dean and a dinner-dance with the student body as a whole, as well as a Minority Brunch and targeted activities.

In development of the applicant pool and support of minority students, the Dean for Admissions works with MSU undergraduates individually and in groups through the Charles Drew Enrichment Program and LANE Scholars Society for select MSU undergraduates from groups

Michigan State University College of Human Medicine, 2006
Applicants and Matriculants by Gender, Race and Ethnicity

Race and Ethnicity	Applicants			Matriculants		
	Women	Men	Total	Women	Men	Total
Hispanic/Latino						
Cuban	10	11	21	0	0	0
Mexican American	47	42	89	2	2	4
Puerto Rican	10	9	19	0	0	0
Other Hispanic	51	41	92	0	0	0
Multiple Hispanic*	7	4	11	0	0	0
Subtotal	125	107	232	2	2	4
Non-Hispanic/Latino**						
Black	146	98	244	10	2	12
Native American/Alaska Native	1	5	6	0	0	0
Native Hawaiian/Other Pacific Islander	8	5	13	0	0	0
White	871	1,216	2,087	40	39	79
Asian	446	558	1,004	4	5	9
Other Race	2	4	6	0	0	0
Multiple Race*	52	53	105	1	1	2
Unknown	12	13	25	0	0	0
Subtotal	1,538	1,952	3,490	55	47	102
Foreign	112	107	219	0	0	0
Total	1,775	2,166	3,941	57	49	106

*Since 2002, students can select more than one race and / or ethnicity. **Those who did not choose Hispanic/Latino' or 'Non-Hispanic/Latino' are counted under 'Non-Hispanic/Latino'.
Data Source: AAMC Data Warehouse: Applicant-Matriculant File, as of 5/9/2007.

underrepresented in medicine. The Office of Admissions contributes to the university in a variety of ways, including writing articles for VOICE, a Center of Excellence-supported student newsletter, and supporting the Tenth Annual Dia De La Mujer Conference, sponsored by the MSU Office of Racial Ethnic Student Affairs.

The College of Human Medicine has demonstrated a strong commitment to the recruitment and retention of applicants from populations currently underrepresented in today's medical profession. Reaching beyond our campus, we routinely make college visits; place ads in relevant publications, both minority student-focused and advisor-focused (such as the National Association of Advisors for the Health Professions, Inc. Annual Directory featuring special programs); and participate in the minority outreach fairs at the AAMC's annual meeting. We support minority student travel to the Annual Student National Medical Association Conferences, University of Michigan's Black Pre-Medical Association's Annual Recruitment Fair, the National Network of Latin American Medical Students Midwest Regional Conference, and the Latino Midwest Medical Student Association Conference. Visits are made to minority pre-medical summer opportunity programs and faculty participate in local, state, and national conferences to discuss our efforts to attract and retain minority students. Emphasis is placed on early discussion of potential careers in medicine.

Admission

The Michigan State University College of Human Medicine seeks a broadly diverse class. The preliminary screening process identifies students with academic potential and experience to support their decision to pursue a medical career. Students from a disadvantaged background and those from underserved groups and groups underrepresented in medicine are given close

scrutiny to discern potential, assess opportunity as well as accomplishment, and to evaluate the many non-cognitive variables addressed in our mission-based admission process. This attention to potential and the experience of the individual continues throughout the admission process as applicants are evaluated by four independent evaluators. Non-cognitive variables include commitment and motivation for medicine, depth and breadth of clinical experience, compassion, communication skills, judgment and problem solving, service and leadership, and potential to contribute to the profession.

In keeping with the above, the Committee on Admissions seeks to admit a class that is not only academically competent but also representative of a wide spectrum of personalities, backgrounds, talents, and motivations. The college does not have a separate review system for minority applicants but strongly encourages applications from students who have the desire and the aptitude to become physicians but have experienced unequal educational opportunities for social, cultural, or racial reasons. Minority and other non-traditional applicants have been very competitive, and the college has shown steadily increasing enrollment. In the past four years, the College of Human Medicine has had underrepresented minority (African American, Spanish-speaking and Native American) enrollment of nearly 20 percent of the entering class.

The requirements for admission are the Medical College Admission Test and the specific course requirements, which are outlined in the AAMC's *Medical School Admissions Requirements* book. Academic major is not a critical factor for admission; a solid background in the arts, humanities, or social sciences is of value to the future doctor along with strong preparations in the biosciences. Completion of B.S., B.A., or equivalent is required.

For information on admissions, please contact Dr. Christine Shafer, Assistant Dean for Admissions, Office of Admissions, Michigan State University, College of Human Medicine, A-239 Life Sciences Building, East Lansing, MI 48824-1317 or visit *(www.mdadmissions.msu.edu).*

Academic Support Programs
The Office of Academic Programs offers a variety of academic support services to medical students. Students are offered skills assessment, skill instruction, tutoring, supplemental instruction, and United States Medical Licensing Examination preparation. These services are meant to train, support, and enhance the presenting skills of first-year students. All students are encouraged to seek assistance early and to constantly assess their skill level, needs, and goals. Student progress is monitored and academic counseling and assistance are provided. Two full-time Academic Support Staff Coordinators are available for students. During Year 1, students have the option of individual tutoring, small-group tutoring, and/or discipline-based small-group supplemental instruction. In the pre-clinical phase, students are given the opportunity to extend their programs. Students are guided by faculty to develop a schedule that extends over a two-year period rather than the customary one year.

The faculty and professional staff of the Office of Academic Programs and the Office of Student Affairs and Services are available to assist in the retention of medical students through personal assistance and counseling.

Enrichment Programs
Post-Baccalaureate Program. The Advanced Baccalaureate Learning Experience (ABLE) is an academic year post-baccalaureate program that is designed to improve the qualifications of students from disadvantaged backgrounds in order to facilitate their

entry into medical school. The program is designed to accommodate a maximum of 15 students. ABLE participants enroll as second baccalaureate degree students in the College of Natural Science, which makes them eligible for campus housing, student privileges, and financial aid, provided they meet the required guidelines.

Admission to the ABLE Program is offered by the College of Human Medicine Committee on Admissions to students from disadvantaged backgrounds who apply to the college in the usual manner (i.e., through the American Medical College Application Service), work their way through the admissions process to the committee level, and are referred to the ABLE Review Committee for consideration. A follow-up application is sent to each ABLE candidate. The ABLE Review Committee then selects the final ABLE Program participants.

Students enroll in selected medical school basic science courses (maximum of two per academic year), which are offered by the College of Human Medicine. Passing medical school courses during this post-baccalaureate year will allow ABLE students, ultimately admitted to the College of Human Medicine, an opportunity to waive a portion of their medical school courses once they begin medical school. They also enroll in upper division and graduate science courses offered by the College of Natural Science.

The ABLE program guarantees admission to the College of Human Medicine for those students who successfully complete the program. Criteria for successful completion are established and defined at the time of acceptance into the program.

For information on the ABLE Program, please contact: Dr. Christine Shafer, College of Human Medicine, A-239 Life Sciences Building, Michigan State University, East Lansing, MI 48824, 517-353-9620.

Another enrichment effort is the *LANE Scholars Society,* which provides preliminary education, enrichment, and motivational experiences for 60 pre-medical students in an academic year.

Student Financial Assistance
The Michigan State University Office of Financial Aid has a staff of health professions advisors to counsel medical students and assist them in financial planning. There are some scholarships and grants available to entering minority students through the Office of admissions. The Michigan State University Urban Affairs Programs awards an Equal Opportunity Program Fellowship for four years of medical education. Most scholarships and grants awarded at Michigan State University are made on the basis of demonstrated financial need. Workshops are conducted during the week of pre-matriculation to encourage students to begin financial planning for their medical school education early. If financial problems are anticipated, students are urged to speak with a health professions counselor at the Office of Financial Aid or with the Assistant Dean for Student Affairs and Services.

Financial aid is not available for student interview trips. The application fee is waived if waived by the American Medical College Application Service (AMCAS), or by individual request with a letter of verification from an undergraduate institution.

Educational Partnerships
The College of Human Medicine has developed alliances with many organizations for mutual benefit. Collaboration has produced workshops on health careers, college admissions, and financial aid. Presentations are made to community constituents and tutorial sessions in math, science, and language arts are available.

Service learning opportunities are also arranged for high school, college, and medical student volunteers.

Linked MSU partners include undergraduate programs and institutions such as the College of Natural Science Charles Drew Laboratory, the Center for Service Learning and Civic Engagement, the Upward Bound Program, and Lansing Community College. Additional local partnerships exist in area public schools in the Lansing School District and the Ingham Intermediate School District Office of Talent Development. Community based organizations include the Black Child and Family Institute, the Cristo Rey Community Center, Greater Lansing African American Health Institute, and Ingham County Health Department.

AAMC

University of Michigan Medical School

Dr. David Mark Gordon
Associate Dean for Diversity
and Career Development
University of Michigan Medical School
1135 Catherine Street
2919C Taubman Medical Library
Ann Arbor, MI 48109-0603
734-764-8185 x0; 734-615-4248 Fax
dgordon@umich.edu
http://www.diversity.umich.edu/
www.med.umich.edu/medschool/diversity

The University of Michigan Medical School has a number of programs and opportunities, described below, that may be of particular interest to students from U.S. populations which are underrepresented in medicine. These programs and opportunities are open to **all** students, regardless of race/ethnicity or gender, and we clearly value the ways in which students of all backgrounds contribute to forming an academically excellent, exciting, and broadly diverse educational environment.

Recruitment

The Medical School has maintained its longstanding commitment to recruit, retain, and graduate members of those minority and disadvantaged groups that have been historically (and continue to be) underrepresented in medicine. This has been accomplished with a number of programs that are coordinated through the Diversity & Career Development Office (DCDO) and the Office of Student Programs' Admissions Office (Diversity & Career Development Web site: *(http://www. med.umich.edu/medschool/diversity/)*. Office of Student Programs Web site: *(http://www. med.umich.edu/medschool/osp/)*. Admissions Web site: *(http://www.med.umich.edu/ medschool/admissions/)*.

These efforts begin at the middle school level (see Enrichment Programs and Educational Partnerships) and continue beyond graduation through assistance in placement of graduating medical students.

The school also has a dual science M.D./ Ph.D. program, either through the Medical Scientist Training Program or individually arranged. Dual degrees are also available in business administration, public health, and law.

Minority and other disadvantaged students in the College of Literature, Science, and the Arts at the University of Michigan and other regional schools are encouraged to develop early linkages with our offices and medical student groups, particularly our Black Medical Association and our Latino American Native American Medical Association for pre-application counseling and support. Additionally, DCDO staff, minority and majority faculty members, medical students, and alumni visit selected health professions summer programs,. regional and national meetings, college career days, etc., to recruit. In addition, medical students who are members of the Black Medical Association, and the Latin American Native American Medical Association, acting on behalf of those student associations, also greet interviewees, conduct school tours, and respond to requests for information from applicants. Our aim is to help any student in need of career advice.

Admissions

All students are considered on the basis of individual qualifications. Cognitive and non-cognitive variables are given careful consideration. Attributes evaluated include motivation, competence, character, and personal fitness for the study of medicine. The academic record and the Medical College Admission Test (MCAT) are used to assess the student's level of academic preparedness. We are also particularly interested in students, minority or

University of Michigan Medical School, 2006
Applicants and Matriculants by Gender, Race and Ethnicity

Race and Ethnicity	Applicants			Matriculants		
	Women	Men	Total	Women	Men	Total
Hispanic/Latino						
Cuban	8	5	13	2	0	2
Mexican American	57	58	115	4	1	5
Puerto Rican	19	14	33	0	0	0
Other Hispanic	57	45	102	5	2	7
Multiple Hispanic*	6	6	12	0	0	0
Subtotal	147	128	275	11	3	14
Non-Hispanic/Latino**						
Black	152	116	268	6	3	9
Native American/Alaska Native	3	6	9	1	0	1
Native Hawaiian/Other Pacific Islander	11	5	16	0	0	0
White	1,119	1,524	2,643	44	52	96
Asian	593	718	1,311	21	22	43
Other Race	1	5	6	0	0	0
Multiple Race*	69	68	137	3	2	5
Unknown	17	17	34	0	1	1
Subtotal	1,965	2,459	4,424	75	80	155
Foreign	40	42	82	0	1	1
Total	2,152	2,629	4,781	86	84	170

*Since 2002, students can select more than one race and / or ethnicity. **Those who did not choose
'Hispanic/Latino' or 'Non-Hispanic/Latino' are counted under 'Non-Hispanic/Latino'.
Data Source: AAMC Data Warehouse: Applicant-Matriculant File, as of 5/9/2007.

Association of American Medical Colleges, 2007

majority, who have overcome major life hurdles in order to achieve what they have, as well as students with a demonstrated commitment to improve the health of underserved and disadvantaged populations. The Admissions Committee is a diverse group that includes medical students and members of the basic science and clinical faculties. Women and members of minority groups are represented on the committee. As a state-assisted institution, the University of Michigan Medical School has a primary responsibility to train future physicians of this state. However, approximately half of the class consists of non-residents.

All applicants must be U.S. citizens or have a U.S. permanent resident visa in order to be considered for admission. A permanent resident must have completed at least one year of pre-medical education at an accredited college in North America.

Our Medical School generally does not accept transfers from other medical schools. If an exception is to be considered, the student must have been previously enrolled in a medical school program leading to the M.D., and he/she must be in good standing and eligible for re-entry to that school.

The school participates in the American Medical College Application Service (AMCAS). The deadline for receipt of the application by AMCAS is November 15th.

Academic Support Programs

Study skills, academic counseling, and tutorial assistance are available in each of the courses for all matriculated students. Assistance is available on an individual and/or group basis. From time to time, students who are having academic difficulty in the medical school are permitted to proceed on a reduced schedule of courses. Plans are generated on an individual as-needed basis and have to be approved by our Academic Review Boards.

The medical school has a very effective counseling program that is available to all students. These various programs account for a high rate of student retention and graduate medical placement.

Pre-matriculation Program Entering students are recommended by the Admissions Committee for participation in the three-week pre-matriculation summer program. This program is designed to facilitate the academic transition to medical school, and is particularly offered to any students who may have been away from a curriculum-intensive environment for some time, or who feel they need supplemental academic enrichment. This program provides a background in study and reading skills to enhance performance in medical school, provides personal development workshops and individual counseling, and orients the students to the faculty, staff, and advanced students, as well as the Medical School and university campus. Students focus on courses in anatomy and molecular and cell biology, study-skills training, and personal development workshops.

Enrichment Programs

Medical School Summer Opportunities for Apprenticeships in Research (MedSOAR) The Medical School also administers the Medical School Summer Opportunities for Apprenticeships in Research Program, which is for Michigan undergraduate residents. The Medical School provides funding to permit hosting a number of local disadvantaged students (including from underserved backgrounds) to attend this ten-week program, for which they receive a stipend. Students work with a member of the faculty involved in an ongoing research investigation. Academic counseling support services are also offered. At the end of the program, students give a poster presentation to their respective laboratories/programs, families and invited guests.

Summer Research Opportunity Program (SROP). Research opportunities are available for disadvantaged undergraduate students (including from underserved backgrounds) from institutions outside the State of Michigan to participate in research projects at the University of Michigan. Several of these research opportunities are within the Medical School, where students work with established investigators in both the basic and clinical sciences. The research work, the SROP seminars, and workshops give participants a realistic groundwork for advanced study, helping them prepare for graduate/professional degrees.~Medicine-oriented students who participate in this program are encouraged to apply to the Medical School. This program is administered by our Rackham School of Graduate Studies *(http://www.rackham.umich.edu/ Recruitment/SROP/index.php).*

Profiles for Success Program (formerly a Health Careers Opportunity Program funded by the federal Health Resources Services Administration). This is a six-week summer program run by the University of Michigan School of Dentistry and the Medical School for economically or educationally disadvantaged individuals, as well as for those who have shown a commitment to working with underserved or disadvantaged populations. This program provides enrichment and skill-building activities for specific pre-medical courses (e.g., chemistry, biology), as well as preparation for the MCAT examination and the medical school admission process. We also provide students opportunities to meet with various medicine specialists and research investigators to talk about their careers *(http://www.dent.umich.edu/ mac/pfs.html).*

Student Financial Assistance

Financial aid at the University of Michigan Medical School is provided on the basis of financial need. The Medical School offers financial assistance in the form of scholarships, loans, and grants. Eligibility is based on current federal, state, and institutional regulations and recruiting goals. The Medical School also administers a Financial Program, funded by the regents of the university, which provides a limited number of tuition scholarships and supplemental grants to economically disadvantaged minority students who encounter unexpected expenses.

Educational Partnerships

The Medical School partners with several of the other health sciences schools at the University of Michigan (i.e., dental, pharmacy, public health, and others) and with the Ypsilanti School District and schools in Detroit, Michigan to provide science education and mentoring to local middle and high school students. The Medical School is committed to creating a strong pipeline to improve the numbers of underrepresented minorities in medicine as well as all sciences. Specific programs run by the Medical School include the following:

Summer Science Academy: This is a two-week summer program for tenth- and 11th-grade students in the State of Michigan who desire educational experiences which showcase careers in medicine and the biomedical sciences. Although open to any student, we especially target disadvantaged students (including from underserved backgrounds) who might not otherwise have access to such an enrichment opportunity. Many of our faculty and trainees participate by giving career talks and providing hands-on activities for the students. We also follow up with students to advise them on the college application process. Over the years of running this program, several such students have gained entry into medical schools, including our own.

Health Occupations Partners in Education (HOPE) Program: This is a partnership among all of our University of Michigan Health Professions Schools.working with the Ypsilanti Public School District to

mentor middle and high school kids towards the health professions and careers in biomedical research. This school district is a relatively disadvantaged district in terms of curriculum offerings, counseling, and presenting career role models, and we do our best to address these unmet needs. This program (including others) also provides a tangible opportunity for our trainees, faculty and staff to "give back" to our local community.

Flint Hurley SCORE: In coordination with the Hurley Medical Center Health Sciences & Medicine of Flint, Michigan, this is a one-day program at our Medical School to expose Flint high school students to careers in medicine. Many of these students are disadvantaged (including from underserved backgrounds).

Association of American Medical Colleges, 2007

AAMC

Wayne State University School of Medicine

Dr. Kertia L. Black
Assistant Dean,
Office of Student Affairs
Wayne State University
School of Medicine
540 East Canfield Avenue
Rm. 1369 Scott Hall
Detroit, MI 48201
313-577-1463; 313-577-0361 Fax
kblack@med.wayne.edu

Recruitment

The Office of Diversity at Wayne State University School of Medicine plans, directs, and implements the medical school's minority recruitment activities. The primary purpose of the Recruitment Outreach Program is to provide an access system for students to the medical school and to aid prospective disadvantaged students in their efforts to become stronger candidates for admission to medical school. The intent of the outreach program is to increase the pool of disadvantaged applicants by strengthening the students' academic and personal background. It is the policy of the Office of Diversity to establish communication and involvement with prospective disadvantaged applicants early in the admissions process.

The School of Medicine Office of Diversity has a Pre-medical Career counseling staff that provides academic and developmental counseling to students. The staff counselors work in the field serving target populations such as the Detroit Public Schools; two- and four-year colleges, other than Wayne State University; and Wayne State University's undergraduate pre-medical program.

Admissions

All students are admitted through the school's Admissions Committee. Membership on the Admissions Committee include minority and female faculty members as well as students. Factors such as a broad educational background, competitive performance in the basic sciences and on the Medical College Admission Test, related experiences in the biomedical field, and personal characteristics are considered by the Admissions Committee.

Academic Support Programs

Tutoring, academic, and personal counseling are available on an individual or group basis to all medical students through the Office of Student Affairs. Faculty and advanced level students serve as tutors.

Enrichment Programs

Pre-Matriculation Program. Entering students are invited to participate in a summer program designed to facilitate the transition to medical school. The students are familiarized with the school and are introduced to the organ systems curriculum. Concepts in biochemistry, anatomy, histology, physiology, and embryology are presented. The students' regular course work begins in the fall. Students are given an opportunity to work on those study skills pertinent to medical school. Counseling and directional work are provided to reinforce confidence. In addition, students are given the opportunity to meet faculty and advanced students.

Post-Baccalaureate Program. This program assists students whose prior academic performances have been compromised by economic and educational disadvantages. The program is restricted to legal Michigan residents. The program offers a year of structured and intensive preparation for medical school. The submission of an application for admission to Wayne State University School of Medicine is one of the prerequisites to candidacy for the school's Post-Baccalaureate Program.

Wayne State University School of Medicine, 2006
Applicants and Matriculants by Gender, Race and Ethnicity

Race and Ethnicity	Applicants			Matriculants		
	Women	Men	Total	Women	Men	Total
Hispanic/Latino						
Cuban	7	9	16	0	1	1
Mexican American	31	19	50	5	1	6
Puerto Rican	5	6	11	0	0	0
Other Hispanic	31	19	50	2	1	3
Multiple Hispanic*	3	5	8	0	0	0
Subtotal	77	58	135	7	3	10
Non-Hispanic/Latino**						
Black	256	123	379	29	11	40
Native American/Alaska Native	1	2	3	0	0	0
Native Hawaiian/Other Pacific Islander	6	3	9	0	0	0
White	670	929	1,599	79	95	174
Asian	363	468	831	20	23	43
Other Race	2	4	6	0	0	0
Multiple Race*	42	42	84	5	2	7
Unknown	10	13	23	3	0	3
Subtotal	1,350	1,584	2,934	136	131	267
Foreign	154	162	316	3	8	11
Total	1,581	1,804	3,385	146	142	288

*Since 2002, students can select more than one race and / or ethnicity. **Those who did not choose Hispanic/Latino' or 'Non-Hispanic/Latino' are counted under 'Non-Hispanic/Latino'.
Data Source: AAMC Data Warehouse: Applicant-Matriculant File, as of 5/9/2007.

Association of American Medical Colleges, 2007

AAMC

Fourteen students participate in the Post-Baccalaureate Program each year. Successful completion of the program assures admission to Wayne State University School of Medicine. The program strengthens the student's academic and non-academic preparation for medical school. The program is divided into three semesters and a summer program. During the fall and winter semesters the students take specific science courses in the university's College of Liberal Arts. Course selection is based on individual needs. Specially designed study skills and reading programs are provided. Students also receive personal counseling. The spring term classes are held at the medical school. Medical school faculty present anatomy, histology, biochemistry, and physiology course material. The intent of this term's work is to facilitate the development of discipline and the necessary mechanisms to handle the volume of work in medical school. During the summer the students participate in the Entering Freshman Summer Program described above.

Student Financial Assistance

All students admitted to Wayne State University School of Medicine who apply for financial aid are awarded assistance based on need and the availability of funds.

Mayo Medical School

Barbara L. Porter, Assistant Dean
for Student Affairs
Mayo Medical School
200 First Street, S.W.
Rochester, MN 55905
507-284-0916; 507-284-2634 Fax
porter.barbara@mayo.edu

Recruitment

Mayo Medical School actively works to encourage and assist underrepresented minority students to pursue careers in medicine and biomedical research. These activities are coordinated by the Office of Minority Student Affairs, which serves the Mayo Medical School, Mayo Graduate School, Mayo School of Health Sciences (allied health), and Mayo School of Graduate Medical Education (residency training programs). Faculty, students, and administrators attend national recruitment meetings, as well as visit selected universities and colleges. Upon request, colleges and universities may arrange to bring groups of students to Mayo for tours and visits. Students who are considering applying to Mayo Medical School may, depending upon availability, tour the school and sit in on classes.

Admissions

Entering class size at Mayo Medical School is 42 students, including six M.D./Ph.D. students, and two O.M.S students. More than 3,400 applications are received each year. The Admissions Committee of Mayo Medical School reviews applications of minority students looking at factors such as grade-point average, Medical College Admission Test scores, as well as non-cogitative attributes of leadership, service, research experiences, health care exploration activities, and commitment to

Mayo Medical School, 2006
Applicants and Matriculants by Gender, Race and Ethnicity

Race and Ethnicity	Applicants			Matriculants		
	Women	Men	Total	Women	Men	Total
Hispanic/Latino						
Cuban	5	14	19	0	0	0
Mexican American	35	30	65	1	2	3
Puerto Rican	6	10	16	0	0	0
Other Hispanic	21	33	54	0	0	0
Multiple Hispanic*	2	1	3	0	0	0
Subtotal	69	88	157	1	2	3
Non-Hispanic/Latino**						
Black	68	43	111	1	1	2
Native American/Alaska Native	7	4	11	0	0	0
Native Hawaiian/Other Pacific Islander	3	1	4	1	0	1
White	781	1,092	1,873	16	16	32
Asian	250	348	598	2	2	4
Multiple Race*	38	41	79	0	1	1
Unknown	6	19	25	0	0	0
Subtotal	1,153	1,548	2,701	20	20	40
Foreign	6	5	11	0	0	0
Total	1,228	1,641	2,869	21	22	43

*Since 2002, students can select more than one race and / or ethnicity. **Those who did not choose Hispanic/Latino' or 'Non-Hispanic/Latino' are counted under 'Non-Hispanic/Latino'.
Data Source: AAMC Data Warehouse: Applicant-Matriculant File, as of 5/9/2007.

medicine. The Admissions Committee is composed of physician and basic science faculty, two student members, one public member, and one administrator. Mayo Medical School actively recruits students from diverse groups underrepresented in medicine. Since 1992, entering classes have averaged about 20 percent underrepresented minority students.

Academic Support Programs
Mayo Medical School does not have a formal program for pre-admission academic reinforcement. Upon entering, each student is paired with a mentor who works to guide them throughout their time at Mayo. For all students, close personal relationships with faculty and administration are maintained, and any student in academic difficulty is offered help as soon as the need is evident. Mayo is prepared to offer whatever academic support is needed including tutoring and repeating a particular course or an entire academic year. It is uncommon for any of Mayo's students to take more than four years to complete the curriculum.

Enrichment Programs
An extensive series of programs and activities are offered to assist minority students in their professional development *(http://www.mayo.edu/msgme/diversity.html.)* These include summer research for undergraduates (SURF) *(www.mayo.edu/mgs/surf.html)*, a post-baccalaureate research program for recent college graduates *(http://www.mayo.edu/mgs/postbacprogram.html)*, summer research (SRF) *(http://www.mayo.edu.msgme/diversity-srf.html)* and clinical preceptorships for medical students *(http://www.mayo.edu/msgme/diversitysep.html)* (not 2007), a career development program (CDP) *(http://www.mayo.edu/msgme/diversitycdc.html)*, and both a one-year Certificate and two-year Masters in Clinical Research. The Clinical Research Training Program (CRTP) allows minority medical students to acquire clinical research skills while taking an appropriate leave of absence from their home school *(http://www.mayo.edu/msgme/crtp.html)*.

All of these programs are coordinated through the Office of Minority Student Affairs and most are supported by the Mayo Clinic's initiative for minority student development, "Training in Translational Research: Bench to Bedsides." This initiative, founded by the National Institutes of Health (NIH), is focused on increasing the number of minority basic science and clinical investigators and addressing the shortage of minority academic physicians.

Student Financial Assistance
Students are admitted to Mayo Medical School without regard to their financial circumstances. If the applicant's American Medical College Application Service (AMCAS) fee is waived. Mayo also waives their application fee. Merit scholarships are available equal to the full cost of tuition. Students may also qualify for other need-based financial aid. Financial aid counseling is available to applicants and is required for accepted students. Mayo also has loan funds available to supplemental federally-sponsored loan and grant programs. These funds, combined with Mayo's generous scholarship program, enable students to avoid excessive debt. Mayo's average debt upon graduation is routinely half the national average for medical student loan debt. Summer and other programs may provide one or more of the following: scholarships, stipends/salaries travel, meals, and housing.

Educational Partnerships
Mayo has ongoing relationships with minority serving high schools, colleges, and universities. Institutional resources are committed to providing minority college students from around the United States with opportunities to learn more about Mayo Medical School and the medical field. Extensive effort is made to bring Mayo programs to the attention of student and to provide high-quality experiences.

Other Pertinent Information
There is an active branch of the Student National Medical Association on campus Mayo Medical School sponsors delegate travel to meetings held elsewhere and occasionally hosts regional meetings.

University of Minnesota Medical School— Twin Cities Campus University of Minnesota Medical School— Duluth Campus

Mary Tate, Director
Office of Minority Affairs and Diversity
University of Minnesota
Medical School-Twin Cites
B-605 Mayo Memorial Building
MMC 293, 420 Delaware Street, SE
Minneapolis, MN 55455-0374
612-626-2173,612-625-1494;
612-626-9340 Fax
minaff@umn.edu
Dr. Joycelyn Dorscher
Director, CAIMH Duluth
218-726-7235
caimh@d.umn.edu
http://www.meded.umn.edu/
minority/index.cfm

Recruitment

The University of Minnesota Medical School strongly believes in the importance of having a culturally diverse student body. Therefore, the university actively seeks the recruitment of competitive and talented students of color interested in pursuing their medical education. Representatives in the Office of Minority Affairs and Diversity (OMA&D) and the Center of American Indian and Minority Health (CAIMH) visit high schools, colleges, and universities and attend local or national pre-health professions student recruitment fairs.

At the University of Minnesota Medical School, faculty, staff, and students assist by spending time with pre-medical students providing clarification regarding the application materials, the application process, and answering general questions or concerns. The Medical School strongly encourages and welcomes interested prospective students to contact the

OMA&D at the address, telephone, and fax numbers, or e-mail address listed above. Prospective students are also encouraged and invited to explore the medical school's Web site at (www.med.umn.edu). Interested students may also visit the CAIMH Web site at (www.caimh.org).

Admissions

Once the Office of Admissions has received a verified application from the American Medical College Application Service, the application is screened by members of the Admissions Committee to determine the applicant's overall qualifications. Qualified applicants are then mailed the University of Minnesota-Twin Cities Medical School supplemental application materials, including a supplemental information form and instructions on how to complete the online portion of the supplemental application. Once all application materials are received and reviewed by the Admissions Committee, competitive applicants are invited for interviews. Limited travel assistance for interviews may be available through the Office of Minority Affairs and Diversity. Applicants are notified of acceptance through a rolling admissions process.

Significant qualifications considered by the Admissions Committee are that an applicant

- is academically qualified to complete the Medical School curriculum;
- demonstrates past experience and commitment of service to others through volunteer or community service activity;
- demonstrates a strong motivation for a career in medicine, excellent interpersonal and communication skills, maturity, and compassion;
- demonstrates the skills and talents necessary to develop mastery of the foundations of a medical education; and
- contributes to the diversity of the medical student body and/or demonstrates a commitment to serving the health needs of a diverse society.

University of Minnesota Medical School, 2006
Applicants and Matriculants by Gender, Race and Ethnicity

Race and Ethnicity	Applicants			Matriculants		
	Women	Men	Total	Women	Men	Total
Hispanic/Latino						
Cuban	2	3	5	0	1	1
Mexican American	20	13	33	1	2	3
Puerto Rican	6	4	10	1	0	1
Other Hispanic	17	19	36	0	1	1
Multiple Hispanic*	2	4	6	0	0	0
Subtotal	47	43	90	2	4	6
Non-Hispanic/Latino**						
Black	41	37	78	1	2	3
Native American/Alaska Native	8	6	14	0	0	0
Native Hawaiian/Other Pacific Islander	2	2	4	0	0	0
White	756	908	1,664	69	59	128
Asian	182	208	390	9	7	16
Other Race	2	2	4	0	1	1
Multiple Race*	31	43	74	0	7	7
Unknown	6	11	17	0	1	1
Subtotal	1,028	1,217	2,245	79	77	156
Foreign	66	93	159	0	3	3
Total	1,141	1,353	2,494	81	84	165

*Since 2002, students can select more than one race and / or ethnicity. **Those who did not choose
Hispanic/Latino' or 'Non-Hispanic/Latino' are counted under 'Non-Hispanic/Latino'.
Data Source: AAMC Data Warehouse: Applicant-Matriculant File, as of 5/9/2007.

Association of American Medical Colleges, 2007

The Admissions Committee is composed of clinical and basic science faculty, physician representatives of medical societies, and student representatives.

Academic Support Programs

The academic success of students is promoted by a number of academic support and student service programs. Highlighted below are some of the programs offered by the school.

Learner Development. Individual assistance and special sessions are provided to assist students in adapting their study techniques, time management, and learning strategies to the unique challenges of medical education, and in developing skills for lifelong learning in medicine. Examples of service include counseling for improving study techniques and test-taking skills, assistance with specific learning for performance problems and (e.g., difficulties in concentration/attention, procrastination, test anxiety, etc.), and assistance with preparation for the United States Medical Licensing Examination (USMLE) Step 1 and Step 2.

Knowledge Co-op: A Student Peer Teaching Program. The year-two students are organized to provide academic peer support for year-one students in the basic sciences, through individual and small-group peer teaching and large-group subject review sessions.

Senior Advisor. Fourth-year medical students are available to counsel students about study strategies, time management, and preparing for the USMLE Step 1 exam.

Careers in Medicine. Programming and advisor services are provided to assist students in understanding medical career options and in selecting and applying to residency programs.

Physician Mentor and Advisor Programs. University faculty and community physicians provide guidance for academic progress and for students' professional development as future physicians.

Confidential Assistance and Referral Program (C.A.R.E.). Counselors are available to meet with students to assist in resolving difficulties that affect academic work and overall well-being (i.e., financial problems, stress, personal and family issues, etc.) C.A.R.E. services may also be utilized by students' families.

Center of American Indian and Minority Health. The University of Minnesota Center of American Indian and Minority Health is one of four Centers of Excellence in Indian Health. The center creates a culturally supportive environment and provides counseling, and academic and research resources to American Indian medical students on both the Duluth and Twin Cities campuses. Interested students may visit the Web site at *(www.caimh.org)* or call 218-726-7235.

Medical School Office of Minority Affairs and Diversity (OMA&D). OMA&D's mission is to create a welcoming and supportive environment for minority medical students and to enhance the student's educational experience at the University of Minnesota Medical School. Students can contact OMA&D for more information about other services available.

Student Financial Assistance

The Medical School's Financial Aid Office is available to assist students in all aspects of the financial aid process including general information, financial counseling, debt management, and loan processing. Questions, comments, or concerns regarding the financial aid process should be directed to this office.

The University of Minnesota Medical School, Office of Minority Affairs and Diversity, or the Financial Aid Office should be contacted for information regarding the University of Minnesota scholarship for the non-resident portion of tuition.

Other Pertinent Information

We in the University of Minnesota Medical School want your educational experience to be a positive and rewarding one. The Medical School faculty and staff are here to serve and assist you in achieving your goal of becoming a Doctor of Medicine.

University of Mississippi School of Medicine

Dr. Jasmine P. Taylor, Associate Vice Chancellor for Multicultural Affairs
University of Mississippi
School of Medicine
University of Mississippi
Medical Center
2500 North State Street
Jackson, MS 39216-4505
601-984-1340; 601-984-1335 Fax
jtaylor@som.umsmed.edu
http://mca.umc.edu

Recruitment

A comprehensive program is designed to accomplish the goals of increased enrollment and retention to assure the academic progression and timely graduation of an increased number of disadvantaged individuals in the fields of medicine, dentistry, and health-related professions. The Health Professional Alliance Partnership (HPAP) consists of formal partnerships with: 1) The University of Mississippi Medical Center and two undergraduate institutions, Alcorn State University and Tougaloo College; 2) Community organizations and the University of Mississippi Medical Center Area Health Education Center (AHEC) Program; and 3) Secondary school systems in the following regions: Southern region (Claiborne and Jefferson County Public School Systems), Central region (Jackson County Public School, Rural Hinds, and Madison Public School Systems), and Philadelphia (Choctaw Indian Reservation).

The University of Mississippi Medical Center (UMMC) and its partner schools, universities, and community organizations has developed a very comprehensive plan to increase the number of disadvantaged students in the state of Mississippi who enter UMMC or other professional schools. This plan will be accomplished by developing an elementary school through post-secondary health science education pipeline. Through the linkages with each partner institution, substantial changes are planned that will improve educational opportunities for and achievement levels of disadvantaged students who are interested in health careers.

The goal of HPAP is to provide students from disadvantaged backgrounds an opportunity to develop skills needed to successfully enter and complete health profession schools. UMMC and its partner schools, universities, and community organizations have developed a comprehensive plan to increase the admission and retention of disadvantaged students in the state of Mississippi in health professions schools.

Admissions

Selection of applicants is made by the Admissions Committee on a competitive basis, without regard to race, age, sex, color, religion, marital status, national origin, veteran status, or handicap. Preference is given to applicants who are legal residents of Mississippi.

The first evaluation of applicants is made on the basis of scholastic record and scores on the Medical College Admission Test (MCAT). Those applicants possessing the scholastic competency necessary to successfully pursue the course of study required of students in the School of Medicine are further evaluated on the basis of character, motivation, and promise of fitness for the practice of medicine. Selection is made on the basis of all these evaluations. The Admissions Committee is composed of members of the faculty of the School of Medicine who are appointed by the Dean. There is minority representation on the committee.

Academic Support Programs

Throughout the academic year, tutorial assistance is available to underrepresented and disadvantaged students on an individual and/or group basis. Academic progress is closely monitored by the Division of Multicultural Affairs for early identification and intervention. The academic year *Tutorial Program* provides tutorial assistance in gross anatomy, histology, neuroanatomy, biochemistry,

University of Mississippi School of Medicine, 2006
Applicants and Matriculants by Gender, Race and Ethnicity

Race and Ethnicity	Applicants			Matriculants		
	Women	Men	Total	Women	Men	Total
Hispanic/Latino						
Puerto Rican	0	1	1	0	1	1
Other Hispanic	1	2	3	0	0	0
Subtotal	1	3	4	0	1	1
Non-Hispanic/Latino**						
Black	29	14	43	12	3	15
Native American/Alaska Native	1	0	1	0	0	0
White	89	116	205	36	46	82
Asian	12	11	23	6	4	10
Multiple Race*	3	1	4	2	0	2
Unknown	0	1	1	0	0	0
Subtotal	134	143	277	56	53	109
Total	135	146	281	56	54	110

*Since 2002, students can select more than one race and / or ethnicity. **Those who did not choose
Hispanic/Latino' or 'Non-Hispanic/Latino' are counted under 'Non-Hispanic/Latino'.
Data Source: AAMC Data Warehouse: Applicant-Matriculant File, as of 5/9/2007.

pharmacology, pathology and microbiology. Assistance with learning skills, test-taking techniques, and academic counseling are also available through the Division of Multicultural Affairs.

You are not alone. When you arrive on this campus, you will have a family watching over you. We offer a formal mentoring program where students are paired with a School of Medicine faculty member whose primary focus will be guiding you through your health professions school experience. Students who are informed and feel connected tend to perform better and are generally happier. Also, each incoming student meets with the Associate Vice Chancellor for Multicultural Affairs for a one-on-one lunch meeting in the fall of the year. The Associate Vice Chancellor will serve as one of your main advocates during your training at the School of Medicine. The URL for these programs is (*mca.umc.edu*).

Enrichment Programs

Summer Enrichment Programs. These programs are offered by the UMMC, through the Division of Multicultural Affairs, to assist disadvantaged students with medical school admission, retention, regular academic progress, and graduation and are conducted under HPAP.

Science Training Enrichment Program (STEP). STEP is a Saturday Science Institute for students in grades six-eight and will consist of ten months of activities that will encourage students to pursue science and math and ultimately choose a career in the health professions or health sciences. The program will offer specialized courses and hands-on-experience in science, mathematics, writing, computer skills, cultural awareness and health careers in collaboration with The University of Mississippi Medical Center, Jackson Public Schools, Madison County Schools, Canton Schools, and Hinds County Schools.

EXCEL Program. The Project EXCEL is conducted at Jackson State University and Alcorn State University. Students are from high schools in the undergraduate linkage school geographic area. High school students (grades 9-12) spend the six-week summer program preparing for college matriculation. College representatives, health care professionals, and students are invited to share information about their college, the admissions process, health care careers, and being a health care professional. Parents are also invited to participate in special activities. The following is the breakdown of participants:

MEDCORP I & II. The MEDCORP I & II program is a six-week summer program designed to provide individuals from disadvantaged backgrounds with mathematics and science education that will enhance their preparation for health profession school. The MEDCORP is conducted at Alcorn and Jackson State Universities. The students at this level of the program are pre-freshman and pre-sophomores.

MEDCORP III & IV. The Facilitating Entry (MEDCORP III & IV) level includes an intense seven-week summer academic enrichment, reinforcement, and motivational program conducted at UMMC. The program provides a concise and thorough review of the knowledge and various skills tested on the MCAT or Dental Admissions Test (DAT).

Clinical correlation and hospital rotations are offered from 1-5 p.m. (or later, depending on rotations) three days per week. Emergency room rotations are on Friday evenings and weekends, including Sundays.

Pre-matriculation Summer Enrichment Program (PRE-MAT). A seven-week program for entering disadvantaged medical and dental students is conducted by the Division of Multicultural Affairs beginning in June. The program affords students a preview of gross anatomy and biochemistry. The program structure is designed to

significantly increase the competitive basis upon which the participants would approach more advanced professional studies and provide an early and controlled measures of their predicted performance in basic science areas.

The Professional Portal Track Program seeks to improve the health care and biomedical education of the underserved citizens of Mississippi. It is a comprehensive two-year mentor based program that offers a non-thesis-requiring Master of Biomedical Science degree. This terminal degree is suitable for preparation for teaching at the community/junior college level, as advanced training for governmental and industrial positions, and as an indication of competitiveness for admission to the University of Mississippi Schools of Medicine (M.D. program), Dentistry (D.M.D. program), and Graduate Studies in the Health Sciences (Ph.D. program). Criteria for admission to the Professional Portal Track include: 1) formal application and denial of admission to either the School of Medicine, School of Dentistry, or School of Graduate Studies in Health Sciences at the University of Mississippi Medical Center; 2) MCAT or DAT scores not more than four years old; 3) belonging to racial or ethnic groups underrepresented in medicine or coming from an environmentally or economically disadvantaged background; 4) recommendation by the medical, dental or graduate school's admission officer; 5) invitation to apply by the Professional Portal Track Program Director; and 6) submission of acceptable Graduate Record Examination (GRE) scores. Residency requirements and time limitations for the Professional Portal Track are the same as those listed in the University of Mississippi Medical Center Bulletin for the Master of Science program. The degree requires the completion of 45 quarter hours of graduate level credit and the maintenance of a B average. The Professional Portal Track Program will begin with the onset of the

004-2005 academic year; a maximum of 5 students will be enrolled in each class.

tudent Financial Assistance
he School of Medicine's financial aid pro-ram is designed to meet the needs of any Mississippi resident admitted to the school whose financial need can be documented.

ducational Partnerships
. comprehensive program is designed to ccomplish the goals of increased enroll-nent and retention to assure the academic rogression and timely graduation of n increased number of disadvantaged ndividuals in the fields of medicine, den-istry, and health-related professions. The Iealth Professional Alliance Partnership onsists of formal partnerships with: 1) he University of Mississippi Medical Center (UMMC) and two undergraduate nstitutions, Alcorn State University and ougaloo College; 2) Community organi-ations and the University of Mississippi Medical Center AHEC Program; and 3) econdary school systems in the following egions: Southern Region (Claiborne and efferson County Public School Systems), Central Region (Jackson Public Schools, Hinds County Public Schools, and Madison County Public School Systems) and the Mississippi Band f Choctaw Indians.

Saint Louis University School of Medicine

Dr. George Rausch
Associate Dean
Office of Multicultural Affairs
Saint Louis University
School of Medicine
1402 South Grand Boulevard, C120
St. Louis, MO 63104-1085
314-977-8730; 314-977-8779 Fax
rauschg@slu.edu
http://medschool.slu.edu/oma

Mission Statement

The Office of Multicultural Affairs (OMA) at Saint Louis University (SLU) is dedicated to ensuring that disadvantaged and underrepresented physicians are reflective of their numbers in the overall population. The office endeavors to assist students from diverse backgrounds to be successful as they progress along the educational

pathway in pursuit of a career as a physician. The focus of the OMA initiatives is prevention rather than crisis intervention.

The OMA is a student-centered, student-friendly office and a resource center for underrepresented and other students who are seeking a diverse and caring environment in which to reach their greatest potential. The charge of the OMA is to support and enhance the academic, educational, social, and cultural interests of the diverse student constituency at Saint Louis University School of Medicine and to maximize the students' abilities in pursuit of a medical career.

The OMA is a first line point of contact for the underrepresented undergraduate student and the secondary student who is in search of information related to a health career in medicine. To this end, the office

Saint Louis University School of Medicine, 2006
Applicants and Matriculants by Gender, Race and Ethnicity

Race and Ethnicity	Applicants			Matriculants		
	Women	Men	Total	Women	Men	Total
Hispanic/Latino						
Cuban	17	15	32	0	0	0
Mexican American	51	55	106	0	1	1
Puerto Rican	7	12	19	0	1	1
Other Hispanic	55	59	114	2	0	2
Multiple Hispanic*	3	3	6	0	0	0
Subtotal	133	144	277	2	2	4
Non-Hispanic/Latino**						
Black	173	81	254	3	0	3
Native American/Alaska Native	3	6	9	0	0	0
Native Hawaiian/Other Pacific Islander	8	12	20	0	0	0
White	1,360	1,945	3,305	41	75	116
Asian	640	749	1,389	20	23	43
Other Race	3	4	7	0	0	0
Multiple Race*	73	81	154	2	1	3
Unknown	8	14	22	1	1	2
Subtotal	2,268	2,892	5,160	67	100	167
Foreign	77	113	190	1	4	5
Total	2,478	3,149	5,627	70	106	176

*Since 2002, students can select more than one race and / or ethnicity. **Those who did not choose
Hispanic/Latino' or 'Non-Hispanic/Latino' are counted under 'Non-Hispanic/Latino'.
Data Source: AAMC Data Warehouse: Applicant-Matriculant File, as of 5/9/2007.

seeks to entice, encourage, enable, and empower students who have medicine as their career goal.

The OMA initiatives are intended to increase the number of disadvantaged and underrepresented students matriculating into the School of Medicine. More specifically, the initiatives are intended to better prepare entering students for the rigors of a medical school curriculum and are designed to improve the probability of underrepresented students successfully completing the course curriculum as expeditiously as possible.

Academic Support Programs

The Skills Enhancement Component is designed to increase the academic opportunities available to currently enrolled underrepresented medical students through individual and group sessions related to time management, auxiliary management (note taking, study skills, memory techniques, etc.), and academic/personal management, (i.e., how to cope in a medical school environment).

The Supplemental Instruction (SI) Initiative is a proactive, participatory, collaborative, approach to learning that utilizes small-group discussion and emphasizes long-term retention of material.

For Males Only and *Woman-to-Woman* are separate informal sessions for underrepresented male and female medical students, respectively. The sessions, facilitated by School of Medicine male and female physicians of color, focus on such pertinent topics as successfully negotiating medical school, being a student of color in a predominantly white medical school, staying focused, and maintaining balance in one's life.

United States Medical Licensing Examination (USMLE) Step 1 Board Review utilizes the SI model, described above, and focuses upon the specific subject areas covered in the Step 1 examination.

The Clinical Survival Skills Booklet is designed as a guide for students while they acclimate themselves to clinical medicine and build their knowledge base.

The Smart Track Support Group is designed to provide a diverse student constituency of high school, undergraduate, and graduate students with the necessary tools to be successful as they progress along the educational pathway in pursuit of a career in medicine.

Enrichment Programs

The Summer Enrichment Program is a three-week experience for 20 St. Louis metropolitan area high school disadvantaged juniors and seniors designed to stimulate and sustain their interest in a career in medicine.

The Summer Research Apprenticeship Program is an eight-week activity that places underrepresented students in a research setting with the intent of stimulating their interest in pursuing a career in academic medicine by giving them an opportunity to participate in a "hands-on" research experience.

Other Pertinent Information

Saint Louis University's School of Medicine is committed to enrolling and graduating disadvantaged individuals and those underrepresented in medicine. To this end, the OMA initiatives delineated above are designed to ensure the matriculation, even progression, and graduation of underrepresented students from the medical school in an expeditious manner.

For information please contact the
Office of Multicultural Affairs
Saint Louis University
School of Medicine
1402 South Grand Blvd.,
St. Louis, MO 63104
Phone: 314-977-8730; Fax: 314-977-8779
(oma@wpogate.slu.edu)

AAMC

University of Missouri— Columbia School of Medicine

Dr. Rachel M.A. Brown
Associate Dean for Student Programs
MA215 Medical Sciences Building
University of Missouri—Columbia
School of Medicine
Columbia, MO 65212
573-882-2923; 573-884-2988 Fax
brownrac@health.missouri.edu
www.muhealth.org/~medicine

Recruitment

The University of Missouri—Columbia School of Medicine is committed to the recruitment of students from underrepresented groups and underserved areas. Recruitment activities occur at the high school and undergraduate levels and include participation in the campus diversity programming. The purpose of these efforts is to provide information on the academic programs offered at the institution and to increase the diverse enrollment at the university. To increase the targeted applicant pool, School of Medicine representatives visit pre-medical clubs and participate in health career programs to provide information and to answer questions. Candidates are invited to schedule campus recruitment and orientation visits. Medical students, staff, and faculty participate in these activities.

Admissions

The Admissions Committee is composed of faculty, students, and alumni. Assessment of all applicants is based upon academic record, pattern of academic performance, personal characteristics, motivation, extracurricular and community activities, interpersonal skills, work experiences, and emotional stability. The goals of the Admissions Committee are two-fold: first, the selection of the most qualified applicants, and second, the selection of a diversified class reflecting the demography of the state.

Academic Support Programs

Academic support activities are designed to meet the needs of the student and may include flexible curriculum scheduling, tutoring, skill development, and counseling. Study-skills instruction is provided in note taking, test taking, time management, and textbook reading. Individualized academic programs are available to students as needed. Students are assigned a faculty advisor to assist with curricular and career planning.

Student Financial Assistance

The School of Medicine's Financial Aid Office provides access to the institutional and federal programs aimed at increasing the attendance of underrepresented and disadvantaged students. Besides traditional need-based scholarships and loans, the University of Missouri-Columbia offers the Professional Degree Assistance Program, which provides significant scholarship assistance to first-year underrepresented medical students. The School of Medicine also participates in the Scholarships for Disadvantaged Students program funded by the federal Department of Health and Human Services. Once students are accepted by the school, they are mailed the necessary forms for applying for financial aid.

Enrichment Programs

High School Mini-Medical School Program. Each summer the School of Medicine conducts a one-week High School Mini-Medical School Program, which is designed to motivate high school students to enter careers in medicine and to give them a sample of the medical student curriculum. Preference is given to students from underrepresented groups and students from underserved areas of Missouri.

University of Missouri - Columbia School of Medicine, 2006
Applicants and Matriculants by Gender, Race and Ethnicity

Race and Ethnicity	Applicants			Matriculants		
	Women	Men	Total	Women	Men	Total
Hispanic/Latino						
Cuban	0	3	3	0	0	0
Mexican American	7	14	21	0	1	1
Puerto Rican	2	2	4	0	0	0
Other Hispanic	10	11	21	0	0	0
Multiple Hispanic*	1	0	1	0	0	0
Subtotal	20	30	50	0	1	1
Non-Hispanic/Latino**						
Black	29	14	43	3	2	5
Native American/Alaska Native	0	2	2	0	0	0
Native Hawaiian/Other Pacific Islander	1	0	1	0	0	0
White	276	360	636	27	44	71
Asian	66	86	152	10	4	14
Other Race	0	1	1	0	0	0
Multiple Race*	10	11	21	2	1	3
Unknown	1	5	6	0	1	1
Subtotal	383	479	862	42	52	94
Foreign	1	3	4	0	0	0
Total	404	512	916	42	53	95

*Since 2002, students can select more than one race and / or ethnicity. **Those who did not choose Hispanic/Latino' or 'Non-Hispanic/Latino' are counted under 'Non-Hispanic/Latino'.
Data Source: AAMC Data Warehouse: Applicant-Matriculant File, as of 5/9/2007.

Excellence in Learning The School of Medicine supports this two-day program, designed to give disadvantaged and underrepresented high school students from St. Louis the opportunity to experience the university environment and to explore health-related careers. Students shadow physicians and work through a problem-based learning case in small groups. *(http://www.missouri.edu/~ingram/excelearn/links.htm)*

Other Pertinent Information

The School of Medicine is strongly committed to the recruitment, enrollment, and graduation of a diverse student body. The Office of Medical Education staff works with all units of the School of Medicine and the university to maintain a high retention rate. There is an active branch of the Student National Medical Association on campus. The association works cooperatively with the Office of Medical Education in their recruitment activities.

University of Missouri— Kansas City School of Medicine

Dr. Reaner Shannon
Associate Dean, Office of Cultural Enhancement and Diversity
University of Missouri—
Kansas City School of Medicine
2411 Holmes Street
Kansas City, MO 64108
816-235-1780; 816-235-5277 Fax
shannonr@umkc.edu

Recruitment

The program at the University of Missouri-Kansas City (UMKC) is a six-year program leading to baccalaureate and M.D. degrees and is designed primarily for high school seniors entering college for the first time. Students who are freshman and have not accumulated more than 24 credit hours are also eligible to apply. In either case, students are required to complete both degrees. A limited number of students already having a baccalaureate degree are admitted at the year-three level to fill any existing vacancies. These students are referred to as, M.D. only.

The Office of Cultural Enhancement and Diversity (OCED) serves as the medical school's central division for diversity initiatives, including community engagement, recruitment, facilitation of admission, and

retention. An Associate Dean directs this office, which provides support in academic, administrative, financial, and personal matters for underrepresented minorities. OCED staff include a Medical Recruiter, who is responsible for recruiting activities that focus on attracting a diverse applicant pool, and a Cultural Competency Curriculum Specialist, who is charged with developing a cultural competency curriculum for the medical school. The OCED also draws attention to minority health through an endowed lectureship that addresses health disparities.

A minority Recruitment Committee works with the Council on Selection at the School of Medicine to identify students interested in health sciences early in secondary schooling. A Summer Scholars Program provides a four-week educational/preparatory realistic exposure to the health professions to selected high school students. Saturday Academy, a core program of the Health Professional Partnership Initiative, provides Saturday didactic sessions on science subjects and topic for students in grades six through 12. Additionally, a Medical Explorer Post provides continuing exposure to the health field.

Admissions

All admissions are the responsibility of the Council on Selection, which is a diverse group of about 18 people. The council consists of ten physicians, two student

University of Missouri - Kansas City School of Medicine, 2006
Applicants and Matriculants by Gender, Race and Ethnicity

Race and Ethnicity		Applicants			Matriculants		
		Women	Men	Total	Women	Men	Total
Non-Hispanic/Latino**							
Unknown		59	40	99	59	40	99
	Subtotal	59	40	99	59	40	99
	Total	59	40	99	59	40	99

*Since 2002, students can select more than one race and / or ethnicity. **Those who did not choose Hispanic/Latino' or 'Non-Hispanic/Latino' are counted under 'Non-Hispanic/Latino'.
Data Source: AAMC Data Warehouse: Applicant-Matriculant File, as of 5/9/2007.

physicians, three basic scientists, and three arts and sciences faculty representatives. The chairman of the council is a physician appointed by the dean. Students seeking admission directly from high school should complete four units of English; three units of social studies; one unit of fine arts; four units of mathematics; three units of science including one unit biology and one unit of chemistry; and two units of a single foreign language. One unit of physics and one-half unit of computer science are highly recommended. Applicants must also submit their scores from the ACT or SAT Test. An initial academic screen to identify applicants for interview is based on class rank and the ACT or SAT composite scores. All applicants not meeting this initial screen are reviewed by a subcommittee of the council. All application information, both cognitive and non-cognitive, is examined for evidence of academic potential.

Academic Support Programs
The university's Center for Academic Development offers a wide range of free services to students. These include tutorial assistance, a writing lab, a math lab, and learning and study skills services in note taking, test taking, reading comprehension, memory, anxiety reduction, and supplemental instruction. The medical school has a strong Academic and Advisory Support Program:

- Education Assistants: Help tailor a curriculum that fulfills individual needs.
- Clinical Medical Librarian: Locates information pertinent to patient care
- Clinical Pharmacologist: Teaches patient-oriented pharmacology at the bedside.
- Supplemental Instruction (SI): Meets weekly in small groups to discuss course content for enhanced learning, application, and retention of basic science disciplines.

Enrichment Programs
Summer Scholars. The medical school sponsors a four-week educational/preparatory program for high school juniors and seniors who are interested in a career in health care. This program is designed to identify and motivate promising minority students toward careers in medicine and other health careers by providing educational experiences to enhance academic performance and supplying realistic information and clinical experiences to clarify their perceptions of health care roles.

Saturday Academy. This is a core program developed for the Health Professionals Partnership Initiative (HPPI). The program is strictly didactic with an emphasis on math and sciences. The curriculum is designed to prepare students to excel in their academic coursework, expand their quest for knowledge, and motivate them to enroll in higher level science and mathematics courses. The program runs concurrently with the school year.

Student Financial Assistance
There are four types of student financial aid. They are scholarships and grants, which are gifts and do not require repayment; long-term loans repayable after termination of schooling at reduced interest rates; short-term loans repayable within the same academic period; and employment in the College Work-Study Program. In general, aid is based on financial need. Gift assistance for minority students is available in years three and four of the six-year curriculum from the National Medical Fellowships, Inc. The out-of-state tuition fee is waived for minorities.

Educational Partnerships
The UMKC had a partnership established through The Robert Wood Johnson HPPI Program. Although the granting period ended in 2003, the school has retained many of those partnerships, particularly with area high schools.

Other Pertinent Information
The medical program at the University of Missouri—Kansas City limits approximately 75 percent of the entering class to residents of Missouri.

Washington University School of Medicine

Dr. Will Ross, Associate Dean for Diversity, Assistant Professor of Medicine
Office of Diversity Programs
660 South Euclid, Box 8023
Washington University School of Medicine
St. Louis, MO 63110
314-362-6854; 314-747-3974 Fax
diversity@msnotes.wustl.edu
medschooldiversity.wustl.edu

Recruitment

The mission of the Office of Diversity Programs is to promote cultural diversity no only within the student body but also within the entire academic workforce as a means of enhancing the educational environment at Washington University School of Medicine.

The recruitment and retention of students from underrepresented and economically disadvantaged groups is our main activity and is accomplished through visits to undergraduate colleges and universities as well as a select science- and medical-exposure programs across the country. Additionally, admissions information is mailed twice yearly to registrants of the Medical Minority Applicant Registry. The associate dean and the director work closely with the Student National Medical Association (SNMA) in welcoming applicants from underrepresented groups to campus during their admission interviews.

In April each year, we sponsor a Revisit Program designed to encourage accepted students who are underrepresented in medicine to enroll at the School of Medicine by taking an in-depth look at the school through a series of activities on campus and in the St. Louis area. The program provides the visiting students with ample opportunity to get to know each other as well as currently enrolled students, faculty, and administrators.

Providing a supportive community for students is an ongoing objective as well. By sponsoring social gatherings throughout the year, the office provides networking opportunities for medical students, residents, and fellows from underrepresented groups. Students are invited to monthly dinners with faculty as well as physicians from the community through the Mound City Medical Forum, a local component of the National Medical Association.

Admissions

The Committee on Admissions consists of faculty and administrators including the Associate Director and the Director of Diversity Programs. Individual attention is given to all applicants of the School of Medicine. All underrepresented minority applicants who apply, or who are considering applying, are encouraged to contact the office. Medical students are selected on the basis of academic performance, aptitude and motivation for the study of medicine, and the personal characteristics required for the effective and compassionate practice of medicine. Selected applicants are invited for a personal interview and tour of the medical center campus. Generally, the Associate Dean for Diversity and the director along with other members meet with minority candidates during their visit to the School of Medicine. The admissions committee consists of several faculty who are from underrepresented groups. Members of the SNMA are also available to meet for breakfast with applicants the day of their interview.

Academic Support Programs

The educational program of Washington University School of Medicine is designed to meet the needs of all students in an individualized and personalized way. The school can provide tutorial aid, on a one-to-one basis, to students at no cost.

Washington University in Saint Louis School of Medicine, 2006
Applicants and Matriculants by Gender, Race and Ethnicity

Race and Ethnicity	Applicants			Matriculants		
	Women	Men	Total	Women	Men	Total
Hispanic/Latino						
Cuban	8	10	18	0	1	1
Mexican American	35	44	79	1	1	2
Puerto Rican	6	19	25	2	2	4
Other Hispanic	34	35	69	0	0	0
Multiple Hispanic*	2	4	6	0	0	0
Subtotal	85	112	197	3	4	7
Non-Hispanic/Latino**						
Black	254	142	396	3	1	4
Native American/Alaska Native	7	4	11	1	1	2
Native Hawaiian/Other Pacific Islander	5	4	9	0	0	0
White	827	1,274	2,101	31	34	65
Asian	426	542	968	16	16	32
Other Race	2	1	3	0	0	0
Multiple Race*	53	60	113	2	1	3
Unknown	16	21	37	1	1	2
Subtotal	1,590	2,048	3,638	54	54	108
Foreign	113	116	229	4	3	7
Total	1,788	2,276	4,064	61	61	122

*Since 2002, students can select more than one race and / or ethnicity. **Those who did not choose Hispanic/Latino' or 'Non-Hispanic/Latino' are counted under 'Non-Hispanic/Latino'.
Data Source: AAMC Data Warehouse: Applicant-Matriculant File, as of 5/9/2007.

Association of American Medical Colleges, 2007

Academic and personal counseling are provided to anyone experiencing academic difficulty. Individualized academic programs can be devised to help students adjust to the medical school curriculum. Individualized programs permit students two years to complete the first year's coursework. Thereafter, it is anticipated that the student would continue his/her regular course work in an uninterrupted fashion, receiving the M.D. degree in five years rather than four.

Enrichment Programs

The Division of Biology and Biomedical Sciences offers BiomedRap, a ten-week summer biomedical research program for undergraduates. Applications can be obtained at *biomedrap.wustl.edu*. Through the Health Care Advocacy Program (HCAP) the Office of Diversity Programs provides Washington University freshman and sophomores with the opportunity to explore the health care setting as part of an eight-week patient care unit assignment at Barnes-Jewish Hospital. For more information, visit *(medschooldiversity.wustl.edu)*.

Research

Summer opportunities in basic science and clinical research are available to undergraduates. Please contact Dr. Koong-Nah Chung, Assistant Dean for Admissions and Student Affairs at Washington University School of Medicine at 314-362-6844 or *(chungkmsnotes.wustl.edu)*. The Division of Biology and Bio-medical Sciences offers BiomedRap, a ten-week biomedical research program for undergraduates. Applications can be obtained online at *(www.biomedrap.wustl.edu)*.

Educational Partnerships

We sponsor a number of outreach programs throughout the educational pipeline to enhance the exposure and preparation of underrepresented students and other students from disadvantaged groups who are interested in careers in medicine:

The Health Professions Fair provides a forum for St. Louis City and County high school students to explore various health related career opportunities. The program is sponsored by the Office of Diversity Programs and the St. Louis Public Schools. Each year approximately 160 students from area schools are selected to participate in the fair.

The Saturday Scholars Program is sponsored by the School of Medicine in collaboration with the St. Louis Public Schools. Students from area high schools are selected by their science teachers to attend this four-week human anatomy and physiology course taught by Dr. Ross with first - and second-year medical students.

The Young Scientist Program is a sponsored by the Washington University Division of Biomedical Sciences and the Office of Diversity Programs. This summer program provides high school students with an eight-week laboratory research experience that introduces them to careers in science.

Cultural Diversity

We promote an atmosphere of multiculturalism on the campus through a variety of activities. Examples include Diversity Week, a lunch-time series that further explores multiculturalism and effective health care delivery. Featured lecturers include faculty from the medical school as well as experts from the St. Louis community. The Fall Orientation retreat begins with an evening diversity workshop that allows students to explore ways to communicate and relate to others in cross-cultural situations through small-group case-based discussions.

Student Financial Assistance

The applicant's ability to finance medical education at Washington University School of Medicine does not influence the selection process. All students accepted have proven scholastic ability. Financial aid, based solely on demonstrated need, is available to all students in the School of

Medicine. Within its financial capabilities, the school is prepared to assist each student with financial aid in the form of loans and grants. Beginning with the 2006-2007 academic year, need-based loans are capped at $20,000 annually. In addition, the secondary application fee of $50 may be waived upon written request documenting financial hardship. Merit-based scholarships are also available and are awarded to candidates presenting exceptional academic and personal credentials.

Other Pertinent Information

Washington University School of Medicine and its faculty believe that the school enters into a partnership with its students in the pursuit of excellence in the medical and scientific educational experience. The Office of Diversity Programs was established to help meet the needs of underrepresented minority students.

The Washington University School of Medicine is committed to recruit, admit, enroll, educate, and graduate an increased number of students from diverse underrepresented racial and cultural groups. Underrepresented minority students in colleges and universities throughout the country are strongly encouraged to file application for admission to the school. Candidates should feel free to contact us at our Web site located at *(http://medicine.wustl. edu/diversity)*.

The school participates in the America Medical College Application Service (AMCAS) of the Association of American Medical Colleges. All applicants must apply through AMCAS by December 1st of the year prior to actually attending the school. The school's AMCAS number is 184.

Creighton University School of Medicine

Dr. Sade Kosoko-Lasaki
Associate Vice President
for Health Sciences—
Multicultural and Community Affairs
Creighton University
School of Medicine
2500 California Plaza
Omaha, NE 68178
Toll Free: 1-877-857-2854;
402-280-2981; 402-280-4030 Fax
skosoko@creighton.edu

Recruitment

The Office of Health Sciences Multicultural and Community Affairs, (HS-MACA), under the direction of an Associate Vice President has a mission to help Creighton University in the training and development of future leaders for an increasingly multicultural society. HS-MACA provides support and retention services to students by providing diversity awareness to the entire campus community. HS-MACA promotes minority affairs through recruiting and retaining underrepresented students in the Creighton University health sciences schools. HS-MACA also promotes local involvement in multicultural communities, civic functions, and community service organizations. HS-MACA coordinates multicultural activities with other areas of the University and works to enhance cultural awareness of health sciences faculty, students, and staff.

HS-MACA's recruiting activities include annual visits to conferences colleges, universities, and organizations with a high concentration of minority students. Pre-college recruitment includes frequent visits to area high schools to educate underrepresented individuals and motivate them to pursue a health professions career. Recruiting materials consist of diversity brochures, fliers, and health sciences program information. The Recruitment & Retention Officer in HS-MACA, distributes recruiting materials and tracks responses from potential applicants to the Health Sciences Schools. Recruitment is through mass mailings, health professional career fairs, national association conferences, college/university campus visits, and invitations to Creighton University campus.

Admission

HS-MACA and Creighton University School of Medicine (CUSOM) work closely to maximize diversity in the medical school. In addition to recruitment by both offices on college campuses and at recruitment fairs, HS-MACA actively encourages applications from students listed in the Association of American Medical Colleges (AAMC) Medical Minority Applicant Registry (Med-MAR). Applications through the American Medical College Application Service (AMCAS) are regularly reviewed by the Assistant Dean for Admissions, and qualified applicants are encouraged to complete their applications by sending references and completing the Secondary Application. Interviews are then offered to qualified applicants.

During the interview, the applicant is invited to stay in the home of a medical student participating in the "Host Program." The applicant may request to stay in the home of an underrepresented medical student. The interviews are conducted on Fridays, and require presence on campus for the full day. Applicants interview with Admissions Committee Members—both student and faculty (or alumni). Both interviews are rated equally and concentrate on motivation for medicine and the applicant's demonstrated activities in service to others. During the campus tour, the applicants visit the HS-MACA. A program, "View HS-MACA," introduces the

Creighton University School of Medicine, 2006
Applicants and Matriculants by Gender, Race and Ethnicity

Race and Ethnicity	Applicants			Matriculants		
	Women	Men	Total	Women	Men	Total
Hispanic/Latino						
Cuban	13	8	21	1	0	1
Mexican American	57	63	120	2	2	4
Puerto Rican	10	9	19	0	0	0
Other Hispanic	52	40	92	2	1	3
Multiple Hispanic*	5	8	13	0	1	1
Subtotal	137	128	265	5	4	9
Non-Hispanic/Latino**						
Black	90	70	160	2	1	3
Native American/Alaska Native	4	2	6	0	0	0
Native Hawaiian/Other Pacific Islander	12	8	20	1	0	1
White	1,235	1,823	3,058	44	51	95
Asian	489	553	1,042	7	6	13
Other Race	6	3	9	0	0	0
Multiple Race*	63	72	135	3	1	4
Unknown	9	17	26	1	0	1
Subtotal	1,908	2,548	4,456	58	59	117
Foreign	70	93	163	0	0	0
Total	2,115	2,769	4,884	63	63	126

*Since 2002, students can select more than one race and / or ethnicity. **Those who did not choose
Hispanic/Latino' or 'Non-Hispanic/Latino' are counted under 'Non-Hispanic/Latino'.

tudent to the diversity program at Creighton University.

Completed applications are reviewed by the Committee on Admissions for scoring. The Committee Score is based on academics, Medical Colleges Application Test (MCAT) scores, and evaluation of the applicant's non-cognitive skills including service to others, involvement in community projects, health care experience as well as academic achievement. Acceptance decisions take into account the committee rating and the interview scores.

Scholarship application is not required for consideration by the Scholarship Committee. Admitted applicants are automatically reviewed for scholarship awards by the Committee. The applicant whose record demonstrates strong commitment to serving others in addition to academic achievement is valued.

Academic Support Programs

The Office of Academic Advancement within the School of Medicine provides formal tutoring for all basic science courses. Assistance with clinical clerkship and elective material is provided on request. This office also coordinates training sessions on study skills, test-taking skills, time management, stress management, and general wellness topics. Each first-year student is assigned a "buddy" from the second-year class who assists in the transition to medical school. A mentoring system is also in place in which all first-year students meet informally with a designated faculty member throughout the year in order to discuss concerns and to build camaraderie. All students are assigned a formal faculty advisor according to his/her curricular, research, and clinical interests.

Enrichment Programs

Cultural Proficiency for Medical Residents, Students, Faculty and Staff. A setting, consisting of didactic presentations on the definition of cultural competency, its benefits

and barriers, is correlated with the changing demographics in the United States. This presentation also includes discussions on the importance of diversity and cultural sensitivity in health care. A diverse group of physicians and community members are invited to discuss their various cultures in small breakout sessions and in a panel discussion. Case studies are presented and discussed in small groups, followed by group interactions. The students are also trained on the effective use of an interpreter in the clinical setting. The seminar concludes with a "reflection" assignment in which students are instructed to submit their own cultural awareness story.

Community Oriented Primary Care (COPC). The program is designed to help reduce health disparities affecting our nation's communities. The mission of the Creighton University Medical Center COPC Public Health Research Endowment program is to increase the number of health professionals who are committed to addressing health disparities through their research and service in medically underserved communities. This mission supports the core values of Creighton University: "service to others, the importance of family life, the inalienable worth of each individual, and appreciation of ethnic and cultural diversity." It also supports the goals of Healthy People of 2010 to eliminate health disparities.

Short-Term Research Training of Minority College Students Program. This program is currently in its fourteenth year at Creighton. The program is designed to offer underrepresented students who are not well represented in the biomedical sciences the opportunity to work with scientists in their labs at Creighton. Every summer, undergraduate students are recruited from all over the United States and are housed at Creighton for six weeks while they perform research with the mentors. A total of 71 students have participated in a variety of cardiovascular,

pulmonary, osteoporosis, and hematological research activities. Many of the trainees have expressed interest in biomedical research, medical, pharmacy, nursing, and allied health professions.

HS-MACA Mentoring Program. The purpose of the program is to provide students in the health science schools formal and informal opportunities for counseling, mentoring, and group support. Short-term results include improvement in academic performance of mentee, enhancement of interpersonal relationships, mutual feelings of honesty and respect, and rewarding and enriching experiences for all involved.

Focus on Health Professions. Creighton University's Focus on Health Professions is a partnership between Creighton's health science schools and Omaha Public Schools. Speakers from the sciences, both faculty and professional students, are on hand in the schools to present, recruit, role model, and demonstrate the different aspects of "becoming a health professional."

HS-MACA Tutoring. This program is designed to provide tutorial assistance in most academic subject areas like math, science, reading, and Spanish for the students from public and private schools. This will enable underrepresented high school students to excel in their academic work, expand their quest for knowledge, and motivate them to strengthen their study skills.

Student Financial Assistance

The School of Medicine's application fee is waived for any student who receives the same waiver from AMCAS. Financial aid and debt management counseling are provided to all students. Two full-tuition Medical Dean's Diversity Scholarships are available to underrepresented minority students each year. In addition, students from economically disadvantaged backgrounds qualify for Disadvantaged Scholarships.

Educational Partnership

Creighton University has a pre-medical Post-Baccalaureate Program. The goal of this program is to increase the number of qualified minority students enrolled in and successfully completing medical school. The Post-Baccalaureate Program was continually funded by federal grants for 25 years. The target population for this program is disadvantaged students who have applied for but failed to qualify for admission to a medical school. The curriculum is designed to correct educational deficiencies and to provide a rigorous academic program that improves the ability of the student to deal with all fundamental concepts necessary for successful completion of a medical school curriculum. This intensive academic program has been highly successful. Since its inception in 1975, 291 minority students have completed the course, and 263 have been admitted to a school of health professions (a success rate of 90 percent). The pre-medical Post-Baccalaureate Program is now fee driven because of the loss of federal funds.

University of Nebraska College of Medicine

Dr. Kristie D. Hayes
Assistant Dean of Student
and Multicultural Affairs
University of Nebraska College of Medicine
984360 Nebraska Medical Center
Omaha, NE 68198-4360
402-559-4307; 402-559-4104 Fax
kdhayes@unmc.edu

Recruitment

Recruitment and career awareness activities at the University of Nebraska Medical Center (UNMC) campus are conducted at the elementary, junior high, high school, and college levels. These activities include, but are not limited to, contact through science clubs, health clubs, minority student organizations, career and/or health fairs, school visits, and by participation in community activities.

Recruitment visits are made annually to colleges in Nebraska that have the largest percentages of minority students enrolled. Contacts with non-resident minorities are made by attending national conferences including the Society for the Advancement of Chicanos and Native Americans in Science, and Minority Access to Research Careers/Minority Biomedical Research Support. In addition, contact is made with students on lists such as the Talent Roster of Outstanding Minority Community College Graduates, the AAMC Medical Minority Applicant Registry, and through correspondence with members of the National Association of Medical Minority Educators. Voluntary recruiters—University of Nebraska faculty members—assist the multicultural affairs office staff with recruitment visits to out-of-state colleges.

University of Nebraska College of Medicine, 2006
Applicants and Matriculants by Gender, Race and Ethnicity

Race and Ethnicity	Applicants			Matriculants		
	Women	Men	Total	Women	Men	Total
Hispanic/Latino						
Cuban	2	0	2	0	0	0
Mexican American	20	14	34	2	2	4
Puerto Rican	0	2	2	0	0	0
Other Hispanic	10	9	19	1	1	2
Multiple Hispanic*	0	3	3	0	0	0
Subtotal	32	28	60	3	3	6
Non-Hispanic/Latino**						
Black	32	21	53	3	1	4
Native American/Alaska Native	4	2	6	0	0	0
Native Hawaiian/Other Pacific Islander	3	2	5	0	0	0
White	355	498	853	43	57	100
Asian	89	104	193	2	4	6
Multiple Race*	20	16	36	1	1	2
Unknown	2	4	6	0	0	0
Subtotal	505	647	1,152	49	63	112
Foreign	7	6	13	0	0	0
Total	544	681	1,225	52	66	118

*Since 2002, students can select more than one race and / or ethnicity. **Those who did not choose
Hispanic/Latino' or 'Non-Hispanic/Latino' are counted under 'Non-Hispanic/Latino'.
Data Source: AAMC Data Warehouse: Applicant-Matriculant File, as of 5/9/2007.

Affiliation agreements exist with several colleges and universities that have a predominant enrollment of students that are underrepresented minorities. These agreements exist to increase awareness of the many academic opportunities available to potential students at the University of Nebraska Medical Center. Summer research opportunities that are fully funded exist for students from these affiliated institutions.

Admissions

Applications should be filed through the American Medical College Application Service (AMCAS), ten to 14 months prior to the proposed matriculation date. Students are selected on the basis of scholarship, appraisals of character, personal interviews, scores on Medical College Admission Test (MCAT), and general motivation and promise. Although a specific minority admissions program does not exist in the medical school, minority applications are encouraged.

Academic Support Programs

All basic science departments at the University of Nebraska College of Medicine offer tutorials to all students. Additionally, student services sponsors an annual *Academic Support Program* for minority students. Activities in this program include workshops on study skills, test-taking skills, stress management, and an introduction to campus resources. Individual and small-group tutorials are provided free of charge in the basic science areas.

Other services of the office include personal development seminars; scholarship, fellowship, and externship reference library; as well as academic and personal advisement and referrals.

A minority faculty preceptorship program is offered to first-year medical students to develop clinical skills and to provide a mentor for freshman and sophomore students.

Enrichment Programs

Summer programs at the University of Nebraska Medical Center are generally contingent upon available grant funds. Currently a *Summer Research Enrichment Program* is being sponsored for juniors and seniors in college. The program is designed to provide academic enrichment in the following areas: communications with an emphasis on technical writing, medical terminology, research skills, clinical and laboratory work experiences, and seminars to explore the health status of minorities. Preference is given to Nebraska residents, but all students are encouraged to apply.

Student Financial Assistance

The University of Nebraska Medical Center is committed to the goal that no student should be forced to withdraw from school because of financial constraints. Financial assistance is offered in the form of scholarships, grants, and loans administered by an experienced financial aid office staff.

The University of Nebraska College of Medicine requires an application fee. Disadvantaged students may apply for an application fee waiver directly through AMCAS. Financial assistance for interview trips is not available.

Association of American Medical Colleges, 2007

University of Nevada School of Medicine

Ann E. Diggins
Director of Recruitment
and Student Services
University of Nevada
School of Medicine
Office of Recruitment/198
Reno, NV 89557
702-784-6063; 702-784-6589 Fax
adiggins@medicine.nevada.edu
www.unr.edu/med

Recruitment

The University of Nevada School of Medicine has a successful history of providing physicians to the state's communities. In continuation of that mission, the school strongly believes in recruiting, retaining, and graduating minority physicians to provide quality medical care for Nevada's increasingly diverse minority communities.

The school is committed to:

- Maintaining diversity among its students by accepting students from a variety of backgrounds, ethnic cultures and experiences.
- Advancing the participation of underrepresented minorities in medicine and science.

Outreach focuses on students in grades seven through 12 and college. Programs for Nevada residents include:

- *Summer of Discovery*—science enrichment programs for Nevada students in grades seven through ten.
  (www.unr.edu/science-partners/htm)
- *High School Medical Scholars*— a three-week residential/academic enrichment program for juniors in high school.
  (www.unr.edu/hs-medsch01.htm)
- *Nevadans Into Medicine*—an admissions preparation program for college juniors and seniors.
  (www.unr.edu/undergrad-nevadans.htm)

Admissions

The School of Medicine's Admissions Selection Committee has adopted a policy that enables applicants from all socioeconomic, sex, racial, religious, and educational backgrounds to be equally considered. All students must meet residency and admissions criteria. Applications from underrepresented minority students are encouraged.
(www.unr.edu/med/admissions).

Academic Support Programs

The medical school offers an intentionally small, personalized atmosphere for students. Services include:

- Tuition scholarships
- Mentoring and colleague programs
- Academic support
- Community service opportunities
- Minority student organizations
- Physician seminars

At the school, students receive personalized instruction and attention from faculty, staff, and colleagues. A class size of only 52 students gives them the opportunity to learn medicine in an environment of caring. The school prides itself on graduating physicians who understand the value of caring for their patients, the importance of receiving a top-notch medical education, and the opportunity to give back to the community.

Mentoring and Colleague Program. First-year medical students are matched with a community physician for an ongoing clinical education and mentoring relationship. Volunteer primary care physicians donate their time and host medical students in

University of Nevada School of Medicine, 2006
Applicants and Matriculants by Gender, Race and Ethnicity

Race and Ethnicity	Applicants			Matriculants		
	Women	Men	Total	Women	Men	Total
Hispanic/Latino						
Cuban	2	3	5	0	1	1
Mexican American	23	17	40	1	0	1
Puerto Rican	3	3	6	1	0	1
Other Hispanic	11	10	21	0	1	1
Multiple Hispanic*	2	2	4	0	0	0
Subtotal	41	35	76	2	2	4
Non-Hispanic/Latino**						
Black	17	9	26	2	0	2
Native American/Alaska Native	3	1	4	1	0	1
Native Hawaiian/Other Pacific Islander	8	6	14	0	0	0
White	226	370	596	19	23	42
Asian	107	117	224	5	3	8
Other Race	0	1	1	0	0	0
Multiple Race*	19	19	38	0	0	0
Unknown	5	3	8	0	0	0
Subtotal	385	526	911	27	26	53
Foreign	4	6	10	0	0	0
Total	430	567	997	29	28	57

*Since 2002, students can select more than one race and / or ethnicity. **Those who did not choose
Hispanic/Latino' or 'Non-Hispanic/Latino' are counted under 'Non-Hispanic/Latino'.
Data Source: AAMC Data Warehouse: Applicant-Matriculant File, as of 5/9/2007.

clinical settings four days each month. This program gives students hands-on experience in clinical care beginning the second week of school.

The Colleague Program matches an incoming student with a veteran second-year student for help in study skills, managing the work of medical school, and balancing his/her personal life with school responsibilities. This program gives students a ready-made "big brother or sister" to help ease the transition into medical school.

Academic Support. The medical school Wellness Program provides an ongoing series of seminars dealing with such issues as study skills, test-taking strategies, and time management. In addition, students are encouraged to seek assistance from faculty. Nevada maintains a very high faculty to student ratio for the purpose of enhancing instruction and support for students.

Community Service Opportunities. The School of Medicine believes in the importance of giving back to the community. Students are involved in caring for patients in clinics for AIDS patients, the medically indigent and homeless, and other populations throughout the state. These activities combine medical education for the students and the need in the community for high-quality health care for those who don't have the ability to pay. Students are also asked to volunteer for mentor programs with high schools and assist in programs designed to provide science enrichment activities for middle and high school minority students.

Physician Seminars. Every six weeks the medical school hosts a luncheon for minority students with minority physicians. During these seminars, the doctors share their experiences and expertise with students. The meetings also give students the chance to discuss practice options and engage in career planning, as well as gather tips for success in medical school.

Student Financial Assistance

The School of Medicine has an increasing endowment for minority student scholarships. In addition, tuition and recruitment scholarships are awarded each year. The school is committed to easing the financial demands of medical school for all students.

Educational Partnerships

The School of Medicine has partnerships with Nevada's two magnet schools for math and science in Las Vegas–Rancho High School and Clark High School. Programs offered by the medical school include science enrichment, career development, and summer outreach programs. In addition, the school has a partnership with Hug High School in Reno. This program includes a high school mentoring program that pairs first-year medical students with underrepresented minority students in the ninth and tenth grades.

Dartmouth Medical School

Dr. Lori Arviso Alvord
Associate Dean of Student
and Multicultural Affairs
Shawn O'Leary
Dartmouth Medical School
301 Remsen Building
Hanover, NH 03755-3833
603-650-1582; 603-650-1169 Fax

Dartmouth Medical School (DMS) is dedicated to advancing health through the dissemination and discovery of knowledge. Our chief responsibility is to select students of exceptional character and accomplishment and prepare them to become superb and caring physicians, scientists, and teachers.

DMS has a strong commitment to diversity. Our Office of Multicultural Affairs takes a leading role in creating a community that honors the diverse backgrounds of our students, faculty, and administrators. We initiate programs that teach our students to be culturally versatile and practice medicine appropriately in the world as it exists today.

Recruitment

A multifaceted approach to minority recruitment is taken at DMS. Faculty, students, and administrators visit a number of summer and health profession career programs, as well as many undergraduate colleges. Information about DMS is sent to select candidates identified through the Medical Minority Applicant Registry (MedMAR) of the AAMC. A student hosting program allows candidates who have been invited to interview to stay overnight in the homes of current students during the interview visit. The Admissions Office is also pleased to respond on an individual basis to inquiries from applicants. Please feel free to contact the Admissions Office at 603-650-1505. The Director of Multicultural Affairs at the Medical School can be reached at 603-650-1553.

Admissions

DMS, the nation's fourth oldest medical school, is committed to making its opportunities available to students from a wide range of backgrounds and experiences. We seek a diverse student body. The admissions process at DMS involves a holistic review of all applications. Though the process is very selective, it does not employ rigid cutoffs in making decisions. All applications are considered carefully, with attention given to the unique qualities, background, and characteristics of each individual. Applications from those underrepresented in medicine are particularly encouraged. The DMS student body is national in scope, with residents from approximately 25 states and 60 undergraduate institutions represented in a typical entering class.

Academic Support Programs

The relatively small class size at DMS permits close and meaningful interaction with faculty and a supportive relationship with classmates on an ongoing basis. Formal academic support programs include a Senior Advising Dean who meets individually with students on an as-needed basis, and a Big Sibling Program, through which each student is matched with a volunteer second-year medical student mentor. In addition, the faculty preceptor, with whom each first- and second-year student works as part of DMS's On-Doctoring course, is an important source of advice and counsel. Students also participate in an active chapter of the Student National Medical

Dartmouth Medical School, 2006
Applicants and Matriculants by Gender, Race and Ethnicity

Race and Ethnicity	Applicants			Matriculants		
	Women	Men	Total	Women	Men	Total
Hispanic/Latino						
Cuban	8	15	23	0	0	0
Mexican American	49	40	89	0	1	1
Puerto Rican	13	15	28	0	0	0
Other Hispanic	40	48	88	0	0	0
Multiple Hispanic*	5	6	11	0	0	0
Subtotal	115	124	239	0	1	1
Non-Hispanic/Latino**						
Black	84	54	138	1	2	3
Native American/Alaska Native	10	5	15	0	0	0
Native Hawaiian/Other Pacific Islander	6	4	10	0	0	0
White	1,138	1,466	2,604	18	29	47
Asian	527	506	1,033	8	9	17
Other Race	2	2	4	0	0	0
Multiple Race*	88	73	161	1	1	2
Unknown	22	25	47	2	0	2
Subtotal	1,877	2,135	4,012	30	41	71
Foreign	179	190	369	6	4	10
Total	2,171	2,449	4,620	36	46	82

*Since 2002, students can select more than one race and / or ethnicity. **Those who did not choose Hispanic/Latino' or 'Non-Hispanic/Latino' are counted under 'Non-Hispanic/Latino'.
Data Source: AAMC Data Warehouse: Applicant-Matriculant File, as of 5/9/2007.

Association of American Medical Colleges, 2007

Association, which addresses the concerns of minority medical students at the campus and national levels.

The Office for Learning and Disability Services (OLADS) at Dartmouth Medical School is committed to helping students live up to their highest potential. In addition to coordinating services for students with disabilities, OLADS assists all DMS students in understanding their learning styles, their strengths and weaknesses, and their individual paths to excellence. The coordinator of that office is both a learning and disabilities specialist and a professional counselor. In addition to working one-on-one with students, a series of Success Seminars are offered in the first year and small-group tutoring is available to students who need assistance in a particular course.

Enrichment Programs

The Advanced Readiness Course (ARC) takes place during the week preceding first-year orientation. ARC is a voluntary course open to any incoming student who feels that he/she could benefit from additional preparation in order to begin medical school with the utmost confidence. Students in ARC are exposed to representative lectures from all the first-term courses and are guided through the advanced skills that insure learning and prepare them to handle the increased workload of medical school. There are also activities during that week designed to help students make the transition to Dartmouth Medical School and to the Upper Valley area.

Student Financial Assistance

DMS is committed to providing an excellent medical education to any accepted student. Students are admitted on a need-blind basis. Once a student accepts the offer of admission, the institution and the student work together to develop a sound approach to financing medical school. We provide institutional need-based financial aid in the form of loans and scholarships to meet the cost of a medical education for those students with documented financial need.

Financial need is defined as the difference between educational costs and the resources that are available from the student and his or her spouse and family. DMS encourages financial aid applicants to complete the Free Application for Federal Student Aid (FAFSA), the Need Access Application, and the free DMS application to be considered for institutional need-based aid. These forms are accessible at *(www.dms.dartmouth.edu/admin/fin_aid/)*.

Other Pertinent Information

In addition to the clinical facilities at Dartmouth, students also participate in Dartmouth-affiliated clerkships in settings as diverse as the Tuba City Indian Health Service Hospital in Arizona; Children's Hospital Orange County, California; Key West, Florida; Connecticut's Hartford Hospital; Kuskokwim Delta Regional Hospital in Bethel, Alaska; Hawkes Bay Regional Hospital in Hastings, New Zealand; and other sites as well. Although many students complete their clerkships in Dartmouth's environs, these off-campus programs ensure that DMS students will have access to a broad variety of patient populations that represent the full spectrum of health care delivery.

UMDNJ—New Jersey Medical School

Dr. Maria L. Soto-Greene
Professor and Vice Dean
UMDNJ—New Jersey Medical School
185 South Orange Avenue C671
Newark, NJ 07103
973-972-9151; 973-972-7104 Fax
sotogrml@umdnj.edu

The New Jersey Medical School (NJMS) is the oldest of eight schools that form the University of Medicine and Dentistry of New Jersey (UMDNJ), the nation's largest freestanding health sciences university. The mission of the NJMS is to educate students, physicians, and scientists to meet society's current and future health care needs.

The NJMS takes pride in the diversity of its faculty, alumni, staff and students, as well as the strengths of its community programs. NJMS is proud of its commitment to recruiting and retaining minority students. The school's commitment to diversity is far reaching with programs beginning at the third-grade level through faculty levels. We are united by our commitment to scholarship, professionalism, and dedication to science, but above all excellence.

Recruitment

The NJMS has an extensive recruitment program. Besides having a full-time recruiter/counselor, selected faculty, administrators, and students also participate in recruitment initiatives by visiting colleges, high schools, health career programs as well as graduate and professional recruitment fairs looking for prospective applicants and disseminating information about the curriculum and life at NJMS.

Admissions

NJMS continues to have a diverse student body and has a strong, dedicated commitment to the recruitment, retention, and graduation of underrepresented minorities. The Board of Trustees of the UMDNJ has committed itself, the university, and its component units to a policy of equal opportunity without regard to race, color, creed or religion, sex, national origin, age, military status, marital status, handicap if otherwise qualified, or other factors prohibited by law. This is the governing principle in student admissions and other student services and employment.

Annually, the NJMS accepts 170 entering students. All applicants must take the Medical College Admission Test (MCAT), either in the spring or fall, the year before their planned matriculation date. It is the responsibility of the applicant to have the results of the test forwarded to the Committee on Admissions. The committee will consider no application for final action until the test results have been received.

NJMS also has a five-year program. This curriculum offers students an opportunity to extend the first two years of coursework over a period of three years, thus completing the requirements for the M.D. degree in five years rather than four. This option is open to accepted students who request it because of family, financial, or education considerations. It is also available to matriculated students who experience academic difficulty during the first year. Further information may be obtained from the Office of Admissions at the time of application.

Academic Support Programs

The New Jersey Medical School Office of Student Affairs provides programs and individual consultations for all medical students. Students can acquire advanced skills needed to achieve optimally in professional-level courses and licensing examinations. All incoming medical students are given direction in how to adapt

UMDNJ - New Jersey Medical School, 2006
Applicants and Matriculants by Gender, Race and Ethnicity

Race and Ethnicity	Applicants			Matriculants		
	Women	Men	Total	Women	Men	Total
Hispanic/Latino						
Cuban	21	23	44	2	2	4
Mexican American	32	38	70	0	0	0
Puerto Rican	34	21	55	4	1	5
Other Hispanic	101	64	165	5	8	13
Multiple Hispanic*	7	10	17	0	1	1
Subtotal	195	156	351	11	12	23
Non-Hispanic/Latino**						
Black	361	163	524	12	7	19
Native American/Alaska Native	3	5	8	0	0	0
Native Hawaiian/Other Pacific Islander	14	12	26	0	1	1
White	834	941	1,775	21	34	55
Asian	685	659	1,344	29	38	67
Other Race	4	2	6	0	0	0
Multiple Race*	51	51	102	1	1	2
Unknown	20	28	48	1	2	3
Subtotal	1,972	1,861	3,833	64	83	147
Foreign	35	25	60	0	0	0
Total	2,202	2,042	4,244	75	95	170

*Since 2002, students can select more than one race and / or ethnicity. **Those who did not choose
'Hispanic/Latino' or 'Non-Hispanic/Latino' are counted under 'Non-Hispanic/Latino'.
Data Source: AAMC Data Warehouse: Applicant-Matriculant File, as of 5/9/2007.

Association of American Medical Colleges, 2007

their study techniques, time management, and learning strategies to the unique challenges of medical education. This guidance begins with an optional pre-matriculation program, continues through orientation in the first year of medical school, and is available throughout the four years of medical education whenever the student requests it.

During the first year, small-group tutorials guided by upper class students provide a rich learning environment outside the traditional curriculum. In addition, a teaching elective is provided for medical students who wish to improve their own educational/teaching skills.

A lending library, stocked by donations from upperclass students, is also available to assist students in deciding which resource materials are best for their individual study. Upper-class tutors, supervised by the Office of Academic Development (OAD), are assigned to help those students who need them.

Customized programs are available for medical board preparation. These include practice examinations, which are given to the second-year medical school class as they prepare for the first step of the United States Medical Licensing Examination.

Enrichment Opportunities

At the New Jersey Medical School, the Office of Special Programs (OSP) develops, implements, and supports, the pre-professional/professional health education and community service programs. The OSP has established educational pipeline programs to address the entire educational spectrum. The educational pipeline programs target pre-college students through the professional level, including their entry at our own institution.

The Hispanic Center of Excellence (HCOE) was established in 1991 with the primary goal of improving the health status of the Latino population by increasing the number of Latinos in the health professions and medicine in particular. Over the past 14 years, there has been a continuous refinement of institutional policies and programs that have permitted the HCOE to implement initiatives aimed at enhancing academic performance, improving the recruitment and retention of faculty, and developing the capacity of the school's graduates to provide culturally competent health care services. HCOE seeks to reduce disparities in health care by supporting individuals committed to advancing the goals of diversity in the medical profession and improved health care to underserved populations.

The Student Health Advocates for Resources and Education (S.H.A.R.E.) Center, founded in 1996, is a student-run organization that promotes community service at NJMS. The S.H.A.R.E. Center serves as the forum for communication between the various community service activities at the medical school.

Robert Wood Johnson Foundation's Summer Medical and Dental Education Program (SMDEP) is a six-week residential summer program designed to provide rising sophomore and junior undergraduate students interested in medicine and dentistry a problem-based learning model of science education. The curriculum has been carefully designed to enhance the students' academic and personal skills required to succeed in medical and dental school. This is accomplished by providing opportunities for the development and practice of critical-thinking skills, problem-based learning skills, and self-assessment.

The Pre-Medical Honors Program is designed to attract promising high school students to medicine and the health sciences and is offered during the fall.

Mini-Med School is a similar program offered to adults. Each program includes 195 minutes of lectures and seminars. The programs address recent findings in medical research and health care, raise consciousness about the routes to medical care, and enhance one of the principle missions of NJMS—to train socially conscious and humane physicians.

Success is Science Tutorial Program, co-sponsored with Rutgers University-New Brunswick, is intended to strengthen the preparation of two-year college transfer educationally/economically disadvantaged students upon entry to a four-year partner undergraduate institution by providing math and science skills development.

Freshman Introduction to Resources and Skills Training (F.I.R.S.T) funded by AmeriChoice provides an early exposure to the rigors of medical school and acclimates incoming NJMS/NJDS students to different teaching techniques and study strategies.

The SMART Initiative (Science, Medicine And Related Topics Pipeline), is a set of pre-college health-related educational enrichment programs for students entering grades eight-12. Its mission is designed to assist participants in acquiring a strong background in the sciences and to cultivate interest in health careers. Programs are offered during the winter and summer.

Mentoring Programs

The mentoring/advising program is a longitudinal program, with a faculty member and student pairing through all four years of medical school. Faculty members volunteer to mentor two to three students from each class. A primary goal of the program is for the faculty and student to develop a relationship during this time. Additional faculty are available for consultation and advising once a student has identified his or her specialty choice. There are four components to the overall program. These include the

Careers in Medicine (CiM) Web site, sponsored by AAMC, the Student and Faculty Manuals for CiM, individual advising by faculty, and a variety of workshops during each class year.

Student Financial Assistance

The UMDNJ Student Financial Aid Office awards financial aid. The amount and type of aid is based on need, specific eligibility requirements, and UMDNJ's financial aid packaging policy, which is a formula developed to determine the amount of aid to be given to the student from university administered aid programs. The total amount of need-based aid awarded to the student cannot exceed his or her financial need.

The primary source of financial assistance at UMDNJ and most other graduate and professional schools is student loans. However, there is also in place an unlimited number of Dean's Academic Excellence Scholarships and other alumni scholarships. Minority students from one of the specific underrepresented minority "target groups," may qualify for assistance from the Minority/Disadvantaged Fund (MDF).

UMDNJ—Robert Wood Johnson Medical School

Dr. Cheryl A. Dickson
Assistant Dean, Student Affairs
Multicultural Affairs
UMDNJ—Robert Wood Johnson
Medical School
675 Hoes Lane
Piscataway, NJ 08854-5635
732-235-2143/2144; 732-235-3972 Fax
dicksoca@umdnj.edu
http://rwjms.umdnj.edu/osap

Robert Wood Johnson Medical School (RWJMS) established the Office of Multicultural Affairs in 1996 to address cultural sensitivity and diversity at RWJMS. The office develops, sponsors, and supports programs and activities that foster cultural awareness and an understanding of diversity. Activities include a multicultural appreciation week, cultural competence workshops, and a presentation on diversity during first-year orientation. Activities are also done in celebration of Asian, Black, and Latin Heritage Months. RWJMS offers several courses addressing multiculturalism that include a complimentary/alternative medicine elective, a medical Spanish elective, a cultural diversity module as part of Introduction to the Patient, and panel presentation on culture, religion and sexuality. The Office of Multicultural Affairs works collaboratively with other departments, offices, and centers within the school that promote the understanding of diversity and delivery of culturally competent health care. Additional resources include a Center for Healthy Families and Cultural Diversity, a Cultural Diversity Committee, and a Student Committee for Multicultural Affairs. For more information contact: Cynthia Ferrer 732-235-3467.

UMDNJ - Robert Wood Johnson Medical School, 2006
Applicants and Matriculants by Gender, Race and Ethnicity

Race and Ethnicity	Applicants			Matriculants		
	Women	Men	Total	Women	Men	Total
Hispanic/Latino						
Cuban	15	11	26	0	0	0
Mexican American	15	11	26	0	0	0
Puerto Rican	20	14	34	2	2	4
Other Hispanic	50	49	99	0	0	0
Multiple Hispanic*	7	7	14	0	0	0
Subtotal	107	92	199	2	2	4
Non-Hispanic/Latino**						
Black	244	131	375	11	2	13
Native American/Alaska Native	2	2	4	0	0	0
Native Hawaiian/Other Pacific Islander	11	7	18	0	0	0
White	653	761	1,414	37	40	77
Asian	521	501	1,022	35	30	65
Other Race	2	1	3	0	0	0
Multiple Race*	32	29	61	0	1	1
Unknown	19	28	47	3	2	5
Subtotal	1,484	1,460	2,944	86	75	161
Foreign	18	9	27	0	0	0
Total	1,609	1,561	3,170	88	77	165

*Since 2002, students can select more than one race and / or ethnicity. **Those who did not choose
'Hispanic/Latino' or 'Non-Hispanic/Latino' are counted under 'Non-Hispanic/Latino'.
Data Source: AAMC Data Warehouse: Applicant-Matriculant File, as of 5/9/2007.

Association of American Medical Colleges, 2007

Recruitment

RWJMS actively seeks to increase the number of underrepresented minority and disadvantaged students who are interested in pursuing careers in medicine. To achieve this goal, RWJMS sponsors enrichment programs for students at the high school and undergraduate levels and has developed articulated admissions programs with several New Jersey undergraduate colleges.

RWJMS welcomes the opportunity to speak with prospective pre-medical students. The Recruiter/Counselors are available to visit high schools, colleges, and universities and to speak with students about the medical school application process and about the diverse programs and opportunities at RWJMS. The school is also delighted to host visits to the RWJMS campus by student groups as this affords an excellent opportunity to meet with students, faculty, and administrators. The Recruiter/Counselors will help to plan such a visit and will arrange for speakers who can address topics of particular interest to the visiting group.

The Recruiter/Counselors also welcome the opportunity to meet individually with prospective applicants. They are very experienced with all aspects of the medical school admissions process, and can discuss with each student his/her individual situation, whether it involves long-range planning and preparation for medical school or the immediate details of the application process.

Admissions

The RWJMS Admissions Committee plays a pivotal role in the school's efforts to increase the number of physicians from disadvantaged and underrepresented minority groups. Every minority/disadvantaged applicant is assured an individualized review of his/her completed application. Admissions Committee members are sensitive to the diverse factors that are important in evaluating medical school applicants. Life experiences, economic background, leadership experiences, and other factors are carefully considered along with the traditional numeric criteria such as GPA and Medical College Admission Test scores. The interview provides the applicant an opportunity to discuss in detail his/her qualifications and to learn about the academic program, environment, and special services offered at RWJMS. Committee membership includes faculty and students (who are full voting members). The Recruiter/Counselors work in the Admissions Office and help to facilitate the admissions process for minority/disadvantaged applicants.

Academic Support Programs

RWJMS is committed to the success of all its students and has developed a variety of programs to help every student achieve his/her goal of becoming a physician. The atmosphere at RWJMS is cooperative and supportive and faculty are accessible and receptive to answering questions and discussing course work. Many first-year courses incorporate faculty-led review periods into the class schedule and some designate a particular faculty member as an academic resource person.

Cognitive Skills Program (CSP). This program provides individual consultation in a variety of learning-related areas, including study strategies, test-taking skills, and time management. The CSP also offers preparation programs for the United States Medical Licensing Examination and academic year tutorials.

RWJMS offers a flexible curriculum option that provides the opportunity for a limited number of students to personalize the sequence of courses. This option accommodates students with special circumstances, including those enrolled in combined degree programs (M.D./M.P.H., M.D./Ph.D.), those who wish to pursue other academic or research interests, and those with particular employment or family needs. Flexible curriculum students pay eight semesters of tuition during their matriculation. Tuition payments are prorated over the duration of their educational program.

As part of its commitment to increasing minority representation in medicine, for nearly 30 years, RWJMS has offered comprehensive academic support programs, a pre-matriculation summer program (discussed in more detail below, Enrichment Programs) and academic year tutorials, as well as individualized assistance with study and test-taking skills are offered. The Office of Special Academic Programs, which administers enrichment programs, also serves as a liaison to effectively present minority students' concerns to the senior administration of RWJMS.

Enrichment Programs

Pre-matriculation Summer Program (PSP). Disadvantaged students, who have been accepted to the first-year class at RWJMS, are invited to attend the seven-week Pre-matriculation Summer Program. The goal of the program is to introduce students to course content they will encounter during their first year of medical school, as well as to give participants the opportunity to familiarize themselves with the RWJMS faculty and staff and the school environment. Cognitive skills seminars and individual cognitive skills assessments are incorporated into the summer program to assist students in identifying efficient and effective methods of studying medical information.

Second-year medical students serve as teaching fellows and also help the new students with such things as locating apartments for the fall. Campus housing is available for students attending the program and scholarships are available to cover tuition, on-campus housing, and living expenses. Contact: Dr. Cheryl Dickson, 732-235-2144 or Cindy Ford 732-235-2808.

Biomedical Careers Program (BCP) For the past 30 years, RWJMS has co-sponsored a summer enrichment program for disadvantaged students with Rutgers, The State University of New Jersey. BCP is designed for undergraduate students interested in pursuing a career in medicine and other health-related professions. This eight-week summer program offers three levels and seven different curricula to meet the academic needs of all participants. Each level offers a set of academic coursework and activities complemented by career-related counseling and life-skills seminars. In order to be eligible, students must have completed one year of college, one semester of biology, and one semester of math. Students enrolled in BCP are eligible for three college credits through Rutgers University, and housing is available. Full and partial need-based scholarships are available to cover tuition, housing, and living expenses. Contact: Sharonda McKinney-Brown, 732-235-2143 *(http://rwjms.umdnj.edu/osap)*

Summer Science Scholars Program (S³A) The academy is a three-week science enrichment program designed for highly motivated and academically committed high school students achieving excellence in the sciences. The curriculum focuses on exploring the human body through a series of lectures, organ laboratories, and clinical experiences. The academy provides a bridge between high school and undergraduate studies in the sciences and ultimately a career in medicine. Students participate in college preparatory workshops, health profession seminars, cognitive skills sessions, and community service opportunities. Additionally, students complete a research project to present at the Summer Science Scholars Academy symposium. S³A classes are small to foster individualized learning and enhance the student's personal experience. Financial assistance is available to cover tuition and housing expenses.

Contact: Sharonda McKinney-Brown, 732-235-2143 *(http://rvjms.umdnj.edu/osap)*

Research in Science and Engineering. This eight-week summer enrichment program is for minority and disadvantaged students interested in pursuing careers in research. Students are paired with research mentors from Rutgers or UMDNJ-RWJMS. Four days per week are spent in the lab with one day spent in classroom preparation for the Graduate Record Exam (GRE) and scientific seminars. The program concludes with a scientific symposium where students present the results of their summer research. There is no tuition charge, housing is available, and a stipend is provided to cover living expenses. Contact: Praxedes Dominguez, 732-235-5016. *(http://RISE.Rutgers.edu).*

Rutgers-UMDNJ Pipeline Project. This academic year program is designed to provide research opportunities to minority and disadvantaged students who are interested in careers in research. A stipend is provided. Contact: Michael Leibowitz, M.D., Ph.D., 732-235-4795.

Student Financial Assistance

The RWJMS application fee will be waived for any student who receives an American Medical College Application Service fee waiver. Overnight accommodations with our medical students can be arranged for applicants coming to interview. To ensure that every student who matriculates at RWJMS has adequate financial support, a financial needs assessment (based on the Free Application for Federal Student Aid form) is made for each student and an individualized financial aid package is developed. The types of financial aid include scholarships and grants (including a special institutional fund for disadvantaged minority students), loans, and college work-study programs. Financial aid counselors are available to assist students in planning effective personal budgets.

Educational Partnerships

RWJMS has articulated admissions programs with Rutgers University and Richard Stockton College. Eligibility for these programs is not restricted to particular racial/ethnic categories. In addition, RWJMS, in conjunction with Rutgers University and Seton Hall University, offers a special articulated admissions program, ACCESS-MED, for disadvantaged students participating in ACCESS-MED in their respective undergraduate institute. Contact: Cheryl Dickson, M.D., 732-235-2144.

Other Pertinent Information

RWJMS was founded in 1966 as a professional school within Rutgers University. Since 1971, RWJMS has been associated with the University of Medicine and Dentistry of New Jersey (UMDNJ), New Jersey's health sciences university. RWJMS continues to enjoy the benefits of its close proximity to, and relationship with, Rutgers University.

RWJMS has facilities at several locations in the central and southern parts of New Jersey. The basic science building, where all students receive two years of pre-clinical instruction, is located in Piscataway, adjacent to the main science campus of Rutgers University. The medical science complex also includes a UMDNJ—Community Mental Health Center and several facilities operated jointly with Rutgers University, including the Library of Science and Medicine, the Center for Advanced Biotechnology and Medicine, and the Environmental and Occupational Health Sciences Institute.

RWJMS offers clinical education at training sites both in central New Jersey (the Piscataway program) and in southern New Jersey (the Camden program). Major teaching affiliations with Robert Wood Johnson University Hospital in New Brunswick and Cooper Hospital/University Medical Center in Camden, plus affiliations with numerous community hospitals in central New Jersey, provide students with a diverse range of clinical training facilities.

Joint Degree Programs

M.D./Ph.D. Students may pursue a Ph.D. degree in the discipline of their choice through one of the graduate programs sponsored by the UMDNJ-Graduate School of Biomedical Sciences (GSBS) or one of the graduate programs sponsored jointly by GSBS and Rutgers University. Tuition remission and stipend support are available. Typically, students take about three years to complete the degree between the second and third year of medical school.

M.D./M.P.H. Students may pursue an M.P.H. through the NJ Graduate Program in Public Health sponsored jointly by UMDNJ-RWJMS and Rutgers University. Students may study in any one of several "tracks" including: Health Care Organization, Family Health, Epidemiology, and Toxicology. Medical-school funded positions for this M.P.H. are available. In addition, a few stipends for living expenses are available to students who take a year off for full-time study in the M.P.H. program. Typically students can complete this degree by taking some courses concurrent with their medical school courses (some courses replace medical school courses) plus an additional year of study.

M.D./J.D. Students may pursue a J.D. degree through either Rutgers Law School (Camden) or Seton Hall Law School (Newark). Typically, two and one-half years of additional study are required. This degree may be taken between years two and three or between years three and four of medical school.

M.D./M.S.J. Students may pursue a Masters of Science in Jurisprudence at Seton Hall Law School. One additional year of full-time study is required. Students would typically complete this degree between years two and three of medical school.

M.D./M.B.A.. Students may pursue a M.B.A. through a joint program sponsored by Rutgers University and RWJMS. Medical-school funded positions are available.

M.D./M.S. in Medical Informatics. Students may pursue the M.S. in Medical Informatics through this joint program with New Jersey Institute of Technology and UMDNJ-School of Health Related Professions. Some scholarships support is available.

Robert Wood Johnson Medical School has a long-standing commitment to increasing access to education for under-represented minority and disadvantaged students. This commitment is evident in institutional policies and procedures, in the programs and services which RWJMS offers, and in the major fiscal commitments that the institution has made to these programs.

Association of American Medical Colleges, 2007

University of New Mexico School of Medicine

Dr. Valerie Romero-Leggott
Associate Dean, Office of Diversity
University of New Mexico
School of Medicine
MSC 08 4680
1 University of New Mexico
Albuquerque, NM 87131-0001
505-272-2728; 505-272-6857 Fax
http://hsc.unm.edu/som/diversity/

Recruitment

The mission of the University of New Mexico School of Medicine Office of Diversity is to promote racial, ethnic, socioeconomic, and geographic diversity in the University of New Mexico Health Sciences Center (UNMHSC) and to develop a variety of opportunities addressing key issues in diversity.

Strategies to achieve this mission include creating college awareness and identifying, recruiting, and supporting students, residents, and faculty from diverse backgrounds. The Office of Diversity addresses the challenges of students from minority groups that are underrepresented in the context of collaborative partnerships and programs. A critical component to the success of our students and programs has been our partnerships with communities, other colleges and entities within the HSC, other educational institutions, community health centers, health professionals and educators.

Recruitment takes place all year round throughout New Mexico at the community level through career fairs, high school and institutions of higher education site visits, and special events. Presentations are given about the School of Medicine's admissions process, UNMHSC colleges and programs, combined B.A./M.D. degree program, and the Health Career Opportunities Programs (HCOP). The programs range from special speakers talking to students about careers to shadowing opportunities and educational events in collaboration with area physicians, local community leaders, medical students, high school teachers, and counselors.

The Office of Diversity also organizes several tours of the UNMHSC for students and educators from all areas of New Mexico. These tours include presentations from faculty and students from a variety of health professions, centers, and institutes, information on student opportunities, and interactive simulated sessions.

The Office of Diversity collaborates in recruitment efforts with other UNMHSC colleges and programs including, the Hispanic and Native American Center of Excellence, the Center for Native American Health, and School Based Health Centers, in addition to UNM main campus recruitment and student support services such as, El Centro de la Raza, American Indian Student Services, African American Student Services, and Minority Science Programs.

Peter Couse, Student Recruiter, or Liliana Sosa, Program Coordinator, 505-272-2728; 505-272-6857 Fax; (http://hsc.unm.edu/som/diversity/)

The School of Medicine's Office of Admissions hosts an Annual Pre Med/Health Day in collaboration with the other UNMHSC programs in an effort to provide pre-med/health students throughout the state an opportunity to visit our campus and learn about all of the opportunities offered by UNM. Pre-med/health students and advisors from two-year community colleges and four-year institutions are invited from all over New Mexico to participate in this event. The program consists of an introduction to all of the

University of New Mexico School of Medicine, 2006
Applicants and Matriculants by Gender, Race and Ethnicity

Race and Ethnicity	Applicants			Matriculants		
	Women	Men	Total	Women	Men	Total
Hispanic/Latino						
Cuban	3	7	10	0	0	0
Mexican American	57	45	102	8	6	14
Puerto Rican	2	3	5	0	0	0
Other Hispanic	23	26	49	2	5	7
Multiple Hispanic*	5	5	10	2	0	2
Subtotal	90	86	176	12	11	23
Non-Hispanic/Latino**						
Black	26	17	43	1	1	2
Native American/Alaska Native	7	2	9	0	0	0
Native Hawaiian/Other Pacific Islander	3	1	4	0	0	0
White	279	345	624	18	26	44
Asian	94	145	239	3	1	4
Other Race	0	1	1	0	0	0
Multiple Race*	17	20	37	1	0	1
Unknown	4	5	9	1	0	1
Subtotal	430	536	966	24	28	52
Foreign	4	11	15	0	0	0
Total	524	633	1,157	36	39	75

*Since 2002, students can select more than one race and / or ethnicity. **Those who did not choose 'Hispanic/Latino' or 'Non-Hispanic/Latino' are counted under 'Non-Hispanic/Latino'.
Data Source: AAMC Data Warehouse: Applicant-Matriculant File. as of 5/9/2007.

UNMHSC programs, information regarding the School of Medicine's curriculum, a presentation on financing medical education, a panel of students from various programs providing a question/answer session, lunch, afternoon tours of the Health Science Center, and mock interviews.

Contact: Marlene Ballejos, Supervisor of Admissions; 505-272-4766; 505-925-6031 Fax; *(http://hsc.unm.edu/som/admissions/)*

The Center for Native American Health (CNAH) partners with Albuquerque-area Indian tribes to target the recruitment of Native-American students and deliver the goals and objectives of Native American Research Centers for Health (NARCH). NARCH is a four-year funded National Institute of Health/Indian Health Service grant aimed to increase a cadre of American Indians into health careers and research. In collaboration with UNMHSC programs, students, and recruiters, the CNAH organizes campus tours and presentations for high school students, school counselors, school administrators and parents from Native-American communities.

Outreach to Native communities involves Native-American medical students and faculty travelling long distances to visit with high school students and their parents within their local communities. This allows potential students to gain insight into the determination and commitment necessary for their journey to becoming healers. Among the undergraduates, CNAH acts as a bridge between the HSC campus, the UNM main campus, and other tribal colleges. This year CNAH co-hosted a Native American Health Science Interest forum for undergraduates at the UNM main campus to encourage and foster interest in health careers. CNAH invites undergraduates interested in medicine to meet other Native-American medical students at the monthly luncheons it sponsors and to visit the HSC campus.

The Native-American medical students receive support to recruit and mentor other native students interested in medical school. Interested students are also connected with Native-American faculty for additional encouragement and guidance.

Contact: Joaquin Baca, Program Specialist; 505-925-4313; 505-272-6019 Fax; *(http://hsc.unm.edu/som/fcm/CNAH/S Development.shtml)*

Admissions
Because the School of Medicine is publicly supported, it has an implied obligation to train students who are likely to serve the state's expanding medical needs. For this reason, residents of New Mexico are given primary consideration for admission. In addition to a 3.0 grade-point average (GPA) and a composite Medical College Admission Test (MCAT) score of 22, the School of Medicine seeks a diverse student body and considers a wide range of factors when evaluating applicants for admission, including but not limited to, demonstrated intellectual capacity, academic achievement, work experiences, life experiences, academic and personal motivation, commitment to public service, the extent to which the applicant has overcome educational and/or economic obstacles, and other indicators that the applicant can succeed in medical studies and make a significant contribution to the School of Medicine community and the state of New Mexico. Furthermore, the UNM School of Medicine seeks the inclusion of students from groups that are underrepresented in medicine in New Mexico. An active minority recruitment program encourages applications from Hispanic, Native American, and African American residents of New Mexico. All applicants meeting the residency, GPA, and MCAT requirements receive individualized consideration and are reviewed competitively in one pool. Applicants who are not residents of New

Mexico, but who have a demonstrated tie to the state or who live in a state with a Western Interstate Commission on Higher Education (WICHE) agreement, must apply through the Early Decision Program (EDP).

The Office of Admissions offers post-admissions workshops to applicants who were not successful in gaining admission into medical school. Students are provided an assessment form to complete regarding various aspects of their application. The Assistant Dean for Admissions, and the Supervisor of Admissions meet with applicants individually to help applicants improve their applications and become more competitive in the application process.

Contact: Marlene Ballejos, Supervisor of Admissions; 505-272-4766; 505-925-6031 Fax; *(http://hsc.unm.edu/som/admissions/)*

Academic Support Programs
Through the Academic Success Center (ASC), the UNM School of Medicine provides assistance to students to enhance their learning skills. Consultation is available regarding study habits, learning skills, test-taking strategies, test anxiety, time management, problem-solving conceptualization, Myers-Briggs Type Indicator administration and interpretation, and other related areas of concern. After initial consultation, students may be directed toward available UNM or community resources, begin working on skills through ASC, or be referred to special courses (Board Review) or diagnostics as needed.

The *Peer Tutorial Program* is a partnership between the ASC and the Office of Diversity funded by the Office of Diversity. This program provides tutoring in basic science courses for medical students in their first and second years. Tutors are third- or fourth-year students who have generally excelled in the disciplines in which they tutor.

Contact: Pamela DeVoe,
Program Manager;
505-272-8972; 505-272-5084 Fax;
(http://hsc.unm.edu/som/excellence)

As part of the counseling program that has emphasis on eventual career choice, the Office of Student Services has established a First Clinician Advisor program to supplement the formal career advisement. This program pairs up four to five Phase I medical students with a practicing clinician at the UNM Hospital or affiliated VA hospital systems. The student meets with the advisor one- on-one, as needed, to assist in developing balance between studies, career, and personal life.

Contact: Cristina Beraun, Program Coordinator, Office of Student Services; 505-272-3414; 505-272-8239 Fax; *(http://hsc.unm.edu/som/oss/)*

The CNAH provides mentoring and role modeling opportunities for Native-American HSC students, as well as high school and undergraduate students interested in health careers and health research. On campus, CNAH shares all announcements of internships, scholarships, etc. with the Native-American students by e-mail. CNAH also offers information on internship possibilities and this year invited a representative from the Los Alamos National Laboratory to speak specifically about their internship programs at one of the CNAH student luncheons.

Contact: Joaquin Baca, Program Specialist; 505-925-4313; 505-272-6019 Fax; *(http://hsc.unm.edu/som/fcm/CNAH/ SDevelopment.shtml)*

Enrichment Programs

The UNM School of Medicine's Office of Diversity offers five distinct, yet inter-related, pipeline programs to increase the disadvantaged applicant pool into health professions in New Mexico. The Office

of Diversity was awarded a $1.6 million federal grant from the Health Resources and Services Administration in 2005 "to assist individuals from disadvantaged backgrounds to enter and graduate from a health or allied health professions program." Although the grant was not renewed, as of 2007 due to Title VII funding cuts, the School of Medicine has committed to continuing the education pipeline programs because of their importance to the people of New Mexico. The other colleges and partners involved in these programs have also committed to their continued participation and support of the following Health Careers Opportunity Programs (HCOP):

Dream Makers. The Dream Makers program is designed to establish and facilitate health career clubs at middle schools in the Albuquerque area, including the Native American Charter Academy and the Native-American community in Ramah, NM. The program's primary goals are to introduce young people to health professions, stimulate interest in science and math, and increase imagination in the areas of medicine and health. Current medical and other UNM Health Sciences Center students regularly assist with Dream Makers workshops in order to give middle school students a realistic sense of opportunities and potential for success in the health sciences fields. The program is offered during the regular school year.

Health Careers Academy (HCA). The Health Careers Academy is a six-week, nonresidential, summer program for rising high school freshmen, sophomores, and juniors. The HCA is designed to help strengthen ACT scores and provide academic enrichment in math, science, English and study skills. The program is also designed to provide exposure to various professions in the health care field. Participants attend presentations by UNM Health Sciences Center professionals, engage

in hands-on activities, and learn about various health careers.

Undergraduate Health Sciences Enrichment Program (UHSEP). The Undergraduate Health Science Enrichment Program is a six-week residential summer program that assists disadvantaged undergraduate students who attend or plan to attend an institution of higher learning in New Mexico. The program is designed to enhance academic preparation and facilitate entry into medical or allied health professions schools. The UHSEP program is separated into two separate residential summer sessions. UHSEP I takes place the summer before a student's freshman year. USHEP II takes place the summer before a student's junior year. UHSEP students attend classes in math, science, English, study skills, and humanities in medicine. They attend health professions seminars and educational and cultural field trips and participate in clinical volunteer job shadowing through community health clinics where preceptors will serve as mentors.

New Mexico Clinical Education Program. The New Mexico Clinical Education Program provides a six-week experience in a rural clinic setting by placing students in primary care facilities and community health centers throughout New Mexico. Students shadow physicians and participate in all areas of the clinic and the community. This program is offered to students who are seriously pursuing a medical or physical therapy career. Prior to placement in a rural clinic, students receive training in CPR/First Aid, intake procedures, and cultural competency and ethics. During the program, students volunteer for a 40-hour work week and are exposed to a variety of different opportunities such as community outreach and patient education; patient intake procedures; physical exams; diagnosis and treatments; emergency medical services and treatments; laboratory, pharmacy, and x-ray; and business management and administration.

Post-Baccalaureate Program (PBP).
Participants in the Post-Baccalaureate Program (PBP) are selected from the pool of medical school applicants by the UNM School of Medicine Admissions Committee. The PBP is a 14-month program where students participate in a summer MCAT preparation course, a two-semester academic program, and a final summer enrichment experience that will help prepare students for the rigors of the curriculum at the UNM School of Medicine. Upon successful completion of the program, students will matriculate into the following fall medical school class. PBP students receive one-on-one mentoring and advisement from School of Medicine admissions faculty on the PBP Advisory subcommittee. The School of Medicine has provided the institutional infrastructure required to assist disadvantaged students with programs including the following: cultural competence training, academic advocacy and counseling, laptop computer loan program, financial aid services, faculty mentorship, lending library, and academic peer tutoring.

Pathways to Pharmacy Program (PPP).
Participants in the Pathways to Pharmacy Program (PPP) are selected from the pool of pharmacy school applicants by the UNM College of Pharmacy (COP) Admissions Committee. PPP is a 12-month program where students will participate in a two-semester academic program, and a final summer enrichment experience that will help prepare students for the rigors of the curriculum at the UNM College of Pharmacy. Upon successful completion of the program, students will matriculate into the following fall pharmacy school class. The PPP participants receive counseling, mentoring, and advising throughout the PPP from UNM

COP faculty and admissions committee members.

Contact: Peter Couse, Student Recruiter, or Liliana Sosa, Program Coordinator, 505-272-2728; 505-272-6857 Fax; *(http://hsc.unm.edu/som/diversity/)*

The Hispanic Center of Excellence (COE) provides enrichment and professional development opportunities for Hispanic medical students and special programs for the general Health Sciences Center student population. The COE sponsors and coordinates the student lending library, the Academic Success Center, and the medical school's USMLE (United States Medical Licensing Exam), Step 1 support program. The COE sponsors Hispanic medical students with off-campus board review programs, as well as professional development experiences through conference travel. In addition, COE sponsors a Junior Faculty Development program which supports selected junior faculty members with research and professional development training and opportunities.

Contact: Pamela DeVoe, Program Manager; 505-272-8972; 505-272-5084 Fax; *(http://hsc.unm.edu/som/excellence)*

The student development program at the Center for Native-American Health is establishing health career clubs in coordination with school counselors within Native-American communities. These students from rural, isolated communities are eligible to receive financial support to attend national conferences where they are exposed to the possibilities in medicine. These students are also given various opportunities to obtain guidance from Native-American health professionals. A one-day session is provided for high school students to shadow a clinician in their local health centers to gain a better understanding of a career in medicine. Currently CNAH is working to get ACT preparatory workshops

delivered to communities by a university-based program.

COLORS is a university-based project designed to (1) familiarize students, teachers, and the community with health career programs and university facilities; (2) offer information on application processes; (3) introduce the numerous university support programs available to Native-American students; (4) introduce role models to attendees; and (5) demonstrate the university's commitment to listening to and addressing community specific needs. CNAH will host a COLORS event inviting students, teachers, and parents to a one-day event to tour the UNM Health Sciences Campus, learn about the CNAH and programs offered for students, learn about the health professions programs and meet individuals form each program, and learn about other programs that support students once they have entered the School of Medicine.

On the Road Program is geared towards familiarizing students and family members within tribal communities about health careers and the need for more Native-American health professionals. Native-American faculty who are role models and potential mentors will be the primary representatives from the university and those who visit the communities. The activities may include students' "shadowing" at a local clinic, hospital, dental office, etc.; a session on how to prepare for a health career; and, a hands-on workshop with UNM faculty presentations.

Work in the community schools has led to the formation of UNM Health Clubs designed to help students keep an interest in health careers and active in research.

Contact: Joaquin Baca, Program Specialist; 505-925-4313; 505-272-6019 Fax; *(http://hsc.unm.edu/som/fcm/CNAH/SDevelop ment.shtml)*

Student Financial Assistance

UNM offers a full range of federal, state and institutional scholarship, loan, and work programs to eligible School of Medicine students. Of particular interest to M.D. students who plan to practice in an underserved area of New Mexico is the Loan-for-Service program. This program provides up to $12,000 in funding per academic year to contracted individuals and is a state-funded program for New Mexico residents only. The School of Medicine has also been the beneficiary over the years of generous funding from the Federal Scholarships for Disadvantaged Students program (approximately $144,485 for the 2006-2007 academic year). Every dollar of this money is awarded to students who meet the federal definition of a student from a disadvantaged background.

In addition, the School of Medicine offers significant scholarship aid to students from its own endowed funds donated by affiliated agencies and groups. This includes a few full tuition scholarships as well as many smaller awards. The school also provides comprehensive loan exit counseling sessions to each graduating class, and with our partner, New Mexico Student Loans, we offer zero percent interest repayment on Stafford Loans for graduates who practice in New Mexico. Applicants to the University of New Mexico School of Medicine normally must remit a $50.00 application fee. Fee waivers will be considered when the applicant indicates he or she is disadvantaged on the American Medical College Application Service (AMCAS) application and writes a brief letter to the Assistant Dean for Admissions describing the reason for the waiver request.

Contact: Janell Valdez, Financial Aid Supervisor, Office of Financial Aid; 505-272-8008; 505-272-8063 Fax; *(http://hsc.unm.edu/som/finaid/)*

Educational Partnerships

The School of Medicine's Office of Diversity facilitates access to medical school for students from minority groups that are underrepresented in medicine in a collaborative effort with various educational partners.

Since August 2006, the Office of Diversity has led in the outreach, recruitment, and admissions for the combined B.A./M.D. Degree Program in partnership with the School of Medicine and College of Arts and Sciences. This program allows New Mexico high school seniors the opportunity to complete their Bachelor of Arts degree and, upon meeting program requirements, students will transfer into the School of Medicine to pursue their Doctor of Medicine (M.D.) degree. The program is an innovative approach to contributing to the diversity of the student body and to growing native New Mexican physicians who are committed to staying in the state and practicing medicine in the areas with the greatest need.

The Office of Diversity has established partnerships regarding educational pipeline and cultural competency issues. Some of our partners within UNM and the Health Science Center include the Colleges of Pharmacy and Nursing, the School of Law, the Southwest Hispanic Research Institute, the Student Services Ethnic Centers and Career Enrichment Programs, Recruitment Services, the Center for Native American Health, the Center of Excellence, and the Institute of Ethics. The Office of Diversity has also partnered with other departments within

UNM and the Health Science Center as well as other New Mexico educational institutions and the Area Health Education Centers.

The Office of Diversity has established several community partnerships to encourage New Mexico's children to consider all the various opportunities available in the health professions fields. The Office of Diversity is collaborating with ENgaging

Albany Medical College

Dr. Assie L. Bishop
Assistant Dean
Student Affairs/Minority Affairs
Albany Medical College
47 New Scotland Avenue
Albany, NY 12208
518-262-5824
518-262-5138 Fax
Bishopa@mail.amc.edu

Recruitment

A full-time Minority Affairs Office, headed by the Assistant Dean of Student Affairs/ Minority Affairs, directly supervises the recruitment process for minority applicants. The process includes visits to pre-medical summer programs, career days, and participation in many conferences with a pre-medical minority focus. Minority applicants receive personal follow-ups from the Minority Affairs Office regarding the status of their application and are encouraged to visit the Medical College. The Minority Affairs office coordinates campus visits and arranges overnight accommodations with minority medical students.

Admissions

All applicants apply through the Albany Medical College Admissions Office. The Assistant Dean for Student Affairs/ Minority Affairs works closely with the Admissions Office to assist them in identifying quality minority applicants. Once students are invited for an interview, the Assistant Dean for Student Affairs/Minority Affairs meets with the students on an informal basis to answer questions or address any concerns the students may have.

In identifying students for interview and for acceptance, Albany Medical College actively looks for other qualities in addition to a good grade-point average, and scores on the Medical College Admission Test (MCAT). We look for qualities such as motivation, persistence, and compassion, and in some cases what the student has had to overcome to get to this point.

All applicants are invited to an informal session hosted by currently enrolled students. In addition, all applicants are invited to attend a luncheon and tour of the school on the day of the interview. Albany Medical College students are present and can at the time give applicants further insight into the school and the admission process.

Academic Support Programs

Science and Technology Entry Program (STEP). This program is designed to provide support for screening, testing, counseling, tutoring, and teaching of New York state residents who are enrolled in secondary school; who exhibit the potential for college-level study, if provided with special services; and are either minority, historically underrepresented in the scientific, technical, health-related, and licensed professions, or economically disadvantaged. Albany Medical College has been involved with the Science and Technology Entry Program for at least 13 years.

Post-Baccalaureate Research Education Program (PREP)

The need to understand diseases that disproportionately affect medically underserved populations in this country has created a large demand for scientists who will commit to a research career to address these diseases. Thus, the Albany Medical College PREP program is a post-baccalaureate program designed to increase the number of underrepresented minorities

Albany Medical College, 2006
Applicants and Matriculants by Gender, Race and Ethnicity

Race and Ethnicity	Applicants			Matriculants		
	Women	Men	Total	Women	Men	Total
Hispanic/Latino						
Cuban	21	15	36	0	0	0
Mexican American	53	61	114	0	1	1
Puerto Rican	19	17	36	1	1	2
Other Hispanic	98	71	169	0	0	0
Multiple Hispanic*	12	9	21	0	0	0
Subtotal	203	173	376	1	2	3
Non-Hispanic/Latino**						
Black	171	118	289	0	1	1
Native American/Alaska Native	1	5	6	0	0	0
Native Hawaiian/Other Pacific Islander	20	12	32	2	0	2
White	1,630	1,958	3,588	35	39	74
Asian	1,135	1,094	2,229	23	15	38
Other Race	5	5	10	0	1	1
Multiple Race*	96	92	188	3	1	4
Unknown	31	36	67	5	1	6
Subtotal	3,089	3,320	6,409	68	58	126
Foreign	180	224	404	4	2	6
Total	3,472	3,717	7,189	73	62	135

*Since 2002, students can select more than one race and / or ethnicity. **Those who did not choose Hispanic/Latino' or 'Non-Hispanic/Latino' are counted under 'Non-Hispanic/Latino'.

Data Source: AAMC Data Warehouse: Applicant-Matriculant File, as of 5/9/2007.

who go on to graduate school to earn the Ph.D. or the M.D./Ph.D. and do research on diseases that disproportionately affect minorities and the medically underserved.

Through employment as Research Apprentices, participants will acquire stronger research skills and will improve the competitiveness necessary for the successful pursuit of a doctoral degree. Research Apprentices will be engaged actively in meaningful, and authentic mentored research, working alongside their mentors who are faculty members in the interdisciplinary research centers of the Graduate Studies Program at Albany Medical College.

Individuals interested in being considered for PREP: Addressing Health Disparities-should send a completed application packet (i.e., application form, all undergraduate transcripts, personal statement, "challenge" essay, and a letter of recommendation from and undergraduate instructor) which can be obtained by e-mail request.

Application Fee: No application fee is required

Application Deadline: Since each applicant's program will be specific and individualized, the application can be made at any time. If you would like more information, do not hesitate to contact the PREP Admissions Coordinator, 518-262-0974, or e-mail *(prep@mail.amc.edu)* with questions or concerns at any time.

Student Financial Assistance

A scholarship is available primarily for minority students. This scholarship is made available by a member of the Albany City Community. All other financial assistance is based on demonstrable need. Applicants may apply for a waiver of the application fee if they consider themselves financially disadvantaged.

Educational Partnerships

Students who participate in the enrichment program are from the local high schools. There are no formal partnerships. Albany Medical College has a partnership with several local colleges in the area. The Medical College has an accelerated B.S./M.D. program where students will do three or four years at the undergraduate institution and then matriculate into Albany Medical College.

AAMC

Albert Einstein College of Medicine of Yeshiva University*

Nilda I. Soto, Assistant Dean
Office of Diversity Enhancement and
Dr. Milton Gumbs, Associate Dean Office
of Diversity Enhancement
Albert Einstein College of
Medicine of Yeshiva University
1300 Morris Park Avenue, Belfer 205
Bronx, NY 10461
718-430-3091; 718-430-8825 Fax
soto@aecom.yu.edu

Recruitment

Minority student recruitment is conducted through the Office of Diversity Enhancement. Faculty members and enrolled medical students also take an active part in these efforts. The College of Medicine participates annually in the National Association of Medical Minority Educators, Inc.'s Student Recruitment Workshop and the Health Careers Conferences sponsored by the various ASPIRA organizations. In addition, visits are made to colleges, both local and out-of-state, in order to speak to student groups interested in medicine as a career. The Office of Diversity Enhancement works closely with pre-medical advisors at various undergraduate institutions.

The Office of Diversity Enhancement and enrolled minority students sponsor an annual recruitment luncheon for prospective applicants.

Admissions

In selecting students for interview and for acceptance, attention is paid not only to the traditional indicators of success, such as grade-point average and Medical College Admission Test scores, but also to those qualities that a student must possess in order to become a good physician. Among these are good character, strong motivation, perseverance, and compassion.

All students are invited to attend a luncheon and tour of the school on the day of the interview. Einstein medical students are present and can, at that time, give applicants further insight into the school and the admissions process.

Academic Support Programs

The Office of Diversity Enhancement, in conjunction with the Associate Dean for Students and Clinical Education and the Academic Support and Counseling Program, closely follows the academic progress of students. Should difficulties arise, students are counseled and may be advised to avail themselves of tutorial assistance or the services of the Cognitive Skills Program. These services are provided to all students free of charge upon their request. Extensive syllabi, which cover the lecture material, are provided for most subjects in the basic sciences.

Since many academic problems arise because of personal difficulties rather than intellectual unpreparedness, a large part of the retention effort involves non-academic supports.

There are chapters of the Student National Medical Association and the Boricua Latino Health Organization at Einstein. Both are quite active in undergraduate advisement, recruitment efforts, and important issues of society and health. The Office of Diversity Enhancement assigns each incoming student a Big Brother/Sister from the second-year class. The support that the students provide to each other, both directly and through their various activities, is invaluable and can, literally, mean the difference between success and failure.

Albert Einstein College of Medicine of Yeshiva University, 2006
Applicants and Matriculants by Gender, Race and Ethnicity

Race and Ethnicity	Applicants			Matriculants		
	Women	Men	Total	Women	Men	Total
Hispanic/Latino						
Cuban	17	19	36	1	0	1
Mexican American	53	48	101	0	0	0
Puerto Rican	20	30	50	2	3	5
Other Hispanic	103	74	177	3	3	6
Multiple Hispanic*	14	11	25	0	0	0
Subtotal	207	182	389	6	6	12
Non-Hispanic/Latino**						
Black	192	120	312	6	3	9
Native American/Alaska Native	1	2	3	0	0	0
Native Hawaiian/Other Pacific Islander	14	10	24	0	0	0
White	1,456	1,665	3,121	55	60	115
Asian	971	993	1,964	19	17	36
Other Race	4	2	6	0	0	0
Multiple Race*	83	72	155	5	1	6
Unknown	27	44	71	0	0	0
Subtotal	2,748	2,908	5,656	85	81	166
Foreign	184	216	400	5	0	5
Total	3,139	3,306	6,445	96	87	183

*Since 2002, students can select more than one race and / or ethnicity. **Those who did not choose 'Hispanic/Latino' or 'Non-Hispanic/Latino' are counted under 'Non-Hispanic/Latino'.
Data Source: AAMC Data Warehouse: Applicant-Matriculant File, as of 5/9/2007.

Association of American Medical Colleges, 2007

Enrichment Programs

The Department of Biochemistry offers a *preparatory course* in medical genetics, immunology, and biochemistry during the two-week period preceding the start of classes. Aside from serving to introduce the students to courses in the first-year curriculum, the course helps to introduce the students to each other, to some faculty members, and to the school environment. Participation is voluntary and is recommended to students whose basic science background is weak or limited in content or scope. In addition, incoming minority students are invited to a special Retreat Weekend prior to the start of classes.

Minority Student Summer Research Opportunity Program. Designed for undergraduates who have completed their sophomore or junior year, this program provides eight and one-half weeks of experience in biomedical research. Students receive a stipend and free housing for students not able to commute.

Hispanic Center of Excellence. The Institute for Community and Collaborative Health of the Albert Einstein College of Medicine was awarded a grant from the Department of Health and Human Services to initiate a Hispanic Center of Excellence. Einstein has submitted a proposal to continue the funding and activities of the Hispanic Center of Excellence. It is the first Center of Excellence in New York State, and it serves to reinforce the participation and presence of the college in all areas of the Bronx community and the Hispanic populations of New York. The Center highlights the college's longstanding institutional commitment to underrepresented minorities in the Bronx and throughout the city and state and provides leadership in research and education on Hispanic health issues and disparities in health care. The Center develops innovative methods to strengthen and enhance the academic performance by minority students, improves educational diversity and cultural competency for all students and faculty, and fosters minority faculty development and promotion.

The center assists with mentoring programs for minority students at Albert Einstein in order to enhance the academic success of the minority students by offering a faculty-mentoring program, which includes office-based experiences with community-based Hispanic physicians. It also provides an annual career-planning workshop for pre-clinical and clinical minority students. The center is active in the development of culturally competent problem-based learning (PBL) seminars in the six-week clerkship in family medicine required of all third-year medical schools. The center provides assistance with the cross-cultural interviewing session that is included in the introduction to clinical medicine course in the first year.

Student Financial Assistance

Application fees are waived for financially-needy students. Financial aid is available to minority students on the basis of financial need and consists of scholarships and awards, in addition to the well-known loan programs. No students should be discouraged from applying due to lack of funds.

Educational Partnerships

The Einstein Enrichment Program (EEP) is an after school program for high school students from the Bronx who are either economically disadvantaged or minorities historically underrepresented in scientific, medical, and health related professions. EEP is funded through the New York State Education Department's Science and Technology Entry Program (STEP). EEP renders a holistic approach and provides support, at all levels, in order to enhance the academic abilities and address the special needs of secondary school students. Academic support is provided in the form of regents review, SAT preparation, cognitive instruction in writing, study skills, and critical thinking. Career advisement and college admission and information workshops, on career paths and options, are presented. Individual and group counseling is offered. The program runs for 30 weeks during the academic year and six weeks in the summer. In the academic year, high school seniors are placed in a laboratory or clinical research setting. During the summer, all students are put in placements. The placements allow students to acquire actual hands-on experiences that provide them with the knowledge and skills necessary for careers in medicine, science, and technology.

AAMC

Columbia University College of Physicians and Surgeons

Dr. Hilda Y. Hutcherson, Associate Dean
Michele Jordan-Davis, Assistant Dean
Office of Diversity
Columbia University College of
Physicians and Surgeons
630 West 168th Street
Third Floor, Suite 401
New York, NY 10032
212-305-4157; 212-305-1049 Fax
www.oda-ps.cumc.columbia.edu

Recruitment

The Office of Diversity assists with the recruitment and nurturing of underrepresented and/or disadvantaged students. Activities include Web and e-mail outreach, participation at recruitment seminars and conferences, and visits to colleges by faculty, administrators and students. Organized visits by prospective applicants are scheduled whenever possible. Such visits feature counseling sessions, opportunities to see the campus, and discussions with medical students. The Office of Diversity regularly provides pre-medical career counseling and advice to individual high school and college students.

The Office of Diversity presents an annual Recruitment Day Conference that provides detailed information to potential underrepresented in medicine students. General topics are covered as well as specific information about the College of Physicians and Surgeons (P&S). P&S has a very active, cohesive, and effective Black and Latino Students Organization (BALSO), which is supported by the Office of Diversity. BALSO is active internally and externally with all Office of Diversity recruitment efforts. BALSO students sponsor pre-enrollment orientation activities for new students, as well as a variety of academic support and social programs.

The Office of Diversity works closely with community outreach programs sponsored by Columbia University Medical Center.

Admissions

Columbia University College of Physicians and Surgeons participates in the American Medical College Application Service (AMCAS) application process. Admission information can be located on the admissions Web site. The Office of Diversity works closely with the Admissions Office. Applicants are encouraged to visit the Office of Diversity at the time of their interviews. Arrangements such as breakfast meetings are made for provision of additional information, tours and meetings with other underrepresented students. Minority faculty serve as active members of the Admissions Committee.

Academic Support Programs

Academic support programs are available to all P&S students, including a student-skills assessment and building program for entering first-year students. During the first year, the program includes the formation of intense, course-oriented study groups, which are popular among students. The Student Success Network (SSN) offers services to help make first-year students' adjustment to medical school a smooth one. SSN promotes a sense of teamwork through regular small-group review sessions, facilitated by second-year students. Tutors are also available free of charge.

Advisory Deans serve as mentors who enhance each P&S student's education by providing support in curriculum, academic progress, professional development, residency choices and all things necessary

Columbia University College of Physicians and Surgeons, 2006
Applicants and Matriculants by Gender, Race and Ethnicity

Race and Ethnicity	Applicants			Matriculants		
	Women	Men	Total	Women	Men	Total
Hispanic/Latino						
Cuban	23	18	41	0	0	0
Mexican American	59	65	124	2	2	4
Puerto Rican	27	27	54	3	5	8
Other Hispanic	93	83	176	2	1	3
Multiple Hispanic*	12	13	25	0	0	0
Subtotal	214	206	420	7	8	15
Non-Hispanic/Latino**						
Black	260	159	419	3	8	11
Native American/Alaska Native	1	7	8	0	1	1
Native Hawaiian/Other Pacific Islander	10	6	16	0	0	0
White	1,307	1,687	2,994	39	52	91
Asian	829	890	1,719	16	10	26
Other Race	3	3	6	0	0	0
Multiple Race*	92	90	182	2	3	5
Unknown	29	39	68	1	1	2
Subtotal	2,531	2,881	5,412	61	75	136
Foreign	204	179	383	3	1	4
Total	2,949	3,266	6,215	71	84	155

*Since 2002, students can select more than one race and / or ethnicity. **Those who did not choose 'Hispanic/Latino' or 'Non-Hispanic/Latino' are counted under 'Non-Hispanic/Latino'.
Data Source: AAMC Data Warehouse: Applicant-Matriculant File, as of 5/9/2007.

to make P&S students even more successful in their careers and personal achievements. In addition, each new student is assigned an advisor from among members of the second-year class.

BALSO students provide extensive counseling with strong ties established between members of the second- and first-year classes. *Brother/Sister* arrangements provide valuable guidance from more senior students. Also, BALSO features several special group tutorials.

Retention rates for underrepresented minority students at P&S are very high. Students are recognized annually as recipients of nationally competitive awards for academic scholarships and are frequently selected for graduation prizes and awards. Students are highly sought after for residency programs.

Enrichment Programs

Summer Medical and Dental Education Program (SMDEP) Columbia is a SMDEP site hosting approximately 80 (60 pre-medical/20 pre-dental) college students for a six-week in-residence program for academic and study skills enrichment, clinical experiences and counseling. Web site: *(www.smdep.org)*

The New York State Science and Technology Entry Program This program supports S-PREP, an innovative, year-long program for underrepresented students who are seriously interested in pursuing a career in medicine or in other health professions. The program, organized and run by the Office of Diversity for over 20 years, features medical science courses taught on Saturdays at P&S with P&S students functioning as teachers and preceptors. Academically talented high school students in grades nine-12 are encouraged to participate in the program.

Web site: *(www.oda-ps.cumc.columbia.edu/ prep.html)*

Student Financial Assistance

Application fees are waived for financially-needy students. Financial aid is available to students on the basis of financial need and consists of scholarships and awards, in addition to the well-known loan programs. No student should be discouraged from applying due to lack of funds. The Student Financial Planning office works closely with the Office of Diversity during the recruiting and post admissions process. All P&S students are assigned a counselor upon entry for their class. This will determine need, financial aid packages, and work closely with that class throughout medical school. Financial Aid Officers have posted walk-in hours each week to handle questions that can be quickly resolved. Intense financial planning and debt management seminars are held regularly for students. All students complete an exit interview upon graduation.

Web site: *(http://cpmcnet.columbia.edu/ student/finaid/aboutus.html)*

Educational Partnerships

P&S is actively involved with community groups, state and national organizations, and partnerships with many local school systems to ensure the achievement of students underrepresented in medicine.

Web sites:
(www.amsny.org)
(www.msiahec.org)
(www.heaf.org)

AAMC

Cornell University Joan & Sanford I. Weill Medical College and Graduate School of Medical Sciences

Dr. Carlyle H. Miller
Associate Dean for Student Affairs
and Equal Opportunity Programs
Weill Medical College
of Cornell University
445 East 69th Street, Room 110
New York, NY 10021
212-746-1057; 212-746-8211 Fax
chm2031@med.cornell.edu
http://www.med.cornell.edu

Recruitment

The faculty at Cornell University's Weill Medical College (WMC) has long recognized that society's needs will be better met by increasing the numbers of men and women in the health science fields from minority groups underrepresented in medicine. Accordingly, a studious effort is made to attract talented minority students to WMC. WMC actively recruits on a nationwide basis to assure that each entering medical school class will be a diverse group of capable, prospective physicians. At WMC, diversity means the inclusion of students representative of populations that are most affected by physician shortages.

Since New York City is one of the great urban academic centers in the United States, the Weill Medical College welcomes visits to its facilities from prospective medical school students who live in the area or who may be visiting. Faculty and students are also eager to participate in pre-medical conferences sponsored by various minority organizations.

Admissions

Weill Medical College does not have a separate admissions committee or subcommittee for applicants from minority groups underrepresented in medicine. Students from minority backgrounds apply to WMC in the same way as other applicants. The Admissions Committee consists of approximately 30 people and, at present, eight members are from underrepresented minority groups.

Academic Support Programs

There is no specific academic support program for students prior to or during their stay at WMC as medical students. When any student encounters academic difficulties, the problem is handled by assistance from faculty.

Enrichment Programs

Travelers Summer Research Fellowship Program for Pre-medical Students. The primary purpose of this program is not to entice students to WMC for their medical education, but to provide pre-medical students from diverse backgrounds with an experience in medical research. It also gives them deeper insights into the field of medicine, including issues that greatly affect the health of traditionally underserved groups. Participants in the program come from a wide range of undergraduate institutions and, to be eligible, must have completed their junior year in a pre-medical curriculum. Through the experiences of laboratory research, classroom lectures, and seminars on public health issues, the fellows gain a clear picture of the demands and opportunities they will encounter in choosing medicine as a career. A popular feature of this seven-week program is the assignment of each participant to a fourth-year medical student, who serves as a clinical tutor and takes the summer student on

Cornell University Joan & Sanford I. Weill Medical College, 2006
Applicants and Matriculants by Gender, Race and Ethnicity

Race and Ethnicity	Applicants			Matriculants		
	Women	Men	Total	Women	Men	Total
Hispanic/Latino						
Cuban	20	20	40	2	0	2
Mexican American	42	47	89	0	1	1
Puerto Rican	22	29	51	1	1	2
Other Hispanic	72	77	149	5	2	7
Multiple Hispanic*	6	13	19	1	0	1
Subtotal	162	186	348	9	4	13
Non-Hispanic/Latino**						
Black	180	122	302	3	3	6
Native American/Alaska Native	4	4	8	1	0	1
Native Hawaiian/Other Pacific Islander	7	4	11	0	0	0
White	1,160	1,415	2,575	20	33	53
Asian	697	778	1,475	12	9	21
Other Race	3	1	4	0	0	0
Multiple Race*	90	77	167	3	1	4
Unknown	23	52	75	2	0	2
Subtotal	2,164	2,453	4,617	41	46	87
Foreign	134	136	270	0	1	1
Total	2,460	2,775	5,235	50	51	101

*Since 2002, students can select more than one race and / or ethnicity. **Those who did not choose 'Hispanic/Latino' or 'Non-Hispanic/Latino' are counted under 'Non-Hispanic/Latino'.
Data Source: AAMC Data Warehouse: Applicant-Matriculant File, as of 5/9/2007.

Association of American Medical Colleges, 2007

weekly rounds at New York Presbyterian Hospital Weill Cornell campus to observe the care of patients. A number of the participants in this program subsequently apply to WMC. The Travelers Foundation funds this summer program.

Tri-Institutional M.D.-Ph.D. Program.
This program sponsors a summer program in biomedical research for college students who have completed their freshman or sophomore years with distinction. This is an opportunity for students to test and develop their interest in pursuing a combined degree program, while providing the student hands-on research experience that is considered highly among the criteria for admission to M.D.–Ph.D. programs. Students should contact Dr. Olaf Anderson, Program Director, 212-746-6023, for further information.

Student Financial Assistance
The application fee will be waived for students with the American Medical College Application Service (AMCAS) fee waiver. Others who would find it extremely difficult financially to pay the application fee should contact the Office of Admissions. There are no special funds set aside specifically for minority group students, but financial aid in the form of grants and loans is made available to all students according to financial need, within the limits of available funds for a given year. Although tuition is high, there is subsidized student housing available for all medical students.

Mount Sinai School of Medicine of New York University

Dr. Gary Butts, Associate Dean for Multicultural Affairs and Director, Center for Multicultural & Community Affairs
Mount Sinai School of Medicine
One Gustave Levy Place—Box 1257
5th Floor Annenberg Building
Room 5-16
New York, New York 10029
212-241-8276; 212-241-3594 Fax
gary.butts@mssm.edu; cmca@mssm.edu
www.mssm.edu/cmca

Center for Multicultural & Community Affairs
The Center for Multicultural and Community Affairs (CMCA), formerly the Office of Multicultural and Community Affairs, was established by the Mount Sinai School of Medicine (MSSM) in 1998 to increase underrepresented minority groups (URMs) in medicine, adding to the diversity of the school and the hospital and to Mount Sinai's effectiveness in serving the ethnically and racially diverse communities of East Harlem, Harlem, the Bronx, Queens, and New York City. CMCA is the interface for educational pipeline programs, minority affairs, institution-wide diversity initiatives, academic supports for medical students, and culture and medicine programs within the School of Medicine. The center's mission is to support improving community health outcomes and reducing race/ethnic health outcome disparities through increasing health care work force diversity and scientific inquiry, which impacts health policy.

Mount Sinai School of Medicine of New York University, 2006
Applicants and Matriculants by Gender, Race and Ethnicity

Race and Ethnicity	Applicants			Matriculants		
	Women	Men	Total	Women	Men	Total
Hispanic/Latino						
Cuban	17	20	37	2	0	2
Mexican American	52	37	89	0	1	1
Puerto Rican	27	25	52	0	1	1
Other Hispanic	101	71	172	8	2	10
Multiple Hispanic*	14	9	23	0	1	1
Subtotal	211	162	373	10	5	15
Non-Hispanic/Latino**						
Black	223	124	347	4	3	7
Native American/Alaska Native	3	7	10	0	0	0
Native Hawaiian/Other Pacific Islander	11	9	20	0	0	0
White	1,528	1,555	3,083	36	30	66
Asian	945	897	1,842	5	10	15
Other Race	6	2	8	0	0	0
Multiple Race*	116	71	187	7	1	8
Unknown	34	44	78	2	1	3
Subtotal	2,866	2,709	5,575	54	45	99
Foreign	158	150	308	4	6	10
Total	3,235	3,021	6,256	68	56	124

*Since 2002, students can select more than one race and / or ethnicity. **Those who did not choose Hispanic/Latino' or 'Non-Hispanic/Latino' are counted under 'Non-Hispanic/Latino'.
Data Source: AAMC Data Warehouse: Applicant-Matriculant File, as of 5/9/2007.

Recruitment

The School of Medicine's recruitment program includes visits by the Center for Multicultural & Community Affairs, faculty, admissions, and students to colleges in the New York metropolitan area, the northeastern states, and selected undergraduate institutions in other areas of the country (i.e., Historically Black Colleges and Universities and Hispanic-Serving Institutions). Information on the MSSM is provided to selected students on the Medical Minority Applicant Registry and from individual requests.

The Center for Multicultural & Community Affairs conducts an annual Open House event for minority student applicants in the fall. The Center for Multicultural & Community Affairs and the Office of Admissions may arrange on-site visits for students in pre-medical clubs and societies. The MSSM conducts a summer internship program and a winter Medical College Admission Test (MCAT) preparation and review program for undergraduate students. On-campus year-round high school science enrichment and internship programs are conducted under the Secondary Education Through Health (SETH) program, the Life Sciences Secondary School, and the Mount Sinai Scholars Program at the Manhattan Center for Science and Mathematics. In a multicultural environment, these programs serve educationally and economically disadvantaged students who have strong interest in careers in medicine and biomedical sciences.

Admissions

All applicants to MSSM are evaluated on the basis of academic performance, MCAT scores, pre-medical committee letters of recommendation, extracurricular activities, and the degree of interest and motivation apparent in the application or evidenced upon interview. The Admissions Committee thoroughly reviews the applications of students from underrepresented minority and educationally disadvantaged backgrounds. Actions are then taken based on these recommendations. Minority faculty and minority student representation are present on the Admissions Committee. Application fees may be waived upon appropriate request.

Academic Support Programs

Summer Enrichment Program. This pre-enrollment program is offered to accepted students who might benefit from such reinforcement. The program includes work in chemistry and mathematics (essential for medicine), cell biology, and introduction to anatomy. Hospital experience is also an integral part of the program. The program is directed by a full-time faculty member and assisted by student tutors. These same students also receive academic counseling and tutoring support through our Learning Center, developed in partnership between CMCA and the Office of Curricular Support, and overseen by the Associate Dean for Undergraduate Medical Education.

During the academic year a retention program exists, consisting of ongoing tutorials by a full-time faculty member as well as tutorials on an individual departmental basis as needed. Review courses in preparation for the United States Medical Licensing Examination (USMLE) Step 1 and Step 2 are given during the academic year. The goals of the retention program are:

- The identification of the student in academic difficulty, as early as possible, so as to assist in improving his/her performance prior to completion of (or failure in) the course;
- The provision of milieu in which students with particular academic difficulty may function in their peer group with a minimum of anxiety; and
- The provision of individual academic support, if needed, to all students admitted to the MSSM so that their medical education may be completed.

Student Financial Assistance

It is the policy of the school to provide as much financial assistance as possible to all students who require such assistance in order to maintain attendance. Students who are accepted for admissions are provided financial assistance applications on which they may document their requests for financial aid. Applications are treated confidentially and awards are made by a faculty committee on financial aid. Each application is considered on an individual basis so that the greatest support for the most needy students may be distributed.

Educational Partnerships

Through the Center of Excellence in Youth Education (CEYE), overseen by the Center for Multicultural & Community Affairs, the majority of educational pipeline programs are administered and directed for high schools and colleges, representing a 30-year institutional commitment. It has a remarkable science enrichment and career exploration infrastructure for educating students from diverse backgrounds. CEYE's year-round programs include: Science Technology Entry Program (STEP), Scholars and Mentoring Program, the Bio-Science Studies Institute, a Collegiate Careers in Medicine and Research Program, and SAT and MCAT Prep Programs.

New York Medical College

Dr. Gladys M. Ayala, Associate Dean
Student and Minority Affairs
New York Medical College
Administration Building, Room 156
Valhalla, NY 10595
914-594-3016; 914-594-4514 Fax
gladys_ayala@nymc.edu

Recruitment

The New York Medical College recruitment strategy includes recruitment visits to undergraduate colleges, participation in career day programs, attendance at professional organization recruitment conferences, and individual counseling of students interested in pursuing a medical career. Also information on the Medical College is provided through individual requests. The Associate Dean, Assistant Dean, medical students, alumni, faculty, and administrators participate in the recruitment efforts.

The College conducts a college preparatory program for minority and disadvantaged high school students, which exposes the students to the academic excellence necessary to pursue career in medicine.

Admissions

The Admissions Committee has no preference as to a major field of undergraduate study, however, any college work submitted must include specified credits in chemistry, physics, biology, and English. Science courses must include substantial laboratory work. The Admissions Committee members consists of faculty from the basic sciences departments, clinical departments and administrators. The Associate Dean of Student and Minority Affairs and Assistant Dean, Minority Affairs are members of the Admission Committee.

Academic Support Programs

The following services are available to all students throughout the year: the decelerated program, individualized tutorial assistance arranged at no cost to the student, personal guidance, career advisement, and the Student Counseling Services.

Student Financial Assistance

Financial aid is awarded on the basis of need; scholarships, based on academic merit and need, are available to entering students. The College provides debt management and loan counseling services.

New York Medical College, 2006
Applicants and Matriculants by Gender, Race and Ethnicity

Race and Ethnicity	Applicants			Matriculants		
	Women	Men	Total	Women	Men	Total
Hispanic/Latino						
Cuban	32	32	64	0	0	0
Mexican American	78	83	161	0	1	1
Puerto Rican	27	30	57	1	1	2
Other Hispanic	140	99	239	6	3	9
Multiple Hispanic*	23	13	36	1	0	1
Subtotal	300	257	557	8	5	13
Non-Hispanic/Latino**						
Black	274	153	427	1	0	1
Native American/Alaska Native	1	6	7	0	0	0
Native Hawaiian/Other Pacific Islander	23	21	44	0	0	0
White	2,224	2,532	4,756	50	60	110
Asian	1,464	1,470	2,934	43	22	65
Other Race	10	4	14	0	0	0
Multiple Race*	138	120	258	1	2	3
Unknown	39	53	92	2	0	2
Subtotal	4,173	4,359	8,532	97	84	181
Foreign	209	219	428	0	0	0
Total	4,682	4,835	9,517	105	89	194

*Since 2002, students can select more than one race and / or ethnicity. **Those who did not choose
'Hispanic/Latino' or 'Non-Hispanic/Latino' are listed under 'Non-Hispanic/Latino'.
Data Source: AAMC Data Warehouse: Applicant-Matriculant File, as of 5/9/2007.

New York University School of Medicine

Mekbib Gemeda
Assistant Dean for Diversity Affairs
and Community Health
550 First Avenue, SLH
New York, NY 10016
212-263 8948; 212-263 6526 Fax
mekbib.gemeda@med.nyu.edu
http://www.med.nyu.edu/diversity_
affairs/index.html

Recruitment

New York University School of Medicine conducts a robust recruitment program in which faculty, students, deans, and administrators of programs are actively involved. The programs include the following:

Presentations at universities and colleges across the United States and Puerto Rico. These visits are coordinated by the Office of Diversity Affairs, the Sackler Institute for Graduate Biomedical Sciences, and the M.D./Ph.D. program, and the presentations are given by the Director of the Institute, Joel Oppenheim, the Director of the M.D./Ph.D. program, Rodney Ulane, and the Director of the Office of Diversity Affairs, Mekbib Gemeda. Contact person: Mekbib Gemeda, *(mekbib.gemeda@med.nyu.edu).*

Visits for student groups from universities and colleges in the Northeast. We organize these visits through minority student clubs, biology and premed clubs and pre-medical offices at institutions in the area. Contact person: Mekbib Gemeda *(mekbib.gemeda@med.nyu.edu).*

Exhibits at national meetings for underrepresented students interested in science and medicine. These meetings include the Annual Biomedical Research Conference for Minority Students (ABRCMS), the Annual Conference of the Society for the Advancement of Chicanos and Native Americans in Science (SACNAS), The Student National Medical Association Meeting (SNMA), the Latino Medical Student Association (LMSA), as well as the AAMC, NAMEE, AMSA, NMA, and AMA conferences.

An *annual career day* for students in the tri-state area interested in pursuing bio-medical careers is also hosted by the school. Contact Person: Martha Laureano, *(martha.laureano@med.nyu.edu).*

A ten-week Summer Undergraduate Research Program for students from institutions across the U.S. and Puerto Rico who are interested in pursuing graduate biomedical and medical training. The program is part of the Leadership Alliance program, a consortium of 29 leading research and teaching institutions. At the end of the program, the students attend a three-day Leadership Alliance Symposium where they present their research findings to deans, faculty, and administrators from Alliance Institutions.

Tours of the school and hospitals and a meeting with current minority students at the medical school are organized for students invited for interviews. We also organize a revisit weekend for students admitted into the medical school.

Bridging the gap is a mentoring program for minority undergraduate students at New York University who are interested in medicine. The program involves minority medical students and faculty at New York University School of Medicine and is coordinated by the Pre-Professional Office and the Black and Latino Student Association at the School of Medicine.

High School Fellows Program is a science enrichment and direct clinical and/or research experience at NYU Medical Center for motivated high school students

New York University School of Medicine, 2006
Applicants and Matriculants by Gender, Race and Ethnicity

Race and Ethnicity		Applicants			Matriculants		
		Women	Men	Total	Women	Men	Total
Hispanic/Latino							
Cuban		25	19	44	3	1	4
Mexican American		55	57	112	0	1	1
Puerto Rican		39	35	74	1	0	1
Other Hispanic		115	84	199	3	2	5
Multiple Hispanic*		11	14	25	0	2	2
	Subtotal	245	209	454	7	6	13
Non-Hispanic/Latino**							
Black		237	157	394	3	2	5
Native American/Alaska Native		5	6	11	0	1	1
Native Hawaiian/Other Pacific Islander		7	8	15	0	0	0
White		1,818	1,957	3,775	46	48	94
Asian		1,171	1,109	2,280	23	17	40
Other Race		6	5	11	0	0	0
Multiple Race*		117	101	218	4	1	5
Unknown		39	59	98	1	0	1
	Subtotal	3,400	3,402	6,802	77	69	146
Foreign		77	90	167	0	1	1
	Total	3,722	3,701	7,423	84	76	160

*Since 2002, students can select more than one race and / or ethnicity. **Those who did not choose 'Hispanic/Latino' or 'Non-Hispanic/Latino' are counted under 'Non-Hispanic/Latino'.
Data Source: AAMC Data Warehouse: Applicant-Matriculant File, as of 5/9/2007.

Association of American Medical Colleges, 2007

in the New York City school system. The program includes an intensive summer semester and a fall/spring session.

Network for minorities in science. The Director of the Office of Diversity Affairs manages the largest online network for minorities in science, (*JustGarciaHill.org*). The site has a growing membership of over 6,000 underrepresented minorities at all levels in the pipeline, from undergraduates to senior scientists.

Admissions
New York University School of Medicine participates in the American Medical College Application Service (AMCAS). The Admissions Committee evaluates applications and selected candidates are invited for an interview. The candidate's academic, professional, and personal experience is evaluated to determine eligibility for admission. This allows candidates to present their best qualities to the admissions committee.

Academic Support Programs
Faculty advisement and tutoring are made available to all students. A "how to navigate" workshop is offered to entering students and students transitioning to the third year. In addition, underrepresented minority students are linked to resident and faculty role-model mentors.

Enrichment Programs
A ten-week Summer Undergraduate Research Program is offered for students from institutions across the United States and Puerto Rico who are interested in pursuing graduate biomedical and medical training. The program is part of the Leadership Alliance program a consortium of 29 leading research and teaching institutions. At the end of the program, the students attend a three-day Leadership Alliance Symposium where they present their research findings to deans, faculty and administrators from Alliance

Institutions. URL: (*http://www.med.nyu.edu/parasitology/training/surp.html*) Contact Person: Mekbib Gemeda (*mekbib.gemeda@med.nyu.edu*).

Science enrichment and direct clinical and/or research experiences at NYU Medical Center are offered for motivated high school students in the New York City school system. The program includes an intensive summer semester and a fall/spring session. Contact Person: Martha Laureano, (*martha.laureano@med.nyu.edu*).

Student Financial Assistance
Financial need-based scholarships and fee waivers are available for students. Students are encouraged to demonstrate financial need in their AMCAS applications. Debt management and financial planning programs and workshops are also offered.

Educational Partnerships
Salk School of Science. Established in 1995 as a joint program of the NYU School of Medicine and New York City's School District 2, the Salk School of Science is an innovative attempt to improve science teaching in a middle school by involving members of the medical/scientific community. The school emphasizes hands-on, in-depth exploration of the physical/ chemical, life, and earth sciences. NYU faculty and students work directly with Salk pupils in a variety of activities that create a connection between biomedical science and the sciences in the Salk curriculum.

Salk students are from all five boroughs of New York City. To gain admission they must complete a competitive four-part assessment process that includes science, math, a written response to a piece of text and a personal interview. As a public school, Salk mirrors its host district in demographics. A third of the 186 students currently enrolled are black or Hispanic; another third are Asian (90 percent of this group are recent immigrants living in nearby Chinatown with non-English speaking parents); 46 percent of students are from low-income households (as indicated by the City's free lunch program); and 40 percent are female, the same percentage as in New York City's three science-oriented high schools.

AAMC

State University of New York Downstate Medical Center College of Medicine

Dr. Constance H. Hill
Associate Dean for Minority Affairs
State University of New York Downstate
Medical Center, College of Medicine
450 Clarkson Avenue, Box 1186
Brooklyn, NY 11201
718-270-3033; 718-270-1929 Fax
chill@downstate.edu
http://sls.downstate.edu/minorityaffairs/
ndro.htm

Recruitment

The State University of New York (SUNY) Downstate's Office of Minority Affairs in the College of Medicine participates in recruitment activities sponsored by the Association of American Medical Colleges, Historically Black Colleges and Universities (HBCUs), the National Association of Medical Minority Educators (NAMME), and local colleges and universities.

The College of Medicine offers students a broad professional education that will prepare them for practice or careers in any location and community. This education provides exceptional opportunities for those students with a commitment to promoting health care in urban communities and addressing the complex challenges of research and preventive care that confront clinicians, educators, and researchers in such an environment. This unique aspect of Downstate's mission is reflected in the students it attracts and selects, the majority of whom are drawn from the New York City Metropolitan area. Many of these students are members of minority and cultural groups underrepresented in the health professions, and/or come from families of first-generation immigrants or from economically disadvantaged backgrounds.

The differences in background and outlook that students bring with them can enhance the quality of the educational experience of all students at SUNY Downstate. The belief that diversity adds an essential ingredient to the educational process is one of the tenets of SUNY Downstate. Many factors, such as race, ethnic or cultural background, academic achievement, geographic location, diversity of experiences, leadership roles, and socioeconomic background, are taken into consideration in the admissions process. A diverse health care work force will be better equipped to provide culturally competent care to an increasingly diverse population.

Admissions

The Committee on Admissions considers the total qualifications of each applicant without regard to sex, race, color, creed, national origin, religion, age, sexual orientation, marital status or disability. Decisions regarding admission are based on multiple factors including prior academic performance, completion of the courses required for admission, the potential for academic success including performance on standardized tests such as the Medical College Admission Test (MCAT), communication skills, character, personal skills, health related experiences, and motivation for a career in medicine. New York State residents are given admissions preference, although well-qualified out-of-state applicants are also accepted. We welcome and encourage applications from women and members of groups underrepresented in medicine.

Academic Support Programs

The Office of Academic Development was established to help ensure that medical students, at every stage of their education,

State University of New York Downstate Medical Center College of Medicine, 2006
Applicants and Matriculants by Gender, Race and Ethnicity

Race and Ethnicity	Applicants			Matriculants		
	Women	Men	Total	Women	Men	Total
Hispanic/Latino						
Cuban	11	8	19	0	0	0
Mexican American	22	19	41	0	0	0
Puerto Rican	21	25	46	2	0	2
Other Hispanic	70	35	105	2	1	3
Multiple Hispanic*	11	13	24	1	0	1
Subtotal	135	100	235	5	1	6
Non-Hispanic/Latino**						
Black	265	125	390	11	4	15
Native American/Alaska Native	2	1	3	0	0	0
Native Hawaiian/Other Pacific Islander	7	6	13	0	0	0
White	925	984	1,909	47	42	89
Asian	566	549	1,115	26	39	65
Other Race	4	1	5	0	0	0
Multiple Race*	58	39	97	1	2	3
Unknown	27	32	59	1	5	6
Subtotal	1,854	1,737	3,591	86	92	178
Foreign	50	40	90	0	1	1
Total	2,039	1,877	3,916	91	94	185

*Since 2002, students can select more than one race and / or ethnicity. **Those who did not choose
'Hispanic/Latino' or 'Non-Hispanic/Latino' are counted under 'Non-Hispanic/Latino'.
Data Source: AAMC Data Warehouse: Applicant-Matriculant File, as of 5/9/2007.

will achieve their full academic potential. Comprehensive and individualized programs of academic assistance are available to all students. A full range of academic services helps students develop optimal study strategies such as time management, study organization, note taking, problem solving, reading, and test-taking skills.

The office also offers programs to help students effectively prepare for the United States Medical Licensing Examination (USMLE) Steps 1 and 2. During the second academic year, a series of general lectures on licensure exam preparation is provided. Students are also able to receive individual counseling on a wide range of academic issues. A three-week preparatory course is sponsored by the medical school at the completion of the second year.

Enrichment Programs

Operation Success. This program is restricted to those students admitted to the next entering class and provides an introduction to basic medical sciences. Operation Success is a six-week residential program directed by medical center faculty with the assistance of rising second-year students. No applications are necessary and information is sent once admission has been granted.

Summer Research. This is an eight-week program designed for undergraduate students who have historically been underrepresented in the biomedical and health related professions. The program is open to all qualified applicants, but it is preferred that students will have completed the sophomore year of college.

Science and Technology Entry Program. The Science and Technology Entry Program at SUNY Downstate Medical Center, funded by the Associated Medical Schools of New York, is designed to encourage minority and economically disadvantaged junior/high school

students to pursue scientific, technological, and health related careers. This program provides mathematics and science enrichment through the use of New York State Board of Education certified teachers, as well as medical students and medical school faculty.

Student Financial Assistance

All students admitted to the SUNY Downstate Medical Center College of Medicine who apply for financial consideration are given financial assistance based on need and available funds. Total financial counseling for the student and his/her parents will be provided during the summer programs and throughout the year.

Educational Partnerships

There is a combined program with the Sophie Davis School of Biomedical Education-City University of New York. The goals of this combined degree program are to train primary care physicians who will work in medically underserved areas and to increase the number of minority physicians.

Students are selected for this pro-gram in the senior year of high school. Only residents of New York are eligible to apply. This seven-year program leads to a baccalaureate degree granted by the City College of New York and to the M.D. degree awarded by one of seven participating New York medical schools.

The Office of Minority Affairs is dedicated to providing students with an opportunity to further their education in the health care field.

Other Pertinent Information

SUNY Downstate Medical Center College of Medicine is a teaching institution educating health care professionals; a research facility seeking answers to the medical problems that beset humankind; a teaching hospital caring for people with special problems; an outpatient facility serving the

health needs of the community; a public service institution; and a unit of the State University of New York.

SUNY Downstate Medical Center is an institution that exists to educate, to do research, and to take care of people. As a large urban medical center, which is part of a large public university system, SUNY Downstate Medical Center College of Medicine is keenly aware of its special obligation for public service and is a vital contributor to the health care needs of the underserved and underprivileged citizens of Brooklyn, the state, and the nation.

AAMC

State University of New York Upstate Medical University College of Medicine

Dr. Greg Threatte, Interim Assistant
Dean of Multicultural Resources
State University of New York
Upstate Medical University
College of Medicine
716 Irving Avenue
215 Weiskotten Hall
Syracuse, NY 13210
315-464-5433; 315-464-5431 Fax
admiss@upstate.edu

Recruitment

The Office of Multicultural Resources provides access for historically underserved students to the College of Medicine. The curriculum adapts to the skills and background of the individual student. This is reflective of the College of Medicine at the State University of New York (SUNY) Upstate Medical University commitment towards increasing the enrollment, retention, and graduation of historically underserved students interested in medicine.

Recruiting activities are geared toward high school and college students. Recruitment visits are made to regional health career meetings and to individual undergraduate schools. Liaison relationships have been established with some undergraduate schools to enable SUNY Upstate Medical University to assist students on a continuing basis to better prepare for medical school.

Admissions

SUNY Upstate Medical University has one Admissions Committee for all applicants to the College of Medicine, including historically underserved applicants. There are historically underserved faculty and staff on the Admissions Committee. Applications from the historically underserved are carefully and thoroughly reviewed by this committee. Every applicant is evaluated on the merits of her/his total application rather than any one specific parameter. Both the academic and clinical faculty have historically underserved individuals.

Academic Support Programs

All students in the College of Medicine, including historically underserved students, participate in a comprehensive program of academic support. The basic components include a summer human anatomy class and faculty- and student-run tutorials in each of the major basic science courses.

There is advisement and counseling to help orient, direct, and guide students throughout their medical education. Each medical student is assigned to an advisory team that includes 12 students, an advisory dean, a clinician, and a senior medical student. First- and second-year students are required to meet once per month in small-group sessions to discuss academic commonalities. Students are also encouraged to meet privately with their advisory deans as needed. This process assures that each student has an advisor who will track the student's progress and serve as a mentor through the four years in medical school.

Enrichment Programs

Summer Programs. Human anatomy is offered for those enrolled as first-year students. The course is eight weeks long. Students successfully completing this summer course are exempt from taking human anatomy during the first year. Students have the opportunity to develop basic learning skills in the context of one of their major academic courses.

State University of New York Upstate Medical University, 2006
Applicants and Matriculants by Gender, Race and Ethnicity

Race and Ethnicity	Applicants			Matriculants		
	Women	Men	Total	Women	Men	Total
Hispanic/Latino						
Cuban	8	8	16	0	0	0
Mexican American	10	12	22	0	0	0
Puerto Rican	10	13	23	0	1	1
Other Hispanic	45	31	76	0	0	0
Multiple Hispanic*	5	6	11	0	0	0
Subtotal	78	70	148	0	1	1
Non-Hispanic/Latino**						
Black	141	70	211	12	8	20
Native Hawaiian/Other Pacific Islander	8	2	10	0	0	0
White	844	997	1,841	48	41	89
Asian	500	509	1,009	14	5	19
Other Race	2	1	3	0	0	0
Multiple Race*	50	41	91	2	1	3
Unknown	20	33	53	3	3	6
Subtotal	1,565	1,653	3,218	79	58	137
Foreign	139	163	302	6	8	14
Total	1,782	1,886	3,668	85	67	152

*Since 2002, students can select more than one race and / or ethnicity. **Those who did not choose Hispanic/Latino' or 'Non-Hispanic/Latino' are counted under 'Non-Hispanic/Latino'.
Data Source: AAMC Data Warehouse: Applicant-Matriculant File, as of 5/9/2007.

Association of American Medical Colleges, 2007

USMLE Step 1 and Step 2. United States Medical Licensing Examination Step 1 and Step 2 preparation is available to students. The preparation includes a three-hour diagnostic test and a questionnaire. The data are computer-analyzed, and each student receives a customized study strategy, test-taking hints, diagnostic exam with computer-assisted feedback, individual study plan, and practice questions with explanations.

Student Financial Assistance

Costs. For 2006-07, the cost of tuition is $18,800 for New York residents and $33,500 for non-residents. Fees for first-year students are $1,090, and books and supplies (including diagnostic kit) cost approximately $2,000 for the year. Students should plan on $1,300 per month for living expenses (rent, food, personal, and travel). Health insurance is required. The total budget for a first-year student is $37,461 for a New York resident, or $52,161 for a non-resident.

Scholarships and grants. Over $1.9 million in scholarship and grant aid was provided to students in the College of Medicine in 2006-07. Many scholarships and grants are need-based, with eligibility based on family circumstances. In general, need-based funds are targeted to those students whose total family incomes are under $70,000 per year. Students are encouraged to provide parents' information on the Free Application for Federal Student Aid. This does not affect the overall eligibility for aid and allows students to be considered for all need- based programs. On average, about 10 percent of the financial aid at SUNY Upstate is in the form of scholarship and grant assistance.

Loans. Borrowing money to pay for medical school is a fact of life for most students. While average debt levels seem high (Upstate's class of 2006 borrowed an average of $124,429 for their pre-medical and medical school education), the amounts

are manageable when compared to average incomes of physicians. The Financial Aid Office staff work closely with students to ensure that each has the information and tools needed to effectively manage their student loan repayments. Students can control the amount of loans that they must borrow by planning and budgeting their finances carefully. The Financial Aid Office staff provides assistance with this also.

Application Process. SUNY Upstate Medical University uses the Free Application for Federal Student Aid (FAFSA). Students are encouraged to file on line at *(www.fafsa.ed.gov)* as soon as possible after January 1. The priority filing date for Upstate is March 1. Admission to Upstate is not required for filing. While completion of income tax returns before filing is helpful, applicants can estimate their income and then provide corrections, if necessary, after tax filing. Applicants are encouraged to provide parental income on the FAFSA so that consideration can be given for need-based scholarships and grants.

Students who have had recent changes in their financial circumstances or their families circumstances are encouraged to send a letter to the Financial Aid Office outlining the changes. Upstate also makes available an optional financial aid application form that applicants can use to report these changes.

Educational Partnerships

Early Decision Program. This program is offered to applicants who are interested in applying only to Upstate. Requirements for the Early Decision Program are the same as for regular admissions, except that the American Medical College Application Service (AMCAS) Early Decision application deadline is August 1, and the deadline to have a complete application on file is August 15. Acceptance decisions are made prior to October 1. Candidates not accepted early decision may apply to other schools and will automatically be considered under the regular admissions process after October 1.

The Early Assurance Program (EAP) offers early acceptance to undergraduate students in their second year of college. Applicants must have sophomore standing and be enrolled at any accredited undergraduate institution. The EAP program is designed to free students from the pressures associated with medical school application and MCAT preparation so they may pursue unique academic interests. It is not intended to accelerate the length of time of the undergraduate education. Accepted students are required to complete their remaining two years of college, maintain a 3.50 science and overall GPA, continue relevant volunteer experiences, and *do not* have to take the MCAT exam. Applicants to the Early Assurance Program must have a minimum GPA of 3.50, a minimum combined SAT score of 1,300 (or ACT composite score of 29) and three of the four science sequences* (see below) completed prior to application:

- General biology or zoology— six-eight semester hours
- General chemistry— six-eight semester hours
- Organic chemistry— six-eight semester hours
- General physics— six-eight semester hours

*All sciences must have the corresponding lab.

The admissions office must have a complete application on file by July 1. Applications are reviewed over the summer, and interviews are scheduled for the end of August into the beginning of September of the junior year.

A completed application consists of:

- EAP Application
- SAT/ACT Score Report
- Official High School Transcript
- Health Professions Committee Letter of Recommendation
- Personal Statement

AAMC

Official College Transcript(s)
$100 Application Fee

Cobleskill Medical School Early Assurance Program. This is a guaranteed acceptance program for first-year students at SUNY Cobleskill who are interested in primary care careers and who meet the following academic requirements:

90 percent high school GPA
1,200 combined SAT scores
or 27 ACT composite
Three years of high school math
& science courses
3.50 Cobleskill OPA

Students enrolled in this program will spend two years at SUNY Cobleskill, two years at either Siena College or Cornell University's College of Agriculture and Life Sciences, and then enter the medical program at SUNY Upstate. For more information on applying to this programs, please contact Anita Wright, Director of Transfer Services at SUNY Cobleskill.

Guthrie Pre-Medical Scholars Program. This is a guaranteed acceptance program involving Wilkes University, SUNY Upstate, the Binghamton Clinical Campus, and the Guthrie Health Care System. This program assures high school seniors of admission to the College of Medicine before they enter Wilkes University for undergraduate course work. To be considered, you must:

- Have a 1,200 combined SAT Scores or 27 ACT
- Obtain a competitive high school GPA rank in the top 10 percent of your high school class
- Reside in a rural county in the southern tier of New York State

Students in this program study the rural health care delivery system by completing clinical coursework and performing basic science research at Guthrie's Robert Packer Medical Center in Sayre, Pennsylvania.

Eligibility information is available from Elleen Sharp, Pre-Health Advisor, Wilkes University.

Blackwell Medical Scholarship Program. This program is for high school students who are from rural areas, from underrepresented minority groups, or are among the first generation in their families to attend college. To be considered, you must:

- Have 1,250 combined SAT Scores (or 27 ACT)
- Have a minimum 90 percent high school GPA
- Demonstrate commitment to a career in medicine

Students accepted into this program will complete their undergraduate degree at Hobart and William Smith Colleges and are guaranteed admission to Upstate's College of Medicine, pending all program standards are met. More information is available from the Admissions Office or Laura Vanniel, Pre-Health Counselor at Hobart and William Smith Colleges.

Elmira College Program. This is a guaranteed acceptance program for first-year students at Elmira College who are interested in pursuing a career in medicine and meet academic and other eligibility requirements. Students accepted into this program will complete their undergraduate degree at Elmira College and then enter the College of Medicine at Upstate. More information is available from Dr. Larry Stevens, Pre-Health Advisor, Elmira College.

The Post-baccalaureate Program is a 19-month program providing students with a Master's Degree in Medical Technology and the opportunity to improve their credentials and skills for entrance into medical school. Students who have been interviewed and denied admission into medical school at Upstate medical university school will be considered for admissions.

The Post-baccalaureate Program provides 45 credit hours of graduate coursework in the basic sciences (i.e., biochemistry, cell and molecular biology, genetics, immunology) and advanced coursework in the clinical laboratory sciences. A thesis proposal and thesis work is also part of the curriculum. Further, the curriculum contains internships in clinical laboratories providing the students with practical experience as well as developing the communication and professional skills needed to deal with patients and other health care professionals. The combination of coursework and clinical experience will be an excellent preparation for students entering medical school.

Stony Brook University Medical School of Medicine*

Dr. Aldustus E. Jordan, Associate Dean for Student and Minority Affairs
Stony Brook University
School of Medicine
Stony Brook, NY 11794-8436
631-444-2341; 631-444-8921 Fax
aldustus.jordan@stonybrook.edu

Recruitment

Recruitment visits are made upon request by undergraduate schools, student groups, and community organizations, or through contacts made by staff and students from Stony Brook University. Staff from the School of Medicine visit undergraduate institutions and summer programs, and also work closely with other campus groups in hosting visits from high school students from the Long Island and New York City area. Faculty, staff, and the Black and Latin Students Association are active participants in these activities.

Admissions

The admissions procedures for minority students are the same as those for all applicants to the School of Medicine. A subcommittee of the Admissions Committee reviews applications and provides an initial evaluation. Final admissions decisions are made by the full Admissions Committee. The subcommittee includes minority members from the Admissions Committee, students, and others.

Academic Support Programs

Academic assistance programs are available for all students. These include faculty advisement, student and faculty tutorials, and small-group seminars, all of which are available upon request by the student or by advisement to the student. Individual arrangements may be made for students who would benefit from different curricular arrangements.

Enrichment Programs

A one-week early academic pre-orientation is provided for entering students who need or desire an orientation to the curriculum. Students work with faculty and upperclass students and focus on anatomy and biochemistry.

Student Financial Assistance

All students admitted, who apply for financial consideration, are given financial assistance based on need and on available funds. Total financial counseling for student and or his/her parents is provided.

Educational Partnerships

The School of Medicine receives funding from the National Institutes of Health for the *Minority High School Student Research Apprenticeship Program* to provide research opportunities for high school students. Students are assigned to a scientific investigator for a six-week period. The *Towards Early Admission to Medicine Program* is a six-week program designed to increase student awareness of medical school and support activities such as academic coursework, research, career advising, and counseling, for minority students in grades 11 and 12. The *Science and Technology Entry Program* is designed for students in grades seven to 12 from local school districts with high enrollments of African American, Latino, and Native American students. The program has a six-week summer component as well as an academic year component.

Stony Brook University Medical School of Medicine, 2006
Applicants and Matriculants by Gender, Race and Ethnicity

Race and Ethnicity	Applicants			Matriculants		
	Women	Men	Total	Women	Men	Total
Hispanic/Latino						
Cuban	4	6	10	0	0	0
Mexican American	9	7	16	0	2	2
Puerto Rican	13	17	30	0	0	0
Other Hispanic	59	38	97	3	2	5
Multiple Hispanic*	4	8	12	0	0	0
Subtotal	89	76	165	3	4	7
Non-Hispanic/Latino**						
Black	181	95	276	5	3	8
Native American/Alaska Native	1	0	1	0	0	0
Native Hawaiian/Other Pacific Islander	7	3	10	0	0	0
White	730	842	1,572	26	34	60
Asian	430	399	829	14	13	27
Other Race	2	1	3	0	0	0
Multiple Race*	32	30	62	0	3	3
Unknown	22	29	51	0	1	1
Subtotal	1,405	1,399	2,804	45	54	99
Foreign	69	55	124	2	0	2
Total	1,563	1,530	3,093	50	58	108

*Since 2002, students can select more than one race and / or ethnicity. **Those who did not choose
Hispanic/Latino' or 'Non-Hispanic/Latino' are counted under 'Non-Hispanic/Latino'.
Data Source: AAMC Data Warehouse: Applicant-Matriculant File, as of 5/9/2007.

Students may receive college credit for successful course completion in selected areas. All of these programs are partnerships between the medical school, undergraduate campus, local school districts, and community-based agencies.

University at Buffalo School of Medicine and Biomedical Sciences State University of New York

Dr. David A. Milling, Assistant
Dean for Multicultural Affairs
University of Buffalo
School of Medicine
and Biomedical Sciences
Office of Multicultural Affairs
3435 Main Street, Room 40 BEB
Buffalo, NY 14214-3013
716-829-2802; 716-829-2798 Fax
dmilling@buffalo.edu

Recruitment

Recruitment of students underrepresented in medicine is coordinated through the Office of Multicultural Affairs. Our efforts focus on undergraduate institutions in New York State and the northeast region. Visits to undergraduate institutions and summer programs are conducted by the Assistant Dean for Multicultural Affairs and minority medical students. Multicultural Affairs staff and University of Buffalo Student National Medical Association members host visitations for local and regional high school and college groups.

Admissions

The SUNY/Buffalo School of Medicine participates in the American Medical College Application Service. All completed applications are evaluated by the Admissions Committee and a determination is made with regard to a personal interview. The interview is a prerequisite to admission and is the final stage of the admissions process. Multiple criteria are used to determine candidate eligibility for admissions. This allows minority students, as well as others, an opportunity to present their very best qualities to the Admissions Committee.

University at Buffalo State University of New York School of Medicine & Biomedical Sciences, 2006
Applicants and Matriculants by Gender, Race and Ethnicity

Race and Ethnicity	Applicants			Matriculants		
	Women	Men	Total	Women	Men	Total
Hispanic/Latino						
Cuban	5	8	13	0	1	1
Mexican American	13	16	29	0	0	0
Puerto Rican	13	15	28	0	2	2
Other Hispanic	39	32	71	1	0	1
Multiple Hispanic*	5	5	10	0	0	0
Subtotal	75	76	151	1	3	4
Non-Hispanic/Latino**						
Black	118	70	188	3	1	4
Native American/Alaska Native	3	1	4	1	0	1
Native Hawaiian/Other Pacific Islander	7	5	12	1	0	1
White	709	840	1,549	43	44	87
Asian	458	487	945	18	19	37
Other Race	2	1	3	0	0	0
Multiple Race*	41	39	80	1	3	4
Unknown	14	23	37	0	2	2
Subtotal	1,352	1,466	2,818	67	69	136
Foreign	52	45	97	0	0	0
Total	1,479	1,587	3,066	68	72	140

*Since 2002, students can select more than one race and / or ethnicity. **Those who did not choose
Hispanic/Latino' or 'Non-Hispanic/Latino' are counted under 'Non-Hispanic/Latino'.
Data Source: AAMC Data Warehouse: Applicant-Matriculant File, as of 5/9/2007.

Academic Support Programs

Faculty advisement, tutoring, counseling, and study skills are offered to all students. Close communication regarding academic progress is maintained between the students, faculty, and Office of Medical Education. Additional academic assistance is always available for students experiencing difficulty.

Enrichment Programs

A ten-week NHLBI (National Heart, Lung and Blood Institute) Summer Research Program is available to undergraduates and students, following their first or second year of medical school. Students in post-baccalaureate programs prior to medical school are also eligible. The goal is to prepare students for careers in research and aims at attracting them to our medical school.

Student Financial Aid

All accepted students are encouraged to apply for a scholarship and/or other financial assistance. Information regarding our scholarship program and other available financial opportunities is mailed to the student at the time of acceptance. Scholarships are awarded based on financial need and academic performance.

Educational Partnership

The Post-Baccalaureate Program is sponsored by the Associated Medical Schools of New York, a consortium of public and private medical schools in New York State. This program is housed at the State University of New York at Buffalo. The program is designed to bridge the gap between undergraduate education and matriculation into medical school. The year-long program addresses weaknesses in the student's preparation for medical school including instruction in study skills. The goal of the program is to increase the enrollment and retention of educationally qualified or economically disadvantaged students in New York State medical schools.

The Science and Technology Entry Program is a New York State initiative sponsored by the Associated Medical Schools of New York. The program is designed to acquaint and academically prepare high school students for subsequent admission into the health related and licensed professions. Students historically underrepresented in the health related and licensed professions in grades nine through 12 from Buffalo area high schools are targeted for participation in the program.

Association of American Medical Colleges, 2007

University of Rochester School of Medicine and Dentistry

Gladys Pedraza Burgos
Director of Educational,
Curricular & Diversity Affairs
Co-Director, The Center for Advocacy,
Community Health, Education,
and Diversity (CACHED)
University of Rochester Medical Center
School of Medicine and Dentistry
Office of Medical Education
601 Elmwood Avenue, Box 601
Rochester, NY 14642
585-275-2175/585-275-2928
585-273-1016 Fax
gladys_pedrazaburgos@urmc.rochester.edu

Recruitment

The Office of Educational, Curricular and Diversity Affairs represents a serious commitment, on the part of the University of Rochester School of Medicine and Dentistry (URSMD), to meet the urgent need for underrepresented minority physicians in all aspects of the medical profession. An active recruitment program seeks applicants for the M.D., Ph.D., and M.D./Ph.D., M.D./M.P.H., and M.D./M.B.A. programs.

In closely coordinated efforts with the Office of Admissions, visits and recruitment trips are made by the Associate Dean for Admissions and the Director of Educational Curriculum and Diversity Affairs to student groups, career programs and activities, summer programs, and pre-medical advisors. In addition, minority medical students, alumni, and administrators participate in recruitment efforts. Undergraduate students are invited to tour the school and meet with faculty and/or students. Contacts are also made by mail and telephone.

Admissions

URSMD is interested in the composite profile of each applicant including his/her academic preparation, performance on the Medical College Admission Test (MCAT), personal background, experiences, commitment, and motivation. Applications are individually reviewed by the Admissions Committee consisting of faculty and students. Applicants invited to the school for interviews typically meet with up to three interviewers, one of whom is a member of the Admissions Committee.

Early application is encouraged. Evaluation of applications is directed by the Office of Educational Curricular and Diversity Affairs in conjunction with the Office of Admissions. The MCAT is required for admission, however.

Academic Support Programs

The URSMD provides academic support for all matriculated students via the Advisory Dean (AD) Program.

The AD Program is designed to enhance the personal and professional development of medical students throughout the course of their undergraduate medical education. This program helps facilitate the many transitions that students face during their medical school tenure, including college student to medical student, classroom to clinic office, and medical school to residency. The interaction of each Advisory Dean with a small cohort of students (25) in each class helps to foster trusting relationships, enhance students' personal development, and ultimately assists in each student's professional growth and development in medicine. The Advisory Dean system is a model advising program for undergraduate medical education.

University of Rochester School of Medicine and Dentistry, 2006
Applicants and Matriculants by Gender, Race and Ethnicity

Race and Ethnicity	Applicants			Matriculants		
	Women	Men	Total	Women	Men	Total
Hispanic/Latino						
Cuban	9	9	18	0	0	0
Mexican American	26	27	53	1	1	2
Puerto Rican	11	9	20	0	0	0
Other Hispanic	52	38	90	1	1	2
Multiple Hispanic*	4	4	8	0	0	0
Subtotal	102	87	189	2	2	4
Non-Hispanic/Latino**						
Black	107	53	160	7	0	7
Native American/Alaska Native	3	0	3	1	0	1
Native Hawaiian/Other Pacific Islander	9	4	13	0	1	1
White	1,002	1,180	2,182	27	44	71
Asian	598	631	1,229	9	4	13
Other Race	3	2	5	0	0	0
Multiple Race*	61	50	111	4	0	4
Unknown	15	28	43	0	0	0
Subtotal	1,798	1,948	3,746	48	49	97
Foreign	23	23	46	0	0	0
Total	1,923	2,058	3,981	50	51	101

*Since 2002, students can select more than one race and / or ethnicity. **Those who did not choose
Hispanic/Latino' or 'Non-Hispanic/Latino' are counted under 'Non-Hispanic/Latino'.
Data Source: AAMC Data Warehouse: Applicant-Matriculant File, as of 5/9/2007.

Association of American Medical Colleges, 2007

Moreover, as part of the institutional effort to nurture and assist students, tutoring and study skills enhancement are provided free of charge. The peer tutorial service has been established to assist students who experience difficulty with pre-clinical courses. In addition to providing an opportunity to meet with individuals who have devised successful approaches to mastering the material, peer tutorial sessions present material in a manner that is consistent with individual students' learning styles.

The Learning Assistance Center is also available to assist students in assessing and enhancing the effectiveness of their study skills and techniques. In particular, assistance is available to help students with organizing information for review, note taking, problem-solving skills, committing information to long-term memory, and preparing for licensure.

Enrichment Programs
The Office of Student Enrichment Programs includes Community Outreach, International Medicine, and Student Research Programs. Together these programs serve to broaden the scope of medical education to include health, social, and academic experiences beyond the classroom. The goal of these experiences is to create cross-culturally competent physicians instilled with the understanding and desire to serve professionally their many communities both locally and globally.

In addition to the above programs, the University of Rochester School of Medicine and Dentistry sponsors enrichment programs designed to support and enhance the preparation of students from underrepresented groups and disadvantaged backgrounds for health and science careers.

Summer Research Fellowship Program (SURF). SURF is an eight-week program designed to enhance the competitiveness of undergraduate students interested in medicine, research, and science who

belong to groups historically underrepresented within these areas. The program is designed to strengthen students' science and research skills and expose them to biomedical research and clinical medicine. Students are individually matched with preceptors (clinicians and scientists) and conduct biomedical and clinically focused research in medical center laboratories. Participants also attend evening presentations, departmental seminars, conferences, and lectures; MCAT prep classes; problem-based learning (PBL) sessions; gross anatomy lectures and labs; and perform weekly rotations in the Emergency Medicine Department. Applicants must have an introduction to their scientific field of interest and must have completed at least two years of college.

Science and Technology Entry Program (STEP). The Science and Technology Entry Program (STEP) is an academic and career development program designed to stimulate and maintain participants' interest in career opportunities in the sciences, medicine, and the health professions. This program targets students in grades eight through 12. STEP participants are exposed to a variety of academic and professional development opportunities to enhance their problem-solving, critical-thinking, and test-taking skills. STEP students have the opportunity to work directly with physicians, technical staff, certified teachers, and medical and graduate students.

Visiting Clerkship Program. With support from the Graduate Medical Education Consortium of Rochester (GMECR), the URSMD invites up to 25 fourth-year medical students (from Liaison Committee on Medical Education-affiliated institutions) to participate in the Visiting Clerkship Program (VCP). Participants have access to a number of clinical electives to afford them exposure to GMECR training programs. GMECR hopes that medical students who have favorable educational

experiences will give consideration to pursuing their post-graduate training in GMECR residency programs. Preference for participating in the program is given to students who have an interest and history in improving the health status of underserved and diverse patient populations via patient care, research, and/or teaching.

Student Financial Assistance
The URSMD offers financial aid on the basis of need and works closely with all granting agencies. The Office of Financial Aid's primary goal is to distribute scholarships and loans so that no student will be deprived of a medical education at Rochester because of unmet financial need. About 80 percent of Rochester students finance their medical education through the use of low-cost student loans. For this reason, a variety of debt management services are provided, designed to support decision making from the beginning to the end of training and, indeed, through the entire repayment process.

Deans scholarships based on merit and future professional potential are available to select students. These fellowships provide partial support for tuition and are renewable for four years.

Consideration will be given to a waiver of the application fee upon appropriate documentation of financial hardship.

Educational Partnerships
Rochester sponsors several limited-access special admissions programs. One program, Rochester Early Medical Scholars Program (REMS), with the undergraduate campus of the university, provides provisional early acceptance to a very select and highly qualified group of high school students who are accepted by the university for undergraduate study. Other affiliations include the Associated Medical Schools of New York and the Bryn Mawr Post-Baccalaureate programs.

The Brody School of Medicine at East Carolina University

Dr. Virginia D. Hardy
Senior Associate Dean,
Academic Affairs
Counseling and Diversity
The Brody School of Medicine at
East Carolina University
Academic Support and Enrichment Center
2N-64 Brody Medical Sciences Building
600 Moye Boulevard
Greenville, NC 27893
252-744-2500; 252-744-2051 Fax
hardyv@ecu.edu
www.ecu.edu/ascc

Recruitment

The Academic Support and Enrichment Center (ASEC) of The Brody School of Medicine plays an integral role in increasing the number of underrepresented minorities in medicine. A recruiter coordinates activities that include providing information about opportunities at The Brody School of Medicine, inviting interested individuals and groups to visit the medical school, visiting undergraduate institutions in North Carolina and Virginia with an emphasis on the Historically Black Colleges and Universities, and assisting prospective minority medical students in completing the application materials for admission to medical school. Medical students, the Dean of Admissions, faculty from the Academic Support and Enrichment Center, and other faculty participate in the various activities on and off campus.

Annual workshops for pre-medical advisors are conducted on the campus of The Brody School of Medicine. Undergraduate students have access to academic assessment, interventions and psychoeducational workshops. Secondary school students are provided with life and career planning opportunities that include skill enhancement workshops and health career education. For additional information, contact the Academic Support and Enrichment Center, Brody School of Medicine, *(www.ecu.edu/ascc)*, 252-744-2500.

Admissions

The Admissions Committee of The Brody School of Medicine includes members who represent a variety of backgrounds and medical school responsibilities. The committee gives serious consideration to applicants who are members of minority groups and/or have disadvantaged backgrounds. Additional contact is available for minority students. The Admissions Committee seeks to admit a class that is educationally competent and represents diverse backgrounds. To achieve this diverse class, different factors, such as intellectual, clinical, personal, and social, are used in the selection process.

As a state-supported medical school, The Brody School of Medicine at East Carolina University has an obligation to educate students who have an interest in serving the medical needs of North Carolina. Therefore, preference is given to qualified residents of North Carolina. The School of Medicine strives to include students from a variety of geographical, economic, and ethnic groups. The application procedure includes the submission of a completed application to the American Medical College Application Service (AMCAS). The application forms may be obtained from the Internet at *(www.aamc.org/ students)*. The Brody School of Medicine may request the applicant to submit a supplementary application. The supplemental application includes an application form, a statement of residence form, at least three academic letters of recommendation or one preprofessional committee evaluation, a recent photograph, and an application

The Brody School of Medicine at East Carolina University, 2006
Applicants and Matriculants by Gender, Race and Ethnicity

Race and Ethnicity		Applicants			Matriculants		
		Women	Men	Total	Women	Men	Total
Hispanic/Latino							
Cuban		2	1	3	0	0	0
Mexican American		3	3	6	0	2	2
Puerto Rican		2	2	4	0	0	0
Other Hispanic		8	5	13	0	1	1
	Subtotal	15	11	26	0	3	3
Non-Hispanic/Latino**							
Black		55	27	82	5	7	12
Native American/Alaska Native		2	3	5	0	0	0
Native Hawaiian/Other Pacific Islander		1	0	1	0	0	0
White		240	281	521	28	23	51
Asian		48	61	109	2	4	6
Multiple Race*		11	5	16	0	0	0
Unknown		0	2	2	0	0	0
	Subtotal	357	379	736	35	34	69
Foreign		3	0	3	0	0	0
	Total	375	390	765	35	37	72

*Since 2002, students can select more than one race and / or ethnicity. **Those who did not choose
Hispanic/Latino' or 'Non-Hispanic/Latino' are counted under 'Non-Hispanic/Latino'.
Data Source: AAMC Data Warehouse: Applicant-Matriculant File, as of 5/9/2007.

fee of $60.00. In addition, a handwritten narrative is requested detailing the following information: the applicant's reason for desiring a career in medicine, a vocational area of interest, reaction to contemporary life, and future professional aspirations.

Applicants are required to take the Medical College Admission Test (MCAT). It should be taken in the spring and no later than the fall semester of the year prior to the desired matriculation date in medical school. Most successful applicants have earned an undergraduate degree. Prior to matriculation, the applicant must have the equivalent of at least three years of acceptable study at an accredited college or university. Regardless of major field of study, applicants must have completed one year of general biology or zoology (including laboratory), general chemistry (including laboratory), organic chemistry (including laboratories), physics (including laboratory), and English. Even though they are not required, courses in genetics, biostatistics, social sciences, humanities, and English are recommended.

Academic Support Programs

Academic support services are available at the Academic Support and Enrichment Center (ASEC). Services include counseling, academic enrichment sessions, reading skills assistance, and learning skills instruction.

Counseling is available in response to the individual needs of the student. Areas of counseling include personal, social, career, financial, and academic concerns. Personal development services and multicultural awareness seminars are offered to all students. The Student National Medical Association collaborates with the Academic Support and Enrichment Center to provide various activities and information. Academic services include assessment, interventions and counseling related to academic performance anxiety, time management, reading and study skills, licensure

preparation, and learning and cognitive development. Academic facilitators or tutors are assigned to students based on academic and attitudinal factors. Reading and learning assistance strengthens reading speed and comprehension, study techniques, note-taking techniques, and test-taking skills.

The Academic Support and Enrich-ment Center has licensed doctoral-level counselors, an administrative assistant, and one secretary. During the summer, School of Medicine faculty members teach in the ASEC Summer Program for Future Doctors. Faculty contributions to the summer program complement, enhance, and expand the work of the ASEC staff.

Enrichment Programs

Summer Program for Future Doctors. The ASEC Summer Program for Future Doctors (SPFD) at The Brody School of Medicine at East Carolina University has an impressive record in preparing students for admission to medical school. The SPFD includes basic sciences as well as cognitive skill development that are necessary for medical school success. The program provides students with a glimpse into the pedagogical style and demands of the medical school curriculum. The Summer Program for Future Doctors introduces participants to the quality and quantity of work that medical schools expect from students. The program helps participants overcome obstacles caused by either educational disadvantage or cultural deprivation, and it improves the students' learning and behavioral skills for success in medical school. Eligible participants for the Summer Program for Future Doctors are students from the sophomore through the graduate level of college. Minority, disadvantaged, and non-traditional students given preference.

The content of the eight-week, tuition-free summer program concentrates on problem-solving experiences that help the

student to identify, analyze, and synthesize concepts relevant to understanding complex subject matter. Instructional modules include basic science courses, medical ethics, MCAT review, along with the opportunity to have practical clinical experience.

The other component of the SPFD is designed for incoming first-year students. The program provides medical students an exposure to the medical school curriculum and the chance to enhance their learning, study, and test-taking skills.

MCAT Review Course. The Academic Support and Enrichment Center sponsors an intensive MCAT review that prepares students for the four sections of the exam. The nine-week course is available to students at the various colleges within the state of North Carolina. Additional effort is made to include students from Historically Black Colleges and Universities.

MCAT Online Review Course. Self-paced MCAT review is also offered via online instruction to any student desiring preparation for testing. Students are able to work at a pace that is suitable for their schedule. Participants have the opportunity to log-in at designated times for chat sessions with course instructors and other course participants to discuss course material or for additional tutoring. The MCAT Online Review is an 11-week preparation leading up to April and August MCAT test dates.

Student Financial Assistance

Financially disadvantaged students should submit an application for financial assistance as soon as applications become available.

Financial needs of economically disadvantaged students can be met through loans and scholarships. The available loans include, but are not limited to, the Federal Perkins Loan; the Federal Stafford Loan; Primary Care Loan; the Scholarship for

Disadvantaged Students; National Health Service Corps; North Carolina Student Loan Program for Health, Science and Mathematics; the North Carolina Academy of Family Physicians Foundation Scholarship Loan; and the Armed Forces Health Professions Scholarship Programs. Other financial aid opportunities are the Board of Governors Medical Scholarship, the Brody Scholarship Program, the Fullerton Scholarship, and the Southern Medical Association of Scholarship.

For additional information about financial aid, contact Kelly Lancaster, Director of Financial Aid and Student Services, Brody School of Medicine at East Carolina University; 252-744-2278; *(lancasterk@mail.ecu.edu)*.

Educational Partnerships

The Brody School of Medicine collaborates with various entities to accomplish its mission. The Brody School of Medicine works closely with the 16 Historically Black Colleges and Universities to provide opportunities and seminars for professional and educational development of pre-medical students. The Brody School of Medicine partners with local school systems to expose both students and educators to the requirements of medical school and other health careers. The Eastern Area Health Education Center plays a significant role in helping to provide educational, clinical, and professional opportunities to prospective and current students.

Duke University School of Medicine

Dr. Delbert R. Wigfall, Associate
Dean of Medical Education
Associate Clinical
Professor of Pediatrics
Director, Multicultural Resource Center
Division of Pediatric Nephrology
Duke University School of Medicine
Box 3005, Rm 0109, DS Purple Zone
Durham, NC 27710
919-668-1670; 919-684-2593 Fax
wigfa001@mc.duke.edu
www.medschool.duke.edu

Recruitment

Duke University School of Medicine is committed to strong minority representation in the student body. Faculty and students visit summer enrichment programs and undergraduate colleges where minority candidates are present in significant numbers. This university offers a *summer program for talented high school students* and a *program for undergraduates* interested in health science careers. All qualified minority candidates are invited to the campus for an interview and formal and informal interaction with minority students and minority faculty. The Dean's Office, the Office of Admissions, and many regional representatives are all involved in helping minority candidates consider Duke University School of Medicine as a place where their academic education will be excellent and their personal needs will be met.

Admissions

All applications are screened by two members of the Committee on Admissions. Attention is paid to evidence of leadership skills, commitment to a medical career, and the candidate's faculty

Duke University School of Medicine, 2006
Applicants and Matriculants by Gender, Race and Ethnicity

Race and Ethnicity	Applicants			Matriculants		
	Women	Men	Total	Women	Men	Total
Hispanic/Latino						
Cuban	19	18	37	0	0	0
Mexican American	42	42	84	0	4	4
Puerto Rican	24	23	47	0	0	0
Other Hispanic	59	73	132	4	0	4
Multiple Hispanic*	5	6	11	0	1	1
Subtotal	149	162	311	4	5	9
Non-Hispanic/Latino**						
Black	285	143	428	12	1	13
Native American/Alaska Native	5	9	14	0	0	0
Native Hawaiian/Other Pacific Islander	5	4	9	0	0	0
White	1,117	1,645	2,762	16	31	47
Asian	505	655	1,160	11	7	18
Other Race	2	4	6	0	0	0
Multiple Race*	77	79	156	1	2	3
Unknown	16	33	49	3	1	4
Subtotal	2,012	2,572	4,584	43	42	85
Foreign	143	128	271	3	1	4
Total	2,304	2,862	5,166	50	48	98

*Since 2002, students can select more than one race and / or ethnicity. **Those who did not choose Hispanic/Latino' or 'Non-Hispanic/Latino' are counted under 'Non-Hispanic/Latino'.
Data Source: AAMC Data Warehouse: Applicant-Matriculant File, as of 5/9/2007.

Association of American Medical Colleges, 2007

recommendations, in addition to, academic record and Medical College Admission Test scores. Students with significant educational disadvantage in grade and high school education are given especially careful consideration as their early academic performance in college may be negatively affected. Evidence of greater success in later college work is favorably reviewed.

Academic Support Program
All medical school matriculants are assigned to an Associate Dean who works with the student during all four years of medical school. Students also obtain academic advice from study track directors and research preceptors during their third year. Individual and group tutors are available to students requesting help. There are no special programs for retention of minority students. The attrition rate is less than 1 percent.

Enrichment Programs
See Recruitment for more information.

Student Financial Assistance
In addition to being eligible for a number of merit awards at Duke University School of Medicine, the following two scholarships are specifically for minority students: The Family Dollar Merit Award is available to a North Carolina minority student enrolled at Duke University School of Medicine and seven Dean's Tuition Merit Awards are available each year to minority students based on prior academic achievement. The scholarships are in the amount of full tuition, and they are annually renewable based on satisfactory academic progress.

Twenty North Carolina Board of Governors Medical Scholarships are awarded each year to financially disadvantaged state residents who enroll in one of the four medical schools in the state. Recipients are selected from qualified nominations submitted by one of the four medical schools

in the state. The award pays full tuition, fees, and a $5,000 stipend each year based on satisfactory academic progress.

The Student Loan Program for Health, Science, and Math provides a $7,500 per year loan to financially needy North Carolinians who enroll in medical school. After completion of residency, the recipient's loan is forgiven on a year-of-service for a year-of-funding basis to those who serve in an eligible practice location within the state. Duke University School of Medicine participates in the federally-funded *First Year Scholarship for Students of Exceptional Need* and *Financial Aid for Disadvantaged Health Professions Students* programs. The school's financial aid package for qualified North Carolinians, who document financial need, is based on a tuition grant up to $11,750. Financial need in excess of $11,750 must come next from a $5,000 Stafford Student Loan. Need in excess of $16,750 comes from one-half school grant and one-half loan. The package for students outside North Carolina is based on a $5,000 *Stafford Student Loan*. Financial need in excess of $5,000 comes from one-half school grant and one-half from loan up to $25,000. Need in excess of $25,000 is funded with three-fourths grant and one-fourth loan.

Educational Partnerships
Duke University has begun specific partnerships with the Durham County School System through its junior and senior high magnet programs. In addition, specific programs are being initiated with Hillside High School and North Carolina Central University to encourage and mentor minority medical students who desire pursuing careers in medical science.Latino Communities for Education (ENLACE); School Based Health Centers; the New Mexico Math, Engineering, and Science Achievement Program (NMMESA); and the Albuquerque Public Schools to name a few. The Office of Diversity also serves on

the Health Careers Workforce Education Alliance, an Albuquerque Public Schools, initiative aimed to develop a health careers pathway program in Albuquerque-area high schools and partners with the Health Occupations Students of America organization. In addition, partnerships with First Choice Community Health Centers and many rural health clinics offer clinical volunteer job shadowing through community health clinics where preceptors will serve as mentors for students.

AAMC

University of North Carolina at Chapel Hill School of Medicine

Larry Keith, Assistant Dean of Admissions and Director of Special Programs
University of North Carolina at
Chapel Hill School of Medicine
322 MacNider Building, CB #7530
Chapel Hill, NC 27599-7530
919-966-7673; 919-966-7734 Fax
Larry_keith@med.unc.edu
www.med.unc.edu/oed/med

Recruitment

The University of North Carolina School of Medicine actively recruits minority students in the state, region, and nation. Primarily, the recruitment of minority students is directed at undergraduate institutions with large numbers of economically disadvantaged North Carolina residents. Information seminars are conducted for many pre-college programs. The Assistant Dean of Admissions and Director of Special Programs, Larry Keith, and Recruitment Specialist, Dr. Nerissa Price, accompanied by volunteer medical students, regularly visit these institutions to conduct group and individual advisory sessions with students enrolled in science and pre-medical programs. Prospective students are encouraged to visit the campus and explore their interests with members of the dean's staff, faculty, and members of the Student National Medical Association.

Workshops for pre-medical advisors from colleges and universities throughout the region are periodically held on campus. Admissions Committee members regularly participate in events sponsored by pre-medical student organizations.

Admissions

The University of North Carolina (UNC) at Chapel Hill School of Medicine is committed to the principle of equal opportunity. It is the policy of the university not to discriminate on the basis of race, sex, color, national origin, religion, or handicap with regard to its students, employees, or applicants for admission or employment. Admission preference is given to North Carolina residents.

It is the duty of the Admissions Committee, acting for the dean and the faculty, to select the students who, in their judgement, will best provide excellence and beneficial diversity in the student body. In making its selections, the committee considers evidence of each candidate's motivation, maturity, industry, and integrity, as well as the scholastic record. To provide a diverse student body, the committee considers a variety of individual qualifications including non-academic accomplishments and special talents; work and service experience; research experience; resourcefulness and a history of overcoming a disadvantaged background; demonstrated compassion and concern for the welfare of others; the ability to establish rapport and communicate with others; and racial, ethnic, and economic background. No single factor is given overriding emphasis.

Members of the Admissions Committee are appointed from the basic science faculty, the clinical faculty, and physicians in private practice. Minority and female representation on the committee is maintained. There is medical student representation on the committee and in the admissions process.

Academic Support Programs

Academic Assistance Program. The Associate Dean for Student Affairs is director of this program, which provides tutorial assistance to students. Advanced graduate students and medical students, or postdoctoral fellows and housestaff officers who are certified by

University of North Carolina at Chapel Hill School of Medicine, 2006
Applicants and Matriculants by Gender, Race and Ethnicity

Race and Ethnicity	Applicants			Matriculants		
	Women	Men	Total	Women	Men	Total
Hispanic/Latino						
Cuban	18	6	24	0	1	1
Mexican American	20	18	38	1	0	1
Puerto Rican	14	10	24	0	0	0
Other Hispanic	47	42	89	1	0	1
Multiple Hispanic*	6	3	9	0	0	0
Subtotal	105	79	184	2	1	3
Non-Hispanic/Latino**						
Black	252	109	361	14	4	18
Native American/Alaska Native	7	8	15	1	1	2
Native Hawaiian/Other Pacific Islander	3	1	4	0	0	0
White	999	1,206	2,205	44	66	110
Asian	286	310	596	7	14	21
Other Race	2	4	6	0	0	0
Multiple Race*	46	44	90	2	2	4
Unknown	10	14	24	0	0	0
Subtotal	1,605	1,696	3,301	68	87	155
Foreign	76	54	130	3	0	3
Total	1,786	1,829	3,615	73	88	161

*Since 2002, students can select more than one race and / or ethnicity. **Those who did not choose 'Hispanic/Latino' or 'Non-Hispanic/Latino' are counted under 'Non-Hispanic/Latino'.
Data Source: AAMC Data Warehouse: Applicant-Matriculant File, as of 5/9/2007.

Association of American Medical Colleges, 2007

the course directors, provide tutoring. Tutors are paid by the Office of Student Affairs. The Associate Dean monitors all students' academic progress, counsels them, and directs them to resources within the medical school and university for academic assistance.

Summer Review Program. This program, directed by the associate dean, is designed for students who have failed a limited number of courses in the first or second year of medical school. Faculty are available during the summer to assist the student in reviewing the courses that were failed. The student is retested in the course at the end of the summer and promoted after successful completion of the program.

The Associate Dean for Student Affairs works directly with class advisors to advise students on academic matters. Students are assigned to Faculty Advisors upon matriculation (ratio of one per four students). Faculty Advisors serve as student advocates and assist students with their academic and non-academic adjustment to medical school. The Associate Dean for Student Affairs reports to class advisors on the academic progress of their assigned students.

A Learning Skills and Assessment Laboratory is available to any student seeking to improve study and other academic skills.

The Associate Dean for Student Affairs identifies and directs students to academic enrichment programs such as research and foreign travel experiences.

Enrichment Program
Medical Education Development (MED) Program. In operation since 1971, with a cumulative total of nearly 2,048 participants as of 2005, this nine-week program is committed to expanding opportunities for students from non-traditional backgrounds. It provides a chance to enhance academic credentials, while preparing for

admission, and increases personal and academic skills for coping with professional training. Approximately 90 percent of former participants have successfully entered health professional schools. Among those who were North Carolina residents, former participants have represented 72 percent of minority matriculants to the UNC Schools of Medicine and Dentistry.

Each summer, the program enrolls 75 to 80 students who show educational and professional promise and a strong commitment to a health career, but who have had limited opportunities in the past that may place them at a disadvantage in competing for admission and in adjusting to medical or dental school. Priority is given to North Carolina residents, typically leaving 12 to 15 spaces for out-of-state applicants. Generally, 10 to 15 percent of participants are new matriculants to the UNC Schools of Medicine and Dentistry. The remainder are rising college seniors or postgraduates preparing to apply to medical or dental school the following fall. A minimum grade-point average of 2.7 is recommended for realistic consideration, and it is highly desirable, although not required, for applicants to take the Medical College Admission Test or DAT in the spring session unless already available for counseling purposes. Financial aid is available on the basis of demonstrated need. A copy of the Financial Aid Form of the College Scholarship Service is required.

The program simulates the experience of beginning medical or dental studies including over 217 hours of basic medical sciences. Courses in gross anatomy, histology, microbiology/immunology, physiology, and clinical biochemistry, taught by regular medical faculty, introduce students to the intense pace and volume of a medical or dental curriculum. These courses are integrated with individualized work or learning, study, reading, and test-taking skills requisite to success in professional education. Other activities include seminars on

clinical or health care issues; pre-professional workshops and counseling; exposure to health facilities; and regular contact with enrolled professional students, faculty, and other members of the professional community.

Support for the program comes from school and state resources. For information contact Georgia Njagu, MED Coordinator, CB# 7530/322 MacNider Building, University of North Carolina School of Medicine, Chapel Hill, NC 27599-7530, 919-966-7673. Application deadline is February 15.

Student Financial Assistance
The Medical School Student Aid Committee, with the approval of the dean, is responsible for recommending the recipients of school scholarships and loans. The University of North Carolina at Chapel Hill School of Medicine has long upheld a tradition of helping individuals of modest financial means to reach their full potential. In accord with this tradition, financial assistance is available in a variety of forms to supplement funds provided by family, savings, summer work, and other sources. The medical school has a well-established scholarship program to supplement state and federal loans. Also, the admissions office may waive the supplementary application fee for disadvantaged students.

To provide increased medical education opportunities for minorities and disadvantaged students, the medical school participates in the Minority Presence Program and the North Carolina Board of Governors' Medical Scholarship Program. Minority presence is need-based for residents of North Carolina and is primarily used as an incentive for recruitment purposes. The Board of Governors was established in the spring of 1974 by the North Carolina General Assembly. It is a four-year scholarship that provides full tuition, fees, and an annual stipend for selected students.

AAMC

Educational Partnerships

The Office of Educational Development at UNC School of Medicine, through a collaborative partnership with UNC School of Dentistry, six undergraduate campuses of the UNC System, an inter-institutional health careers program at the UNC system, a medical student organization, three public school systems, and nine regional Area Health Education Centers (AHECs), will conduct activities to increase the number of disadvantaged students entering the health professions with the ultimate aim of improving access to and quality of health care for disadvantaged North Carolinians.

Wake Forest University Health Sciences, School of Medicine

Dr. Brenda Latham-Sadler
Director, Office of Diversity
& Development Initiatives
Wake Forest University Health Sciences,
School of Medicine
Medical Center Boulevard
Winston-Salem, NC 27157-1037
336-716-4271; 336-716-5807 Fax
www1.wfubmc.edu/MDProgram/
studentservices/diversity

Recruitment

The director and staff of the Office of Diversity and Development Initiatives, as well as students, participate in special career day programs and panel discussions at high schools, colleges, and universities. Historically Black Colleges and Universities (HBCUs) are also visited. Wake Forest University Health Sciences, School of Medicine annually hosts a Medical and Allied Health Professions Seminar for minority students from colleges throughout North Carolina. An extensive recruitment program is maintained at the community, middle and high school, and undergraduate levels through the Office of Diversity and Development Initiatives. Wake Forest University School of Medicine, Office of Student Services, composed of the Offices of Medical Student Admissions, Diversity and Development Initiatives, and Student Services, strives to provide the best service to prospective medical students by recruiting and selecting from medical school applicants a diverse population representative of our society who best reflect the core mission of Wake Forest University School of Medicine and who desire to learn according to the goals defined by the curriculum.

Wake Forest University School of Medicine, 2006
Applicants and Matriculants by Gender, Race and Ethnicity

Race and Ethnicity	Applicants			Matriculants		
	Women	Men	Total	Women	Men	Total
Hispanic/Latino						
Cuban	20	12	32	0	0	0
Mexican American	28	49	77	0	0	0
Puerto Rican	21	11	32	1	0	1
Other Hispanic	80	58	138	0	1	1
Multiple Hispanic*	7	7	14	0	0	0
Subtotal	156	137	293	1	1	2
Non-Hispanic/Latino**						
Black	256	115	371	6	5	11
Native American/Alaska Native	8	12	20	1	0	1
Native Hawaiian/Other Pacific Islander	13	9	22	0	0	0
White	1,762	2,288	4,050	31	49	80
Asian	631	713	1,344	6	7	13
Other Race	6	4	10	0	0	0
Multiple Race*	76	71	147	1	3	4
Unknown	18	27	45	0	1	1
Subtotal	2,770	3,239	6,009	45	65	110
Foreign	162	208	370	2	0	2
Total	3,088	3,584	6,672	48	66	114

*Since 2002, students can select more than one race and / or ethnicity. **Those who did not choose Hispanic/Latino' or 'Non-Hispanic/Latino' are counted under 'Non-Hispanic/Latino'.
Data Source: AAMC Data Warehouse: Applicant-Matriculant File, as of 5/9/2007.

Association of American Medical Colleges, 2007

Admissions

Wake Forest University Health Sciences, School of Medicine participates in the American Medical College Application Service (AMCAS) of the Association of American Medical Colleges. Formal application to the first-year class must be submitted through AMCAS. Applications are received from AMCAS from July 1 through the November 1 deadline. Upon receipt, the applications are considered by the Committee on Admissions (COA), composed of 20 voting members and five advisory members selected by the dean from a variety of disciplines and clinical areas. All faculty members hold either a Ph.D. or M.D. degree. Diversity is also sought for composition of this committee.

All applicants are screened, using a formula that considers GPA, MCAT scores, and the undergraduate institution attended. Competitive applicants are sent a secondary application and non-competitive applicants are rejected. The secondary application asks for more detailed information, demographics, pre-college test scores, a processing fee, and evaluations from either a pre-medical committee or two professors–one science and one non-science. Completed applications are then reviewed and placed in interview pools according to the competitiveness of the completed application. Applicants are then selected from the top interview pool for interview. After the interview, the interviewers make recommendations and vote. These votes and recommendations are taken to the Admissions Committee that then considers each interviewed applicant and votes. Final decisions are then made from the committee's cumulative vote report and offers made.

An applicant, who is accepted, is asked to respond in writing within two weeks. Upon acceptance of an offer, a holding place fee must be submitted. This fee, which is credited towards tuition, is refundable until May 15th.

Factors considered for admissions include academic achievement, personal qualifications, evaluation by the pre-medical evaluators, state of residence, and with appropriate attention to diversity with regard to race, creed, age, and sex.

Academic Support Programs

Comprehensive academic counseling, personal counseling, and tutoring are offered at no cost to the student. In addition, the Office of Student Services provides test-taking, study skills, and time-management counseling. Second- year students attend seminars to prepare for the United States Medical Licensing Examination Step 1.

Enrichment Programs

Post-Baccalaureate Pre-medical Program: Wake Forest University campus. The purpose of the program is to identify, encourage, and support minority/disadvantaged students in order to facilitate their entry into medical school. The curriculum includes microbiology, gross anatomy, and Phys/Pharm graduate level science courses. Workshops in study skills and problem solving are among the support services offered.

- *Cost*: There is a small fee and participants are responsible for their own living expenses, books, etc.
- *Eligibility*: Underrepresented minority/disadvantaged college graduates; cumulative GPA of 2.5; a score of seven on each section of the MCAT; "N" or better on MCAT writing sample.
- *Duration*: ten months.
- *Enrollment*: seven-ten students.
- *Application deadline*: March 1st.

CERTL Summer Research Program. The purpose of this program is to increase interest in science and mathematics research among high school students. The program provides hands-on research experience with distinguished faculty from Winston-Salem State University and Wake

Forest University School of Medicine.

- *Cost*: None. Program participants receive a stipend.
- *Eligibility*: High school students from Winston-Salem/ Forsyth County Schools. *Duration*: Six weeks.
- *Enrollment*: 15 students.
- *Application deadline*: February 18th.

CERTL Science and Mathematics Summer Camp. A hands-on, interactive, fun look at science and mathematics. The purpose of the program is to enhance students' interest in science and mathematics. The students attend problem-based learning sessions daily. In these sessions, students work in teams and use resource materials to discover potential solutions to problems presented in their cases.

- *Cost*: None.
- *Eligibility*: Kindergarten through eighth graders from Winston-Salem/Forsyth County Schools.
- *Duration*: Two weeks.
- *Enrollment*: 90 students per session.
- *Application deadline*: February 18th.

Student Financial Assistance

Wake Forest University School of Medicine attempts to assure that every student's needs for financial aid are met. Federal, state, and institutional resources are available through both scholarship and loan sources. Tuition scholarships are awarded to minority students on the basis of financial need and academic standing. On the day of the interview, applicants meet with the Financial Aid Officer and are provided general information about financial aid and appropriate application materials.

The Office of Financial Aid provides individual debt management counseling to all students annually. Students are provided estimated repayment plans based on their current level of educational debt and projections of repayment plans estimating their repayment amounts at graduation. Financial planning workshops are conducted annually.

Application fees are waived for students validating financial hardship. A letter of support from the undergraduate financial aid office is adequate.

Educational Partnerships

Winston-Salem/Forsyth County Schools and Winston-Salem State University. This educational partnership was developed among the Winston-Salem/Forsyth County Schools, Winston-Salem State University, and Wake Forest University School of Medicine to develop the Winston-Salem Center of Excellence for Research, Teaching, and Learning (CERTL). The goals of the partnership are to improve students' problem-based learning (PBL) skills and increase the number of kindergarten through 12th-grade students who sustain their interest in science and mathematics.

Other Pertinent Information

Wake Forest University School of Medicine offers all the advantages of a small school and is affiliated with an excellent progressive medical center that maintains state-of-the-art technology. In addition, Wake Forest University School of Medicine has a strong commitment to providing equal access to medical education for minority students. This commitment is expressed in the distribution of resources to minority students.

These resources include not only financial aid but also the availability of advisors and special programs to provide support so that, once enrolled, students are retained through graduation.

University of North Dakota School of Medicine and Health Sciences*

Eugene DeLorme, Director
Indians Into Medicine
Program (INMED)
University of North Dakota School
of Medicine and Health Sciences
501 North Columbia Road
Grand Forks, ND 58203
701-777-3037; 701-777-3277 Fax
gdelorme@medicine.nodak.edu

Recruitment

The Indians Into Medicine (INMED) Program recruits American-Indian students for health careers and assists these students in completing health professions degrees. The University of North Dakota (UND) School of Medicine and Health Sciences adds slots in its entering class each year for fully qualified INMED students.

Program participants come from throughout the United States, but INMED's most intensive recruitment efforts focus on the 24 reservations in North and South Dakota, Montana, Nebraska, and Wyoming. This primary service area was designated, at the time of INMED's inception in 1973, because of severe and continuing staffing problems at Indian health facilities within this 24-reservation, five-state area. The program maintains an all-Indian Tribal Advisory Board with representatives from these tribes.

INMED serves students from junior high school through medical school. Staff members make recruitment visits to high schools and community colleges with large Indian populations, provide health career workshops, and set up recruitment booths at Indian health and minority education conferences.

INMED contacts Indian students who are listed each year in the Medical Minority Applicant Registry. The program also receives referrals from educators and from tribal organizations. INMED distributes a newsletter and recruitment and motivational publications. The INMED Web site provides valuable information regarding programs to rural reservation communities.

University of North Dakota School of Medicine and Health Sciences, 2006
Applicants and Matriculants by Gender, Race and Ethnicity

Race and Ethnicity		Applicants			Matriculants		
		Women	Men	Total	Women	Men	Total
Hispanic/Latino							
Mexican American		0	1	1	0	1	1
Other Hispanic		0	1	1	0	0	0
	Subtotal	0	2	2	0	1	1
Non-Hispanic/Latino**							
Black		0	1	1	0	0	0
Native American/Alaska Native		11	8	19	4	2	6
White		117	109	226	26	26	52
Asian		6	3	9	1	1	2
Multiple Race*		1	5	6	0	1	1
Unknown		0	1	1	0	0	0
	Subtotal	135	127	262	31	30	61
	Total	135	129	264	31	31	62

*Since 2002, students can select more than one race and / or ethnicity. **Those who did not choose Hispanic/Latino' or 'Non-Hispanic/Latino' are counted under 'Non-Hispanic/Latino'.
Data Source: AAMC Data Warehouse: Applicant-Matriculant File, as of 5/9/2007.

Admissions

The UND School of Medicine and Health Sciences adds up to seven positions in its entering class each year for Indian students who are enrolled members of federally recognized tribes. INMED applicants are expected to meet the same admissions criteria as non-Indian applicants to the School of Medicine. The deadline for application to the UND School of Medicine and Health Sciences is November 1st each year.

Applicants must complete a standardized form that requests basic personal and academic information and submit a personal statement, letters of recommendation, academic transcripts, and Medical College Admission Test (MCAT) scores.

Candidates who meet basic admissions requirements are granted interviews with the school's 11-member admissions committee. The committee members are both appointed by the Dean of the School of Medicine and elected by the faculty or the student body. The committee includes basic science and clinical faculty members, medical students, and a consumer. The Dean of Student Affairs and Admissions and the INMED Director are available to the committee throughout the interview process.

Most INMED medical students at UND earn their medical degrees in the state. Due to the limited number of clinical placement sites, however, some INMED students transfer to the University of South Dakota School of Medicine for third- and fourth-year clinical training. INMED maintains a South Dakota Satellite Office at the School of Medicine in Sioux Falls, and South Dakota transfer students are designated at the time of matriculation.

Academic Support Programs

The UND School of Medicine and Health Sciences and INMED provide academic support and retention services for medical students at the University of North Dakota. These services can include faculty advisement, computer-assisted instruction, and study-skills courses. UND has recently instituted a patient-centered learning curriculum. All biomedical sciences are incorporated and integrated in this approach.

INMED's additional support services for Indian undergraduate and medical students include a Learning Resource Center library, study centers, and a student computer room. The program also provides counseling and academic tutoring.

Enrichment Programs

Med Prep. INMED offers Med Prep, an annual summer academic enrichment program with two separate tiers. One tier is for up to ten college juniors and seniors who participate in a six-week Med Prep course designed to assist students who are planning to take or retake the MCAT. These students are offered sessions focusing on the basic sciences and on verbal reasoning and writing to establish a solid academic foundation in the medical sciences in preparation for medical school. The course is taught by medical school faculty and Indian medical students and may include course work in the areas of biochemistry, histology, neurology, embryology, microbiology, and study skills.

The second tier is for up to ten Med Prep participants who are entering medical school in the fall. The program is designed to enhance study skills, introduce patient-centered learning, and provide clinical experiences and independent, life-long learning skills.

Pathway. INMED also offers Pathway, a six-week summer enrichment program for up to ten tribal community college students transferring to the university in health care or pre-health care fields. University instructors teach Pathway courses in the areas of anatomy, physiology, biology, and physics.

A learning skills component promotes successful study habits and learning styles.

The Summer Institute. In addition, INMED offers this six-week academic enrichment program for 90 junior high and high school students. The program can also assist college and medical students in applying for summer Indian Health Service (HIS) externships at health facilities.

Student Financial Assistance

The University of North Dakota School of Medicine and Health Sciences does not assess an application fee to Indian students who apply for admission through INMED. Once accepted into medical school, the Office of Student Financial Aid and INMED can assist students in applying for financial aid through a variety of sources.

Most of INMED's medical students utilize IHS scholarships. These scholarships fund tuition and fees, travel, and textbook expenses, and include a monthly stipend for living expenses. IHS scholarship students, enrolled in professional degree programs, are obligated to year-for-year service paybacks in the Indian Health Service.

INMED also maintains a student emergency loan fund for two-month, interest-free loans to students.

Educational Partnerships

The UND School of Medicine and Health Sciences and INMED entered into a Satellite Office Agreement with the University of South Dakota School of Medicine in 1990. The agreement enabled an increase in the number of Indian students who are admitted each year through the INMED program with some medical students designated at the time of enrollment for transfer to USD for third- and fourth-year clinical training.

The UND School of Medicine and Health Sciences also maintains placement linkages with several IHS clinical facilities. Most Indian students at the UND School of Medicine and Health Sciences complete Phase III and Phase V clinical clerkships at IHS facilities as part of their medical curricula.

INMED staff members maintain contact with health and Indian education organizations throughout the country. Since the program's inception in 1973, INMED has received recruitment assistance, support, and guidance from an all-Indian Tribal Advisory Board, which includes representatives from 24 tribal governments.

Case Western Reserve University School of Medicine*

Dr. Robert C. Haynie
Associate Dean for Student Affairs
Joseph Williams,
Director, Multicultural Programs
Case School of Medicine
2109 Adelbert Road, Room E 421
Cleveland, OH 44106-4920
216-368-2212; 216-368-8597 Fax
joseph.williams@case.edu

Recruitment

The recruitment of minority students to the Case Western Reserve University (CWRU) School of Medicine is under the direction of the Office of Multicultural Programs. Visits are made on a regular basis to colleges throughout the United States and to graduate school Career Day Fairs. High schools in greater Cleveland and health professions fairs are also visited regularly.

The office also works with the Office of Graduate Education to recruit minority students into graduate programs in the medical school.

Admissions

The Admissions Committee is composed of a diverse group of faculty and students. Any minority student can request a meeting with the Director of the Office of Minority Programs.

Academic Support Programs

The Director of the Office of Multicultural Programs, the Society Deans, and other staff organize programs, monitor progress of the students, counsel, and maintain the main support system for minority students. All students have access to a school-wide tutorial program. Tutors are available

Case Western Reserve University School of Medicine, 2006
Applicants and Matriculants by Gender, Race and Ethnicity

Race and Ethnicity	Applicants			Matriculants		
	Women	Men	Total	Women	Men	Total
Hispanic/Latino						
Cuban	7	8	15	0	1	1
Mexican American	44	40	84	0	3	3
Puerto Rican	13	14	27	2	0	2
Other Hispanic	54	41	95	0	3	3
Multiple Hispanic*	9	4	13	1	0	1
Subtotal	127	107	234	3	7	10
Non-Hispanic/Latino**						
Black	219	135	354	7	4	11
Native American/Alaska Native	2	5	7	0	0	0
Native Hawaiian/Other Pacific Islander	4	4	8	0	0	0
White	1,178	1,640	2,818	34	51	85
Asian	659	767	1,426	21	32	53
Other Race	4	3	7	0	0	0
Multiple Race*	75	60	135	1	0	1
Unknown	20	22	42	0	0	0
Subtotal	2,161	2,636	4,797	63	87	150
Foreign	118	146	264	6	4	10
Total	2,406	2,889	5,295	72	98	170

*Since 2002, students can select more than one race and / or ethnicity. **Those who did not choose 'Hispanic/Latino' or 'Non-Hispanic/Latino' are counted under 'Non-Hispanic/Latino'.
Data Source: AAMC Data Warehouse: Applicant-Matriculant File, as of 5/9/2007.

to all students at any time the student or faculty feels one is needed. This service is provided at no cost to the recipient. Many upperclass minority students serve as tutors.

Physician Mentors. All entering minority students are matched with a minority alumnus or faculty person. The mentor serves as a role model and is available to counsel and advise the student. This one-on-one interaction enhances the student's adjustment to medical school life.

Student National Medical Association. There is a very active chapter of the Student National Medical Association. Its members mentor undergraduate minority pre-medical students and students in the public schools. Study aids have also been developed for its members.

Enrichment Programs
Short Term Research. With funding from the National Institutes of Health, we are able to provide summer biomedical research opportunities for students interested in research or academic medicine. A stipend and other support are provided. We strongly encourage all students to undertake summer research.

Over the past 18 years, the Case Western Reserve University School of Medicine (CWRU) has conducted a six-week summer enrollment program designed to assist highly motivated and capable minority students in preparing for a career in medicine and in dentistry. Our Summer Medical and Dental and Education Program (SMDEP) is designed to enrich students who are completing their freshman or sophomore year of college and are considering professional careers in medicine and dentistry. SMDEP targets those from communities that are historically underrepresented in medicine and dentistry: African Americans, Latinos, Native Americans, and those who are economically disadvantaged. All are welcome to apply. SMDEP is a FREE summer program. We provide campus housing and

meals at no cost to students. We will also assist with travel expenses.

Student Financial Assistance
The School of Medicine may waive the application fee. No student is denied admission because of financial incapability. Over 85 percent of all students at the School of Medicine receive some form of financial assistance.

AAMC

Northeastern Ohio Universities College of Medicine*

Ms. Yvonne Mathis
Director for Diversity
and Multicultural Affairs
Northeastern Ohio
Universities College of Medicine
4209 State Route 44
Rootstown, OH 44272-0095
330-325-6222; 330-325-5909 Fax
ym@neoucom.edu

Recruitment

One of the goals of Northeastern Ohio Universities College of Medicine (NEOUCOM) is to recruit and support qualified medical school applicants from underrepresented minority groups. In addition to the traditional recruitment activities such as mailings, high school visits, college fairs, and receptions, NEOUCOM has several outreach programs that have been developed to increase the enrollment of medical minority students. These programs include telephone calls to medical minority candidates, scholarship mailings, program development luncheons with current medical minority students, and receptions with prospective medical minority students and their families. Contact Person(s): Tihida Simmons and Stephen Manuel, Ph.D.

Admissions

NEOUCOM accepts applications for admissions to the medical school through two separate programs: The *Combined B.S./M.D. Degree Program*, which offers high school seniors a reserved seat in medical school, and the traditional *M.D. Degree Program Direct Entry*. Admission to the *Combined B.S./M.D. Degree Program* is limited to students who have not taken college course work following high school graduation. Requirements for consideration to this program include high school transcripts and the results of the ACT (American College Test) or SAT (Scholastic Aptitude Test). Applications may be requested after August 1st. The Early Action (non-binding) application deadline is October 1st, and the application deadline is December 15th.

Admission requirements for consideration to the *M.D. Degree Program Direct Entry* include completion of at least three years of undergraduate study, one year of both university-level organic chemistry and physics, and the results of the MCAT (Medical College Admission Test). Applicants to the *M.D. Degree Program Direct Entry* should request the American Medical College Application Service (AMCAS) application in April of the year preceding anticipated enrollment. The deadline for the AMCAS application is November 1st, and the NEOUCOM Supplemental Application should be submitted by December 1st. Early decision is also available. NEOUCOM's Admission Office can be reached via the internet at *(www.neoucom.edu)*.

Contact Person(s): Tihida Simmons and Stephen Manuel.

Academic Support Programs

The Office of Professional Development coordinates and provides most of the advising efforts during the four years of medical school. Personnel in this office provide services that encourage and enhance students' professional, career, academic, and personal development. Orientations specifically tailored to students' needs precede each year of medical school, including such activities as a "White Coat Ceremony" during the freshman year and the longitudinal development of each class's individual oath. Efforts

Northeastern Ohio Universities College of Medicine, 2006
Applicants and Matriculants by Gender, Race and Ethnicity

Race and Ethnicity	Applicants			Matriculants		
	Women	Men	Total	Women	Men	Total
Hispanic/Latino						
Cuban	5	6	11	0	0	0
Mexican American	7	7	14	0	0	0
Puerto Rican	2	4	6	0	1	1
Other Hispanic	16	19	35	2	0	2
Multiple Hispanic*	1	2	3	0	0	0
Subtotal	31	38	69	2	1	3
Non-Hispanic/Latino**						
Black	45	39	84	0	1	1
Native American/Alaska Native	0	2	2	0	0	0
Native Hawaiian/Other Pacific Islander	2	0	2	0	0	0
White	408	524	932	38	35	73
Asian	204	251	455	23	15	38
Other Race	0	2	2	0	0	0
Multiple Race*	22	23	45	1	0	1
Unknown	7	4	11	1	0	1
Subtotal	688	845	1,533	63	51	114
Foreign	10	15	25	0	0	0
Total	729	898	1,627	65	52	117

*Since 2002, students can select more than one race and / or ethnicity. **Those who did not choose Hispanic/Latino' or 'Non-Hispanic/Latino' are counted under 'Non-Hispanic/Latino'.
Data Source: AAMC Data Warehouse: Applicant-Matriculant File, as of 5/9/2007.

are concentrated on fostering and assessing students professional development; promoting leadership through student government, activities, and organizations; encouraging personal development; and inculcating the lifelong learning habits and skills required by the profession of medicine.

The Learning Specialist offers a learning skills program to help students study more efficiently and effectively. Learning skills assistance is offered in large-group meetings, small-group "Brown Bag" lunches, and individual sessions. Print materials such as Users' Guides, newsletters, and a Web page containing study tips are supplied. Peer tutoring is available for most basic science courses.

Career development is encouraged through the utilization of the MedCAREERS materials and the efforts of a Coordinator of Student Advising and the Assistant Dean for Student Affairs. Within the Professional Development Advising Teams (PDAT), a continuous advising program is offered that spans all four years of a student's medical education experience and incorporates students and basic scientists. The Coordinator of Student Advising oversees the PDAT program, a Peer Mentor program, and is also the Student Personal Advisor.

Students are assisted in residency planning by the Coordinator of Student Professional Development. Types of assistance available include support in writing resumes and personal statements, maintenance of fellowship and residency materials, and individual consultation. This year the Pathway Evaluation Program for Medical Professionals will be initiated to aid in residency decision-making process.

Enrichment Programs

NEOUCOM offers several recruitment programs aimed to encourage young people interested in the sciences from the sixth grade through high school graduation.

These programs include *MEDCAMP, MedSuccess, and Project Health Quest.*

- MEDCAMP is a three-day intensive experience designed to stimulate students' interests in the basic sciences and medicine and to expose them to opportunities for careers in the science and medicine fields. The program is fashioned after the SPACECAMP Program, and includes biomedical science workshops involving research, problem solving, computers, and an introduction to the field of clinical medicine.

- MEDCAMP is held in the summer and is designed for students who will enter the ninth grade when they begin school in the fall. Preference is given to minorities, females, rural students, and other underrepresented groups in medicine, who have demonstrated achievement in science and an interest in medicine as a possible career. Contact Person: Debbie Frank.

- *MedSuccess* is an enrichment program for ninth- through 12th-grade students from underrepresented groups medicine. MedSuccess was developed to better prepare minority students for careers in medicine early in their education. Students gain college readiness skills and medical school preparation through their participation in various activities and workshops. Students have an opportunity to explore careers in medicine, interact with medical students and physicians, tour associated hospitals, and attend college planning and test-taking workshops. The MedSuccess program is held from January to May of each year, and students participate in activities once a month. Students can remain in the program through their senior year in high school. Contact Person: Tihida Simmons.

- *Project Health Quest* is a yearly program designed to stimulate students' interest in careers in the field of health care. Selected students begin the program in grade six and have the opportunity to participate yearly through grade 12.

Project Health Quest activities are held primarily during the summer on the Youngstown State University campus. While participating in the summer camp each year, students will have the opportunity to visit the medical school, area hospitals, and universities where they will have contact with area physicians, allied health professionals, and medical students who serve as role models. Students do not have to pay to participate in the program. Project Health Quest is sponsored by the college's Area Health Education Center (AHEC), Office of Diversity and Multicultural Affairs, and the Eastern Ohio Area Health Education Center. Contact Person: Yvonne Mathis.

Student Financial Assistance

The following are scholarship funds that exist in support of minority medical students at Northeastern Ohio Universities College of Medicine who demonstrate financial need. Contact Person: Anita Miller.

- The *Eleanor Smith Bozeman, M.D., Minority Endowment Fund* was personally established by Dr. Bozeman, an internist from Akron, for the purpose of assisting a financially deserving female minority medical student.

- The *Kenneth L. Calhoun Trust Scholarship* was created through a bequest by Mr. Calhoun. The fund distributes annual restricted scholarship funds of $5,000 to a minority medical student attending NEOUCOM who demonstrates financial need.

The *Dr. Melvin and Mrs. Leona Farris Minority Scholarship* was established for Dr. Melvin Farris, a family physician, who served as a Member of the Board of Trustees for both the Northeastern Ohio Universities College of Medicine and The University of Akron. These scholarship funds are designated for underrepresented medical minority students admitted through the traditional four-year Direct Entry Admissions Program at NEOUCOM. The underrepresented medical minority students must demonstrate financial need and meet eligibility criteria. This scholarship is renewable for the four years of the student's enrollment and renewal mounts will remain consistent with the original award, but new award amounts may vary annually.

The *John D. Finnegan Foundation Minority Medical Student Scholarship Fund* was provided by the Finnegan Foundation as a $10,000 gift for scholarship support over two years, to a financially underrepresented minority medical student from Youngstown State University. Contingent upon good academic standing, the student will receive the second award for the following academic year.

The *Clarence E. Josephson Minority Medical Student Scholarship Endowment* was established by Dr. Josephson for minority medical students attending NEOUCOM. A former president of Heidelberg College, Dr. Josephson was concerned about the future of the American health care system and equality among all races.

- The *Minority Scholarship Fund* was established to attract a more diverse student body to the College of Medicine. This scholarship is available to underrepresented minority medical students demonstrating financial need. Students entering through the Direct Entry Admissions Program will be given top priority, followed by students entering through the B.S./M.D. program.

- The *NEOUCOM Minority Scholarship Matching Fund* was created in 1999 to support minority medical students attending NEOUCOM. All non-endowment gifts to the NEOUCOM Foundation in support of minority medical scholarships will be matched by the college for this award.

- The *NEOUCOM Foundation Minority Student Aid Fund* is used for scholarship support for minority students, as well as a minority student recruitment and retention program.

- The *Luther H. Robinson Memorial Endowment Fund* was established by staff physicians at Children's Hospital Medical Center of Akron in memory of Dr. Luther Robinson, who was a pediatrician at Children's Hospital and one of the original members of the NEOUCOM Admissions Committee. Dr. Robinson passed away in 1989. The Luther H. Robinson Memorial Scholarship provides scholarship aid to financially deserving minority medical students entering their junior year of medical school who rank in the top quartile of their class academically.

- The *Links Scholarship Fund* was established by the Kent, Ohio, chapter of The Links, Inc. The scholarship benefits a minority medical student attending NEOUCOM.

- The *Shirali Family Scholarship Endowment* Drs. Sudheer and Charulata Shirali, pediatricians in Canton, Ohio, and parents of Swati Shirali M.D. ('90), established the Shirali Family Scholarship Fund to benefit NEOUCOM medical students. The scholarship provides aid to a financially deserving underrepresented minority student from Stark County.

Educational Partnerships
- Area Health Education Network (AHEC), Rootstown, Ohio
- Akron Public Schools, Akron, Ohio
- Akron City Hospital (SUMMA), Akron, Ohio
- Eastern Ohio Health Education Network, Youngstown, Ohio
- Forum Health, Youngstown, Ohio
- Kent State University, Kent, Ohio
- Links, Inc., Akron/Kent Chapter
- National Medical Association (NMA), Akron/Canton Chapter
- St. Elizabeth Health Center, Youngstown, Ohio
- Youngstown Public Schools, Youngstown, Ohio
- Youngstown Community Health Center, Youngstown, Ohio
- Youngstown State University, Youngstown, Ohio
- Upward Bound, University of Akron, Akron, Ohio

Ohio State University College of Medicine

Muntagima Furgan
Associate Director
Office for Diversity and Cultural Affairs
Ohio State University College
of Medicine and Public Health
066 Meiling Hall
370 West Ninth Avenue
Columbus, OH 43210-1238
614-688-8489; 614-292-2556 Fax

Recruitment

Active recruitment of underrepresented minority students at the community, junior high school, high school, and undergraduate levels is conducted by members of the Ohio State college administration, faculty, students, and alumni. Recruitment is coordinated through the Admissions Office, the Office for Diversity and Cultural Affairs, and the other health professional schools at the Ohio State University (OSU).

Graduate and Professional Schools Visitation Days. The OSU Office of Minority Affairs, the Graduate School, and Professional Colleges invite five to eight high-ranking seniors and an administrative or faculty representative from a college or university to visit the Ohio State University's campus to explore graduate and professional study opportunities: *(http://medicine.osu.edu/odca).*

Admissions

All applicants for admission are evaluated by the Admissions Committee of the College of Medicine and Public Health. Every effort is made to include individuals representative of all segments of society with a variety of backgrounds, medical career goals, and aspirations. Applications from underrepresented minority students are encouraged and every effort is made, by the Admissions Committee to assist students in becoming successful applicants. The committee is made up of faculty members of the College of Medicine. See *(http://medicine.osu.edu/futurestudents/ admissions).*

Academic Support Programs

A strong academic support program is available to all students enrolled in the OSU College of Medicine and Public Health. The MEDPATH Office staff can assist students experiencing academic difficulty with assistance in learning strategies and test-taking development and provides academic advising. The Medical Student Advisory Center offers students test preparation guidance, academic advising, and general counseling services. The Academic Program Committees, for first through fourth year, also offer a variety of academic support options for students as they progress through each of the four years of the curriculum. *(http://medicine.osu.edu/odca)*

Enrichment Programs

Summer Pre-Entry Program. The College of Medicine and Public Health offers a six-week summer enrichment program for entering medical students in order to strengthen their academic background and skills prior to starting the first year. The program is designed for students who are non-science majors, students who may need special preparation prior to beginning medical school, or students who have been out of school for a period of time. Instruction in human gross anatomy, neuroanatomy, and immunology are offered. In addition, learning strategies and test-taking seminars are included in the curriculum.

The program allows students to meet and become acquainted with their faculty and classmates. It also gives students time to acclimate to the medical school environment and the surrounding community.

Ohio State University College of Medicine, 2006
Applicants and Matriculants by Gender, Race and Ethnicity

Race and Ethnicity	Applicants			Matriculants		
	Women	Men	Total	Women	Men	Total
Hispanic/Latino						
Cuban	8	11	19	0	2	2
Mexican American	41	33	74	1	2	3
Puerto Rican	6	15	21	0	3	3
Other Hispanic	44	39	83	0	1	1
Multiple Hispanic*	7	4	11	0	0	0
Subtotal	106	102	208	1	8	9
Non-Hispanic/Latino**						
Black	211	111	322	14	6	20
Native American/Alaska Native	3	6	9	0	0	0
Native Hawaiian/Other Pacific Islander	3	6	9	0	0	0
White	903	1,528	2,431	65	75	140
Asian	377	500	877	12	19	31
Other Race	2	1	3	0	0	0
Multiple Race*	45	47	92	2	6	8
Unknown	11	21	32	2	1	3
Subtotal	1,555	2,220	3,775	95	107	202
Foreign	37	54	91	0	0	0
Total	1,698	2,376	4,074	96	115	211

*Since 2002, students can select more than one race and / or ethnicity. **Those who did not choose Hispanic/Latino' or 'Non-Hispanic/Latino' are counted under 'Non-Hispanic/Latino'.
Data Source: AAMC Data Warehouse: Applicant-Matriculant File, as of 5/9/2007.

limited number of stipends for the program will be allotted to underrepresented minority and disadvantaged students in financial need.

Post-Baccalaureate Program. The College of Medicine and Public Health offers a four-quarter Post-Baccalaureate Program that is aimed at developing the academic knowledge base and skills of students prior to their entry into medical school so that they will be more competitive for, and successful in, medical school. The program is designed for individuals who have received a bachelor's degree and who need more in-depth science coursework. The curriculum begins with a two-week, intensive science review and testing of biology, chemistry, and physics. Students are also provided with an assessment and instruction in reading, study strategies, and problem-solving. This first phase of the program is intended to give students a profile of their academic strengths and weaknesses, learning style, and comprehension ability.

Phase II of the program, beginning in the fall term, consists of lecture, laboratory, and computer-assisted instruction in biochemistry, genetics, histology, medical terminology, microbiology, pathology, pharmacology, and physiology. Courses are selected according to individual student's backgrounds and academic records.

The College of Medicine and Public Health Admissions Committee will grant up to 15 conditional acceptances into medical school to underrepresented minority and disadvantaged applicants upon the applicants successful completion of the Post-Baccalaureate Program. Tuition scholarships are available to students in the program.

One of the aims of the program is to increase the number of underrepresented minority and disadvantaged students accepted into medical school. Nationally, African Americans, Native Americans, Mexican Americans, mainland Puerto Ricans, and individuals from low-income families are not adequately represented in medicine. This underrepresentation in medicine adversely affects the health care of these populations and the country.

Student Financial Assistance

The OSU Office of Financial Aid has a staff to counsel medical students and assist them in financial planning. There are need-based university scholarships and grants available to underrepresented minority students. The National Medical Fellowships Inc. provides assistance to some first- and second-year students. All scholarships and grants awarded at the OSU are made on the basis of demonstrated financial need. Financial aid, in the form of loans, is also available (e.g., Stafford Student Loan, the Perkins Loan, and the Primary Care Loan). Students are encouraged to begin financial planning for their medical school education early. If financial problems are anticipated, students are urged to contact the Office of Medical Student Affairs.

University of Cincinnati College of Medicine*

Dr. Charles W. Collins
Assistant Dean
University of Cincinnati
College of Medicine
231 Albert Sabin Way, Suite E251
P.O. Box 670552
Cincinnati, Ohio 45267-0052
513-558-4898; 513-558-1100 Fax
charles.collins@uc.edu
www.med.uc.edu

Recruitment

The University of Cincinnati College of Medicine (UCCOM) actively recruits minority, disadvantaged, and non-traditional students. The college encourages individuals from diverse backgrounds to consider the many exceptional educational programs that are offered. Commitment to recruiting, admitting, and graduating students begins with several enrichment programs for middle school, high school, and college students, and extends through medical school graduation.

Under the umbrella of Pathways to Health Careers, the Office of Student Affairs sponsors programs for high school and college students/graduates, one program for high school teachers, and one year-round program for middle school students. All programs introduce students to the sciences, facilitate the development of their critical thinking skills, and expose them to health careers through research and clinical experiences. *Note: Middle and high school programs are for students in the Cincinnati area.*

Pathways Programs

Saturday Science Academy. Seventh- and eighth-grade students and their parents meet once a month to explore health careers via a hands-on, interactive approach to the sciences.

Health Careers Exploration (HCARE). Eleventh- and twelfth-grade students focus on critical thinking skills and problem-solving skills while learning biology and chemistry and exploring health related careers.

Excellence in Science Education and Learning (ExSEL). This is a summer program for 11th- and 12th grade students. This program is for gifted and academically talented students who are interested in the sciences.

Teachers' Initiative Program in Biomedical Research. Middle and high school teachers complete research with UC faculty members, present their research, and share ideas for teaching science courses and promoting careers in the sciences, particularly the medical sciences in their schools.

Summer Premedical Enrichment Program. This program exposes rising college juniors and seniors and recent college graduates from all over the country to clinical experiences, medical school curriculum, and to the medical school admissions process.

Summer Research Scholars is for students who are interested in research, in preparation for medical or graduate school. They are matched with faculty mentors and placed in laboratories to complete bench and translational research in an area of interest.

For further information or applications to the above programs, please contact: Pathways to Health Careers, University of Cincinnati College of Medicine, P.O. Box 670552, Cincinnati, OH 45267-0552, (P) 513-558-7212,(F) 513-558-6259. *(www.med.uc.edu/admissions/summer enrich.cfm).*

University of Cincinnati College of Medicine, 2006
Applicants and Matriculants by Gender, Race and Ethnicity

Race and Ethnicity	Applicants			Matriculants		
	Women	Men	Total	Women	Men	Total
Hispanic/Latino						
Cuban	9	7	16	0	0	0
Mexican American	21	25	46	0	1	1
Puerto Rican	7	6	13	0	0	0
Other Hispanic	38	31	69	0	0	0
Multiple Hispanic*	3	5	8	0	0	0
Subtotal	78	74	152	0	1	1
Non-Hispanic/Latino**						
Black	183	92	275	2	7	9
Native American/Alaska Native	1	2	3	0	0	0
Native Hawaiian/Other Pacific Islander	7	4	11	0	0	0
White	970	1,353	2,323	55	69	124
Asian	404	498	902	10	13	23
Other Race	4	2	6	0	0	0
Multiple Race*	47	50	97	0	1	1
Unknown	12	14	26	0	0	0
Subtotal	1,628	2,015	3,643	67	90	157
Foreign	24	27	51	0	0	0
Total	1,730	2,116	3,846	67	91	158

*Since 2002, students can select more than one race and / or ethnicity. **Those who did not choose
Hispanic/Latino' or 'Non-Hispanic/Latino' are counted under 'Non-Hispanic/Latino'.
Data Source: AAMC Data Warehouse: Applicant-Matriculant File, as of 5/9/2007.

AAMC

Admissions

All applicants to the University of Cincinnati College of Medicine are selected on the strength of their credentials. A preliminary screening based on academic qualifications will determine applicant ranking for interviews. Undergraduate grade-point average, post-baccalaureate/graduate work, and Medical College Admission Test (MCAT) scores are considered in this evaluation. The secondary application fee is $25.

Applicants invited for an interview will meet with one member of the admissions committee and participate in a 2.5 hour program introducing them to the college, including a session with the Director of Financial Aid, lunch, and a tour.

Final decisions are based on a combination of academic achievement and personal attributes. The academic assessment may include but is not limited to competitive science and cumulative GPA, honors course work, independent study, research, and performance on the MCAT. Personal qualities may include but are not limited to interpersonal skills, leadership abilities, evidence of commitment to helping others, clinical experiences, the ability to establish priorities, coping skills, motivation, and maturity.

Early Decision Admissions Program (EDP). The University of Cincinnati encourages students to consider this process if the College of Medicine is their first choice for medical school. There are no special requirements such as higher MCAT scores or grade-point averages. A competitive applicant for regular admissions will be competitive for EDP.

For further information, please contact: Admissions, University of Cincinnati College of Medicine, P.O. Box 670552, Cincinnati, OH 45267-0552, (P)513-558-7314, (F) 513-558-1165. (www.med.uc.edu/).

Academic Support Programs

Extensive support programs are available for all students. Tutorial services, learning skills development (including test taking, note taking, study, and reading strategies), and counseling are available. Preparation for the United States Medical Licensing Examination Step 1 is available through the Office of Student Affairs working closely with the faculty. The pass rate for the college has been very high; over the past five years, an average of 98 percent of students pass Step 1 on their first attempt.

Minority Mentoring Program enhances the medical school experience for minority students. This program includes personal, academic, and career counseling. Support groups introduce students to each phase of the medical education experience, prepare them for residency, and discuss gender issues (women's support group). The program also provides students with a supportive link to and interaction with minority physicians in the community. For more information on recruitment and retention services, please contact: Office of Diversity and Community Affairs, University of Cincinnati College of Medicine, P.O. Box 670552, Cincinnati, OH 45267-0552, (P) 513-558-4898, (F) 513-558-1100.

Special Programs

Physician Scientist Training Program (PSTP). The Physician Scientist Training Program integrates graduate and clinical education to develop physician-scientists who are interested in combining clinical and research careers. Students are awarded an M.D./Ph.D. degree upon completion of the seven to eight year program. The program matriculates up to six students each year. To learn more about this exciting career, please contact: Physician Scientist Training Program, University of Cincinnati College of Medicine, P.O. Box 670555, Cincinnati, OH 45267-0555, (P) 513-558-2380, (www.med.uc.edu/pstp).

M.D./M.B.A. Program. A five year Medical Degree and Masters in Business Administration is available. This combined experience provides unique preparation for a career in medicine and business in the 21st century. Students apply to the MBA program after their first year in medical school.

High School Dual Admissions Program. Outstanding high school students who are interested in a career in medicine are invited to explore this exciting program. The University of Cincinnati College of Medicine has formed a partnership with five universities in the state of Ohio to accept academically talented high school seniors into medical school when they are accepted to their undergraduate college. The universities who currently participate in the program are John Carroll University, University of Dayton, Miami University, Xavier University, and University of Cincinnati. The University of Cincinnati has two programmatic tracts to medical school, one for students in engineering and one for any undergraduate student regardless of their major. For additional information, please contact Dual Admissions Program, University of Cincinnati College of Medicine, P.O. Box 670552, Cincinnati, OH 45267, (P) 513-558-5581, (www.med.uc.edu/hs2md/).

Enrichment Programs

See Recruitment and Academic Support Programs.

Student Financial Assistance

The Director of Financial Aid is extremely proactive in working with students to finance their medical education. Financial Aid at the University of Cincinnati College of Medicine is awarded on the basis of need. The secondary application fee can be waived if the applicant makes a written request and supplies documentation of financial need.

During the interview day program, the Director presents financial aid information and is available to meet with applicants individually if appointments are made in advance. Financial aid is not available for interview trips.

The debt management and financial planning programs offered by the College of Medicine are designed for all students. These programs extend throughout student matriculation.

In addition to a group Entrance Interview, first-year students are invited to take part in one-on-one counseling sessions, which include personal financial planning advisement. Seminars on budgeting, financial planning, and debt management are presented during each academic year. Students receive a quarterly financial aid newsletter.

A series of financial planning programs are presented to graduating seniors in the weeks following Match Day. Senior students also receive one-on-one debt management counseling as a part of their financial aid Exit Interview. Graduates are encouraged to contact the financial aid office for debt management assistance whenever necessary.

Educational Partnerships
See High School Dual Admissions Programs.

Other Pertinent Information
University of Cincinnati College of Medicine offers an exciting medical education program. Beginning early in year I and continuing through year II, students work with patients to develop a proficiency in interviewing, history taking, and physical diagnosis. This early clinical experience is designed to facilitate the transition to the third year. In addition, there are several enrichment opportunities available the first two years of medical school (e.g., Maternal Healthcare—an opportunity to work with a pregnant patient and follow

her progress through delivery; Homeless Healthcare—an opportunity to work with the homeless in an inner city clinic, and the Family Medicine Scholars Program—for students who wish to explore career opportunities in Family Medicine). Other unique experiences include participation in the Urban Health Project and the Leadership in Medicine selective.

The University of Cincinnati College of Medicine has a national reputation for providing excellent clinical training. The Clinical Biennium (third and fourth year) includes core clerkships in internal medicine, surgery, pediatrics, psychiatry and obstetrics/gynecology. Other required clerkships include primary care, radiology, and specialty clerkships. Students gain valuable learning experiences by working with faculty in several clinical settings (e.g., The University Hospital, Veterans' Administration Hospital, the nationally known Cincinnati Children's Hospital Medical Center, urban and rural health clinics, geriatrics facilities, private physician offices and other community hospitals).

In the fourth year, students complete an eight-week Acting Internship. This experience is designed to allow students to assume greater responsibility in patient care management, further preparing them for the demands of residency. If a student's interest is highly specialized, students may select to rotate in outstanding subspecialty electives at The University Hospital. Students spend 12 weeks of electives at the College of Medicine. The remaining electives may be taken anywhere in the United States or in a variety of international health care settings.

University of Toledo College of Medicine*

Dr. Samuel H. Hancock
Assistant to the President
for Institutional Diversity and
Assistant Clinical Professor
Department of Medicine
University of Toledo College of Medicine
3045 Arlington Avenue
Toledo, OH 43614-5805
419-383-3609; 419-383-6450 Fax
shancock@mco.edu

Recruitment

The Office of Institutional Diversity supports the Office of Admissions by visiting high schools, community organizations, and colleges. High school and college students are invited to visit the medical school either individually or in groups. The Associate Dean of Admissions makes a number of recruiting trips on a national basis. The recruitment program is administered by the Office of Admissions with participatory support from medical students and faculty. The Student National Medical Association (SNMA) is an integral part of this effort.

Admissions

Minority and educationally disadvantaged applicants are evaluated by the Admissions Committee. The committee considers relevant cognitive and non-cognitive factors in their evaluation of applicants. The committee reviews the academic background of applicants, as well as the non-academic responsibilities, stated interest in medicine, manifestation of that interest, and potential contribution to the field.

The Five Year Program. The medical school initiated this five-year program in 1988. Students spend three years in the basic sciences and two years in the clinical sciences. Five students are admitted to the program each year. The University of Toledo, College of Medicine is committed to the goal of student body diversity. Minority faculty and students are represented on the Admissions Committee and its related activities. Eligibility is based upon academic and socioeconomic disadvantage.

Academic Support Programs

The Academic Enrichment Center is available to assist students in optimizing performance. This program offers comprehensive support through activities related to study and test-taking skills, a tutorial program, and coordinating of academic advising.

Student Financial Assistance

The application fee is waived if requested and documented through American Medical College Application Service or the undergraduate institution. The institution has established The Medical University of Ohio Scholarship Program. The scholarships are renewable for a four-year period. Individuals from diversified backgrounds, who demonstrate the potential for academic excellence, will be considered.

Educational Partnerships

The SNMA has established an outstanding mentoring program with community schools, whose student bodies are predominantly minority. In addition to social activities, the medical students assist in the academic development of their mentees through career counseling and tutorial support. For the past several years the Office of Institutional Diversity has participated in the University of Toledo Excel Program's Summer Institute, assisting this program with lectures and tours of the campus to minority high school students in the Toledo community.

University of Toledo College of Medicine, 2006
Applicants and Matriculants by Gender, Race and Ethnicity

Race and Ethnicity	Applicants			Matriculants		
	Women	Men	Total	Women	Men	Total
Hispanic/Latino						
Cuban	3	7	10	1	0	1
Mexican American	18	15	33	0	0	0
Puerto Rican	5	7	12	0	0	0
Other Hispanic	27	26	53	1	1	2
Multiple Hispanic*	3	1	4	1	0	1
Subtotal	56	56	112	3	1	4
Non-Hispanic/Latino**						
Black	73	59	132	8	2	10
Native Hawaiian/Other Pacific Islander	6	3	9	0	0	0
White	707	973	1,680	51	63	114
Asian	341	435	776	9	12	21
Other Race	2	2	4	0	0	0
Multiple Race*	29	31	60	2	1	3
Unknown	7	12	19	0	3	3
Subtotal	1,165	1,515	2,680	70	81	151
Foreign	24	28	52	0	0	0
Total	1,245	1,599	2,844	73	82	155

*Since 2002, students can select more than one race and / or ethnicity. **Those who did not choose Hispanic/Latino' or 'Non-Hispanic/Latino' are counted under 'Non-Hispanic/Latino'.
Data Source: AAMC Data Warehouse: Applicant-Matriculant File, as of 5/9/2007.

Other Pertinent Information

The University of Toledo, College of Medicine Department of Family Medicine has been awarded a federal grant, "Multicultural Predoctoral Training in Family Medicine," to facilitate the development of cultural competence in medical students. First- and second-year students are presented with the clinical significance of cultural factors. Additionally students have the opportunity to gain clinical experience in community health centers serving underserved populations.

Wright State University Boonshoft School of Medicine

Dr. Gary LeRoy
Assistant Dean of Minority Affairs & Student Affairs
Wright State University
School of Medicine
P.O. Box 1751
Dayton, OH 45401-1751
937-775-2934; 937-775-3322 Fax
gary.leroy@wright.edu
http://www.med.wright.edu

Recruitment

The academic medical community at Wright State is intensely interested in the maintenance of a diverse student body. Wright State University Boonshoft School of Medicine is a strong supporter of equality in educational opportunities. Every

effort is made to recruit qualified minority students who wish to pursue a medical career. The school's philosophy is to seek students with diverse social, ethnic, and cultural heritages. This includes not only minority students, but also the older and non-traditional student.

The School of Medicine offers a number of programs intended to increase the number of minority students entering the medical profession. To reach minority students as early as possible, one summer program is aimed at high school juniors and seniors. *Horizons in Medicine* provides exposure to the medical sciences as well as work experiences in area health care settings. In association with the Student National Medical Association chapter, the Office of Student Affairs and Admissions has supported the establishment of an undergraduate Minority Association of Pre-Health

Wright State University Boonshoft School of Medicine, 2006
Applicants and Matriculants by Gender, Race and Ethnicity

Race and Ethnicity	Applicants			Matriculants		
	Women	Men	Total	Women	Men	Total
Hispanic/Latino						
Cuban	5	7	12	0	0	0
Mexican American	31	18	49	0	0	0
Puerto Rican	8	8	16	0	0	0
Other Hispanic	27	28	55	0	0	0
Multiple Hispanic*	2	3	5	0	1	1
Subtotal	73	64	137	0	1	1
Non-Hispanic/Latino*						
Black	157	90	247	9	1	10
Native American/Alaska Native	4	1	5	0	0	0
Native Hawaiian/Other Pacific Islander	3	1	4	0	0	0
White	724	862	1,586	45	30	75
Asian	298	366	664	9	3	12
Other Race	0	4	4	0	0	0
Multiple Race*	31	33	64	2	0	2
Unknown	10	11	21	0	0	0
Subtotal	1,227	1,368	2,595	65	34	99
Foreign	14	19	33	0	0	0
Total	1,314	1,451	2,765	65	35	100

*Since 2002, students can select more than one race and / or ethnicity. **Those who did not choose Hispanic/Latino' or 'Non-Hispanic/Latino' are counted under 'Non-Hispanic/Latino'.
Data Source: AAMC Data Warehouse: Applicant-Matriculant File, as of 5/9/2007.

students (MAPS) chapter at Wright State University that is made up of minority students interested in health careers and assists them in developing seminars and workshops throughout the year on topics concerning the medical profession and the process of applying to medical school.

Admissions
Admission to the Boonshoft School of Medicine is guided by a philosophy dedicated to increasing the number of students from racial, ethnic, and socioeconomic backgrounds underrepresented in medicine. The Admissions Committee considers not only the academic record, but also the biographical and personal comments of all applicants. The School of Medicine does not set quotas or numerical goals. We select students who have the qualities that will make excellent, dedicated physicians no matter what specialty they choose. The membership of the Admissions Committee includes not only full-time faculty, but also medical students, practicing physicians, and undergraduate instructors as representatives of the local community. There is significant minority representation on the committee. Twice each year interview days that allow minority students to meet currently enrolled minority students, minority faculty, and alumni in order to address issues unique to students of color are scheduled. These interview days are planned in consultation with current students and provide applicants the opportunity to hear firsthand about academics and student life at Wright State University. Not all minority applicants are interviewed on these days and applicants are given the option of interviewing on a regular interview day if preferable.

Academic Support Programs
Strong academic support is provided jointly by the Office of Academic Affairs and the Office of Student Affairs and Admissions. First-year students are offered group and individualized programs

that help improve skills such as time management, note taking, organization, and test taking. Support in mastering subject material of the freshman year is provided by a peer tutorial system that is available to all students. For the individual who experiences difficulty with a particular subject, an opportunity to remediate usually exists in courses during the basic science biennium.

Enrichment Programs
In addition to *Horizons in Medicine*, which is available to high school students, a short-term research training program is held each summer for minority undergraduate, graduate, and health professional students. This is an eight-week program that matches underrepresented minority undergraduate students from around the country with basic science faculty to provide the opportunity to participate in laboratory research focused on the cardiovascular system. This allows students to develop a sound research base as well as hone scientific writing and presentation skills with the faculty of an academic medical center that ranks near the top nationally in the amount of research funding received by community-based medical schools. A four-week summer program is available to students who have been accepted and will enroll in the next freshman class at the School of Medicine. This *pre-matriculation program* emphasizes preparation for gross anatomy, a major topic covered in the first year curriculum. This program, which is available to all matriculating students, also helps develop strong study skills and smooth transition to medical school.

Student Financial Assistance
Applicants whose American Medical College Application Service fee has been waived may request a waiver of the Wright State application fee at the time they submit their supplemental applications. The Office of Student Affairs and Admissions of the School of Medicine in cooperation with the Office of Financial Aid of the university administer financial aid. Information concerning available loans and scholarships can be obtained from the Office of Student Affairs and Admissions. Each year, the local minority medical professional society awards several scholarships specifically to minority students.

University of Oklahoma College of Medicine*

Michelle English
Director of Student Services
University of Oklahoma
College of Medicine
P.O. Box 26901
Oklahoma City, OK 73190
405-271-2316; 405-271-3032 Fax
michelle-english@ouhsc.edu

Recruitment

The University of Oklahoma Health Sciences Center (HSC) Student Affairs Office helps develop a Sooner community of health care professionals through recruitment, retention, and recreational programs and services. The HSC Student Affairs staff is responsible for student recruitment and student services; provides oversight for all campus student organizations and student government; coordinates student development and community-based programs for health professions awareness; oversees Union and fitness facilities; and provides counseling services for Health Sciences Center students through HSC Counseling Services.

HSC Student Affairs outreach and recruitment programs strive to reach all populations throughout the state of Oklahoma by introducing them to the excitement and rewards awaiting a health care profession. Through our transfer advising services, recruiters visit higher education institutions across the state assisting students through the matriculation and admissions process. Our Summer Academy and Discovery programs give first-generation and at-risk high school students an early introduction into the various health care professions through programs that span anywhere from two-weeks to a full academic year.

Admissions

The Admissions Committee is designed to include representatives from underrepresented groups in medicine and to select students that will contribute to a diverse educational environment. The academic potential of the successful applicant is complimented by self-awareness, self-discipline, empathy, personal competence, and social competence.

Academic Support Programs

The college retains the services of an academic counselor and a counselor with special expertise in study skills, time management, and test taking. Students may self refer or be referred if difficulties are recognized. Five sessions may be conducted at no cost to the student. Access to services is coordinated through the Office of Student Affairs. Faculty and Course Directors are available to students for advice, counseling, and assistance with course work.

With support from the college, African American and Hispanic student groups sponsor health fairs in communities as well as pre-medical advising programs/workshops.

Student Financial Assistance

All College of Medicine students, including minority students, are invited each spring to apply for college scholarships to be applied the following academic year. Disadvantaged students are also invited to apply for the Scholarships for Disadvantaged Students (SDS) each spring through the Office of Financial Aid.

There are various state and federal monies available, both as stipends and loans. Information regarding financial assistance may be obtained from: Office of Financial Aid, University of Oklahoma Health Sciences Center, P.O. Box 26901, Oklahoma City, OK 73190, 405-271-2118.

The College of Medicine does not provide financial help to any students for expenses associated with interviews.

University of Oklahoma College of Medicine, 2006
Applicants and Matriculants by Gender, Race and Ethnicity

Race and Ethnicity	Applicants			Matriculants		
	Women	Men	Total	Women	Men	Total
Hispanic/Latino						
Cuban	2	1	3	0	0	0
Mexican American	17	10	27	0	1	1
Puerto Rican	5	1	6	0	0	0
Other Hispanic	11	16	27	0	0	0
Multiple Hispanic*	0	1	1	0	0	0
Subtotal	35	29	64	0	1	1
Non-Hispanic/Latino**						
Black	35	16	51	2	0	2
Native American/Alaska Native	23	17	40	4	4	8
Native Hawaiian/Other Pacific Islander	2	0	2	0	0	0
White	266	388	654	43	80	123
Asian	76	125	201	7	10	17
Other Race	0	2	2	0	1	1
Multiple Race*	25	22	47	4	2	6
Unknown	0	4	4	0	0	0
Subtotal	427	574	1,001	60	97	157
Foreign	3	7	10	0	0	0
Total	465	610	1,075	60	98	158

*Since 2002, students can select more than one race and / or ethnicity. **Those who did not choose 'Hispanic/Latino' or 'Non-Hispanic/Latino' are counted under 'Non-Hispanic/Latino'.
Data Source: AAMC Data Warehouse: Applicant-Matriculant File, as of 5/9/2007.

Oregon Health & Science University School of Medicine

Dr. Ella Booth
Associate Dean, Diversity
Oregon Health & Science University
School of Medicine
3181 SW Sam Jackson Park Rd. L-102
Portland, OR 97239
503-494-8089; 503-494-3400 Fax
boothe@ohsu.edu
http://www.ohsu.edu/ohsuedu/academic/som/diversity

Recruitment

Oregon Health & Science University (OHSU) has a long history of dedication to providing community services while improving access to health care for underserved and disadvantaged communities. In addition, OHSU has offered outreach programs for at least 22 years to increase the number of underrepresented and disadvantaged individuals entering medicine, dentistry, and biomedical research. The university-wide Center for Diversity and Multicultural Affairs (CeDMA) participates in career fairs, hosts campus visitations, and maintains ties statewide with counselors in secondary schools, community colleges, and universities. These activities help us recruit students from underserved areas. These include the *YO Science* summer program, which provides 40 disadvantaged middle school students with hands-on experience in health care professions over a week. CeDMA also sponsors the *CURE* project, giving most participants their first exposure to a laboratory. The well known AHEC MedStars program gives 30 disadvantaged high school students from urban and rural settings a chance to experience medicine at OHSU for three days in the summer. In partnership with OHSU's academic schools, the Health and Science Careers Conference serves as a catalyst for academic programs to identify prospective underrepresented and/or disadvantaged college students by introducing the health and science tracks offered by OHSU. This conference attracts more than 100 students annually.

The OHSU School of Medicine also has an Associate Dean of Diversity, who meets with students individually to provide career advice. The OHSU Student National Medical Association (SNMA) also provides information for prospective students through the Diversity Affairs Web site. Current medical students list their career and extracurricular interests and can be e-mailed for more information about student life through the Office of Diversity Affairs Web site.

For information on CeDMA programs the Multicultural Resource Guide, see *(http://www.ohsu.edu/academic/diversity/)*.

OHSU SNMA Student Directory: *(http://www.ohsu.edu/som/dean/oma/)*.

Admissions

The Admissions Committee seeks students who have demonstrated academic excellence and who will contribute to the diversity necessary to enhance the medical education of all students. Applicants are selected on the basis of demonstrated motivation for medicine, humanistic qualities, and a realistic understanding of the role of the physician in providing health care to all communities in need of it. The School of Medicine Admissions Committee fully recognizes the importance of diversity in its student body and in the physician workforce in providing effective delivery of health care to all. The Admissions Committee strongly encourages applications from people from all socioeconomic, racial, ethnic, religious,

Oregon Health & Science University School of Medicine, 2006
Applicants and Matriculants by Gender, Race and Ethnicity

Race and Ethnicity	Applicants			Matriculants		
	Women	Men	Total	Women	Men	Total
Hispanic/Latino						
Cuban	3	5	8	0	0	0
Mexican American	57	52	109	2	1	3
Puerto Rican	6	6	12	0	0	0
Other Hispanic	44	44	88	2	2	4
Multiple Hispanic*	6	6	12	0	0	0
Subtotal	116	113	229	4	3	7
Non-Hispanic/Latino**						
Black	48	25	73	1	0	1
Native American/Alaska Native	9	9	18	0	2	2
Native Hawaiian/Other Pacific Islander	13	6	19	0	1	1
White	1,122	1,389	2,511	50	44	94
Asian	441	430	871	9	5	14
Other Race	2	4	6	0	0	0
Multiple Race*	91	69	160	0	1	1
Unknown	14	13	27	0	0	0
Subtotal	1,740	1,945	3,685	60	53	113
Foreign	10	16	26	0	0	0
Total	1,866	2,074	3,940	64	56	120

*Since 2002, students can select more than one race and / or ethnicity. **Those who did not choose Hispanic/Latino' or 'Non-Hispanic/Latino' are counted under 'Non-Hispanic/Latino'.

Data Source: AAMC Data Warehouse: Applicant-Matriculant File, as of 5/9/2007.

and educational backgrounds, particularly those groups that are underrepresented in medicine.

Academic Support Programs
The OHSU School of Medicine believes in enabling all of its students to discover their individual career paths in medicine. We encourage and work with students in the pursuit of away rotations, rural rotations, and endeavor to be flexible with the academic curriculum in order to help its students succeed. We also offer tutors and an OSHU learning specialist for students in need as well as an extremely dedicated faculty available to students throughout their entire medical career.

Enrichment Programs
In addition to the programs sponsored through the Center for Diversity and Multicultural Affairs, the School of Medicine offers enrichment programs. Each of these programs is designed to assist educationally and economically disadvantaged students achieve degrees as physician assistants or physicians.

The Health Professions Testing Program provides up to 20 disadvantage juniors with a no-cost Medical College Admission Test (MCAT/GRE). This is a summer enrichment program designed to identify, develop, and enhance the competitive profiles of undergraduate college students for the health professions. Students also work with a learning specialist, receive mentoring on study skills and career choice, and receive a stipend. Room and board are also included.

The Post-Baccalaureate Conditional Acceptance Program contains an MCAT/GRE program (depending on if the student is applying for physician assistant or medical school), an academic year at neighboring Portland State University taking upper-level science and math coursework, clinical shadowing, and entrance into the Completion Program (below).

Six students are accepted into the program and receive stipends. With successful completion of the program, students are offered acceptance to the P.A. or M.D. programs. Students must interview successfully with the School of Medicine Admissions Committee, and have been refused from all medical schools or physician assistant programs to be eligible for this program.

Completion Program. This program is a four-week pre-matriculation to medical school course, with early work in anatomy and physiology. It provides study groups, tutoring, mentoring, and assessment of study skills and time management.

Equity Summer Research is an 8-10 week summer research internship through the Graduate Studies Program. Students receive a stipend to work on a research project alongside, a faculty principal investigator. They also meet with basic science faculty, attend lectures, and learn about the M.D./Ph.D. program from medical and graduate students.

Program information and applications are available at *(http://www.ohsu.edu/ohsuedu/ academic/som/diversity/index.cfm.)*

Student Financial Assistance
Underrepresented minority and disadvantaged students are considered for four Diversity Achievement Scholarships offered annually by the School of Medicine. These awards are available to both Oregon residents and non-residents. Other scholarships that provide assistance for disadvantaged students come from endowed scholarship programs. The Office of Diversity Affairs offers a database of national, state, and local scholarships that are accessible for students at our Web site: *(http://www.ohsu.edu/ academic/diversity/medicalscholarships.html)*

In assistance to those students who need financial management, CeDMA offers a financial management workshop in which students learn and implement a checkbook management system that allows the users to simultaneously save as they spend money. The focus outcome is to assist students to better manage their spending and saving to ease their monetary concern during their tenure at medical school.

Educational Partnerships
Both the Office of Diversity Affairs and the Center for Diversity and Multicultural Affairs partner with Portland and Oregon schools. These partnerships include Benson, Jefferson, Roosevelt, Century, and Woodburn high schools; Oregon State University; Willamette University; and Portland State University. The large majority of these schools have formal agreements to promote student success and diversification. Both the office and the center also have formal, longstanding partnerships with Oregon Area Health Education Centers as well.

AAMC

Drexel University College of Medicine (Formerly MCP Hahnemann School of Medicine)

Dr. Anthony R. Rodriguez
Associate Dean, Student Affairs & Diversity
Drexel University College of Medicine
2900 Queen Lane
Philadelphia, PA 19129-1096
215-991-8265; 215-843-1766 Fax
Anthony.Rodriguez@DrexelMed.edu

Recruitment

Two institutions with a rich history of excellence and diversity in medical education, the Medical College of Pennsylvania and Hahnemann University, have joined their strengths to create a single school with a common goal—providing expanded educational opportunities for minorities in the field of medicine.

Drexel University College of Medicine (formerly MCP Hahnemann School of Medicine) is committed to providing each of its graduates with superior clinical skills, combined with an in-depth understanding of, and dedication to, community needs.

The school draws on traditions of diversity that extend back almost 150 years. Hahnemann University was founded in 1848 and the Medical College of Pennsylvania was founded in 1850. Over their histories, the schools have educated hundreds of minority physicians, including the second African American woman in the United States to become a physician, in 1867. In the past 25 years, more than 400 minority physicians have graduated from the schools.

Through the Office of Diversity, the medical school continues its historical mission by devoting major energies in the identification, admission, retention, and graduation of students who are members of racial/ethnic groups traditionally underrepresented in the medical profession (i.e., African American, Puerto Rican, Mexican American, and Native American). Recruitment activities include visitation to colleges and graduate and professional career awareness conferences. In addition, orientation visits to the medical school are encouraged and provided to pre-medical advisors and student groups. In cooperation with the campus chapters of the Student National Medical Association and the Latin Medical Student Association, a Minority Applicant Host Program has been established. Preceding, during, and after the interview day, members of the program serve as an important student link between the applicant and the medical school. Individuals are encouraged to contact the Office of Diversity regarding pre-application information or to request a campus visit.

Program for Integrated Learning. All students entering the medical school have the opportunity to complete their first two years of medical school in a curriculum that is an alternative to the traditional lecture-based, large-group, faculty-directed curriculum. Under this alternate curriculum, students meet in small groups to pursue self-directed, problem-based learning. Guided by a faculty facilitator, they learn the basic science principles of medical ethics and community and preventive medicine, as well as elements of patient communication, physical diagnosis, and history-taking in this integrated interactive format.

Admissions

All applicants must apply through the American Medical College Application Service (AMCAS) and request their application, letters of recommendation, and Medical College Admission Test (MCAT) results be forwarded to the Office of Admissions, Drexel University

Drexel University College of Medicine, 2006
Applicants and Matriculants by Gender, Race and Ethnicity

Race and Ethnicity	Applicants			Matriculants		
	Women	Men	Total	Women	Men	Total
Hispanic/Latino						
Cuban	32	30	62	0	0	0
Mexican American	84	89	173	2	1	3
Puerto Rican	41	30	71	1	0	1
Other Hispanic	151	101	252	4	2	6
Multiple Hispanic*	18	14	32	1	0	1
Subtotal	326	264	590	8	3	11
Non-Hispanic/Latino*						
Black	425	204	629	5	1	6
Native American/Alaska Native	10	9	19	0	0	0
Native Hawaiian/Other Pacific Islander	23	25	48	0	1	1
White	2,640	2,987	5,627	68	74	142
Asian	1,582	1,532	3,114	38	40	78
Other Race	9	8	17	0	0	0
Multiple Race*	159	134	293	6	7	13
Unknown	45	47	92	2	2	4
Subtotal	4,893	4,946	9,839	119	125	244
Foreign	29	43	72	0	0	0
Total	5,248	5,253	10,501	127	128	255

*Since 2002, students can select more than one race and / or ethnicity. **Those who did not choose Hispanic/Latino' or 'Non-Hispanic/Latino' are counted under 'Non-Hispanic/Latino'.
Data Source: AAMC Data Warehouse: Applicant-Matriculant File, as of 5/9/2007.

College of Medicine. All applications are reviewed by a member or members of the Admissions Committee.

All applicants must complete the application process prior to consideration for an admission interview. The successful applicant will show evidence of a caring personality, leadership skills, service-oriented activities, and a true commitment to a medical career, in conjunction with strong academic credentials. The Associate Dean for Diversity, College of Medicine, the Director of Minority Affairs, and minority faculty members serve as advocates for the minority applicants.

Academic Support Services

At Drexel University College of Medicine there is a university-wide commitment to the retention and graduation of underrepresented minority (URM) students. The administration, Office of Diversity personnel, faculty, and the Director of Enrich-ment and Assessment are all an integral part of a comprehensive retention effort. Students have the option of participating in several enrichment and support programs, which have been implemented to assist in the academic success of each student.

These programs include individual and group tutorial assistance, academic and personal counseling, structured study groups, workshops on stress management, standardized test management, effective study techniques, and diagnostic testing to identify learning styles and academic strengths and weaknesses. Departments in the basic sciences provide regularly scheduled review sessions, and pre-clinical faculty are assigned as advisors to members of the first-year class. First-year students are encouraged to attend the weekly Medical Scholars Review Program. This program is designed to assist the student in the review of course content and information presented the previous week.

United States Medical Licensing Examination Step 1 Review. The Director of Academic Enrichment administers an 18-week Board Review Program, cost free, to second-year students preparing for this examination. The review program is offered from January through May of each academic year. It includes diagnostic testing, faculty volunteers who present weekly two-hour lectures that are videotaped for student use, accompanying practice question sessions, and strategies for taking this standardized examination.

Enrichment Program

Drexel Pathway to Medical School Program (DPMS). The program is designed for students from a lower socioeconomic/disadvantaged background. Students are required to have at least the minimum courses required of medical school acceptance; one year each of biology, chemistry, organic chemistry, and physics, (each with laboratory); and one year of English literature and behavioral science courses. In addition, a 2.90 undergraduate math/science GPA and a minimum MCAT score of 20, with no section below a 6, is necessary.

If an applicant meets these requirements, they may be granted an interview with Drexel University College of Medicine. If, after the interview, they are granted provisional acceptance into the School of Medicine, the applicant will be accepted into this Early Assurance Program.

Student Financial Assistance

The Office of Student Financial Planning administers a comprehensive financial assistance program. Financial assistance eligibility is determined on the basis of need as assessed by Free Application for Federal Student Aid. The Director of Financial Planning provides counseling to each student and develops a financial assistance package commensurate with the needs of the individual student. The office assists students in obtaining funds from

private sources and counsels students on locating additional resources. Waiver of the application fee is granted to students who have been approved for American Medical College Application Service (AMCAS) fee waivers. The university provides Academic Merit Scholarships. In order to be considered for the Academic Merit Scholarship, an applicant must meet the criteria established by the Admissions Committee.

Educational Partnerships

Faculty Development Program. This program was established to increase the number of underrepresented faculty and to assist in the academic development and progress of each minority faculty member.

Transitions to Medicine Programs. In order to increase the opportunity for underrepresented minority students to gain entrance into medical school, this program offers each student an MCAT review and one year of medical curriculum course work prior to making re-application to medical school.

Middle School Project. This program provides summer and year-round academic activities for middle school students.

Youth Mentoring Program. This program matches high school students interested in health care careers with university-wide employees.

Health Start. This is a year-round program in which medical students facilitate groups of high school students in problem-based learning instruction and research.

AAMC

Jefferson Medical College of Thomas Jefferson University

Dr. Edward B. Christian, Associate Dean
Ms. Luz Ortiz, Assistant Dean
Office of Diversity and Minority Affairs
Jefferson Medical College of
Thomas Jefferson University
1020 Locust Street, Suite 163
Philadelphia, PA 19107-6799
215-503-4795; 215-503-4096 Fax
edward.christian@jefferson.edu
Luz.Ortiz@jefferson.edu

Recruitment

The Office of Diversity and Minority Affairs (ODAMA) invites you to visit Jefferson Medical College (JMC) of Thomas Jefferson University, one of the oldest and largest academic health centers in the country. At Jefferson Medical College, we are committed to the active recruitment and retention of a diverse student population. The staff of ODAMA provides information on opportunities at Jefferson as well as assistance with the application process for students who are underrepresented in the field of medicine. Throughout the year, recruiting opportunities are provided through attendance at regional and national conferences and visits to college campuses nationwide. The ODAMA staff attends recruitment fairs and conferences to meet, seek, and recruit potential students. In addition, any group that desires to visit Jefferson Medical College or wishes to have an ODAMA representative visit your home campus should contact our office for arrangements.

Admissions

Jefferson Medical College participates in the American Medical College Application Service (AMCAS). Minority students from all states are encouraged to apply for admissions and are urged to identify themselves on the AMCAS application form. All underrepresented applications are reviewed and qualified students receive an invitation for an interview. Individuals of diverse social, racial, and economical backgrounds are encouraged to apply. Jefferson Medical College has a strong commitment to matriculating a diverse student body to take care of a diverse patient population.

Only completed applications, both the AMCAS and Jefferson secondary application, are processed and considered by the Admissions Committee. The criteria for selection are those that will produce competent and compassionate physicians. Selection factors include, but are not limited to, academic record, Medical College Admission Test (MCAT) scores, recommendations, breadth of medical and community exposure and knowledge-base, personal characteristics, and communication skills. The Admissions Committee takes actions on all applicants.

Academic Support Programs

Jefferson Medical College encourages its students to utilize the numerous resources and faculty that are available to them. The Offices of Undergraduate Medical Education and Student Affairs and Career Counseling are two of the major support service areas for all students. There are a wide variety of skilled personnel, faculty, and materials to assist students throughout their four years.

Computerized and traditional tutorial programs are available for those who need academic reinforcement. Mentoring programs are provided in conjunction with the Office of Student Affairs and Career Counseling.

Additional support is provided to underrepresented students through organizations such as the JMC Diversity Council,

Jefferson Medical College of Thomas Jefferson University, 2006
Applicants and Matriculants by Gender, Race and Ethnicity

Race and Ethnicity	Applicants			Matriculants		
	Women	Men	Total	Women	Men	Total
Hispanic/Latino						
Cuban	17	16	33	0	0	0
Mexican American	42	45	87	1	0	1
Puerto Rican	20	24	44	0	2	2
Other Hispanic	103	72	175	5	4	9
Multiple Hispanic*	13	11	24	0	0	0
Subtotal	195	168	363	6	6	12
Non-Hispanic/Latino**						
Black	219	128	347	2	1	3
Native American/Alaska Native	4	3	7	0	0	0
Native Hawaiian/Other Pacific Islander	21	16	37	0	0	0
White	1,987	2,169	4,156	93	76	169
Asian	1,126	1,070	2,196	32	21	53
Other Race	5	3	8	0	0	0
Multiple Race*	104	94	198	5	4	9
Unknown	29	32	61	2	1	3
Subtotal	3,495	3,515	7,010	134	103	237
Foreign	190	199	389	3	3	6
Total	3,880	3,882	7,762	143	112	255

*Since 2002, students can select more than one race and / or ethnicity. **Those who did not choose 'Hispanic/Latino' or 'Non-Hispanic/Latino' are counted under 'Non-Hispanic/Latino'.
Data Source: AAMC Data Warehouse: Applicant-Matriculant File, as of 5/9/2007.

Student National Medical Association (SNMA), Jefferson African American Student Society (JAASS), and Jefferson Boricua Latino Health Organization (JBLHO).

Student Financial Assistance

JMC students who demonstrate financial need are considered for financial assistance from the school's institutional financial aid programs. Minority and disadvantaged students have additional funding options available to them through the Algernon B. Jackson Scholarship Program.

If AMCAS has previously granted a fee waiver, Jefferson's admissions application fee is waived as well.

Other Pertinent Information

Whether your interest is clinical medicine, academic medicine, or research, Jefferson can meet your academic and social needs. Three dual degree programs are offered in academic medicine: M.D./Ph.D., M.D./ M.B.A., and M.D./M.P.H. Participation in research and community opportunities are plentiful. Students are eligible to apply for research programs and gain experience in research in the summer between the first and second years. We provide hands on clinical experience in the first and second years in addition to a wide range of hospital sites in the third and fourth years. Opportunities to participate in research, community outreach, and global health programs are plentiful.

Jefferson Medical College maintains its focus on the recruitment, retention, and graduation of underrepresented students, while simultaneously advancing the diversity initiatives.

Pennsylvania State University College of Medicine*

Dr. Alphonse E. Leure-duPree
Associate Dean for
Academic Achievement
Pennsylvania State
University College of Medicine
P.O. Box 850, 500 University Drive
Hershey, PA 17033
717-531-6411; 717-531-4045 Fax
djL11@psu.edu

Recruitment

The Pennsylvania State University College of Medicine is actively involved and strongly committed to the recruitment of minority groups who are underrepresented in medicine.

The recruitment program includes:

- Visitations by faculty and students to high schools and universities in Pennsylvania and neighboring states.
- Orientation visits to medical schools. Students, faculty, and administrators host groups of interested minority students who visit the campus.
- National minority conferences and workshops. Faculty and students are registrants and participants in national conferences and workshops.
- Career days. School representation is apparent at selected career day programs.

Admissions

Although there is neither a separate Admissions Committee nor a separate policy employed in the selection of minority

Pennsylvania State University College of Medicine, 2006
Applicants and Matriculants by Gender, Race and Ethnicity

Race and Ethnicity	Applicants			Matriculants		
	Women	Men	Total	Women	Men	Total
Hispanic/Latino						
Cuban	20	12	32	0	0	0
Mexican American	32	36	68	0	0	0
Puerto Rican	20	17	37	0	1	1
Other Hispanic	67	53	120	0	0	0
Multiple Hispanic*	11	7	18	0	0	0
Subtotal	150	125	275	0	1	1
Non-Hispanic/Latino**						
Black	171	102	273	3	8	11
Native American/Alaska Native	2	4	6	0	0	0
Native Hawaiian/Other Pacific Islander	9	10	19	0	0	0
White	1,503	1,773	3,276	51	57	108
Asian	777	772	1,549	12	8	20
Other Race	5	2	7	0	0	0
Multiple Race*	74	69	143	3	2	5
Unknown	14	22	36	0	0	0
Subtotal	2,555	2,754	5,309	69	75	144
Foreign	158	144	302	4	3	7
Total	2,863	3,023	5,886	73	79	152

*Since 2002, students can select more than one race and / or ethnicity. **Those who did not choose Hispanic/Latino' or 'Non-Hispanic/Latino' are counted under 'Non-Hispanic/Latino'.
Data Source: AAMC Data Warehouse: Applicant-Matriculant File, as of 5/9/2007.

students, the Committee recognizes and gives consideration to special features of an applicant's background and experience. There is minority representation on the Medical Selection Committee, and both minority faculty and currently enrolled students are participants in the candidate's interview schedule. No student is admitted who cannot, in the judgment of the Committee, complete the graduation requirements and fulfill the school's academic standards.

Academic Support Programs

The Associate Dean of Academic Achievement, the Director of Special Programs, and the course directors work together to identify students who may be experiencing academic difficulty. Students can obtain individual tutorial assistance or group tutorial help. Computerized assistance is also available in selected courses. In addition, each student has a faculty advisor who is an important part of the educational system. The faculty advisor is a source of general support for students in the areas of academic, personal, and social counseling. Study skills, time management, and stress management programs are also available. A restructuring of the student's curriculum may also be employed to assist in mastery of course material.

Enrichment Programs

The Pennsylvania State University College of Medicine does not offer a summer academic reinforcement program. Individual employment opportunities may be available.

Student Financial Assistance

In addition to need-based financial aid, the school provides four-year Dean's Scholarships to competitive minority applicants who have been accepted to the College of Medicine.

Temple University School of Medicine

Dr. Raul A. DeLa Cadena
Assistant Dean & Director Recruitment
Admissions and Retention Program
Director, Center of Excellence
for Research and Training
on Health Disparities
Temple University School of Medicine
3400 North Broad Street
Philadelphia, PA 19140
2150-707-3595; 215-707-3597 Fax
cadena@temple.edu

Recruitment

The Recruitment, Admissions and Retention (RAR) Program at Temple University School of Medicine is meeting the challenge of providing opportunities for the medical education of students underrepresented in the health profession of medicine. The RAR Program has a legacy of over 30 years of ongoing support services. Temple is concerned with more than the facade of equal opportunity. It is devoted to its substance—the effort to help disadvantaged students overcome the academic and economic obstacles that are the reasons for their under representation among our nation's physicians.

Admissions

The RAR Program has a full-time Counselor responsible for increasing the number of RAR Program applicants to our medical school, maintaining a high level of RAR Program enrollment, helping promote students' academic successes, and ensuring retention and on-time graduation.

Academic Support Programs

As the students' advocate, the RAR Program Counselor works closely with our faculty

Temple University School of Medicine, 2006
Applicants and Matriculants by Gender, Race and Ethnicity

Race and Ethnicity	Applicants			Matriculants		
	Women	Men	Total	Women	Men	Total
Hispanic/Latino						
Cuban	26	28	54	0	2	2
Mexican American	53	67	120	1	4	5
Puerto Rican	35	31	66	0	0	0
Other Hispanic	131	85	216	1	2	3
Multiple Hispanic*	16	15	31	2	0	2
Subtotal	261	226	487	4	8	12
Non-Hispanic/Latino**						
Black	480	234	714	12	3	15
Native American/Alaska Native	4	7	11	0	0	0
Native Hawaiian/Other Pacific Islander	16	18	34	0	0	0
White	2,000	2,259	4,259	45	54	99
Asian	1,235	1,170	2,405	19	18	37
Other Race	9	5	14	0	0	0
Multiple Race*	119	102	221	5	5	10
Unknown	31	34	65	1	1	2
Subtotal	3,894	3,829	7,723	82	81	163
Foreign	43	43	86	0	0	0
Total	4,198	4,098	8,296	86	89	175

*Since 2002, students can select more than one race and / or ethnicity. **Those who did not choose Hispanic/Latino' or 'Non-Hispanic/Latino' are counted under 'Non-Hispanic/Latino'.
Data Source: AAMC Data Warehouse: Applicant-Matriculant File, as of 5/9/2007.

Association of American Medical Colleges, 2007

and administrative offices, such as Financial Aid and Student Affairs. The Counselor serves on medical school committees that monitor students' academic progress and coordinate support services to meet individual student's needs. If necessary, particular help is provided with sharpening students' learning skills. Counseling is also available to students should personal issues adversely affect their academic performances. Once an underrepresented student in the health profession of medicine is admitted to Temple, the RAR Program staff seeks to academically support each and every student by helping them through difficulties as well as sharing in their academic successes.

Enrichment Programs

We provide a wide range of year-round student support services for enrolled underrepresented medical students and conduct a voluntary two-week Summer Program during July for qualified students who will enroll in the first-year class. In keeping with Temple's goal to academically retain all students it enrolls, our RAR Program Counselor and the faculty of the medical school have long agreed that entering first-year students who participate in our Summer Program, called SERA (Summer Educational Reinforcement Activity) better their chances for an academically successful first year.

The SERA is a no-penalty simulation of what it is like to experience the first year of medical education. In the first week, students are introduced to the faculty, staff, upper-class students, and the facilities of the medical school. During the remaining week, medical school faculty present lectures, conferences, and laboratory experiences from segments of the first-year courses in gross anatomy, biochemistry, and physiology. Students attend seminars designed to sharpen their learning skills; participate in Learning Teams with their

new classmates; experience a variety of early patient care activities; and have Clinical Conferences about medical topics presented by physicians, many of whom are graduates of Temple.

Throughout the two-week SERA, the RAR Program Counselor assists students with planning for their enrollment in the fall, with particular attention directed to their initial adjustment to the first-year curriculum, financial planning, and housing. Year-round student support services provided by our RAR Program help with students' concerns in many areas including adjustment to the rigors of the first-year medical school curriculum and, in subsequent years, timely preparation for taking the licensure examinations as well as residency selection in the fourth year.

The RAR Program Counselor also works very closely with the Office of Admissions to assist in the timely processing of applications from students underrepresented in the health profession of medicine. We provide follow-up communications with applicants when necessary and are advocates for applicants at all stages of their admissions process, including the medical school's Admissions Committee.

Applicants meet with members of the RAR Program staff at the time of their Personal Interview and talk with currently enrolled medical students in order to obtain a realistic picture of what is like to be a medical student at Temple University.

Student Financial Assistance

Student financial aid awards at Temple are based primarily on need established by the use of the Temple University Medical Financial Aid application and the Free Application for Federal Student Aid (FAFSA), which detail financial resources of students (and/or their families). They are balanced against a standard educational expenses budget including special

need factors. The bulk of financial aid is derived from federally-guaranteed sources such as Stafford Loans. The medical school may provide some funding through private loan and scholarships sources, depending upon need and availability. Application procedures and eligibility requirements vary for each financial program. Our medical school's Financial Aid Counselor is available to provide information and assistance to all applicants.

AAMC

University of Pennsylvania School of Medicine

Dr. Karen E. Hamilton, Assistant Dean for Diversity and Community Outreach in Undergraduate Medical Education
University of Pennsylvania School of Medicine
3450 Hamilton Walk, Suite 100 Stemmler Hall, Philadelphia, PA 19104
215-898-4409; 215-898-0833 Fax
odco@mail.med.upenn
http://www.med.upenn.edu/diversityume

Recruitment

The University of Pennsylvania School of Medicine is committed to sustaining a diverse student body in keeping with the view that interaction among students from different backgrounds enriches the educational experiences of all students, faculty, and the Penn community at large.

In 1968, it established the Office of Minority Affairs, now known as the Office of Diversity and Community Outreach in Undergraduate Medical Eduction. Among its many responsibilities are efforts to recruit and retain students from groups that are underrepresented in medicine. Currently, 119 students from underrepresented groups compose approximately 16.5 percent of the student body. The recruitment and subsequent graduation of 571 students from these groups since 1968, reflects the School of Medicine's contribution to diversity within the school and within the medical profession.

The office hosts student groups from various undergraduate colleges and community-based organizations in order to provide general information about medical school preparation and details of the School of Medicine's admissions process,

curriculum, student life, research opportunities, and financial aid. Similarly, students and office staff participate in outreach activities at local high schools, undergraduate colleges, summer enrichment programs, as well as at the annual career fairs of the Association of American Medical Colleges and the National Association of Medical Minority Educators (NAMME).

The most significant recruitment effort on the part of the office has been coordinating the publication of *Getting into Medical School: A Planning Guide for Minority Students*. This book was conceived of and written by Penn Medical minority students. To date, it is the only commercially published book of its kind written by and for minority students.

During the admissions season, the office and the Penn Medical chapters of the Student National Medical Association and the Boricua Latino Health Organization sponsor informational sessions about their programs and activities. Applicants from underrepresented groups and those interested in minority health issues and health care delivery for underserved communities are encouraged to attend these sessions.

Admissions

The Committee on Admissions is composed of a diverse group of faculty and students, some of whom are from groups underrepresented in medicine. In its mission to enroll a student body reflective of cultural diversity, consideration is given to an applicant's special features of background and experiences that may contribute to a candidate's potential for a career in medicine. The committee evaluates applicants whom it admits on the basis of their academic potential, service, and leadership.

Applications for admission must be submitted through the American Medical

University of Pennsylvania School of Medicine, 2006
Applicants and Matriculants by Gender, Race and Ethnicity

Race and Ethnicity		Applicants			Matriculants		
		Women	Men	Total	Women	Men	Total
Hispanic/Latino							
Cuban		16	16	32	0	0	0
Mexican American		34	45	79	0	1	1
Puerto Rican		23	21	44	4	0	4
Other Hispanic		67	59	126	3	5	8
Multiple Hispanic*		6	7	13	0	2	2
	Subtotal	146	148	294	7	8	15
Non-Hispanic/Latino**							
Black		229	133	362	4	4	8
Native American/Alaska Native		2	4	6	0	0	0
Native Hawaiian/Other Pacific Islander		8	3	11	0	0	0
White		1,379	1,688	3,067	50	56	106
Asian		744	775	1,519	11	5	16
Other Race		3	2	5	0	0	0
Multiple Race*		81	82	163	0	2	2
Unknown		30	38	68	0	2	2
	Subtotal	2,476	2,725	5,201	65	69	134
Foreign		121	114	235	0	2	2
	Total	2,743	2,987	5,730	72	79	151

*Since 2002, students can select more than one race and / or ethnicity. **Those who did not choose 'Hispanic/Latino' or 'Non-Hispanic/Latino' are counted under 'Non-Hispanic/Latino'.

Data Source: AAMC Data Warehouse: Applicant-Matriculant File, as of 5/9/2007.

Application Service (AMCAS) between June 1 and October 15. The Committee on Admissions will begin processing the application when all supplemental materials have been received, including the application supplemental, application fee or AMCAS fee waiver, Medical College Admission Test (MCAT) scores, and letters of recommendation. In addition to the M.D. program, students may pursue the M.D./Ph.D. degree or the M.D. and Master's degree. The Master's programs most commonly combined with the M.D. degree are the M.B.A., the Master's in Bioethics, and the Master's in Clinical Epidemiology.

Academic Support Programs

Curriculum flexibility is maintained to assure meeting students' individual needs in preparing for a future career. All students will have at least one and one-half years of elective time available to develop a personalized educational program. While most students will enter clinical clerkships at the midpoint of the second year, some are permitted to arrange an alternative schedule.

Counseling is an integral part of the School of Medicine's retention efforts. It is offered in all areas: personal, financial, residential, and academic. The summer prior to matriculation, each entering first-year student is assigned to an upper-class student peer advisor. Moreover, the Student Affairs administrators, the Associate Dean, Assistant Dean, and Associate Director for Diversity and Community Outreach in Undergraduate Medical Education Programs also serve as advisors.

With guidance from the Office for Diversity and Community Outreach in Undergraduate Medical Education, the Student National Medical Association (SNMA) and the Boricua Latino Health Organization (BLHO) have developed academic enrichment activities that include review sessions for the basic

sciences, tutoring, cultural competency lectures, and health education projects for underserved communities. These two student organizations also produce an ethnic guide to Philadelphia as part of the larger *Guide to the First Year,* an on-line publication sponsored by the Penn Med Student Government with the Office for Diversity and Community Outreach in Undergraduate Medical Education. The SNMA and BLHO also organize the Case Presentation Seminar Series in which minority faculty and residents give advice about successful academic performance for each required clerkship. These sessions, open to all, are continuous and facilitate interaction among students, minority faculty, and residents.

Enrichment Programs

Summer Internships in the Biological Sciences. This internship program offers hands-on research experience in a laboratory setting for undergraduate students interested in the biological sciences. Each undergraduate intern is matched with a faculty member and participates for ten weeks in the on-going research of the investigator's laboratory or performs a specific and supervised research project related to the goals of the laboratory. A weekly seminar provides an overview of the breadth of contemporary biomedical science. Formal courses are not offered.

Applicants may specify their research interest: biochemistry and molecular biophysics, cell and molecular biology, developmental biology, genetics, genomics and computational biology, immunology, microbiology, parasitology, and virology neuroscience and pharmacological sciences. Previous research experience is not necessary.

The program is open to students of all racial and ethnic backgrounds. Approximately 30 college sophomores and juniors participate each year. The stipend is $250/week, round-trip transportation to Philadelphia, and on-campus housing. February 1st is the application deadline.

For an application or further information contact (*http://www.med.upenn.edu/bgs/suip.shtml*) Summer Internship Coordinator, Biomedical Graduate Studies, 160 BRB 2/3, Currie Blvd., University of Pennsylvania, Philadelphia, PA 19104-6064.

Undergraduate Student Scholars Program. The Undergraduate Student Scholars Program in the NIH Center for Molecular Studies in Digestive and Liver Disease at the University of Pennsylvania is an organized program of summer lectures and presentations combined with basic research experience in the laboratory of an expert investigator. This program is open to students from the University of Pennsylvania as well as outside of the university. The curriculum is designed specifically for undergraduate students with an interest in biomedical research, with the eventual goal of M.D., Ph.D., or M.D.-Ph.D. degrees. Applications from women and members of underrepresented minorities are strongly encouraged.

During the program, students attend weekly seminars on introductory topics in biomedical research. At the end of the course, all participants present their research to members of the Center for Molecular Studies in Digestive and Liver Disease in a focused seminar and receive a certificate recognizing their completion of the program. For the research experience, students are paired with individual mentors. The research program is thus individualized to each student and each laboratory. Research interests of program faculty are available at (*http://www.med.upenn.edu/molecular/*)

The stipend this year is expected to be $3500 for the ten-week program. Applications, may be obtained at (*http://www.med.upenn.edu/molecular/*) or by contacting Ms. Daphne Jolly at the address below:

Daphne Jolly
Administrative Assistant
Gastroenterology Division
University of Pennsylvania
School of Medicine
600 Clinical Research Building
415 Curie Boulevard
Philadelphia, PA 19104
Email: *djolly@mail.med.upenn.edu*

Student Financial Assistance

The School of Medicine is committed to assisting students to fund their medical educational, minimizing debt, and providing financial counseling. The school awards both need based and merit scholarships. Need is documented after a financial analysis of the student's financial situation, including the parents' and spouse's financial situation. This data is requested on the financial aid application.

A successful applicant must be a United States citizen or hold a permanent residence visa, or an immigrant visa to be eligible for financial aid. The types of aid available include the following:

- School of Medicine scholarships
- School of Medicine loans
- MSTP funding (for M.D./Ph.D. program candidates)
- Federal loan programs
- Federal programs emphasizing primary care careers
- Alternative loan programs

Educational Partnerships

In partnership with the School of Medicine, the School of Dental Medicine, School of Veterinary Medicine, and the School of Nursing, along with the Office of Career Services Review have developed the *Pre-health Professions Mentor Program*. The goal of the program is to increase the number of undergraduates admitted to highly competitive health professional

schools. Although the program is a structured network of support for undergraduates who are from groups underrepresented in the health professions, its workshops and other programmatic activities are open to all Penn undergraduates. These include:

- Academic monitoring, counseling, and advising
- Medical College Admissions Test (MCAT) preparation
- Dental School Admissions Test (DAT) preparation
- Graduate Record Exam (GRE) preparation
- Mentoring by faculty; medical, dental, veterinary, and nursing students; and peers
- Interaction with faculty and professionals in the field
- Research experience
- Educational programs and workshops
- Tutoring

Association of American Medical Colleges, 2007

University of Pittsburgh School of Medicine

Dr. Chenits Pettigrew, Jr.
Assistant Dean of Student Affairs/Director
of Diversity Programs
University of Pittsburgh
School of Medicine
M-247 Scaife Hall
3550 Torrace Street
Pittsburgh, PA 15261
412-648-8987; 412-624-2516 Fax
Diversityaffairs@medschool.pitt.edu
http://www.medschoolpitt.edu/future/
future_03.asp

Recruitment

The Office of Student Affairs/Diversity Programs was instituted in 1979 to enhance and support the increasingly diverse student body of the school and to assist the Office of Admissions in recruiting underrepresented, underprivileged, and non-traditional students. Office staff and members of the Student National Medical Association (SNMA) participate in recruitment visits (fairs and small-group presentations) to various campuses nationwide during the school year and to summer programs. Visits are made to majority as well as Historically Black Colleges and Universities and Hispanic-serving campuses. Staff actively utilize the Medical Minority Applicant Registry (Med-MAR) to identify and contact prospective applicants. High school students are contacted via guidance counselors and during recruitment for the university's summer and enrichment programs (see Enrichment Programs). Staff have a great deal of interaction with the University of Pittsburgh undergraduate population through active involvement with the Pre-health Organization for Minority Students, a Student National Medical Association MAPS chapter.

Admissions

The school's student body represents many states of residence, differing undergraduate majors, and many for whom medicine was not a first career choice. All of these perspectives blend to create a diverse and enriching community. All candidates are considered via a common admissions process. An applicant's entire application is evaluated holistically when being considered for admission. Community service and other demonstrations of caring for others are extremely important. Additionally, first generation status and socioeconomic status are considered. Grade-point averages in conjunction with letters of recommendation and Medical College Admission Test (MCAT) scores contribute in making the admission decision.

Academic Support Programs

The curriculum is a blend of basic sciences, organ system studies, small-group learning, lectures, field experience, and self-directed learning. Significant emphasis is placed upon the physician/patient relationship; students begin interacting with patients in the first week of the first year. Course syllabi and study guides are distributed prior to the beginning of each course. The curriculum is quite effective, as evidenced by a 100 percent pass rate on United States Medical Licensing Examination (USMLE) Steps 1 and 2 in most recent years. New students are assigned to FAST (Faculty and Students Working Together) groups led by faculty and peer advisors who are available for advice and guidance. In addition, the Student Academic Resource Consortium, a team of second-year students, helps first-year students adjust to the rigors of medical school.

For students who need additional support, the University of Pittsburgh School of Medicine has a proactive program of assistance, including faculty retention committees that monitor student progress on an ongoing basis and recommend

University of Pittsburgh School of Medicine, 2006
Applicants and Matriculants by Gender, Race and Ethnicity

Race and Ethnicity	Applicants			Matriculants		
	Women	Men	Total	Women	Men	Total
Hispanic/Latino						
Cuban	13	12	25	1	0	1
Mexican American	40	36	76	3	0	3
Puerto Rican	14	16	30	0	0	0
Other Hispanic	55	47	102	2	0	2
Multiple Hispanic*	4	7	11	0	0	0
Subtotal	126	118	244	6	0	6
Non-Hispanic/Latino**						
Black	219	116	335	4	6	10
Native American/Alaska Native	3	4	7	0	0	0
Native Hawaiian/Other Pacific Islander	9	9	18	0	0	0
White	1,262	1,691	2,953	34	44	78
Asian	706	760	1,466	15	32	47
Other Race	2	4	6	0	0	0
Multiple Race*	82	77	159	1	2	3
Unknown	21	29	50	1	2	3
Subtotal	2,304	2,690	4,994	55	86	141
Foreign	27	32	59	0	0	0
Total	2,457	2,840	5,297	61	86	147

*Since 2002, students can select more than one race and / or ethnicity. **Those who did not choose Hispanic/Latino' or 'Non-Hispanic/Latino' are counted under 'Non-Hispanic/Latino'.
Data Source: AAMC Data Warehouse: Applicant-Matriculant File, as of 5/9/2007.

Association of American Medical Colleges, 2007

interventions. The Office of Academic Development provides assistance in learning strategies, time management, test taking, and coordinates a peer tutorial service. Faculty are always available for assistance on a group review and individual basis. The Office of Academic Development also works with students on pretest assessment and study plans for the USMLE Step 1 in the Spring of the second year.

A staff psychologist who has intimate knowledge of the curriculum and medical student life is available to assist students with personal issues that might arise.

Physician Partners Mentoring Program. The program links underrepresented, first-generation, and non-traditional medical students with faculty and community physicians in supportive relationships.

Enrichment Programs
For further information on any of the following programs, contact Dr. Chenits Pettigrew, Assistant Dean of Student Affairs/ Director of Diversity Programs at 412-648-8987, or visit *(http://www. medschoolpitt.edu/future/future_03.asp)*

Medical Explorers. Hosted in cooperation with the Boy Scouts of Southwestern Pennsylvania, this program provides high school students with exposure to the field of medicine through presentations given by physicians and medical students clinical pathology conferences, field trips, and laboratory experiences. The program operates through the academic year. Students meet twice per week in the Fall semester and once per week in the Spring semester. Planning for the programs is done by the Explorer student body at the end of each Spring. While designed for high school students, middle school students are welcome to attend.

Summer Pre-medical Academic Enrichment Program (SPAEP) Level I is a seven-week program offered to underrepresented and first-generation rising college freshmen

and sophomores. Its purpose is to 1) expose students to the pre-medical basic sciences through studying diseases that affect underserved communities (e.g., AIDS, sickle-cell anemia, hypertension); 2) motivate students to pursue careers in medicine; and 3) familiarize students with the medical school environment, and academic preparation and application processes for medical school. Students participate in lectures, presentations, research and a course in scientific communication. They shadow physicians and are responsible as a group for planning a portion of a community health fair. Study-skills diagnostics and tutorials are included. Physicians speak about their fields of practice at a weekly "Brown Bag Lunch" series. At the end-of-program forum each student gives an oral presentation of research on a selected disease. Preference in admission is given to Pennsylvania students, particularly those from Pittsburgh. However, students from across the nation can (and do) participate. Room, board, and travel are included. The application deadline is March 1st.

SPAEP Level II is a seven-week summer research program. Participants spend four days per week engaged in mentored laboratory research. Fridays are dedicated to study skills, medical school admissions workshops, and physician shadowing. Room, board, travel, and MCAT preparation are included.

Pre-matriculation Program. This program is offered only to students who have been accepted into the first-year class of the University of Pittsburgh School of Medicine. In addition to providing a look at the curriculum, the program seeks to help students adapt to the medical school, the city, and the university. Participants begin to form support networks during the program. Lectures are given by School of Medicine faculty. Study skills diagnostics are administered, and survival skills

workshops are held bi-weekly. Students meet weekly with the school's administrative deans and participate in problem-based learning small-group sessions with the director of medical education.

Medical Crossroads. A day-long medical school preparation program co-sponsored by the University of Pittsburgh School of Medicine chapter of the SNMA. Medical students provide all the lectures and focus on pre-medical academic preparation: the MCAT, the American Medical College Application Service (AMCAS) application, and interview skills. Students participate in a problem-based learning group and sample physical diagnosis sessions facilitated by medical students. All pre-medical students in the state of Pennsylvania are invited to attend.

Student Financial Assistance
The University of Pittsburgh works diligently to help students to overcome the obstacles created by finances. Secondary application fees are waived for those who have received AMCAS fee waivers. Other requests for waivers are considered on an individual basis. For students who have been invited to interview, overnight housing is available through student hosts (this request must be made in advance of the interview day).

Financial aid is awarded based on financial need, as determined from information supplied on the Free Application for Federal Student Aid (FAFSA), and other school-specific documents. Locally-funded aid for underrepresented or first-generation students includes grants and emergency loans through the Negro Educational Emergency Drive (NEED), which are available to residents of Southwestern Pennsylvania. Contact NEED at 412-566-2760.

Students are counseled throughout their matriculation on the types and amount of loans they have borrowed. To facilitate financial planning and awareness, a debt-counseling session is offered for students in the second semester of the first year. Fourth-year students participate in "Your Financial Rx," a debt-counseling seminar co-sponsored by the Association of American Medical Colleges, the Pennsylvania Medical Society, and the School of Medicine. Sessions include information on negotiating residency contracts, managing student loan repayment, budgeting, investing, and handling stress during residency. Students may participate in "Your Financial Rx" or have an individual debt-counseling exit interview.

Other School of Medicine resources include Dean's Scholarships (available to all students); the alumni-funded Charles M. Hefflin Medical Student Scholarship; The Gateway Medical Society Award; and the Chi Delta Mu Award. The Medical Alumni Scholarship is awarded on a competitive basis to three freshmen from Pennsylvania who demonstrate exceptional academic achievement.

Educational Partnerships
The Office of Student Affairs/Diversity Programs maintains an active relationship with the City of Pittsburgh Public School System. This relationship allows the School of Medicine to involve students with its Medical Explorers Post and Summer Pre-medical Academic Enrichment Program. The school of medicine also partners with the Boy Scouts of Southwestern Pennsylvania. The Medical Explorers Post is the largest and longest existing Exploring post in the nation.

The Office of Admissions of the University of Pittsburgh identifies potential candidates for its Guarantee Program whereby a limited number of undergraduate students accepted to the university may be considered for guaranteed admission, should they attain set academic standards.

Ponce School of Medicine*

Arvin Báez, Assistant
Dean for Student Affairs
Ponce School of Medicine
PO Box 7004
Ponce, PR 00732-7004
787-840-2575; 787-259-1931 Fax

Recruitment
Ponce School of Medicine actively recruits highly qualified students who have completed the pre-medical requirements. The medical student body's composition is diversified, consisting primarily of Puerto Ricans and students from the mainland who are bilingual.

Recruitment efforts and academic programs are designed to ensure equal opportunity. Specific information about requirements for admission at Ponce School of Medicine is provided to all public and private colleges and universities, particularly those with pre-medical programs. The same information is provided to any applicant within Puerto Rico or the continental United States.

Admissions
The following criteria are considered by the Admission Committee to evaluate all applicants:

1) grade-point average,
2) grade-point average in science courses,
3) Medical College Admission Test (MCAT) scores,
4) Ability to communicate in English and Spanish,
5) Interview reports by Admissions Committee members, and
6) Letters of recommendation.

Ponce School of Medicine, 2006
Applicants and Matriculants by Gender, Race and Ethnicity

Race and Ethnicity	Applicants			Matriculants		
	Women	Men	Total	Women	Men	Total
Hispanic/Latino						
Cuban	24	19	43	2	1	3
Mexican American	22	13	35	1	0	1
Puerto Rican	171	154	325	23	24	47
Other Hispanic	57	36	93	2	2	4
Multiple Hispanic*	10	7	17	0	0	0
Subtotal	284	229	513	28	27	55
Non-Hispanic/Latino**						
Black	17	14	31	0	1	1
Native American/Alaska Native	2	1	3	0	0	0
Native Hawaiian/Other Pacific Islander	1	1	2	0	0	0
White	66	85	151	3	3	6
Asian	32	36	68	0	1	1
Other Race	0	2	2	0	0	0
Multiple Race*	4	2	6	0	0	0
Unknown	1	5	6	0	0	0
Subtotal	123	146	269	3	5	8
Foreign	10	12	22	1	2	3
Total	417	387	804	32	34	66

*Since 2002, students can select more than one race and / or ethnicity. **Those who did not choose Hispanic/Latino' or 'Non-Hispanic/Latino' are counted under 'Non-Hispanic/Latino'.
Data Source: AAMC Data Warehouse: Applicant-Matriculant File, as of 5/9/2007.

Minority status and economic factors are not used as criteria for admission. Puerto Rican students account for about 85 percent of the student population.

Academic Support Programs

Students identified to have special educational needs during the first semester of the first year are offered the choice of a decelerated schedule. This schedule allows students to take three years for the completion of the basic science curriculum, therefore, allowing five years to complete the degree.

The different student associations are active in student support. Both male and female students could be members of the organizations.

The Office of Student Affairs coordinates a program of student tutorships in conjunction with the basic sciences departments. Also, students receive counseling in study strategies and test-taking skills at the Office of Student Affairs. Activities directed toward career counseling are scheduled along the academic year. Counseling Program is available to students. The program offers professional counseling, and psychological or psychiatric services.

The physiology and biochemistry departments offer summer courses for students who need to do remedial work in these subjects.

Enrichment Programs

Medical Student Summer Research Program (MSSRP). This program is intended to increase the number of medical students participating in biomedical research activities. This allows students to integrate and develop skills necessary for research in the basic sciences through active research participation.

Student Financial Assistance

To be eligible for assistance, students must be U.S. citizens, be registered on a full-time basis, be in good standing, and have demonstrated financial need.

The following loans are currently available: Federal Stafford, Alternative Loans, and Unsubsidized Stafford Loan. The Student Financial Aid Office assists all qualified students with their applications to available state and federal financial aid programs. Scholarships for U.S. Army, U.S. Navy, and National Health Service Corps are available. Students receive all information about financial aid upon being admitted to the school.

Educational Partnerships

Ponce School of Medicine has a program with the Pontifical Catholic University of Puerto Rico and Interamerican University-Ponce Campus called the *Binary Program.* This program allows for academically exceptional students to complete their pre-medical requirements in two years, finishing their college and medical education in six years. The students receive a Bachelor in Science degree from their respective university after completing the second year of medical studies.

Other Pertinent Information

The Ponce Medical School Foundation is a non-profit organization responsible for the operation of the Ponce School of Medicine. The Foundation took over the operation of the school July 1, 1980, under the government of a Board of Trustees.

The Ponce School of Medicine is located in Ponce, Puerto Rico, the second largest city of the island. Applications for admission are considered based on the qualifications of the applicants without regard to race, age, creed, sex, national origin, or physical handicaps. Students, faculty, and staff are assured of participation in programs and the use of facilities without discrimination.

San Juan Bautista School of Medicine

Carretera 172
URB Turabo Gardens
Caguas, PR, 00725-4968
787-743-3038 x227

San Juan Bautista School of Medicine was founded in 1978 in San Juan, Puerto Rico. It is a non-profit corporation, incorporated under the laws of the Commonwealth of Puerto Rico. It has been in continuous operation since being granted authorization by the Council of Higher Education of Puerto Rico to offer studies pertinent to the M.D. degree. Starting in the 2007-2008 academic year, the Liaison Committee on Medical Education (LCME) granted accreditation to the educational program leading to the M.D. degree for a period of four years.

For more information about this institution, visit *(http://www.universities.com/ OnCampus/www.San_Juan_Bautista_School_Of_ Medicine.html).*

Universidad Central del Caribe School of Medicine

Dr. Areliz Quiñones Berríos
Guidance Counselor
Universidad Central del Caribe
School of Medicine
P O Box 60327, Bayamón
Puerto Rico, 00960
787-798-3001 ext. 2405
787-269-7550 Fax
aquinones@uccaribe.edu
www.uccaribe.edu

Recruitment

UCC School of Medicine is a private, non-profit institution that has been committed to primary care medical education, serving in local communities and Hispanic populations in the United States. Our mission aims at preparing high quality physicians to practice in Puerto Rico and the U.S.

mainland. As a result, Hispanic, primarily Puerto Ricans, or Spanish-speaking U.S. citizens, constitute the majority of our student body.

The Hispanic population is the fastest growing minority group in the U.S., creating the need for more Hispanic-oriented institutions, particularly in the health-related professions. The significance of Hispanic needs within the health professions is an important factor contributing to the School of Medicine's explicit social contract, which depends to some degree upon enrolling Puerto Ricans and other Hispanics in our educational program.

Recruitment efforts emphasize visits to public and private colleges and universities in Puerto Rico. Tours and orientation sessions on campus, particularly with the medical students' association and counselors of universities and high schools, are

coordinated with our faculty members. Also, state educational fairs, community clinics, and open houses are available throughout the year.

Admissions

The admission process is implemented by the Admissions Committee. This is an Advisory Committee composed of faculty members who are responsible to the Office of the Dean of the Medical School. The process is designed to assure that each applicant is evaluated in terms of his/her academic qualifications and potential. Fluency in both English and Spanish is essential.

The admissions process relies on a combination of objective factors such as performance on the Medical College Admission Test, undergraduate record, and the personal qualifications of the applicant as conveyed by letters of recommendations and a personal interview. There is no discrimination on the basis of sex, color, race, religion, physical disability, economic status, political ideology, or national origin.

Academic Support Programs

New Student Orientation Program. Each summer, the UCC-SOM offers orientation activities for new medical students. This program aims at facilitating the students' transition to the new academic responsibilities and environment. It includes intensive workshops to enhance students' skills in time and stress management, study habits, learning styles, effective communication, spirituality and health, self-care and problem solving. Emphasis is placed on helping students to identify high-risk situations that might hinder their academic performance and how to obtain adequate assistance to prevent them.

Fellow medical students (peer counselors) assume a significant role during orientation activities in sharing their stories of success and failure in order to encourage new students to seek help, become

Universidad Central del Caribe School of Medicine, 2006
Applicants and Matriculants by Gender, Race and Ethnicity

Race and Ethnicity	Applicants			Matriculants		
	Women	Men	Total	Women	Men	Total
Hispanic/Latino						
Cuban	15	12	27	3	2	5
Mexican American	21	17	38	0	0	0
Puerto Rican	159	128	287	14	29	43
Other Hispanic	45	30	75	5	2	7
Multiple Hispanic*	8	8	16	2	0	2
Subtotal	248	195	443	24	33	57
Non-Hispanic/Latino**						
Black	19	36	55	0	0	0
Native American/Alaska Native	1	4	5	0	0	0
Native Hawaiian/Other Pacific Islander	3	2	5	0	0	0
White	117	167	284	1	1	2
Asian	78	103	181	1	1	2
Other Race	0	2	2	0	0	0
Multiple Race*	11	16	27	0	0	0
Unknown	2	7	9	0	1	1
Subtotal	231	337	568	2	3	5
Foreign	20	8	28	1	0	1
Total	499	540	1,039	27	36	63

*Since 2002, students can select more than one race and / or ethnicity. **Those who did not choose Hispanic/Latino' or 'Non-Hispanic/Latino' are counted under 'Non-Hispanic/Latino'.
Data Source: AAMC Data Warehouse: Applicant-Matriculant File, as of 5/9/2007.

Association of American Medical Colleges, 2007

motivated and gain self-confidence. This is with the purpose of showing them how to cope with the challenges and opportunities they will face during their medical education. The program also includes activities of integration with faculty, introduction the academic program and classes, the methods of evaluation and promotion, and training in computers for the learning supports system.

Guidance and Counseling Program. All medical students have access to confidential guidance and counseling services with a professional counselor on a self-referred basis. Any student in need of mental health services not available in the UCC-SOM, may be referred to other professionals within the community, with the student's consent and authorization. The guidance and counseling program includes individual and group meetings with the students to discuss issues related to their success in the medical school. This issue includes personal and family problems, academic difficulties, or other daily-life aspects that may interfere in the health and performance of the student.

Academic Monitoring and Tutoring Program. The Coordinators for each medical school year submit an academic monitoring report to the Dean of Students. This report includes the progress of each student and identifies the ones that have academic problems. Those students are referred to the Guidance and Counseling Program to be interviewed and make a work plan to remediate their low performance. This plan may include, but is not limited to, tutoring services, individual counseling, and referrals. The tutoring services are conducted by outstanding fellow medical students who are previously identified by the faculty and Dean of Students as potential tutors. Tutoring sessions (individual or group) are coordinated by the counselor and this service is free for the students.

P.U.E.D.O. (I CAN) Program. This is a longitudinal program to enhance the performance of the medical students in the United States Medical Licensing Examination (USMLE) Steps 1 and 2. The P.U.E.D.O. program includes individual and group tutoring, reviews, online resources, books, workshops, the USMLE comprehensive exam, and other relevant activities to promote the success of the students in the USMLE.

Enrichment Programs

Prevention and Integral Health Program. This institutional well-being and prevention program includes workshops, health clinics, and lectures throughout the academic year. The program is directed at helping the students develop healthy attitudes and behavior regarding the use of alcohol, tobacco, and other drugs. Also, activities focused on healthy sexual activities, dealing with stress, violence and aggression, and achieving overall well-being among the student body.

Summer Preceptorships Program. Research activities and programs are offered for medical students, both in the UCC-SOM and other universities and health-related agencies.

Co-Curricular Program. Each academic year, the Dean of Students plans and offers co-curricular activities that include social, community, and service activities.

Student Financial Assistance

Commonwealth of Puerto Rican Scholarship. These scholarships are allocated to needy students, who are enrolled in Puerto Rican institutions. These funds are to support good standing and economically needy students enrolled in the UCC.

Novo Nordisk Diabetes Scholarship Fund. The Novo Nordisk Fund was established to recognize excellence in academic achievements among minority medical students. The fund's purpose is to support diversity within the medical profession and to encourage leadership in improving overall health care and diabetes care among minority population and in underserved communities. This fund is designated to a third-year student.

Educational Partnership

The UCC-SOM maintains an educational partnership with many health-related agencies and programs in Puerto Rico. For example, an academic partnership is available with two private universities (Sacred Heart University and Pontifical Catholic University) to recruit undergraduate students to our Biomedical Sciences and Substance Abuse Counseling programs. Also, an agreement is taking place with "Hogar Padre Vernard," a non-profit organization that offers primary care services to underrepresented communities.

University of Puerto Rico School of Medicine*

Dr. América Facundo, Director
Hispanic Center of Excellence
University of Puerto Rico
School of Medicine
Office A-865, P.O. Box 365067
San Juan, PR 00936-5067
787-756-6343; 787-765-9182 Fax
afacundo@rcm.upr.edu

Recruitment

The School of Medicine's recruitment activities are divided into two major areas according to the target population: high school and college students. High school recruitment activities are centered around the Medicine Clubs, which are organized in public high schools in underserved areas. These clubs are sponsored by a Health Resources and Services Administration Hispanic Center of Excellence (HCOE) grant. College recruitment, done in collaboration with the Office of the Dean of Students of the Medical Sciences campus, consists of an annual career day, a week-long summer program, and visits to colleges and universities.

Admissions

Candidates are admitted to the first-year class on a competitive basis. The admissions process utilizes a formula that takes into consideration academic and non-academic factors. The academic factors include the general and science grade-point averages and the Medical College Admission Test scores. To assess the applicant's skills and attributes, the Admissions Committee requires an evaluation by pre-medical advisors or recommendations from three professors and a personal interview conducted, according to established guidelines, by a School of Medicine faculty member. Fluency in Spanish is required as the patient population is mainly Spanish-speaking.

The Admissions Committee is composed of faculty members, representing both basic and clinical sciences, and student representatives. The admission process is through the American Medical College Application Service.

Academic Support Programs

Pre-orientation Activities. These activities for new matriculants are typically offered in June, and they include an Orientation Week. They are designed to acquaint the first-year class with the school's academic program, the methods of evaluation, the different services available to students, and with the faculty, administration, and student body.

Introduction to Medical Studies Program. This one-month duration enrichment program is offered to students from disadvantaged backgrounds with the support of the HCOE grant. It includes minicourses in the basic sciences, as well as workshops on study skills, anxiety management, communication, professionalism, group building, among others.

The Office of Student Affairs, also supported by the Hispanic Center of Excellence staff, provides tutoring services, orientation, and counseling services to all students whose academic or interpersonal problems might interfere with their performance. Study-skills services are made available to interested students.

Psychological testing and psychiatric consultation are also available through the Student's Health Service.

The academic performance of each student is followed throughout the year by a Committee on Advancement, appointed by the dean, for each educational level. These committees recommend the student's promotion or advise on other alternatives.

University of Puerto Rico School of Medicine, 2006
Applicants and Matriculants by Gender , Race and Ethnicity

Race and Ethnicity		Applicants			Matriculants		
		Women	Men	Total	Women	Men	Total
Hispanic/Latino							
Cuban		3	1	4	0	0	0
Puerto Rican		137	129	266	52	46	98
Other Hispanic		2	1	3	0	0	0
Multiple Hispanic*		4	1	5	0	1	1
	Subtotal	146	132	278	52	47	99
Non-Hispanic/Latino**							
Black		1	0	1	0	0	0
White		0	2	2	0	1	1
Asian		0	1	1	0	0	0
Multiple Race*		2	0	2	0	0	0
Unknown		0	2	2	0	0	0
	Subtotal	3	5	8	0	1	1
	Total	149	137	286	52	48	100

*Since 2002, students can select more than one race and / or ethnicity. **Those who did not choose Hispanic/Latino' or 'Non-Hispanic/Latino' are counted under 'Non-Hispanic/Latino'.
Data Source: AAMC Data Warehouse: Applicant-Matriculant File, as of 5/9/2007.

AAMC

Student Financial Assistance

Financial assistance is available for eligible, qualified students from university, state, and federal government loan funds and other special trust funds. Educational costs covered by financial aid include tuition and fees, books, supplies and equipment, room and board, transportation, and personal expenses. In order to qualify, students must meet the following requirements: U.S. citizen/permanent resident; accepted for enrollment or enrolled in the School of Medicine; in need of financial aid; and in good academic standing.

In addition, medical students benefit from summer employment opportunities and work-study programs.

Warren Alpert Medical School of Brown University

Dr. Alicia D. Monroe, Associate Dean of Medicine (Minority Affairs)
Office of Minority Medical Affairs
Division of Biology and Medicine
Brown Medical School
97 Waterman Street, Box G-222C
Providence, RI 02912
401-863-3335; 401-863-3801 Fax
Email: Alicia_Monroe@Brown.edu
http://med.brown.edu/omma

Recruitment

The Associate Dean of Medicine (Minority Affairs) and the Associate Dean of Medicine (Minority Recruitment and Retention) are directly involved in the recruitment of minority applicants through multiple routes of admission (see Admissions section). The

Associate Dean of Medicine (Minority Affairs) directly supervises the recruitment process for minority applicants through the Brown–Tougaloo Early Identification Program. The Associate Dean of Medicine (Minority Recruitment and Retention) directly supervises the recruitment process of applicants to the Program in Liberal Medical Education.

Each year approximately two to four promising, second-semester sophomore students, enrolled at Tougaloo College, are selected to participate in the Medical School's Early Identification Program (EIP). Admission to the Medical School is contingent upon sustained academic achievement at Tougaloo College, satisfactory completion of all pre-medical course requirements, continued recommendation by the pre-medical advisor at Tougaloo College, and documented verification of

Warren Alpert Medical School of Brown University, 2006
Applicants and Matriculants by Gender, Race and Ethnicity

Race and Ethnicity	Applicants			Matriculants		
	Women	Men	Total	Women	Men	Total
Hispanic/Latino						
Cuban	13	9	22	0	0	0
Mexican American	49	40	89	1	0	1
Puerto Rican	11	13	24	1	0	1
Other Hispanic	54	46	100	1	2	3
Multiple Hispanic*	8	7	15	0	0	0
Subtotal	135	115	250	3	2	5
Non-Hispanic/Latino**						
Black	113	82	195	8	4	12
Native American/Alaska Native	1	8	9	0	0	0
Native Hawaiian/Other Pacific Islander	6	4	10	1	0	1
White	893	1,159	2,052	18	24	42
Asian	558	545	1,103	7	11	18
Other Race	3	3	6	0	0	0
Multiple Race*	78	59	137	0	0	0
Unknown	20	26	46	5	4	9
Subtotal	1,672	1,886	3,558	39	43	82
Foreign	176	167	343	3	1	4
Total	1,983	2,168	4,151	45	46	91

*Since 2002, students can select more than one race and / or ethnicity. **Those who did not choose Hispanic/Latino' or 'Non-Hispanic/Latino' are counted under 'Non-Hispanic/Latino'.
Data Source: AAMC Data Warehouse: Applicant-Matriculant File, as of 5/9/2007.

Association of American Medical Colleges, 2007

completed academic record. In the Spring of the senior year, the Dean of Biological Sciences and Medicine reviews the students' applications for formal admission into the Medical School.

The Office of Minority Medical Affairs is a major driving force in the continuous effort to increase the number of underrepresented minority students matriculating to the college and the Medical School. The office not only plays a crucial role at the Medical School level, but also serves as a vital link with undergraduate medical students and participates in several activities to encourage prospective minority students to attend Brown.

Admissions
The Warren Alpert Medical School continues to offer a number of admission routes to the M.D. program. The majority of first-year entrants are from the *Program in Liberal Medical Education*, or PLME, in which students enter Brown University in their freshman year and commit to an eight-year continuum leading to both the bachelor's degree and the M.D. degree. Brown accepts applications from qualified graduates of any college or university, through the standard route of admission. Students enrolled as undergraduates at Providence College, Rhode Island College, the University of Rhode Island, and Tougaloo College may apply through the EIP, a cooperative venture between the Medical School and these institutions. The remaining places in the class are reserved for students applying to the M.D./Ph.D. Program and those who enter through special programs at institutions with which the Medical School has a formal linkage (the pre-medical post-baccalaureate programs). Occasionally, students are admitted to the Medical School with advanced standing.

The Admissions Committee is composed of clinical and basic science faculty, administrators, and medical students, all with equal screening and ranking privileges.

Applicants are selected on the basis of academic achievement, faculty evaluations,

and evidence of maturity, motivation, leadership, integrity, and compassion. Applicants to the M.D./Ph.D. program are also evaluated on the basis of their research accomplishments and potential as well.

The Associate Dean of Medicine (Minority Affairs) is a voting member of the Program in Liberal Medical Education Selection Advisory Council, the M.D. Admissions Committee, and the Early Identification Selection Committee.

Academic Support Programs
The Office of Minority Medical Affairs implements pre-orientation programs focused on academic enhancement and building a spirit of community for underrepresented first- and second- year medical students. This program complements general orientation programs available for all medical students. In addition, the Medical School has a formal tutorial program for all enrolled students. The program provides content tutors for basic science courses required in Years I and II, as well as study skills instruction. Students needing tutorial assistance in any basic science course may self-refer for a content tutor, or may be referred for content tutoring by an academic advisor or course leader. Students experiencing academic difficulties related to ineffective learning approaches or test-taking strategies can also be referred by one of the deans to receive study skills instruction. Tutorial assistance is provided to students from certified learning specialists as well as faculty and student tutors. The Associate Dean of Medicine (Minority Affairs) and the Associate Dean of Medical Minority Recruitment and Retention use a proactive approach in advising and counseling students to ensure that students utilize all available resources to maximize academic success.

United States Medical Licensing Examination (USMLE) Step 1 Preparation. Although passage of USMLE Step 1 is not required for promotion into Year III at Brown, individual and group academic coaching is available to all students preparing for their board exams. The Learning Specialist is available to help students develop their board study plans, identify potential weaknesses, hone their test-taking skills, and provide positive reinforcement during the preparation process. In addition, the Medical School offers Step 1 workshops, one-on-one tutoring, and USMLE study groups proctored by senior medical students who have been trained in appropriate study techniques.

Enrichment Programs
Summer Research Early Identification Program (EIP). This program is designed to help members of underrepresented minority groups consider research careers in the biological and medical sciences. The program introduces undergraduates to research under the guidance of Brown faculty who serve as mentors. EIP consists of three major components: research—mentorship; academic enrichment; and seminars and field trips.

The program is ten weeks long, beginning in early June and ending in mid-August. Each student is assigned a research project at the beginning of the program. The research is conducted both on the Brown campus and in laboratories at Brown-affiliated hospitals. EIP students are assigned to laboratories by research preference and space availability. Students accepted will receive $2,500 in summer research fellowships, and funds are available for travel and partial housing allowances. At the end of the ten weeks, students are required to present a written report of their summer research activity and give a ten-minute presentation of their data in a mini-symposium. The scholars also meet with the director of the program, at regular inter-als, to discuss scientific research, as a career option, and to review their progress. Eight special seminars are presented during the program to expose the students to other Brown faculty and their fields of research. Field trips are conducted to various scientific sites.

Student Financial Assistance

Before students may be considered for financial aid from Brown University, they must apply for a federally-insured, guaranteed student loan. Financial aid may then be offered in the form of scholarships, loans, or both. Over 70 percent of the students receive financial aid. Financial aid may be awarded to foreign national students on a limited basis. M.D./Ph.D. students are eligible for a graduate fellowship (tuition and stipend), during the Ph.D. portion of their studies, and a full tuition scholarship for the last two years of medical school following successful completion of the Ph.D. work.

Medical University of South Carolina College of Medicine

Dr. Deborah Deas
Associate Dean
College of Medicine Admissions
Medical University of South Carolina
67 President Street, CDAP/4 North
Charleston, South Carolina 29425
843-792-5214; 843-792-7353 Fax
deasd@musc.edu

Recruitment

The Medical University of South Carolina (MUSC) is committed to increasing the number of minority students. The Associate Deans for Admissions and the Director of Admissions, along with selected medical students, travel statewide to colleges and universities to recruit students. In addition to regular recruitment visits, the recruiters attend career fairs at all Historically Black Colleges and Universities in South Carolina.

The College of Medicine collaborates with the College of Graduate Studies at MUSC to sponsor the Ernest E. Just annual symposium to present contributions of Just, current science, and topics on diversity. The Ernest E. Just symposium attracts undergraduate students and their advisors from South Carolina, North Carolina, Georgia, and Florida. Students attend information sessions during the afternoon to meet Dr. Reves, Dean of the College of Medicine, associate deans, admissions staff, and current medical students to learn about the medical school requirements and resources available to enhance their applications for admission.

Medical University of South Carolina College of Medicine, 2006
Applicants and Matriculants by Gender, Race and Ethnicity

Race and Ethnicity		Applicants			Matriculants		
		Women	Men	Total	Women	Men	Total
Hispanic/Latino							
Cuban		6	7	13	0	1	1
Mexican American		12	3	15	2	0	2
Puerto Rican		5	4	9	0	0	0
Other Hispanic		20	11	31	1	1	2
Multiple Hispanic*		1	3	4	0	0	0
	Subtotal	44	28	72	3	2	5
Non-Hispanic/Latino**							
Black		100	41	141	11	8	19
Native American/Alaska Native		0	5	5	0	0	0
Native Hawaiian/Other Pacific Islander		1	2	3	0	0	0
White		532	662	1,194	48	67	115
Asian		80	114	194	4	3	7
Other Race		1	0	1	0	0	0
Multiple Race*		18	24	42	1	1	2
Unknown		6	12	18	0	1	1
	Subtotal	738	860	1,598	64	80	144
Foreign		2	7	9	0	1	1
	Total	784	895	1,679	67	83	150

*Since 2002, students can select more than one race and / or ethnicity. **Those who did not choose Hispanic/Latino' or 'Non-Hispanic/Latino' are counted under 'Non-Hispanic/Latino'.

Data Source: AAMC Data Warehouse: Applicant-Matriculant File, as of 5/9/2007.

Post-baccalaureate Reapplication Education Program (PREP). The Medical University of South Carolina (MUSC) established the Post-baccalaureate Reapplication Education Program (PREP) in a committed effort to increase the number of qualified South Carolina applicants who are representative of the medically underserved population in the state. The year-long program is jointly administered by the College of Medicine at MUSC and the College of Charleston. It is an integrative, individually tailored course of undergraduate study prescribed for underprepared but promising students who seek admission to MUSC's College of Medicine. The PREP program provides enriched academic assistance to students who come from historically medically underserved groups (minority, rural, low income) to prepare them to enter and succeed in medical school.

Students selected for the program must attend the College of Charleston for two semesters and take at least 15 semester hours of science courses each semester. Student must maintain a minimum cumulative grade-point average of 3.0 in science coursework and retake the Medical College Admission Test (MCAT) in April to improve scores. If a student fulfills all requirements, he or she is admitted into College of Medicine's first-year class beginning with the Summer Gross Anatomy course at MUSC. Tuition for PREP is paid by the College of Medicine.

Summer Institute Program. Since 2000, the Office of Student Diversity has sponsored a Summer Institute Program for students interested in health care. In 2005, The College of Medicine assumed sponsorship of this program, which is designed for recent baccalaureate graduates who have applied to the College of Medicine for admission but were not selected.

Additionally, a few highly motivated junior and senior college students who have been identified as having the academic potential for medicine are eligible. The eight-week institute includes intensive courses in organic chemistry, physics, and biochemistry, as well as a MCAT preparation, test-taking skills, verbal reasoning, and mock interviews.

Admissions

The Admissions Committee consists of 25 members —17 of whom are basic science and clinical faculty members who are appointed by the Dean of the College of Medicine serving staggered three-year terms and two student members appointed at the end of their first year serving until graduation. Regular meetings are held from September through March. Special meetings may be called any time during the academic year. All decisions are made by a simple majority of those attending and are presented to the dean as recommendations. The criteria for admission to the regular M.D. program are the same for all students seeking enrollment in the College of Medicine. Consideration is given to the applicant's grade-point average (GPA), MCAT scores, interviews, and accomplishments (i.e., leadership, volunteer efforts and shadowing experiences). Students are also screened for personal qualities and accomplishments that are considered valuable in adding diversity to a class: cultural experiences, research or graduate degrees, significant artistic or athletic achievements, overcoming adversity or some type of disability, a pattern of significant improvement in coursework, or any type of extended post-baccalaureate career experiences. An Added Value subcommittee reviews all applicants considered for these qualities and accomplishments and assigns an adjustment to the applicant's overall ranking index.

Academic Support Programs

The College of Medicine established the Office of Academics and Student Affairs to assist students with academic and personal challenges. Proactive intervention strategies, such as early detection, collaborative consultation, and appropriate referrals to campus resources are utilized to enhance students' academic performance and decrease stress related to personal issues. The Director of Academics and Student Support provides academic counseling and facilitates the referral process for supplemental instruction. The Center for Academic Excellence is a centrally located university resource, which provides supplemental instruction, test-taking skills, study skills, and time management

Enrichment Programs

Since 2000, the Office of Student Diversity has sponsored a Summer Institute Program for students interested in health care. This program is designed for rising junior and senior college students who have been identified as having academic potential for the health professions and who are highly motivated for a career in health care. Also, recent baccalaureate graduates who have applied to the College of Medicine for admission but did not make a competitive MCAT score have been selected as Summer Institute participants. The eight-week institute includes intensive courses in organic chemistry, physics, and biochemistry, as well as, a MCAT preparation, test taking skills, verbal reasoning, and mock interviews.

Student Financial Assistance

State and federal loans, specialized scholarships, and fellowships are arranged individually through the University Financial Aid Office. The Graduate Incentive Scholarships coordinated by the Office of Student Diversity and University Financial Aid Office are available to all entering

rofessional and minority medical stu-
ents. The fellowship is available to all
uth Carolinians who agree to practice in
uth Carolina one year for each $5,000 or
rtion received. Grants and scholarships
e also available from an endowment in
e Medical University's Health Sciences
undation and from the Earl B. Higgins
cholarship Fund.

University of South Carolina School of Medicine*

Dr. Carol McMahon
Assistant Dean for Minority Affairs
Assistant Professor of Pathology
University of South Carolina
School of Medicine
Medical Library Building, Room 304
Columbia, SC 29208
803-733-3319; 803-733-1513 Fax
cmcmahon@dcsmserver.med.sc.edu

Recruitment

Minority applicants for admission to the School of Medicine are identified through site visits to college campuses; the *Role Models for Medicine Program*; career day activities and seminars for high school and college students; collaboration with under-graduate pre-medical advisors, minority

physicians/mentors, and health care agencies; and correspondence from the Assistant Dean for Minority Affairs to referred students and those identified in relevant regional and national databases. The primary goal of the Office of Minority Affairs is to increase the number of minority applicants, matriculants, and graduates by informing minority students of the School of Medicine's interest in them through participation in new and established recruitment activities.

The School of Medicine's Student National Medical Association (SNMA) chapter also plays an active role in the recruitment of minority students by conducting seminars and workshops about medical school, the application and admissions process, Medical College Admission Test (MCAT) preparation, and interviewing skills. SNMA members provide academic assistance and

University of South Carolina School of Medicine, 2006
Applicants and Matriculants by Gender, Race and Ethnicity

Race and Ethnicity	Applicants			Matriculants		
	Women	Men	Total	Women	Men	Total
Hispanic/Latino						
Cuban	11	10	21	0	0	0
Mexican American	4	6	10	0	0	0
Puerto Rican	4	5	9	0	1	1
Other Hispanic	20	17	37	0	0	0
Multiple Hispanic*	2	2	4	0	0	0
Subtotal	41	40	81	0	1	1
Non-Hispanic/Latino**						
Black	100	40	140	2	3	5
Native American/Alaska Native	2	2	4	0	0	0
Native Hawaiian/Other Pacific Islander	0	2	2	0	0	0
White	477	616	1,093	25	41	66
Asian	128	165	293	4	3	7
Other Race	3	1	4	0	0	0
Multiple Race*	21	31	52	1	0	1
Unknown	4	8	12	0	0	0
Subtotal	735	865	1,600	32	47	79
Foreign	18	13	31	0	0	0
Total	794	918	1,712	32	48	80

*Since 2002, students can select more than one race and / or ethnicity. **Those who did not choose 'Hispanic/Latino' or 'Non-Hispanic/Latino' are counted under 'Non-Hispanic/Latino'.
Data Source: AAMC Data Warehouse: Applicant-Matriculant File, as of 5/9/2007.

personal support to enrolled students and participate in health education programs for middle school through college-age students as well as community groups.

Minority students are encouraged and invited to visit the campus of the University of South Carolina School of Medicine to acquaint themselves with its facilities and programs, to participate in the *Day in the Life of a Medical Student* program, and to meet the Assistant Dean for Minority Affairs and currently enrolled students.

Admissions

All qualified applicants are admitted through the regular admissions process with the selection involving comparative evaluation and review of all available data. These data include MCAT scores, academic record, letters of recommendation, and results of personal interviews with Admissions Committee members. The Admissions Committee is a diverse group, inclusive of minorities, composed of faculty members, community physicians, administrators, and medical students. Its representative nature assures a thorough and sensitive review of the credentials of every applicant. The opportunity for admission is greatest for legal residents of South Carolina.

Academic Support Programs

All students accepted into the medical program will find that, because of the small class size, close interpersonal relationships are maintained between students and faculty members. These relationships facilitate individualized teaching and mentoring relationships and permit early identification of any potential or real academic difficulties, so that help may be offered as soon as necessary. In addition, an extensive orientation program, prior to matriculation in

the first year, and small-group educational activities throughout the curriculum, ensure the development of cooperative working relationships among all students. Each incoming student is assigned to an advisory group consisting of first-through fourth-year students and faculty advisors who monitor the student's academic progress and act both as counselors and advisors to the student. Although no special tutorial programs have been established, interested faculty are always available to provide individual attention to students who encounter academic difficulty.

Extended Curriculum Program. This program is available to students with compelling personal reasons. It is an appropriately sequenced and individually scheduled track that permits completion of the first two years of medical school in three years.

Student Financial Assistance

The Office of Student Services makes every effort to provide information and assistance to help students with their financial obligations. All minority students are nominated for Graduate Incentive Fellowships—state-supported grants that require students to work one year in the state following completion of training for every $5,000 of fellowship money granted. Conventional routes of funding (loans, scholarships, etc.) may be available to those who apply for financial consideration. Such assistance is provided on the basis of need and availability of funds.

Educational Partnerships

Through its *Role Models for Medicine Program*, the School of Medicine has established partnerships with students enrolled in public and private high schools throughout the state, and with their science teachers and guidance counselors.

Other Pertinent Information

The School of Medicine admitted its first class of 24 students in August 1977 and has a current entering class size of 80 new students.

The Office of Minority Affairs was created in 1996 as a result of the School of Medicine's strategic planning efforts and its commitment to diversity. The Assistant Dean for Minority Affairs serves as an advisor to all prospective and enrolled students.

Sanford School of Medicine of the University of South Dakota

Dr. Gerald J. Yutrzenka, Associate
Professor, Director of Minority Affairs
Assistant Director
INMED Satellite Office
of the University of South Dakota
Sanford School of Medicine
414 East Clark Street
Vermillion, SD 57069
605-677-5156; 605-677-6381 Fax
yutrzen@usd.edu
www.usd.edu/med

Recruitment

In 1990, the Sanford School of Medicine (SSOM) established a satellite office of the Indians into Medicine (INMED) program located at the University of North Dakota School of Medicine. Through this agreement two additional Native American students are accepted into the University of North Dakota School of Medicine INMED program each year with the intent of transferring into the third year of the medical school curriculum at SSOM. Upon completion of the requirements for graduation these students receive their medical degree from the Sanford School of Medicine of the University of South Dakota. The INMED satellite office at SSOM serves the educational and cultural needs of the INMED transfer students, promotes health career opportunities for Native Americans in South Dakota and surrounding states, is involved in the recruitment and retention of Native American students in health career programs at the University of South Dakota, and serves as a valuable resource to the faculty and students of the School of Medicine and the university.

In addition, SSOM faculty are involved in summer enrichment programs designed to enhance recruitment of Native Americans into careers in health and/or biomedical research. SSOM faculty work in concert with the Undergraduate Admissions Office, the TRIO Program, and with other departments and disciplines in efforts to enhance the diversity of the medical school and the university.

Admissions

The Sanford School of Medicine gives priority to applicants who are legal residents of South Dakota and to non-residents who have close personal ties to South Dakota. Applications from Native Americans who are enrolled members of tribes located in South Dakota and states bordering onto South Dakota are also placed in the priority pool. The INMED Satellite Office and the Office of Medical Student Affairs are available to offer assistance to minority and other disadvantaged applicants.

The Admissions Committee, composed of 15 faculty from the School of Medicine, evaluate all applicants for admission on the basis of intellect, character, and motivation. Information considered in the evaluation of an applicant includes academic achievement, Medical College Admission Test (MCAT) scores, evaluations by former instructors and others who know the individual well, assessment of interpersonal factors and communication skills, and interest in and understanding of medicine and health care, especially as it relates to South Dakota and the mission of SSOM. All applicants being considered for admission are offered two one-on-one personal interviews with members of the Admissions Committee. Any applicant with questions about admission is encouraged to contact the Dean of Student Affairs, SSOM.

Sanford School of Medicine of the University of South Dakota, 2006
Applicants and Matriculants by Gender, Race and Ethnicity

Race and Ethnicity	Applicants			Matriculants		
	Women	Men	Total	Women	Men	Total
Hispanic/Latino						
Cuban	1	3	4	0	0	0
Mexican American	7	5	12	0	0	0
Puerto Rican	1	0	1	0	0	0
Other Hispanic	8	8	16	0	0	0
Multiple Hispanic*	1	1	2	0	0	0
Subtotal	18	17	35	0	0	0
Non-Hispanic/Latino**						
Black	6	9	15	0	0	0
Native American/Alaska Native	5	1	6	0	0	0
White	245	322	567	23	25	48
Asian	52	68	120	1	1	2
Other Race	0	2	2	0	0	0
Multiple Race*	12	20	32	0	1	1
Unknown	3	7	10	0	0	0
Subtotal	323	429	752	24	27	51
Foreign	20	14	34	0	0	0
Total	361	460	821	24	27	51

*Since 2002, students can select more than one race and / or ethnicity. **Those who did not choose
Hispanic/Latino' or 'Non-Hispanic/Latino' are counted under 'Non-Hispanic/Latino'.
Data Source: AAMC Data Warehouse: Applicant-Matriculant File, as of 5/9/2007.

Academic Support Programs

All students who matriculate at SSOM are assigned a basic science faculty advisor for Year 1 and Year 2 and a clinical faculty advisor for Year 3 and Year 4 who advise the student on academic and career issues. The Longitudinal Follow-up Committee and the Student Progress and Conduct Committee are both involved with assessing the progress of medical students throughout the curriculum and recommending action, when needed, to help the student successfully complete the curriculum. The INMED Satellite Office is available to help address needs of Native American students. The Office of Student Affairs with its Student Professional Support Services Office is available to all students. The Student Professional Support Services office coordinates training in study skills, referrals for counseling and planning review programs for United States Medical Licensing Examination (USMLE) preparation.

Enrichment Programs

The School of Medicine has established the Research Apprentice Program (RAP) designed to provide opportunities for up to eight disadvantaged high school students from South Dakota, to become engaged in seven weeks of hands-on, mentored research activities within the medical school and other departments within the university. RAP participants are selected with the assistance of the University of South Dakota Upward Bound program. The RAP students participate in after hours social and other learning activities along with Upward Bound students. *(www.usd.edu/rap)*

The NIH-funded IDEA Networks of Biomedical Research Excellence (INBRE) project has been established at the University of South Dakota. Part of INBRE's efforts are directed toward working with some of the South Dakota tribal colleges

to enhance educational, research, and mentoring opportunities for Native-American and other disadvantaged students attending these tribal colleges. *(www.usd.edu/brin)*

Several School of Medicine faculty members are involved in providing mentoring experiences, with an emphasis on health professions and biomedical research, to high school as well as undergraduate students. *(www.usd.edu/biomed)* and *(www.usd.edu/med/research)*.

The INMED (Indians into Medicine) Satellite office is directly involved in providing mentoring and educational opportunities relative to exposing Native American middle school and high school students to careers in the health professions. The INMED Satellite office has worked to establish the Native American Scholars Program (NASP) designed to provide assistance with enhancing the academic skills and career advising of Native American students who express interest in pursuing careers in medicine and other health care professions. *(www.usd.edu/med/md/diversityopp.cfm)* *(www.usd.edu/med/md)* *(www.med.und.nodak.edu/depts/inmed/)*

SSOM has established a four-week elective (ASNIYA) available to fourth-year medical students that is designed to give students the opportunity to interact with the Native-American tribes in South Dakota. Medical students provide career mentoring and health education instruction to middle school and high school students on one of the several reservations in the state. Medical students are required to obtain at least 20 hours of experience in the local health care facility and must submit a paper in which they reflect upon the experience. ASNIYA provides medical students with the opportunity to become more aware of the health care opportunities and challenges found within the reservations as well as to

enhance their own competency in working with Native-American colleagues and in providing health care to Native-American patients. *(www.usd.edu/med/md/diversityopp.cfm)*

School of Medicine faculty members have been actively involved in a variety of enrichment programs at the University of South Dakota including among others: Upward Bound, Math Science Initiative Program, Talent Search, Research Apprentice Program, Lawrence Brothers Summer Science Camp, Health Careers Summer Camp, and the Governors Camp for the Gifted. *(www.usd.edu/events)* *(www.usd.edu/trio)* *(www.usd.edu/lbc)* *(www.usd.edu/rap)*

Student Financial Assistance

The medical school will waive the $35 application fee upon request and presentation of reasonable evidence of need. A limited number of scholarships, from local sources, are designated especially for American Indian students. The INMED Satellite Office can assist with application for Indian Health Service scholarships.

The Financial Aid officer is responsible for financial aid counseling and debt management counseling for all medical students. *(www.usd.edu/med/md)*

Educational Partnerships

SSOM has partnered with a number of local, state, and national entities to enhance the opportunities for South Dakota minority students to gain access to medical school and other health professions programs. These partnerships include the Talent Search, Upward Bound, and Student Support Services components of the USD TRIO programs, the INMED program, and the Dakota Native American Health Collaborative (DNAHC). DNAHC is a state-wide consortium of representatives from SSOM, Native American tribes, the Indian Health Service, Aberdeen Area Tribal Chairman's Health Board, hospitals, and others with the purpose of addressing global health concerns, health professions mentoring, and educational opportunities in order to positively impact the health care needs of the tribes in South Dakota.

Stanford School of Medicine has taken a leadership role in helping to establish the Pathways into Health (PIH) collaborative. This effort is designed to provide enhanced opportunities for American Indian/Alaskan Native peoples to enter careers in medicine and other health care professions. PIH acts as a mechanism for providing mentoring and role modeling relative to health care careers, development of education and training utilizing Web-based and distance-education technology, development of "pipeline" programs, and serving as a resource for information on health care professions and health care education opportunities. (www.usd.edu/trio/home.cfm) (www.med.und.nodak.edu/depts/inmed) (www.pathwaysintohealth.org.)

East Tennessee State University James H. Quillen College of Medicine

Mr. Steve C. Ellis, Assistant Dean
East Tennessee State University
James H. Quillen College of Medicine
Office of Student Affairs
Post Office Box 70580
Johnson City, TN 37601
423-439-6181; 423-439-6616 Fax
ellis@etsu.edu

Recruitment

The James H. Quillen College of Medicine of East Tennessee State University actively seeks applications from minority and disadvantaged groups. Representatives from the Office of Student Affairs conduct visitation and career day programs at many college campuses across the region. This institution is also an active participant in Pre-medical Enrichment Programs at East Tennessee State University and other institutions.

Admissions

The application and admissions process for all prospective students is the same. The Admissions Committee looks at demonstrations of ability to succeed academically, motivation for and knowledge of the profession, and personal skills believed to be desirable in a physician. In addition to grades and test scores, the Admissions Committee considers evidence of an individual's integrity, leadership ability, motivation, maturity, and intellectual curiosity. Applicants are urged to ensure that their American Medical College Application Service (AMCAS) application provides broad preliminary information in these areas.

East Tennessee State University James H. Quillen College of Medicine, 2006
Applicants and Matriculants by Gender, Race and Ethnicity

Race and Ethnicity	Applicants			Matriculants		
	Women	Men	Total	Women	Men	Total
Hispanic/Latino						
Cuban	0	3	3	0	0	0
Mexican American	5	6	11	0	0	0
Puerto Rican	2	5	7	0	0	0
Other Hispanic	9	8	17	0	0	0
Multiple Hispanic*	2	1	3	1	0	1
Subtotal	18	23	41	1	0	1
Non-Hispanic/Latino**						
Black	79	32	111	2	3	5
Native American/Alaska Native	2	4	6	0	0	0
Native Hawaiian/Other Pacific Islander	0	1	1	0	0	0
White	334	488	822	21	28	49
Asian	77	109	186	1	3	4
Other Race	1	1	2	0	0	0
Multiple Race*	16	15	31	0	1	1
Unknown	2	2	4	0	0	0
Subtotal	511	652	1,163	24	35	59
Foreign	11	10	21	0	0	0
Total	540	685	1,225	25	35	60

*Since 2002, students can select more than one race and / or ethnicity. **Those who did not choose Hispanic/Latino' or 'Non-Hispanic/Latino' are counted under 'Non-Hispanic/Latino'.
Data Source: AAMC Data Warehouse: Applicant-Matriculant File, as of 5/9/2007.

The Admissions Committee is composed of representatives from a diverse group of people with a variety of backgrounds. Medical school and undergraduate faculty and professional staff, hospital staff, students, and local community representatives make up the committee. Training exercises, such as simulated admissions, are conducted to help committee members improve their skills in analyzing the applications of minority students, utilizing both cognitive and non-cognitive indicators.

Academic Support Programs

The College of Medicine has an effective system of student advisement to help students transition to medical school. Upon matriculation, entering students are assigned a faculty advisor. In addition, all faculty maintain open-door policies and are available to assist students in any way possible. The Offices of Student Affairs and Academic Affairs have staff available to assist students in academic and personal areas. Professional counselors are also available to serve students who may have need of confidential counseling and/or treatment.

Enrichment Programs

The College of Medicine operates a summer enrichment program for students interested in pursuing medicine or other professional health careers.

The Pre-health Reinforcement and Enrichment Program is a summer program for college students from traditionally underrepresented groups who are considering a professional health career. The primary goal of this program is to increase the number of such students applying to and gaining entrance into professional health schools. This is accomplished through a rigorous schedule that strengthens

participants' basic science foundation, enhances their academic and reasoning skills, and provides pre-professional career information and guidance.

Further information can be found on the College of Medicine's Web site at *(http://com.etsu.edu/sacom)* and clicking on Outreach Programs.

Educational Partnerships

The College of Medicine is a partner in the Tennessee Institutes of Pre-professionals (TIP). The Tennessee Institutes for Pre-Professionals (TIP), which is operated by the University of Tennessee Health Sciences Center, is open to members of underrepresented groups who are residents of Tennessee who are interested in a career in medicine, dentistry, pharmacy, or veterinary medicine. The program is designed to promote and to nurture student's interest in the health professions through an array of structured activities. The program's ultimate goal is to increase the representation and active participation of under represented groups in health professions training and practice. More information on the program can be found at *(www.utmem.edu/tip)*.

Student Financial Assistance

The James H. Quillen College of Medicine is authorized to provide state and federal financial assistance to minorities under the guidelines set forth by the various programs. The supplemental information fee (application fee) may be waived by action of the Assistant Dean for Admissions upon the written request of the applicant, provided that an AMCAS fee waiver has been granted. In recent years, the Tennessee Higher Education Commission has also provided scholarships to a limited

number of African-American students. Other scholarships may be available on a limited basis.

The administration of the College of Medicine is keenly aware of the financial burden that medical students bear. As such, Financial Services strives to aid students in making wise financial decisions to limit students' overall indebtedness by conducting debt management and financial planning workshops throughout the year.

Meharry Medical College School of Medicine

Mr. Allen D. Mosley, Director Admissions
and Recruitment
Meharry Medical College
School of Medicine
1005 Dr. D.B. Todd Jr. Boulevard
Nashville, TN 37208
615-327-6223; 615-327-6228 Fax
amosley@mmc.edu

Recruitment

Recruitment is done primarily at the undergraduate college level. Visitations, seminars, and interviews are conducted on various college campuses and in communities as requested by the institutions or organizations. Visits are accepted from pre-med clubs of both undergraduate colleges and high schools. Two summer programs [Health Careers Opportunities Program (HCOP) and Summer Neuroscience Apprentice Program (SNAP)] are offered yearly to prepare undergraduate students for careers in medical education and research.

The School of Medicine directs the recruitment program that is coordinated by the Office of Admissions and Records. Participation in the recruitment program involves faculty, administrators, and students. All three groups conduct visitations.

Admissions

Students are selected for admission to Meharry Medical College by the Admissions Committee, which is charged with selecting students who will make suitable candidates for the study and eventual practice of their profession. The number of applicants greatly exceeds the capacity. All applications are considered on a competitive basis from the standpoint of scholarship, intelligence, aptitude, character, and general fitness. In the final selection of applicants comparing most favorably on these factors, the current policy of the institution is to give preferential consideration to applicants who: 1) come from areas with inadequate health care as measured by the medical population ratio, 2) have underserved backgrounds, 3) are from Southern Regional Education Board (SREB) states having contracts with Meharry, 4) are from schools that have special contracts with Meharry to admit students who have been in special courses, and 5) have a history of community activities, especially in the health care area. Special consideration is given to minority groups and disadvantaged applicants of all origins.

Academic Support Programs

Any student who experiences difficulty at Meharry can expect assistance, as necessary, from the faculty. At the end of the first month, students are evaluated and advised as to whether or not they should accept a reduced load. Also, at the end of each scheduled examination, each department checks to see if any student is having difficulty. If so, the student is assigned to a faculty advisor for tutorial sessions or referred to the Epps Center for Educational Development and Support Services (CEDSS). The CEDSS is devoted to improving the teaching and learning environment. It assists students in developing a variety of skills that can help to improve their learning. Examples of the types of programs offered by the CEDSS include time and stress management; study, test and note-taking skills; analytical reasoning; problem-solving skills; peer tutoring services; small-group instruction; and a comprehensive review program for licensure in medicine.

Meharry Medical College, 2006
Applicants and Matriculants by Gender, Race and Ethnicity

Race and Ethnicity	Applicants			Matriculants		
	Women	Men	Total	Women	Men	Total
Hispanic/Latino						
Cuban	15	10	25	0	0	0
Mexican American	39	27	66	1	0	1
Puerto Rican	20	14	34	1	0	1
Other Hispanic	70	51	121	0	1	1
Multiple Hispanic*	6	3	9	0	0	0
Subtotal	150	105	255	2	1	3
Non-Hispanic/Latino**						
Black	976	440	1,416	53	25	78
Native American/Alaska Native	4	8	12	0	0	0
Native Hawaiian/Other Pacific Islander	10	7	17	0	0	0
White	374	538	912	2	4	6
Asian	425	439	864	3	3	6
Other Race	4	4	8	0	0	0
Multiple Race*	49	43	92	0	0	0
Unknown	11	8	19	0	0	0
Subtotal	1,853	1,487	3,340	58	32	90
Foreign	112	129	241	0	0	0
Total	2,115	1,721	3,836	60	33	93

*Since 2002, students can select more than one race and / or ethnicity. **Those who did not choose 'Hispanic/Latino' or 'Non-Hispanic/Latino' are counted under 'Non-Hispanic/Latino'.

Data Source: AAMC Data Warehouse: Applicant-Matriculant File, as of 5/9/2007.

The Office of the College Chaplain and Counseling Services provides counseling services to students in the following areas:

• Spiritual and theological concerns
• Interpersonal relationships
• Pre-marital concerns
• Family problems/marital counseling
• Grief
• Stress management
• Conflict resolution
• Adjustment problems
• Self-esteem problems
• Time management

These concerns and others, which are of interest to the students, may be discussed in confidence in the Office of the College Chaplain and Counseling Services.

Enrichment Programs
The Summer Neuroscience Apprentice Program (SNAP) offers minority undergraduates an opportunity to experience the excitement of brain research. Meharry Medical College and Vanderbilt University recently formed a partnership to help develop and promote the scientific careers of underrepresented minorities. SNAP is the first stage of that process and is linked to opportunities for advanced training in graduate school. SNAP consists of 10 weeks of directed research in the laboratory of a successful scientist supplemented by minicourses in the ethics of science and "survival" skills for young aspiring scientists. A variety of enrichment activities include faculty seminars and a closing celebration with individual presentations of research by students. The program provides a stipend and support for housing and travel.

The Health Careers Opportunity Program (HCOP) offers minority undergraduates from disadvantaged backgrounds a challenging academic opportunity to realize their dream of becoming a physician, dentist, or public health professional.

One of the most exciting aspects of the HCOP at Meharry is the opportunity to shadow a professional in the discipline the student is pursuing. Students in the dental program will gain exposure to dental specialties through shadowing experiences in the campus clinic. Students in the medical program will shadow physicians, residents, and medical students and spend two evenings in a hospital emergency room. Public health students will spend time with local experts throughout Nashville. Each participant earns a stipend. The program finances travel, room, meals, and tuition.

Rising juniors and seniors are eligible to apply to both programs (SNAP or HCOP). For application forms or additional information write to the Admissions and Records Office at the address above or send e-mail to *(admissions@mmc.edu)*.

Student Financial Assistance
Meharry Medical College is committed to making its programs available to qualified students from diverse backgrounds and thus offers a variety of financial assistance programs through scholarships, financial aid, and financing options to families of all income levels.

The Director of Admissions considers application fee waiver requests on an individual basis, provided that an AMCAS fee waiver has been granted.

University of Tennessee, Health Science Center, College of Medicine

Dr. Gerald J. Presbury
Associate Professor
Department of Pediatrics
University of Tennessee, Health Science
Center, College of Medicine
62 South Dunlap, Memphis, TN 38163
901-572-5394; 901-572-3122 Fax

Recruitment

The College of Medicine maintains a long-term, continuing program for the recruitment of underrepresented minority and disadvantaged students. As a means of identifying students, referral information is requested from high school principals, counselors, college pre-med advisors, and other educational referral agencies. Further, admissions and financial aid representatives for each of the six health professions colleges of the University of Tennessee (UT), Memphis make regular high school and college visits throughout Tennessee and adjoining states. Once students are identified, they are tracked throughout their educational experience. Academic progress is monitored; counsel and reinforcement are provided regarding career decisions; and close association with faculty and students from the College of Medicine is encouraged through numerous on-campus educational enrichment experiences. Students developing interest, motivation, and knowledge about the health profession are stimulated by periodic health profession publications and newsletters; on-campus visitation programs, including tours, seminars, and study-skills workshops; and summer work experience in laboratories and clinics of the College of Medicine.

The College of Medicine is committed to increasing the number of underrepresented minority students who will enter the medical profession.

Admissions

To support the work of the Admissions Committee in selecting highly qualified minority students, a select subcommittee, composed of the Assistant Dean for Admissions and Students and other members of the Admissions Committee, carefully review the applications of all minority students prior to their presentation to the full committee.

Academic Support Programs

The Student Academic Support Service at UT, Memphis provides academic support for medical students throughout their training. This program offers individual laboratory assessments of learning difficulties, as well as an integrative program of skill development in reading, time management, problem solving, note taking, test taking, and memorizing. Computer-assisted instruction, based on the curriculum, is available in large-group, small-group, and individual sessions. Tutorial assistance is also available at no charge. In addition, the college sponsors a variety of other support programs that include:

- *The Faculty Advisory System* facilitates interaction among faculty and students. Each entering student becomes a member of a faculty advisor group composed of five first-year students, five second-year students, two faculty advisors, and two student advisors. The faculty share their perspective on medical education and the profession and serve as resource persons for specific questions or problems. The M-2 student advisors coordinate the activities of the group, and the M-4 student advisors share perspectives of those further advanced in the curriculum.

University of Tennessee Health Science Center College of Medicine, 2006
Applicants and Matriculants by Gender, Race and Ethnicity

Race and Ethnicity		Applicants			Matriculants		
		Women	Men	Total	Women	Men	Total
Hispanic/Latino							
Cuban		2	2	4	0	0	0
Mexican American		4	2	6	0	1	1
Puerto Rican		2	2	4	0	1	1
Other Hispanic		8	7	15	1	0	1
	Subtotal	16	13	29	1	2	3
Non-Hispanic/Latino**							
Black		111	49	160	9	6	15
Native American/Alaska Native		2	4	6	1	0	1
White		356	531	887	43	72	115
Asian		63	63	126	3	12	15
Other Race		1	0	1	0	0	0
Multiple Race*		13	17	30	0	0	0
Unknown		0	3	3	0	1	1
	Subtotal	546	667	1,213	56	91	147
Foreign		1	1	2	0	0	0
	Total	563	681	1,244	57	93	150

*Since 2002, students can select more than one race and / or ethnicity. **Those who did not choose
'Hispanic/Latino' or 'Non-Hispanic/Latino' are counted under 'Non-Hispanic/Latino'.
Data Source: AAMC Data Warehouse: Applicant-Matriculant File, as of 5/9/2007.

Association of American Medical Colleges, 2007

- *Big Brother/Big Sister Program.* Each entering student is assigned a Big Sib. The Big Brother or Big Sister offers invaluable insight into the ropes of the first year: which books are best, the first test, best grocery store, where to get a haircut, where to relax and have fun, how to sign up for intramurals, et cetera. Close and lasting relationships often develop through this program.
- *Career Counseling and Residency Placement.* Choosing the specialty most congruent with students' interests, talents, and long-term personal and professional goals is a major life decision. Programs and activities are available to support students as they contemplate this decision and choose their specialties and residencies, beginning in the second year and continuing through the National Residency Match Program (NRMP) Match in the fourth year.
- *Peer Counseling Program.* Peer Counselors are trained, carefully selected volunteers who offer a confidential personal support system to students in all classes. This program teaches physicians-to-be that it is acceptable to need help, to turn to one another for help, and to know how to offer it. This program fosters positive development and a sharing, cooperative approach to education.

Enrichment Programs

The College of Medicine and the UT, Memphis sponsor a host of summer enrichment activities that are designed to promote a greater interest in the health profession, enhance students' competitiveness as applicants, and contribute to their success in the medical curriculum. The following listing is representative of the interest and commitment of the college.

Summer High School Research Apprenticeships. Opportunities for employment in research settings for high school and college students. Generally eight weeks in duration.

Tennessee Preprofessional Fellowship Program (PFP). African American residents of Tennessee, who have completed two years of undergraduate study with demonstrated interest in medicine, participate in two required eight-week summer enrichment programs following junior and senior years. Students who successfully complete the programs receive an assurance of medical school admission if, by the time of their application, they meet or exceed minimum admission requirements.

Early Admission. The Committee on Admissions invites applications from outstanding minority applicants at the beginning of their junior year. Students may begin their medical study during their senior year or complete their undergraduate training while having a space reserved for them in the next entering class.

All of the above summer programs carry a stipend to replace lost income.

Student Financial Assistance

Financial aid for all students at UT, Memphis is based on need. These needs are met through scholarships, grants, loans, and work-study. The financial aid officers, through a combination of these means, have been successful in supplying enough assistance to complete degree programs. The College of Medicine is very pleased to sponsor scholarship programs for minority students. Scholarships in the amount of $10,000 annually have been available to all minority students accepted for admission.

AAMC

Vanderbilt University School of Medicine

Dr. George C. Hill, Associate Dean
and Levi Watkins, Jr., Professor
for Diversity in Medical Education
and Professor in the Department
of Microbiology and Immunology
Vanderbilt University
School of Medicine
301 Light Hall
Nashville, TN 37232-0190
615-322-7498; 615-322-4526 Fax

Recruitment

The Vanderbilt University School of Medicine is committed to a diversified student population. To this end, the school administers an active recruitment program that involves visits by students and staff to other campuses and encourages contacts between applicants and matriculating students. Applicants that have been invited to Vanderbilt are encouraged to return for the "second visit" weekend that occurs each April. Currently enrolled minority students and alumni are actively involved in the school's recruitment program.

Vanderbilt University School of Medicine has organized an Office for Diversity in Medical Education under the leadership of an Associate Dean in Medical Education reporting to the Dean of the School of Medicine. This office will focus on increasing the diversity of the medical and graduate students, housestaff, and faculty and enhancing an evolving environment that recognizes and embraces diversity.

The regional Student National Medical Association at Vanderbilt University School of Medicine is extremely active in student affairs and received the region award for excellence in 2004. We also have an active Asian Pacific American Medical Student Association (APAMSA) organization, National Network of Latin American Medical Students (NNLAMS), and a Minority Association of Pre-medical Students (MAPS) chapter.

Admissions

The admissions process at Vanderbilt School of Medicine does not use mathematical formulas for choosing applicants. All parts of the American Medical College Application Service (AMCAS) application and secondary application are of value in making selections. There is a stated goal to matriculate a highly diverse class in terms of race, gender, geography, and other elements. The first priority of the process is to ensure that academic credentials suggest that students can graduate from a highly competitive environment. All aspects of the applications are considered to accomplish the goals of diversity, which enhances the educational experience of our students.

Academic Support Programs

The Vanderbilt University School of Medicine provides a supportive, positive environment in which students are treated individually in their pursuit of excellence in careers in medicine. Individual tutoring and counseling, as needed, are provided to all students. There has been minimal attrition.

Enrichment Programs

Accepted students are given special assistance in locating funded summer research positions with Vanderbilt faculty.

Vanderbilt Summer Science Academy
The Vanderbilt Summer Science Academy (VSSA) hosts over 70 undergraduates from institutions all over the country who conduct research in one of the basic science research laboratories at Vanderbilt. Each student has an opportunity to present their research at the Summer Symposium held on the last day of the program. The VSSA also organizes

Vanderbilt University School of Medicine, 2006
Applicants and Matriculants by Gender, Race and Ethnicity

Race and Ethnicity	Applicants			Matriculants		
	Women	Men	Total	Women	Men	Total
Hispanic/Latino						
Cuban	10	6	16	0	0	0
Mexican American	22	26	48	0	0	0
Puerto Rican	14	9	23	1	0	1
Other Hispanic	45	54	99	0	0	0
Multiple Hispanic*	2	4	6	0	0	0
Subtotal	93	99	192	1	0	1
Non-Hispanic/Latino**						
Black	215	107	322	7	4	11
Native American/Alaska Native	4	7	11	0	0	0
Native Hawaiian/Other Pacific Islander	2	3	5	0	0	0
White	1,106	1,572	2,678	28	41	69
Asian	371	421	792	8	6	14
Other Race	2	4	6	0	0	0
Multiple Race*	57	47	104	2	0	2
Unknown	12	22	34	0	2	2
Subtotal	1,769	2,183	3,952	45	53	98
Foreign	113	116	229	3	4	7
Total	1,975	2,398	4,373	49	57	106

*Since 2002, students can select more than one race and / or ethnicity. **Those who did not choose Hispanic/Latino' or 'Non-Hispanic/Latino' are counted under 'Non-Hispanic/Latino'.
Data Source: AAMC Data Warehouse: Applicant-Matriculant File, as of 5/9/2007.

orientation, a research seminar series, a Graduate Record Examination (GRE) preparatory course, enrichment seminars, and social activities. The research seminars cover many of the major areas of investigation in the biomedical sciences and expose students to the newest technology used in these areas of study. In addition, the enrichment seminars provide useful information for working in the laboratory, applying to graduate program, and exposure to the many career options open to individuals with a Ph.D. in the biomedical sciences. This is an excellent opportunity for undergraduates to experience research at a major academic research center and to understand what graduate life would be like were they to decide on a research career. It is also an excellent opportunity for them to network with students at other institutions from across the country.

Our Summer Academy students have the opportunity to work in one of over 200 laboratories in any of the departments or programs affiliated the Office of Biomedical Research Education and Training. These include those affiliated with the Interdisciplinary Graduate Program (biochemistry, biological sciences, cancer biology, cell & developmental biology, human genetics, microbiology & immunology, molecular physiology & biophysics, neurosciences (molecular & cellular, cognitive/integrative), pathology, and pharmacology) and the Chemical and Physical Biology Program (all Interdisciplinary Graduate Program participating departments and programs as well as chemistry, physics, and mathematics). Students are matched with mentors based on research interest as well as with mentors who have an excellent track record of mentoring students during the summer.

More information can be found at: (*https://medschool.mc.vanderbilt.edu/ summer_academy/*)

For questions, please contact:
Michelle Grundy, Ph.D. Director
Vanderbilt Summer Science Academy
michelle.grundy@vanderbilt.edu

Initiative for Maximizing Student Diversity
The Office of Biomedical Research Education and Training provides opportunities for individuals holding a bachelors degree to prepare for PhD training through the Initiative for Maximizing Student Diversity (IMSD) training grant funded by the National Institutes of Health. The Vanderbilt Initiative for Maximizing Student Diversity (IMSD) is an NIH-funded program geared toward students who contribute to diversity, and who have a real interest in biomedical research and would like to enter a first-rate graduate program in the biomedical sciences. The Vanderbilt IMSD program is a very highly flexible approach that involves extensive and careful mentoring at all stages. The Vanderbilt IMSD offers a one-year training opportunity (pre-Interdisciplinary Graduate Program) prior to the traditional first or Interdisciplinary Graduate Program year of graduate school. Students will be selected to matriculate into the pre-Interdisciplinary Graduate Program program on a holistic basis. Although applicants will be required to submit GPA and GRE scores, future potential for success as evidenced by recommendation letters and a personal interview will be the key basis for selecting applicants. We anticipate that students who complete the two year pre-Interdisciplinary Graduate Program/Interdisciplinary Graduate Program will be fast tracked for success in their later years in research.

More information can be found on the following website: (*https://medschool.mc. vanderbilt./imsd*)
or contact:
Linda Sealy, Ph.D.
Associate Director
Initiative for Maximizing Student Diversity
linda.sealy@vanderbilt.edu

Vanderbilt Emphasis Program
The Emphasis Program is a unique mode of self-directed study that takes place during the first two years of medical school. This program aims to harness the student's skills, talents, and passions by allowing them to pursue a project of their choosing.

Perhaps one of the greatest advantages of the Emphasis Program is the opportunity for students to learn more about themselves and what type of physicians they would like to become.

We will match students' areas of interest with those of committed, excellent faculty mentors. Students will cultivate knowledge and skill through these mentorship experiences, as well as hands-on research and study in desired areas of focus.

Program Director
Denis O'Day, MD
denis.oday@vanderbilt.edu
615-936-2100

Program Coordinator
Tamie Swah
tamie.swah@vanderbilt.edu
615-343-0410

More information can be found at: (*www.mc.vanderbilt.edu/emphasis*).

AAMC

Student Financial Assistance

The school grants application fee waivers for students for whom the American Medical College Application Service has granted a fee waiver.

Vanderbilt uses a needs-analysis system for awarding need-based scholarships. There are Dean's Scholarships awarded to students in order to encourage diversity in the medical student population. In addition, there are merit scholarships, based on academic and leadership potential, for which all Vanderbilt students are eligible.

Educational Partnerships

Vanderbilt faculty participate in special programs in community middle and high schools that are designed to enrich the schools' science curricula and to encourage student interest in the sciences and the health professions. Students and teachers are, in turn, accommodated in summer enrichment programs at the medical center.

Baylor College of Medicine

Dr. James L. Phillips, Senior Associate Dean and Professor of Pediatrics
Baylor College of Medicine
One Baylor Plaza, M108
Houston, TX 77030
713-798-6598; 713-798-8449 Fax
phillips@bcm.edu
www.bcm.edu/osa/osa-minority.html

Recruitment

Baylor has an active program of visiting colleges and secondary schools to seek out and inform individuals, from groups underrepresented in medicine, about career opportunities. Faculty, medical students, administrators, and alumni participate in these recruitment efforts. The career fairs for underrepresented minority students at the annual meetings of the

Association of American Medical Colleges (AAMC), Society for the Advancement of Chicanos and Native Americans in Science (SACNAS), the National Association of Medical Minority Educators (NAMME) are attended by our faculty and students. Individuals and school groups are also encouraged to visit the campus and participate in organized tours conducted by medical students.

Admissions

The Admissions Committee is composed of faculty and students, several of whom are members of groups underrepresented in medicine. Applicants are evaluated on both cognitive and non-cognitive strengths, including review of one's complete academic record. Since 1971, a significant percentage of each year's entering classes has been minority group students

Baylor College of Medicine, 2006
Applicants and Matriculants by Gender, Race and Ethnicity

Race and Ethnicity	Applicants			Matriculants		
	Women	Men	Total	Women	Men	Total
Hispanic/Latino						
Cuban	8	5	13	0	0	0
Mexican American	92	81	173	11	8	19
Puerto Rican	18	19	37	0	0	0
Other Hispanic	66	54	120	4	4	8
Multiple Hispanic*	4	7	11	0	1	1
Subtotal	188	166	354	15	13	28
Non-Hispanic/Latino**						
Black	239	124	363	14	1	15
Native American/Alaska Native	8	12	20	0	1	1
Native Hawaiian/Other Pacific Islander	11	6	17	0	0	0
White	867	1,242	2,109	25	40	65
Asian	531	587	1,118	24	27	51
Other Race	5	6	11	0	0	0
Multiple Race*	56	67	123	3	3	6
Unknown	15	15	30	0	1	1
Subtotal	1,732	2,059	3,791	66	73	139
Foreign	100	81	181	0	1	1
Total	2,020	2,306	4,326	81	87	168

*Since 2002, students can select more than one race and / or ethnicity. **Those who did not choose Hispanic/Latino' or 'Non-Hispanic/Latino' are counted under 'Non-Hispanic/Latino'.
Data Source: AAMC Data Warehouse: Applicant-Matriculant File, as of 5/9/2007.

underrepresented in medicine. Baylor as an institution is committed to diversity. In addition to having an underrepresented minority enrollment in each class that ranges from 16-22 percent, several enroll in our Medical Scientist Training Program (MSTP), Baylor's M.D./Ph.D. program, and the M.D./MBA program, which is operated in conjunction with Rice University. The faculty and staff at Baylor focus on helping our students maximize their potential, with some being Howard Hughes Scholars and some recipients of other research fellowships.

Applicants should submit their applications as early as possible (June), since admissions are granted on a rolling basis following interviews in the fall semester.

Academic Support Programs
Each basic science department offers tutorial assistance and individual conferences for all students. Tutors and review sessions are available for students, faculty are readily accessible, and videotapes of the lectures may be checked out from the Learning Resource Center. An innovative mentoring program that utilizes clinical and basic science faculty, plus fellows and residents, is also in place.

Enrichment Programs
Michael E. DeBakey Summer Surgery Program. The Michael E. DeBakey Summer Surgery Program provides students with an opportunity to work with faculty, residents, medical students, and nurses in a surgical hospital environment. During the eight-week program, students become familiar with the hospital environment, the operating room, and the lifestyle of a surgeon through participation in surgical team routines, making daily rounds with an attending physician, observing surgeries, and attending brown bag lunches and conferences.

Saturday Morning Science Program. This program targets students in grades seven-12 from our underserved communities. Lectures and labs are presented by our faculty, who are assisted by our medical students. Careers in the biosciences for the students constitute the goal of this initiative, which concludes each semester with a career/college fair.

Several High Schools for the Health Professions throughout the state are affiliated with Baylor College of Medicine.

The SMART Program. The 10-week, Summer Medical and Research Training Program is open to undergraduate college students. In addition to a major laboratory experience, there is a daily seminar series and career development workshops and activities. Contact Gayle Slaughter, Ph.D., Program Director, 713-798-5915.

Student Financial Assistance
Significant financial aid is available for students with demonstrated financial need. Applicants may also request waiver of the application fee on the basis of financial need.

The Texas A&M University System Health Science Center College of Medicine

Dr. Wanda J. Watson, Director of Recruitment and Special Programs
Texas A&M Health Science Center
College of Medicine
159 Joe H. Reynolds Medical Building
College Station, TX 77843-1114
979-845-7743; 979-845-5533 Fax
Wwatson@medicine.tamhsc.edu
www.medicine.tamhsc.edu

Recruitment

The recruitment program at The Texas A&M Health Science Center College of Medicine is an integrated series of activities and efforts primarily focused at Texas residents. As part of its commitment to recruit and graduate qualified disadvantaged students, the College of Medicine throught the Office of Student Affairs and Admissions and Office of Special Programs, administer several summer enrichment programs are very special opportunities. The College of Medicine hosts and sponsors enrichment programs which identify and support promising disadvantaged college students by providing guidance, information, and activities designed to encourage graduation and subsequent application to the university's pre-medical programs.

The College of Medicine, in partnership with the Application Center for Medical/Dental/Undergraduate Research Summer Programs in Texas, also has a program of annual recruiting visits to undergraduate institutions throughout the state of Texas.

Admissions

Disadvantaged student applications are considered along with other applicants.

Admission to the College of Medicine is competitive. The College of Medicine considers for enrollment only individuals who are U.S. citizens or permanent residents of the United States, and who have completed their undergraduate coursework at a fully accredited college or university in the United States or its territories. By state mandate, enrollment of of individuals from states other than Taxas may not exceed 10 percent. Applicants must demonstrate better than average ability to master a challenging educational experience. Assessment of applicants is based on academic record, pattern of academic performance, extracurricular activities, motivation, and background. The Admissions Committee consists of faculty from the basic and clinical sciences. Eighty students matriculate each year.

Academic Support Programs

Students in academic difficulty receive assistance from faculty members and students. Review sessions are periodically scheduled in particular disciplines. Specific remedial work if necessary, is assigned on an individual basis. Workshops on learning strategies and time management techniques are conducted during the first year. Assistance in these areas, upon request or referral, is provided on an individual basis. During the third and fourth years on the Temple clinical campus, students select a faculty advisor with whom they can meet and discuss choices of electives, residency training, and career opportunities.

Student Financial Assistance

Scholarship and loan funds are available for disadvantaged students with financial need from local, state, and national sources. Financial need of the applicant is not a consideration in the admission process. After acceptance, every effort is made to assist disadvantaged students in meeting their financial requirements.

Texas A&M Health Science Center College of Medicine, 2006
Applicants and Matriculants by Gender, Race and Ethnicity

Race and Ethnicity	Applicants			Matriculants		
	Women	Men	Total	Women	Men	Total
Hispanic/Latino						
Cuban	6	4	10	0	0	0
Mexican American	154	125	279	2	3	5
Puerto Rican	6	6	12	0	0	0
Other Hispanic	49	46	95	3	0	3
Multiple Hispanic*	2	6	8	0	0	0
Subtotal	217	187	404	5	3	8
Non-Hispanic/Latino**						
Black	128	56	184	2	1	3
Native American/Alaska Native	7	9	16	1	0	1
Native Hawaiian/Other Pacific Islander	2	2	4	0	1	1
White	648	785	1,433	23	15	38
Asian	367	355	722	15	17	32
Other Race	26	27	53	0	0	0
Multiple Race*	21	16	37	0	2	2
Unknown	2	1	3	0	0	0
Subtotal	1,201	1,251	2,452	41	36	77
Foreign	26	27	53	0	0	0
Total	1,444	1,465	2,909	46	39	85

*Since 2002, students can select more than one race and / or ethnicity. **Those who did not choose 'Hispanic/Latino' or 'Non-Hispanic/Latino' are counted under 'Non-Hispanic/Latino'.
Data Source: AAMC Data Warehouse: Applicant-Matriculant File, as of 5/9/2007.

Approximately 90 percent of the students currently in the program are receiving some form of financial aid.

Educational Partnerships

The Partnership for Primary Care Program. The Texas A&M Health Science Center College of Medicine entered into agreements with member institutions of the Texas A&M University Systems to develop and implement the Partnership for Primary Care Program. This program is designed to recruit and jointly admit a select group of students with a guaranteed admission to the COM. The College of Medicine and A&M system's member institutions work together to develop programs of recruitment, admission, augmentation of undergraduate studies, and targeted opportunities for exposure to medicine during undergraduate years.

A specific Primary Care or Rural Medicine Track provides students with enrichment experiences over the four years of medical school. Also, students will be provided with the opportunity for a significant portion of their clinical training during medical school in the geographic vicinity of either their hometown or the A&M System University of their undergraduate experience. The program is targeted to provide primary care physicians for rural and/or underserved areas and areas of Texas with a disproportionately low number of primary care physicians.

The Joint Admissions Medical Program (JAMP). The Joint Admissions Medical Program (JAMP) is a program created by Senate Bill 940 of the 77th Texas Legislature to provide services to support and encourage highly qualified, economically disadvantaged students pursuing a medical education. The program awards undergraduate and medical school scholarships and guarantees admission to those students who satisfy both academic and non-academic requirements to one of the eight

participating medical schools. The Texas A&M health Science Center College of Medicine is one of the eight medical schools participating in the program. As part of its commitment to the program, the COM provides JAMP students with stipends, summer enrichment internships; and mentoring and personal assistance to facilitate preparation for medical school while attending college.

The summer enrichment experience is rather intense by design. Part of the experience requires clinical exposure or clinical observational experiences. The bulk of that experience has been worked out with Scott & White Clinic College Station. However, the COM also provides the participants with an all day clinical experience at Scott & White in Temple shadowing physician faculty.

The Texas A&M University System Prairie View A&M University Undergraduate Medical Academy(UMA). The Texas A&M Health Science Center College of Medicine has entered into an agreement with the Prairie View A&M University to create the Undergraduate Medical Academy. The College of Medicine Office of Special Programs in the Office of Student Affairs and Admissions coordinates the summer enrichment experience for the Academy students. The COM faculty members are highly involved in the program.

As with all of our summer enrichment programs, the Academy students are required to participate in clinical exposure or clinical observational experiences. The bulk of that experience is with Scott & White Clinic in College Station. They participate in all day clinical experience as Scott & White in Temple shadowing physician faculty.

The academy was created through legislation to increase skills needed for students to enter medical school or other health professions schools, to create a cooperative network between the Academy faculty

members, students, and the medical community; and to foster and encourage interest in science and mathematics.

The South Texas College. The Texas A&M Health Science Center College of Medicine has entered into an agreement with the South Texas College (STC) in McAllen, Texas. Through the College of Medicine Partnership for Primary Care Program, qualified students are recruited for simultaneous admissions to the STC Valley Scholars Program and to the CCOM, provided students transfer successfully to the Texas A&M University BIMS or Biology programs. Students are expected to complete the associate of science degree at STC a baccalaureate degree in BIMS or Biology at Texas A&M University, and the M.D. degree at the College of Medicine.

This program is for the purpose of recruiting, enrolling, and graduating significantly greater numbers of physicians to serve the designated health professions shortage areas of south Texas, to correct disproportions in physician distribution, and to meet the health care needs of rural and underserved south Texas.

AAMC

Texas Tech University Health Sciences Center School of Medicine

Dr. Bernell K. Dalley, Associate Dean for Admissions and Minority Affairs
Texas Tech University Health Sciences Center School of Medicine 3601 4th St.
MS6216
Lubbock, TX 79430
306-743-2297; 806-743-2725 Fax
bernell.dalley@ttuhsc.edu

Recruitment

Texas Tech University Health Sciences Center (TTUHSC) School of Medicine is responsive to both the health care needs of the area it serves and to the need for involvement of minority and disadvantaged groups in the health professions. The School of Medicine has a sincere desire to identify, at the earliest stage of high school and undergraduate training, highly motivated and academically qualified students.

The Office of Border Health on the El Paso campus was created to recruit students from the border counties of Texas, with emphasis on the undergraduate programs in those areas, including San Antonio. The effort is supplemented by identifying high school students in the El Paso County area. Due to increased grant support from the Texas Tech University School of Medicine and Hispanic Center of Excellence and Office of Rural and Community Health initiatives, the number of applicants as well as matriculants from underrepresented groups has steadily increased. The Offices of Border Health and Rural and Community Health work in coordination with the Office of Admissions and Minority Affairs and the Office of Student Affairs.

Admissions

The Admissions Committee of Texas Tech University Health Sciences Center School of Medicine is composed of basic science faculty, clinical faculty, and medical students. Minorities are represented on the committee. It is the policy of the TTUHSC School of Medicine to select from a pool of applicants those students who have demonstrated strong academic ability and motivation for medicine. The goal of the institution is to recruit a diverse medical class exhibiting the personal experiences and the qualities promising academic success and to meet the needs of an increasingly diverse population. To that end, race/ethnic background as well as interest in the region will be among the many factors considered in the admissions process. All potentially acceptable minority applicants are invited for interviews and receive full committee consideration. While all applicants are subjected to standard admission procedures and policies, each applicant is reviewed with careful attention to background and extenuating circumstances.

Students enrolled in the School of Medicine act as recruiters and promoters by talking with potential applicants when they visit the school and at pre-medical organization meetings. Applicants, especially those from underrepresented groups, are always encouraged to visit the medical school and talk with faculty and students. Representatives of the Admissions Committee annually attend the Texas Association of Advisors for the Health Professions Meeting. There is also regular participation in recruitment workshops. Visits are scheduled to campuses with significant numbers of minority students.

Academic Support Programs

The Admissions Committee accepts students considered to be capable of proceeding through the curriculum. In addition, students have the opportunity for individual instruction, remediation, and extra

Texas Tech University Health Sciences Center School of Medicine, 2006
Applicants and Matriculants by Gender, Race and Ethnicity

Race and Ethnicity		Applicants			Matriculants		
		Women	Men	Total	Women	Men	Total
Hispanic/Latino							
Cuban		6	5	11	0	0	0
Mexican American		158	133	291	4	5	9
Puerto Rican		3	7	10	0	0	0
Other Hispanic		47	48	95	0	2	2
Multiple Hispanic*		2	6	8	0	0	0
	Subtotal	216	199	415	4	7	11
Non-Hispanic/Latino**							
Black		123	55	178	1	3	4
Native American/Alaska Native		6	10	16	0	1	1
Native Hawaiian/Other Pacific Islander		2	2	4	0	1	1
White		616	780	1,396	36	50	86
Asian		354	352	706	16	15	31
Other Race		28	27	55	3	2	5
Multiple Race*		20	17	37	1	0	1
Unknown		2	1	3	0	0	0
	Subtotal	1,151	1,244	2,395	57	72	129
Foreign		22	24	46	0	0	0
	Total	1,389	1,467	2,856	61	79	140

*Since 2002, students can select more than one race and / or ethnicity. **Those who did not choose Hispanic/Latino' or 'Non-Hispanic/Latino' are counted under 'Non-Hispanic/Latino'.
Data Source: AAMC Data Warehouse: Applicant-Matriculant File, as of 5/9/2007.

help from the faculty. A faculty mentoring program in which faculty serve as advisors to a small group of first- and second-year students is designed to assist in the adjustments to the medical school environment. For those students who do experience difficulty, there is also special assistance offered through the Academic and Career Advisor in the Office of Student Affairs. These programs and individuals help to identify student difficulties at an early period, so that academic and other help will be profitable. Flexible programs, when appropriate, may be designed for students encountering academic difficulties.

Enrichment Programs

Summer enrichment internships are available for disadvantaged and rural high school, undergraduate, and medical students. One of these, the Summer Pre-medical Academy, consists of an all expenses paid six-week intensive course designed for students with 60 or more college credits. It includes shadowing experiences, a short course in gross anatomy, written and oral communication courses, community service activities and a full Medical College Admission Test review course (Stanley Kaplan). Information is available at the following Web site: *(www.ttuhsc.edu/som/admissions).* Please inquire through the TTUHSC School of Medicine Office of Admissions (806-743-2297) or the Office of Border Health (915-545-6552) for information related to enrichment programs.

Student Financial Assistance

TTUHSC School of Medicine personnel believe that no student should be denied a medical education due to lack of funds. A needs-based scholarship fund has been established for assistance during the first year of medical school. No student or prospective student shall be excluded

from participation in, or be denied the benefits of any financial aid program on the basis of race, color, national origin, religion, or sex.

All students receive financial assistance in accordance with demonstrated need. Financial capability does not enter into the student selection process, neither is the lack of personal funds permitted to interfere with the completion of medical school education. The needs analysis is determined through the use of the Free Application for Federal Student Aid (FAFSA).

Educational Partnerships

The Offices of Admissions and Minority Affairs, Student Affairs, Rural and Community Health, and Border Health coordinate and administer partnership initiatives. The regional campuses at Lubbock, Amarillo, and El Paso have joined the independent school systems of the respective communities via available magnet high schools for the health professions. Undergraduate programs in all three cities are also involved in mentoring programs with the School of Medicine students. In addition, summer employment and community-based elective opportunities for medical students are provided in these areas, especially in the largely Hispanic rural areas of the Lower Valley outside of El Paso.

Other Pertinent Information

TTUHSC School of Medicine particularly maintains a commitment to well-qualified students who are residents of Texas, eastern New Mexico, and southwestern Oklahoma.

University of Texas Medical Branch University of Texas Medical School at Galveston

Dr. Lauree Thomas, Associate Dean
for Student Affairs and Admissions
The University of Texas Medical
School at Galveston
Ashbel Smith Building, Suite 1.208
301 University Blvd.
Galveston, TX 77555-1307
409-772-1442; 409-772-5148 Fax
lauthoma@utmb.edu
www.utmb.edu/somstudentaffairs

Recruitment

The Office of Student Affairs and Admissions facilitates the recruitment, admissions, and matriculation of a medical school class that is of the highest quality and is proportionally representative of the state's population. The School of Medicine recruits primarily throughout the state as well as on a national level. The Director of Recruitment, faculty, and medical students visit with pre-medical students and advisors at universities in Texas and other states with a significant enrollment of Texas residents from educationally and economically disadvantaged backgrounds. During these visits, presentations on the medical school admission process, academic preparation, curriculum, student life, and financial aid are discussed at length as well as the rigorous and demanding expectations of medical school.

The University of Texas Medical Branch (UTMB) has committed substantial institutional resources towards our core institutional value of diversity. To achieve this goal, UTMB has established partnerships with several Texas colleges and universities, community organizations, and school districts to enhance the recruitment, matriculation, retention, and graduation of educationally and economically disadvantaged pre-medical and medical students. Every year the school of medicine hosts a number of recruitment programs both on and off campus, which are designed to facilitate acceptance into medical school. These programs include the Interview Day Night Before Social, the annual Premedical Conference, the Early Medical School Acceptance Program (EMSAP), the Joint Admission Medical Program (JAMP), The Research and Academic Enrichment Training Program (RACE), and the Prematriculation Reinforcement and Enrichment Program (PREP).

It is praiseworthy to note that UTMB strongly adheres to its core values of diversity in training a cadre of workforce physicians who mirrors the population of the State of Texas.

Admissions

The major goals of the UTMB Medical School include the recruitment, retention, and graduation of students from educationally and economically disadvantaged backgrounds and correcting the physician shortage among medically underserved populations. Therefore, UTMB is well known for its student body diversity. The Admissions Committee makes sure that all applicants are given adequate consideration when reviewing applications for medical school. All minority and disadvantaged applications are screened by members of the Admissions Committee where special attention is given to the cognitive and noncognitive attributes of each applicant. Consideration is given to all applicants from disadvantaged backgrounds and rural and medically underserved areas. The following factors are considered: educational level of parents, occupation of parents, family income and household in

University of Texas Medical Branch University of Texas Medical School at Galveston, 2006
Applicants and Matriculants by Gender, Race and Ethnicity

Race and Ethnicity	Applicants			Matriculants		
	Women	Men	Total	Women	Men	Total
Hispanic/Latino						
Cuban	6	5	11	2	1	3
Mexican American	185	155	340	12	18	30
Puerto Rican	5	7	12	0	1	1
Other Hispanic	58	56	114	3	5	8
Multiple Hispanic*	2	6	8	0	0	0
Subtotal	256	229	485	17	25	42
Non-Hispanic/Latino**						
Black	175	72	247	17	0	17
Native American/Alaska Native	9	13	22	1	0	1
Native Hawaiian/Other Pacific Islander	2	2	4	0	0	0
White	752	936	1,688	59	67	126
Asian	403	418	821	17	20	37
Other Race	29	28	57	1	1	2
Multiple Race*	23	22	45	1	1	2
Unknown	2	2	4	0	0	0
Subtotal	1,395	1,493	2,888	96	89	185
Foreign	33	33	66	0	2	2
Total	1,684	1,755	3,439	113	116	229

*Since 2002, students can select more than one race and / or ethnicity. **Those who did not choose Hispanic/Latino' or 'Non-Hispanic/Latino' are counted under 'Non-Hispanic/Latino'.
Data Source: AAMC Data Warehouse: Applicant-Matriculant File, as of 5/9/2007.

Association of American Medical Colleges, 2007

which applicant grew up, high school and college attended, percentage of college expenses earned by applicant, hometown, geographic region of state from a medically underserved community as defined by the Texas Higher Education Board, and English as a second language. Each interviewee receives two separate interviews while on campus, and a special effort is made to introduce minority applicants to currently enrolled minority students. As authorized by the Board of Regents, the University of Texas System has granted UTMB permission to use race and ethnicity as one of several factors that are considered for admission into medical school and in awarding scholarships.

Academic Support Programs

The *Academic Counseling Program* has been developed specifically to aid medical students so that they can achieve academic success. Students are assisted in defining and addressing learning styles and any academic or personal problems that may impact their academic performance. Workshops are conducted for groups of students or they are seen on an individual basis for an assessment of their reading and comprehension ability, learning skills, study skills, time management, and test-taking strategies.

An *Early Academic Identification Warning System* assesses the student's level of academic performance throughout the basic science curriculum so that proactive interventional strategies can prevent failure. Performance in the problem-based learning small-group discussions, quizzes, and block exams are closely followed. Once a student is identified, they are placed in an automatic academic monitoring tracking system and the student is immediately counseled. An individualized, discipline-specific academic plan is created based upon a thorough assessment of the student's needs. Several workshops are given that cover a variety of topics such as

stress management, handling personal relationship issues, relaxation, time management, and dealing with stress and test anxiety.

Tutorial assistance in the basic sciences courses is offered through the *Peer Tutorial Program*. Some students receive individual assistance, but most meet in small groups. In the *For Students by Students Program*, students that have completed an academic year develop a book for the upcoming class which provides insights into studying for different courses that cover textbooks, labs, Web sites, practice tests, and learning tools.

Step Prep is a formal United States Medical Licensing Examination Step 1 intensive board preparation program consisting of several components. A comprehensive manual is distributed to each second-year student in January. In the Spring, a free board review course is taught over a three-week period. Two Comprehensive Basic Science Examinations (CBSEs) are also given to provide feedback to students as to their progress in board preparation. Additionally, a mentoring component allows senior students to advise and/or tutor the sophomores throughout their preparation.

Enrichment Programs

A variety of enrichment programs are offered at UTMB that promote the professional development of perspective candidates so that they become more competitive for Medical School entrance.

Research and Academic Enrichment Training Program (RACE). UTMB supports basic and clinical research directed to the causes, prevention, and treatment of cardiovascular, pulmonary, and hematological diseases. Summer research training opportunities in these areas are available at UTMB School of Medicine for 15 talented, underrepresented minority undergraduate and medical students. Each student will work closely with a National Institutes of

Health funded faculty member at UTMB on an exciting research project directed to these specific areas. In order to bolster the already short supply of minority biomedical researchers, we believe that by providing this opportunity, underrepresented students may become interested in pursuing a career in medical or biomedical research. All trainees will participate in scientific seminars, workshops, or clinical conferences that will be held throughout the summer. At the conclusion of the program, each student will present their research at a scientific symposium held on campus.

Prematriculation Reinforcement Enrichment Program (PREP). This program provides a smooth transition from college to the rigorous and demanding expectations of the medical school curriculum. This six-week program gives a realistic preview of selected courses in the first-year curriculum that are taught by UTMB faculty. The demands of the courses, including the pace and examinations are identical to that of courses taught during the academic year. The program provides the opportunity to make the academic, psychological, emotional, and physical adjustments necessary to adapt to the work load of the medical school curriculum.

Early Medical School Acceptance Program (EMSAP). This program is a formal partnership and contractual agreement for conditional acceptance into medical school between UTMB and six public universities (UT Brownsville, UT el Paso, UT Pan American, Texas A&M, International University at Laredo, Prairie View A&M and Texas Southern University). A maximum of 30 college students are accepted each year and are offered conditional acceptance to UTMB's Medical School provided they maintain an overall and science GPA of 3.25 and a MCAT score of 24. Five students are selected from each of the partnership universities. EMSAP enhances the competitiveness of underrepresented nd disadvantaged college students for admission into medical school. The students participate in a comprehensive, integrated, six-week intensive summer program at UTMB that provides academic support services, MCAT preparation, clinical exposure, and mentoring. The main objectives of the program are to increase the number of bilingual and bicultural physicians in Texas, to support the drive to cultivate and produce medical professionals with a passion for delivering health care to the underserved, and to offer outstanding college students an opportunity to prepare for the competitiveness of the medical school admissions process.

Student Financial Assistance

UTMB falls in the bottom quartile of all medical schools for tuition and fees; tuition has been raised only once in a ten-year period. It has made significant strides in awarding scholarships to underrepresented minority students. With the establishment of the Herzog Foundation in 1994, UTMB has more than $8,000,000 in endowments that provide scholarships for students from minority and disadvantaged backgrounds. Several other scholarship programs are available and new ones are added each year. Minority students are encouraged to apply for National Medical Fellowships, the National Hispanic Scholarship Fund, scholarships offered through local medical societies, and any of the other state funded initiatives. Two years ago, UTMB embarked upon a Capital Campaign, which designated scholarships for minority students as a top priority. UTMB's need-based scholarships are primarily awarded to low income minority students.

To assist students with financial planning and debt management, Enrollment Services has specialists who are available for counseling. In addition to this service, students may use the online tools provided on the Enrollment Services Web site to assist them with managing their loan debt and planning a budget. All financial aid students are required to complete online entrance interviews prior to receiving any loan funds.

Association of American Medical Colleges, 2007

University of Texas Medical School at Houston

Dr. R. Andrew Harper
Assistant Dean
for Educational Programs
University of Texas
Medical School at Houston
6431 Fannin, JJL 304
Houston, TX 77030
713-500-5140; 713-500-0603 Fax
r.andrew.harper@uth.tmc.edu
http://med.uth.tmc.edu/administration/
edu_programs/index.htm

Recruitment

The University of Texas Medical School at Houston (UTMS-H) sponsors several substantive recruitment programs. The UTMS-H Office of Admissions sponsors between five and ten Admissions Workshops each year at colleges and universities throughout the state of Texas. Medical students frequently attend career fairs at high schools in the greater Houston metropolitan area to distribute information and promote careers in medicine to high school juniors and seniors.

The UT Medical Summer Research Program is a ten-week hands-on research program for undergraduate and medical students interested in biomedical research. Administered by the Office of Educational Programs, this program offers students opportunities to do basic science research under the direction of UTMS-H faculty and to be introduced to the medical environment. More information about this program can be found at *(http://med.uth.tmc.edu/administration/edu_programs/ep/summer_research_program/).*

The University of Texas Medical School at Houston currently has affiliation agreements for assured acceptance programs with several Texas universities. Two agreements of note are with the University of Houston, which has the most culturally diverse student population in the nation, and the University of Texas at El Paso, the only major research university in the nation with a predominately Mexican-American student body. More information about assured acceptance programs can be found at: *(http://med.uth.tmc.edu/administration/admissions/assured-acceptance.html).*

Admissions

All applicants participate in the same admissions process. Each applicant's file is screened, and those applicants that indicate a potential for success in medicine are invited for an interview. The applicant obtains an interview and subsequent matriculation into medical school based upon a number of criteria. Ethnicity is considered in the evaluation of applicants to medical school, but it is considered in conjunction with many additional criteria.

The Admissions Committee is composed of a richly diverse cross section of the school's faculty membership and represents several cultural and ethnic backgrounds. These basic science and clinical faculty evaluate each interviewed applicant. The committee takes into consideration the following criteria in reviewing applicants: Medical College Admission Test (MCAT) scores; non-cognitive variables, such as potential for service, determination, and independence; and commitment of the applicant to practicing in the state of Texas in a needed area or specialty.

The Admissions Committee is frequently apprised of the mission and purpose of the admissions process and the goals for our institution. These goals include attention to underrepresented minorities as well as to candidates from health professions

University of Texas Medical School at Houston, 2006
Applicants and Matriculants by Gender, Race and Ethnicity

Race and Ethnicity	Applicants			Matriculants		
	Women	Men	Total	Women	Men	Total
Hispanic/Latino						
Cuban	6	5	11	0	1	1
Mexican American	191	151	342	13	8	21
Puerto Rican	7	9	16	0	0	0
Other Hispanic	60	60	120	4	1	5
Multiple Hispanic*	2	6	8	1	2	3
Subtotal	266	231	497	18	12	30
Non-Hispanic/Latino*						
Black	178	74	252	5	2	7
Native American/Alaska Native	8	13	21	2	0	2
Native Hawaiian/Other Pacific Islander	2	2	4	0	0	0
White	765	937	1,702	63	98	161
Asian	421	428	849	10	11	21
Other Race	29	27	56	1	1	2
Multiple Race*	26	25	51	1	1	2
Unknown	3	8	11	1	0	1
Subtotal	1,432	1,514	2,946	83	113	196
Foreign	41	36	77	0	0	0
Total	1,739	1,781	3,520	101	125	226

*Since 2002, students can select more than one race and / or ethnicity. **Those who did not choose
'Hispanic/Latino' or 'Non-Hispanic/Latino' are counted under 'Non-Hispanic/Latino'.
Data Source: AAMC Data Warehouse: Applicant-Matriculant File, as of 5/9/2007.

Association of American Medical Colleges, 2007

AAMC

shortage areas, and to those candidates who may be likely to return to these areas of our state.

Information about admissions requirements and criteria can be found at: *http://med.uth.tmc.edu/administration/ admissions/*)

Academic Support Programs

UTMS-H sponsors several programs that are designed to increase the retention rate of all medical students. A five-week summer *Pre-Entry Program* is designed to enhance the performance of students in the basic science years. The program is for students who, for a variety of reasons, might benefit from such a program. Services, administered by the Assistant Dean for Education Programs, include the *Peer Tutoring Program*, which provides tutelage for first- and second-year students by second- and fourth-year student tutors; academic monitoring; and academic and non-academic counseling. An *Alternate Pathway Program* (*http://med.uth.tmc.edu/ students-current/policies.htm#altpath*) offers students the option to complete the first-year basic science curriculum in two years. The *Master Advisor Program* is designed to facilitate interactions between students and members of the medical school faculty and administration. Several organizations whose members are interested in service to historically underserved communities and in recruitment of minority students, such as the *Student National Medical Association*, have chapters at UTMS-H.

Enrichment Programs

Elementary School Science Enrichment Program
UTMS-H coordinates an enrichment project designed to spark elementary school students' interest in science. Approximately 700 hours of science enrichment activities are presented to a group of 120 African-American and Hispanic elementary school students during the academic year. This program is organized by first-year medical

students with administrative support from the Office of Admissions.

Program Contact: UTMS-H Office of Admissions

Anatomy Enrichment Program
This program is administered through the Office of Admissions. High school students from the greater Houston metropolitan area are invited to participate in a day-long workshop in the Human Anatomy Facility of the UTMS-H. Students are presented with a hands-on lesson in human anatomy and physiology in the morning and tour the medical school facility in the afternoon.

Program Contact: Nancy Murphy *Nancy.D.Murphy@uth.tmc.edu*

Summer Medical and Dental Education Program (SMDEP)
This program is presented in collaboration with The University of Texas Dental Branch (UTDB) and funded by a grant from the Robert Wood Johnson Foundation. The mission of SMDEP is to assist rising sophomore and junior undergraduate students from backgrounds that are historically underrepresented in dentistry and medicine. The program also aims to enhance the students' knowledge, skills and attitudes to make them more competitive and improve their chances of becoming successful applicants to either a medical or dental school of their choice.

SMDEP serves to advance our institutions' core missions of providing the highest quality education, conducting the highest caliber or research in biomedical and health sciences, and providing exemplary clinical care in a diverse and culturally competent environment.

Students experience academic enrichment in five core areas: microbiology, anatomy and physiology, pre-calculus and calculus, physics, and organic chemistry. In addition, students participate in study and communication skills classes, financial

planning and career development workshops, and academic counseling sessions. Students are involved in clinical experiences in emergency medicine, family practice, internal medicine, restorative dentistry, and oral surgery. All SMDEP scholars participate in admission discussions and simulated interviews as preparation for the formal application process. Social interactions with other SMDEP scholars, currently enrolled medical and dental students, and faculty complete the experience. (*http://www.smdep.org/progsites/houston.htm*), (*http://www.db.uth.tmc.edu/ SMDEP/index.htm*). Program Coordinator: Cynthia Santos *Cynthia.Santos@uth.tmc.edu*

Summer Research Program
This program serves to foster a greater understanding of biomedical research among both undergraduate and medical students. Administered by the Office of Educational Programs, this ten-week summer program offers students opportunities to do intensive, hands-on biomedical laboratory research under the direct supervision of a selected UTMS-H faculty sponsor. These preceptorships are in the basic science and clinical departments. The program provides science training workshops, a weekly seminar series featuring top scientists, and enrichment series and special facility/laboratory tours. Participants are awarded $2,500 scholarships funded through a National Institutes of Health (NIH) training grant and by the Dean of the Medical School.

(*http://med.uth.tmc.edu/administration/ edu_ programs/ep/summer_research_program/*)
Program Coordinator: Jimmie Pope *summer.research@uth.tmc.edu*

Summer Pre-Entry Program
This five-week program, administered through the Office of Educational Programs, is offered each year for new matriculants to the UTMS-H. The purpose of the program is to strengthen academic performance of participants by providing

a rigorous academic program, tutorial sessions, computer and study-skills workshops, and by establishing support networks with students and faculty. Approximately 30 students who are judged most likely to benefit from enhanced academic preparation and/or an early adjustment to medical school are invited to participate. Scholarships are available for students who require financial assistance.

(http://med.uth.tmc.edu/administration/ edu_programs/ep/pre-entry_program.htm)
Program Contact: Elizabeth Green
Elizabeth.Green@uth.tmc.edu

Student Financial Assistance
Financial aid is available primarily in the form of loans. Students with outstanding credentials are automatically considered for a Faculty Scholarship Award.

Other additional scholarships may be funded by benefactors within the community.

University of Texas Medical School at San Antonio

Dr. David J. Jones, Associate
Dean for Medical School Admissions
University of Texas
School of Medicine at San Antonio
7703 Floyd Curl Drive
San Antonio, TX 78229
210-567-6080; 210-567-6962 Fax
jonesd@uthscsa.edu

Recruitment
An active recruitment program is currently underway. This effort involves visits by faculty, administrative staff, and students to a variety of undergraduate campuses within the state of Texas. Visits to the School of Medicine campus are encouraged in order that the disadvantaged student may become familiar with available opportunities.

These visits are coordinated by the Coordinator of Recruitment and Science Outreach (210-567-3941). Inquiries from Texas residents attending undergraduate school outside the state are encouraged.

Admissions
The University of Texas School of Medicine at San Antonio seeks to admit a class that reflects the diversity of the population of the state of Texas. Minority applicants and socioeconomically disadvantaged applicants, as with all applicants, are reviewed holistically in an active effort to determine which of these candidates will be able to successfully complete the medical education curriculum. While the grade-point average (GPA) and the Medical College Admission Test (MCAT) score are important ingredients in the assessment process, many other factors

University of Texas Medical School at San Antonio, 2006
Applicants and Matriculants by Gender, Race and Ethnicity

Race and Ethnicity	Applicants			Matriculants		
	Women	Men	Total	Women	Men	Total
Hispanic/Latino						
Cuban	8	6	14	1	0	1
Mexican American	190	162	352	12	14	26
Puerto Rican	5	8	13	2	0	2
Other Hispanic	58	60	118	5	2	7
Multiple Hispanic*	2	6	8	0	0	0
Subtotal	263	242	505	20	16	36
Non-Hispanic/Latino**						
Black	167	72	239	7	1	8
Native American/Alaska Native	9	14	23	2	1	3
Native Hawaiian/Other Pacific Islander	2	2	4	0	0	0
White	768	932	1,700	65	59	124
Asian	409	412	821	28	13	41
Other Race	28	29	57	3	1	4
Multiple Race*	26	22	48	3	1	4
Unknown	3	1	4	0	0	0
Subtotal	1,412	1,484	2,896	108	76	184
Foreign	32	26	58	0	0	0
Total	1,707	1,752	3,459	128	92	220

*Since 2002, students can select more than one race and / or ethnicity. **Those who did not choose Hispanic/Latino' or 'Non-Hispanic/Latino' are counted under 'Non-Hispanic/Latino'.
Data Source: AAMC Data Warehouse: Applicant-Matriculant File, as of 5/9/2007.

nter into the consideration. Early educa-
ional experiences, parental influences,
ocioeconomic factors, clinical/volunteer
ctivities, and life experiences of the appli-
ant are all relevant issues to be reviewed.
vidence of leadership capacities, excep-
ional motivation, and record of past
chievement, whether academic or in other
ife areas, are also among the factors con-
idered. The records of all applicants are
eviewed. Promising candidates are offered
nterviews. The candidates are interviewed
y two members of the Admissions Committee. At the completion of the interview
rocess, the applicants are then discussed
n detail. The ultimate selection is by the
Dean of the School of Medicine, upon
ecommendation by the Selection Sub-
Committee of the Admissions Committee.

Academic Support Programs

The Medical Dean's Office has developed
an extensive Faculty Advisor System. The
Faculty Advisor functions as a student
advocate and will aid the student in find-
ng help should problems, academic or
otherwise, occur. Additionally, the Health
Science Center Counseling Service provides a full range of educational and learning-skills development services. The
Counseling Service also coordinates
an extensive peer advisor system for
all students.

The primary mission of the Office of
Academic Enhancement is to promote the
retention and advancement of medical students through their four year curriculum.
This mission is primarily accomplished by
using the experiences and resources of the
UTHSCSA medical student population.
The input helps to develop and implement
projects with the consumer in mind—the
medical student. Currently the Office of
Academic Enhancement offers group
tutoring programs for medical students, a
pre-matriculation program for incoming
medical students, a tutoring elective for
those interested in academic medicine, a

USMLE preparation course and consultation services for study skills, time management issues, and test-taking assistance.

Student Financial Assistance

Scholarship assistance is available. The
Office of Student Financial Assistance
works closely with all students in order to
identify the most effective aid package for
each student.

Financial assistance is not routinely available for interviews. Application fee waivers
are not granted.

Educational Partnership

*Facilitated Admissions for South Texas
Scholars.* The University of Texas-Pan
American, Texas A&M International
University and St. Mary's University in
partnership with the University of Texas
School of Medicine at San Antonio offer
programs to provide for early acceptance
to medical school. The objectives of this
program are to: 1) select outstanding students from these universities to a program for facilitated acceptance to the
School of Medicine, 2) support students
who are accepted to the program during
their undergraduate studies by providing
academic enrichment and MCAT and
medical school preparation courses, 3)
provide early acceptance to medical
school based on academic/MCAT performance, and finally, 4) offer the opportunity to return to South Texas for clinical training in their third and fourth
years of medical school at the Regional
Academic Health Center-associated clinical facilities.

University of Texas Southwestern Medical Center at Dallas Southwestern Medical School

Dr. Byron Cryer, Associate
Dean for Minority Student Affairs
University of Texas Southwestern Medical
Center at Dallas
Southwestern Medical School
5323 Harry Hines Boulevard
Dallas, TX 75235-9006
214-648-2168; 214-648-7517 Fax
byron.cryer@utsouthwestern.edu

Recruitment
Members of the faculty make numerous visits to the undergraduate campuses throughout the state of Texas each year. During these visits, meetings with pre-medical students are held to discuss questions and problems of both general and specific natures. These visits may include a meeting with groups of under-represented minority (URM) pre-medical students. Several of these visits are to historically Black colleges in the state of Texas as well as to South Texas where there is a large Hispanic population.

Additionally, every effort is made to arrange opportunities for minorities to visit the Southwestern Medical School campus to see the facilities and to talk with faculty and students. Once a year a conference for pre-medical students is held on the campus to accomplish this goal.

Admissions
All admissions decisions are made by a single Admissions Committee. This committee participates in all screening of applications and decides which candidates should be invited for interviews and which ones will be offered places. The admissions policies dictate that a decision be reached for each applicant separately, taking into account the breadth of considerations for each application.

The Admissions Committee carefully considers the complete background of each applicant as well as their specific future medical career aspirations.

Academic Support Programs
Academic or tutorial assistance at Southwestern is an individually tailored program. Students are advised that there are many avenues open to them should they encounter problems of any sort. They are encouraged to use them and, from all indications, they respond. A center composed of specialists in medical education offer students training in study habits and test-taking skills. Students in academic difficulty are most often identified early and tutorial or special programs are arranged to meet the individual needs of the students. Recently, modifications in the curriculum have been incorporated to assist and accommodate students having serious difficulty. There is ample flexibility in the curriculum to meet students' needs on an individual basis. Student mental health services provides psychological support to students.

Enrichment Programs
The Medical School conducts several programs that target minority high school and undergraduate students. The Health Professions Recruitment and Exposure Program (HPREP) is a collaborative agreement between University of Texas (UT) Southwestern and Dallas Independent School District that enrolls approximately 150 ninth- through 12th-grade minority students in a program designed to stimulate their interests in health and science careers. A Pre-medical Conference is conducted

University of Texas Southwestern Medical Center at Dallas Southwestern Medical School, 2006
Applicants and Matriculants by Gender, Race and Ethnicity

Race and Ethnicity	Applicants			Matriculants		
	Women	Men	Total	Women	Men	Total
Hispanic/Latino						
Cuban	6	4	10	0	0	0
Mexican American	171	139	310	13	13	26
Puerto Rican	3	7	10	1	0	1
Other Hispanic	48	51	99	8	12	20
Multiple Hispanic*	2	7	9	0	1	1
Subtotal	230	208	438	22	26	48
Non-Hispanic/Latino**						
Black	171	65	236	10	7	17
Native American/Alaska Native	8	11	19	0	0	0
Native Hawaiian/Other Pacific Islander	2	2	4	0	0	0
White	752	922	1,674	38	49	87
Asian	416	404	820	33	34	67
Other Race	26	26	52	0	0	0
Multiple Race*	22	26	48	2	1	3
Unknown	4	3	7	0	0	0
Subtotal	1,401	1,459	2,860	83	91	174
Foreign	35	37	72	4	2	6
Total	1,666	1,704	3,370	109	119	228

*Since 2002, students can select more than one race and / or ethnicity. **Those who did not choose Hispanic/Latino' or 'Non-Hispanic/Latino' are counted under 'Non-Hispanic/Latino'.
Data Source: AAMC Data Warehouse: Applicant-Matriculant File, as of 5/9/2007.

each year at UT Southwestern. The conference is designed to increase college students' awareness of the application process and of medical school experience.

Enrichment Programs

UT Southwestern offers a Summer Enrichment Program (SEP) for 20 incoming students admitted to the medical school. During the seven weeks prior to the start of classes, the SEP features in-depth instruction in biochemistry and anatomy, and a guided self-study in embryology. Learning assessment is offered in areas that include, but are not limited to, reading, critical thinking, and learning styles. In addition, seminars are presented on learning skills, financial management, stress management, and library resources. The SEP is a challenging academic program designed to promote participants' academic, social, and environmental adjustment relative to the first year of medical school.

Student Financial Assistance

Waiver of the application fee to University of Texas Medical Schools can be solicited from the Medical and Dental Application Center and is granted in extreme cases. Southwestern is unable to provide financial assistance for interview trips to any students.

In conjunction with the financial aid application process and prior to entering any financial commitment, all financial aid applicants are provided access to an annual publication of the Office of Student Financial Aid entitled, *Meeting College Expenses: A Guide for Seeking Financial Assistance.* Much of this publication is designed to provide each student with debt management and budgeting tools for use throughout the student's enrollment. Prior to the disbursement of each student's financial aid, formal counseling is required and made available through the use of established video and Web-based

productions. Three full-time financial aid counselors and the director are available throughout the academic year for personal student consult and guidance.

Prior to a student's official separation from the campus by means of withdrawal, leave of absence, or dismissal, financial aid recipients are subject to a financial aid exit. Financial aid exits are available in individual or group settings, depending on the time of year and volume of students needing to complete the process. During the financial aid exit, each student is provided with detailed information related to each loan received, including the lending agency to whom the student will be processing repayment, a projected payment schedule, and terms and conditions specified in the promissory note.

Educational Partnerships

UT Southwestern Medical School has an educational partnership with Paul Quinn College, a historically Black university located in Dallas. Undergraduate students enrolled in this partnership primarily focus on preparation for the Medical College Admission Test (MCAT).

University of Utah School of Medicine

Candi Ramos, Director
Diversity and Community Outreach
University of Utah School of Medicine
30 N. 1900 E. 1C117
Salt Lake City, UT 84132-2101
801-585-2430; 801-585-3300 Fax
candi.ramos@hsc.utah.edu
www.uuhsc.utah.edu/som/diversity

Recruitment

The University of Utah School of Medicine is committed to recruiting a diverse student body. The School of Medicine believes that students from a broad range of cultural, ethnic, economic, and experiential backgrounds bring different perspectives to the learning environment and enhance the educational experience of the student body. The Office of Diversity and Community Outreach works closely with students from minority groups identified by the state of Utah as underrepresented. These are Africans and African Americans; American Indians; Alaska Natives; Polynesians and Pacific Islanders including Native Hawaiians, Tongans, Samoans, Filipinos, Tahitians, Maoris, Fijians, Niueans, Palauans; and Chicanos/as and Latinos/as including Mainland Puerto Ricans, Mexican Americans, Central Americans, and South Americans. The office provides academic advising and assistance to these students in their preparation for and application to medical school. The Office of Diversity and Community Outreach also offers support for out-of-state interviewees such as student hosting, rides to and from the airport, and mock interviews. Visit our Web site at: *(www.uuhsc.utah.edu/som/diversity/)*.

Recruitment of out of state students takes place through targeted mailings and selected on-site visits to pre-medical events within the region. The office will arrange visits for students wanting to check out Utah, with hosting from current medical students. We will also provide application assistance and advice. In-state students are recruited in a similar manner, with visits and seminars to students at various venues and forums around the state. The Association of Minority Medical Students is very active in supporting and assisting in recruitment of students from diverse backgrounds. The group helps with hosting, answering student e-mail inquiries, and anything else applicants need.

Admissions

The University of Utah School of Medicine carefully considers each applicant on the basis of individual merit. The School of Medicine is looking for well-rounded students with a demonstrated commitment to serving people. Some of the characteristics the School of Medicine looks for in students include integrity, composure, maturity, independence, compassion, self-knowledge, interpersonal skills, problem-solving ability, leadership, and intellectual curiosity. The school has eight formal categories for evaluating applicants, which are: Medical College Admission Test (MCAT), GPA, extracurricular activities, leadership, research, medical exposure, physician shadowing, and volunteer service. Applicants are expected to meet minimum performance standards in each category and be average or above average in at least five. We should also mention that we have strict GPA and MCAT minimums—3.0 in both science GPA and cumulative GPA (as calculated by American Medical College Application Service), and 7 in each section of the MCAT (not total score). These minimums are balanced out by the total weight of MCAT and GPA being only 20 percent of the final selection score. Interviewers and selection committee members are not given MCAT and GPA information on applicants. The non-cognitive criteria listed

University of Utah School of Medicine, 2006
Applicants and Matriculants by Gender, Race and Ethnicity

Race and Ethnicity	Applicants			Matriculants		
	Women	Men	Total	Women	Men	Total
Hispanic/Latino						
Cuban	5	3	8	0	0	0
Mexican American	28	34	62	0	0	0
Puerto Rican	5	8	13	0	1	1
Other Hispanic	24	33	57	1	0	1
Multiple Hispanic*	3	4	7	0	1	1
Subtotal	65	82	147	1	2	3
Non-Hispanic/Latino**						
Black	37	31	68	0	0	0
Native American/Alaska Native	1	4	5	0	0	0
Native Hawaiian/Other Pacific Islander	2	6	8	0	0	0
White	181	600	781	25	57	82
Asian	42	50	92	6	4	10
Other Race	0	1	1	0	0	0
Multiple Race*	19	17	36	4	1	5
Unknown	2	7	9	1	1	2
Subtotal	284	716	1,000	36	63	99
Foreign	12	10	22	0	0	0
Total	361	808	1,169	37	65	102

*Since 2002, students can select more than one race and / or ethnicity. **Those who did not choose 'Hispanic/Latino' or 'Non-Hispanic/Latino' are counted under 'Non-Hispanic/Latino'.

Data Source: AAMC Data Warehouse: Applicant-Matriculant File, as of 5/9/2007.

Association of American Medical Colleges, 2007

...bove are 80 percent of the applicant's final ...core. Please see the admissions Web site at *www.uuhsc.utah.edu/som/admissions/)* or con-...act the admissions office if you have ...ny questions.

Academic Support Programs

Tutorial programs are available to all stu-...dents in both basic and clinical sciences. Peer counseling is available to all freshman ...nd sophomore students, and physician ...mentors are assigned to all students, upon ...request, for the duration of their study at ...Utah. An extensive program of academic ...nd personal counseling is made available ...o all students. The director of student ...counseling, a licensed psychologist, sees ...students and their families by request to ...resolve personal or academic issues. ...Students may also access the counseling ...center on the main campus as an addi-...tional resource. The Director of Learning ...Resources meets with students individually ...to discuss test-taking strategies, board ...study and preparation, and learning strate-...gies and tools.

The Office of Diversity and Community ...Outreach informs students of research, ...fellowship, internship, and externship ...opportunities offered both locally and ...nationally and assists them with their ...applications for these programs. ...Additionally, the office disseminates ...information on scholarships locally ...and nationally to eligible students. ...Assistance with curriculum vitas and ...personal statements for residency appli-...cations is also provided to students.

Enrichment Programs

The School of Medicine offers over 20 con-...tinuous outreach programs over the course ...of the school year and summer months. ...Please see our Web site for program ...descriptions and photos: *(www.uuhsc.utah. edu/som/diversity/).*

We whole-heartedly follow a symbiotic programming and partnership model to ensure continuity and appropriate benefit for all involved. Our school has a strong culture of service, as evidenced by our admissions standards, and we try to pro-vide an outlet for medical students after matriculation. The outreach programs offer medical students a chance to become more acquainted with communities of color in and around Salt Lake City. It is our hope that through programming we can increase the cultural awareness and inter-action skills of medical students thereby improving their competence as future practitioners. The students we serve with our programs are gaining exposure to medicine and can begin the planning process of pursuing a career involving higher education in the health sciences.

Some of our programs are community based partnerships that do not fit into grade categories, such as the Calvary Baptist Youth Science Outreach Program, which is a partnership with the African American community through the church. We also have some programming for rural students to reach into Utah's many rural communities, and assist medical students with grants they've received in Glaucoma Screening, Diabetes care, etc.

Programming for elementary aged youth focuses on hands-on exposure to medicine and anatomy, preventive health, and safety. We currently have an outreach program at Edison Elementary School and partner with National Youth Sports Program, Gear-Up, and Club Ute for summer activi-ties. The office also supports science fairs and community events, by invitation, at schools that align with our outreach goals.

Junior high-aged students are served through on-site outreach at Glendale and Northwest Intermediate schools. Students are taught slightly more advanced anatomy

and physiology by volunteer medical stu-dents. Glendale's partnership is a *Youth Teaching Youth* grant model through the Utah Museum of Natural History, where students advance in the program toward teaching responsibilities of younger stu-dents. At Northwest our partnership is with the MESA Club, which has been active for over five years. We also have an interdisciplinary program at the School of Medicine called Science Power, which is for junior high-age women interested in sci-ence. This program expands hands-on activities through campus partnerships with engineering, math, genetics, etc. Women faculty and students from across campus volunteer to mentor and teach participants throughout the year.

High school student programming is focused on college preparation, more exposure to health sciences careers—par-ticularly medicine—and mentoring. *Future Doctors*, which began in 1997, is a free after-school program open to all students across the Salt Lake Valley. Each session includes a lecture from a physician in a medical discipline followed by a related hands-on activity. In the past we have cov-ered dermatology/suturing, pathology/ gram staining, cardiology/cow heart dis-section, and more. The other high school program is specifically for Native American students. *Expanded Indian Nations* began in 1998 as a program focused on recruiting students to the University of Utah and into higher education in general. Each year more than 25 students from tribes across the state visit the campus for lectures on health sciences careers, hands-on labs and activities, campus activities and tours, and shadowing. Students get an in-depth pic-ture of college life and the medical profes-sion. Specific focus is given to financial aid strategies, the importance of high school advising, the process of applying to college, and the ACT or SAT.

The pre-medical and college outreach programs focus on making students aware of the admissions process and helping students prepare to be successful applicants. Two, day-long seminars are offered each year—one for minority students and one for women students. At each of these seminars, the Associate Dean of Admissions and the Assistant Vice President for Diversity in the Health Sciences candidly talk with participants about admission policies and procedures. Students openly ask questions and find out about the selection process and ultimately what makes a great applicant. The day also includes a medical student experiences panel, a workshop on personal statements, interviewing, or the AMCAS application, and of course, hands-on labs. The Office of Diversity and Community Outreach also advises students throughout the year, offering one-hour appointments to help students tackle issues specific to their individual preparation strategies.

The Summer MCAT Preparation and Research/Clinical Training Program, which began in 2001, selects ten students each year. The program is limited to students who meet Utah's admission standards, and who have an interest in applying to Utah's medical school. Eligibility is based on economic, social, and educational disadvantage. Designed to strengthen each student individually, the program places students in unfilled requisite areas, or areas of the student's application that need to be strengthened. For ten weeks students engage in a Kaplan MCAT prep course, supplemental group and individual tutoring, learning and test-taking assessments, and either a research or clinical medicine placement. In addition to these basic tenets, students also receive instruction in application strategies, personal statement writing, the AMCAS application, mock interviewing, financial aid, and more. Weekly seminar lunches are provided for students as a chance to meet current medical students, residents, and faculty at the

University of Utah. Although preference is given to Utah residents, the program does accept students from out of state and provides room and board for the summer. All participants receive a stipend for June, July, and August.

Student Financial Assistance

The University of Utah School of Medicine and the Financial Aid and Scholarships Office at the University of Utah assist students in meeting the costs of medical school. The school makes every effort to meet the financial needs of admitted students. Student financial assistance packages may consist of loans, scholarships, and loan repayment programs.

Educational Partnerships

Health Professions Magnet School. The Health Professions Magnet School is a partnership between the Salt Lake City School District and the University of Utah Health Sciences Center. The Health Professions Magnet School began as the Health Professions Academy in 1999. Over the years the program has grown and expanded into a magnet school for students in the Salt Lake City area.

Students are recruited for the program in junior high school and begin the program once in high school. The students' curriculum includes health science courses and opportunities for field trips to the University Hospital and clinics. Additionally, throughout the four years of the Health Professions Magnet School, the students participate in hands-on activities including dissection, first aid, lab experiments, shadowing, and community service projects.

Health Sciences LEAP. Begun in 2001, Health Sciences LEAP is a four-year-long pipeline program designed to assist students interested in careers in medicine, nursing, pharmacy, or health who come from populations traditionally underrepresented in the health professions in Utah. This population includes students from minority

backgrounds, but also those who meet definitions of educational, social, or economic disadvantage. We currently have four cohorts of students in the program, with 96 percent from minority backgrounds.

In the first year of Health Sciences LEAP, students take two humanities seminars of three credit hours each, thereby fulfilling their general education humanities requirement. In the first semester, they study American autobiography in a course that also fulfills their diversity requirement and in the second they read ethical philosophy and apply it to current issues in health care delivery. They are also eligible for three one-credit-hour add-ons: a library research skills class, a service learning class, and a course on how minority students can better succeed on a white majority campus.

The second year of Health Sciences LEAP begins with a two-credit-hour fall semester course in "Health Professions Exploration," called UUHSC 2500. Students shadow professionals in their future fields for two hours per week, and then write about and discuss their experiences in light of reading they've done and lectures they've heard on cultural competency in medicine, complementary and alternative medicine, professionalism, collegiality, collaboration, and medical ethics. Wherever possible, arrangements are made for students to shadow minority providers, who add a mentoring aspect to the course. Guest lecturers for the seminar are also drawn from a group of minority and/or women experts. In their second semester, students take a two-credit-hour course in "Basic Lab Technique" (Biology 2115), taught by a biology professor, which prepares them to work in research laboratories during their third year.

Third year Health Sciences LEAP consists of two semesters that together make up UUHSC 3000 and 3001: "Research eminar for Advanced LEAP Students." tudents are placed with faculty as research ssistants for eight months, working en hours per week in a paid position. Vhenever possible, they are placed with Principal Investigators from minority backgrounds and can choose either basic cience or social science areas of study. tudents reflect on this work in the two eminars, which require them to give oral presentations on their research, first to lassmates, then to other Health Sciences LEAP students, and finally to the university as a whole in the context of the Under- graduate Research Symposium. They also visit each other's research labs and learn to write up their research in a form appropri- te to a medical or scientific journal.

The final Health Sciences LEAP year asks tudents to research, design, implement, and evaluate an extended service project n cooperation with the University of Jtah's Bennion Center, the Huntsman Cancer Center's Special Populations Office, or the University Neighborhood Partners. The course sequence, "Service Learning Through Community Partnerships," is two semesters long and carries one credit hour each semester. Students are required to meet regularly as a class and with their service partners. Working alone or in pairs, they contribute at least 100 hours to their community partnerships, 80 of which are n direct service. The course emphasis is on higher education's responsibility to com- munity, and establishing viable partner- ships with symbiotic rewards.

Upon completion of all four years of the program, students receive the designation of *Health Science Scholar* on their diplo- mas. Over the course of the program, stu- dents are supported by personal advising, peer mentors, library skill and study skills courses, and biannual celebrations of their accomplishments.

University of Vermont College of Medicine*

Tiffany J. Delaney, Director of Admissions and Minority Affairs Officer
University of Vermont
College of Medicine
E-215 Given Building
89 Beaumont Avenue
Burlington, VT 05405-0068
802-656-2154; 802-656-9663 Fax
medadmissions@uvm.edu

Recruitment
The University of Vermont College of Medicine (UVMCOM) prides itself on its goal to select successful individuals from many cultures with unique life experiences to promote diversity among future physi- cians. Active recruitment of minority stu- dents to the College of Medicine is under the leadership of the Director of Admissions with assistance from medical students,

faculty, and staff. Information on UVM-COM is sent to targeted candidates identified through the Medical Minority Applicant Registry (Med-MAR) of the AAMC. In addition, minority candidates are encouraged to visit the campus prior to applying. Please contact the Office of Admissions at 802-656-2154 for informa- tion on arranging a visit.

Admissions
Applicants are reviewed for admission on the basis of their personal essays, Medical College Admission Test scores, letters of reference, and grade-point averages. Significant direct human service experi- ence is desirable. The university makes a particular effort to identify applicants who will enhance the overall diversity of the student body. Applicants considered to be promising candidates, based on a review of

University of Vermont College of Medicine, 2006
Applicants and Matriculants by Gender, Race and Ethnicity

Race and Ethnicity	Applicants			Matriculants		
	Women	Men	Total	Women	Men	Total
Hispanic/Latino						
Cuban	16	11	27	0	0	0
Mexican American	44	39	83	1	1	2
Puerto Rican	11	10	21	0	1	1
Other Hispanic	63	55	118	2	0	2
Multiple Hispanic*	8	5	13	0	0	0
Subtotal	142	120	262	3	2	5
Non-Hispanic/Latino**						
Black	55	34	89	0	0	0
Native American/Alaska Native	4	3	7	0	0	0
Native Hawaiian/Other Pacific Islander	9	9	18	0	0	0
White	1,529	1,759	3,288	48	36	84
Asian	640	620	1,260	9	2	11
Other Race	8	3	11	0	0	0
Multiple Race*	81	67	148	1	2	3
Unknown	23	26	49	0	0	0
Subtotal	2,349	2,521	4,870	58	40	98
Foreign	136	172	308	1	3	4
Total	2,627	2,813	5,440	62	45	107

*Since 2002, students can select more than one race and / or ethnicity. **Those who did not choose Hispanic/Latino' or 'Non-Hispanic/Latino' are counted under 'Non-Hispanic/Latino'.
Data Source: AAMC Data Warehouse: Applicant-Matriculant File, as of 5/9/2007.

the application materials, are invited for an interview. The interview takes place at the University of Vermont College of Medicine. It includes an orientation session with the Associate Dean of Admissions, an opportunity to meet informally with medical students, a tour of the College of Medicine, an opportunity to meet with the financial aid counselor, and an interview with a member of the Admissions Committee and a third- or fourth-year medical student when available. The Admissions Committee is composed of 38 faculty members plus the Associate Dean for Admissions, who chairs the committee. Committee membership varies annually. The committee is seeking applicants who are mature, who are highly motivated for a career in medicine, and who relate well to others.

Academic Support Programs

Initial advisement is provided by the Associate Dean for Student Affairs. The structure of the freshman curriculum allows multiple opportunities for contact with faculty in small-group teaching sessions, thus providing additional opportunity for the development of close relationships with faculty. Tutoring is available for students in academic difficulty, and other academic support services are available. Involvement in clinical medicine from the first week of medical school provides a significant stimulus to academic performance throughout the basic science years. In the third year, students select formal advisors based on their career preferences at that point in their education. The College of Medicine has a tradition of a flexible policy for leaves of absence for students who need to depart from the traditional four-year sequence.

Enrichment Programs

During the summer following the freshman year, medical students may participate in *Summer Research Fellowships* or *Preceptorship Placements* with practicing physicians. The remaining summer periods of the student's medical education are committed to clinical educational experiences.

Student Financial Assistance

The secondary application fee is waived for those applicants who qualify for a fee waiver from the American Medical College Application Service. The College of Medicine Financial Aid Office provides some low-interest loans to eligible students, as well as grant and scholarship aid to those students from high-need backgrounds. Most students meet the majority of their expenses through these institutional funds (the dollar amount varies from year to year), federal loans, and personal resources.

Educational Partnerships

No such partnerships are in place at this time.

AAMC

Eastern Virginia Medical School

Gail C. Williams
Assistant Dean for Student Affairs
and Director of Minority Affairs
Eastern Virginia Medical School
700 West Olney Road
Norfolk, VA 23507-2000
757-446-5869; 757-446-5817 Fax
williagc@evms.edu/www.evms.edu
www.evms.edu/minority/index.html

Recruitment

Eastern Virginia Medical School (EVMS), Virginia's only privately funded medical school, accepted its first class in October 1973. EVMS offers exciting and challenging opportunities for aspiring physicians through its excellent programs in medical education, research, and clinical care. EVMS has one of the 10 largest Clinical Skills Centers in the United States and Canada for teaching and assessment. The Medical School's affiliation with over 33 community based health care facilities across the Hampton Roads area allows students to gain clinical training that is both broad and culturally diverse. Although EVMS provides outstanding training and experience for students entering the full range of medical specialties, the school is committed to help meet the nation's need for producing more primary care physicians.

EVMS is also committed to the recruitment, admission, education, and retention of minority group students who are underrepresented in medicine, as well as students from disadvantaged backgrounds. The recruitment activities are coordinated through collaborative efforts between the Office of Admissions and the Office of Minority Affairs.

EVMS faculty, administrators, and students make visits to area high schools, upon request, and participate fully in career day activities. Counselors, students, and science teachers make periodic visits to the EVMS campus for tours and orientation. Qualified minority high school students attending Norfolk public schools are actively recruited for admission into the EVMS/Norfolk Public Schools Magnet High School for the Sciences and Health Professions.

Primarily in-state undergraduate institutions, as well as select out-of-state institutions, are visited each year by the Associate Dean for Admissions and/or the Director of Minority Affairs. A pre-health coalition of advisors has been established to afford the exchange of information and professional services between EVMS and the undergraduate schools. Special efforts are also made to meet with pre-medical clubs and pre-medical advisors. On-campus visitations are arranged upon request.

The Director of Minority Affairs and the Associate Dean for Admissions are available for individual on-campus meetings, by appointment, with students.

Admissions

EVMS seeks to produce a diverse physician workforce to advance medical education, patient care, and research. The school does not discriminate on the basis of race, color, national origin, gender, age, sexual orientation, citizenship, religion, political affiliation, or handicap.

Early completion of the American Medical College Application Service (AMCAS) application and EVMS supplemental application is strongly encouraged. It is also recommended that the Medical College Admission Test (MCAT) be taken as early as possible. All applications are carefully screened, and an interview is granted to applicants being considered for admission to the medical school. On the

Eastern Virginia Medical School, 2006
Applicants and Matriculants by Gender, Race and Ethnicity

Race and Ethnicity	Applicants			Matriculants		
	Women	Men	Total	Women	Men	Total
Hispanic/Latino						
Cuban	13	14	27	0	0	0
Mexican American	21	29	50	0	2	2
Puerto Rican	14	10	24	0	0	0
Other Hispanic	49	51	100	0	0	0
Multiple Hispanic*	5	3	8	0	0	0
Subtotal	102	107	209	0	2	2
Non-Hispanic/Latino**						
Black	200	72	272	4	1	5
Native American/Alaska Native	1	5	6	0	0	0
Native Hawaiian/Other Pacific Islander	9	11	20	0	0	0
White	1,052	1,248	2,300	37	43	80
Asian	526	563	1,089	5	11	16
Other Race	2	4	6	0	1	1
Multiple Race*	64	60	124	2	3	5
Unknown	10	17	27	0	0	0
Subtotal	1,864	1,980	3,844	48	59	107
Foreign	87	94	181	1	0	1
Total	2,053	2,181	4,234	49	61	110

*Since 2002, students can select more than one race and / or ethnicity. **Those who did not choose
Hispanic/Latino' or 'Non-Hispanic/Latino' are counted under 'Non-Hispanic/Latino'.
Data Source: AAMC Data Warehouse: Applicant-Matriculant File, as of 5/9/2007.

day of the interview, minority candidates routinely meet with the Director of Minority Affairs in a one-to-one setting.

The Admissions Committee is composed of basic science faculty members, clinical science faculty, and students. Members of minority groups are represented on the committee. All applicants are evaluated on the basis of several factors including science and overall grade-point average (GPA), MCAT scores, medical exposure, community/volunteer work, the personal interview, and letters of recommendation.

Academic Support Programs

The advisor system is coordinated through the Office of Academic Affairs. Each entering student is assigned a faculty advisor, as well as a second-year student advisor through the *Big Brother, Big Sister Partnership Program*. During the clinical years, each student selects a faculty advisor for consultation concerning fourth-year electives and choices of medical specialty. An academic support seminar is offered during the fall for all entering students. The foci are on test-taking skills, study and time management, stress management, and processing information and monitoring text comprehension.

Special tutorial sessions are arranged for M1 and M2 students through departmental course directors and through the Office of Academic Affairs. Flexible curriculum schedules may be devised at the request of the student or, if deemed necessary, by the Student Progress Committee.

Ongoing counseling and advising are available through the Offices of Minority, Women, Student, and Academic Affairs, as well as through the Human Values in Medicine Program. In addition, the EVMS Chapter of the Student National Medical Association, and the Committee on Minority Group Affairs, actively address minority issues and/or concerns.

Enrichment Programs

The Office of Minority Affairs at EVMS sponsors three enrichment programs, which include an MCAT Workshop and an On-Campus Visitation Day Program. Both programs have received excellent evaluations by past participants.

MCAT Workshop. The workshop is offered in February of each year. An intensive review, incorporating problem-solving exercises, is offered in each of the MCAT subtest areas on the first two days of the workshop. A mock MCAT exam is administered on the third day. The workshop allows students to assess their strengths and weaknesses in preparation for the MCAT exam.

On-Campus Visitation Day Program. The on-campus program, "Enhancing Diversity in Medicine," is held in the spring of each year. A few of the day's scheduled activities include a tour of the school's basic educational facilities; a review of the admission selection factors and interview assessment variables; mock admission interviews conducted by members of the EVMS Admissions Committee; and panel presentations by medical students, residents, and physicians. The panel presentations allow students to get a realistic view of each level of the medical education spectrum, including both the rewards and challenges of practicing medicine.

EVMS Summer Scholars Research Program EVMS supports the mission of the Virginia-Nebraska Alliance (*vanealliance.com*) in promoting better health outcomes for minorities by increasing the numbers of health care professionals and researchers from traditionally underrepresented minority groups. EVMS will provide summer research experiences (ten-12 weeks) for students from the Alliance member schools. The program will combine didactic sessions with mentored research projects, including community health, clinical, and bench research.

Participating research programs in the EVMS Medical Center include the Center for Pediatric Research, Streliz Diabetes Institute, and the Glennan Center for Geriatrics and Gerontology, to name a few.

For enrichment program dates and registration information, interested students should visit the Web site at *(www.evms.edu/ minority/index.html)*.

Student Financial Assistance

EVMS participates in the Federal Student Loan Program for undergraduate, graduate, and professional studies. There are scholarship opportunities as well, including funds for individuals from socioeconomic and disadvantaged backgrounds who demonstrate financial need. Institutional financial aid is awarded on the basis of demonstrated need without regard to race or ethnicity. Waiver of the admissions application fee will be graded on the basis of an AMCAS application fee waiver.

It is the mission of the Office of Financial at EVMS to provide students the tools and resources to obtain assistance to fund their education. The Office of Financial Aid assists students with debt management and financial planning. This is accomplished through mini sessions offered throughout the year including topics of establishing good credit, information about identity theft, managing student loan debt, and preparing an efficient spending plan. A mandatory Entrance Interview is conducted upon entry into school. This session provides the students pertinent information about their rights and responsibilities. A financial seminar including topics of insurance, investments, and a savings plan, is hosted as the student is entering the last semester at EVMS.

It is the intent of the Office of Financial Aid at EVMS to provide all students the opportunity to gain insight to financial management and planning. We are ready to assist students in areas that are of importance to their particular needs.

Educational Partnerships

EVMS has formal joint B.S./M.D. programs in medicine with nine Virginia undergraduate institutions (including each of the state's Historically Black Colleges and Universities): the College of William and Mary, Hampden-Sydney College, Hampton University, Norfolk State University, Old Dominion University, Saint Paul's College, Virginia Wesleyan University, Virginia State University, and Virginia Union University.

Students are selected from the sophomore class by the pre-health committee of the undergraduate institutions and the EVMS Admissions Committee based on the merit of their academic performance, including competitive SAT scores, and non-academic factors such as extracurricular and volunteer activities, leadership experience, and health care exposure. Students who meet the continued eligibility requirements will not be required to take the Medical College Admission Test and are given early assurance of positions into medical school. Interested students should contact the pre-medical advisors at the participating institutions for more program information and an application.

University of Virginia School of Medicine

Dr. Norman Oliver
Associate Dean for Diversity
Associate Professor of Family Medicine
University of Virginia Health System
Office for Diversity
P.O. Box 800739
Charlottesville, VA 22908-0739
434-924-1867; 434-924-8387 Fax
www.healthsystem.virgina.edu/itemet/diversity

Recruitment

All predominantly African-American schools in the state of Virginia are invited each year to participate in the *Day at the Medical Center* sponsored by the Medical Alumni Association. Some schools are visited by members of the Admissions Committee for the purpose of recruiting students. Representatives from the School of Medicine also visit summer programs to recruit students. Pre-medical societies may request a visit by the Associate Dean for Diversity throughout the year.

Admissions

Minority students invited for interviews have an opportunity to meet with the Associate Dean for Diversity and a minority faculty member who are able to answer questions informally as well as give advice to prospective students.

Academic Support Programs

Each entering student is assigned a faculty member and a second-year student as advisors. During the clinical years, each student selects a faculty member whom he/she consults about such matters as fourth-year electives program and career choice. The School of Medicine provides academic support services for medical

University of Virginia School of Medicine, 2006
Applicants and Matriculants by Gender, Race and Ethnicity

Race and Ethnicity	Applicants			Matriculants		
	Women	Men	Total	Women	Men	Total
Hispanic/Latino						
Cuban	9	5	14	1	0	1
Mexican American	23	23	46	0	0	0
Puerto Rican	11	8	19	1	0	1
Other Hispanic	39	43	82	3	2	5
Multiple Hispanic*	3	3	6	0	0	0
Subtotal	85	82	167	5	2	7
Non-Hispanic/Latino**						
Black	170	72	242	4	2	6
Native American/Alaska Native	4	3	7	0	0	0
Native Hawaiian/Other Pacific Islander	3	3	6	0	0	0
White	1,038	1,295	2,333	44	54	98
Asian	345	389	734	7	17	24
Other Race	4	3	7	0	0	0
Multiple Race*	49	35	84	1	1	2
Unknown	12	20	32	1	1	2
Subtotal	1,625	1,820	3,445	57	75	132
Foreign	57	53	110	0	1	1
Total	1,767	1,955	3,722	62	78	140

*Since 2002, students can select more than one race and / or ethnicity. **Those who did not choose 'Hispanic/Latino' or 'Non-Hispanic/Latino' are counted under 'Non-Hispanic/Latino'.
Data Source: AAMC Data Warehouse: Applicant-Matriculant File, as of 5/9/2007.

students including structured *Peer Tutorial Programs* in biochemistry, cell and tissue structure, genetics, gross anatomy, human behavior, introduction to clinical medicine, microbiology, neuroscience, pathology, pharmacology, physiology, and psychopathology. Tutoring is provided by faculty teaching the courses, by fourth-year medical students, and graduate students. Preparatory workshops for Step 1 of the United States Medical Licensing Examination and workshops on time management, stress management, study skills, and test-taking strategies are offered. Academic and personal counseling and resources for students with special learning needs are also provided. During the clinical experience, individual assistance is available when necessary. The student academic support program is directed by the Associate Dean for Student Academic Support. When necessary, the curriculum can be adjusted to allow additional time for completion by the student with special requirements.

Enrichment Programs
Summer Medical and Dental Education Program (SMDEP). This six-week program, funded by The Robert Wood Johnson Foundation, is offered each summer to enhance opportunities for minority and other students from disadvantaged backgrounds to enter, remain in, and graduate from medical school. SMDEP is aimed at increasing acceptance rates into medical school for minorities and other students from disadvantaged backgrounds and is designed for students who have completed at least one year of college. SMDEP offers academic enrichment and clinical experience with faculty mentors; lectures by eminent scientists in biomedical research; exposure to the *real*

world of medicine through a clinical medicine lecture series; academic and personal counseling; and sessions on admission procedures, financial planning, study skills, time management, and interviewing skills.

Student Financial Assistance
The admission application fee may be waived for financially disadvantaged applicants. The Minority Affairs and Financial Aid offices work closely with minority students to ensure that no applicant is denied access to medical school due to lack of funding.

AAMC

Virginia Commonwealth University School of Medicine

Donna H. Jackson
Office of Student Outreach Programs
Virginia Commonwealth University
School of Medicine, P.O. Box 980565
Richmond, VA 23298-0565
804-828-9630; 804-828-1246 Fax
donna.jackson@vcu.edu

Recruitment

The School of Medicine has undertaken a variety of recruitment efforts for prospective medical school applicants. Admissions representatives, the Director of Diversity Access Programs, along with selected medical students and faculty members annually visit with pre-medical advisors and student groups on the medical campus and at the undergraduate institutions. On-campus recruitment visits include a tour of the medical facilities by medical students. All recruitment sessions conducted include information about the unique and desirable features that the institution offers as well as the medical school curriculum, financial aid, student life-style, and student organizations. Recruitment visits are made to most colleges and universities in the state of Virginia and to most out-state schools that have a large enrollment of Virginia residents. Groups who wish to visit the campus should contact the School of Medicine Admissions Office. Individual tours are not provided; however, interested individuals are welcomed to visit the Admissions Office and pick up a self-guided tourbook. Science clubs and other special groups are also invited to tour the facilities.

Recruitment visits are also provided at the middle and high school levels. School of Medicine representatives and selected medical students participate in school career days and college fairs.

The Office of Student Outreach Programs sponsors a "Second Look" Program to accepted students from backgrounds underrepresented in medicine. These students are invited back to the medical campus to meet and speak with medical students, residents, and faculty and learn more about the facilities and opportunities.

Admissions

The School of Medicine has an institutional goal to educate and train students who will meet the health needs of our state and nation. Two important objectives are to increase the population of students from backgrounds underrepresented in medicine and graduate 50 percent of the medical school class who are interested in primary care.

An initial screening is conducted on all applications. The Admissions Committee, who makes the decision to grant interviews, reviews those applicants who are provided with secondary applications. All interviews are conducted on the Medical College of Virginia Campus and are one-on-one interaction. Selection factors include, but are not limited to: Medical College Admission Test (MCAT) scores, GPA, letters of recommendations, essays, and exposure to medicine. No factor is weighted. Acceptances are made to those candidates who clearly demonstrate an ability to be successful students as well as exhibit compassion and other important interpersonal qualities of a physician.

The Admissions Committee is composed of School of Medicine administrators, physicians, and fourth-year medical students. All are full voting members.

Virginia Commonwealth University School of Medicine, 2006
Applicants and Matriculants by Gender, Race and Ethnicity

Race and Ethnicity		Applicants			Matriculants		
		Women	Men	Total	Women	Men	Total
Hispanic/Latino							
Cuban		13	9	22	0	0	0
Mexican American		27	27	54	1	1	2
Puerto Rican		15	11	26	0	1	1
Other Hispanic		65	48	113	2	1	3
Multiple Hispanic*		8	3	11	0	0	0
	Subtotal	128	98	226	3	3	6
Non-Hispanic/Latino**							
Black		194	93	287	11	4	15
Native American/Alaska Native		2	4	6	0	0	0
Native Hawaiian/Other Pacific Islander		11	10	21	0	0	0
White		1,251	1,496	2,747	53	49	102
Asian		623	681	1,304	21	29	50
Other Race		5	5	10	0	1	1
Multiple Race*		65	61	126	3	4	7
Unknown		13	12	25	1	1	2
	Subtotal	2,164	2,362	4,526	89	88	177
Foreign		11	12	23	1	0	1
	Total	2,303	2,472	4,775	93	91	184

*Since 2002, students can select more than one race and / or ethnicity. **Those who did not choose 'Hispanic/Latino' or 'Non-Hispanic/Latino' are counted under 'Non-Hispanic/Latino'.

Data Source: AAMC Data Warehouse: Applicant-Matriculant File, as of 5/9/2007.

Association of American Medical Colleges, 2007

Academic Support Programs

The Associate Dean of Student Affairs, Director of Student Outreach Programs, Director of Curriculum, the Diversity Access Program Director, and professionals in the University Counseling Center are concerned with the progress and maturation of individual medical students. Students who have academic problems are identified early in the academic year, and these individuals are provided with tutorial assistance. A variety of tutorial services are available: individual and group tutoring based upon a personal needs assessment; educational resources such as computer disks, co-op notes, review material, audio tapes of first- and second-year lectures; and study-skills sessions.

The Office of Student Affairs provides all students with a School of Medicine faculty advisor. In addition, the Office of Student Outreach Programs works with Student Affairs to provide students with a minority physician mentor.

Enrichment Programs

There are a number of enrichment programs available to prospective and matriculating medical students.

Health Careers/Education and Special Services for Students (HC/ESSS). Virginia Commonwealth University hosts various programs to encourage and educate high school and college-level students about health careers. The programs currently serve students ranging from fourth grade to undergraduate and post-baccalaureate grade levels. In addition, HC/ESSS provides support and resources to enrolled VCU health profession students. For more information, visit *(www.vcuhealth.org/vp/sassdss/programs/).*

VCU Acceleration Program. The VCU Acceleration Program provides college students early exposure to the math and science curriculum of pre-health sciences and opportunities for internships and volunteer work in various clinical health service provider settings. The VCU Acceleration Program offers many unique and valuable learning experiences for students. Upon acceptance into the program the students will participate in the four-week Summer Health Sciences program, which exposes them to the math and science curriculum of health sciences. Prior to the start of the sophomore year, a stipend will be given to each student while participating in the summer programs. They also will do internships in various clinical health service provider settings. Other program features include Supplemental Instruction in math and science, and academic and health professions advising.

Project Inquisitive Minds. This one-week program is designed to encourage and educate high school students about the many interdisciplinary programs of health careers. Through activities and educational experiences, high school students in the program will develop and understand the roles and responsibilities of diverse health careers. The program targets underrepresented minority students within the Richmond area who have an interest in pursuing a health career beyond high school graduation.

Diversity Access Programs. This program is designed to provide bachelor and post-bachelor students with the resources, skills, and exposure needed to successfully complete college level work and gain entrance into one of VCU's health professions schools. The programs include a skills development workshop series focusing on topics such as preparing for professional school admissions, improving learning skills, and financial planning and wellness. This program operates through the Office of the Vice President of Health Sciences under the Office of Students Academic Support Services for Students with Disabilities.

Area Health Education Centers (AHEC). The Virginia Statewide AHEC Program is located within HC/ESSS and develops health careers recruitment programs for Virginia's students, especially underrepresented and disadvantaged students. The AHEC programs support community-based training of primary care health professions students, residents, and other health professions students in Virginia's underserved communities. AHEC also provides educational and practice support systems for the Commonwealth's primary care providers. The Virginia AHEC regularly collaborates with health, education, and human services organizations to achieve the shared goal of improved health and disease prevention for the citizens of the Commonwealth.

Post-Baccalaureate Program. The School of Medicine offers a one-year pre-medical basic health sciences certificate for individuals seeking to enhance their background in the basic health sciences. This is an opportunity for advanced graduate-level training prior to entry into a professional program. Interested individuals should contact VCU's School of Graduate Studies at 804-828-6916.

Foundations of Clinical Medicine. All first- and second-year medical students must participate in the Foundations of Clinical Medicine course, which is designed to provide the students with patient exposure to help prepare them for their clinical years. Within the course, components address the importance of getting to know the patient individually and gaining an effective history with cultural issues in mind. Cases are provided and students practice with simulated patients.

Project ACEe. The School of Medicine sponsors an educational experience for inner-city minority high school students who have an interest in the medical field. Beginning in January of each year, selected students are provided with educational

AAMC

workshops that will help them to become self-sufficient learners in college. They are matched with physicians to gain exposure in their field of interest. This is a major pipeline program.

Cultural Competence. The School of Medicine currently addresses cultural competence at all levels. Students have cultural competencies integrated into their coursework through both lecture and electives during all years. In addition, courses and seminars are given regarding professionalism and ethics. Cultural competency for faculty is addressed through the Office of Faculty and Instructional Development. Diversity Awareness and other training sessions are also provided for all faculty.

Student Financial Assistance
A detailed evaluation of financial aid for each student with a need is conducted after the student has been accepted into the School of Medicine. Available scholarship monies and loans vary in amount and distribution each year. Every effort is made to meet the financial needs of all students.

Full-Time Student Expenses. Average expenses for the first year of medical school include tuition and fees, loan fees, room and board, books and supplies, transportation, and personal. These factors are used in the determination of need for financial aid.

In order to serve its student body efficiently and correctly, the School of Medicine maintains its own Office of Financial Aid. Policies for the awarding of institutional financial aid are made by the School of Medicine Scholarship Committee, composed of administrators, faculty, and appointed doctors from various areas of medicine. Financial aid is awarded on the basis of financial need, which is determined through use of the Free Application for Federal Student Aid (FAFSA) financial statement and/or merit.

Applicants seeking consideration for institutional scholarships are requested to report on the FAFSA statement their own income and assets, that of their parents, and, where applicable, their spouse. In addition, applicants are asked to complete the needs access on-line form. Students must also complete a Web-based scholarship application. Students seeking loan assistance only are not required to provide parental financial information.

The foundation of all financial aid awards is the presumption of a reasonable level of borrowing, beginning with a federally-subsidized Stafford Student Loan of $8,500. Applicants who have financial need, after factoring in both family resources and loans, may receive institutional scholarship assistance to help meet remaining need. Since aid is based upon financial need, aid recipients are required to notify the Financial Aid Office of changes in their financial resources.

Applicants who anticipate borrowing as a means of financing medical education are advised to assure that their personal credit record has no adverse credit history. The establishment of good credit is not a requirement for obtaining student loans, but the absence of poor credit history is a requirement.

Financial assistance is not available to students who are not U.S. citizens or permanent resident aliens. Financial need is not a factor in decisions regarding admission. Financial aid applications are made available to all students who are invited to the school for admissions interviews.

About 88 percent of Virginia Commonwealth University medical students receive financial aid. Of these students, approximately 38 percent receive some form of school-based aid. School-based aid is composed of revolving loan monies and scholarship funds. Federal funds consist of the subsidized and unsubsidized Stafford

student loans. A variety of other outside sources are utilized, such as the Alternative Loan Program (ALP).

The School of Medicine will waive application fee requirements for all students for whom that fee will be a financial hardship as determined by the American Medical College Application Service.

Educational Partnerships
Guaranteed Admissions Program. The Virginia Commonwealth University's Honors Program offers a Guaranteed Admissions Program to qualified high school seniors. This is an opportunity to gain a guarantee of future admissions to highly selective graduate and professional programs at VCU.

Preferred Admissions Program. Similar to the Guaranteed Admissions Program, Virginia Commonwealth University's Honors Program offers a Preferred Admissions Program to sophomore students currently enrolled at VCU. These students, who have performed well academically for the first years of undergraduate school, are given the opportunity to gain a guarantee of future admissions to VCU's highly selective graduate and professional programs.

Mason Scholar Program. The George Mason University (GMU) chooses 10 Mason Scholars each year. They are high school graduates who have shown superior academic accomplishment, civic involvement, and leadership potential. Each year, a selected number of these scholars are given the opportunity to gain admission to the VCU School of Medicine. In the past, VCU has admitted one to four Mason Scholars to each medical school class. Individuals apply for the GMU Scholars program as they apply for admissions to GMU. The selections are made solely by the GMU Scholars Program administration.

University of Washington School of Medicine

Dr. David Acosta, Associate Dean
for Multicultural Affairs
T-545 Health Sciences Center
Box 357430
Seattle, WA 98195
206-685-2489; 206-543-9063 Fax
http://www.uwmedicine.org/Education/
MDProgram/

Recruitment

Founded in 1946, the UW medical school is recognized for its excellence in training primary-care physicians and for advancing medical knowledge through scientific research. It's nationally known for its commitment to community service through the volunteer activities of its students, staff, faculty and alumni. The Office of Multicultural Affairs (OMCA) *(http://depts.washington.edu/omca/)* was established in 1980 by the Dean of the School of Medicine as a reaffirmation of the medical school's efforts and intent to matriculate and graduate a diverse group of individuals who are traditionally underrepresented in medicine.

The University of Washington (UW) School of Medicine serves as the regional school for the five WWAMI states (Washington, Wyoming, Alaska, Montana, and Idaho – for more information, go to *(http://www.uwmedicine.org/Education/WWAMI/)*. Students outside of the region who are from disadvantaged backgrounds or who have a demonstrated commitment to work with the underserved populations are encouraged to apply. The OMCA staff coordinates activities that are designed to encourage, assist and support students who have an interest in pursuing a career in medicine.

OMCA works directly with K-12 schools, colleges, universities, and established community organizations in the Pacific Northwest to identify, encourage, recruit, and train a diverse medical student body. A medical student advisory board and a community advisory board participate in the development of program activities and strategies to help achieve the goals established in our mission statement.

Admissions

The School of Medicine is committed to building and sustaining a diverse academic community of faculty, staff, fellows, residents, and students and to assuring that access to education and training is open to learners from all segments of society, acknowledging a particular responsibility to the diverse populations within the WWAMI region. Given this mission of the School of Medicine, the Admissions Committee is committed to selecting students with the goal of meeting the needs and demands of our local and regional communities. Applicants are considered on the basis of academic performance, Medical College Admission Test (MCAT) scores, letters of recommendation, their motivation to pursue medicine, maturity, and demonstrated humanitarian qualities and experiences. Extenuating circumstances in an applicant's background are evaluated as they relate to these selection factors.

All five states in the region offer annual Pre-Admissions Workshops for potential applicants. The workshops are designed to provide in-depth information on the medical school and the WWAMI model (for more information, see *(http://www.uwmedicine.org/Education/WWAMI/Medical+School.htm)*, the application process, interview skills, and financial aid.

University of Washington School of Medicine, 2006
Applicants and Matriculants by Gender, Race and Ethnicity

Race and Ethnicity		Applicants			Matriculants		
		Women	Men	Total	Women	Men	Total
Hispanic/Latino							
Cuban		6	5	11	0	1	1
Mexican American		65	58	123	4	0	4
Puerto Rican		13	9	22	1	0	1
Other Hispanic		51	46	97	1	2	3
Multiple Hispanic*		5	6	11	0	0	0
	Subtotal	140	124	264	6	3	9
Non-Hispanic/Latino**							
Black		78	50	128	1	1	2
Native American/Alaska Native		15	10	25	3	1	4
Native Hawaiian/Other Pacific Islander		12	7	19	0	0	0
White		1,004	1,254	2,258	70	64	134
Asian		389	437	826	16	10	26
Other Race		2	5	7	0	0	0
Multiple Race*		76	82	158	5	2	7
Unknown		13	16	29	0	0	0
	Subtotal	1,589	1,861	3,450	95	78	173
Foreign		32	29	61	0	0	0
	Total	1,761	2,014	3,775	101	81	182

*Since 2002, students can select more than one race and / or ethnicity. **Those who did not choose
'Hispanic/Latino' or 'Non-Hispanic/Latino' are counted under 'Non-Hispanic/Latino'.
Data Source: AAMC Data Warehouse: Applicant-Matriculant File, as of 5/9/2007.

Academic Support Programs

The School of Medicine offers a variety of services for minority and/or disadvantaged students. A learning specialist is available to assist students with learning skills, study skills, and test-taking strategies for the U.S. Medical Licensing Examination Boards and medical school courses. Individual and small-group tutoring services are offered during the academic year for all students. Stipends are available for students who are eligible for Board preparation courses. A research advisor is available to provide assistance with research projects, such as the required Independent Investigative Inquiry project that all medical students are required to complete. Counseling staff provide free, short term, confidential counseling services to all students and can help the student cope with a variety of personal and/or professional issues surrounding the demands of medical school. An optional expanded curriculum is also available for students requiring more than the traditional four years to complete the curriculum.

Pre-Matriculation Program (http://depts. washington.edu/omca/PREMATI). This five-week summer program is offered for new medical school matriculants from minority and/or disadvantaged backgrounds. It provides an introduction to the medical school curriculum (histology); exposure to local health care systems; and workshops in study skills, test-taking skills, stress management, and clinical skills. Eligible students receive stipends for the duration of the program. Contact: *Mary Walls, mwalls @u.washington.edu*, 206-616-3047.

Student Organizations. The School of Medicine has a variety of student organizations for minority medical students. These include PALANA (Pacific Islander, Asian, Latino, African American, Native American), the Student National Medical Association (Region I: *(http://www.snmaregion1.org/)*; contact: Muyiwa Awoniyi, *mu7@u.washington.edu*), the Latino Medical Student Association *(http://students.washington.edu/lmsa/officers.html)*; contact: Lili Peacock-Villada, *lilip05@alum.dartmouth.org*; Christina Arredondo, *arredonc@u.washington.edu*); Medicine Wheel Society *(http://faculty.washington.edu/dacosta/nacoe/mws.html)*; contact: Amanda Bruegl, *asbruegl@u.washington.edu*) and the Asian Pacific American Medical Student Association (Region VII contact: Catherine Delostrinos, *cathetr @u.washington.edu*; Duc Ngo, *ducngo@u. washington.edu*) These student organizations not only provide support, social activities, and cultural events for students, they also provide students with the opportunities to participate in recruitment, community outreach, and peer mentoring among local K-12 schools, high school and college students. Student groups work actively with the UW Medical Alumni Association and other campus and community-based organizations in providing information to others regarding the health needs of local underserved communities.

Mentoring Networks. Structured mentoring networks for medical students have been established and are active with local minority community health professionals: African American Mentoring Network *(http://faculty. washington.edu/dacosta/aamn/index.html)*, Chicano/Latino Mentoring Network, and the Medicine Wheel Society. Students participate in support activities with community mentoring networks designed to provide social, moral and academic support. They meet regularly to discuss and address student needs, issues and activities. In addition, the mentors provide career-counseling in medicine.

Enrichment Programs
UDOC. This is a free summer enrichment program for high school students that is offered in Seattle, WA (three weeks; *http:// depts.washington.edu/omca/UDOC/)* and Anchorage, AK (six weeks; *http://biomed. uaa.alaska.edu/UDOC.htm)*. This program

encourages high school students from minority and/or disadvantaged backgrounds to pursue a career in the health professions and fosters their development in academics, leadership and community service. Contact: Felicity Abeyta, 206-685-2489, *fabeyta@u.washington.edu.*

The Robert Wood Johnson Foundation Summer Medical and Dental Education Program (SMDEP). This is a free six-week summer enrichment program offered to college freshman and sophomores from minority and/or disadvantaged backgrounds that have a demonstrated interest in pursuing a career in medicine or dentistry. The program is located in Seattle, WA *(http://depts.washington.edu/omca/SMDEP/ index.html)* and offers academic preparation in the basic sciences, clinical immersion experiences with an individually assigned physician/dentist mentor, exposure to the local health care system and community, including opportunities for emergency room, surgery observation and dental procedures and biomedical science research. Participants receive free room and board, travel assistance, and a stipend. Other amenities include textbooks, access to the university's many educational and recreational resources, mentorship and advising. Contact: Dan Olson, *dano@u.washington.edu*, 206-543-9733.

Student Financial Assistance
Provide as much information as possible concerning financial aid for students. Please indicate if the application fee is waived and if financial aid is available for interview trips. Emphasis should be placed on opportunities available only at your institution (that is, non-need-based awards, fellowships, grants, local loan possibilities, state scholarships or loan programs, and so on).

Educational Partnerships
WWAMI. WWAMI is an enduring partnership between the UW School of Medicine (SOM) and the states of Wyoming, Alaska, Montana and Idaho.

The UWSOM is the only medical school in the five-state WWAMI region, and has established partnerships with the University of Wyoming *(http://uwadmnweb.uwyo.edu/wwami/)*, Washington State University *(http://www.wsu.edu/~wwami/)*, University of Alaska-Anchorage *(http://biomed.uaa.alaska.edu/)*, Montana State University *(http://www.montana.edu/wwwami/)*, and University of Idaho *(http://www.webs.uidaho.edu/wwami/)*. It collaborates closely with community and regional organizations to implement its programs, community outreach and mentoring networks to help support students in their pursuit of their medical career. Students from Alaska, Montana, Idaho, and Wyoming take their initial year at state universities in their home states.

Post-Baccalaureate Pre-Medical Certificate Program—Montana State University *(http://www.montana.edu/dhs/hpa/Post-bacc.advising.htm)*. This program is offered for those students who have completed their bachelor's level work at a four-year institution who are interested in taking the science courses traditionally required for application to medical and dental schools. These requisite courses include general chemistry, introductory biology, organic chemistry, introductory physics and biochemistry. Post-baccalaureate students completing 36 of the suggested 45 credits available will receive a Certificate of Completion. Students will be advised in their curricular choices and medical school applications by Jane Cary, Director of Health Professions Advising, at *hpa@montana.edu*, 406-994-1670.

National Institute of Diabetes and Digestive and Kidney Diseases—Charles Drew University of Medicine and Sciences National High School Student Summer

Research Apprentice Program (http://www2.niddk.nih.gov/Funding/Funding Opportunities/Minority_Health_Research_Coordination/stusummer.htm). In partnership with UCLA, this program is designed to provide high school students with an opportunity to work in a biomedical laboratory in their state. Each student is paired with an established researcher and assigned to a research team to work on a specific biomedical research project. The eight-week program provides students with real experiences working in a laboratory and learning research protocols. In the last week the students travel to Washington, DC to present their research. The purpose of the program is to increase the number of ethnic minorities involved in biomedical research. Contact: Felicity Abeyta, 206-685-2489, *fabeyta@u.washington.edu*. Project H.O.P.E. (Health Occupations Preparatory Experience; *(http://www.wwahec.org/WWAHEC_HOPE.htm)*. In partnership with Western Washington Area Health Education Center (AHEC), this program provides high school students with a six-week paid internship to learn and be exposed to health careers in local health facilities in their communities. The students spend part of their time at the UW SOM and the OMCA and are exposed to the health sciences.

AAMC

Joan C. Edwards School of Medicine at Marshall University

Dr. Marie C. Veitia
Associate Dean for Student Affairs
Joan C. Edwards School of Medicine
at Marshall University
1600 Medical Center Drive,
Huntington, WV 25701
304-691-1730; 304-691-1744 Fax
veitia@marshall.edu

Recruitment

The Joan C. Edwards School of Medicine does not have a special recruitment program for minority students. An admissions counselor does visit all colleges in West Virginia to discuss medical school opportunities and current medical students are invited to participate. Every effort is made to recruit minority students.

Admissions

The admissions process is the same for all applicants. The Admissions Committee considers the grade-point average for undergraduate studies, particularly in science and related courses; Medical College Admission Test scores; and character qualifications such as motivation, enthusiasm, emotional stability, mature judgment, integrity, leadership, and scope of interests as is evident from letters of recommendation and two interviews with members of the Admissions Committee. Minorities are represented on the Admissions Committee.

Academic Support Programs

All medical school matriculants can receive tutorial assistance and advisement from a particular course professor, an assigned faculty advisor, and/or a student-selected faculty advisor. Academic achievement

as well as personal and emotional needs are monitored closely, and the Office of Student Affairs intervenes as is indicated. A Peer-Tutoring Program is available upon request to first-year students at no charge. A U.S. Medical Licensing Exam (USMLE) Step 1 Review Course is offered on campus to all second-year students at no charge. Financial assistance is provided for other review materials. The main campus of Marshall University also provides extensive learning resources through the Higher Education for Learning Problems program.

Enrichment Programs

Several programs are conducted annually with high school and college students designed to stimulate interest in the medical professions. Most notably is the Southwestern West Virginia Area Health Education Center (SWAHEC). This federally funded program aims to recruit disadvantaged students from rural communities and increase retention among those who are educated in the medical professions. The Concord Summer Academy, which partners with Concord University, is an enrichment program aimed at exposing high school students to the health professions. Finally, college students are invited to participate in stipend-supported summer programs. Every effort is made to meet the needs of all students, including especially minority and disadvantaged students.

Student Financial Assistance

Those students receiving a fee waiver from the American Medical College Application Service will also receive a waiver of the application fee for the School of Medicine. Debt management and financial planning are currently offered on a one-on-one basis. Plans are underway to provide more opportunities for students in this area.

Other Pertinent Information

There is no discrimination because of race, gender, religion, age sexual orientation,

Joan C. Edwards School of Medicine at Marshall University, 2006
Applicants and Matriculants by Gender, Race and Ethnicity

Race and Ethnicity		Applicants			Matriculants		
		Women	Men	Total	Women	Men	Total
Hispanic/Latino							
Cuban		3	7	10	0	0	0
Mexican American		6	8	14	0	0	0
Puerto Rican		1	3	4	0	0	0
Other Hispanic		22	28	50	0	0	0
Multiple Hispanic*		0	2	2	0	0	0
	Subtotal	32	48	80	0	0	0
Non-Hispanic/Latino**							
Black		35	34	69	0	0	0
Native American/Alaska Native		0	3	3	0	0	0
Native Hawaiian/Other Pacific Islander		1	1	2	0	0	0
White		384	519	903	24	33	57
Asian		195	241	436	3	3	6
Other Race		0	2	2	0	0	0
Multiple Race*		13	26	39	0	1	1
Unknown		6	8	14	0	0	0
	Subtotal	634	834	1,468	27	37	64
Foreign		11	14	25	0	0	0
	Total	677	896	1,573	27	37	64

*Since 2002, students can select more than one race and / or ethnicity. **Those who did not choose
Hispanic/Latino' or 'Non-Hispanic/Latino' are counted under 'Non-Hispanic/Latino'.
Data Source: AAMC Data Warehouse: Applicant-Matriculant File, as of 5/9/2007.

Association of American Medical Colleges, 2007

handicap, or national origin. Qualified members of minority groups are encouraged to apply. The Joan C. Edwards School of Medicine is committed to developing mechanisms by which to enhance diversity. By working with the Office of Multicultural Affairs at Marshall University, the School of Medicine strives to provide fairness and equity in the distribution of opportunity and in the treatment of individuals. Objectives and strategies for doing so are established and/or reviewed annually.

West Virginia University School of Medicine*

Dr. G. Anne Cather, Associate Dean
Student Services and
Professional Development
West Virginia University
School of Medicine
Room 1146, HSCN Box 9111
Morgantown, WV 26506-9111
304-293-2408; 304-293-7814 Fax

Recruitment

The School of Medicine participates in a yearly program, on a university-wide basis, to interest secondary school students in health science careers. This program is especially oriented toward minority students. In addition, personnel from the Office of Admissions and Records, and the Office of Student Services, make yearly visits to colleges in the state. These visits are

prearranged, and special invitations are sent to students who are interested in health science careers, especially minority students. During these visits, discussions are held on a one-to-one basis with the student, and they are encouraged to pursue their interest. Also, periodic visits are made to high schools within the state holding career day activities; and, again, individual students are counseled regarding their questions and concerns for health science careers. Intermittently, the Office of Student Services holds a one-half day seminar in which pre-medical advisors from the state's colleges are invited. During this seminar, discussions and programs are carried out to help the advisors in their work with students interested in health science careers. Minority advisors are especially welcomed, and every effort is made to indicate our interest in helping needy students. Special tours and seminars are

West Virginia University School of Medicine, 2006
Applicants and Matriculants by Gender, Race and Ethnicity

Race and Ethnicity	Applicants			Matriculants		
	Women	Men	Total	Women	Men	Total
Hispanic/Latino						
Cuban	6	1	7	0	0	0
Mexican American	14	8	22	1	0	1
Puerto Rican	1	6	7	0	0	0
Other Hispanic	22	26	48	0	1	1
Multiple Hispanic*	4	4	8	0	0	0
Subtotal	47	45	92	1	1	2
Non-Hispanic/Latino**						
Black	39	28	67	0	1	1
Native American/Alaska Native	3	5	8	0	0	0
Native Hawaiian/Other Pacific Islander	4	2	6	0	1	1
White	539	727	1,266	28	61	89
Asian	214	274	488	2	12	14
Other Race	0	2	2	0	0	0
Multiple Race*	20	27	47	1	0	1
Unknown	6	2	8	1	0	1
Subtotal	825	1,067	1,892	32	75	107
Foreign	28	25	53	0	0	0
Total	900	1,137	2,037	33	76	109

*Since 2002, students can select more than one race and / or ethnicity. **Those who did not choose Hispanic/Latino' or 'Non-Hispanic/Latino' are counted under 'Non-Hispanic/Latino'.
Data Source: AAMC Data Warehouse: Applicant-Matriculant File, as of 5/9/2007.

arranged, on request, for individual students or groups wishing to have additional exposure to the requirements for medical school or health science careers.

Admissions

The School of Medicine has no differences in requirements for minority students. Every effort is made to select minority students who are felt to have proper motivation and capabilities for professional school. There is no special screening panel or admissions committee devoted to minority applicants. The criteria used for selection are the same for all students, and these include the grade-point averages, Medical College Admission Test scores, personal interviews, letters of recommendation, and student's motivation and interpersonal skills. The Admissions Committee is made up of both of basic science and clinical faculty. In addition, there are senior students who are full members of the committee. Every effort is made to obtain minority students and faculty for membership on the Admissions Committee.

Academic Support Programs

Every effort is made to make an early identification of students in academic difficulty, regardless of their minority or socioeconomic status. This is done through close supervision, cooperation, and communication among the course instructors, course coordinators, and Office of Student Services. Assistance is routinely given to students with special needs. This assistance may take several forms, such as identification and help with personal problems, improvement in study techniques, and tutorial guidance on a one-to-one basis by faculty members. The Health Sciences Center Campus has a branch Learning Resources Center with learning tutorials, time and stress management help, and overall study-skills enhancement available. Every attempt is made to individualize students' needs, and special arrangements for scheduling are, at

times, made on an individual basis. All students are encouraged to communicate with the Office of Student Services if they need assistance in the areas of academic achievement, health, or matters of personal concern.

Enrichment Programs

Health Careers Opportunity Program (HCOP). West Virginia University (WVU) recognizes the underrepresentation of health care providers from minority and other underrepresented backgrounds practicing in the state. We have established a program aimed at increasing the number of qualified applicants applying to and graduating from medical, dental, pharmacy, and allied health programs. This program, known as the Central Appalachian Health Careers Opportunity Network (CAHCON), has three components:

- Preliminary Education: supports students as they transition from high school to college.
- Facilitating Entry: supports students applying to health and allied health professions schools.
- Retention: supports students in health and allied health professions schools.

Highlights
- Award of $1.86 million in federal funds.
- Over 500 students helped since 1985; all but a handful are WV residents.
- Very high retention rate of at risk participants (only seven students have dropped out of college from this program in the past ten years).
- Students from all WV institutions of higher education are eligible for this program and do participate.

HSS – Health Sciences Seminar has been supported by WVU since 1981 with the purpose of trying to encourage sixth to ninth grade disadvantaged youths to

examine career possibilities in the health sciences. Nearly 1,100 seventh, eighth, and ninth graders from all over West Virginia along with their parents have participated in this overnight, two-day, cost-free event. The university will provide this seminar free to students and parents/ guardians. West Virginia's Division of Student Affairs and HCOP sponsor this program. These students are given hands-on experiences with health care professions illustrating health career opportunities, tours of the extensive health care facilities at WVU, a chance to learn about financial aid opportunities, educational and skill requirements for multiple health professions, and much more. This program has a special emphasis on recruiting financially disadvantaged, first generation, and underrepresented minority participants.

Educational Partnerships

The Health Sciences and Technology Academy (HSTA) reaches out to ninth- to 12th-grade underrepresented students and follows them to college and toward professional school to help them prepare for health care careers. The goal is to nurture the ambitions of talented students who, for economic or other reasons, might not ordinarily achieve these career goals. HSTA is a partnership among the numerous units of West Virginia University, West Virginia Rural Health Education Partnership, and many Appalachian communities. The program brings minority and disadvantaged students and their teachers to campus each summer for clinic, laboratory, and classroom training and enrichment activities, and then provides the infrastructure and support for community-based science projects mentored by teachers, health professions students, and volunteer community leaders during the school year. HSTA aims to share the resources and talent of the partnership, to encourage public school teachers' and community leaders' mentoring of students.

The ultimate goal is to increase the college-going rate among underrepresented students in the Appalachian region, to improve science and math education, to empower communities through leadership development of their youth, and, ultimately, to increase the number of health care providers in West Virginia's currently underserved rural communities.

- Total number of students served by HSTA—2,100
- Total number of students currently served by HSTA—760
- Retention of students who begin the program in high school—64 percent
- Number of graduates to date, academic years 1998-2004—580 (currently 26 counties)
- Percent of graduates to enter college—99 percent
- Average high school GPA of graduates—3.57
- Average college GPA of graduates reporting—3.01

Student Financial Assistance

Weir Foundation. Scholarship awarded to disadvantaged minority student in the School of Medicine. Must complete Free Application for Federal Student Aid (FAFSA) by March 1.

Robert D'Alessandri Medical Fund. Scholarship awarded to a medical student with financial need and academic promise. Preference given to minority/underrepresented students who completed the HSTA, HSS, or HCOP programs. Applicants must be U.S. citizens. To be considered, the FAFSA must be filed by March 1. There is no cost to file the FAFSA. The scholarship is not available for interview trips.

Medical College of Wisconsin

Dr. Dawn St. A. Bragg
Assistant Dean, Student Affairs/Diversity
Assistant Professor, Pediatrics
Medical College of Wisconsin
8701 Watertown Plank Road
Milwaukee, WI 53226
414-456-8734; 414-456-6506 fax
dbragg@mail.mcw.edu
www.mcw.edu/diaplay/router.asp?
docid=619

Recruitment

The Medical College of Wisconsin (MCW) recognizes the importance of allowing its medical students the opportunity to exchange ideas with others who have talents, backgrounds, viewpoints, experiences, and interests different from their own. To this end, the Medical College is committed to the recruitment,

admission, and graduation of talented students from diverse backgrounds. Specifically, students who demonstrate experiences in one or more of the following categories will be deemed to contribute to the diversity of the MCW student body:

- Growing up in poverty or in a disadvantaged socioeconomic status;
- Being the first person from one's family to attend college or graduate school;
- Overcoming educational disadvantage (graduating from a high school with little resources or with a high drop out rate);
- Having a primary language other than English;
- Living in a rural area; or
- Overcoming a significant handicap.

The Office of Student Affairs/Diversity provides support service to enhance

Medical College of Wisconsin, 2006
Applicants and Matriculants by Gender, Race and Ethnicity

Race and Ethnicity	Applicants			Matriculants		
	Women	Men	Total	Women	Men	Total
Hispanic/Latino						
Cuban	12	13	25	0	0	0
Mexican American	47	57	104	3	7	10
Puerto Rican	10	4	14	0	1	1
Other Hispanic	56	43	99	0	1	1
Multiple Hispanic*	4	6	10	2	0	2
Subtotal	129	123	252	5	9	14
Non-Hispanic/Latino**						
Black	124	70	194	9	2	11
Native American/Alaska Native	2	6	8	0	1	1
Native Hawaiian/Other Pacific Islander	9	11	20	0	0	0
White	1,452	2,165	3,617	80	74	154
Asian	568	688	1,256	4	12	16
Other Race	3	5	8	0	0	0
Multiple Race*	65	69	134	3	4	7
Unknown	17	22	39	1	0	1
Subtotal	2,240	3,036	5,276	97	93	190
Foreign	94	130	224	0	0	0
Total	2,463	3,289	5,752	102	102	204

*Since 2002, students can select more than one race and / or ethnicity. **Those who did not choose Hispanic/Latino' or 'Non-Hispanic/Latino' are counted under 'Non-Hispanic/Latino'.
Data Source: AAMC Data Warehouse: Applicant-Matriculant File, as of 5/9/2007.

Association of American Medical Colleges, 2007

students' academic learning. Among the services provided are academic counseling, test-taking strategies, and other services to help students manage all aspects of their student life.

Admissions

The Assistant Dean of Student Affairs/Diversity discusses career options at MCW with all students who are invited for an interview. After the interview process, the Admissions Committee reviews all applications for admissions. Attempts are made to select students who are not only academically talented, but who also demonstrate non-cognitive characteristics believed to predict successful completion of medical school (i.e., motivation, leadership qualities, commitment to helping others, realistic understanding of medicine, and other personal traits). The committee interviewers include basic science and clinical faculty as well as medical students. Application fees may be waived by MCW when requested by the applicant after obtaining an American Medical College Application Service fee waiver. Students are notified of their acceptance to MCW within two weeks after their interview.

Academic Support Programs

The Medical College of Wisconsin provides academic support for all students. In addition to the faculty, there are large- and small-group tutoring sessions as well as study skills workshops. The college offers a decelerated five-year program where students can complete the first two years over a three-year period. Several events are facilitated throughout the year to introduce the medical students to cultural and professional resources within the greater Milwaukee Metropolitan area.

Enrichment Programs

Academic programs are offered to high-school and college-level students through a series of educational pipeline programs.

Sixty percent of students who participate in summer enrichment programs at the Medical College of Wisconsin go on to medical school or graduate studies in biomedical fields. The two programs currently offered are the Apprenticeship in Medicine (AIM) and the Multicultural Summer Research Training Program (MSRTP)

High School Program-Apprenticeship In Medicine (AIM). The AIM program offers 16 local high school students from diverse backgrounds the opportunity to engage in a variety of clinical hands-on experiences. An intensive six-week program has been designed to increase awareness of common medical problems in underserved communities and career opportunities in fields of medicine. This program offers a stipend upon completion of the program

Multicultural Summer Research Training Program (MSRTP). A ten-week summer fellowship for 14 students interested in the areas of cardiovascular, pulmonary, and hematological research is available to undergraduate and graduate students from diverse backgrounds. The program is sponsored by the National Institutes of Health, Lung and Blood Institute and offers a monthly stipend to participants.

Student Support Groups and Community Outreach Programs. Students of diverse backgrounds are encouraged to become active in community outreach programs, which are sponsored by student-led organizations such as the Student National Medical Association (SNMA), LaRaza Medical Student Association (LaRaMA), and the Physicians for Social Responsibility (PSR). Students utilize their creative energies to sponsor health fairs, high school career day visits, and are available to participate in the numerous programs and activities sponsored by the Office of Student Affairs/Diversity.

Student Financial Assistance

Several major competitive scholarships are available to students who contribute to the diversity of the student body and have outstanding academic credentials. For Wisconsin residents, the Dean's Scholarship reflects the college's commitment to ensure that students from diverse backgrounds have an opportunity to pursue their career goals in medicine. Other scholarships available and open to both Wisconsin and out-of-state residents include the Presidential Scholarship and the Advanced Medical Opportunity Scholarship. In addition to these, the Wisconsin Energy Corporation Foundation Endowment and the Hearst Foundation Endowment provide financial support to deserving students.

Scholarships are also funded through several clinical departments for students from diverse backgrounds who possess outstanding academic credentials. Students who would like to be considered for any of these scholarships should contact the Assistant Dean for Student Affairs/ Diversity. Other institutional financial assistance is comprised of need-based scholarships, interest-deferred loans and federal loans (i.e., Stafford loan program). The Office of Student Financial Services provides assistance to students completing their financial aid application. Application fee waivers for financially disadvantaged applicants are available for those who have received an AMCAS fee waiver. Students are encouraged to contact the Office of Admissions as questions or concerns arise. In addition, students do not have to be accepted to begin the financial aid process; however, a clean credit report is required of all students prior to matriculation.

Educational Partnerships

Realizing the need to stimulate an interest in math and science at an early age, students are encouraged to strive for academic excellence so that they may become more competitive for college. MCW has established a collaborative program with the University of Wisconsin-Milwaukee, called the Center for Science Education, which places strong emphasis on science and math education, starting as early as middle school. Through these initiatives, MCW has strengthened its community ties. Other educational partnerships include the Center for Healthy Communities, Center for the Advancement of Urban Children, and undergraduate higher education institutions throughout the regional area, (i.e., Marquette University, University of Wisconsin Milwaukee, etc.). Thus, underrepresented students in medicine have an ample opportunity to pursue their dream of becoming physicians.

University of Wisconsin School of Medicine and Public Health

Dr. Gloria Hawkins, Assistant
Dean for Multicultural Affairs
University of Wisconsin-Madison
750 Highland Ave, Room 2146-HSLC
Madison, WI 53705
608-263-3713; 608-262-4226 Fax
gvhawkin@facstaff.wisc.edu

The mission of the Multicultural Affairs Office in the School of Medicine and Public Health is to provide academic opportunities that will yield an increase in students historically underrepresented in medicine and to work toward the development of learning environments that will foster academic success. To carry out this mission, the Office has outreach programs/activities for pre-college and college students; works

collaboratively with undergraduate programs, pre-medical organizations, students, and advisors; as well as works closely with the school's Office of Admissions. The Multicultural Affairs staff advises and counsels medical students, monitors their academic progress, and makes appropriate academic and counseling referrals. Partnerships have been forged with internal and external constituent groups to provide a climate that embraces diversity and supports the professional development of all students, especially students from diverse backgrounds.

Recruitment
The Office of Admissions and Multicultural Affairs Office work collaboratively to recruit students from diverse backgrounds, especially those who are from groups historically underrepresented in higher education and medicine. Visits are made during the year to colleges and universities

University of Wisconsin School of Medicine and Public Health, 2006
Applicants and Matriculants by Gender, Race and Ethnicity

Race and Ethnicity	Applicants			Matriculants		
	Women	Men	Total	Women	Men	Total
Hispanic/Latino						
Cuban	5	3	8	0	0	0
Mexican American	31	35	66	1	2	3
Puerto Rican	6	8	14	0	0	0
Other Hispanic	25	20	45	0	0	0
Multiple Hispanic*	4	3	7	0	0	0
Subtotal	71	69	140	1	2	3
Non-Hispanic/Latino**						
Black	78	47	125	6	1	7
Native American/Alaska Native	4	4	8	0	0	0
Native Hawaiian/Other Pacific Islander	2	4	6	0	0	0
White	872	1,141	2,013	50	58	108
Asian	234	300	534	11	13	24
Other Race	1	1	2	0	0	0
Multiple Race*	35	36	71	3	3	6
Unknown	7	15	22	1	1	2
Subtotal	1,233	1,548	2,781	71	76	147
Foreign	22	31	53	0	0	0
Total	1,326	1,648	2,974	72	78	150

*Since 2002, students can select more than one race and / or ethnicity. **Those who did not choose Hispanic/Latino' or 'Non-Hispanic/Latino' are counted under 'Non-Hispanic/Latino'.
Data Source: AAMC Data Warehouse: Applicant-Matriculant File, as of 5/9/2007.

in the state and throughout the country. High school students who are residents of Wisconsin are encouraged to become familiar with the school through the Summer Research Apprentice Program. The program provides opportunities for students to participate as research apprentices in the laboratories of university faculty. Working collaboratively with faculty within the school, research opportunities are available to undergraduates who are interested in medicine. Inquiries about undergraduate research opportunities should be made to the Assistant Dean of Multicultural Affairs.

Admissions

The Admissions Committee is composed of faculty and students, some of whom are minority, and considers several factors when reviewing applicants. These factors include: 1) undergraduate and graduate academic performance and the Medical College Admission Test (MCAT) scores; 2) extracurricular activities; 3) the applicant's employment record, volunteer experience, and medical exposure; 4) the personal, educational, and socioeconomic background of the applicant and the response of the applicant to any challenges; 5) the applicant's character with reference to honesty and integrity, empathy, maturity, leadership, self-discipline, and emotional stability; 6) motivation to pursue a career in medicine; and 7) the interest and suitability of the applicant for special programs and/or future specific careers.

Furthermore, in the interests of both enriching the educational environment for all students and better meeting the future medical, educational, and scientific needs of society, the committee makes a special effort to select a class whose members represent a broad range of diverse life experiences, backgrounds, and interests. This diversity may include 1) ethnic or racial background, 2) socioeconomic background, 3) educational background, 4)

regional and geographic background, 5) interests and/or aptitudes for different medical careers, and 6) other cultural experiences. Therefore, non-residents in addition to Wisconsin residents who are from diverse backgrounds are strongly encouraged to apply.

All applicants must take the following courses to be given consideration for admission: 1) one semester of general biology with lab; 2) one semester of advanced biology with lab; 3) two semesters of inorganic/general chemistry with lab; 4) one semester of organic chemistry; 5) one semester of biochemistry; 6) two semesters of physics with lab; and 7) two semesters of mathematics with statistics and calculus recommended to meet this quantitative requirement.

Campus interviews are arranged by the Admissions staff, and the Multicultural Affairs Office plans special outreach activities for minority and disadvantaged applicants on some of the interview days. Applicants who receive acceptance offers from the school are invited to attend the Second Visit Program, sponsored by the Multicultural Affairs Office, for a more in-depth look at the school.

Academic Support Programs

The Multicultural Affairs Office works closely with the Student Academic Development Office in the school to insure that students are provided with the academic support required for success. The Student Academic Development Office has a highly trained staff to conduct self-assessment tests, study-skills workshops, and exam-preparation sessions. Other services include study materials and tutors for medical school classes and for the United States Medical Licensing Examination Steps 1 and 2. Additionally, both offices may periodically consult with other campus and community services in an effort to provide appropriate and effective support for students.

Summer Human Gross Anatomy Course.
Students holding an acceptance into the entering class may matriculate in the summer and enroll in the eight credit human gross anatomy course. The student-instructional staff ratio in this summer class provides opportunities for students to work closely with faculty and teaching assistants. The summer course also helps students smoothly transition into medical school during a less demanding time of the year.

Careers in Medicine and Mentoring.
Careers in Medicine is a comprehensive program that connects medical students with clinical faculty through career advising, mentoring, and workshops/seminars. This program is available to first-year medical students and culminates with residency placement. Faculty mentors help students assess their goals and interests, explore their options, choose a specialty, and prepare for residency placement.

Student Support and Community Outreach

Students are encouraged to explore their interests through organizations within the school and community outreach activities. These organizations include Medical Students for Minority Concerns (MSMC), Asian Pacific American Medical Student Association (APAMSA), American Medical Student Association (AMSA), Medical Students for the Arts (MFA), National Network of Latin American Medical Students (NNLAMS), Student National Medical Association (SNMA), and Student Physicians for Social Responsibility (PSR). Community outreach activities include the middle school Mentorship Achievement Program (MAP) and the Health Professions Mentoring Program (HPMP) for high school students. The Native American Health Working Group (NAHWG), a committee within the health sciences, focuses on educational and community issues. All of the organizations and groups have a diverse and active student membership.

Student Financial Assistance

The university makes available financial aid in the form of grants, scholarships, and low-interest loans to all students who demonstrate financial need. These funds are awarded based on the availability of funds and information the student provides on the university financial aid application. The school is committed to helping competitive students from diverse, as well as economically disadvantaged, backgrounds identify resources to finance their education.

Educational Partnerships

The University of Wisconsin School of Medicine and Public Health works closely with the University of Wisconsin-Madison and the University of Wisconsin-Milwaukee in preparing students for medical education. The Multicultural Affairs Office has pipeline programs and outreach initiatives ranging from middle school through undergraduate studies. These initiatives include a summer research program, hosting campus visits, pre-medical activities for merit-based and special support program students, and a long-standing partnership with the AHANA Pre-Health Society at the University of Wisconsin-Madison.

Other Pertinent Information

The American Medical College Application Service (AMCAS) application must be filed with AMCAS by November 1. Prospective applicants are strongly encouraged to apply early for consideration for admission to the University of Wisconsin School of Medicine and Public Health.

Association of American Medical Colleges, 2007

Enrichment
Programs

Summer Medical and Dental Education Program

In November 2005, the Association of American Medical Colleges and the American Dental Education Association announced the selection of 12 institutions that will be funded by the Robert Wood Johnson Foundation to provide summer academic enrichment programs for undergraduate college students from minority groups, from rural areas, and from economically disadvantaged backgrounds. This new medical and dental education collaboration replaces the Summer Medical Education Program. If you are interested in a career in medicine or dentistry, please contact representatives from these programs, or visit the SMDEP Web site for more information *(www.smdep.org)*.

	Pre-K to Kindergarten	Elementary/Junior High School Level	High School Level	Undergraduate College Level	Pre-matriculants to *Their* Medical School	Combined College/MD Programs for HSS[1]	Post-Baccalaureate	Educational Partnerships	Extended Programs	Other
AL University of Alabama School of Medicine	✓	✓	✓				✓			
University of South Alabama College of Medicine			✓				✓			NCRR K-12 Science Reduction Program
University of Arizona College of Medicine	✓	✓	✓				✓	✓		INMED[2]
University of Arkansas for Medical Sciences College of Medicine	✓	✓	✓	✓			✓			
Keck School of Medicine of the University of Southern California	✓	✓	✓	✓			✓			
Loma Linda University School of Medicine	✓	✓	✓	✓		✓	✓			MSEAP[1]
Stanford University School of Medicine			✓	✓				✓		
University of California, Davis, School of Medicine		✓	✓	✓		✓				
University of California, Irvine, School of Medicine	✓	✓	✓				✓	✓		
University of California, LA, David Geffen School of Medicine at UCLA			✓	✓			✓	✓	✓	SMDEP[3]
University of California, San Diego, School of Medicine	✓	✓	✓	✓			✓	✓		
University of California, San Francisco, School of Medicine			✓							
Charles R. Drew University School of Medicine and Science			✓	✓						
CO University of Colorado School of Medicine	✓	✓	✓	✓	✓	✓	✓			
CT University of Connecticut School of Medicine	✓	✓	✓	✓	✓	✓	✓			
Yale University School of Medicine			✓	✓				✓		SMDEP[3]
DC The George Washington University School of Medicine and Health Sciences			✓						✓	Upward Bound, AHEC, AMSA STATS, ISCOPES
Georgetown University School of Medicine	✓	✓				✓	✓			
Howard University College of Medicine		✓	✓	✓	✓	✓	✓		✓	SMDEP[3]
FL Florida State College of Medicine	✓	✓	✓			✓	✓			
University of Florida College of Medicine	✓	✓	✓		✓		✓			
University of Miami Leonard M. Miller School of Medicine			✓	✓	✓		✓			
University of South Florida College of Medicine			✓	✓						Master of Science MedSci degree
GA Emory University School of Medicine	✓	✓	✓							
Medical College of Georgia School of Medicine	✓	✓	✓	✓			✓			
Mercer University School of Medicine			✓	✓			✓			
Morehouse School of Medicine	✓	✓	✓	✓		✓	✓	✓		
HI University of Hawaii John A. Burns School of Medicine			✓			✓				
IL Loyola University of Chicago Stritch School of Medicine			✓	✓						
Northwestern University, The Feinburg School of Medicine		✓	✓	✓	✓	✓	✓			
Rosalind Franklin U. of Medicine and Science/Chicago Medical School			✓	✓			✓			
Rush Medical College of Rush University Medical Center			✓							

[1]High School Students

[2]Indians Into Medicine

[3]Summer Medical Dental and Education Program

[4]Early Assurance

[5]Limited to State Residents

Additional Note: 1) Many schools offer other types of programs that are not identified on the grid. These are programs such as USMLE preparation, elementary and middle school, and combined degree. 2) We have made every attempt to compile the list of enrichment programs on this chart based on the information reported in the school entries and on the checklist. However, we cannot guarantee the complete accuracy of each entry. Some schools may offer programs listed on the grid but did not identify them. (✓) It is advised that you contact the medical schools for more information. Source: Minority Student Opportunities in United States Medical Schools. L.M.I. Johnson, ed. Washington, DC: Association of American Medical Colleges, 2007.

Enrichment Programs

State	School	Pre-K to Kindergarten	Elementary/Junior High School Level	High School Level	Undergraduate College Level	Pre-matriculants to *Their* Medical School	Combined College/MD Programs for HSS[1]	Post-Baccalaureate	Educational Partnerships	Extended Programs	Other
IL	Southern Illinois University School of Medicine		✓	✓	✓	✓		✓	✓		MEDPREP
IL	University of Chicago Pritzker School of Medicine				✓						
IL	University of Illinois at Chicago College of Medicine		✓	✓	✓	✓	✓	✓			
IN	Indiana University School of Medicine		✓	✓	✓	✓			✓		Master of Science
IA	University of Iowa Roy J. and Lucille A. Carver College of Medicine		✓	✓	✓	✓					
KS	University of Kansas School of Medicine	✓	✓	✓	✓	✓	✓	✓	✓		
KY	University of Kentucky College of Medicine			✓	✓	✓	✓	✓			
KY	University of Louisville School of Medicine		✓	✓	✓	✓		✓	✓		SMDEP[3]
LA	Louisiana State University School of Medicine in New Orleans	✓	✓	✓	✓	✓			✓		
LA	Louisiana State University HSC School of Medicine in Shreveport		✓	✓	✓	✓			✓		
LA	Tulane University School of Medicine		✓	✓	✓				✓		
MD	Johns Hopkins University School of Medicine		✓	✓	✓				✓		
MD	Uniformed Services University of the Health Sciences, F. Edward Hébert School of Medicine			✓	✓			✓	✓		
MD	University of Maryland School of Medicine		✓	✓	✓	✓			✓		
MA	Boston University School of Medicine			✓					✓	✓	EMSSP
MA	Harvard Medical School		✓	✓	✓	✓			✓		
MA	Tufts University School of Medicine		✓	✓	✓	✓					
MA	University of Massachusetts Medical School		✓	✓	✓	✓		✓	✓	✓	International Program
MI	Michigan State University College of Human Medicine		✓	✓	✓	✓	✓	✓	✓	✓	
MI	University of Michigan Medical School		✓	✓	✓	✓			✓	✓	
MI	Wayne State University School of Medicine			✓	✓			✓			
MN	Mayo Medical School			✓				✓	✓	✓	
MN	University of Minnesota Medical School		✓	✓	✓	✓					
MS	University of Mississippi School of Medicine	✓	✓	✓	✓	✓			✓		
MO	Saint Louis University School of Medicine		✓	✓	✓						
MO	University of Missouri - Columbia School of Medicine		✓	✓	✓						
MO	University of Missouri - Kansas City School of Medicine		✓	✓	✓		✓				
MO	Washington University in St. Louis School of Medicine		✓	✓	✓				✓	✓	
NE	Creighton University School of Medicine		✓	✓	✓	✓		✓	✓		
NE	University of Nebraska College of Medicine		✓	✓	✓				✓		SMDEP[3]
NV	University of Nevada School of Medicine		✓	✓	✓				✓		

[1]High School Students
[2]Indians Into Medicine
[3]Summer Medical Dental and Education Program
[4]Early Assurance
[5]Limited to State Residents

Additional Note: 1) Many schools offer other types of programs that are not identified on the grid. These are programs such as USMLE preparation, elementary and middle school, and combined degree. 2) We have made every attempt to compile the list of enrichment programs on this chart based on the information reported in the school entries and on the checklist. However, we cannot guarantee the complete accuracy of each entry. Some schools may offer programs listed on the grid but did not identify them. (✓) It is advised that you contact the medical schools for more information. Source: Minority Student Opportunities in United States Medical Schools. L.M.I. Johnson, ed. Washington, DC: Association of American Medical Colleges, 2007.

richment Programs

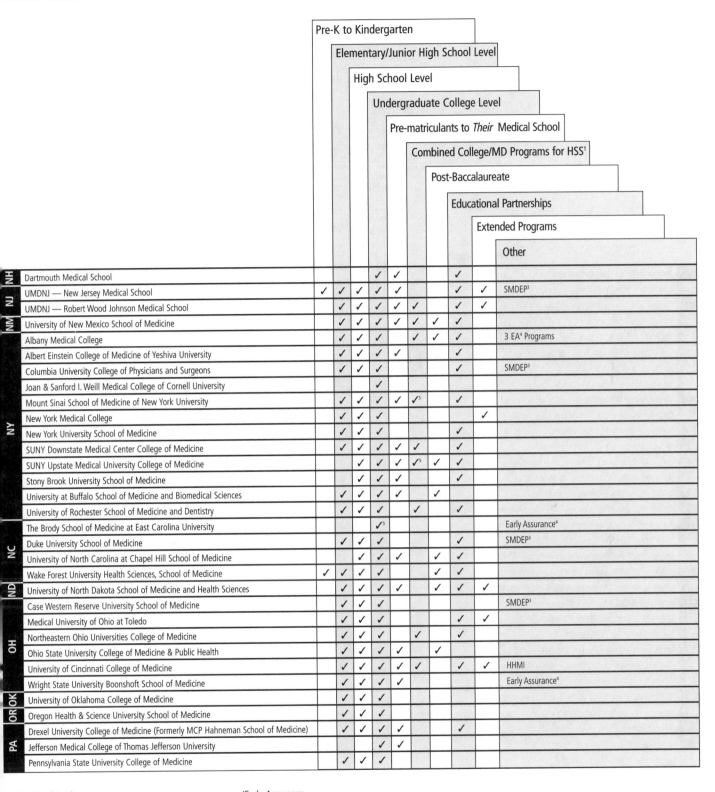

State	School	Pre-K to Kindergarten	Elementary/Junior High School Level	High School Level	Undergraduate College Level	Pre-matriculants to Their Medical School	Combined College/MD Programs for HSS[1]	Post-Baccalaureate	Educational Partnerships	Extended Programs	Other
NH	Dartmouth Medical School			✓	✓			✓			
NJ	UMDNJ — New Jersey Medical School	✓	✓	✓	✓	✓		✓	✓		SMDEP[3]
NJ	UMDNJ — Robert Wood Johnson Medical School		✓	✓	✓	✓	✓	✓	✓		
NM	University of New Mexico School of Medicine		✓	✓	✓	✓	✓	✓			
NY	Albany Medical College		✓	✓	✓		✓	✓			3 EA[4] Programs
NY	Albert Einstein College of Medicine of Yeshiva University		✓	✓	✓	✓		✓			
NY	Columbia University College of Physicians and Surgeons		✓	✓	✓			✓			SMDEP[3]
NY	Joan & Sanford I. Weill Medical College of Cornell University			✓							
NY	Mount Sinai School of Medicine of New York University	✓	✓	✓	✓	✓	✓[5]	✓			
NY	New York Medical College		✓	✓	✓				✓		
NY	New York University School of Medicine		✓	✓	✓			✓			
NY	SUNY Downstate Medical Center College of Medicine		✓	✓	✓	✓	✓	✓			
NY	SUNY Upstate Medical University College of Medicine		✓	✓	✓	✓	✓[5]	✓			
NY	Stony Brook University School of Medicine		✓	✓	✓			✓			
NY	University at Buffalo School of Medicine and Biomedical Sciences	✓	✓	✓	✓	✓			✓		
NY	University of Rochester School of Medicine and Dentistry	✓	✓	✓			✓	✓			
NC	The Brody School of Medicine at East Carolina University			✓[5]							Early Assurance[4]
NC	Duke University School of Medicine		✓	✓	✓			✓			SMDEP[3]
NC	University of North Carolina at Chapel Hill School of Medicine		✓	✓	✓	✓		✓	✓		
NC	Wake Forest University Health Sciences, School of Medicine	✓	✓	✓	✓			✓	✓		
ND	University of North Dakota School of Medicine and Health Sciences		✓	✓	✓	✓		✓	✓	✓	
OH	Case Western Reserve University School of Medicine		✓	✓	✓						SMDEP[3]
OH	Medical University of Ohio at Toledo		✓	✓	✓			✓	✓		
OH	Northeastern Ohio Universities College of Medicine		✓	✓	✓		✓	✓			
OH	Ohio State University College of Medicine & Public Health		✓	✓	✓	✓	✓				
OH	University of Cincinnati College of Medicine		✓	✓	✓	✓	✓	✓	✓		HHMI
OH	Wright State University Boonshoft School of Medicine		✓	✓	✓	✓					Early Assurance[4]
OK	University of Oklahoma College of Medicine		✓	✓	✓						
OR	Oregon Health & Science University School of Medicine		✓	✓	✓						
PA	Drexel University College of Medicine (Formerly MCP Hahneman School of Medicine)		✓	✓	✓	✓		✓			
PA	Jefferson Medical College of Thomas Jefferson University			✓	✓						
PA	Pennsylvania State University College of Medicine		✓	✓	✓						

[1] High School Students
[2] Indians Into Medicine
[3] Summer Medical Dental and Education Program
[4] Early Assurance
[5] Limited to State Residents

Additional Note: 1) Many schools offer other types of programs that are not identified on the grid. These are programs such as USMLE preparation, elementary and middle school, and combined degree. 2) We have made every attempt to compile the list of enrichment programs on this chart based on the information reported in the school entries and on the checklist. However, we cannot guarantee the complete accuracy of each entry. Some schools may offer programs listed on the grid but did not identify them. (✓) It is advised that you contact the medical schools for more information. Source: Minority Student Opportunities in United States Medical Schools. L.M.I. Johnson, ed. Washington, DC: Association of American Medical Colleges, 2007.

Association of American Medical Colleges, 2007

Enrichment Programs

State	School	Pre-K to Kindergarten	Elementary/Junior High School Level	High School Level	Undergraduate College Level	Pre-matriculants to *Their* Medical School	Combined College/MD Programs for HSS[1]	Post-Baccalaureate	Educational Partnerships	Extended Programs	Other
PA	Temple University School of Medicine				✓	✓					NIH-T35
PA	University of Pennsylvania School of Medicine			✓		✓					
PA	University of Pittsburgh School of Medicine	✓	✓	✓	✓	✓		✓			
PR	Ponce School of Medicine			✓				✓	✓		
PR	Universidad Central del Caribe School of Medicine			✓				✓			
PR	University of Puerto Rico School of Medicine	✓	✓	✓	✓						
RI	Brown Medical School			✓			✓	✓			
SC	Medical University of South Carolina College of Medicine			✓			✓	✓			
SC	University of South Carolina School of Medicine	✓	✓	✓	✓			✓	✓		
SD	University of South Dakota School of Medicine	✓	✓	✓							INMED[2] Satelite Office – co-op agreement w/ UNDSM
TN	East Tennessee State University James H. Quillen College of Medicine			✓				✓			
TN	Meharry Medical College School of Medicine	✓	✓	✓	✓	✓	✓	✓	✓		
TN	University of Tennessee, Health Science Center College of Medicine	✓	✓	✓	✓						
TN	Vanderbilt University School of Medicine			✓			✓	✓			
TX	Baylor College of Medicine	✓	✓	✓							
TX	Texas A & M University System Health Science Center College of Medicine			✓				✓			
TX	Texas Tech University Health Sciences Center School of Medicine	✓	✓	✓				✓	✓		
TX	University of Texas Medical School at Galveston				✓	✓	✓	✓			NIH-T35
TX	University of Texas Medical School at Houston	✓	✓	✓	✓	✓		✓			SMDEP[3]
TX	University of Texas Medical School at San Antonio			✓				✓			
TX	University of Texas Southwestern Med. Cntr. at Dallas Southwestern Medical School	✓	✓	✓	✓			✓	✓		
UT	University of Utah School of Medicine	✓	✓	✓	✓			✓			
VT	University of Vermont College of Medicine										
VA	Eastern Virginia Medical School	✓	✓	✓				✓			
VA	University of Virginia School of Medicine			✓				✓			SMDEP[3]
VA	Virginia Commonwealth University School of Medicine	✓	✓	✓	✓	✓	✓	✓	✓		
WA	University of Washington School of Medicine	✓	✓	✓	✓		✓	✓	✓		SMDEP[3]
WV	Marshall University Joan C. Edwards School of Medicine	✓	✓	✓				✓			
WV	West Virginia University School of Medicine	✓	✓	✓				✓			WEIR, ALESSANDRI
WI	Medical College of Wisconsin	✓	✓	✓	✓			✓	✓		
WI	University of Wisconsin Medical School	✓	✓	✓				✓			

[1] High School Students
[2] Indians Into Medicine
[3] Summer Medical Dental and Education Program
[4] Early Assurance
[5] Limited to State Residents

Additional Note: 1) Many schools offer other types of programs that are not identified on the grid. These are programs such as USMLE preparation, elementary and middle school, and combined degree. 2) We have made every attempt to compile the list of enrichment programs on this chart based on the information reported in the school entries and on the checklist. However, we cannot guarantee the complete accuracy of each entry. Some schools may offer programs listed on the grid but did not identify them. (✓) It is advised that you contact the medical schools for more information. Source: Minority Student Opportunities in United States Medical Schools. L.M.I. Johnson, ed. Washington, DC: Association of American Medical Colleges, 2007.

Association of American Medical Colleges, 2007

Selected
AAMC Data

Association of
American Medical Colleges

Applicants by Race and Ethnicity within Sex, 2003-2006

Race and Hispanic Origin of Applicants 2003 - 2006	2003			2004			2005			2006		
	Hispanic or Not*			Hispanic or Not*			Hispanic or Not*			Hispanic or Not*		
	N	Y	Total	N	Y	Total	N	Y	Total	N	Y	Total
Women												
American Indian or Alaska Native	35	7	42	47	22	69	45	13	58	74	22	96
American Indian or Alaska Native, Black or African American	26	2	28	28	4	32	34	4	38	17	2	19
American Indian or Alaska Native, White	108	4	112	91	12	103	106	16	122	60	15	75
Asian	3,093	43	3,136	3,429	50	3,479	3,699	56	3,755	3,798	49	3,847
Asian, White	266	9	275	324	10	334	341	16	357	297	11	308
Black or African American	1,906	22	1,928	1,940	65	2,005	1,917	68	1,985	2,007	61	2,068
Black or African American, White	42	13	55	54	24	78	51	26	77	35	20	55
Native Hawaiian or Other Pacific Islander	13	3	16	23	7	30	23	3	26	64	11	75
White	9,749	600	10,349	10,017	767	10,784	10,143	889	11,032	10,373	846	11,219
White, Other	116	67	183	7	12	19	1	2	3	3	2	5
Other	280	436	716	43	205	248	20	63	83	40	37	77
Unknown	86	52	138	96	122	218	140	238	378	209	353	562
Non U.S. Citizen/Permanent Resident	497	.	497	516	.	516	627	.	627	794	.	794
Multiple Race, N<300	158	39	197	87	16	103	74	11	85	74	19	93
Total for Women	16,375	1,297	17,672	16,702	1,316	18,018	17,221	1,405	18,626	17,845	1,448	19,293
Men												
American Indian or Alaska Native	50	10	60	60	12	72	50	17	67	72	19	91
American Indian or Alaska Native, Black or African American	11	1	12	16	2	18	11	2	13	4		4
American Indian or Alaska Native, White	80	9	89	115	14	129	109	18	127	79	15	94
Asian	3,060	25	3,085	3,306	44	3,350	3,596	55	3,651	3,734	35	3,769
Asian, White	223	6	229	278	7	285	302	12	314	271	11	282
Black or African American	835	21	856	862	38	900	893	31	924	899	41	940
Black or African American, White	25	10	35	37	27	64	30	16	46	20	6	26
Native Hawaiian or Other Pacific Islander	10	6	16	16	9	25	19	5	24	47	8	55
White	10,487	522	11,009	11,028	717	11,745	11,612	813	12,425	12,296	783	13,079
White, Other	159	59	218	5	12	17	1	3	4	1	.	1
Other	328	422	750	67	174	241	30	71	101	44	40	84
Unknown	81	67	148	125	160	285	137	249	386	228	351	579
Non U.S. Citizen/Permanent Resident	462	.	462	510	.	510	578	.	578	733	.	733
Multiple Race, N<300	115	35	150	62	14	76	74	13	87	64	14	78
Total for Men	15,926	1,193	17,119	16,487	1,230	17,717	17,442	1,305	18,747	18,492	1,323	19,815
All Applicants												
American Indian or Alaska Native	85	17	102	107	34	141	95	30	125	146	41	187
American Indian or Alaska Native, Black or African American	37	3	40	44	6	50	45	6	51	21	2	23
American Indian or Alaska Native, White	188	13	201	206	26	232	215	34	249	139	30	169
Asian	6,153	68	6,221	6,735	94	6,829	7,295	111	7,406	7,532	84	7,616
Asian, White	489	15	504	602	17	619	643	28	671	568	22	590
Black or African American	2,741	43	2,784	2,802	103	2,905	2,810	99	2,909	2,906	102	3,008
Black or African American, White	67	23	90	91	51	142	81	42	123	55	26	81
Native Hawaiian or Other Pacific Islander	23	9	32	39	16	55	42	8	50	111	19	130
White	20,236	1,122	21,358	21,045	1,484	22,529	21,755	1,702	23,457	22,669	1,629	24,298
White, Other	275	126	401	12	24	36	2	5	7	4	2	6
Other	608	858	1,466	110	379	489	50	134	184	84	77	161
Unknown	167	119	286	221	282	503	277	487	764	437	704	1,141
Non U.S. Citizen/Permanent Resident	959	.	959	1,026	.	1,026	1,205	.	1,205	1,527	.	1,527
Multiple Race, N<300	273	74	347	149	30	179	148	24	172	138	33	171
Total for Women and Men	32,301	2,490	34,791	33,189	2,546	35,735	34,663	2,710	37,373	36,337	2,771	39,108
Total	32,301	2,490	34,791	33,189	2,546	35,735	34,663	2,710	37,373	36,337	2,771	39,108

Source: AAMC: Data Warehouse: Applicant Matriculant File as of 10/27/2006.

Association of American Medical Colleges, 2007

Hispanic Ethnicity and Non-Hispanic Race by Acceptance Status, 2004-2006

		Applicants from 2004 on	2004 Appli-cants	2004 Time Appli-cants	2004 Accep-tees	2004 Matricu-lants	2005 Appli-cants	2005 Time Appli-cants	2005 Accep-tees	2005 Matricu-lants	2006 Appli-cants	2006 Time Appli-cants	2006 Accep-tees	2006 Matricu-lants
Women	Hispanic	Mexican American	420	297	190	177	463	356	213	198	491	365	228	218
		Puerto Rican	280	233	150	146	272	232	157	152	294	251	147	145
		Cuban	65	56	40	37	74	68	42	40	106	84	48	46
		Other Hispanic	450	341	186	176	495	367	201	193	489	372	208	203
		Multiple Hispanic	101	74	40	38	101	78	39	36	68	49	32	29
		Subtotal	1,316	1,001	606	574	1,405	1,101	652	619	1,448	1,121	663	641
	Non-Hispanic	Black	1,940	1,369	772	718	1,917	1,324	703	665	2,007	1,417	804	760
		Asian	3,429	2,684	1,659	1,589	3,699	2,832	1,730	1,658	3,798	2,948	1,720	1,633
		Native American (incl AK)	47	41	27	24	45	33	15	13	74	59	37	35
		Native Hawaiian/OPI	23	15	7	7	23	13	6	6	64	45	17	17
		White	10,017	7,850	5,188	4,867	10,143	7,929	5,045	4,713	10,373	8,067	5,117	4,818
		Other	43	29	13	12	20	9	10	9	40	25	11	11
		Unknown	96	84	73	66	140	128	114	109	209	200	153	145
		Multiple Race	591	450	291	268	607	482	317	301	486	375	255	242
		Subtotal	16,186	12,522	8,030	7,551	16,594	12,750	7,940	7,474	17,051	13,136	8,114	7,661
	Non-U.S.	Foreign	516	409	132	110	626	506	174	146	794	647	182	143
		Unknown Citizenship	.	.	.	.	1	1	.	.	.	.	.	.
		Subtotal	516	409	132	110	627	507	174	146	794	647	182	143
	Total for Women		18,018	13,932	8,768	8,235	18,626	14,358	8,766	8,239	19,293	14,904	8,959	8,445
Men	Hispanic	Mexican American	390	266	213	200	416	281	216	207	464	355	238	230
		Puerto Rican	225	187	140	136	254	206	163	160	266	224	156	149
		Cuban	79	62	44	43	93	77	57	54	100	86	44	42
		Other Hispanic	439	300	198	184	461	331	198	191	446	326	207	194
		Multiple Hispanic	97	74	41	38	81	55	39	38	47	39	27	27
		Subtotal	1,230	889	636	601	1,305	950	673	650	1,323	1,030	672	642
	Non-Hispanic	Black	862	599	388	368	893	637	418	403	899	619	415	395
		Asian	3,306	2,456	1,575	1,505	3,596	2,650	1,728	1,655	3,734	2,749	1,705	1,609
		Native American (incl AK)	60	40	26	24	50	30	23	20	72	47	33	33
		Native Hawaiian/OPI	16	14	4	4	19	12	12	12	47	32	16	16
		White	11,028	8,320	5,779	5,476	11,612	8,683	5,881	5,582	12,296	9,071	6,073	5,723
		Other	67	37	31	26	30	13	11	10	44	26	13	12
		Unknown	125	108	73	68	137	122	81	81	228	214	136	131
		Multiple Race	513	377	242	230	527	369	240	234	439	318	221	210
		Subtotal	15,977	11,951	8,118	7,701	16,864	12,516	8,394	7,997	17,759	13,076	8,612	8,129
	Non-U.S.	Foreign	510	417	140	111	578	468	154	117	733	573	199	154
		Subtotal	510	417	140	111	578	468	154	117	733	573	199	154
	Total for Men		17,717	13,257	8,894	8,413	18,747	13,934	9,221	8,764	19,815	14,679	9,483	8,925
All Applicants	Hispanic	Mexican American	810	563	403	377	879	637	429	405	955	720	466	448
		Puerto Rican	505	420	290	282	526	438	320	312	560	475	303	294
		Cuban	144	118	84	80	167	145	99	94	206	170	92	88
		Other Hispanic	889	641	384	360	956	698	399	384	935	698	415	397
		Multiple Hispanic	198	148	81	76	182	133	78	74	115	88	59	56
		Subtotal	2,546	1,890	1,242	1,175	2,710	2,051	1,325	1,269	2,771	2,151	1,335	1,283
	Non-Hispanic	Black	2,802	1,968	1,160	1,086	2,810	1,961	1,121	1,068	2,906	2,036	1,219	1,155
		Asian	6,735	5,140	3,234	3,094	7,295	5,482	3,458	3,313	7,532	5,697	3,425	3,242
		Native American (incl AK)	107	81	53	48	95	63	38	33	146	106	70	68
		Native Hawaiian/OPI	39	29	11	11	42	25	18	18	111	77	33	33
		White	21,045	16,170	10,967	10,343	21,755	16,612	10,926	10,295	22,669	17,138	11,190	10,541
		Other	110	66	44	38	50	22	21	19	84	51	24	23
		Unknown	221	192	146	134	277	250	195	190	437	414	289	276
		Multiple Race	1,104	827	533	498	1,134	851	557	535	925	693	476	452
		Subtotal	32,163	24,473	16,148	15,252	33,458	25,266	16,334	15,471	34,810	26,212	16,726	15,790
	Non-U.S.	Foreign	1,026	826	272	221	1,204	974	328	263	1,527	1,220	381	297
		Unknown Citizenship	.	.	.	.	1	1	.	.	.	.	.	.
		Subtotal	1,026	826	272	221	1,205	975	328	263	1,527	1,220	381	297
	Total for Women and Men		35,735	27,189	17,662	16,648	37,373	28,292	17,987	17,003	39,108	29,583	18,442	17,370

Source: AAMC: Data Warehouse: Applicant Matriculant File as of 10/27/2006.

Association of American Medical Colleges, 2007

Matriculants by Race and Ethnicity within Sex, 2003-2006

Race and Hispanic Origin of Matriculants 2003 - 2006	2003 Hispanic or Not* N	Y	Total	2004 Hispanic or Not* N	Y	Total	2005 Hispanic or Not* N	Y	Total	2006 Hispanic or Not* N	Y	Total
Women												
American Indian or Alaska Native	16	2	18	24	8	32	13	3	16	35	7	42
American Indian or Alaska Native, Black or African American	6	.	6	7	2	9	12	1	13	5	1	6
American Indian or Alaska Native, White	54	2	56	45	5	50	48	6	54	27	5	32
Asian	1,545	11	1,556	1,589	15	1,604	1,658	21	1,679	1,633	16	1,649
Asian, White	139	5	144	146	2	148	174	10	184	171	7	178
Black or African American	700	10	710	718	20	738	665	22	687	760	15	775
Black or African American, White	25	7	32	32	14	46	34	17	51	13	7	20
Native Hawaiian or Other Pacific Islander	2	.	2	7	2	9	6	1	7	17	5	22
White	4,779	284	5,063	4,867	351	5,218	4,713	401	5,114	4,818	397	5,215
White, Other	53	30	83	1	7	8	1	1	2	2	.	2
Other	90	176	266	12	88	100	9	32	41	11	17	28
Unknown	62	21	83	66	54	120	109	101	210	145	156	301
Non U.S. Citizen/Permanent Resident	110	.	110	110	.	110	146	.	146	143	.	143
Multiple Race, N<300	69	14	83	37	6	43	32	3	35	24	8	32
Total for Women	7,650	562	8,212	7,661	574	8,235	7,620	619	8,239	7,804	641	8,445
Men												
American Indian or Alaska Native	19	3	22	24	6	30	20	7	27	33	9	42
American Indian or Alaska Native, Black or African American	5	.	5	5	.	5	5	.	5	2	.	2
American Indian or Alaska Native, White	38	3	41	46	8	54	53	6	59	34	7	41
Asian	1,519	11	1,530	1,505	15	1,520	1,655	17	1,672	1,609	14	1,623
Asian, White	121	6	127	129	4	133	129	5	134	133	8	141
Black or African American	360	8	368	368	20	388	403	13	416	395	17	412
Black or African American, White	15	6	21	21	17	38	17	12	29	8	4	12
Native Hawaiian or Other Pacific Islander	3	2	5	4	1	5	12	2	14	16	3	19
White	5,345	234	5,579	5,476	342	5,818	5,582	423	6,005	5,723	376	6,099
White, Other	57	30	87	3	4	7	.	1	1	.	.	.
Other	117	186	303	26	96	122	10	30	40	12	16	28
Unknown	54	26	80	68	82	150	81	128	209	131	183	314
Non U.S. Citizen/Permanent Resident	102	.	102	111	.	111	117	.	117	154	.	154
Multiple Race, N<300	45	14	59	26	6	32	30	6	36	33	5	38
Total for Men	7,800	529	8,329	7,812	601	8,413	8,114	650	8,764	8,283	642	8,925
Matriculants												
American Indian or Alaska Native	35	5	40	48	14	62	33	10	43	68	16	84
American Indian or Alaska Native, Black or African American	11	.	11	12	2	14	17	1	18	7	1	8
American Indian or Alaska Native, White	92	5	97	91	13	104	101	12	113	61	12	73
Asian	3,064	22	3,086	3,094	30	3,124	3,313	38	3,351	3,242	30	3,272
Asian, White	260	11	271	275	6	281	303	15	318	304	15	319
Black or African American	1,060	18	1,078	1,086	40	1,126	1,068	35	1,103	1,155	32	1,187
Black or African American, White	40	13	53	53	31	84	51	29	80	21	11	32
Native Hawaiian or Other Pacific Islander	5	2	7	11	3	14	18	3	21	33	8	41
White	10,124	518	10,642	10,343	693	11,036	10,295	824	11,119	10,541	773	11,314
White, Other	110	60	170	4	11	15	1	2	3	2	.	2
Other	207	362	569	38	184	222	19	62	81	23	33	56
Unknown	116	47	163	134	136	270	190	229	419	276	339	615
Non U.S. Citizen/Permanent Resident	212	.	212	221	.	221	263	.	263	297	.	297
Multiple Race, N<300	114	28	142	63	12	75	62	9	71	57	13	70
Total for Women and Men	15,450	1,091	16,541	15,473	1,175	16,648	15,734	1,269	17,003	16,087	1,283	17,370
Total	15,450	1,091	16,541	15,473	1,175	16,648	15,734	1,269	17,003	16,087	1,283	17,370

*Not Hispanic includes those designating themselves as Not Hispanic, those who did not respond to the ethnicity question, and Non U.S. Citizen/Permanent

Source: AAMC: Data Warehouse: Applicant Matriculant File as of 10/27/2006.

Total Graduates by Race/Ethnicity within Sex, 2002-2006

Graduates - All U.S. Medical Schools		Class of 2002	Class of 2003	Class of 2004	Class of 2005	Class of 2006
Women	Race/Ethnicity					
	Black	689	670	642	691	733
	Native American (incl AK)	63	47	43	46	78
	Asian	1,350	1,429	1,458	1,465	1,630
	Native Hawaiian/OPI	22	17	15	21	22
	White	4,237	4,256	4,447	4,539	4,638
	Mexican American	162	161	191	146	175
	Puerto Rican	131	144	152	142	159
	Cuban	0	0	0	0	40
	Other Hispanic	135	143	142	139	168
	Foreign	48	76	76	73	98
	Unknown	88	90	96	153	214
	Total for Women*	6,925	7,033	7,262	7,415	7,746
Men	Race/Ethnicity					
	Black	398	343	391	356	389
	Native American (incl AK)	60	54	56	50	60
	Asian	1,692	1,739	1,713	1,654	1,602
	Native Hawaiian/OPI	33	16	13	25	19
	White	5,808	5,647	5,675	5,495	5,392
	Mexican American	221	188	198	197	185
	Puerto Rican	153	134	154	131	129
	Cuban	0	0	0	1	31
	Other Hispanic	157	180	170	182	176
	Foreign	97	80	77	98	86
	Unknown	136	126	121	161	256
	Total for Men*	8,755	8,507	8,568	8,349	8,179
All Graduates	Race/Ethnicity					
	Black	1,087	1,013	1,033	1,047	1,122
	Native American (incl AK)	123	101	99	96	138
	Asian	3,042	3,168	3,171	3,119	3,232
	Native Hawaiian/OPI	55	33	28	46	41
	White	10,045	9,903	10,122	10,034	10,030
	Mexican American	383	349	389	343	360
	Puerto Rican	284	278	306	273	288
	Cuban	0	0	0	1	71
	Other Hispanic	292	323	312	321	344
	Foreign	145	156	153	171	184
	Unknown	224	216	217	314	470
	Total for Women & Men*	15,680	15,540	15,830	15,764	15,925

Source: AAMC: Data Warehouse: Applicant Matriculant File (DW:AMF) as of 4/18/2007 and
SRS_READ_STUDENT_ENROLL_STATUS as of 11/9/06.

* Starting in 2002-03, applicants could indicate races and ethnicities in combination or alone, thus the counts may not be equal to total individual count.

Association of American Medical Colleges, 2007

Distribution of U.S. Medical School Faculty by Sex and Race/Hispanic Origin

Asian	10,449	5,395	15,844
Black	1,958	1,810	3,768
Native American/Alaskan	82	53	135
Native Hawaiian/OPI	116	58	174
White	59,779	26,930	86,709
Other	180	82	262
Unknown	4,915	3,059	7,974
Multiple Races	1,811	1,013	2,824
Cuban	39	26	65
Mexican American	444	241	685
Puerto Rican	537	408	945
Other Hispanic	2,136	1,091	3,227
Multiple Hispanic	114	82	196
Total	**82,560**	**40,248**	**122,808**

Note: This table excludes 472 faculty with missing sex data.

Data Source: AAMC Faculty Roster, as of October 3, 2007.

Association of American Medical Colleges, 2